# PRONOUNCING VOCABULARY

OF

# GEOGRAPHICAL AND PERSONAL NAMES.

THE GEOGRAPHICAL LIST

EMBRACES ALL THE NAMES WORTHY OF NOTE IN THE KNOWN WORLD, ACCOMPANIED WITH SUCH DESCRIPTIVE AND STATISTICAL FACTS AS ARE USUAL IN GAZETTEERS.

THE PERSONAL NAMES

COMPRISE THOSE OF THE MOST CELEBRATED MEN OF ANCIENT AND MODERN TIMES, DOWN TO THE PRESENT DAY, WHICH ARE LIKELY TO BE MET WITH IN GENERAL READING; APPENDED TO EACH NAME ARE SUCH BIOGRAPHICAL FACTS AS ARE NECESSARY IN A BOOK OF REFERENCE.

TO WHICH IS ADDED

A COMPLETE LIST OF SCRIPTURAL NAMES.

CONCLUDING WITH TABLES

WHICH SHOW AT A GLANCE THE POPULATION OF THE SEVERAL STATES, THE TIME OF THEIR ELECTIONS, THE MEETING OF THEIR LEGISLATURES, THE SUCCESSION OF THE PRESIDENTS, AND A LIST OF ALL THE COLLEGES AND PROFESSIONAL SCHOOLS IN THE UNITED STATES.

---

BY ELIAS LONGLEY.

---

CINCINNATI:
LONGLEY BROTHERS, PUBLISHERS,
168 VINE STREET, ABOVE FOURTH.
1857.

# INTRODUCTION.

---

## PECULIAR FEATURES OF THE WORK.

A WANT has long been felt, in every community, for a cheap Vocabulary of Geographical and Personal Names, as a book of reference for pronunciation, mainly, but secondarily as a brief guide to the leading items of information connected with those names. This want has been experienced, perhaps often unconsciously, by pupils in our common schools, by the poorer portion of students in high schools and colleges, and by the mass of newspaper readers who invest very little money in books. The thorough student, and the general reader who has plenty of means with which to supply every convenience, can obtain the information desired in such works as "*Lippincott's Gazetteer*," "*Appleton's Biographical Encyclopedia*," etc.; but they are too expensive for the classes mentioned, and in many cases too voluminous to be convenient.

In regard to personal names, so far as the publishers are aware, there has never before been an attempt made to give their pronunciation in an extended list. [For remarks on the importance of calling men by their right names, see pages 128—9.]

But there is another feature of the work here presented, which, in the minds of the publishers and of the many school teachers and friends of education who have examined the subject, is of more value than either of the considerations above mentioned, and demands more than a passing notice. The methods of representing pronunciation in the ordinary dictionaries and gazetteers, either by marked letters or by figures in connection with them, is so imperfect and unsatisfactory as to be a constant source of annoyance to all who are necessitated to use them. That the reader may understand the full merits of the system of notation employed in this book, we propose to notice briefly some of the circumstances that call for its introduction.

The first principle of alphabetic writing or printing was the representation of each sound by a simple *character* or *letter*, so that these letters or *elemental parts*, when combined, would be the counterpart of the spoken word—a picture of the word itself. Such was the Sanscrit, and such, it is evident to every intelligent mind, should be the principle of *all* alphabetic writing, for thus the acquisition of written or printed language would be as easy as that of spoken, and there would be no necessity for Pronouncing Dictionaries and Gazetteers, while a disregard of this principle renders the represented language, if not hieroglyphical, at least ideagraphic; that is, the written or printed word represents an idea, and can not, as a general thing, be considered as representing the sounds of a spoken word. For example, take the word *cough*, and what relation does either of the letters bear to the three sounds heard, as indicated by the Pronouncing Dictionary, *kof?* *C* can not definitely represent *k*, because in *cent* it is supposed to stand for *s*, in *suffice* for *z*, in *vicious* for *sh*, etc.; and how can *o* be a representative of the vowel sound in *cough*, when it has such different sounds in *no*, *son*, *woman*, *women*, etc.; and *u* is not any better a representative of this sound, and the two uncertainties together can not make the matter more clear, especially when we see them called so differently in *count*, *cousin*, *pour*, *tour;* while *g* is a poor representative of *f*, and *h* is no better, and the two together are no improvement, when we view their varying sounds in *lough*, *ghost*, and want of sound in *dough* and *weigh*. Any other word, almost, would answer just as well to show the utter deficiency of English orthography to represent the spoken words of the language. There are only 60 words, in the 90,000 used by English speakers, whose spellings are in accordance with the true principle of alphabetic writing.*

Primarily, then, an insurmountable difficulty in the way of accurately representing by means of the Roman alphabet any words whatever, is, in its consisting of but *twenty-three* representative letters, while the spoken language consists of upwards of *forty* distinct sounds! And secondarily, even were there a uniformity in the notation used by the different authorities in supplying the deficiency caused by employing the Romanic semi-alphabet, it is still open to the charge of complexity and inaccuracy, and therefore unfit to be used in teaching children a correct pronunciation.

There are other serious objections to our present orthography as it regards teaching a correct pronunciation, only one of which we shall mention in this connection, and which has a bearing on the remarks above. It is that it gives rise to a slip-shod manner of pronunciation or *enunciation*. Who that has paid the least attention to the pronunciation of the middle and upper classes, as well as that of public speakers, has not noticed the great want of care, the inaccuracies and diversities prevalent, and particularly how utterly regardless of all rules and taste they are in the enunciation of unaccented syllables? The words fall from their lips robbed of all their beauty and interest—shapeless and repulsive to the educated ear. The fault with the better educated class of people is chargeable, to a great extent, to themselves, but with those less fortunate there can be no such plea, and the present English or Johnsonian orthography, absurd as it is in structure, becomes responsible here. Good pronunciation is in giving the *whole* word, with all its parts perfect; *every unaccented syllable should be enunciated clearly and distinctly—not* with emphasis but with *distinctness*. Speakers who are thus accurate are seldom found, nevertheless there are such, and it is probable that when phonology

---

*For further illustrations of this subject, see "Plea for Phonetic Spelling."

shall have been generally taught the number will be increased; nay, more, good speech will come to be "a common heritage."

A word further in reference to elemental speech. "It is rare," says Mr. A. J. Ellis, whose authority is unquestioned on this subject, "to meet with a single elemental work which contains even a tolerably correct account of this important subject, and even scholars and professed teachers of pronunciation and elocution are generally very ignorant of the latter. Nay, more, the very teachers and best investigators of the subject are at variance. Let any one peruse the works of the greatest authorities we possess, those of Amman, Johannes Müller, Willis, Wheatstone, Lepsius, Max. Müller, Latham, etc., and he will see differences on fundamental points which are irreconcilable. If he turn to works of minor pretence, as Bell, Smart, Walker, Worcester, and the numerous works on elocution, he will find confusion partly arising from ignorance, and partly from a partial view of the subject. While in common grammars, and in the common treatises of travelers, and Pronouncing Vocabularies and Dictionaries, he will find that one person has copied from another without understanding him, till words are repeated and sense entirely lost."* So long as we have for guides the clumsy system of notation of Webster, the "obscure" vowel sounds of Worcester, and the common imperfect works on phonology, we may expect no better results. The remedy clearly is the *general introduction, into all our primary schools, of works based upon a strictly phonetic principle*, and in time there will be a total revolution and a harmony in pronunciation.

By the application, then, of the phonetic principle, that every distinct element in speech shall have its distinct symbolic exponent, to the representation of the pronunciation of geographical words, we have a work that at once combines the three things desirable, *simplicity*, *accuracy*, and *reliability*.

It may be urged in opposition, that the introduction of this without being accompanied or preceded by primary works will prove inexpedient, and, eventually, a failure. We reply that if this were the first work of the kind offered to the public there might be some ground for apprehension, but *phonotypy is a fixed fact;* and its promulgation for several years past, and its introduction into primary schools in different parts of the country as a means of teaching to read romanically, in the common print, and the generally increasing demand for teachers qualified to teach it, have wrought a complete change in our system of primary instruction, and stamp phonetics as an indispensable adjunct in teaching to read, and the knowledge of it a prerequisite to a qualified teacher. When, previous to the introduction of phonetics, did we hear of the first principles of language, the elemental sounds, being taught in schools? Or where were the teachers who were well acquainted with them? Even now, in many sections of the West and South, instructors as well as pupils are greatly deficient in this respect; but the light of the phonetic principle is opening their eyes; and whether it reach them directly through the phonotypic alphabet or by means of Charts of the Elementary sounds, newly arranged spelling books and readers, or some other channel, it matters not, they will soon all be

* Introduction to Phonetic Dictionary, p. xxiv.

theoretical phoneticians, and will not object to a philosophical alphabet for the representation of pronunciation in Dictionaries, Vocabularies, etc., if for no other purpose.

In regard to the availability of the Phonetic alphabet for teaching children to read the common spelling in shorter time and in a better manner, than by the ordinary method, the reader is referred to the Primer and Readers advertized at the close of this work, or for the philosophy of the fact, to the Introduction to the Phonetic Dictionary, by the same publishers.

The phonetic alphabet will be found on page 12, facing the first page of the Vocabulary, where, by examining the *key words* the sounds of the new letters will be readily learned, the old letters having the sounds they usually represent in the old spelling, which are also designated.

## PRONUNCIATION OF FOREIGN NAMES.

In accordance with the established custom of the best Geographers, we have given the pronunciation of the names of cities, towns, rivers, etc., as nearly as English mouths can speak them, as they are pronounced by the best educated people of the countries in which they are situated. To do this it has frequently been necessary to give two pronunciations, as the same printed word is often spoken differently in different countries; as, LIMA, *Lé-mq*, a province in Peru, but *Lį-ma*, towns in the United States; PARIS, *Pq-ré*, a city in France, but *Pár-is*, towns in this country.

In carrying out this plan we have been compelled to represent a few sounds not provided for in the English Phonetic Alphabet, because not heard in the English language. The most frequent is that of the German and Scotch *ch* and German *g* at the end of a syllable, which represent the same sound, namely, a strongly aspirated *h*, which we indicate by using the italic of that letter. Thus, METTERNICH, Mét-er-ni*h*; LOCHABER, Lo*h*-q́-ber; HAMBURG, Hq́m-burr*h*.

Next is the trilled *r*, which in French, German, and indeed most of the European languages, is often sounded more roughly, even, than in such English words as *crash*, *terror*, etc., which we indicate by the italic *r*. Thus, LIERRE, Lɛ-ą́*r*; PERNAU, Pẹ́*r*-nȣ.

The Welsh *l*, too, we represent by the italic of that letter, which may be called the whisper of the English vocal *l*, an approximation to which the reader may make by sounding *hl*. Thus, LLANELLY, *L*an-é*l*-ɛ.

Lastly, is the sign of the French orinasal vowels, or, as some phoneticians regard it, the whispered ŋ. It can only be produced by sounding some vowel through the nose and mouth at the same time, to do which is indicated by affixing the letter ṅ; thus, MONT BLANC, Mωṅ Bloṅ.

The French *u* or *eu* being very difficult to produce by English mouths, we have not attempted to represent it accurately, but give the nearest English approximation, namely ẹ́ as the vowel in *sir*, or *earth*, which is at least as near the proper sound as "*u* in *tub* or *fur*," which Baldwin gives.

# GENERAL PRINCIPLES OF PRONUNCIATION OF THE LEADING EUROPEAN LANGUAGES.

As a guide to the pronunciation of such unimportant names, or names that may hereafter come into sudden notoriety, as are not to be found in this book, we give the following rules, which are more specific, by far, than can be found in any ordinary dictionary. The letters in parentheses, in the Phonetic alphabet, have the sounds referred to immediately preceding.

*A.*—Always has the sound of *a* in the English word *arm*, (ɑ) in modern Greek, Italian, Norwegian, Polish, Portugese, Spanish, Swedish and usually Welsh.

In German it generally has the above sound, but when followed by *h* it frequently has the sound of *a* in *all*, (ɵ).

In Danish, in addition to the above, it sometimes has the sound of *a* in *at*, (a).

In French, its first sound is like *a* in *arm*, (ɑ); its second like the vowel in *at*, (a), with a circumflex, â, it is sounded very nearly like *a* in *all* (ɵ).

In Dutch, it is similar to the French.

In Hungarian, it is like *o* in *not*, (o); with an accent, á, like *a* in *arm*, (ɑ).

*E.*—In Danish is sounded like *i* in *ill*, (i), at the end of an accented syllable; in other situations like *e* in *ell*, (e), or like *ea* in *earth*, (ẹ).

The Norwegian is similar to the Danish.

In French, marked thus, é, it is sounded like *a* in *ale*, (a); thus, è, like *ea* in *pear*, or *ai* in *air*, (ą); thus, ê, like *e* in *very*, (e), and unmarked, like *u* in *up*, (u.)

In Dutch and Flemish, similar to the French.

In German, when long, it is like *a* in *ale* (a); it is, however, more frequently short like *e* in met, (e), and sometimes like *ea* in *earth*, (ẹ).

Swedish, the same as in German.

In Greek, (modern,) it has the sound of *a* in *ale*, (a).

In Hungarian, like *e* in *met*, (e); with an accent, é, more like *i* in *sir*, (ẹ).

In Italian it has two sounds, like *a* in *ale*, (a), and like *e* in *ell*.

In Polish, without an accent, like *e* in *ell*, (e); with an accent, é, like *a* in *ale*, (a).

In Portugese and Spanish, it is like *a* in *ale*, (a).

In Welsh, like *e* in *met*, (e); when circumflexed, è, like *ai* in *air*, (ą).

*I.*—In Portugese, Spanish and Polish is sounded like *ee* in *eel*, (ɛ).

In Danish, Dutch, Flemish, French, German, Greek, Hungarian, Italian, Norwegian, Swedish and Welsh, it has two sounds; first, as in *eel*, (ɛ), second as in *ill*, (i.)

O.—In Danish, Greek, Hungarian, Norwegian, Portugese and Spanish, is sounded as in English.

In French, Dutch, Flemish, German, Italian and Welsh, it has two sounds; first, as *o* in *note*, (ɷ), and second, as *o* in *rob*, (o).

In Polish, unaccented, like *o* in *note*, (ɷ), with an accent, like *oo* in *good*, (ɯ).

In Swedish, at the end of a syllable, it is like *oo* in *fool*, (ɷ); otherwise like *o* in *not*, (o.)

*U.*—In Danish, Hungarian, Italian, Norwegian, Polish, Portugese and Spanish, is sounded like *oo* in *fool*, (ꝏ).

The French sound of *u* is not heard in English. It seems to be an attempt to pronounce *ee* and *oo* at the same time. We have represented it in this work by the phonetic ẹ, which is, perhaps, the nearest approximation to the true sound English mouths can make, without much vocal teaching.

Greek and Dutch are similar to the French.

In German, *u* has two sounds, long like *oo* in *fool*, (ꝏ), short like *u* in *full*, (ɯ).

In Swedish we have represented *u* by the phonetic ꝏ, though this is not the exact sound.

In Welsh, the sound of *u* is like *i* in *ill*, (i), circumflexed, û as *ee* in *eel*, (ɛ).

*Y.*—In Danish and Swedish, is like the French *u*, (ẹ).

In Dutch and Flemish, like long *i* in English, (ị) in *ice*.

In French, German, Hungarian, (when a vowel) Portugese and Spanish, like *ee* in *eel*, (ɛ).

In Greek, when a consonant and before a vowel or a liquid sound, is like the English *v;* otherwise like *f*.

In Polish, like *i* in *ill*.

In Welsh, in a monosyllable or final syllable, as in *ill*, (i); in the penult or antipenult, like *u* in *up*, when circumflexed, like *ee* in *feet*, (ɛ).

*Aa.*—In Danish, sounds like *o* in *ope*, (ɷ).

*Ae.*—In Danish and German, like *a* in *ale*, (a).

In Dutch and Flemish, like *a* in *arm*, (ạ).

*Ai.*—In French and Greek, like *a* in *ale*, (a).

In German, Spanish and Italian, like *i* in *ice*, (ị).

*Au.*—In French, like *o* in *ope*, (ɷ).

In German, Italian and Spanish, like *ow* in *owl*, (ȣ).

*Ei.*—In French, sounds like *a* in *fate*, (a).

In German, like *i* in *ice*, (ị).

In Spanish, *ei* and *ey* are pronounced a-ɛ.

In Greek, like *ee* in *see*, (ɛ).

*Eu.*—In French, is the same as *u*, (ẹ́).

In German, it is sounded like *oi* in *oil*, (ơ).

*Ia.*—In French, is pronounced like *ia* in *medial*, (i-a).

*Ie.*—In Danish, Dutch, Flemish, French and German, sounds like *ee* in *see*, (ɛ).

*Oe.*—In Danish, German and Hungarian, has no English equivalent; the sound, however, approaches very near the phonetic ẹ.

In Dutch and Flemish, it sounds like *oo* in *food*, (ꝏ).

*Oi.*—In French, is nearly like *wa* in *was*, (wạ).

In Greek, like *ee* in *eel*, (ɛ).

*Oo.*—In Dutch, is like *o* in *ope*, (ɷ).

*Ou.*—In French, is like *oo* in *fool*, (ꝏ).

*Ua*, *ue*, *ui*, *uo* in French, and *ue* in German, are like the French *u*, (ẹ).

*Ui*, or *uy* in Dutch, sound like *oi* in *oil*, (ơ).

*Ão.*—In Portugese, are pronounced almost *owng*, (ȣŋ.)

☞ Nearly all of the letters in French are silent in different positions.

Most of the consonants are sounded as in English; the following are exceptions:

*B.*—In German, at the beginning of words as in English, but at the end of a word it is pronounced like *p.*
In Greek it is sounded as *v.*
In Spanish, between two vowels, it is sounded like *v* modified by *w.*

*C.*—In French, with a cedilla, ç, always has the sound of *s.*
In German, before *e, i* and *y,* like *ts.*
In Hungarian *c* is not used except in connection with some other consonant.
In Italian, *c* and *cc,* before *a, o* and *u,* are sounded as *k;* before *e, i* and *y* as *ch,* or *tsh,* (ꞔ);—*cc* and all double letters, more strongly than single *c,* followed by *e* or *i,* or *i* and another vowel, has the sound of *ch.*
In Spanish, before *e* and *i,* as *th* in *thin,* (ŧ).

*Ch.*—In French and Portugese, like *sh* in *shall,* (ʃ).
In German, like a strongly aspirated *h.*
In Italian, before *e* and *i,* like *k.*

*Cs.*—In Hungarian, is sounded like *ch* in *cheap,* (ꞔ).

*Cz.*—In Hungarian, like *ts;* in Polish like *ch,* (ꞔ).

*D.*—In Danish and Spanish, between two vowels, or at the end of a syllable following a vowel, is sounded like *th* in *this,* (đ).

*G.*—In Danish, at the end of a word, has the sound of *h.*
In Dutch, like a strongly aspirated *h.*
In German, except at the beginning of words, when it is always heard as in *go,* (g), it generally has the same sound as in Dutch.
In Spanish, before *e* and *i,* the same.
In French, before *e, i* and *y,* like *zh,* or *s* in *measure,* (ʒ).

*H.*—In German, is only pronounced when it begins a word.
In Italian it is never sounded.
In Portugese it is silent except when following *l* or *n,* when it becomes *y.*

*J.*—In French and Portugese, is like *zh,* (ʒ).
In Hungarian, like *ee.*
In Spanish like strongly aspirated *h.*
In the other languages like consonant *y.*

*Kj.*—In Swedish is sounded as *ch* in English.

*L.*—When it ends a word in French, preceded by *i,* it takes the sound of *y;* or when *ll* follows *i* in any position, the last *l* becomes *y.*
The same in Spanish.

*Ñ.*—In Spanish, or in Polish with an accent (*ń*), is sounded as *ny,* (consonant).

*Q,* and *qu,* in French and Portugese, are sounded as *k.*
In Spanish, *qu* before *e* and *i* is sounded as *k,* unless *u* be marked with a diæresis, in which case it is *kw.*

*R.*—In Danish, French, German, Hungarian, Italian, Polish, Portugese, and Spanish, has a stronger trill than in English.

*S.*—In French, between two vowels, has the sound of *z.*
In German, at the beginning of a word or between two vowels, it is like *z.*
In Hungarian, like *sh,* (ʃ).
In Polish, with an accent, (*ś*) like *sy* (consonant.)

*Sc.*—In Italian, before *e* and *i*, is like *sh*, (ʃ).
*Sch.*—In German, is like *sh*, (ʃ).
*Sz.*—In Hungarian, is like *s*.
In Polish, like *sh*, (ʃ).
*Th.*—In German, is pronounced like *t*.
*Ts*, and *ty* in Hungarian, are like *ch* in English, (ç).
*V.*—In German, except when betwen two vowels, has the sound of English *f*.
*W.*—In Danish, Dutch and German, is sounded very nearly like English *v*, except that the upper teeth should not touch the lower lip.
*X.*—In French, sometimes has the sound of *s* or *z*.
In Portugese, like *sh*, (ʃ).
In Spanish, like the strongly aspirated *h*.
*Z.*—In German, is sounded as *ts*.
In Polish, like *zh*, (ʒ).
In Italian, like *dz*.
*Zs.*—In Hungarian, is like *zh*, (ʒ).
*Zz.*—In Italian, is like *ts*.

ACCENT.—The French language cannot be said to have any accent, yet there is seemingly a stress of the voice on the last syllable in a word, and when any accent has been given in this work, it is on the last syllable. Great care should be taken, however, in not making so great a difference as in English, but to pronounce each syllable with such a force as will let each glide smoothly into that which follows it.

No rule can be given for the accent of the German words. And the same may be said of the Hungarian, yet with this difference, while the German names have a distinct accent, the Hungarian are distinguished by *quantity*. In Italian, Spanish and Portugese, words ending in a vowel are accented on the penult; Spanish words ending in a consonant are accented on the last syllable. Polish words or names of more than one syllable are always accented on the penult. Russian words are always accented on the last syllable. Welsh words are always accented either on the penult or the last syllable.

---

Of course, in the preparation of a work of this kind at the present day, there can be but little originality, and we have to acknowledge our indebtedness to most of the Gazetteers that have heretofore been published, not having relied exclusively upon any one.

The compiler also acknowledges valuable aid received from Mr. William Henry Smith, especially in the preparation of the list of Personal Names, to obtain the pronunciation of which was often attended with considerable investigation and trouble.

Conscious that there may be some blunders and inaccuracies in the pages thus prepared, for we have found many such in the most carefully compiled books we have consulted, we commend our labors to the leniency of those who may seek to be benefited by them, with the request that they will assist us in making it more perfect, by forwarding to the publishers a note of such errors as they may discover.

# CONTRACTIONS EMPLOYED IN THIS WORK.

As a general thing the contractions will suggest the reading intended. The populations of towns, cities and islands, are represented by figures and fractions that give the number of thousands; thus, 5½ immediately following any such name is to be read 5,500; but if a fraction only, then the population is only that portion of a thousand. In the sentence, "*l*, *càn* and *t* Switz., 7½," and similar ones, the figures apply only to the place last mentioned.

Abys. for Abyssinia.
Af. ...... Africa.
Afg. ..... Afghanistan.
Ala. ..... Alabama.
Am. .... America.
Ara. ..... Arabia.
Ark. ..... Arkansas.
Aus. ..... Austria.
Aust. .... Australia.
Ba. ...... Baden.
Bav. ..... Bavaria.
Bel. ...... Beloochistan.
Belg. ..... Belgium.
Ben. ..... Bengal.
Bo. ....... Bolivia.
Boh. ..... Bohemia.
Br. Ind. .. British India.
Bra. ...... Brazil.
Bur. ...... Burmah.
Cal. ...... California.
Can. ..... Canada.
Cen. Am. . Cen. America.
Chi. ...... China.
Con. .... Continent.
Conn. .... Connecticut.
Dal. ...... Dalmatia.
Dan. ..... Danish.
Del. ...... Delaware.
Den. ..... Denmark.
E. Ind. ... East India.
Ec. ...... Ecuador.
Eg. ...... Egypt.
Eng. ..... Eng.
Eu. ...... Europe.
Fa. ...... Florida.
Flan. ..... Flanders.
Fr. ...... France, French.
Ga. ...... Georgia.
Ger. ...... Germany.
Gr. *or* Gre. Greece.
Gr. Br. ... Great Britain.
Green. .... Greenland.
Gua. ..... Guinea.
Gui. ...... Guiana.
Han. ..... Hanover.
Hind. .... Hindoostan.
Hol. ...... Holland.
Hun. ..... Hungary.
Ia. ....... Indiana.
Ill. ....... Illinois.
Ind. ...... India, Indies.
Io. ....... Iowa.
Ir. ....... Ireland.
It. ....... Italy.

Ky. ...... Kentucky.
Ka. ...... Kansas.
Kam. .... Kamtchatka.
La. ...... Louisiana.
Lab. ..... Labrador.
Lap. .... Lapland.
L. I. ..... Long Island.
Lom. .... Lombardy.
Lux. .... Luxemburg.
Mad. .... Madagascar.
Mass. .... Massachusetts.
Md. ...... Maryland.
Me. ...... Maine.
Mex. .... Mexico.
Mi. ...... Mississippi.
Min. ..... Minnesota.
Mo. ...... Missouri.
Mt. ...... Mount.
N-B. .... N. Brunswick.
N. C. .... North Carolina.
N-H. .... N. Hampshire.
N-J. ..... New Jersey.
N-Y. ..... New York.
Neth. .... Netherlands.
Neb. ..... Nebraska.
N-Eng. ... New England.
N-Gra. ... New Granada.
N-Zeal. ... New Zealand.
N. W. .... North Wales.
Nor. ..... Norway.
Oc. ....... Ocean.
Oca. ...... Oceanica.
O. ........ Ohio.
Or. ....... Oregon.
Pa. ....... Pennsylvania.
Pac. ...... Pacific.
Pan. ...... Panama.
Par. ...... Paragua.
Pat. ...... Patagonia.
Per. ...... Persia.
Phil. ...... Philippine.
Po. ....... Poland.
Port. ...... Portugal.
Pru. ...... Prussia.
R. I. ...... Rhode Island.
Rus. ...... Russia.
Swe. ...... Sweden.
Swit. ..... Switzerland.
S. C. ..... S. Carolina.
Sp. ....... Spain.
Ter. ...... Territory.
Tenn. ..... Tennessee.
Tex. ...... Texas.
Tran. ..... Transylvania.

Trin. ..... Trinidad.
Tus. ...... Tuscany.
Tur. ...... Turkey.
U. S. ..... United States.
Va. ...... Virginia.
Vt. ....... Vermont.
Wis. ...... Wisconsin.
Yu. ...... Yucatan.
Zeal. ..... Zealand.

---

*anc* ....... ancient.
*b* ......... bay.
*ba* ........ bayou.
*bo* ........ borough.
*c* ......... city.
*cap* ....... capital.
*co* ........ county.
*com* ...... commercial.
*con* ....... continent.
*cr* ........ creek.
*cy* ........ country.
*dep* ....... department.
*dis* ....... district.
*fr* ........ free.
*ft* ........ feet.
*gar* ...... garrison.
*gov* ....... government.
*gr* ........ group.
*h* ......... houses.
*har* ...... harbor.
*i* ......... island.
*in* ........ inhabitants.
*ist* ....... isthmus.
*l* ......... lake.
*m* ........ mountain.
*mil* ...... military.
*nav* ..... navigable.
*p* or par .. parish.
*pen* ..... peninsula.
*p o* ..... post office.
*pop* ..... population.
*prin* ..... principality.
*prov* ..... province.
*r* ........ river.
*reg* ...... region.
*s-pt* ..... seaport.
*st* ........ strait.
s. m. ..... square miles.
*sub* ...... suburb.
*t* ........ town.
*ter* ...... territory.
*v* ........ village.
*val* ...... valley.
*vol* ...... volcano.

# PHONETIC ALPHABET OF THE ENGLISH LANGUAGE.

**Each letter has the sound of the *italicized* letter or letters in the illustrative words.**

| Letters. | Illustrative Words. | Name. |
|---|---|---|
| | *Long Vowels.* | |
| Ɛ ɛ | *ee*l | ɛ |
| E ẹ | *ea*rth | ẹ |
| Ⱥ a | *a*le | a |
| Ą ą | *ai*r | ą |
| Ɑ ɑ | *a*rms | ɑ |
| Θ θ | *a*ll | θ |
| Ω ω | *oa*k | ω |
| Ꙍ ꙍ | *oo*ze | ꙍ |
| | *Short Vowels.* | |
| I i | *i*ll | it |
| E e | *e*ll | et |
| A a | *a*m | at |
| Ɑ ɑ | *a*sk | ɑt |
| O o | *o*n | ot |
| U u | *u*p | ut |
| Ɯ ɯ | w*oo*d | ɯt |
| | *Diphthongs.* | |
| Ɨ ɨ | *i*ce | ɨ |
| Ɵ ɵ | *oi*l | ɵ |
| Ȣ ȣ | *ow*l | ȣ |
| Ʉ ʉ | d*u*pe | ʉ |
| | *Coalescents.* | |
| Y y | *y*ea | ya |
| W w | *w*ay | wa |
| | *Breathing.* | |
| H h | *h*ay | ha |

| Letters. | Illustrative Words. | Name. |
|---|---|---|
| | *Explodents.* | |
| P p | *p*ale | pɛ |
| B b | *b*ale | bɛ |
| T t | *t*ame | tɛ |
| D d | *d*ame | dɛ |
| Ȼ ç | *ch*eer | ça |
| J j | *j*eer | ja |
| K k | *k*ing, came | ka |
| G g | *g*ame | ga |
| | *Continuants.* | |
| F f | *f*ain | ef |
| V v | *v*ain | vɛ |
| Ƕ ŧ | *th*igh | iŧ |
| Ɖ đ | *th*y | đɛ |
| S s | *s*eal | es |
| Z z | *z*eal | zɛ |
| Σ ʃ | *sh*all | iʃ |
| Ʒ ʒ | vi*s*ion | ʒɛ |
| | *Liquids.* | |
| L l | *l*u*ll* | el |
| R r | *r*a*r*e | ɑr |
| | *Nasals.* | |
| M m | *m*ai*m* | am |
| N n | *n*i*n*e | en |
| Ŋ ŋ | si*ng* | iŋ |

☞ The marks of punctuation are the same as in the old orthography, excepting the following changes and additions: the mark of interrogation ¿ is placed before the first word in a sentence that indicates a query, ? at the end of a sentence indicates doubt, ‽ laughter, ! surprise. ¡ sorrow; the inverted ' signifies the omission of a letter.

## *Rules of Accent.*

1. Words of two syllables are accented on the first.

2. Words of three or more syllables are accented on the third from the end; *Unless* the last syllable *but one* contain a long vowel or dipthong, or the *last* syllable begin with *ʃ*, *ʒ*, or *y*,—in which case the accent falls on the last syllable but one.

Exceptions to these rules are marked with the sign ′ placed over the vowel to be accented.

Words wholly printed in capitals, and French words, (which have no regularly accented syllables,) are not thus marked.

# PRONOUNCING

# GEOGRAPHICAL VOCABULARY.

---

Aa, Ā-q, or Ā; contraction of old German *Ahha; rs* in Ger., Neth., Fr.
Aach, Āh, *t* and *r* Bad.
Aachen, Āh'en, See *Aix-la-Chapelle.*
Aagard, Ω'gqrd, *v* Den.
Aal, Ol or Θl, *t* Nor.
Aalborg, Ol'bωrg, *c* Den., 7½.
Aalesund, Ω'le-sωnd, *t* Nor.
Aalst, Ālst, *v* Neth., *t* Belg.
Aar, Ār, *r* Swit., *rs* G.
Aarau, Ā'rɤ, *t* Swit., 4¾.
Aarberg, Ār'berg, *t* Swit.
Aargau, Ār'gɤ, [Fr. Argovie, Ār-gω-vē,] *can* Swit.
Aarhuus, Or'hωs, *s-pt t* Den., 8.
Aaron, Ā'ron, *p* Fr.; -burg, *p o* N. Y.
Aasy, El, El-Ā'sε, *r* Syr.(See Orontes.)
Aath, or Ath, Āt, *t* Bel., 8¾.
Abacaxis, Ā-bq-kq-ʃéz, *r* Bra.
Abaco, Ā'bq-kω, Bahama island.
Abaite, Ā-bị-ta, *r* Bra.
Abakan, or Abakane, Ā-bq-kqn, *r* Si.
Abakansk, Ā-bq-kqnsk, *ft t* Si.
Abancay, Ā-bqn-kị, *t* Peru, 5.
Abanilla, Ā-bq-nél-yq, *t* Sp., 3¾.
Abano, Ā-bq-nω, *t* Lom., 2½.
Abany, A-bqny, *t* Hun. 7¾.
Abaran, Ā-bq-rqn, *c.* As. Rus.
Abasa, Ā-bq-sq, As. ter. sub. to Rus.
Abatis Villa, Latin of Abbeville.
Aba Uj Var, O-bó-ω-ε-vqr, dis. Up. Hun.
Abba-Jaret, or Abba-Yaret, Ā-bq-yq-ret, *m* Abys., 14,918.
Abbaye Point, Ab-á Pθnt, upper pen. of Mich.
Abbeokoota, Ā-bε-ω-kω-tq, or Abbekuta, Ā-bε-kω-tq, *t* W. Af., 50.
Abbeville, Āb-vél, *ft t* Fr., 19¼; Ab'ε-vil, *dis* and *t* S. C.; *vs* Ala., La.
Abbeyfeale, Ab-ε-fál, *p* and *v* Ir.
Abbeyleix, Ab-ε-lás, *p* and *t* Ir.
Abbeyville, Ab'ε-vil, *v* O.
Abbitibbe, or Abbitibbie, Ab-ε-tib-ε, *l, r, s* Brit. N. Am.
Abbotsford, Ab'ots-ford, Sir W. Scott's seat, Scot.
Abd-El-Curia, Ābd-el-kω-ri-q, or Abd-Ul-Kooree, or Kouri, *is* In. Oc.
Abenberg, Ā'ben-berg, *t* Bav.
Aberdeen, Ab-er-dén, *c* Scot., 41½; *ts* Miss., Ark., Tenn., O., Ind.
Aberdeenshire, Ab-er-dén-ʃεr, *co.* Scot.
Aberfeldie, Ab-er-fél-dε, *v* Scot.
Aberffraw, Ɛ-ber-frɤ, *s-pt* and *p* Wales.
Aberford, Ab'er-ford, *p* and *t* Eng.
Aberfoil, Ab-er-fθl, *p o* Ala.
Aberfoyle, Ab-er-fθl, *v* and *p* Scot.
Abergavenny, Ab-er-gá-nε, *t* Wales.
Abergeley, Ab-er-gé-lε, *t* Wales.
Abergwilly, Ab-er-gwiθ-lε, *p* Wales.
Aberlady, Ab-er-lá-di, *v* Scot.
Abernethy, Ab'er-neθ-i, *t* and *p* Scot., *v* Mo.
Abert, Ɛ'bert, *l* Oregon.
Aber-Ystwith, Ab-er-ist-wiθ, *bor* and *s-pt* Wales.
Abher, or Ebher, *t* Per.
Abilin, Ā-bε-lén, *v* Syr.
Abimes, Les, Laz Ā-bém, *t* Gaudeloupe.
Abingdon, Ab'iŋ-don, *bor* and *t* Eng.; *t* Va.; *vs* Md., Ill., Iowa.
Abington, Ab'iŋ-ton, *p* Eng.; *v* Scot.; *ts* Ill., Mass., Conn., Pa., Ind.
Abiquiu, Ā-bε-kε-ω, *t* N-Mex.
Abistada, Āb-is-tq-dq, *l* Afg.
Abkasia, Ab-kq-ʃi-q, Abasia, or Abascia, Ā-báʃ-i-q, *ter* Asia.
Abo, Ā'bω, *c* and *s-pt* Rus., 14.
Aboh, Ā'bω, Ibo, or Eboe, Ɛ'bω, *t* Af.
Aboite, A-bθt, *r* and *v* Ind.
Abomey, Ab-ω-má, *t* Af., 24.
Aboo-Arish, or Abu-Arisch, Ā'bω-q-riʃ, *t* Ar., 5.

Aboo-Girgeh, Abou-, *or* Abu-, A-bω-jír-je, *t* Eg.
Abookeer, *or* Aboukir, A-bω-kér, *b* and *v* Eg.
Aboolonia, A-bω-ló-ni-q, *v* and *l* As. Minor.
Abrantes, A-brq́n-tez, *ts* Port. and Brazil.
Abries, A-brε-á, *v* Fr.
Abrolhos, A-bról-yωs, rocky *is* Bra.
Abrud-Banya, Ob-rωd-bq́n-yo, *t* Transylvania.
Abruzzo, A-brót-sω, *prov* Naples.
Abscota, Ab-skó-ta, *p o* Mich.
Absecum, Ab-sé-kum, *or* Absecom, Absecombe, Absecon, *v* N. J.
Abydos, A-bí-dos, *c* As. Minor.
Abyssinia, Ab-i-sin-i-a, *cy* E. Af.
Acadia, A-ká-di-a, first name of Nova Scotia.
Acaponeta, A-kq-pω-ná-tq, *t* Mex.
Acapulco, A-kq-pól-kω, main *s-pt t* Mex., 5.
Acari, A-kq-ré, *t* Peru, 6.
Acarnania, Ak-qr-ná-ni-a, *dep* Greece.
Acra, Accra, *or* Accrah, A'krq, *cy* Af., belonging in pqrt to England.
Accumoli, A-kó-mω-lε, *t* Italy, 3¾.
Acebo, A-tá-bω, *v* Sp., 2⅓.
Acerenza, A-ça-rén-zq, *c* Naples, 3½.
Achaia, A-ká-yq, *or* A-kí-yq, *dep* Gr.
Acheen, Atcheen, Achen, Atchin, Atçén, *king* and *t* Sumatra.
Achelous, Ak-ε-ló-us, *r* Gr.
Achen, A'ḣen, *r* Bavaria.
Acheron, Ak'ε-ron, *r* ancient Greece.
Achill, Ak'il, (*or* Eagle Island,) *i* Ir.
Achor, Ak'or, *v* O.
Achtyrka, Aḣ-tír-kq, *r* and *t* Eu. Rus. 14¼.
Aci, *or* Aci Reale, A'çε-ra-q́-la, *t* and *s-pt* Sicily, 19¾.
Aconcagua, A'kon-kq́-gwq, *m* Chili, 23,910; *r*, *prov* and *t* Chili.
Acquackanonck, A-kwák-a-noŋk, *t* N. J., 3.
Acqui, A'kwε, *t* Piedmont, 7¾.
Acre, A'ker, *or* E'ker, *or* Akka, A'kq, *or* St. Jean D'Acre, Sań-ʒoń-dq́k-r, *c* and *s-pt* Syria, 10.
Actopan, Ak-tω-pq́n, *t* and *dis* Mex.
Aculco, A-kól-kω, *l* Chili.
Acworth, Ak'wurth, *vs* N-H., and Ga.
Ada, A'dq, *v* Mich.
Adafoodia, A-dq-fó-di-q, *t* W. Af., 24.
Adair, A-dq́r, *cos* Ky., Mo., Iowa.
Adaja, A-dq́-ḣq, *r* Sp.
Adalia, A-dq́-li-q, *or* Satalieh, Sq-tq́-li-ye, *g* and *s-pt* As. Min.
Adams, Ad'amz, *cos* in seven States; *tps* twenty-one; *vs* seven.
Adams, Mount, Ad'amz, Mσnt, *m* Or., near Colombia river.
Adana, A-dq́-nq, *c* Asia Minor, 10.
Adario, A-dq́-ri-ω, *p os* O., Wis.
Adda, A'dq, *r* nor. Italy; *prov* Af.
Addison, Ad'i-son, *vs* N-Y., Pa., &c.
Adelaide, Ad'ε-lad, *c* and *r* Australia.
Ad-el-Ji-vas, Ad-el-ji-vq́s, *t* As. Tur.
Aden, A'den, *or* E'den, *s-pt*. Ar., 20; cape and gulf.
Adenara, A-den-q́-rq, *i* Malay, Arch.
Aderno, A-dér-nω, *t* Sic., at foot of Mt. Etna, 6¾.
Adije, A'dε-ja, *r* nor. Italy 220.
Adirondack, Ad-i-rón-dak, *v* N. Y., 2000 feet above the sea; *ms*, highest, Tahawus, 5460 ft.
Adjyghur, Ad-jí-gúr, *t* Bengal.
Admiralty, Ad'mi-ral-ti, *b* S. Am.; *is* Rus. Am.; Pac. Oc.; N. Zeal.; *sound*, Terre del Fuego.
Adony, A-dóny, *t* Hun., on Danube, 3.
Adorf, A-dórf, *t* Sax., on Elster, 2¾.
Adour, A-dór, *r* Fr. 200.
Adowa, A'dω-wq, (*or* Adova,) cap. of Tigré, Abys., 8.
Adra, A'drq, *s-pt t* Sp., 7⅓.
Adramyti, A-drq-mé-ti, *s-pt t* Asia Minor, 5.
Adria, A'dri-q, *t* Lomb., 10.
Adrian, E'dri-an, *t* Mich., 4.
Adriance, E'dri-ans, *v* N. Y.
Adrianople, Ad-ri-an-ó-pl, *c* Eu. Tur. 160.
Adriatic, Ad-ri-át-ik, or Gulf of Venice, arm of Med. Sea, 500 m. long, 100 wide.
Adro, A'drω, *cap* Venetian Lom., 2¼.
Adur, E'dur, *r* Eng., 25.
Ægades, E'ga-dεz, *is* w. coast Sic.
Ægean, E-jé-an, sea, or Grecian Arch., part of Mediterranean, 400 by 200 m.
Ægina, Egina, E-jí-na, *or* Engia, En' ji-a, *i* Greece, 16; *t* 10; gulf 50 by 30.
Aeroe, E'rę-e, (*or* Arroe,) *i* Den., 10¾.
Aeroeskiobing, E'rę-es-kyę́-biŋ, *s-pt t* of above island.
Aerzen, Art'sen, *t* Hanover, 1.
Æthiopia, *or* Ethiopia, E-ti-ó-pi-a, countries s. of Eg.
Ætna, *or* Etna, Et'na, *vol* Sicily, 10¾ ft. above the sea.
Ætolia, E-tó-li-a, guv. of k. of Gr.
Afganistan, Af-gq́n-is-tq́n, cy. of Asia.
Afioom, Afioum, Afium, A-fi-óm, *or* Afium-Karahissar, -Kq-rq́-his-q́r, (Black-Castle of Opium,) *c* As. Min. 60.
Afragola, A-frq-gó-lq, *t* Naples, 13.
Africa, Af'ri-ka, great division of the globe, third in extent; 5,000 by 4,800 miles; pop. 60,000,000, speaking 150 languages.

Afrikiah, A-fré-ki-q, (*or* Mahadiah,) *s-pt t* Tunis.
Afshars, *or* Afschars, Af-ʃqrz, *tr* Per. 20,000 houses.
Agably, *or* Aghably, A-gq-blɛ, *t* Af.
Agadez, *or* -es, A'gq-dez, *c* Cen. Af., formerly 50 now 8.
Agamenticus, Ag-a-mén-ti-kus, *m* Maine.
Agate, Ag'at, Harbor, n. part Mich.
Agawam, Ag-a-wóm, *v* Mass.
Agawan, Ag-a-wón, *r* Mass.
Agdas, *or* Aghades. Same as Agades.
Agde, Agd, *t* Fr. 9.
Agen, A-ʒáṅ, *t* Fr. 16.
Aggershuus, Ag'erz-hɷz, *prov* Nor. 592½.
Aghmat, A*h*-mqt, *r* and *t* Morocco, 6.
Aghor, A*h*'or, (*or* Hingól) *r* Bel.
Aghrim, *or* Aughrim, Θg'rim, *p* Ir.
Agincourt, A-ʒáṅ-kɷr, (*or* Azincourt) *v* Fr.
Agio Strati, A'jɷ Strq-tɛ, *i* Gr. Arch.
Aglie, Al'ya, *or* Aglia, Al'yɑ, *t* Pied., 4⅓.
Agly, A-glé, *r* Fr.
Agno, An'yɷ, *r* Lomb., 50; *v* Swit.
Agnone, An-yó-na, *t* Naples, 7.
Agoa de Pao, A'gwq-da-pq-ɷṅ, *v* and *m* peak of the Azores.
Agogebic, A-gó-jɛ-bik, *l* n. part Mich.
Agogna, A-gón-yq, (*or* Gogna,) *r* Pied.
Agoona, A-gɷ́-nq, *st* w. part Af.
Agosta, A-gós-tq, *or* Augusta, Ɤ-gɷ́s-tq, *c* Sicily, 10.
Agows, A'gɤz, people of Abyssinia.
Agra, A'grq, *prov* Hind., 23,800,549; the city of the same name has been held by Eng., since 1803; pop. 96½.
Agram, Og-róm, (*or* Zagrab,) *cap* Croatia, Aus., 14¾.
Agreeb, Agrib, A-grèb *or* Agarrib, A-gq-réb, *m.* Eg. off gulf Suez. Can be seen 100 m.
Ague Caliente, A'gwq, Kq-lɛ-én-ta, *set* Cal.
Aguas Calientes, A'gwqs Kq-lɛ-én-tes, *st* Mex., 81¾; *c* 20.
Aguachapa, A-gwq-qq-pq, *t* Gua.
Aguadilla, A-gwq-dél-yq, *s-pt t* Antilles, Porto Rico.
Agua Dulce, A'gwq Dɷ́l-sa, *cr* Texas.
Agua Fria, A'gwq Fré-q, *v* N-Mex.; *t* and *cr* Cal.
Agua Nueva, A'gwq Nwá-vq,
Aguapehi, A-gwq-pa-hé, *r* Bra.
Agua, Volcan de, Vol-kqn-da A'gwq, *m.* Cen. Am.
Agueda, A-gá-đq, *r* Sp.
Aguila, A'gɛ-lq *or* Ag'wil-ɑ, *cr* Tex.

Ahanta, A-hqn-tq, *k* At.
Ahascragh, As'krq, *or* As'krq*h*, *t* and *p* Ir.
Ahmedabad, A'med-q-bqd, *dis* and *c* Hin., 100.
Ahmednuggur, A-med-núg-ur, *dis* and *c* Hin., 20.
Ahmood, A-mɷ́d, *t* Brit. Ind.
Ai, Ɨ, *p o* O.; *r* Rus.; *t* Fr.
Aidin, Ɨ-dén, (Iden *or* Guzzel-Hissar,) *t* As. Tur.
Aigash, Ɛ-gqʃ, *or* Aigas, Ɛ-gqs, *i* Scot.
Aigues Mortes, Ɛg'mort, *t* Fr. 4.
Aiguille, La-géy, *m* Fr.
Ain, Aṅ, *r* and *dep* Fr.
Aintab, Ɨn-tqb, *t* As. Tur., 20.
Air, Ar, *t* Pa.; *p o* Mo.
Airdrie, Ar'drɛ, *bor* and *t* Scot., 14½.
Aire, Ar, *t* Fr.; *r* Eng.
Aisne, Ɛn, *or* En, *r* and *dep* Fr.
Aitkin, Ɛt'kin, *l* and *ferry* Min.
Aix, Ɛks, *c* Fr., 27¼; *t* Sar.
Aixe, Ɛks, *t* Fr. 2¾.  m
Aix Ile d', Ɛl-dáks, *i* and *mil ft* and *vs* Fr.
Aix-La-Chapelle, Ɛks-lq-ʃq-pél, *c* of Prus., 45½.
Ajaccio, A-yqt-ɡɷ, *or* Ajazzo, A-yqt-sɷ, *s-pt* and *cap* Corsica, 11¾; Napoleon Bonaparte's birth place, 1769.
Ajan, A-ʒqn, country of Af.
Ajeho, Ɨ-ye-hó, *c* Mantchooria, 60.
Ajmeer, Aj-mér, (*or* Rajpootana) *prov* and *c* India, 25.
Akerman, A'ker-mqn, *t* Bessarabia, 26.
Akhalzikh, *or* Akalzik, A-*h*ql-zɛ*h*, *c* As. Rus., 10.
Ak-Hissar, Ak'his-a*r*, *t* As. Minor, 6.
Akootan, *or* Akutan, A-kɷ-tqn, *i* and *vol* Aleutian series.
Akowaay, A-kɷ-wj, *t* Guin., 8.
Akron, Ak'ron, *v* N-Y. *t* O., 4½.
Aksai, Ak-sj, *r* and *v* Circassia.
Akshehr, *or* Akscher, Ak-ʃá-her, *c* and *l* As. Tur.
Aksoo, *or* -ou, Ak-sɷ́, *t* and *r* Chinese Toorkistan.
Akstafa, Ak'stq-fq, *r* and *val* As. Geo.
Alabama, Al-a-bq-mɑ, Am. *st* 50,772 s. m.; pop., in 1850, 426½ whites, 2¼ free blacks, 342¾ slaves, total, 771¾; representative pop., 634½; *cap* Mobile; *r* navigable 460 m.
Alabama, (*or* Big Sandy Creek) and *v* Texas.
Alachua, A-láq-q-ɑ, *co* in Florida.
Alacrane, Al-a-krán, *is* Gulf Mex.
Alaculsa, Al-a-kúl-sɑ, *cr* Ga.
Ala-Dagh, A'lq-dqg, *m* As. Tur.
Alaghez, A-lq-géz, (*or* Ali-) *vol m* Arm.

Alagoa, Ȧ-lạ-gṓ-ạ, *t* and *dis* island St. Michael.
Alagoas, Ȧ-lạ-gṓ-ạs, *prov* Bra., 220; *c* 4.
Alagon, Ȧ-lạ-gṓn, *r* Sp., 120.
Alais, Ȧ-lá, *t.* Fr. 18¾.
Alajuela, Ȧ-lạ-hœ-á-lạ, *c* Costa Rica, 10.
Alamance, (*or* Alle-) Ȧ'la-mans, *cr* and *co* N. C.
Alameda, Ȧ-lạ-má-dạ, *t* Sp.; *co* Cal.; *t* N-Mex. [*ft.* Tex.
Alamo, Al'a-mœ, *v* Ia., Mich., Cal.;
Alamos, Los, Lœs Ȧ'lạ-mœs, *t* Mex. 10.
Alan, Al'an, (*or* Camel) *r* Eng.
Aland, Ȧ'land, *or* Oland, Ȯ'land, eighty islands Gulf Bothina, 15.
Alapaha, A-láp-a-he, *v* and *r* Ga., 100 m.
Alaqua, Al'a-kwe, *v* and *r* Florida.
Alasea, Ȧ-lạ-sá-ạ, (*or* Alasey, -ej) *r* Sib.
Ala-Shehr, Ȧ-lạ́-ʃẹr, *or* Ala-Schehr, Ȧ-lạ-ʃá-her, *c* As. Mi., 15.
Alaska, *or* Aliaska, Ȧl-yạ́s-kạ, *pen* Rus. Am.
Alatamaha. See Altamaha.
Alausi, Ȧ-lɤ-sé, *vol* Andes, *t* Ecuador.
Alava, A-lạ́-vạ, *prov* n. part Sp.
Alba, Ȧl'bạ, *ts* Pied., Nap.; Al'ba *t* Pa.
Alba Longa. See Albano.
Albania, Al-bá-ni-a, [*Turk.* Arnaoodlik, -tleck, -outlik,] country Eu. Tur., 1,600,000.
Albano, Ȧl-bạ́-nœ, *c* It. 5½; *t* Nap.; *l* and *m* It.
Albany, Ɵl'ba-ni, *co* and *cap* N-Y., 60; *r ft* and *dis* Br. N. Am.; div. Cape of Good Hope; *ts* Ga., Ill., and *vs* in many states.
Albay, Ȧl-bj, *v* and *t* Philippine Is., 13.
Albemarle, Al-bɛ-mạ́rl, *t Fr.*; *co* Va.; —Sound, N. E. part N. C.
Alberche, Ȧl-bạ́*r*-ꞔa, *r* Sp. 148 m.
Alberes, Ȧl-bạ́r, *ms* part of Pyrenees.
Albia, Al'bi-a, *co t* Iowa.
Albion, Al'bi-on, anc. name Gr. Britain; *co ts* N-Y., Ia., Ill., and numerous *vs.*
Albuera, Al-bœ-á-rạ, *r* Sp.
Albufeira, Ȧl-bœ-fá-ɛ-rạ, *s-pt* Port.
Albufera, Ȧl-bœ-fá-rạ, *l* Sp.
Albuquerque, Ȧl-bœ-ké*r*-ka, *t* N-Mex. *is* Car. Sea.
Alburg, Ɵl'burg, *p o;* -Springs, Vt.
Alby, *or* Alby, Ȧl'bɛ, *or* Ȧl-bé, *c* Fr., where, on account of the religious wars, the Protestants received the name of *Albigenses.* 13¾.
Albyn, *or* Albinn, Ȧl'bɛn, anc. name Sc.
Alcala de Henares, Ȧl-kạ-lạ́-da En-ạ́-res, *c* Sp., in 1768, 22, now 3½; —la-Real, lạ-Ra-ạ́l, *c* Sp. 11½.

Alcamo, Ȧl'kạ-mœ, *t* Sic. 15.
Alcantara, Ȧl-kạ́n-tạ-rạ, *ft t* Sp.; *r* Sic.; *t* Bra.
Alcaraz, Ȧl-kạ-rạ́ŧ, *t* Sp. 7¼.
Alcazar, (*or* Alcacer) de San Juan, Ȧl-kạ́-ŧer da Sạn-hœ-ạ́n, *t* Sp., 7½.
Alcester, (*or* Awlster) Ɵl'ster, *t* Eng. 2¼.
Alcona, Al-kṓ-na, *co* Mich.
Alcovy, Al'kœ-vi, *r* Ga. (Ulcofauhachee.
Alcoy, Ȧl-kṓ-ɛ, *t* Sp., 27; also *r.*
Aldan, Ȧl-dạ́n, *r* 300, and *ms* Siberia.
Aldborough, (*or* Aldburg) Ɵld'bur-œ, *s-pt t* Eng., 1½; also, market *t* 2½.
Alde, Ɵld, *r* Eng.
Alden, Ɵl'den, *t* N-Y. 2½; *v* Ill.
Aldenville, Aldenbrook, and similar combinations, have the first syllable pronounced alike.
Alderney, (*or* Aurigny,) Ɵl'der-ni, *i* Eng. Channel, 1.
Aldstone, Ɵld'ston, (*or* Alston-Moor) *t* Eng. [Port.
Alemtejo, (*or* -en) Ȧ-loṅ-tá-ʒœ, *prov*
Alençon, Ȧ-loṅ-sṓṅ, *c* Fr. 14¾.
Aleppo, A-lép-œ, (Haleb *or* Haleb es Shabba) *c* As. Tur.; prev. to earthquake 1822, pop. 200, now 60 to 80.
Alessandria, Ȧ-les-ạ́n-dri-ạ, *c* Piedmont, 19, with suburbs 40.
Aleutian, A-lụ́-ʃi-an, *is* (volcanic) Rus. Am.
Alexander, Al-eks-án-der, various *cos* and *ts* U. S.
Alexandria, Al-eks-án-dri-a, *s-pt c* Eg.; before the war with Cæsar, and the burning of the libraries, its population was 600,000 when it went down to 6,000; it has now 80,000.
Alexandria, *c* Va., 8¾; various *ts* and *vs* U. S.
Alford, Ɵl'ford, *t* Eng., 2.
Alfordsville, Ɵl'fordz-vil, *ts* N. C., Ia.
Alfred, Al'fred, *ts* and *vs* Me., O., N-Y., &c.
Alfreton, Al'frɛ-ton. *t* Eng., 8¼.
Algarve, (*or* -bia) Ȧl-gá*r*-va, *prov* Port.
Algeciras, (*or* -zi,) Al-jez-é-ras, [Sp. Ȧl-*ha*-ŧé-ras,] *s-pt t* Sp., 11.
Algeria, Al-jé-ri-a, [Fr. Ȧl-ʒa-ré] *ter* Nor. Af., Fr. colonial province; 90,000 s. m.; native pop. 2 mil.; European, 119¼.
Algiers, Ȧl-jérz, *cap.* Algeria, 94½, half European; *v* op. N-Orleans, La.
Algoa, Al-gṓ-a, *b* S. E. coast Af.
Algoma, Al-gṓ-ma, *v* Wis.
Algonac, Al-gœ-nák, *t* Mich.

Algonquin, Al-gón-kwɛn, Am. Indians nearly extinct; *vs* O., Mich., Ill.
Alhama, Al-hq́-mq, *t* Sp., 6.
Alhambra, Al-hám-brɑ, *v* Ill.
Aliaska, Al-yq́s-kq, *pen* Rus. Am.
Alicante, A-lɛ-kq́n-ta, *prov* and *s-pt c* Sp., 19.
Alicata, (*or* Licata) A-lɛ-kq́-tq, *s-pt t* Sic., 13½.
Alicudi, A-lɛ-kó-dɛ, w. Lipari Islands, 1.
Alida, A-li-dɑ, *t* Ill.
Alipee, A-li-pé, *s-pt t* Hin. 13.
Alixan, A-liks-óṅ, *v* Fr., 2½.
Alkaisareeyeh, (*or* -seria) Al-ki-ser-ɛ-ye, *t* Mor. 8.
Alkmaar (*or* -maer) Alk-mq́r, *t* Hol., 9.
Alkosh, Al-kóʃ *ft t* As. Tur., 3.
Allahabad, A-lq-hq́-bq́d, *t* Hin., in 1832, 64¾.
Allaire, A-lq́r, *v* Fr., 2.
Allamuchy, (*or* -chee) Al-a-mó-qi, *v* N-J.
Allan, Al'an, two *rs* Scot.
Alle, A'lɛ, *r* East Prus., 115.
Allegan, Al'ɛ-gan, *co* and *v* Mich.
Alleghany,* Al-ɛ-gá-ni, *r* Pa.; range *ms* Pa., Md., Va.; *cos* Pa., N-Y., Md., Va.; *vs* N-Y., and Pa.
Alleghany City, opposite Pittsburg, Pa., 21¼.
Allen, Al'en, numerous *cos* and *ts* in the U. S., with various combinations.
Allentown, the most prominent, *co t* Pa., 6.
Alliance, A-li-ans, *t* O.
Allier, A-lɛ-á, *r* Fr., 260 m.
Alligator, Al-i-gá-tor, *r* N. C.; *t* Fa.
Allisonia, Al-i-só-ni-ɑ, *t* Tenn.
Alloa, Al'ɷ-ɑ, *s-pt t* Scot., 5½.
Allomakee, Al-ɷ-ma-ké, *co* Iowa.
Alloway, Al'ɷ-wa, *v* N-Y.
All-Saints Bay, Θl-Sants Ba, on the coast of Brazil.
Alma, Al'mq, *r* Rus., in the Crimea.
Almaden, Al-mq-dén, *t* Sp., 8½.
Almagro, Al-mq́-grɷ, *c* Sp., 12½.
Almalee, (*or* -li) Al-mq-lé, *t* As. Tur. 20.
Almas, Ol'moʃ, *t* Hun, 8½.
Almazarron, Al-mq-tq-rón, *t* Sp., 6¾.
Almeida, Al-má-ɛ-dq, *ft t* Por., 6¼; *t* Bra., 4.
Almeria, Al-ma-ré-q, *s-pt c* Sp., 17¾.
Almond, A'mond, two *rs* Scot.; *vs* N-Y., Ala., Wis.
Almont, Al-mónt, *v* Mich.
Alne, Aln, three *rs* Eng.
Alnwick, *or* Alenwick, An'ik, *t* Eng., 7½.
Alost, A'lost, *t* Bel., 15.
Alpena, Al-pé-nɑ, *co* Mich.
Alps, Alps, *m* Eu.; extending through part of Swit., Fr., It., Bav., Aus., and Tur., varying from 10,000 to 15,800 ft. in height.
Alsace, Al-sq́s, one of the old German prov., ceded to France 1648.
Alsen, Al'sen, *is* Den., in the Baltic 22½.
Alstead, Al'sted, *t* New Hampshire.
Alsten, Al'sten, *i* Norway.
Alster, Al'ster, *r* Den.
Altai, Al-ti, *m* Sib., rich in gold, silver, copper, &c.
Altamaha, Θl'ta-ma-hé, *r* Geo., navigable 140 miles.
Altamira, Al-tq-mé-rq, *t* Mex.
Altamont, Al'ta-mont, *v* Ten.
Altamura, Al-tq-mó-rq, *t* Naples, 16.
Altenburg, Al'ten-bɷrg, duchy and *c* Ger., 13½.
Alton, Al'ton, *t* Eng., 3¼; *c* Ill., 4; *ts* Maine, N-H., N-Y., Tex., O., Mich.
Altona, Al'tɷ-nɑ, (*or* Altena,) second *c* Den., 37.
Altoona, Al-tó-nɑ, *v* Pen., 2½.
Altorf, Al'torf, (*or* Altdorf,) *t* Swit.
Alvarado, Al-vq-rq́-dɷ, *t* and *r* Mex.
Alzey, Alt'si, *t* Hesse Darmstadt, 4½.
Amacura, A-mq-kó-rq, *r* S. Am.
Amager, A'mq-ger, (*or* Amak,) *i* Den.
Amalfi, A-mq́l-fɛ, *c* and *s-pt* Naples, pop. once, 50 now 4.
Amambahi, A-mqm-bq-é, *or* Amambay, A-mqm-bi, *m* and *r* S. Am.
Amanda, A-mán-dɑ, various *ts* and *vs* U. S.
Amarante, A-mq-rq́n-ta, *t* Port., 4.
Amarapoora, Amarapura, Am-q-ra-pó-ra, *ft c* Burm., in 1800 175; now much reduced.
Amasia, Amasieh, *or* Amasiyah, A-mq́-sɛ-ɑ, *c* As. Min., 25.
Amatitlan, A-mq-tɛ-tlq́n, *or* Amititan, A-mq-tɛ-tq́n, *t* Gua. 12.
Amaxichi, A-mqks-é-kɛ, *s-pt t* Ionian Island, Santa Maura, 6.
Amazon, Am'a-zon, largest *r* not only of S. Am., but of the globe; length 4000 miles; breadth of the largest mouth, 96 miles; but the two, with the island included, cover a width of 250 m.; *v* Ill.
Ambato, Am-bq́-tɷ, (*or* Hambato,) *t* Ec., 12.

---

* All considerate persons will unite with the editors of Lippincott's Gazeteer in giving but one orthography to this name.

Amberg, Ām'berg, *t* Bav., 11.
Ambert, Oṅ-bąr, *t* Fr., 8¼.
Amboise, Oṅ-bwąz, *t* Fr., 4¾.
Amboy, Am-bó, various *vs* U. S.
Amboyna, *or* Amboina, Ām-bó-na, *i* Malay Arch., 29½; *cap t* 8¾.
Ambriz, Am'briz, *or* Ām-bréz, ind. Negro kingdom Af.
Ambrosia, Am-bró-ʒi-a, *p o* Iowa.
Amelia, A-mé-li-a, *t* and *co* Vir., *v* O.
Amenia, A-mé-ni-a, *v* N-Y.
America, A-mér-i-ka, with the exception of Asia, the largest division of the globe. — North, entire coast line 22,800 m; area 8,000,000 s. m.; divided into six political organizations, viz., Danish America or Greenland; Brit. Am., Rus. Am., U. S., Mex., and Cen. Am.; entire pop., in 1854, exceeded 40,000,000. — Central, is the narrow strip of land uniting North and South Am.; length 800 or 900 m.; its breadth from 20 to 400 m.; area 200,000 s. m.; the states of Gua., San Sal., Hon., Nic., and Costa Rica, though nominally republican, are ruled by military despots; total pop. 2,146,000. — South, is a vast peninsula, of about 6,500,000 s. m.; comprising the republics of N. Gran., Ven., Ec.; Brit., Fr., and D., Gui.; Pe., Bol., Ch., the United Prov. of La Plata, Par., Ura., Bra., Pat., Ter. del Fue., the Falk. and other islands; entire pop. 16,000,000. *r* central Cal.
Americus, A-mér-i-kus, *vs* Geo., Ind.
Amersfort, *or* Amersfoort, Ā'mers-fort, *t* Neth., 13.
Ames, Āmz, *v* N-Y.
Amga, Ām-gą, *r* Si., 460 m.
Amhara, Ām-hą-rą, *k* Abys.
Amherst, Am'erst, *s-pt t* Brit. Ind., 5.; *co* and *t* Vir., *ts* Me., N-H., Mass., (seat of Amherst College,) 3.; *v* O.
Amhertsburgh, Am'erst-burg, *gar t* C. W., 1⅓.
Amicalola, A-mik-a-ló-la, *p o* Geo.
Amicu, Ā-me-kó, *or* Amucu, Ā-mo-kó, *l* South Am.
Amiens, Ā-me-áṅ, *t* Fr., 52¼.
Amite, Am-ét, *r* Miss., Lou., *co* Miss.
Amity, Am'i-ti, various *vs* U. S.
Amlwch, Am'lok, *s-pt t* N. W.
Ammer, *or* Amper, Ām'per, *r* Ger.
Ammonoosuck, Am-o-nó-suk, upper and lower, *r* N-H.
Amol, Ā-mól, *c* Per., 35 to 40.
Amoo, Amou, *or* Amu, Ā-mó, *r* Cen. As., 1300 m.
Amoor, Amour, Amur, Ā-mór, *r* E. As., 2200 m.
Amorgos, *or* Amorgo, Ā-mór-go, *i* Gre. Arch., 2¾.
Amoskeag, Am-os-kég, *v* N-H.
Amoy, Ā-mó, (*or* Emoui,) *s-pt t* China, pop. 250.
Amphila, Ām-fé-la, *b* and *i* Red Sea.
Amphitrite, Am-fi-trį-te, *is* China Sea.
Amrawutti, Ām-ra-wút-e, *or* Amaravati, Ām-a-ra-vą-te, *t*. Ind.
Amritseer, Amritsir, Ām-rit-sér, *c* of Punjab, Hind., 115.
Amsterdam, Ām-ster-dąm, *c*, *cap* Hol., 228¾; *v* N-Y., Vir., O., Ia., Iowa.
Anabara, Ā-nq-bq-rą, *r* Si. 400 m.
Anachuana, Ā-nq-ço-ą-nq, *v* and *b* Isthmus of Panama.
Anacoca, An-a-kó-ka, *p o* La.
Anacostia, An-a-kós-ti-a, *p o* Dis. Col.
Anadarco, An-a-dąr-ko, *p o* Tex.
Anadeer, Anadir, *or* Anadyr, Ā-nq-dér, *r* N. E. Asia, in Siberia.
Anagni, Ā-nąn-ye, *t* It.
Anagua, Ā-ną-gwq, *p o* Tex.
Anahuac, Ān-q-wąk, *table-land*, *m* and *v* Tex.
Anam *or* Annam, Ā-nąm, Empire of Cochin China, pop. 12,000,000.
Anamaboe, Ā-nq-ma-bó, Brit. *ft* Af., 4½.
Anamirapucu, Ā-nq-mi-rq-po-kó, *r* Bra., 200 m.
Anamosa, An-a-mó-sa, *v* Iowa.
Anandale, An'an-dal, *vs* Pen., Vir.
Anapa, Ā-nq-pą, *s-pt t* Russian Cir.
Anaquasscook, An-a-kq-ás-kuk, *p o* N-Y. [Fa.
Anastasia, An-a-stá-ʃi-a, *i* e. coast
Anatolia, Ān-a-tó-li-a, *or* Anadolia, Ā-nq-dó-li-a, (written also Anadoli and Natolia,) *pen.*; pashalic of Tur. in As., identical with Asia Minor, area 270,000 sq. m.; pop. 4,500,000.
Anava, Ā-nq-vą, *or* Guanahau, Gwq-nq-hą, *r* Brazil, 200 m.
Anazo, Ā-ną-zo, (*or* Hanazo,) *r* Abys.
Ancach, Ān-kąç, *dep* North Peru.
Ancaster, An'kas-ter, *v* Canada West.
Ancholme, An'çolm, *r* Eng.
Anchor, Aŋ'kor, *i* N-Zeal.; *is* Bra.
Ancober, An-kó-ber, *r* Af.; *t* Abys.
Ancona, Ān-kó-nq, a free port *c* Papal States, in two parts, Citta Vechia, (Ci-tą Vék-i-q,) Citta Nuova, (Ci-tą Nwó-vq;) pop. 36.
Andalusia, An-da-lų-ʃi-a, (Sp. Andalucia, Ān-dq-lo-té-a,) division of the s. of Spain; *vs* Penn., Ala., Ten., Illinois.

Andaman, An-da-mán, *i* Bay of Ben.
Andaya, Ȧn-dą́-yą, *or* Andaia, Ȧn-dį́-ą, *r* Bra., 120 m.
Andelle, Oṅ-dél, *r* Fr.
Andelys, Les, Laz-oṅ-dlé, *t* Fr. 5¼.
Anderson, An'der-son, *dis* S. C.; *cos* Tex., Ten., Ken.; *vs* N-J., S. C., Geo., Tex., Ill.; *t* Ia.
Andersonville, An'der-son-vil, *vs* S. C., [Ia.
Andes, An'diz, range of *ms* extending parallel to the Pacific coast, the entire length of S. A., 4500 miles; and under different names, traverses the whole N. American continent, about 9000 m.; the ridges and peaks varying from 2 to 22,000 ft. above the sea.
Andkhoo, Ȧnd-kó, Ankkoui, Ȧn-kó-ɛ, (*or* Ankoi,) *t* ind. Tartary, 25.
Andorra, Ȧn-dór-ą, (Valley of) *ind cy*, a republic on the s. slope of the Pyrenees, pop. 6; *t*, *cap* of the above, 2¾.
Andover, An'dɷ-ver, *t* Eng.; *vs* Maine, N-H., Ver., Mass., 7; Con., N-Y., N-J., O., Mich., Ill.
Andraix, Ȧn-drą́-ɛ*h*, *s-pt t* island of Majorca, 4¾.
Andreeva, Ȧn-dra-e-vą́, *t* Rus., 12.
Andrew, An'drɷ, *co* Mo.; *v* Iowa.
Andro, Ȧn'drɷ, (*or* An'dros,) *i* Gre. Arch., 15¼.
Androscoggin, An-dros-kóg-in, *r* N-H., Maine; *co* Maine. [Sp., 9⅓.
Andujar, *or* Anduxar, Ȧn-dó-*h*ar, *t*
Anegada, Ȧ-na-gą́-da, *t* of the Antilles.
Angara, Ȧŋ-gą-rą́, *r* of Siberia, 1000.
Angelica, An-jél-i-ka, *co t* N-Y.
Angelina, An-je-lé-na, *r* and *co* Tex.
Angermann, Oŋ'er-man, *nav r* Swed., 120 m. [Swed.
Angermannland, Oŋ'er-mąn-ląnd, *prov*
Angermunde, Ȧŋ'er-men-de, *t* Prus., 4⅓.
Angerona, An-jɛ-ró-na, *p o* Va.
Angers, An'jerz, (Fr. Angiers, Oṅ-ʒá,) *ft c* Fr., 46½.
Anglesey, *or* Anglesea, Ȧŋ'gl-sɛ, *i* N. W., 51.
Angola, Aŋ-gó-la, *cy* w. coast of Africa, notorious for its slave trade: pop. 2,000,000; *p os* N-Y., Del., N-C., Ia.
Angora, Aŋ-gó-ra, *t* As. Tur., 35.
Angornou, *or* Angornu, Ȧn-gor-nó, *t* Cen. Africa, 30.
Angosta, Ȧn-gós-ta, *dis*, *r* and three *i* s. e. of Africa.
Angostura, Ȧn-gos-tó-rą, (*or* Bolivar City) *t* Venezuela, 8½.
Angouleme, Oṅ-gɷ-lám, *c* Fr., 21⅙.
Angra, Ȧn'grą, *s-pt t* of Port., on the island of Terceira, 10.
Angrab, Ȧn-grą́b, *r* Abys., 120 m.
Angra dos Reis, Ȧŋ'grą-dɷs-rá-ɛs, *s-pt* and *b* Brazil, 3.
Anguilla, Ȧn-gé-lą, *i* Br. West Ind., 3.
Anhalt, Ȧn'hąlt, three duchies Central Germany.
Anhanduhy-Mirim, Ȧn-yąn-dɷ-é-mi-rɛṅ, two rivers in Brazil.
Anholt, Ȧn'holt, *i* Den., *t* Prus., 2.
Aniooy, Ȧ-ni-ó-ɛ, *or* Aniuj, Aniuy, Ȧn-yó-ɛ, two rivers in Siberia.
Anklam, *or* Anclam, Ȧn'kląm, *t* Pr. 8½. [Abys., 12.
Ankober, (*or* Ankobar,) Ȧn-kó-ber, *t*
Ankova, Ȧn-kó-vą, *k* Madagascar.
Annaberg, Ȧ'ną-be*rg*, *t* Saxony, 6¾.
Annagh, Ȧ-ną́, two islands Ireland.
Annan, An'an, *r* and *s-pt* Scot.
Annapolis, An-áp-ɷ-lis, *cap* Md., 3; *vs* O., Ia.; *r* and *ft s-pt t* Nova Scotia.
Ann Arbor, An-ą́r-bor, *c* Mich., 4¾.
Annawaika, An-a-wį́-ka, *p o* Ala.
Anne Arundel, An-a-rún-del, *co* Md.
Annecy, Ȧn-sé, *t* and *l* Savoy.
Annisquam, An-is-gwą́m, *p o* Mass.
Annobon, Ȧ-nɷ-bón, *i* w. coast of Af.
Annonay, Ȧ-nɷ-ná, *t* Fr., 13¼.
Anoka, A-nó-ka, *v* Minnesota.
Anselm, An'selm, *p o* O.
Anson, An'son, *co* N. C.
Ansonia, An-só-ni-a, *v* Conn.
Anspach, Ȧn'spą*h*, *ft c* Bavaria, 16.
Antang, Ȧn-tą́ŋ, *v* and *dis* isl. Java, 10.
Antarctic, Ant-ą́rk-tic, *oc*, the expanse of water around the South Pole.
Antequera, Ȧn-ta-ká-rą, *c* Sp., 17.
Anthony, An'tɷ-ni, *p os* R. I., Ia.
Antibes, Oṅ-téb, *ft s-pt t* Fr., 6⅛.
Anticosti, An-ti-kós-ti, *des i* C. E.
Antietam, An-té-tam, *cr* Penn.
Antigua, Ȧn-té-gą, Brit. W. I. Island, 36; *station*, *ft* and *arch* in the Philippine Islands.
Antilles, Ȧn-tél, West India Islands.
Antioch, An'ti-ok, *c* and *anc cap* Syria, the place where the name of *Christians* was first given to the followers of Jesus Christ. Founded 300 B. C. Ancient pop., 400,000, time of Chrysostrom, 200,000, at present, 10,000; *vs* S. C., Ga., Ala., Tenn., O., Ill.
Antioch College. See Yellow Springs.
Antioco, Ȧn-té-ɷ-kɷ, *i* Med., 2¼.
Antioquia, Ȧn-ti-ɷ-ké-a, *t* S. Am. 4.
Antipodes, An-típ-ɷ-dɛz, *i* S. Pac. Oc.
Antisana, Ȧn-ti-są́-ną, *vol* in Ecuador, 19,140 feet high.
Antivari, Ȧn-té-vą-rɛ, *t s-pt* of Albania.

Antoin, An-tŏn, *p o* Arkansas.
Antrim, An'trim, *cos* Ir., Mich.; *vs* N-H., Penn., O., Mich.
Antuco, Ä-tó-kō, *vol* (16,000 ft) and *val* of Chilian Andes.
Antwerp, Ant'wẹrp, *ft c* Belgium, 79; *prov* do.; *vs* N-Y., O.
Aonia, Ā-ó-ni-a, *p o* Ga.
Aosta, Ä-ós-tä, *t* Pied., 7.
Apache Indians, Ä-pä-ça In'di-anz, Texas and N-Mexico.
Apennines, Ap'en-īnz, a mountain chain traversing the Italian peninsula, 800 miles, embracing Mounts Albano, Vesuvius and Etna.
Apollonia, Ä-pol-ó-ni-ä, (*or* Amanahea,) *dis, cape* and *fort* Africa.
Apostles' Islands, A-pós-lz Ī'landz, Straits of Magellan.
Appalachee, Ap-a-lä-çē, *r* Ga.; *b* Fa.
Appalachian, Ap-a-lá-çi-an, the Alleghany Mountains.
Appalachicola, Ap-a-laç-ïē-kó-la, *r, b* and *t* Fa.
Appalachin, Ap-a-lä-çin, *p o* N-Y.
Appanoose, Ap-a-nōs, *co* Iowa; *v* Ill.
Appenzell, Ä-pent-sél, *can* and *t* Swit.; *cap* Inner Rhodes, 3.
Appleby, Ap'l-bi, *bor* and *t* Eng., 2½.
Appleton, Ap'l-ton, *vs* O., Ill., Wis.
Appling, Ap'liŋ, *co* Ga.; *vs* N-Y., Ga.
Appomattox, Ap-ō-mát-oks, *co* and *r* Va., 150 m.
Appoquinnimink, Ap-ō-kwin-i-miŋk, *cr* Del.
Apsheron, Äp-ʃa-rón, (*or* Abcheron,) *pen* Russian dominions.
Apulia, Ä-pū-li-a, *anc prov* Southern Italy; *p o* N-Y.
Apure, Ä-pó-ra, *r* Venezuela.
Apurimac, Ä-pō-ri-mäk, *r* S. Am. 500.
Aquapim, Ä-kwä-pém, *st* Africa.
Aquasco, A-kwás-kō, *p o* Md.
Aquia, Ak'wi-a, *p o* and *cr* Va.
Aquila, Ä'kwi-lä, *ft c* Naples, 11⅛.
Aquileja, Ä-kwi-lá-yä, *t* Nor. It., 1½.
Aquokee, A-kwó-kē, *r* Ga., Tenn.
Aquone, A-kwó-nē, *p o* N. C.
Arabgheer, Arabgir, Ä-räb-gér, (*or* Arabkir,) *t* As. Tur., 6000 houses.
Arabia, A-rá-bi-a, s. w. part of Asia, 750,000 square miles, mainly desert.
Arabian Sea, A-rá-bi-an Sē, on the s. w. coast of Asia.
Aracan, *or* Arracan, Ar-a-kán, British prov. Farther India; *t* do., 10.
Aracati, *or* Aracaty, Ä-rä-kä-té, *r* and *port*, Brazil, 5.
Araguahi, Ä-rä-swä-hé, *r* Bra.
Arad, Or-ód, *t* Hun., old and new, 20.
Arafat, Ä-rä-fät, Mount, granite hill, Arabia.
Aragon, Arragon, Är-ä-gón, *r* and *anc k* Sp.
Araguay, Är-ä-gwī, *r* Brazil, 1000 m.
Aral, Ar'al, *sea* Ind. Tartary.
Aranda-de-duero, Ä-rän-dä-da-dwá-rō, *dis* and *t* Spain.
Aranjuez, Ä-rän-ħwéθ, *t*, royal res., of Spain.
Aransas, Ar-án-sas, *r, b* and *v* Texas.
Arapahoe, A-ráp-a-hō, Indians, *tribe* between the s. fork of Platte river and the head waters of the Arkansas.
Ararat, Ar'a-rat, *vol m* Western Asia, 17,323 ft; *r* and *m* N. C.; *vs* Pa., Va.
Aras, Ä-räs, (*or* Araxes,) *r* Arm. 500m.
Arasaig, Är-a-ság, *v* and *dis* Scot.
Arator, *or* Arrator, A-rá-tor, *v* Mo.
Araucania, Ä-ro-kä-ni-ä, *ind ter* s. part of Chili, 70.
Arauco, Ä-rō-kō, *ft* Chili.
Araure, Ä-rō-ra, *c* Venezuela, 10.
Arba, Är'ba, *p o* Ia.
Arbacoochee, Är-ba-kó-çē, *p o* Ala.
Arbe, Är'ba, *i* Adriatic, 5.
Arbela, Är-bé-la, *p o* Mo.
Arboga, Är-bó-gä, *t* Sweden, 2.
Arbois, Är-bwä, *t* Fr., 7.
Arbroath, Är-bróθ, *s-pt t* Scot., 8⅓.
Arbuthnot, Är'buθ-not, *par* Scot.
Arcabutla, Är-ka-bút-lä, *p o* Miss.
Arcade, Är-kád, *v* N-Y.
Arcadia, Är-ká-di-a, *anc prov* Greece, in the Gulf of Morea; *vs* R. I., N-Y., La., Tenn., Ia., Ill., Mo.
Arcanum, Är-ká-num, *p o* O.
Archaig, Loch, Loħ-är-kág, *l* Scot.
Archangel, Ärk-án-jel, *ter* and *s-pt t* Russia in Europe, 24½; also a bay.
Archipelago, Är-ki-pél-a-gō, signifies a sea interspersed with numerous *is*.
Arcola, Är-kó-lä, *anc t* Piedmont, 2¼; *vs* Va., N. C., O.
Arcos de la Frontera, Är-kōs da lä Fron-tá-rä, *t* Spain, 11¼.
Arcot, Är-kót, (Arucati, *or* Arookatee,) *c* South Hindostan, 40.
Arctic Ocean, Ärk'tic Ō'ʃan, the Northern Sea, containing Greenland, Spitzbergen, Iceland and many other islands.
Ardèche, Är-dáʃ, *r* and *dep* France.
Arden, Är'den, *p o* Va.
Ardennes, *or* Arden, Är'den, *dep* Fr.
Ardrah, Är'drä, *t* and *prov* Africa.
Aremberg, Ä'rem-bẹrg, *div* Hanover.
Arena, A-ré-na, *v* Wis.
Arenac, Ar-ē-nák, *co* Mich.
Arequipa, Ä-ra-ké-pä, *dep* and *c* Peru, 35; *vol* 20,300 ft high.
Arezzo, Ä-rét-sō, *prov* and *c* It., 11¾.

Argentan, Ar-zoṅ-tóṅ, *t* Fr., 5¾.
Argentaro, Ar-jen-tá-ro, *m* Turkey in Europe; *prom* Western Italy.
Argenteuil, Ar-zoṅ-túl, *t* Fr., 4¾.
Argentine, Ar'jen-tin, Republic of S. American countries, comprising Buenos Ayres, Santa Fé, Entre Rios, Corrientes, Cordova, La Rioja, Santiago del Estero, Tucuman, Catamarca, Salta and Jujuy, San Luis, Mendoza, San Juan. Total pop. 820.
Argo, Ar'go, *i* in the Nile; *p o* Ga., Ill., Mo., Iowa.
Argoon, *or* Argun, Ar-góon, *r* separates the Russian and Chinese Empires; *r* in Circassia.
Argos, Ar'gos, *t* Greece, 8.
Argostoli, Ar-gós-to-le, *s-pt t* Ionian Is.
Argyle, *or* Argyll, Ar-gil, *co* Scot.; *co* New South Wales; *vs* Me., N-Y., N. C., Ga., Ill., Miss., Wis.
Arica, A-ré-ka, *dis* and *t* Peru, 3½.
Ariége, A-re-áz, *dep* Fr.
Ariel, A'ri-el, *p o* Penn.
Arienzo, A-ri-én-zo, *t* Naples, 10.
Arigal, A'ri-gel, *m* Ireland, 2,462.
Arispe, A-rís-pa, *t* of Sonora, Mexico; *v* Ill.
Arjish, Ar-jéʃ, *t* and *r* Eu. Turkey.
Arkadelphia, Ark-a-dél-fi-a, *v* Ark.
Arkansas, Ar-kán-sas, (formerly Ar'kan-se,) *r* U. S., 2000 m. in length, navigable by steamboats 800 m. from its mouth in the Mississippi; one of the United States, containing 52,197 s. m.; pop. in 1854, 253,117, of whom 199,224 were white, 60,279 slaves, and 614 free colored.
Arkansas Post, *co t* Ark.
Arlanza, Ar-lán-tha, *r* Sp.
Arlanzon, Ar-lán-thon, *r* Sp.
Arles, Arl, *c* and *r-port* Fr., 23¼.
Arlington, Ar'liŋ-ton, *p os* Vt., O., Mich., Ill., Wis.
Armacolola, Ar-ma-ka-ló-la, *cr* in Ga.
Armada, Ar-má-da, *p o* Mich.
Armagh, Ar-má, *bor* and *c* Ir., 9; *t* Pa.
Armançon, Ar-móṅ-soṅ, *r* Fr.
Armenia, Ar-mé-ni-a, a mountainous country of Western Asia, now politically defunct; *v* Ga.
Armentières, Ar-moṅ-ti-ár, *t* Fr., 8⅓.
Armuchee, Ar-móo-ce, *p o* Ga.
Arnheim, Arn'him, *or* Arn'him, *v* O.
Arnhem, Arn'hem, (also Arnheim) *ft t* Neth., 16¾; *b* Australia.
Arno, Ar'no, *r* Tuscany.
Arnon, Ar-nóṅ, *r* Fr.; Ar'non, *v* Ill.
Arnsberg, Arnz'berg, *t* and *gov* Ger.
Aroa, A-ró-a, *t* and *r* Venezuela.
Arok-Szallas, A'rok-sa-láʃ, *v* Hun., 9.
Aroma, A-ró-ma, *v* Ill.
Aron, A-róṅ, *r* and *v* Fr.; *t* Pied. 5.
Arooat, Arouat, Aruat, A-ro-át, *st* and *t* N. Africa.
Aroostook, A-róos-tuk, *r* U. S., 120 m.; [*co* and *p o* Me.
Arpino, Ar-pé-no, *t* Naples, 11.
Arqua, Ar'kwa, *t* Mexico, 4.
Arques, Ark, *r* and *t* Fr.
Arran, Ar'an, *i* w. coast of Scotland; *is* w. coast of Ireland.
Arras, Ar'as, *ft c* Fr., 24⅓.
Arrifana, Ar-i-fá-na, *ft*, *b* and *i* s. w. coast of Portugal.
Arroas, A-ró-as, *is* Straits of Malacca.
Arroe, A-ró, *is* in the Red Sea.
Arroo, Arco, Aru, A-róo, *is* n. of Australia; also, n. w. coast of Wash. Ter.
Arrow, Ar'o, *r* Wales and Eng.; *cr* Eng.; *l* and *r* Ireland.
Arta, Ar'ta, *r* Eu. Tur.; *ts* Albania and Majorca, *gulf* Ionian Sea.
Artas, Ar-tás, (*or* Artoss,) a beautiful fertile valley of Palestine, near Bethlehem.
Artaxata, Ar-taks-á-ta, former cap. of Armenia, with a pop. of about 190,000, now a mass of ruins.
Artois, Ar'twa, *old prov* Fr.
Aruba, A-róo-ba, (*or* Oruba,) *i* Dutch Antilles.
Arun, Ar'un, *r* Eng.
Arundel, Ar'un-del, *t* Eng. [*dis* Hun.
Arva, Ar'va, *rs* Sp. and Hun.; *v* and
Arve, Arv, *r* Sardinia.
Averni. See Auvergne.
Asahan, *or* Assahan, As-a-hán, *t*, *dis* and *r* Sumatra. [pan.
Asama-Yama, A-sá-ma-yá-ma, *vol* Ja-
Asbury, Az'ber-i, *vs* N-J., Ga., Ala., Tenn., O., Ill.
Ascalon, As'ka-lon, *or* Asculan, As-koo-lán, ruined *s-pt c* Syria.
Ascension, A-sén-ʃon, *i* n. w. of St. Helena; *par* La.; *b* Yucatan. [8½.
Aschaffenburg, A-ʃáf-en-burg, *t* Bav.,
Aschersleben, Aʃ-erz-lá-ben, *t* Prus., 10.
Ascoli, As'ko-le, *c* It., 3.
Aseer, (*or* Asir,) A-sér, *ind st* Arabia.
Ashangee, Aʃ-án-ge, *l* Abys.
Ashantee, Aʃ-an-té, *k* W. Af.
Ashapoo, (*or* Ashepoo,) Aʃ-a-póo, *r* S. C.
Ashborough, Aʃ'bur-o, *v* N. C.
Ashby, Aʃ'bi, *v* Ill.
Ashbyburg, Aʃ'bi-burg, *v* Ky.
Ashe, Aʃ, *co* N. C.
Asheville, Aʃ'vil, *vs* Pa., N. C., Ala.
Ashfield, Aʃ'feld, *t* Mass.
Ashford, Aʃ'ford, *t* and *par* Eng., 5; *ts* Conn., N-Y., Wis.

Ashland, Aʃ'land, *co* O.; *ts* Mass., N-Y., Pa., Va., N. C., Ga., Tenn., O., Ia., Iowa; residence late Henry Clay, Ky.
Ashley, Aʃ'li, *r* S. C.; *co* and *v* Ark.; *vs* O., Mo.; *l* Utah Ter.
Ashley City, Aʃ'li Sít-i, (*or* New Baltimore,) *v* Mich.
Ashleyville, Aʃ'li-vil, *vs* Mass., Mich.
Ashpetuck, Aʃ-pɛ-túk, *r* Conn.
Ashtabula, Aʃ-ta-bú-lq, *r*, *co* and *v* O.
Ashton, Aʃ'ton, *vs* Pa., La., Mo., Wis.
Ashton-under-Lyne, Aʃ'ton-un-der-lįn, *t* and *par* Eng., 30¾.
Ashuelot, Aʃ'wɛ-lot, *r* N-H.
Asia, Ɛ'ʃi-ɑ, largest of the great divisions of the globe. Its greatest length, 7,500 m., breadth, 5,166 m.; pop., 480,000,000, considerably more than half the entire pop. of globe.
Asia Minor. See Anatolia.
Asiatic Archipelago. See Malay Arch.
Asimagomy, Ɑ-si-mq-gó-mɛ, *l* U. C.
Asirmintar, Ɑ-sɛr-min-tq́r, *vol i* Onekotan.
Askeaton, As-ká-ton, *t* Ir.
Asnieres, Ɑs-ni-ą́r, several *vs* Fr.
Aspalaga, As-pa-lq́-ga, *v* Fa.
Aspe, Ɑs'pa, *t* Sp., 6¾. [2½.
Aspinwall, As'pin-wel, *s-pt* Cen. Am.,
Aspropotamo, Ɑs-prɷ-pót-q-mɷ, largest river of Greece, 100 m.
Assabet, As'a-bet, *cr* and *v* Mass.
Assal, Ɑ-sq́l, *l* Eastern Africa.
Assam, *or* Asam, A-sq́m, *cy* India.
Assamoonick, As-a-mɷ́-nik, *p o* Vir.
Assatchinskaya, Ɑ-sqt-çin-skį-yq, *vol* Kamtchatka.
Assiniboin, A-sín-i-bɵn, *r* N. Am.
Assisi, Ɑ-sɛ́-sɛ, *t* It., 6. [C. E.
Assuapmoussoin, Ɑ-swqp-mɷ-swáṅ, *l*
Assumption, A-súmp-ʃon, *v* and *r* C. E.; *p* and *v* La.
Assumption, (Sp. Ɑ-sɷṅ-si-ɷ́n, *c* S. Am., *cap* Par.
Assyria, A-sír-i-ɑ, modern Koordistan.
Asti, Ɑs'tɛ, *prov* and *c* of Alessandria, 20.
Astonville, As'ton-vil, *v* Penn.
Astor, As'tor, *r* and *ft* of Cen. Asia; *v* Wis. [Or.
Astoria, As-tɷ́-ri-ɑ, *v* N-Y., Ill., Mo.,
Astrabad, Ɑs-trq-bád, *c* and *prov* Per.
Astrakhan, Ɑs-trq-*h*q́n, *gov* and *c* of Rus.
Astura, Ɑs-tɷ́-rq, *v* and *r* It.
Asturias, Ɑs-tɷ́-ri-qs, *anc div* Spain.
Asuay, *or* Assuay, Ɑ-sɷ-į, *or* Ɑ-swį, *dep* Ec.
Atabapo, Ɑ-tq-bq́-pɷ, *r* Ven.
Atacama, Ɑ-tq-kq́-mq, *prov* Bol.
Atalanta, At-a-lán-tɑ, *v* Ill.
Atascosa, At-as-kó-sɑ, *cr* Tex.
Atauai, A-tɤ-į, (Atooi, Atui, *or* Tauai,) Sandwich Islands.
Atbara, Ɑt-bq́-rq, *ter* and *r* Nubia.
Atchafalaya, Aç-af-a-lį-ɑ, Bayou Lou., 250 m.
Atchison, Aç'i-son, *co* Mo.
Atchison City, *t* of Kanzas.
Aterno, Ɑ-tér-nɷ, *r* Naples.
Atessa, Ɑ-tés-q, *t* Naples, 7½.
Ath *or* Aath, Ɑt, *ft t* Belgium, 8¾.
Athabasca, Aŧ-a-bás-kɑ, (*or* Athapescow,) *l* and *r* British N. Am.
Athens, Aŧ'enz, *cap* Gr., founded B. C. 1336, 30; *co* in O.; *ts* in N. Y., Pa., Ga., O., &c.
Athlone, Aŧ-lón, *t* Ir., 6⅓.
Athol, Athole, *or* Atholl, Ɑ'ŧol, *dis* Scot.; Ɛ'ŧol, *vs* Mass., N-Y.
Athos, Aŧ'os, (Mount,) Holy *m* Gr.
Atitlan, Ɑ-ti-tlq́n, *l*, *t* and *vol* Central Am. [Ky.
Atkinson, At'kin-son, *ts* Me., N-H.,
Atlanta, At-lán-ta, *c* Ga., 4.
Atlantic, At-lán-tik, *co* and *t* N-J.
Atlantic Ocean, the largest of the five great hydrographical divisions of the globe; its extreme breadth is 5000 m., and its area 25,000,000 s. m.
Atlas Mountains, At'las Mɤ́n-tenz, in N. Af.
Atlixco, At-líks-kɷ, *t* Mex.
Atrato, Ɑ-trq́-tɷ, *r* N-Gran.
Atsion, At'si-on, *r* and *v* N-J.
Attakaspa, A-túk-a-pe, fertile *dis* s. part La.
Attakembo, Ɑ-tq-kém-bɷ, one of the Feejee Islands.
Attala, A-tq́-la, *co* Miss.
Attawal, Ɑ-tq-wél, *is* Red Sea.
Attersee, Ɑ-ter-sá, *l* Upper Aus.
Attica, At'i-kɑ, *div* of Gr.; *vs* N-Y., O., Mich., Ia., Iowa, Wis.
Attleborough, At'l-bur-ɷ, *ts* Mass., Pa.
Attoo, Attou, *or* Attu, Ɑ-tɷ́, largest of the Aleutian Islands.
Attoyac, At-ɵ-ák, *r* Tex.
Aubagne, ɷ-bq́ny, *t* Fr.
Aube, ɷb, *r* and *dep* Fr.
Aubenas, ɷb-nq́, *t* Fr.
Auburn, Ɵ'burn, *c* N-Y., 11; *vs* in half the States of the Union.
Auch, ɷʃ, *c* Fr., 12¼.
Aucheahachee, Ɵ-çɛ-háç-ɛ, *r* Ga., sometimes called Little Ocmulgee.
Auchtermuchty, O*h*-ter-mú*h*-tɛ, *burg* and *par* Scot., 2¾.
Auckland, Ɑk'land, *pt* of N-Zeal., group of *is* in S. Pac. Oc.

Aude, Od, *r* and *dep* Fr.
Audrain, O-drán, *co* Mo.
Audubon, O'du-bon, *co* Iowa; *vs* Tenn., Ill. [O.
Auglaize, O-gláz, *rs* O., Mo.; *co* and *t*
Augsburg, Ogs'burg, (Ger. Ogz'burg,) *c* Bav., 38.
Augusta, O-gús-ta, *co* Va.; *c* Me., 10. *c* Ga., 12; *vs* in over a dozen states.
Augustowo, O-gos-tó-vo, *prov*, *t* Pol.
Aullagas, Ol-yá-gas, *l* of Bol.
Aulne, On, *r* Fr.
Auraria, O-rá-ri-a, *v* Ga.
Auray, O-rá, *r-pt* Fr.
Aure, Or, *r* Fr.
Aurelius, O-ré-li-us, *t* N-Y., O.
Aurich, O'rih, *t* Hanover.
Aurillac, O-rel-yák, *t* Fr., 11.
Aurora, O-ró-ra, *ts* Maine, N-Y., Ken., O., Ind., Ill., Wis., *i* Red Sea.
Aurungabad, O-rung-ga-bád, *c* Hind., 60.
Au Sable, O-sá-bl, *r* N-Y.; *v* Ill.
Austerlitz, Os'ter-litz, *t* Mor., *vs* N-Y., Mich. [ous *vs*.
Austin, Os'tin, *cap* Tex., 3; numer-
Australasia, Os-tral-á-ʃi-a, *div* of the globe, consisting of the continent of Australia, Van Diemen's Land, N-Zeal., and numerous other islands.
Australia, Os-trál-ya, *or* New Holland, the largest island in the world, lies between the Indian and Pacific Ocs.; greatest length 2400 m., breadth 1700 to 1900 m. including an area of 3,000,000 s. m. The British colonies are directed by a governor appointed by the crown, and a legislative council, partly elective and partly appointed by government; white pop. 500,000.
Australian Alps, *ms* of Australia.
Austria, Os'tri-a, one of the most extensive of the European monarchies; comprising 258,000 s. m.; pop. in 1850, 36,514,466. The government is vested in the emperor, who exercises supreme control in all the provinces, excepting Hungary and Transylvania.
Autauga, O-té-ga, *cr* and *co* Ala.
Auterive, O-te-rév, *t* Fr.
Auteüil, O-tély, *v* enclosed within the new walls of Paris.
Authie, O-té, and Authion, O-ti-oñ *rs* of Fr.
Autun, O-túñ, *c* Fr., 12.
Auvergne, O-várny, *prov* and *ms* Fr.
Auxerre, O-sár, *c* Fr., 14¼.
Auxonne, Ok-són, *ft t* Fr. 6¼.
Ava, A'va, *c* Burmah, 30; principality of Japan; *v* N-Y., Ga., Ill.
Avallon, A-va-lóñ, *t* Fr.
Avalon, Av'a-lon, *pen* Newfoundland; *p o* Md.
Avant, A-vánt, *p o* Tex.
Avares, A-vá-res, political *div* Cir.
Avatcha, A-vát-ça, *t* and *b* Kam.
Avatchinskaya, A-vaç-in-ski-ya, *vol* Kam.
Aveiro, A-vá-e-ro, *s-pt t* Port.; *t* Bra.
Avellino, A-ve-lé-no, fortified episcopal *c* Naples, 22¾.
Aven Loch, Loh A'ven, *l* Scot. Aven or Avon, several Scotch rivers.
Averno, A-vér-no, *l* Naples.
Aversa, A-vér-sa, *t* Naples, 16¼.
Avery, A'ver-i, *vs* Ill., Iowa.
Avesnes, A-ván, *ft t* Fr., 3¾.
Aveyron, A-va-róñ, *r* and *dep* Fr.
Avigliano, A-vel-yá-no, *t* Naples, 9¾.
Avignon, A-ven-yóñ, *c* Fr. 35.
Aviston, Av'is-ton, *v* Ill.
Avlona, Av-ló-na, *t* Albania, 8.
Avo, A'vo, *v* Va.
Avoca, A-vó-ka, (*or* Ovoca,) *val* and *r* Ir.; *vs* N-Y., Ala., Ill., Mo., Wis.
Avola, A-vó-la, *s-pt t* Sic., 6¾.
Avon, A'von, *rs* Wales, W. Australia; numerous *vs* U. S.
Avondale, A'von-dal, (*or* Avendale,) *par* of Scot.; *v* Penn. [*rs* in Eng.
Avon (Hampshire,) (Lower,) (Upper,)
Avoyelles, Av-o-élz, *par* La.
Avranches, Av-róñʃ, *t* Fr.
Awe, Loch, Loh O, *l* Scot.
Axbridge, Aks'brij, *t* Eng.
Axe, Aks, *rs* Eng.
Axholme, Aks'olm, Isle of, Eng.
Axoom, Axoum, Ak-sóm, anc. *t* Abys.
Ayacucho, I-a-kó-ço, *dep* S. Peru.
Ayamonte, I-a-món-ta, *s-pt t* Sp.
Ayasoolook, I-a-so-lók, *v* As. Min.; site of the ancient Ephesus.
Ayersville, Arz'vil, *p o* N. C., O.
Aylesbury, Alz'ber-i, *bor* and *t* Eng.
Ayletts, I'lets, *v* Vir.
Aylmer, Al'mer, *l* Brit. N. Am.; *ts* C. E., C. W.
Aylsham, Al'ʃam, *t* Eng.
Ayora, I-ó-ra, *t* and *r* Sp.
Ayr, Ar, *r* and *s-pt t* Scot., 10.
Ayrshire, Ar'ʃer, *co* Scot.
Aysville, Az'vil, *p o* Ia.
Azalia, A-zá-li-a, *v* Ia.
Azerbaijan, Az-er-bi-ján, *prov* Persia.
Azimghur, Az'im-gur, *dis* Brit. Ind.
Azio, Ad'zi-o, *dis* and *prom* Gr.
Azof, Az'of, (Azoph, *or* Azov,) *sea* e. part of Europe.

Azores, Az'ωrz, *or* A-zórz, *or* Western Islands, in the N. Atlantic Oc., belonging to Portugal.

Azpeytia, *or* Azpeitia, Ās-pá-i-tε-ą, *t* Spain.

Aztalan, Az'tal-an, *v* Wis.

# B.

Baagöe, Bó-gę-e, *i* Denmark.

Baalbec, Bą́l-bek, ruined *t* of Syria, 2.

Bababeg, Bą-bą-bég, *t* Persia.

Baba-dagh, Bą-bą-dą́g, *t* Eu. Tur., 10; *m* As. Min. [10.

Babakanda, Bą-bą-ką́n-dą, *t* W. Af.,

Babba, Bą́-bą, *i* As. Arch.

Bab-el-mandeb, Bąb-el-mą́n-deb, *str* and gulf of the Arabian Sea.

Babelthuap, Bą-bel-tω-ą́p, Pelew *is.*

Babylon, Báb-i-lon, anc. *cap* Babylonio-Chaldean Empire, whose walls were 60 m. in circumference, 87 thick, and 350 high.

Babylonia, Bab-i-ló-ni-ą, anc. *prov* Middle As., now called Bagdad.

Bacalar, Bą-ką-lár, *s-pt t* Yucatan, 4.

Back's River, Brit. N. Am.

Bacolor, Bą-kω-lór, *t* on *i* Luzon, 8½.

Badajos, Bad-a-hós, *ft c* Sp. 11¾.

Bad Axe, *co, p o* and *r* Wis.

Baden, Bą́-den, grand duchy of the German Confederation; *t* in Baden, 6; *ts* Swit., Lower Aus.; Bá-den, *v* Pa. [Arch.

Badong, Bą-dóŋ, *st* and *s-pt t* Malay

Badoor, Bą-dωr, (*or* Bhugwar,) *r* Bel.

Baena, Bą-á-ną, (*or* Vaena,) *t* Sp., 13.

Baeza, Bą-á-ŧą, (*or* Baeça,) *t* Sp., 10¾. [N. Am.

Baffin's Bay, Báf-inz Ba, inland *sea*

Baganga, Bą-gą́ŋ-gą, *s-pt t* and *b* Mal. Arch.

Bagaria, Bą-gą-ré-ą, *or* Bagheria, Bą-ga-ré-ą, *t* Sicily.

Bagdad, Bąg-dą́d, *c* As. Tur., 65; Pashalic of, *ter* As. Tur.; Bág-dad, *vs* Tenn., Mo.

Baghul, Bą-gúl, Sikh states, Hind.

Baglen, Bąg-lén, *or* Bagaleen, Bą-ga-lán, Dutch residency on *i* of Java.

Bagnères-de-bigorre, Bąn-yą́r-dę-bε-gor, *t* Fr., watering-place.

Bagnères-de-luchon, Bąn-yą́r-dę-lų-ʃωń, watering-place, Fr.

Bagnoli, Bąn-yó-lε, *t* Naples.

Bagnolo, Bąn-yó-lω, *t* Piedmont.

Bahala, Ba-há-lą, *cr* Miss.

Bahama Channel, Ba-há-mą Ͼán-el, *or* Gulf of Florida, sea between Florida coast and Bahama Islands.

Bahama Islands, 500 islands belonging to Great Britain, n. e. of Cuba, 28.

Bahar, Ba-hą́r, *t* British India, 30.

Bahia, Bą-é-ą, *prov* Bra.

Bahia, *or* Sao Salvador, Są́-ωŋ Sąl-vą-dωr, *s-pt c* Brazil.

Bahia Honda, Bą-é-ą ón-dą, *har* Cuba.

Bahlingen, Bą-liŋ-en, *t* Würtemberg.

Bahrein, Bą-rán, (*or* Aval Island,) *i* in the Persian Gulf.

Baiboot, Bį-bωt, *t* Asiatic Turkey.

Baikal, Bį-kąl, *l* or Holy Sea, Siberia.

Bailleul, Bą-yę́, *t* Fr., 7.

Bainbridge, Bán-brij, many *vs* U. S.

Bains-du-Mont-d'Or, Bań-dę-mωń-dωr, *v* Fr., celebrated for mineral baths.

Bairdstown, Bą́rdz-tɜn, *v* Ga.

Baireuth, Bį-ręŧ, *c* Bav., 17.

Baise, *or* Bayze, Baz, *r* Fr.

Baja, Bó-yo, *t* Hun., 14½.

Bajada-de-Santa-Fe, Bą-hą́-dą-da-są́n-tą-fa, *c* Entre Rios, 6.

Bajibo, Bą-jé-bω, *ts* Western Africa.

Bajoor, *or* Bajour, Bą-jωr, *dis* and *t* of Northern Afghanistan.

Bakel, Bą-kél, *v* Western Africa.

Baker, Bá-ker, *co* Ga.; *v* O.

Baker's Falls, Hudson River, N-Y.

Bakhtchissarai, Bąh-çis-a-rį, *t* Russia.

Bakhtegan, Bah-ta-gą́n, *l* Persia.

Bakhtiyari, Bąh-ti-yą́-rε, *ms* Persia.

Bakony-Wald, Bo-kóny-vąlt, *m* Hun.

Bakoo, Bakou, or Baku, Bą-kω, *s-pt t* Rus., 5⅓; *t* Mol.

Balabac, Bą-lą-bąh, *i* Malay Arch.

Balaguer, Bą-la-gą́r, *ft t* Sp.

Balakhna, Bą-lą́h-ną, *t* Rus.

Balaklava, Bą-lą-klą́-vą, *t* Rus., 3½.

Balasore, Bąl-a-sωr, *dis* British India; *t* and *cap*, 11½.

Balatony, Bą́-lą-tony, *l* Hun.

Balbriggan, Bal-bríg-an, *t* Ir., 3.

Balças, *or* Balsas, Bą́l-sąs, *r* Brazil, 200.

Bald Eagle Mountain, Pa.

Baldo, Monte, Món-ta Bél-dω, *m* Lom.

Baldwin, Béld-win, *cs* and *ts* U. S.

Balearic Isles, Ba-lé-rik Īlz, *is* Med.

Balfurosh, Bąl-fur-óʃ, *t* Per., pop. in 1822, 200,000, but since devastated by the plague and cholera.

Balize, Belize, Ba-léz, (*or* British Honduras,) British colony e. of Yucatan; *cap* Honduras; *v* and pass at the mouth of the Mississippi river.
Balkan, Bql-kán, *m* Eu. Tur.
Balkash, Bql-káʃ, *l* Central Asia.
Balkh, Bql*h*, *prov* and *c* Cen. Asia.
Ballinahinch, Bal-in-a-hínq, *l*, *r* and *t* Ir.
Ballina, Bal-ε-ná, *t* Ir., 5⅓.
Ballinasloe, Bal-in-a-sló, *t* Ir.
Ballon D'Alsace, Bq-lóṅ-Dql-sás, *m* of the Vosges chain in France.
Ballon de Guebwiller, — Geb-vε-lá*r*, *m* Vosges chain, Fr.
Ballston Spa, Bél-ston Spq, *v* N-Y.
Ballymena, Bal-i-mé-na, *t* Ir.
Baltic, Bél-tik, inland sea of N. Eu.
Baltic Provinces, Russian governments of Courland, Esthonia, Livonia, St. Petersburg, and Finland.
Baltimore, Bél-ti-mor, *s-pt t* Ir.; numerous *vs* in U. S.; *c* Md., 200.
Bambarra, Bam-bár-a, *ind st* W. Af.
Bambecque, Boṅ-bék, *v* Fr.
Bamberg, Bám-be*rg*, *t* Bav., 19⅓.
Bambook, Bambouk, Bqm-bók, *cy* Af.
Bamian, Bq-mi-án, (*or* Baumeean,) valley and pass of Afghanistan.
Banalbufar, Bqn-yql-bo-fá*r*, *t* island of Majorca, 5.
Banana, Bq-ná-nq, *is* n. w. of Africa.
Bananal, Bq-ná-nal, *i* of Brazil in the river Araguay.
Banas-Chai, Bán-ás-ʃí, *r* Asia Minor.
Banat, Bq-nát, *prov* Austria.
Banca, *or* Banka, Báŋ-kq, *i* in Malay Arch., 35.
Bancroft, Bán-kroft, *co* Iowa; *ts* Me., [Mass., Ga.
Banda, Bán-dq, Isles, twelve small islands in the Molucca Arch.
Banditti, Ban-dít-i, Isle, Malay Arch.
Bandon, Bán-don, *r* and *t* s. of Ir., 9.
Banela, Ba-né-la, *v* Miss.
Banff, Bqmf, *bor* and *s-pt t* Scot.
Bangalore, Baŋ-ga-lór, *ft t* s. Ind., 60.
Bangkok, *or* Bankok, Ban-kók, *cap c* Siam, 400.
Bangor, Báŋ-gor, *c s-pt* and *par* North Wales; *s-pt t* and *par* Ir.; *c* Me., 20.
Bang-pa-kung, Bqŋ-pq-kúŋ, *r* Siam.
Banguey, Boŋ-gá, *i* Malay Arch.
Baniak, Bq-ni-ák, Islands, Ind. Oc.
Banialuka, Bq-ni-q-ló-ka, *ft t* Eu. Tur., 7¾.
Banister, Bán-is-ter, *r* and *v* Vir.
Banjermassin, *or* Banjarmassin, Bqn-yer-mq-sín, *cy* of Borneo.
Banjoemas, Bqn-yo-más, *t* Dutch East Indies, 9.



Bann, Bqn, *r* Ir.
Bannacks, Bán-aks, (*or* Boonaks,) indians in Oregon.
Bantallan, Bqn-tq-lán, *i* Malay Arch.
Bantam, Bqn-tám, *k* Dutch East Indies; *t* and *r* of Java; Bán-tam, *v* O.
Baracoa, Bq-rq-kó-q, *s-pt t* W. Ind.
Barak, Bq-rák, *r* Farther Ind.
Baranca, Nueva, Nwá-vq Bq-rán-kq, *t* New Granada.
Barataria, Bar-a-tá-ri-a, *b* s. e. La.
Barbados, *or* Barbadoes, Bqr-bá-doz, eastern of the Carribbee Islands; Bq*r*-bá-dos, *r* Brazil.
Barbary, Bár-ba-ri, division of Af.
Barbour, Bár-bur, *v* Ala.
Barboursville, *co ts* Va., Ky.
Barcelona, Bq*r*-sa-ló-nq, *prov* and *s-pt t* Sp., 121¾; *t* and *port* Ven.; *v* N-Y.
Bardstown, Bárdz-tεn, (*or* Bairdstown,) *t* Ky.
Bareily, Bar-á-lε, *dis* and *c* Brit. Ind.
Barge, Bá*r*-já, *t* Piedmont, 7.
Bargoozeen, (*or* Bargouzin,) Ba*r*-go-zén, *r* Siberia.
Bari, Bá-rε, *ft c* Naples, 27¼.
Bark River, Wis.
Bar-le-Duc, Bq*r*-le-dék, *t* Fr., 14¾.
Barletta, Ba*r*-lét-q, *s-pt c* Naples, 20.
Barmen, Bá*r*-men, *t* Prussia, 35.
Barnaul, Ba*r*-nál, *t* w. Siberia, 10.
Barnegat, Bqr-nε-gát, *v* N-Y.; *b* and *t* N-J.
Barnsley, Bárnz-li, *t* Eng., 15.
Barnstable, Bárn-sta-bl, *co* and *t* Mass.
Barnstaple, Bárn-sta-pl, *s-pt t* Eng.
Barnwell, Bárn-wel, *dis* and *t* S. C.
Baro, Bq-ró, *r* Africa.
Baroach, Bq-róq, *dis* of British India.
Baroda, Ba-ró-da, *c* Hindostan. [12.
Barquesimeto, Bq*r*-ka-si-má-to, *c* Ven.
Barraboo, Bar-a-bó, *r* and *t* Wis.
Barrada, (*or* Burada,) Ba-rá-dq, *r* Syr.
Barra, Bár-q, Islands, w. coast Scot.
Barre, Bár-ε, *t* Vt.
Baréges, Bq*r*-áz, watering place of Fr.
Barren River, Tenn.
Barriers Reef, n. e. coast of Australia.
Barrow, Bár-o, (*or* Borragh,) *r* Ir.
Bartholomew, Bqr-tól-o-mq, *bayou* Ark. and La., nav. 250 miles; *co* Ind.
Barton, Bár-ton, num. *vs* U. S.; *r* Vt.
Bartsch, Bq*r*q, *r* Prus.
Baseelan, (*or* Basilan,) Bq-sé-lqn, *i* Sooloo Arch.
Basel, Bá-zel, *canton* and *t* Swit., 27¼.
Bashkeers, *or* Bashkirs, Báʃ-kεrz, people of Russia, inhabiting the plains adjoining the South Uralian Mts.
Basiento, Bq-si-én-to, *r* Naples.

Baskahegan, Bas-ka-hé-gan, *r* and *l* Me.
Basque, Bask, Provinces, Sp.
Bassano, Bq-sq́-nɷ, *c* n. Italy, 12.
Basse-Terre, Bqs-tą́r, *s-pt t* W. I., 12⅓.
Bassorah, Bq́s-ɷ-rq, *c* As. Tur., 60.
Bastia, Bqs-tḗ-q, *s-pt t* Corsica, 12½.
Bastrop, Bás-trop, *co* and *t* Tex.
Batavia, Ba-tá-vi-ɑ, (Dutch Bq-tq́-vi-q,) *c* Java, 118¼; *vs* N-Y., O., Ill.
Bath, Bqŧ, *c* Eng., 54¼; *c* Me., 12; numerous *vs* U. S. [Va.
Bath Alum Springs, watering place,
Bathurst, Báŧ-urst, *t* N-B.; *i* N. Australia; *l* Newfoundland.
Batignolles-Monceaux, Bq-tɛn-yól-mɷń-só, *t* 19¼.
Baton Rouge, Bat-on Rőʒ, *cap* La., 4½.
Batoo, Bq-tő, *vol is* Malay Arch.
Batoom, Bq-tőm, *s-pt t* Tur. in As., 25.
Batsɷ, Bát-sɷ, *r* and *v* N-J.
Battahatchee, Bat-a-háç-ɛ, *r* Ala. See Buttahachie.
Battam, Bq-tq́m, *i* Malay Arch.
Battenkill, Bát-en-kil, *r* Vt.
Battle Creek, *cr* and *t* Mich.
Baubaugo, Be-bé-gɷ, *cr* Ia.
Baubula, Bɤ-bő-lq, *r* Sp.
Baughman, Bé-man, *v* O. [livia.
Baure, Bɤ́-ra, (Baurus, Bɤ́-rɷs,) *r* Bo-
Bautzen, Bɤ́t-sen, *t* Saxony, 12.
Bavaria, Ba-vá-ri-ɑ, (Kingdom of,) part of Ger. confederation, 4,559,442; its government is a constitutional monarchy.
Bavispe, Bq-vís-pa, *t* and *r* Mex.
Bay, Bį, *l* island of Luzon.
Bayamo, Bq-yq́-mɷ, (or San Salvador,) *t* Cuba, 14.
Bayan, Bį-q́n, mountain range Asia.
Bayazeed, Bį-a-zéd, *ft t* Tur. Armenia.
Bayeux, Bq-yę́, *c* Fr., 9¼.
Bay Islands, in the Bay of Honduras.
Baylique, Bį-lé-ka, *i* coast of Brazil.
Bayonne, Bq-yón, *ft c* Fr., 18¾.
Bayou, Bį-ɷ, *or* Bį-ɷ, a term confined chiefly to La., Tex., and Ark., signifies a stream which is derived from some other stream or from a lake.
Bayou Bœuf, — Bęf, — Chicot, Σé-kɷ, — Goula, Gő-lq, — Pierre, Pɛ-ą́r, — Ramois, Rq-mɷ́, — Sara, Sá-rɑ, *vs* La.
Baza, Bq́-ŧq, *c* Sp., 10.
Bear Lake, Bąr Lak, *l* Brit. N. Am.
Bear, *or* Utah River, Utah and Oregon Ter.; also California.
Beas, Bé-as, *or* Beypasha, Bá-paʃ-q, *r* Punjab, 220 miles.
Beaucaire, Bɷ-ką́r, *t* Fr. 11.
Beaufort, Bɷ-fór, *ts* Fr.
Beaufort, Bq́-fort, *co* and *t* N. C.
Beauharnais, Bɷ-hqr-ná, *v* C. E.
Beaulieu, Bɷ-li-ę́, *t* Fr.; Bq́-li, *r* Eng.
Beauly, Bó-li, *r* Scot.
Beaumaris, Bɷ-má-ris, *s-pt t* N. W.
Beaumont, Bɷ-móń, *ts* Fr., Bel.
Beaumont, Bó-mont, *vs* U. S.
Beaune, Bɷn, *anc t* Fr., 11.
Beauvais, Bɷ-vá, *c* Fr., 14¼.
Beaver, Bé-ver, and numerous compounds; *crs* and *ts* U. S.
Beaver Islands, Lake Michigan.
Beaver Lake, Jasper co., Ia. [Pa.
Beaver River, different *rs* N-H., N-Y.,
Becancour, Ba-koń-kőr, *v* C. E.
Bechuanas, Bet-çɷ-q́-naz, a nation of S. Af.
Bedford, Béd-ford, *t* Eng., 11¾; numerous *cos* and *ts* U. S.
Bedouin, Ba-dwáń, *t* Fr.
Bedouin, *or* Beduin, Béd-ɷ-in, inhabitants of the desert, supposed to be derived from Ishmael, the population of Arabia.
Beemah, Bé-mq, *r* S. Ind. 400 m.
Beersheba, Bɛ-ę́r-ʃɛ-bɑ, a ruined *t* of Palestine.
Begsheher, Beg-ʃéh-her, *l* and *r* As. Min.
Behring, Bé-riŋ Sea, N. Pac. Oc.; *str* between Asia and Am.
Beilan, Ba-lq́n, *t* and *pass* of Syria.
Beit-el-Fakih, Bát-el-Fq́-kɛh, *t* Ar., 3.
Beja, Bá-ʒq, *t* Port., 5½.
Bejapoor, Bɛ-ja-pőr, *c* S. Ind. [19.
Bekes, Ba-kéʃ, (*or* Bekesvar,) *t* Hun.,
Bela, Belah, Beila, *or* Beylah, Bá-lq, *t* Beloochistan, 5.
Belaia, Ba-lį́-q, *or* Bielaja, Bya-lq́-yq, *r* Rus., 550 m.
Belair, Bɛ-ląr, *v* Vt.
Bel Air, Bel Ąr, *v* Md., Ga., Ill.
Beled-el-Jereed, Bɛ-léd-el-Jer-ḗd, sterile region of Af.
Belfast, Bel-fást, *s-pt t* Ir., 120; *s-pt t* Me.
Belgium, Bél-ji-um, a *k* of Cen. Eu., divided into 9 prov.; Antwerp, S. Brabant, E. Flanders, W. Flanders, Hainaut, Liege, Limbourg, Luxembourg, and Namur; having a total pop. of 4,359,090, who for the most part, speak the Fr. language; government is a constitutional monarchy.
Belgrade, Bel-grád, *ft c* of Servia, pop. 30.
Bellechasse, Bel-ʃq́s, *co* C. E.
Bellefontaine, Bel-fón-tan, "fine fountain," *ts* O., Ia., Mo., Iowa.

Bellefonte, Bel-fónt, *vs* Pa., Ala., Mo.
Bellemont, Bel-mónt, *v* Tenn.
Bellemonte, *vs* Pa., Mo.
Belle River, *stream* Mich.
Belleview, Bel-vų́, numerous *vs* U. S.
Belleville, Bél-vil, numerous *vs* U. S.
Bellevue, Bel-vų́, *vs* Ga., O., Mich., Iowa.
Bellona, Be-ló-na, *v* N-Y. [*vs* U. S.
Belmont, Belmonte, Bel-mónt, *cos* and
Beloit, Bε-lót, *v* Wis.
Beloochistan, Bel-œ-kis-tán, mountainous *cy* of S. As.; the government is despotic; pop. uncertain, estimated at from 450,000 to 2,000,000.
Belvidere, Bel-vi-dér, *ts* U. S.
Benares, Ben-ą-rez, *c* of Hind.; stationary pop. est. at from 200, to 600.
Ben-Aven, Ben-á-ven, *m* Scot.
Bencruachan, Ben-krœ́-*h*an, *m* Scot.
Benevento, Ben-ε-vén-tœ, *c* S. It., 16½.
Bengal, Ben-gél, *prov* Brit. Ind., consisting mainly of the immense valley of the Ganges; pop. 57,985,656.
Bengal, Bay of, part of the Indian Oc.
Benguela, Ben-gá-lą, *cy* of W. Af.
Beni, Ba-né, *dep* and *r* of Bol.; 2000 m.
Benicia, Bε-niʃ-i-a, former *cap* Cal., 2.
Benin, Ben-én, a negro *cy*, *r* and *t* W. Af., 15.
Benlawers, Ben-lé-erz, *m* Scot.
Benledi, Ben-léd-i, *m* Scot.
Ben-Lomond, Ben-ló-mond, *m* Scot., also of Vandiemen's Land.
Ben-Macdhui, Ben-mak-dœ́-i, *m* Scot.
Ben-More, Ben-mór, *m* Scot.
Ben-Nevis, Ben-né-vis, *m* Scot., also Van Diemen's Land.
Bennington, Bén-iŋ-ton, various *cos* and *ts* U. S.
Bentevoglio, Ben-tε-vól-yœ, *t* Va.
Benton, Bén-ton, numerous *cos* and *ts* U. S.
Berbice, Ber-bés, *dis* and *r* Brit. Gui.
Berdiansk, Ber-di-ánsk, *t* S. Rus., 10.
Berditchev, Ber-di-ćév, *t* Rus. Pol., 20.
Berea, Bε-ré-a, *ts* N. C., O.
Beresina, Ber-i-zé-ną, *r* Rus., 200 m.
Bergamo, Bér-gą-mœ, *ft c* Lom., 32¾.
Bergen, Bér-gen, *ft c* Nor., 25¾; *ts* Prus., Neth.; Bér-gen, *co* N-J.; *vs* N-Y., N-J. [Neth., 10.
Bergen-op-zoom, Bérg-en-op-zœm, *ft t*
Bergerac, Ber-ʒe-rák, *t* Fr., 10½.
Bergholtz, Bérg-holts, *v* N-Y., 2.
Bergues, Berg, *ft t* Fr., 6.
Berhampoor, Ber-ąm-pœ́r; *t* Brit. Ind.
Berja, Bér-*h*ą, *t* Sp., 9¾.
Berkeley, Bérk-li, *t* Eng.; *cos* U. S.

Berkshire, Bérk-ʃεr, *cos* and *vs* U. S.
Berlin, Bér-lin, (Ger. Ber-lén,) *c* Ger., *cap* Prussian monarchy; except Vienna, Berlin is the largest *t* in Ger., pop. in 1852, 442,000.
Bermuda, Ber-mœ́-da, (*or* Bermudas,) *is* N. Atlantic Oc., belonging to Great Britain, 15.
Bern, *or* Berne, Bern, *canton* and *t* of Swit., 27¾.
Bernadotte, Ber-na-dót, *v* Ill.
Bertie, Ber-té, *co* N. C.
Berwick, Bér-ik, *co* and *t* Scot.
Berwick, Bér-wik, *vs* U. S.
Besançon, Be-zoṅ-sóṅ, *ft c* Fr., 41¼.
Bessarabia, Bes-a-rá-bi-a, *prov* S. Rus.
Bethany, Béθ-a-ni, *vs* Pal., and of U. S.; seat of College established in 1841 by Alexander Campbell.
Bethel, Béθ-el, *t* Pal.; and *vs* U. S.
Bethlehem, Béθ-lε-hem, *c* of Pal., birth place of the Founder of Christianity; *vs* U. S.
Bethune, Ba-tén, *ft t* Fr., 8.
Betisbooka, *or* Betisbouka, Ba-tis-bœ́-ką, *r* Madagascar.
Bettws, Bét-œs, *pars* Eng., and Wales.
Betwah, Bét-wą, *r* Hind.
Beulah, Bų́-la, *ts* N. C., Iowa.
Bevedero, Ba-va-dá-rœ, *l* La Plata.
Beverly, Bér-er-li, *ts* Mass., N-J., Vir., Ohio. [Ga., Ala.
Bexar, Ba-ár, *or* Ba-*h*ár, *co* Tex.; *vs*
Beyroot, Beyrout, Beirout, Bá-rœt, *s-pt t* of Syria, 30.
Beziers, Ba-zi-á, *c* Fr., 19½.
Bhadrinath, Bhad-rin-áth, *t* N. Hind., in a valley of the Himalayas, 10,294 ft. above the sea, remarkable for a temple visited annually by 50,000 Hindoo pilgrims.
Bhamo, Bhą-mó, *or* Bhanmo, Bhąn-mó, large *t* Burmah.
Bhawlpoor, Bhel-pœ́r, *ind st* N. W. Hind.; *cap c* 20.
Bheels, Bεlz, mountaineers of Hind.
Bhirjan, Bεr-ján, Beerjoon, Bεr-jœ́n, *ts* Pers.
Bhooj, Bhœj, *ft c* Hind., 30.
Bhurtpoor, Bhurt-pœ́r, *or* Bhartpoor, Bhąrt-pœ́r, *state* and *c* Hind.
Bialystok, Bi-ál-is-tok, *prov* and *c* Eu. Rus.
Bickaneer, Bicanere, *or* Bicanir, Bik-an-ér, *state* Hind.; *ft t cap*, 70.
Bidais, Bε-dá, *cr* Tex.
Bidschow, Béç-ov, *t* Bohemia.
Bielopol, Bε-a-ló-pol, *t* Rus., 9.
Bienne, Bε-én, *l* and *t* Swit.
Bienville, Bε-én-vil, *par* La.; *p o* Miss.

Bigelow's (mills,) Bíg-ɛ-lɷz, *p o* Ia.
Bighton, Bị-ton, *par* Eng.
Big Plover, Plúv-er, *r* Wis.
Bijawar, Bejawer, Bɛ-jé-er, *or* Bejour, Bɛ-jɤ-er, *state* Hin.
Bilbao, Bil-bą́-ɷ, (often written and pronounced, in English, Bilboa, Bil-bɷ-ɑ, *c* and *port* Sp., 12.
Billerica, Bíl-er-ik-ɑ, *v* Mass.
Biloxi, Bi-lóks-i, *v* and *b* Miss.
Bingham, Bíŋ-ham, *ts* Me., Penn., Mich.
Binghamton, Bíŋ-am-ton, *c* N-Y.
Bingtang, Biŋ-táŋ, *i* Malay Arch.
Biobio, Bé-ɷ-bé-ɷ, *r* Chili, 200 m.
Biorneborg, Bi-ór-ne-borg, *s-pt t* Fin.
Birioossa, Bɛ-ri-ɷ́-sɑ, *r* Siberia.
Birkenhead, Bẹ́rk-en-hed, *t* Eng., opposite Liverpool, 24¼.
Birket-el-Hadji, Bér-ket-el-Hád-jị, ("lake of pilgrims,") 10 m. n. e. of Cairo.
Birmingham, Bẹ́r-miŋ-am, *c* Eng.; 232-¾; Bẹ́r-miŋ-ham, manufacturing *ts* Conn., N-Y., Pa., and numerous *vs*.
Birnee, Bẹ́r-nɛ, (Birnie, old,) *t* Cen. Af., 10, once 200.
Bisayas, Bɛ-sị-ɑs, Philippine Islands, excepting Luzon.
Biscay, Bís-ka, *or* Biscaya, Bis-kị-ɑ, *prov* of N. Spain; (Bay of,) w. coast of France.
Bisceglia, Bɛ-ʃél-yɑ, *s-pt t* Naples.
Bischwiller, Bíʃ-vil-er, *t* Fr., 6¾.
Bisignano, Bɛ-sɛn-yą́-nɷ, *t* Nap., 10.
Bissagos, Bɛ-są́-gɷs, *or* Bijooja Islands, Bɛ-jɷ́-ja, *arch* off the w. coast of Af., densely peopled with a savage negro race.
Bissao, Bɛ-są́-ɷń, *i* W. Af.
Bistineau, Bis-tin-ɷ́, *l* La.
Bistritz, Bís-trits, *r* and *c* Tran.
Bitioog, Bɛ-ti-ɷ́g, *r* Rus.
Bizerta, Bɛ-zér-tɑ, *ft s-pt* Tunis, 10.
Blackfeet Indians, n. and w. portions of Mo. Territory.
Black Hills, *m* range Mo. Ter.
Black Hole. See Calcutta.
Black Lake, La., formed by a bayou of its own name.
Black log Mountain, Pa.
Black River, *rs* Cornwall, Ir., Vt., N-Y., N-J., S. C., La., Mo., O., Mich., Wis., Mo. Ter.
Black, *or* Euxine, Yɥk'sin, inland sea between Europe and Asia, length 700 m., breadth, 380 m.
Black Warrior River, Ala.
Blackwater, *r* Ir., 100 m.; three *rs* Eng.; (River,) N-H., Va.
Blackwell's Island, Blák-welz, in the East River, opposite N-Y., seat of the city penitentiary.
Blanche, Blɑnɑ, *v* Mo.
Blaye, Bla, *ft s-pt t* Fr.
Blegno, *or* Blenjo, Blén-yɷ, *r* Swit.
Blenheim, Blén-im, *or* Blén-hịm, *v* Bav.; *v* N-Y.
Bligh, Blị (Islands,) Feejee Arch.
Block Island, belonging to Rhode Is.
Blois, Blwɑ, *anc c* Fr., 17¾. [U. S.
Bloomfield, *ts* Me., N-J.; and many *vs*
Bloomington, *t* Ia., 2; and other states.
Bloomsburg, Blɷ́mz-burg, *t* Pa.
Blount, Blɤnt, *cos* Ala., Tenn.
Bluefields, *or* Blewfields, Blɷ́-fɛldz, *r* and *t* Mosquito Ter.
Blue Mountains, in Pa., Or., Jamaica, Australia. [ghany *ms*.
Blue Ridge, easterly ridge of the Ale-
Blue River, three streams of Ia., one of Wis.
Bluestone, *r* s. w. part Vir.
Blyth, *or* Blythe, Blịθ, three *rs* Eng.
Boavista, Bɷ-ɑ-vés-tɑ, (*or* Bonavista,) *i* Af.
Bocchetta, Bo-két-ɑ, *m* W. Apennines.
Bockenheim, Bók-en-hịm, *t* Hesse Cassel. [n. w. La.
Bodcau, Bód-kɤ, (Lake and Bayou,)
Bodega, Bɷ-dé-gɑ, *v* and *b* Cal.
Bœotia, Bɛ-ó-ʃi-ɑ, *dep* of Gr.
Boglipoor, Bó-gli-pɷ́r, (*or* Bhaugulpoor,) *dis* Brit. Ind., *cap* same, 30.
Bogota, Bɷ-gɷ-tą́, (formerly Santa Fe de Bogota,) *c cap* New Granada, 40.
Bohemia, Bɷ-hé-mi-ɑ, *div* Austrian Empire, forming the e. part of the Germanic Confederation, 20,000 s. m.; pop. in 1850, 4,409,900.
Böhmerwald, Bẹ́-mer-vɑlt, *m* Ger. between, Bohemia and Bavaria.
Bohol, Bɷ-hól, one of the Phil. Is.
Bois Blanc, Bwɑ Blɒń, *i* Lake Huron.
Bois D'ark, Bɷ Dɑrk, *v* Mo.; *r* Tex.
Bois-le-duc, Bwą́-lẹ-dẹ́k, *ft c* Neth., 21¾.
Bojana, Bɷ-yą́-ną́, *r* Eu. Tur.
Bokhara, Bɷ-*h*ą́-rɑ, (called also Great Bucharia,) state of Central Asia, in Ind. Toorkistan, pop. 2,000,000; *c*, *cap* of same, 150.
Bolabola, Bɷ-lɑ-bɷ́-lɑ, (*or* Borabora,) one of the Society Islands, Pac. Oc.,
Bolbec, Bol-bé*h*, *t* Fr., 9½.
Bolingbroke, Bɷ́l-iŋ-brɥk, *t* Eng. 1.
Bolivar, Ból-i-vɑr, various *ts* U. S.
Bolivia, Bɷ-lé-vi-ɑ, *or* Upper Peru, *st* South America. Area, 374,480 s. m. pop. 1,030,000.

Bolivia, Bo-lív-i-a, *vs* Miss., Mo.
Bologna, Bo-lón-yq, *c* It., 75.
Bolonchen, Bo-lon-qén, *v* Yucatan, 7.
Bolor-Tagh, Bo-lór-tqg, mountain chain of Central Asia.
Bolsas, Ból-sqs, *r* Mexico.
Bomarsund, Bó-mar-sond, *ft* island of Aland, Russia.
Bombay, Bom-bá, most westerly Presidency of British India. Area, 68,074 s. m., pop. 7,240,277; *c*, *s-pt* and *cap* of the above presidency, 500.
Bona, *or* Bonah, Bó-nq, *ft s-pt* Algeria, 9¾.
Bonaparte, Bó-na-pqrt, *vs* Ill., Iowa.
Bon Aqua, Bon Ă'kwa, *p o* Tenn.
Bonaventure, Bon-q-vón-tęr, *co* C. E.
Bondoo, *or* Bondou, Bon-dó, *cy* Senegambia.
Bongay, *or* Bangey, Bon-gá, *i* Malay Arch.
Bon Homme, Bon-om, *t* Mo.
Bonite, Bo-nét, *p o* Tex.
Bonn, Bon, *t* Rhenish Prussia, 14¼.
Bonne Femme, Bon Fem, *cr* Mo.
Bonpland, Bóń-plóń, *l* Cal.
Bonsecours, *or* Bonesecour, Bon-se-kór, *b* Ala.
Boom, Bom, *t* Belgium, 6¼.
Boondee, Bón-de, *st* and *c* Hindostan.
Boone, Bon, *cos*, -ville, *ts* U. S.
Boorghas, Bor-gqs, *s-pt t* Eu. Tur., 6.
Boorhanpoor, Bor-han-pór, *c* India.
Booro, *or* Bouro, Bó-ro, *i* Malay Arch.
Boosempra, Bo-sém-pra, *r* Wes. Af.
Boossa, *or* Boussa, Bó-sa, *t* Cen. Af., 18.
Bootan, *or* Boutan, Bo-tqn, *ind st* N. India.
Boothia, Bó-thi-q Fé-liks, insular portion Brit. N. Am., — Gulf, Brit. Am.
Boquet, Bo-ká, *r* N-Y.
Bordeaux, Bor-dó, *c* Fr., 131.
Borgia, Bór-jq, *t* Naples.
Borgne, Born, *l* or *b* s. e. part of La.
Borgoo, *or* Borgou, Bor-gó, two *ks* Af.
Borinage, Bo-ri-nqz, *dis* Belgium.
Borneo, Bór-ne-o, *i* Malay Arch., excepting Australia the largest island on the globe. The greatest length is 850, width 600 miles; area, 280,000 s. m., pop. 2,000,000. [22.
Borneo, *or* Brunai, Bró-nj, *t* Borneo,
Bornholm, Bórn-holm, *i* Denmark, in the Baltic Sea, 26½.
Borodino, Bor-o-dj-no, *v* N-Y.
Borovsk, Bo-róvsk, *t* Russia.
Boscawen, Bós-ka-wen, *t* N-H.
Bosco Tre-case, Bós-ko Tra-kq-sa, *t* Naples, 8½. [60.
Bosna Serai, Bós-nq Ser-j, *t* Eu. Tur.,
Bosnia, Bóz-ni-q, *prov* Eu. Tur.

Bosporus, Bós-po-rus, (less correctly, Bosphorus,) called also the Strait of Constantinople, a passage connecting the Black Sea with the Sea of Marmora, and separating Europe from Asia, 17 miles long.
Bossier, Bos-i-á, *par* La.
Boston, Bós-ton, *s-pt t* and *par* Eng., 15½; second commercial city of the U. S., *cap* Mass., 137.
Böszörmeny, Bęz-ęr-mány, *t* Hun., 17.
Botany, Bót-a-ni, Bay, Pacific Ocean.
Botetourt, Bót-e-tort, *co* Va.
Bothelle, Bo-thél, *p o* Wis.
Bothnia, Bóth-ni-q, *cy* Nor. Eu.; *g* nor. part of Baltic Sea. [Fr.
Bouches-du-Rhone, Bosh-dę-ron, *dep*
Bouchoux, Les, La Bo-shó, *v* Fr., 1¼.
Bouckville, Bók-vil, *p o* N-Y.
Bougainville, Bo-gań-vél, *b* in S. Am.; *i* in the Pacific.
Bouguenais, Bog-ná, *t* Fr.
Bouie, Bó-e, *r* Miss.
Bouillon, Bol-yóń, *or* Bo-yóń, *t* Bel.
Bouin, Bo-áń, *or* Bwań, *i* w. coast Fr.
Boulogne, Bo-lón, *or* Bo-lóny, *s-pt t* Fr., 30¾.
Bourbeuse, Bor-bęz, *or* Bor-bóz, *r* Mo.
Bourbon, Bor-bóń, *i* Indian Ocean, Fr., 108; Búr-bon, *co* Ky. [12.
Bourg-en-Bresse, Borg-oń-Brés, *t* Fr.,
Bourges, Borz, *c* Fr., 25, built six centuries before the Christian era.
Bourne, Born, *t* and *par* Eng.
Bourneville, Bórn-vil, *v* O.
Boutonne, Bo-tón, *r* Fr.
Bouvignes, Bo-vény, *v* Bel.
Bouxviller, Bo-vel-ąr, *t* Fr.
Bovina, Bo-vj-na, *ts* N-Y., Miss.
Bovino, Bo-vé-no, *t* Naples.
Bowdark, Bo-dqrk, *v* Mo.
Bowditch, Bó-diq, *i* S. Pac. [Me.
Bowdoin, Bó-din, College, Brunswick,
Bowdon, Bó-don, *p os* Ga., Ala.
Bowenville, Bó-en-vil, *v* Ga.
Bowersville, Bó-erz-vil, *v* O.
Bowie, Bó-e, *co* Tex.
Bowlesville, Bólz-vil, *p o* Va.
Bowling Green, numerous *vs* U. S.
Bowman, Bó-man, *p o* Va.
Boyaca, Bo-yq-kq, *v* New Granada.
Boyana, Bo-yq-nq, *b* and *t* Madagascar.
Boydton, Bód-ton, *p o* S. C.
Boyer, Bó-er, River, Iowa.
Boyne, Bon, *r* Ir.
Bozzolo, Bót-so-lo, *t* N. Italy, 5.
Bra, Brq, *t* Piedmont, 8.
Brabant, Brq-bqnt, North, *prov* Netherlands; — South, *prov* Belgium.
Braga, Brq-gq, *c* Port., 16.

Bragança, Brq-gq́n-sq, *ts* Port., Bra.
Brahe, Brq́-ę, *r* Prus.
Brahilov, Brq-hi-lóv, Brailoff, *or* Brailow, Brq-i-lóv, *ft t* Wallachia, 6.
Brahmapootra, *or* Brahmaputra, Brqma-pó-tra, (*or* Burrampooter,) *r* South Asia, 1500 miles.
Brailes, Bralz, *par* Eng.
Brambanan, Brqm-bq-nq́n, *dis* island of Java.
Branco, Brq́ŋ-kɷ, one of the Cape de Verd Islands; *r* Brazil.
Brandenburg, Brq́n-den-burg, *prov* and *t* Prussia; Brán-den-burg, *t* Ky.
Brandywine, Brán-di-wįn, *cr* Pa., and Del.
Brathay, Brá-ŧa, *r* Eng.
Brattleborough, Brát-l-bur-ɷ, *v* Vt.
Braunau, Brɤ́-nɤ, *ts* Upper Austria and Bohemia.
Braunfels, Brɤ́n-felz, *t* Wis.
Braunsberg, Brɤ́nz-bęrg, *t* Prus.
Bray, Bra, *r* Fr.
Brazil, Bra-zíl, *or* Brq-zél, empire of South America; area, 3,956,800 s. m. It is divided into 18 provinces, pop. 6,065,000.
Brazoria, Bra-zó-ri-a, *co* and *t* Tex.
Brazos, Brq́-zos, *co* and *r* Tex., 900 m.
Brazos Santiago, — San-ti-q́-gɷ, *v* Tex.
Brazza, Brq́t-sq, *i* Dalmatia, 15½.
Breafy, Bré-fi, *or* Brá-fi, (Breaghwee, Brá-wɛ,) *par* Ir.
Breathitt, Bréŧ-it, *co* Ky.
Breda, Bra-dq́, *ft t* Netherlands, 12¾.
Breede, Brá-dę, *or* Brɛd, *r* S. Africa.
Brejo, Brá-ʒɷ, *t* Brazil.
Bremen, Brá-men, free city of Ger., 53; Bré-men, *vs* U. S.
Breneau, Bre-nó, *r* Oregon Ter.
Brenta, Brén-tq, *nav r* Lom.
Brescelia, Bra-ʃél-a, (*or* Bregella,) *t* Nor. Italy, 2.
Brescia, Bréʃ-i-a, *or* Bréʃ-q, *c* Lom., cap. of the province, 35.
Breslau, Brés-lɵ, *or* Brés-lɤ, *c* Prus., cap. of Silesia, 112¼.
Brest, Brest, *ft c* Fr., 61¼.
Breton, Cape, Bré-ton, *i* Brit. N. Am.
Briançon, Brɛ-óṅ-sɷṅ, *t* Fr., 4½.
Bridgeport, Bríj-pɷrt, *s-pt c* Conn., &c.
Bridgeton, Bríj-ton, port of entry, N-J.
Bridgetown, Bríj-tɤn, *cap i* Barbados, 19½.
Bridgewater, Bríj-wɵ-ter, *bor* and *r-pt* Eng., 11; numerous *vs* U. S.
Brieg, *t* Brɛ*h*, Prus. Silesia, 12¼.
Brighton, Brį-ton, *bor s-pt t* and watering place, Eng., 69¾.
Brignoles, Brɛn-yól, *t* Fr.
Brihueja, Brɛ-wá-gq, *t* Spain.
Brindisi, Brín-di-sɛ, *ft c* Naples, 6¼.
Brioni, Brɛ-ó-nɛ, Islands, in Adriatic.
Brioude, Brɛ-ɷ́d, *t* Fr., 5.
Brisbane, Bríz-ban, *r co* and *t* East Australia.
Bristol, Brís-tol, *s-pt c* and *co* Eng., 137⅓; port of entry, R. I.; *vs* U. S.
Bristol Channel, s. w. arm of the Atlantic, Great Btitain.
British America, Brít-iʃ A-mér-i-ka, northern portion of North America, comprising the Canadas, New Brunswick, Nova Scotia, Cape Breton, Prince Edward's Island, Newfoundland, North-west Territory, and Hudson's Bay Territory; 2,684,000.
British Empire, The, Brít-iʃ Em'pįr, in many respects the greatest that has ever existed, comprehends the following colonies and dependencies:—*Europe* — British Isles, Helgoland, Gibraltar, Malta and Gozo, Ionian Islands. *Africa*—Gambia, Sierra Leone, Gold Coast Possessions, Fernando Po, Ascension, St. Helena, Cape Colony, Natal, Maŭritius, Seychelles. *Asia*—Aden, India, (British,) India, (Dependencies,) Tenasserim Provinces, Ceylon, Penang, Malacca, Singapore, Laboоan, Hong Kong. *America*—Canada East, Canada West, New Brunswick, Nova Scotia and Cape Breton, Prince Edward Island, Newfoundland, Hudson's Bay Territory, Labrador, West India Islands, Bermudas, Honduras, Guina, Falkland Islands. *Australasia*—New South Wales, South Australia, Western Australia, Victoria or Port Philip, Australia, (not settled,) Van Diemen's Land, New Zealand, Norfolk Island, Auckland Islands. Area, 8,356,781 s. m., pop. 205,884,357.
Britannia, Bri-tán-i-a, Islands, Pac. Oc.
Brixham, Bríks-am, *s-pt t* Eng., 6.
Brody, Bró-di, *t* Aus. Gallicia, 17¾.
Bromberg, Bróm-bęrg, *t* Prus. Pol., 9½.
Bromley, Brúm-li, *t* Eng. m
Brompton, Brómp-ton, western suburb of London, Eng.
Bromsgrove, Brómz-grɷv, *t* Eng., 10¼.
Bronte, Brón-ta, *t* Sicily, 9¼.
Brooklyn, Brúk-lin, *s-pt c* N-Y., 125.
Brookville, Brúk-vil, *ts* Ia., Ill., Iowa.
Broughton, Bré-ton, *t* Eng.
Broughty, Bre-ti, Ferry, *v* Scot.
Brownsville, Brɤ́nz-vil, *ts* N-Y., Pa., Tex., Ark.

Bruche, Brȩʃ, *r* Fr.
Bruchsal, Brú*h*-sql, *t* Ger., 7⅓.
Bruges, Brǿ-jiz, *ft c* Bel.; pop. once 200, now scarcely 49¾.
Brunn, Brȩn, *ft c* Austrian Em.; *cap* Moravia and Silesia, pop. 45
Brunswick, Brúnz-wik, *duchy* and *c* Ger.; *ts* Me., Ga.
Brusa, *or* Broussa, Brǿ-sq, (also Bursa,) *c* As. Min., pop. 60.
Brussels, Brús-elz, *c, cap* Bel., 123¾.
Brüx, Brȩks, (*or* Brix,) *t* Bohemia, 3.
Brzesc Litewski, Bʒets Lɛ-tév-skɛ, *ft t* Rus., 8. [icia, 7.
Brzezany, Bʒa-ʒq́-nɛ, *t* Austrian Gal-
Brzezyn, Bʒá-zin, *t* Pol. 3¼.
Buagie, Bꝏ-q-gé, Sikh state Ind.
Bubrooah, Bub-rǿ-q, *t* Hind., 2000 houses.
Buccaneer, Buk-q-nér, *arch* Ind. Oc.
Buccari, Bꝏ-kq́-rɛ, *s-pt t* Aus.
Buccino, Bꝏt-çé-nꝏ, *t* Nap., 5½.
Buccleuch, *or* Buccleugh, Bu-klq́, *par* Scot.
Buchanan, Buk-án-an, *cos* and *vs* U. S.
Bucharest, *or* Bukharest, Bꝏ-kq-rést, *cap* Wallachia, pop. 60¾.
Bucharia, Bq́-ká-ri-ɑ, *ter* Cen. Asia.
Buchholz, Bǿ*h*-hꝏlts, *t* Sax.
Buckatawny Buk-a-tó-ni, *r* Miss.
Bückeburg, Bȩ́k-e-bú*r*g, *t* N. Ger.
Buckingham, Búk-iŋ-am, *t* Eng.
Bucyrus, Bq-sį-rus, *t* O., 2½.
Buda, Bq́-do, free *c, cap* Hun., 40½.
Budeaux, Bǿ-dꝏ, *par* Eng.
Büdos-Hegy, Bȩ-dóʃ-hej, *m* Tran.
Budukhshan, Bud-u*h*-ʃq́n, (*or* Badakhshan,) *ter* Cen. Asia; *t, cap* of the same.
Budweis, Búd-wįs, *or* Budwitz, Búdvits, *t* Bohemia, 8¾.
Buech, Bȩ-áʃ, *or* Bweʃ, *r* Fr.
Buenaventura, Bwa-nq-ven-tǿ-rq, *t* Mex.
Buena Vista, Bwá-nq Vés-tq, battlefield Mex.; and 36 *vs* U. S.
Buen Ayre, Bwen Ɏ'ra, (*or* Bon Air,) Dutch West India Island.
Buenos Ayres, Bó-nos Ꞩrz, (Sp. Bwánꝏs Ɏ'res,) *c cap* Buenos Ayres, pop. 85.; *prov* S. Am., area, 75,000 s. m., pop. 320.
Buffalo, Búf-a-lꝏ, *c* N-Y., 80.
Buffalo Bayou, nav. *stream* Tex.
Buffalo Lake, Wis.; three lakes of Brit. N. Am.
Buffalo River, Tenn., Mo., Wis.
Bug, Boug, Bꝏg, (*or* Bog,) *r* Rus., 340 m.
Bugis, Bǿ-gɛz, people of Malay Arch.
Bujalance, Bꝏ-*h*q-lq́n-ꞇa, *t* Sp., 9.
Bukharia, *or* Bucharia, Bꝏ-ká-ri-ɑ, *ter* Cen. Asia.
Bulacan, Bꝏ-lq-kq́n, *t* Phil. Is., 9¾.
Bulama, Bꝏ-lq́-mq, *is* w. coast of Af.
Bulga, Bǿl-gq, *m* and *t* Abys.
Bulgaria, Bul-gá-ri-ɑ, *prov* Eu. Tur.
Bullina, Bꝏl-yé-nq, *rs* Mex., Yuc.
Bullion, Búl-yon, *t* Wis.
Bullit, Búl-it, *co* Ky.
Bullock, Búl-ok, *co* Ga.
Bulti, Búl-tɛ, Baltee, Bq́l-tɛ, *or* Bultistan, Bul-ti-stq́n, (called also Little Thibet,) *state* Central Asia.
Bunawe, Bun-ó, *v* Scot.
Bunchiom, Bun-çi-óm, *t* Siam, 5.
Buncombe, Búŋ-kom, *co* N. C.
Bundelcund, Bun-del-kúnd, *ter* Hind.
Bund-Emeer, Bund-ɛ-mér, *r* Per.
Bunker Hill, celebrated height near Boston, Mass.
Bunpoor, Bun-pǿr, *ft* and *dis* W. Bel.
Buntzlau, Búnts-lɤ, *t* Silesia 6⅓; *t* Bohemia, 5.
Burdette, Bur-dét, *v* N-Y.
Burdwan, Burd-wón, *dis* Brit. Ind.; *t cap* above dis., 54.
Bureau, Bq́-rꝏ, *co* and *creek* Ill.
Burg, Bur*h*, *t* Saxony, 14½.
Burgau, Bú*r*-gɤ, *t* Bav.
Burgdorf, Bú*rh*-dor*f*, *t* Swit.
Bürglen, Bȩ́*rh*-len, *v* Swit.
Burgos, Bǿ*r*-gꝏs, *prov* and *c* Sp., 16.
Bürgstein, Bȩ́*rh*-stįn, (*or* Birkstein) *v* Bohemia.
Burgundy, Bur-gún-di, former *prov* Fr.
Burhampoore. See Burhanpoor.
Burhampooter River. See Brahmapootra.
Burke, Burk, *cos* and *ts* U. S.
Burkha, *or* Burka, Bú*r*-ka, *t* Ar.
Burleson, Búr-lɛ-son, *co* Tex.
Burlington, Búr-liŋ-ton, most populous *t* Vt., 6¼; *c* N-J., 4½; *c* Iowa, 7.
Burmah, Burma, *or* Birmah, Bȩ́r-mq, state in Farther India; area 200,000 s. m., pop. in 1826, 4,230,558.
Burnley, Búrn-li, *t* Eng., 14¾.
Burriana, Bꝏ-rɛ-q́-nq, *t* Sp., 6¼.
Burslem, Búrs-lem, *t* Eng., 16.
Burtscheid, Bú*r*t-ʃįt, *or* Borcette, Borsét, *t* Prus.
Bury, Bér-i, *t* Eng., 31½.
Bury St. Edmund's, *t* Eng., 14.
Burzen, Bú*r*t-sen, *r* Tran.
Burzenland, Bú*r*t-sen-lqnt, *dis* Hun.
Busca, Bǿs-kq, *t* Pied., 9.
Buseo, Bꝏ-sá-ꝏ, *r* and *t* Wal., 4½.
Busheab, Bꝏ-ʃɛ-q́b, *i* Persian Gulf.
Bushi, Bq́-ʃį, *p o* Ala.

Bushire, Bo-ʃér, *s-pt c* Persia, 20.
Bush River, S. C.
Bussaher, Bús-q-her, Sikh state, Ind.
Bussero Bús-ɛ-rɷ, *cr* Ia.
Busto-Arsizio, Bɷ́s-tɷ-ar-séd-zi-ɷ, *t* It., 9¾.
Busvagon, Bɷs-vq-gɷ́n, Phil. Is.
Bute, Bųt, *i* Scot., 9½.
Butow, Bé-tov, *t* Prus.
Buttahatchie, But-a-háq-ɛ, *r* Ala., Miss.
Butte, Bųt, *r*, *t* and *co* Cal. [Wis.
Butte des Morts, Bųt da Mert, *l* and *v*
Buttigliera, Bɷ-tɛl-yá-rq, *t* Pied.
Buycksville, Bįks-vil, *p o* Ala.
Büzancais, Bę-zoñ-sá, *t* Fr., 5.
Bylaugh, Bį-le, *p* Eng.
Byram River, Bį-ram, Conn.
Byrne, Bęrn, *p o* Tenn.
Byrneville, Bęrn-vil, *vs* N. Y., Iowa.
Byske, Bés-ka, *or* Bís-ke, *r* Swed.
Bytown, Bį-tɤn, *t* C. W., 8.
Byturney, Bi-tɷ́r-nɛ, *or* Vaiturani, Vį-tɷ-rq́-nɛ, *r* Hind., 400 m.
Byzantium, Biz-án-ʃi-um, ancient *c* on the site of modern Constantinople.

# C.

Cababuri, Kq-bq-bɷ-ré, *r* Brazil.
Cabagan, Kq-bq-gq́n, *t* Phil. Is., 11¼.
Cabapuana, Kq-ba-pɷ-q́-nq, *r* Bra.
Cabes, Kq́b-es, *gulf* Med.
Cabool, Kq-bɷ́l, (*or* Caboul, Cabul,) Afg., 60.
Cabra, Kq́-brq, *t* Sp., 11½.
Cabrera, Kq-brá-rq, *is* Med.
Cabriel, Kq-brɛ-él, *r* Sp.
Cacapon, Kák-a-pon, (often Cáp-on,) *r* Va., 140 m.
Caceres, Kq́-ŧa-res, *prov* and *t* Sp., 12.
Caceres, Nueva, Nɷ-á-vq Kq́-sa-rez, *t* Phil., 12.
Cache, Kaʃ, *r* and *t* Ark.; *cr* Cal.
Cachemaso, Kaʃ-ɛ-mq́-sɷ, *p o* Ark.
Cachimayo, Kq-ɕɛ-mį-ɷ, *r* Bol., 340 m.
Cachoeira, *or* Caxoeira, Kq-ʃɷ-á-i-rq, *c* Bra., 15.
Caddo, Kád-ɷ, (Lake,) Tex., La.
Cadereita, Kq-de-rá-i-tq, *t* Mex. 4.
Cadiz, Ká-diz, (Sp. Kq́-dɛŧ,) *prov* and *c* Sp., pop. 54.
Cadwallader, Kad-wól-a-der, *p o* O.
Caen, Koñ, *c* Fr.
Caerleon, Kęr-lé-on, *t* Eng.
Caernarvon, Kęr-nq́r-von, *v* Pa.
Caerwys, Kįr-wis, *t* Wales.
Cæsarea, Ses-a-ré-a, haven of Palestine, once a place of note, now a mass of ruins.
Cagayan, Kq-gį-q́n, *prov* of Is. Luzon.
Cagli, Kq́l-yɛ, *t* It., 9¾.
Cagliari, Kq́l-yq-rɛ, *c cap* Is. Sar., 30.
Cagnano, Kqn-yq́-nɷ, *t* Naples, 4.
Cagua, Kq́-gwq, *t* Ven., 5¼.
Cahawba, Ka-hé-ba, *r* Ala., nav. 100 m.; *t* Ala.
Cahete, Kq-á-ta, *t* Bra., 6.
Cahir, *or* Caher, Ká-her, *t* Ir.
Cahokia, Ka-hó-ki-a, *v* and *cr* Ill.
Cahors, Kq-ór, *t* Fr., 13½.
Cailloma, *or* Caylloma, Kįl-yɷ́-mq, *prov* and *t* S. Am.
Caillou, Ka-yɷ́, *or* Ka-lɷ́, *l* La.
Caiiriris, Kį-rɛ-rés, *m* Brazil.
Cairn, Karn, *v* and *r* Scot.
Cairo, Kį-rɷ, *cap c* Egypt, pop. 250.
Cairo, Ká-rɷ, *t* Ill., at junction O. and Miss. *rs*.
Caitawistky, Kat-a-wíst-ki, *cr* N. C.
Cajazzo, Kq-yq́t-sɷ, *or* Caiasso, Kį-q́-sɷ, *t* Naples. [Nap.
Cajeta, Kq-yá-tq, (*or* Caieta,) *s-pt c*
Calabar, Kq-lq-bq́r, (*or* Cross River,) *r* Af., nav. 200 m.
Calabria, Ka-lá-bri-a, *or* Kq-lq́-bri-q, part of Naples.
Calahorra, Kq-lq-ór-q, *c* Sp., 5¾.
Calais, Kál-is, (Fr. Kq-lá,) *s-pt t* Fr., 100; *c* Me., 6.
Calaisis, Kq-la-zé, *dis* Fr.
Calamianes, Kq-lq-mɛ-q́-nes, *is* Malay Arch. [Sumatra.
Calantiga, Kq-lqn-té-gq, *is* N. E.
Calapooya, Kal-a-pɷ́-ya, *p o* Oregon.
Calasparra, Kq-lqs-pár-q, *t* Sp., 5¼.
Calata Bellota, Kq-lq́-tq Bel-ɷ́-tq, *t* and *r* Sicily, 4¾. [10.
Calata Fimi, Kq-lq́-tq Fé-mɛ, *t* Sicily,
Calata-Scibetta, Kq-lq́-tq-ʃɛ-bét-q, *t* Sicily, 4¾.
Calatayud, Kq-lq-tq-yɷ́đ, *t* Sp., 8½.
Calaveras, Kal-a-vá-ras, *r* California.
Calayan, Kq-lq-yq́n, *i* Malay Arch.
Calbuco, Kql-bɷ́-kɷ, *or* El Fuerte, El Fɷ-ér-ta, *t* Chili.
Calcasieu, Kál-ka-ʃɷ, *r* and *l* La.
Calci, Kq́l-ɕɛ, *v* Tuscany.
Calcinaja, Kql-ɕɛ-nq́-yq, *t* Tuscany.

Calcio, Kq́l-ço, *t* Lombardy.
Calcken, Kq́l-ken, *t* Belgium.
Calcutta, Kal-kút-ɑ, *c* Hindostan, seat of gov. British India, 230.
Calder, Kél-der, *r* Eng.
Caldera, Kql-dá-rq, *port* Costa Rica; *s-pt* Hayti.
Calder, Kq́l-der, *r* Scot.
Caldewgate, Kél-dŋ-gat, suburb of the city of Carlisle, Eng., 5½.
Caldwell, Kéld-wel, *cos* U. S.
Caledonia, Kal-ɛ-dó-ni-ɑ, anc. name of Scotland.
Caledonian Canal, Scot., connects the North and Irish Seas, 60½ miles.
Caledonia, New, *cy* British N. Am.; *i* Australia.
Calhoun, Kal-hɵ́n, *vs* Ga., &c.
Cali, Kq-lé, *t* New Granada, 4.
Calicut, Kál-i-kut, *s-pt t* Brit. Ind., 25.
California, Kal-i-fór-ni-ɑ, *st* U. S., area, 188,982 s. m., pop. in 1852, 264,435.
California, Gulf of, arm of the Pacific, w. of Cal., length, 700 miles.
California, Lower or Old, *dep* Mex.
Calk's Ferry, Keks, *p o* S. C.
Callaghans, Kál-a-hanz, *p o* Va.
Callao, Kq-lɤ́, *i* China Sea; Kq-lq́-ɷ, *s-pt t* Peru, 8½. [gon.
Callapooya Indians, Kal-a-pɵ́-yɑ, Ore-
Calmina, Kal-mé-nɑ, *t* Africa, 15.
Calmucks, *or* Calmacks, people of Upper Asia.
Caln, Kqn, *p o* Pa.
Calne, Kqn, *t* Eng.
Calore, Kq-ló-ra, *r* Naples.
Calpentyn, Kql-pen-tịn, *pen* and *s-pt* Ceylon.
Caltagirone, Kql-tq-ji-ró-na, (*or* Calatagirone,) *c* Sicily, 21¾. [17¼.
Caltanisetta, Kql-tq-ni-sét-q, *c* Sicily,
Caltonica, Kql-tón-i-kq, *t* Sicily, 7.
Calumet, Kál-yụ-met, (*or* Calumick,) *r* Ind., and Ill.
Calvados, Kql-vq-dós, *dep* Fr.
Calvary, Kál-va-ri, *t* Ohio.
Calventura, Kql-ven-tɵ́-rq, *is* Bay of Bengal.
Calvert, Kél-vẹrt, *co* Md.
Calw, *or* Kalw, Kqlv, *t* Ger., 4½.
Calzada, Kql-ŧq́-đq, *t* New Castile, 4.
Cam, *or* Granta, *r* Eng. [Bra.
Camacho, *or* Camaxo, Kq-mq́-ʃɷ, *ls*
Camacuan, Kq-mq-kwq́n, *r* Brazil.
Camanche, Ka-mán-çɛ, *v* Iowa.
Camanche Indians, (*or* Comanche,) Mexico and Texas.
Camaranca, Kq-mq-rq́ŋ-kq, *r* Africa.
Camargo, Kq-mq́r-gɷ, *t* Mex., *vs* U. S.
Camargue, La, Lq Kq-mq́rg, *pop i* Fr.
Camarines, Kq-mq-ré-nes, *two provs* Philippines, island of Luzon.
Cambay, Kam-bá, *gulf* and *s-pt t* Hindostan, 10.
Cambodia, Kam-bó-di-ɑ, (Camboge, *or* Camboja,) *t* Siam. [Fr., 21¼.
Cambrai, *or* Cambray, Kam-brá, *ft t*
Cambria, Kám-bri-ɑ, ancient name of Wales; *cos* U. S.
Cambridge, Kám-brij, *t* Eng., 28; *c* Mass., 15¼; numerous *vs* U. S.
Camden, Kám-den, *c* N-J., 15; *ts* S. C., Ala., Miss., Ark., &c.
Camenz, Kq́-ments, *t* Saxony, 4.
Camerino, Kq-ma-ré-nɷ, *c* Italy.
Cameron Kám-er-on, *co* and *v* Texas.
Cameroons, Kam-er-ɵ́ns, (*or* Camerones,) *r* and *ms* West. Africa.
Camiguin, Kq-mi-gén, Malay Arch.
Camogli, Kq-mól-yɛ, *t* Sardinian States, 5¾.
Campagna, Kqm-pq́n-yq, *t* Naples, 6¾.
Campbell, Kám-el, *cos* and *vs* U. S.; *i* South Pacific Ocean.
Campbello, Kam-bél-ɷ, *v* Mass.
Campbelton, Kám-el-ton, *s-pt t* Scot.
Campeachy, *or* Campeche, Kam-pé-çi, *gulf* and *s-pt t* Yucatan, 18.
Campinas, Kqm-pé-nqs, *c* Brazil, 6.
Campobasso, Kq́m-pɷ-bq́-sɷ, *ft c* Naples, 7¾.
Camtoos, Kqm-tɵ́s, *or* -tɵ́s, *r* S. Af.
Cana, Ká-nɑ, ruined *t* Pal.; *p o* Ia.
Canaan, Ká-nan, *or* Ká-na-an, "Promised Land" of the Israelites; *vs* U. S.
Canada, Kán-a-dɑ, two British provinces in N. America; area, 357,822 s. m., pop. 1,842,265.
Canaderaga, Kan-a-dɛ-ré-gɑ, *l* N-Y.
Canadian, Kan-á-di-an, (*or* North Channel,) passage in St. Lawrence; *r* New Mexico, 900 m.
Canajoharie, Kan-a-jɷ-hár-ɛ, *v* N-Y.
Canandagua, Kan-an-dá-gwɑ, *v* and *l* N-Y.
Cananore, Kan-a-nór, *s-pt t* Brit. Ind.
Canaries, Ka-ná-riz, (*or* Canary Islands,) *arch* Atlantic Ocean, 257¾, belonging to Spain.
Canasauga, Kan-a-sé-gɑ, *v* Tenn.
Canaseraga, Kan-a-sɛ-ré-gɑ, *v* N-Y.
Canastota, Kan-as-tó-tɑ, *v* N-Y.
Canastra, Kq-nq́ȝ-trq, *ms* Brazil.
Cancale, Koṅ-kq́l, *b* and *s-pt t* Fr., 6.
Cancao, Kqn-kɤ́, *s-pt t* Farther India.
Candahar, *or* Kandahar, Kqn-dq-hár, *ft c* and *cap* Central Afghanistan, pop. from 25 to 100.
Candeish, Kan-dáʃ, *dis* India.

Candia, Kán-di-a, (*or* Crete,) *i* Med.; *s-pt c* and *cap* island of Crete, 12; *t* Sardinia; *ts* U. S.
Cane, Kan, (*or* Ken,) *r* India.
Canete, Kqn-yá-ta, *prov* and *s-pt t* Peru.
Cangallo, Kqn-gql-yo, *prov* and *t* Peru.
Cangozima, Kqn-go-zé-mq, (*or* Kangozima,) *s-pt t* Japan.
Canguçu, Kqn-go-só, *r* and *t* Brazil.
Caniapuscaw, Kan-i-áp-us-ko, *r* and *l* Labrador.
Canicatti, Kq-ni-kq-tε, *t* Sicily, 18.
Caninde, Kq-nén-da, *r* Brazil, 200 m.
Canisteo, Kan-is-té-o, *co, r* and *v* N-Y.
Cannes, Kqn, *s-pt t* Fr.
Cannon River, Minn. Ter.
Cannouchee, *or* Canoochee, Ka-nó-çε, *r* Ga.
Canoma, Kq-nó-mq, *r* Brazil.
Canonsburg, *t* Pa.
Canquaga, Kan-kwq-ga, *cr* N-Y.
Canso, *or* Canseau, Kán-so, Gut of, passage bet. Nova Scotia and Cape Breton.
Cantabrian, Kan-tá-bri-qn, *ms* Sp.
Cantal, Koṅ-tql, *dep* Fr.
Canterbury, Kán-ter-ber-i, *c, bor* and *co* Eng.; pop. of *c* 18¾; *vs* U. S.
Canton, Kán-ton, *r* and *c* China; pop. estimated by Balbi at 500,000, by others at 1,500,000; *ts* U. S.
Canturio, Kqn-tó-ri-o, (*or* Cantu,) *t* Italy.
Canuma, Kq-no-mq, *l* Brazil.
Cap au Gray, Kap o Gra, *p o* Mo.
Cape Agulhas, A-gól-yas, s. coast Af.
Cape Aia, A'yq, s. coast Russia.
Cape Anguilla, An-gwíl-q, coast Newfoundland.
Cape Apsheron, Ap-ʃε-rón, e. Georgia, Caspian Sea.
Cape Béarn, Ba-árn, *prom* Fr.
Cape Beaufort, Bó-fort, Rus. America; Brit. America.
Cape Boeo, Bo-á-o, w. point of Sicily.
Cape Breton, Bré-ton, *i* Brit. N. Am.; length 100 miles; breadth 85 miles; pop. 54,880.
Cape Coast Castle, *ft t* Africa, 10.
Cape Cod, Mass., 65 miles long, from 1 to 20 miles wide.
Cape Colony, *or* Cape of Good Hope, territory of Great Britain, the southern extremity of Africa, pop. 166,408, of whom 70,000 are colored.
Cape Domesne, *or* Domesnes, Do-mán, Russia.
Cape Fear River, N. C., nav. 120 m.
Cape Girardeau, Jε-rqr-dó *co* and *t* Mo.
Cape Grisnez, Grε-ná, France, point nearest Britain.
Cape Haytien, Há-ti-en, (formerly Cape Français, Froṅ-sá,) *s-pt t* Hayti. Pop. in 1789, 18,500; in 1851, 6,000.
Cape Horn, Horn, most s. point Amer., on last island of the Fuegian Arch.
Cape Island, *c* watering place, N. J.
Cape Malabar, Mal-a-bqr, s. e. extremity of Mass.
Cape Matapan, Mq-tq-pqn, s. extremity, Morea, Greece.
Cape May, s. extremity of N. J.
Cape Maysi, *or* Maisi, Mi-sé, e. extremity of Cuba.
Cape of Good Hope, see Cape Colony.
Cape River, *or* Rio de Segovia, *r* Cen. America, 300 miles long.
Capernaum, Ca-pęr-na-um, *anc c* Pal.
Cape Town, *ft s-pt t* S. Africa, 22½.
Cape Trafalgar, Traf-al-gqr, headland of Spain.
Cape Verd, (*or* Verde,) *is* w. Africa, Atlantic Ocean, pop. in 1834, 55,838.
Cape Vincent, Vín-sent, port of entry, N-Y.
Capibaribe, Cq-pε-bq-ré-ba, *r* Brazil.
Capiz, Kq-pés, *c* Philippines, 11¼.
Cappadocia, Kap-a-dó-ʃi-a, *anc prov* Asia Minor; *v* Naples.
Capsali, Kqp-sq-lε, *s-pt t* Ionian Is., 5.
Capua, Kq-po-q, *ft c* Naples, 8.
Caqueta, Kq-ká-tq, *r* S. Am.
Caracas, Kq-rq-kqs, *c* and *cap* Ven., 63.
Caraglio, Kq-rql-yo, *t* Piedmont, 6¼.
Caramnassa, Kq-rqm-nq-sq, *r* Br. Ind.
Carangamite, Kq-rqn-gq-mét, salt water lake, Australia.
Caravaca, Kq-rq-vq-kq, *t* Sp., 10.
Caravaggio, Kq-rq-vqd-jo, *t* Italy, 6.
Caravellas, Kq-rq-vél-qs, *s-pt t* Bra., 5.
Carbondale, Kqr-bon-dal, *c* Pa.
Carcajente, Kqr-kq-hén-ta, *t* Sp., 6¼.
Carcassonne, Kqr-kq-són, *c* Fr., 20.
Cardenas, Kqr-da-nqs, *s-pt t* Cuba, 6.
Cardiff, *or* Caerdiff, Kqr-dif, *s-pt t* South Wales, 18¼.
Cardigan, Kqr-di-gan, *co, t* and *b* S. Wales.
Cardington, Kqr-diŋ-ton, *v* O.
Cariaco, Kq-ri-q-ko, *gulf* and *t* Venezuela, 7.
Caribbean, Kar-i-bé-an, Sea, portion of the North Atlantic Ocean.
Caribees, Kár-i-bεz, part of the West India Islands.
Carignano, Kq-rεn-yq-no, *t* Pied., 8.
Carinhenha, Kq-rεn-yén-yq, *r* and *t* Brazil.
Carini, Kq-ré-nε, *r* and *t* Sicily, 7.
Carleton, Kqrl-ton, *v* Iowa.

Carlisle, Kqr-lįl, *c* Eng.. 26½; *t* Pa., 6; *vs* Ky., O., Ind., &c.
Carlow, Kq́r-lœ, *co, par* and *t* Ir., 8¾.
Carlowitz, *or* Karlowitz, Kq́r-lœ-vits, *t* Austria, 5½.
Carlsbad, Kqrlz-bqt, *t* Bohemia, watering-place.
Carlscrona, *or* Karlskrona, Kqrls-krǿ-nq, *ft s-pt t* Sweden, 12½.
Carlshamn, Kq́rls-hqm, *ft s-pt t* Swed., 5.
Carlsruhe, *or* Karlsruhe, Kq́rlz-rœ, *c* cap. of Baden, 25¾.
Carlstad, Kq́rl-stqt, *prov* and *t* Swed.
Carlyle, Kqr-lįl, *vs* Ala., Ill.
Carmagnola, Kqr-mqn-yǿ-lq, *t* Pied.
Carmarthen, Kqr-mq́r-then, *s-pt t* S. Wales, 10½.
Carmel, Kq́r-mel, *m* Palestine.
Carmen, Kq́r-men, *i* Gulf of Cal.
Carmi, Kq́r-mi, *v* Ill.
Carmoe, Kq́r-mę-e, *i* Norway, 6¼.
Carmona, Kqr-mǿ-nq, *c* Sp., 13.
Carnarvon, Ka-nq́r-von, (*or* Caernarvon,) *b* and *s-pt t* North Wales, 8¾.
Carolina, Kar-œ-lį-na, *vs* Miss., Tex., Tenn.
Caroline Islands, (*or* New Philippines,) *arch.* of Oceania.
Carondelet, Ka-rón-dε-let, *v* Mo.
Carony, *or* Caroni, Kq-rœ-nέ, *r* Venezuela, 400 miles.
Carora, Kq-rǿ-rq, (*or* Caroro) *t* Ven., 9.
Carouge, Kq-rǿʒ, *t* Swit., 5.
Carpathian, (*or* Kar-) Kqr-pá-thi-an, mountain range in Europe, chiefly in Austria.
Carpentaria, Kqr-pen-tq́-ri-a, *gulf* in S. Pac. Oc., n. coast of Australia.
Carpentras, Kqr-poṅ-trq́s, *c* Fr., 10¾.
Carrara, Kq-rq́-rq, *c* It. 8¼.
Carrick-on-Suir, Kár-ik-on-sεr, *t* Ir.,
Carrollton, *vs* Ga., Ala., Miss., La., &c.
Carson's Lake, w. part Utah Ter.
Cartagena, Kqr-ta-jέ-na, *c* Sp., 27¾.
Cartagena, *or* Carthagena, Kq́r-ta-jέ-na, New Granada, 18.
Cartago, Kqr-tq́-gœ, *r* and *b* Mosquito Coast; *cap* Costa-Rica; *t* New Gran.
Cartaya, Kqr-tį-yq, *t* Sp., 4.
Carthage, Kq́r-thaj, *anc cap* of a famous country of the same name in Northern Africa; numerous *vs* U. S.
Carthagena, Kqr-tha-jέ-na, *p o* O.
Carupano, Kq-rœ-pq́-nœ, *s-pt t* Venezuela, 5.
Carvin-Epinoy, Kqr-váṅ-Ɛ-pε-nwq́, *t* Fr., 4.
Casale, Kq-sq́-la, *prov* and *t* Sardinian States, 21.
Casanare, Kq-sq-nq́-ra, *r* N-Granada.
Casas-Grandes, Kq́-sqs-Grq́n-des, *t* Chihuahua, 3.
Cascade, Kás-kad, City, Wash. Ter.
Cascade Range, *ms* w. part of Oregon.
Casco, Kás-kœ, Bay, Me.
Caserta, Kq-sę́r-tq, *t* Naples, 25¾.
Cashel, Káʃ-el, *c* Ir., 8.
Cashie, Káʃ-i, *r* N. C.
Cashmere, Kashmir, Kachemir, *or* Cachemire, Kqʃ-mέr, *cy* Hindostan, under the protection of Eng.; pop. 200,000, having been reduced, in twenty years, from 800,000, by earthquakes, pestilence, and famine.
Cash River, s. extremity of Ill.
Casoria, Kq-sǿ-ri-q, *t* Naples, 8.
Caspe, Kq́s-pa, *t* Sp., 7½.
Caspian Kq́s-pi-an, Sea, inland sea bet. Europe and Asia; length, 760 m., breadth, 270 m.
Cassadaga, Kas-a-dá-ga, *l* and *v* N-Y.
Cassandra, *or* Kassandra, Kq-sq́n-drq, *pen* and *gulf* Eu. Turkey.
Cassay, Kq-sá, (Kathee, *or* Munnipoor,) *ind cy* Farther Ind., 75¾.
Cassel, *or* Kassel, Kq́-sel, walled city of Germany, cap. of Hesse-Cassel, pop. 34½; also *ft t* Hesse-Darmstadt, pop. 2¼; Kq-sél, *t* Fr., 4¼.
Cassiquiare, Kq-si-kε-q́-ra, (*or* Cassiquiari,) *r* Venezuela.
Cass Lake, central Mich.
Cass River, Mich.
Cassville, *ts* N-Y., Pa., Ga., Mo., &c.
Castalia, Kas-tá-li-a, *v* O.
Castel-a-Mare, Kqs-tél-q-mq́-ra, *c* Naples, 16; *t* Sicily, 6.
Castellon de la Plana, Kqs-tel-yǿn dá lq Plq́-nq, *c* Sp., 17.
Castelnaudary, Kqs-tel-nœ-dq-rέ, 10.
Castel Nuovo, Kqs-tél Nœ-ǿ-vœ, *ft t* Dalmatia, 7.
Castiglione, Kqs-tεl-yǿ-na, *ts* Italy, Naples, Sicily, &c.
Castile, Kqs-tέl, former kingdom of Spain, (Old and New,) *ts* U. S.
Castine, Kas-tέn, port of Entry, Me.
Castlebar, Kas-l-bq́r, *r* and *t* Ir.
Castlereagh, Kas-l-rá, *r* Australia.
Castleton, Kás-l-ton, *vs* Vt., N-Y., &c.
Castletown, Kás-l-tʊn, *cap* Isle of Man, Eng., 2¼.
Castor, Kás-tor, *bayou* La.; *r* Mo.
Castres, Kq́s-tr, *t* Fr., 20¾.
Castro, Kq́s-trœ, *s-pt t* Naples, 7; *t* As. Turkey, 6½; *ts* Brazil, Chili.
Castro-del-Rio, Kq́s-trœ-del-Rέ-œ, *t* Sp., 9.
Castrogiovanni, Kq́s-trœ-jœ-vq́-nε, *c* Sicily, 11½.
Castro-Urdiales, Kq́s-trœ-Œr-di-q́-les, *t* Sp., 3.
Catahoula, Kat-a-hǿ-la, *l* La.

Catalamet, Kat-a-lá-met, *v* Wash. Ter.
Catalonia, Kq-tq-ló-ni-a, *old prov* Sp.
Catamarca, Kq-tq-mq́r-kq, *dep* and *t* La Plata, 4.
Catanduanes, Kq-tqn-dœ-q́-nes, one of the Philippine Islands. [54¼.
Catania, Kq-tq́-ni-q, *g* and *c* Sicily,
Catanzaro, Kq-tqn-zq́-rœ, *c* Nap., 11½.
Catapuliche, Kq-tq-pœ-lé-qa, *r* S. Am.
Catasauqua, Kat-a-sé-kwa, *v* Pa.
Catatonk, Kat-a-tóŋk, *p o* N. Y.
Cataula, Ka-té-la, *cr* and *p o* Ga.
Catawba, Ka-té-ba, *r* N. and S. C.
Catawissa, Kat-a-wis-a, *m*, *cr* and *v* Pa.
Cateau, Le, Lę Kq-tó, *t* Fr., 8¼.
Catfish River, Wis.
Catorce, Kq-tér-ŧa, *t* Mex.
Catrimani, Kq-tri-mq́-ne, *r* Brazil.
Catrine, Ká-tren, *v* Scot.
Catskill, Káts-kil, *ms* and *t* N-Y.
Cattaraugus, Kat-a-ré-gus, *cr* and *v* N-Y.
Cattaro, Kq́-tq-rœ, *s-pt t* Austria.
Cattegat, Kát-e-gat, arm of North Sea, w. Sweden.
Cauambe, Kɤ-q́m-ba, *or* Gaume, Gɤ́-ma, *r* Brazil.
Cauca, Kɤ́-kq, *r* New Gran.
Caucasus, Ké-ka-sus, range of mountains forming the boundary bet. Europe and Asia, 700 m. in length.
Caucasus, portion of the Russian Empire contiguous to Caucasian Mts.
Caudebec-lès-Elbeuf, Kœd-bék-laz-El-bęf, *t* Fr., 7¼.
Caughdenoy, Ke-de-nó, *p o* N. Y.
Caughnawaga, Ke-na-wé-ga, *v* N-Y.
Cauquenes, Kɤ-ká-nes, min. springs, Chili.
Caura, Kɤ́-rq, *r* Venezuelan Gaiana.
Cauten, Kɤ-tén, (*or* Imperial,) *r* Chili.
Cauto, Kɤ́-tœ, *r* Cuba.
Cava, Kq́-vq, *t* Naples 13.
Cavaillon, Kq-va-yóń, *t* Fr., 7½.
Cavanas, Kq-vq́-nqs, port of Cuba.
Cavery, Ké-ver-i, (*or* Cauvery,) *r* Ind.
Cavesa, Ka-vá-sa, *cr* Tex.
Cave Spring, Ga., seat of state asylum for the deaf and dumb.
Cavité, Kq-ve-tá, *ft s-pt t* Phil. Is.
Cawnpoor, Caunpoor, Ken-pór, (*or* Caunpore,) *dis* and *t* Hindostan.
Caxamarca, *or* Cajamarca, Kq-*h*q-mq́r-kq, *c* Peru, 8. [Bra.
Caxias, *or* Cachias, Kq-ʃé-qs, com. *t*
Cayambe, Kį-q́m-ba, (*or* Cayambeurcu, Kį-qm-ba-œr-kó, *m* in Ecuador, 19,535 feet high. [*i* At. Oc.
Cayenne, Kį-én, *s-pt cap* Fr. Guiana;
Caymans, Kį-mq́nz, three *is* Brit. W. Ind.
Caymites, Kį-mét, two *is* West Ind.
Caymito, Kį-mé-tœ, *r* New Gran.
Cayo Cocas, Kį-œ Kó-kqs, *i* Carribean Sea, belonging to Cuba; — Largo, Lq́r-gœ, ditto; — Romano, Rœ-mq́-nœ, ditto.
Cayuga, Ka-yq́-ga, *l*, *v* and *co* N-Y.; *vs* Miss., Mich., Can. West.
Cayuse, Kq-yq́s, Indians, Oregon.
Cayuta, Ka-yq́-ta, *v*, *cr* and *l* N-Y.
Cazembe, Kq-zém-be, *cy* Africa.
Cazenovia, Kaz-en-ó-vi-a, *v* N-Y., 5.
Cazorla, Kq-ŧér-lq, *c* Sp., 7¼.
Cea, Ħá-q, *r* Sp.
Ceccano, Ɵek-q́-nœ, *v* It., 6.
Cecina, Ɵa-qé-nq, *r* Tus.
Cedar Bluff, *v* Ala.
Cedar Rapids, *t* Iowa.
Cedarville, *ts* N-J., O., &c.
Cefalu, Ɵa-fq-ló, *ft s-pt t* Sicily, 9.
Ceglie, Ɵál-ya, *c* Naples, 7¼.
Cehegin, Ħa-a-*h*én, *t* Sp., 9½.
Celebes, Sél-e-bes, *i* Malay Arch., government federal and republican, pop. 2,000,000. [12.
Celle, Tsél-e, *or* Zell, Tsel, *t* Hanover,
Centenary College, Jackson, La.
Central America. See America.
Central Falls, *v* R. I.
Central Village, *or* North Plainfield, manufacturing *v* Conn.
Centreville, Sén-ter-vil, *ts* Mass., R. I., Conn., O., Ia., &c., &c.
Cephalonia, Sef-q-ló-ni-q, *i* Med.; length 32 m., breadth 12 m.; under protection of Eng., pop. 63¼.
Ceram, *or* Zeram, Se-rq́ŋ, *i* Malay Arch., 226.
Cerea, Ɵa-rá-q, *t* Lom., 5¾.
Ceresco, Se-rés-kœ, *vs* Mich., Wis.
Cerignola, Ɵa-ren-yó-lq, *t* Nap., 10¼.
Cerigo, Ɵér-i-gœ, s. Ionian Is., pop. 9.
Cerro-de-Pasco, Sér-œ da Pq́s-kœ, *t* Peru, 16.
Cerro Gordo, Sér-œ Gér-dœ, battlefield, 60 m. n. w. city Mex.; *vs* U. S.
Cesena, Ɵa-sá-nq, *t* It., 12.
Cesenatico, Ɵa-sa-nq́-ti-kœ, *s-pt t* Pontifical States.
Cette, Set, *ft s-pt t* Fr., 19¼.
Cettina, Tse-té-nq, *r* Austria.
Ceuta, Sq́-ta, *s-pt t* Af., belonging to Sp., 8¼.
Cevennes, Sa-vén, *ms* Fr.
Ceylon, Sé-lon, *i* Ind. Oc., belonging to Great Brit., length 270 m. breadth 100 m., pop. 1,507,000.
Cezimbra, Sa-zém-brq, *s-pt t* Port., 5.

Chabeuil, Σq-bely, *t* Fr., 4½.
Chablais, Σq-blá, *prov* Savoy, 54¾.
Chachacomani, Єq-çq-kɷ-mq-nɛ, *m* peak Andes, in Bolivia, 20,235 ft.
Chachapoyas, Єq-çq-pó-yqs, (*or* Chacapoyas,) *t* Peru.
Chadda, Єád-ɑ, *r* Guinea. [Plata.
Chadi-Leubu, Єq-dɛ-Le-ɷ-bɷ́, *r* La
Chæronea, Ker-ɷ-né-ɑ, ruined *c* of Gr.
Chagres, Єq-gres, *s-p t* New Granada.
Chagres River, Isthmus of Panama.
Chagrin Falls, Σa-grin Fɵlz, *v* and *r* O.
Chalcis, Kál-sis, (*or* Negropont) *t* Gr.
Chaldea, Kal-dé-ɑ, *anc div* As., on the Euphrates.
Chaleur, Σq-lɷ́r, *b* Gulf of St. Law.
Chalonnes-sur-Loire, Σq-lón-sęr-lwq́r, *t* Fr. [*c* Fr., 15¾.
Chalons-sur-Marne, Σq-lɷ́n-sęr-mqrn,
Chalon-sur-Saone, -sɷn, *t* Fr., 16½.
Chama, Єq-mq, *r* Ven.
Chamahatchie, Єam-a-háç-i, *p o* Ala.
Chambersburg, Єám-berz-burg, *t* Pa., 5; *vs* O., Ia.
Chambersia, Єam-bęr-ʃi-ɑ, *v* Tex.
Chambery, Σoṅ-ba-ré, *c*, *cap* Savoy, 16.
Chambly, Σám-bli, *co* and *v* C. E.
Chamouni, Σq-mɷ-né, (*or* Chamonix,) picturesque *val* and *t* Sar. States.
Champagne, Σóṅ-pqny, old *prov* Fr.
Champagnolle, Σam-pan-yól, *cr* and *v* Ark.
Champaign, Σam-pán, *cos* U. S.
Champlain, Σam-plán, *l* bet. N-Y., and Vt., 130 by ½ to 10 m.; *t* N-Y., 5; *v* C. E.
Chanahachee, Єan-a-háç-ɛ, *p o* Ala.
Chandeleur, Σan-dɛ-lɷ́r, *b* s. e. La.
Chandernagore, Σqn-der-nq-gɷ́r, Fr. *t* Bengal, 35¾.
Chandlersville, Єánd-lerz-vil, *t* O.
Changchoofoo, Єqŋ-çɷ-fɷ́, *c* China, pop. from 800,000 to 1,000,000.
Chang-Mai, Єqŋ-mį, *t* Laos, 25.
Chang-Sha, Єqŋ-ʃq, *c* China.
Channahon, Єán-a-hon, *v* Ill.
Channel Єán-el (Islands,) group in the Eng. Chan., belonging to the Eng. crown.
Chao-Tchoo, Єq-ɷ-çɷ́, *or* Tchao-Cheou-Fou, Єq-ɷ-ça-ɷ́-fɛ, *c* China.
Chapala, Єq-pq-lq, *l* Mex.
Chapari, Єq-pq-ré, *r* Bol.
Chapelle Agnon, La, Lq Σq-pél Ꭿn-yɷ́n, *t* Fr.
Chapelle St. Denis, La, Saṅ Da-né, *t* Fr., 18¾.
Chapola River, Єa-pó-lɑ, Fa., Ala.
Chapoo, Єq-pɷ́, *or* Σq-pɷ́, *t* China.
Chappaqua, Єa-pé-kwɑ, *v* N-Y.
Chapultepec, Єq-pɷl-ta-pék, fortress of Mex., 2 m. s. w. of the capital.
Charbar, Єqr-bqr, (*or* Choubar,) *b* Bel.
Chard, Єqrd, *t* Eng., 5¼.
Chardon, Єqr-don, *v* O., 1.
Charikar, Єar-i-kqr, *t* Afg., 5.
Chariton, Єár-i-ton, *r* Iowa, and Mo., *vs* Mo., Iowa.
Charlemont, Єqr-lɛ-mont, *v* Mass.
Charleroi, Σqr-lɛ-rɷ́, *ft t* Bel., 6⅓.
Charles River, Mass.
Charleston, *c* and port of entry, S. C., 43; *ts* and *vs* Ill., Iowa, &c.
Charleston, Єqrlz-tɤn, *c* and *s-pt* adjoining Boston, Mass., pop. 17¼; *vs* N-H., Pa., Va., Ia.
Charleville, Σqr-le-vél, *t* Fr., 9¼.
Charlevoix, Σqr-lɛ-vɷ́, *co* Mich.
Charloe, Єqr-lɷ, *v* O.
Charlotte, Σqr-lot, *ts* Vt., N-Y., N. C.
Charlotte Amalie, -Ꭿ-mq-lɛ-ę, *t*, *cap* of the Is. St. Thomas, 10.
Charlotte Harbor, (*or* Boca Grande,) w. coast of Fa. [Prus., 7¼.
Charlottenburg, Σqr-lót-en-bɷrh, *t*
Charlotte River, N-Y. [Va., Ia.
Charlottesville, Σqr-lots-vil, *ts* N-Y.,
Charlotte-town, *cap* Pr. Edward Is., Brit. Am., 4¾.
Charties, Єqr-tɛrz, *t* Pa.
Chartres, Σqr-tr, *c* Fr., 18¼.
Chateaugay, Σɘ-tɷ-gá, *r*, *l* and *t* N-Y.; *v* and *r* C. E.
Chateauroux, Σɘ-tɷ-rɷ́, *t* Fr., 16.
Chatham, Єát-am, *r-pt*, *naval arsenal* and *t* Eng., pop. 28½; *vs* Mass., Conn., N-Y., N-J., Ill., C. E., C. W., N-Brunswick.
Chatham Harbor, e. ex. Cape Cod.
Chatham Islands, S. Pac., e. N-Zeal.
Chattahoochee, Єat-a-hɷ́-çɛ, *r* Ga., length 550 m., nav. 350 m. from the Gulf; *v* Fa. containing U. S. ars.
Chattanooga, Єat-a-nɷ́-gɑ, *v* Tenn.
Chattooga, Єa-tɷ́-gɑ, *r* bet. S. C. and Ga., also *r* Ala.
Chaudeire, Σɷ-dɛ-ą́r, *r* C. E.
Chaumont, Σɷ-móṅ, *t* Fr., 6⅓.
Chaumont, Σɷ-mó, *v* N-Y.
Chauncey, Єqn-si, *v* O.
Chautauque, Σa-tó-kwɛ, *co* and *l* N-Y.
Chaux-de-fond, La, Lq Σɷ-dę-fóṅ, *t* Swit.
Chazy, Σaz-é, *r*, *l* and *v* N-Y.
Cheadle, Єé-dl, *t* Eng., 4¾.
Cheat River, Va. and Pa.
Cheduba, Єɛ-dɷ́-bq, *i* Far. Ind., 8½.
Cheektowaga, Єɛk-tɷ-á-gɑ, *p o* N-Y.
Chehaw, Єɛ-hé, *r* S. C.
Chehalis, Єɛ-há-lia, *co* Wash. Ter.

Chelmsford, Cémz-ford, *t* Eng., 7¾.
Chelsea, Cél-se, *t* Eng., 56½.
Chelsea, Cél-se-a, *vs* Vt. 2; Mass., 6¾, Mich., &c.
Cheltenham, Célt-nam, *t* and watering place, Eng., 35.
Chemnitz, *Hém*-nits, *t* Sax., 28¾.
Chemung, Σe-múŋ, *r*, *co* and *v* N-Y.; *v* Ill.
Chenango, Σe-náŋ-gω, *r* and *co* N-Y.
Chenook, Ce-nώk, (*or* Chinook,) *v* Wash. Ter.
Chepachet, Ce-pák-et, *v* R. I.
Chepillo, Ca-pél-yω, *i* off the s. coast of the Isthmus of Panama.
Chepo, Cá-pω, *r* and *t* N-Gran.
Chepstow, Cép-stω, *t* and *r-pt* Eng.
Cher, Σqr, *r* Cen. Fr.
Cherasco, Ka-rqs-kω, *t* Pied., 8¾.
Cheraw, Ce-ró, *v* S. C., 1.
Cherbourg, Σér-burg, *ft s-pt t* naval station, Fr., 28.
Cheribon, *or* Sheribon, Σér-i-bon, *s-pt t* Java, 11.
Cherokee, Cer-ω-ké, (Indians) a noble tribe who formerly occupied the southern portion of the Appalachian Mountains, and contiguous ter., now nearly extinct; *cos* and *vs* U. S.
Cherry Valley, *vs* N-Y., Pa., Tenn., Ill., &c.
Cherso, Kér-sω, *i* of Illyria, in the Adriatic, pop. 14.
Chersonesus, Ker-sω-né-sus, anc. name of several peninsulas.
Chertsey, Cés-i, *t* Eng., 6.
Chesapeake, Cés-a-pek, largest *b* in U. S., length, 200 m.
Chesapeake City, *v* Md.
Chesham, Céſ-am, *t* Eng., 6.
Cheshire, Céſ-er, *vs* Mass., Conn., O., [&c.
Chestatee, Ces-tá-te, *r* Ga.
Chester, Cés-ter, *c* Eng., 27¾; *vs* N-H., Vt., Mass., Conn., N-Y., Pa., Ill.
Chesterfield, Cés-ter-feld, *t* Eng., 7¼; *v* N-H., Mass., S. C., &c.; — Inlet, Brit. N. Am., length, 250 m.
Chester River, Del., and Md. [O., &c.
Chestertown, *vs* N-Y., Md., Pa., S. C.
Chesuncook, Ce-sún-kuk, *l* Me.
Chetachee, Ce-tq-çe, *cr* Ala.
Chetimaches, Cet-im-áç-ez, *or* Σet-máſ, *l* La. [*m* Eng.
Cheviot, Cív-i-ot, *or* Cév-i-ot, *v* O.;
Chiantla, Ce-qnt-lq, *r* and *t* Gua.
Chiapq, Ce-q-pq, s. state Mex. Con., pop. 162. [7.
Chiaramonte, Ke-q-rq-món-ta, *t* Sic.,
Chiari, Ke-q-re, *t* Lom., 9. [10⅓.
Chiavari, Ke-q-vq-re, *t* Sar. States,
Chicago, Σi-ké-gω, com. *c* Ill., on Lake Mich. and Chicago River, remarkable for its rapid growth. It contained in 1840, 4¾ inhabitants, 1850, 30; 1853, 60⅔; 1855, 87½.
Chicapa, Ce-kq-pq, *r* and *t* Mex.
Chichester, Cíç-es-ter, *c* Eng., 8¾.
Chickahominy, Cik-a-hóm-i-ni, *r* Va.
Chickamauga, Cik-a-mó-ga, *cr* Ga. and Tenn.
Chickasaw, Cík-a-se, *r* Ga.; *v* Ala.; Indian tribe originally occupying portions of Mississippi and Alabama.
Chickopee, Cik-ω-pé, *r* Mass.
Chickopee Falls, *v* Mass., 2½.
Chico, Cé-kω, *p o* Cal.
Chicot, Σé-kω, *co* Ark.
Chicsoi, Cek-sώ-e, *r* Guatemala.
Chictawaga, Cik-ta-wé-ga, *tp* N. Y.
Chienne *or* Cheyenne, Σe-én, Indian tribe Mo.
Chieri, Ke-á-re, *t* Pied., 13¼.
Chieti, Ke-á-te, *ft c* Naples, 17¾.
Chignecto, Σig-nék-tω, *b* bt. N. S. and N. B.
Chihauhau, Ce-wq-wq, *c* and *st* Mexican Confederation, 14.
Chikiri, Cheekeeree, *or* Tchikiri, Ce-ke-ré, *r* Mantchooria, China.
Chila, Cé-lq, *r* Perū, 105 m.
Chilapa, Ce-lq-pq, *and* Chilapilla, Ce-lq-pél-yq, *rs.* Mex.
Chilhowee, Cil-hɤ-e, *m* and *p o* Tenn.
Chili, Cíl-e, *ind rep* S. A., area 170,000 s. m., pop. mostly of Spanish and Indian descent; *vs* N-Y., O., Ind., Ill., &c.
Chillicothe, Cil-i-kót-e, *c* O., 7¼; *vs* Ill., Mo., Iowa.
Chillisquaque, Cil-is-kwé-kwe, *v* and *cr* Pa.
Chillitecaux, Σil-i-te-kώ, *p o* Mo.
Chilo, Cí-lω, *v* O.
Chiloe, Ce-lω-á, *i* w. coast S. A., 42.
Chilpanzingo, Cel-pqn-sín-gω, *t* Mex. Confederacy, 27.
Chiltepec, Cel-ta-pék, *r* Mex. Con.
Chimbarongo, Cem-bq-rón-gω, *r* Chili.
Chimborazo, Cim-bω-rq-zω, *m* S. A. Height, 21,424 ft.
Chimepanipestick, Σem-pq-nep-sték, *r* Canada East.
China, (see Chinese Empire) *vs* Me., N-Y., Mich., &c.
China Sea, portion of the Pacific Oc.
Chincha Islands, Cín-çq Ɨlandz, tre small *is* Pac. Oc. near Peru, noted for their guano.
Chinchilla, Cin-çél-yq, *c* Spain, 12⅓.
Chinchon, Cen-çώn, *t* Spain, 5⅓.

Chin-choo, ɕin-ɕǿ, region and *c* China.
Chincoteague, ɕiŋ-kɷ-tég, *p o* Va.
Chinendega, ɕɛ-nen-dá-gq, New and Old *ts* Nicaragua.
Chinese Empire, extensive ter. of Asia. Area, 5,000,000 s. m.; pop., 400,-000,000. Divided into China Proper and the dependencies: Corea, Mantchooria, Mongolia, Elee, including Soongaria, East Toorkistan, Kokonor, Thibet, and various islands.
China Proper, area 1,297,999 s. m.; pop. 387,632,907.
Ching-Hai, ɕiŋ-hí, seaport *t* China.
Ching-Kiang, ɕiŋ-kɛ-q́ŋ, *c* China.
Ching-Kiang-Foo, ɕiŋ-kɛ-q́ŋ-fǿ, *ft c* China.
Chingleput, ɕiŋ-gl-pút, *dis* and *c* Br. [India.
Chiobbe, ɕɛ-ób-a, *t* China, 300.
Chioggia, Kɛ-ód-ja, *ft t* N. Italy, 27.
Chipicani, ɕɛ-pɛ-kq́-nɛ, *m p* Andes. Height, 19,740 ft.
Chipola, ɕi-pó-la, *r* Ala., 150 m.
Chippenham, ɕip-num, *t* Eng.
Chippewa, ɕip-ɛ-wa, *rs* O., Mich., Wis.; *vs* Pa., O., Ia., Ill., C. W. [Wis.
Chippeway *or* Ojibbeway, *Indian tr*
Chiquimula de la Sierra, ɕɛ-kɛ-mǿ-lq da lq Sɛ-ér-q, *t* Cen. A.
Chiquimula, *ist.* Cen. A.
Chiquitos, ɕɛ-ké-tɷs, *ter* Bolivia.
Chiriqui, ɕɛ-rɛ-ké, *r, lagoon* and *arch* Costa Rica.
Chirripo, ɕɛ-*ré*-pɷ, *vol* and *r* Costa Ri.
Chisago, ɕi-sé-gɷ, *co* Minnesota.
Chiswick, ɕiz-ik, *par* Eng. [Y.
Chittenango, ɕit-en-áŋ-gɷ, *cr* and *v* N-
Chivasso, Kɛ-vq́-sɷ, *c* Piedmont, 7¾.
Chocolochee, ɕɷ-kɷ-ló-ɕɛ, *cr* Ala.
Choctaw, ɕók-tɵ, *Ind tr* Miss. [and Fa.
Choctawhatchee, ɕok-tɵ-háɕ-ɛ, *r* Ala.
Choestoe, ɕó-stɷ, *p o* Ga.
Choiseul, Σwq-zél, *i* S. Pac. Oc.
Choleechel, ɕɷ-la-ɕél, *i* La Plata.
Cholet *or* Chollet, Σɷ-lá, *t* France, 10⅓
Cholmondeley, ɕúm-li, *seat of a marquis*, Eng. [Indians.
Cholula, ɕɷ-lǿ-lq, *t* Mex., 10, wholly
Chonos, ɕó-nɷs, *arch* W. Patagonia.
Choo-Kiang, ɕɷ-kɛ-q́ŋ, Chinese for Canton River.
Choptank, ɕóp-taŋk, *r* Del. and Md.
Chorley, ɕór-li, *t* Eng., 12¾.
Chorolque, ɕɷ-ról-ka, *m* Bolivia. Elevation, 16,548 ft.
Chowan, ɕɷ-wén, *r* N. C. [Pa., Wis.
Christiana, Kris-ti-q́-na, *r* Mich.; *vs*
Christiania, Kris-ti-q́-ni-q, *cap c* Norway, 26¼. [*t* Norway, 8⅓.
Christiansand, Krís-ti-qn-sq́nd, *ft s-pt*
Christianstadt, Krís-ti-qn-stqt, *ft t* S. Sweden. [St. Croix.
Christiansted, Krís-ti-qn-sted, *t* island
Christiansund, Krís-ti-qn-sɷnd, *s-pt t* Norway.
Chuapa, ɕɷ-q́-pq, *r* Chili.
Chucuito, ɕɷ-kwé-tɷ, *t* Bolivia.
Chulafinne, ɕɷ-la-fín, *p o* Ala.
Chulahoma, ɕɷ-la-hó-ma, *v* Miss.
Chumbul, ɕum-búl, *r* India, 500 m.
Chuprah, ɕúp-ra, *t* Br. India, 50.
Chuqueapo, ɕɷ-ka-q-pó, *r* Bolivia.
Chuquibamba, ɕɷ-kɛ-bq́m-bq, *t* Peru; *m*, elevation 21,000 ft.
Chuquisaca, ɕɷ-kɛ-sq́-kq, (*or* La Plata,) *cap* Bolivia, 12.
Churchill, ɕúrɕ-il, (*or* Missinnippi,) *r* Brit. Am., 700 m. [U. S.
Churubusco, ɕɷ-rɷ-bǿs-kɷ, *vs* Mex.,
Cibolo, Sɛ-bó-lɷ, *r* Texas.
Cicero, Sís-er-ɷ, *vs* N-Y., O., Ind.
Cicola, ɕɛ-kó-lq, *r* Austria.
Cienfuegos, Sɛ-en-fwá-gɷs, *t* Cuba, 4¾.
Cieza, Ћɛ-á-ђq, *t* Spain, 7.
Cinaloa *or* Sinaloa, Sin-q-ló-q, *st* and *t* Mex., 9½.
Cincinnati, Sin-sin-á-ti, *c* O., fifth in size in the Union, 160¼; *vs* Ia., Mo., Iowa, Or. Terr.
Cinque (Siŋk) Ports, *s-pts* Eng., endowed with various privileges, in consideration of furnishing ships of war for the king's use, when demanded.
Circassia, Sɛr-káʃ-i-a, *cy* s. e. cor. of Eu.; area 40,000 s. m., pop. 650,000.
Circleville, Sér-kl-vil, *t* O., 4½; *vs* Ia.,
Cirencester, Sis-ɛ-ter, *t* Eng. [Ill.
Cisalpine (Sis-ál-pin) Republic, a former *st* Italy.
Citronelle, Sit-rɷ-nél, *v* Ala. [ta.
Citta Vecchia, ɕi-tq́ Vék-i-q, *ft c* Mal-
Ciudadela, Sɛ-ɷ-dq-dá-lq, *c* and *s-pt* island of Minorca, 7¾. [6½.
Ciudad Real, Sɛ-ɷ-dq́d Ra-q́l, *t* Mex.,
Ciudad Real, Ћɛ-ɷ-đq́đ Ra-q́l, *c* Sp., 10¼.
Civita Vecchia, ɕé-vɛ-tq Vék-ɛ-q, *s-pt c* Pontifical States.
Clackamas, Klák-a-mas, *r* Oregon.
Claiborne, Klá-burn, sev. *cos* U. S.; *vs* Ala., Miss.
Clara, Klq́-rq, *t* Cuba.
Clare, Klqr, *r* Ir.; *i* off w. coast of Ir.
Claremont, Klqr-mónt, *v* N-H.
Clarence, Klár-ens, *i* S. A.; *r* Australia.
Clarendon, Klár-en-don, *vs* Vt., N-Y.
Clarion, Klár-i-on, *r* and *v* Pa.
Clarke's *or* Flathead, *r* Wash. Terr.
Clarkesville, Klq́rks-vil, *v* Ga., ½.

Clarksburg, *t* Va., 1¼; *vs* Ky., O., &c.
Clarks, *r* w. part of Ky.
Clarkston, Klqrks-ton, *v* Mich.
Clarksville, *t* Va., 1; *vs* Ala., Tex., Ark., Tenn., &c.
Clausthal (*or* Klaus-), Klŏs-tql, *t* Han.
Clay, Kla, *cos* and *tps* U. S. [&c.
Claysville, Kláz-vil, *vs* Ky., O., Ind.,
Clayton, Klá-ton, *vs* N-Y., Ill., &c.
Clearfield, Klér-fɛld, *v* Pa., ¾. [*v* Wis.
Clearwater, Klér-we-ter, *r* Br. N. A.;
Cleckheaton, Klék-ɛ-ton, *v*. Eng.
Clerkenwell, Klẹr-ken-wel, *out-par* of London, 56¾.
Clermont, Klẹr-mónt, *vs* O., Ind.
Clermont-Ferrand, Kler-móṅ-Fer-óṅ, *c* France, 33½.
Cleveland, Klév-land, *c* and *l pt* O., 41; *vs* N-Y., Tenn., Ind., Ill.
Cleves, Klɛvz, *ts* Prussia, Ohio.
Clifton, Klif-ton, *watering-place*, Eng., 14; sev. *vs* U. S.
Clinch, Klinç, *r* Va. and Tenn.
Clinton, Klín-ton, *ts* Me., Mass., Conn., N-Y., N-J., La., &c.
Clinton - Golden (Klín-ton-Gól-den) Lake, Br. N. A.
Clinton River, Mich., 50 m.
Clintonville, *vs* N-Y., &c.
Clio, Klį-ɷ, *vs* S. C., Ky., O.
Clitheroe, Klíđ-er-ɷ, *t* Eng., 11½.
Clonmel, Klon-mél, *t* Ir., 13½.
Cloverdale, Kló-ver-dal, *v* Ia.
Cloverport, Kló-ver-pɷrt, *v* Ky.
Clwyd, Klwid, *r* N. Wales.
Clyde, Klįd, *r* Scotland; *t* N-Y.; *v* O.
Clymer, Klį-mer, *v* N-Y.
Coahoma, Kɷ-a-hó-ma, *co* Miss.
Coanza, Kɷ-q̇n-za, *r* Lower Guinea.
Coast Range, Kɷst Ranj, *m* Cal.
Coatesville, Kóts-vil, *v* Pa. [Mex.
Coatzacoalco, Kɷ-qt-sq-kɷ-q̇l-kɷ,
Coban, Kɷ-bq̇n, *c* Guatemala, 14.
Cobbessecontee, Kob-es-kón-tɛ, *r* Me.
Cobija, Kɷ-bé-*h*q, (*or* Port la Mar,) *s-pt* Bolivia.
Coblentz, Kób-lents, *ft c* Prus., 18¾.
Cobourg, Kó-burg, *port of entry* C. W.
Coburg, Kó-bur*g*, *t* Cen. Ger., 10.
Cochabamba, Kɷ-çq-bq̇m-bq, *or* Condorillo, Kon-dɷ-rél-yɷ, *r* Bolivia.
Cochabamba, (*also* Oropesa, Ō-rɷ-pá-sq,) *c* Bolivia.
Cochin, Kó-çin, *or* Kɷ-ʃén, *s-pt t* Hin.
Cochin China, Kó-çin Ȼį-na, s. e. portion of Anam.
Cochituate, Kɷ-çit-yq-at, *v* and *l* Mass.
Cochran's Grove, Kók-ranz Grɷv, *v* Ill.
Cocle, Kó-kl, *r* N-Grenada.
Cocolamus, Kɷ-kól-a-mus, *cr* Pa.
Cocos, Kó-kos, *is* Indian Ocean.
Codogno, Kɷ-dón-yɷ, *t* Lombardy, 9½.
Codorus, Kɷ-dó-rus, *v* and *cr* Penn.
Coepang *or* Koepang, Kɷ-pq̇ŋ, *t* island of Timor, 5.
Coeslin, Kẹs-lén, *t* Prus., 8¼.
Coesse, Kɷ-és, *p o* Ind.
Coeyman's, Kwé-manz, *v* N-Y.
Coffeville, Kóf-ɛ-vil, *v* Miss.
Coffin's, Kóf-inz, *i* Gulf of St-Law.
Coggeshall, Kóg-ʃal, *t* Eng.
Cognac, Kɷn-yq̇k, *t* Fr.
Cohahuila, Kɷ-q-wé-lq, *or* Montelovez, Mon-ta-ló-ves, *t* Mex.
Cohahuila, Kɷ-q-wé-lq, *st* Mex.
Cohansey, Kɷ-hán-si, *r* N-J.
Cohasset, Kɷ-hás-et, *v* Mass.
Cohoes, Kɷ-hóz, (*or* Cahoos *and* Cahoes,) *v* N-Y.
Coila, Kó-la, *p os* N-Y., Miss.
Coimbatoor, Kɷm-ba-tɷ́r, *dis* and *t* Hindostan.
Coimbra, Kɷ-ém-brq, *c* Portugal.
Coin, Kɷ-én, *t* Sp.
Cojutepeque, Kɷ-*h*ɷ-ta-pá-ka, *t* San Salvador; also *l*.
Colair, Kɷ-lq̇r, *l* Hind.
Colaparchee, Kɷ-la-pq̇r-çɛ, *p o* Ga.
Colberg *or* Kolberg, Kól-ber*h*, *t* Prussian Pomerania.
Colbert, Kól-bert, *v* Miss.
Colchagua, Kol-çq̇-gwq, *dep* Chili.
Colchester, Kól-çes-ter, *t* Eng., 19½; *vs* Vt., Conn., &c. [N-J., &c.
Cold Spring, Kɷld Spriŋ, *vs* N-Y. 1¼,
Cold Spring Harbor, *v* N-Y.
Coldwater, Kóld-we-ter, *t* Mich., 2; *r* Miss.
Coleborne, Kól-born, *v* C. W. [&c.
Colebrook, Kól-brɷk, *v* N-H., Conn.,
Coleraine, Kɷl-rán, *s-pt t* Ir.; *vs* U. S.
Colima, Kɷ-lé-mq, *ter* and *t* Mex., 31¾; *vol* 12,000 ft.
Collamer, Kól-a-mer, *vs* Conn., Ill., &c.
College of St. James, *v* Md.
Colliers, Kól-yerz, *v* N-Y. [*vs*.
Collinsville, Kól-inz-vil, *t* Conn., 1; sev.
Colmar, Kol-mq̇r, *c* Fr., 23½.
Colne, Kɷln *or* Kɷn, *rs* and *t* Eng.
Cologna, Kɷ-lón-yq, *t* N. It., 6½.
Cologne, Kɷ-lón, *c* Prus., 92¼.
Cololo, Kɷ-ló-lɷ, *m p* Andes, 17,930 ft.
Coloma, Kɷ-ló-ma, *p os* Ala., Ill.
Colombia, Kɷ-lóm-bi-q, former name of the republic of S. A.
Colombo, Kɷ-lóm-bɷ, *or* Columbo, Kɷ-lúm-bɷ, *s-pt t* and *cap* Ceylon, 31½.
Colonia do Santissimo Sacramento, Kɷ-ló-ni-q dɷ Sqn-té-si-mɷ Sq-krq-mén-tɷ, *ft t* Uruguay.

Colorado, *or* Rio Colorado, Ré-ω Kol-ω-rq́-dω, (to distinguish it from the Colorado of Texas,) *r* U. S., w. of the Rocky Mountains.
Colossæ, Kω-lós-ɛ, *ruined c* As. Minor.
Colquitt, Kól-kwit, *v* Ga.
Colton, Kól-ton, *v* N-Y.
Coluguape, Kω-lω-gwq́-pa, *l* Patagonia.
Columbia, Kω-lúm-bi-a, (*or* Oregon,) largest *r* entering Pacific Ocean from American continent; entire length 1200 m.; *c, cap* S. C., 7; *ts* Pa., Tenn., Mo.; *vs* Me., N-H., Conn., N-Y., O., Ind., Tex., &c.
Columbiana, Kω-lum-bi-án-a, *co* and *v* O.; *v* Ill.
Columbia Village, Kω-lúm-bi-a Víl-aj, *v* N-Y. [Med.
Columbretes, Kω-lωm-brá-tes, *vol is*
Columbus, Kω-lúm-bus, *c, cap* O., 25; *c* Ga., 9; *t* Miss.; *vs* Tex., Ind., Wis.
Colusi, Kω-ló-sɛ, *co* and *t.* Cal.
Colzean, Kol-zán, Castle, Scot.
Comacchio, Kω-mq́-ki-ω, *ft t* It.
Comal, Kω-mál, *co* and *t* Tex.
Comanche, Kω-mán-ça, *or* Comanches, Kω-mán-çes, (*also* Camanches,) *Am. Ind.* Mex. and Tex.
Comayagua, Kω-mi-q́-gwq, (formerly Valladolid,) *c* Cen. Am., 12.
Combaconum, Kom-ba-kó-num, *or* Combooconum, Kom-bω-kó-num, *t* Hind., 40.
Combahee, Kom-ba-hé, *r* S. C.
Comitan, Kω-mɛ-tq́n, (*or* Comitlan, Kω-mɛt-lq́n, *t* Mex., 10.
Comite, Kω-mét, *r* La.
Communipaw, Ko-mq́-ni-pe, *v* N-J.
Como, Kó-mω, *l, prov* and *c* Lom., 18½; *vs* U. S.
Comodo, Kó-mω-dω, *i* Malay Arch.
Comorn, Kó-morn, *fr t* Hun., 18.
Comoro, Kóm-ω-rω, Isles, *vol is* Mozambique Channel; pop. 80,000, Arabs and Negroes.
Competition, Kom-pɛ-tí-ʃon, *v* Va.
Compiano, Kom-pɛ-q́-nω, *t* It.
Compiegne, Koṅ-pɛ-any, *t* Fr., 10¾.
Compotine, Kom-pó-tɛn, *p o* Io.
Compton, Kómp-ton, *v* Ga.
Comstock, Kóm-stok, *v* Mich., 1¼.
Concentaina, Kon-ϑen-ti-nq, *t* Sp.
Concepcion, Kon-sep-sɛ-ón, (*or* Conception,) *i* n. side Panama.
Concepcion, Kon-sep-sɛ-ón, *pt* Chili, 10; *ts* Bol., N-Grenada, &c.
Conception, Kon-sép-ʃon, Bay, *inlet* Newfoundland. [Salvador.
Conchagua, Kon-çq́-gwq, *g* and *vol* San
Conchardee, Kon-çq́r-dɛ, *p o* Ala.

Conchas, Kón-çqs, (*or* Conchos,) *rs* Mex. and Braz. [Peru.
Conchucos, Kon-çó-kωs, *prov* and *t*
Concord, Kóŋ-kord, *c* N-H., 8½; *t* Vt.; *vs* Mass., Ky., Mich., &c.
Concordia, Kon-kór-di-a, *par* La.; sev. *vs* U. S.
Concord River, Mass.
Condé, Kωṅ-dá, *t* Fr., 5¼.
Conde, Kón-da, *ts* Braz.
Condé-sur-Noireau, Kωṅ-dá-sęr-nwq-ró, *t* Fr., 6½.
Condom, Kωṅ-ɗóṅ, *t* Fr., 7¼.
Conecocheague, Kon-ɛ-kω çég, *cr* Pa.
Conecuh, Kω-né-ku, *r* Ala.
Conedogwinit, Kon-ɛ-dog-wín-it, *cr* Pa.
Conegliano, Kω-nal-yq́-nω, *t* It., 6½.
Conemaugh, Kón-ɛ-me, *r* Pa. [Pa.
Conequenessing, Kon-ɛ-kwe-nés-iŋ, *cr*
Conestoga, Kon-es-tó-ga, *cr* and *v* Pa.
Conesus, Kω-né-sus, *v* and *l* N-Y.
Conewago, Kon-ɛ-wá-gω, *cr* Pa. [N-Y.
Conewango, Kon-ɛ-wáŋ-gω, *cr* and *v*
Coney, Kó-ni, Island, s. w. of Long Island, N-Y.
Congaree, Koŋ-ga-ré, *r* S. C.
Congleton, Kóŋ-gl-ton, *t* Eng.
Congo, Kóŋ-gω, *or* Zaire, Zq́-é-ra, *r* S. Af.; extensive *cy* W. Af.
Congrehoy, Kon-gra-hó-ɛ, *r* Guat.
Congress, Kóŋ-gres, *v* O.
Conhoeton, Kon-hók-ton, *r* N-Y.
Coni, Kó-nɛ, *or* Cuneo, Kω-ná-ω, *t* Piedmont, 18¾.
Conki, Kón-kɛ, *r* Hind.
Connasauga, Kon-a-sé-ga, *r* Ga.
Connaught, Kón-et, *prov* Ir.
Conneaut, Kon-ɛ-ét, *cr* Pa.; *v* O.
Conneautville, Kon-ɛ-ét-vil, *v* Pa.
Connecticut, Kon-ét-i-kut, *r* N-Eng., 400 m.; one of the U. S., area 4674 s. m., pop. 370,792.
Connemara, Kon-ɛ-már-a, *dis* Ir.
Connersville, Kón-erz-vil, *t* Ind.
Conoloway, Kω-nól-ω-wa, *cr* Pa.
Conotten, Kω-nót-en, *cr* and *v* O.
Conseca, Kon-sá-kq, walled *t* Sierra Leone, 20.
Conseguina, Kon-sa-gé-nq, *vol* Nic.
Conshatte Chute, Kωṅ-ʃq́t Σωt, *p o* La.
Conshohocken, Kon-ʃω-hók-en, *v* Pa.
Constance, Kón-stans, *ft c* Baden; *l* Cen. Eu.
Constantia, Kon-stán-ʃi-a, *v* N-Y.
Constantina, Kon-stqn-té-nq, *t* Sp., 7.
Constantine, Kon-stqn-tén, (*or* Constantina,) *ft c* Algeria, 21.
Canstantine, Kón-stan-tɛn, *v* Mich.
Constantinople, Kon-stan-ti-nó-pl, *c* Tur., *cap* Ottoman Empire, 787.

Contentny, Kon-tént-ni, *cr* N. C.
Contoocook, Kón-tœ-kuk, *r* N-H.
Contra Costa, Kón-tra Kós-ta, *co* and *p o* Cal.
Contreras, Kon-trá-rqs, bat. field, Mex.; *is* s. w. of Guatemala.
Contreras, Kon-tré-ras, *p o* O.
Conversano, Kon-ver-sq-nœ, *t* Nap., 7¾.
Conway, Kón-wa, *or* Conwy, Kón-we, *r* North Wales.
Conway, Kón-wa, *r* Va.; *v* Mass. [C.
Conwayborough, Kón-wa-bur-œ, *v* S.
Conyersville, Kón-yerz-vil, *v* Tenn.
Conyngham, Kún-iŋ-ham, *v* Pa.
Coobcabia, Kœb-kq-bi-q, *t* Cen. Af.
Coodoonia, Kœ-dœ-ni-a, *r* N. W. Af.
Coogee, Kœ-ge, *s-pt t* N-S. Wales.
Cook Inlet, Rus. Am.
Cook Islands, Pac. Oc., s. of Polynesia, pop. 50,000, Malay.
Cookstown, *t* Ir.; *vs* N-J., C. W.
Cooksville, *vs.* Miss., Ind., Wis., C. W.
Coomassie, Kœ-más-e, *t* Guinea, 18.
Coonewar, Kœ-ne-wér, *p o* Miss.
Cooper, Kúp-er, River, S. C.
Cooperstown, *vs* N-Y., N-J., Pa., Wis.
Cooper's Wells, watering-place, Miss.
Coos, Kœ-ós, *co* N-H.
Coosa, Kœ-sa, *r* Ga. and Ala.
Coosauda, Kœ-sé-da, *v* Ala.
Coosawattee, Kœ-sa-wót-e, *r* Ga.
Coosawhatchie, Kœ-sa-hwóç-e, *v* S. C.
Cootehill, Kœt-hil, *t* Ir., 2½.
Copan, Kœ-pqn, *r* and ruined *c* Guat.
Copano, Kœ-pq-nœ, *v* Tex.
Copeland, Kóp-land, Islands, n. w. Ir.
Copenhagen, Kœ-pen-há-gen, *cap* Denmark, 133¼; *vs* N-Y., N. C.
Copiah, Kœ-pj-a, *cr* and *co* Miss.
Copiapo, Kœ-pe-q-pœ, *r* Chili.
Copiapo *or* San Francisco de Selva, *t* Chili.
Coppermine, Kóp-er-mjn, *ms* and *r* Brit. N. Am.
Coquago, Kœ-kwq-gœ, *or* Oquago, Œ-kwq-gœ, branch Delaware *r*, N-Y.
Coquet, Kók-et, (*or* Cocket,) *r* Eng.
Coquimbo, Kœ-kém-bœ, *prov.* and *s-pt t* Chili, 8.
Cora, Kœ-rq, *cap* island of Samos; *v* Iowa.
Coral, Kœ-rql, *i* Brazil; Kór-al, *v* Ill.
Coral Sea, part Pac. Oc., w. Australia.
Corannas, Kœ-rqn-qs, *tribe* S. Af.
Corato, Kœ-rq-tœ, *c* Nap., 11½.
Corbeau, Ker-bœ, *v* N-Y.
Corcobado *or* Corcovado, Ker-kœ-vq-dœ, *vol* Patagonia; *g* w. coast S. Am.
Corcovado, Ker-kœ-vq-dœ, *m* Brazil, height 2000 ft.

Cordillera, Kor-dil-e-ra, (Sp. Ker-del-yá-rq,) Spanish name of Andes *ms.*
Cordova, Kér-dœ-vq, *prov* Sp.; also *c.*, 42, in the tenth century nearly 1000.
Cordova, Kér-dœ-va, *t* Mex., 6; *prov* and *c* La Plata, 13. [Ill.
Cordova, Kér-dœ-va, *p os* Tenn., Ky.,
Corea *or* Korea, Kœ-ré-a, *cy* N.-E. As.
— Archipelago of, *is* w. Corea.
Corea, Strait of, connecting Sea of Japan with Yellow Sea.
Corentyn, Kœ-ren-tjn, *r* S. Am.
Core Sound, coast N. C.
Corfu, Kor-fœ *or* Kér-fœ, one of Ionian *is*, 75; *cap* same, 20.
Corigliano, Kœ-rel-yq-nœ, *t* Nap., 8¼.
Corinaldo, Kœ-re-nql-dœ, *t* It., 6.
Coringa, Kœ-riŋ-gq, *s-pt* Brit. India.
Corinna, Kœ-rin-a, *v* Me.
Corinth, Kór-inð, anc. *c* Greece, on isthmus of Corinth, 2; *g* arm Med.; *vs* Me., Vt., Ga.
Corisco, Kœ-rís-kœ, *b* and *i* w. Af.
Cork, Kerk, *c* Ir., 84½.
Corniglio, Ker-nél-yœ, *t* It.
Corning, Kérn-iŋ, *v* N-Y., 4.
Corno, Monte, Món-ta Kér-nœ, *m* Nap.
Cornucopia, Ker-nq-kœ-pi-a, *p o* Ind.
Cornwall, Kérn-wel, *co* Eng.; *vs* Vt., Conn., N-Y., Nova Scotia, C. W.
Cornwall, New, portion w. coast N. A.
Coro, Kœ-rœ, *c* Ven., 4.
Coromandel, Kor-œ-mán-del, *har* e. coast N-Zeal.
Coronata, Kœ-rœ-nq-tq, *i* Adriatic.
Coronation, Kor-œ-ná-ʃon, *is* N-S. Shetland and Rus. Am.
Coronda, Kœ-rón-dq, *t* Santa-Fé.
Coroora, Kœ-rœ-rq, *i* N. Pac. Oc.
Carowaugh, Kór-œ-we, *p o* Va.
Corpus Christi, Kér-pus Krís-ti, *v* Texas, 1¼; *b* Texas.
Corrib, Lough, Lo Kór-ib, *l* Ir.
Corrientes, Kor-e-én-tes, *dep* La Plata.
Corsica, Kér-si-ka, *i* Med., 110 by 53 m., pop. 236,251; *vs* Pa., O.
Corsicana, Ker-si-ká-na, *v* Texas.
Corté, Ker-tá, *t* Corsica, 4¾.
Cortetz, Ker-téts, *i* in the Dnieper.
Cortland, Kórt-land, *co* and *v* N-Y.
Cortona, Ker-tœ-nq, *t* Tuscany.
Corunna, Kœ-rún-a, *ft c* Sp., 19½; *v* Mich.
Corvo, Kér-vœ, *i* Azores, 1.
Corycian, Kœ-riʃ-i-an, Cave, in Bœotia.
Corydon, Kór-i-don, *vs* Pa., Ky., Ia., Iowa.
Cos, Kos, *or* Stanchio, Stqn-ke-œ, *i* Med.; *g* near island.
Cosala, Kœ-sq-lq, *t* Cinaloa, Mex.

Cosenza, Kω-sén-zą, *c* Nap., 14.
Coshocton, Kω-ʃók-ton, *co* and *v* O.
Cossatot, Kós-a-tot, *cr* Ark.
Cosi, Kώ-sε, *or* Koose, Kώ-sε, *r* Hind.
Cosiguina, Kω-si-gé-ną, *vol* Nic.
Cosihuiriachi, Kω-si-wε-ri-ą-çε, *t* Chihauhau.
Cosmoledo, Kos-mω-lá-dω, *is* Ind. Oc.
Cosne, Kωn, *t* Fr.
Cossacks, Kós-aks, (Country of the Don,) vast plain S. Rus.
Costa Rica, Kos-tą Ré-ką, southern *st* Cen. Am.; area 16,250 s. m., pop. 150,000.
Cosumne, Kós-um-nε, *p o* Cal.
Cote Blanche, Kωt Bląṅʃ, *b* s. La.
Cote D'Or, Kωt Der, *ms* and *dep* Fr.
Cotile, Kω-tél, *p o* La.
Cotindiba, Kω-tεn-dé-bą, *r* Brazil.
Cotoma, Kω-tώ-mα, *p o* Ala.
Cotopaxi, Kω-tω-páks-ε, *vol* Ecuador, height 18,875 ft.
Cotosa, Kω-tώ-sα, *p o* Ga.
Cotrone, Kω-trώ-na, *t* Naples, 5½.
Cotta, Kót-ą, *v* Ceylon. [8¼.
Cottbus *or* Kottbus, Kót-bus, *t* Prus.,
Cottica, Kot-é-ką, *r* Dutch Guiana.
Cotuit, Kót-yą-it, *v* Mass.
Cotuy *or* Cotui, Kω-twé, *t* Hayti, 2.
Couche's (Kɤ́ç-ez) Gap, *v* Tenn.
Coudersport, Kɤ́-derz-pωrt, *v* Pa.
Coudoonia, Kω-dώ-ni-ą, *r* Soodan.
Coudres, Kώd-r, *i* St. Lawrence.
Coulson's, Kól-sonz, Mills, *p o* Mo.
Council Bluffs, Kɤ́n-sil Blufs, *v* Io., 4.
Council City, *v* Kanzas.
Courbevoie, Kωr-bę-vwą́, *v* Fr., 5.
Courland *or* Kurland, Kώr-lqnd, a gov. Russia.
Courtableau, Kωr-tą-blώ, Bayou, La.
Courtais, Kωr-tá, *cr* Mo.
Courtesy, Kúr-tε-si, *v* Ga.
Courtland, Kórt-land, *vs* Ala., Ia., Wis.
Courtrai *or* Courtray, Kωr-trá, *ft t* Belgium, 19¾. [La.
Coushattee Chute, Kω-ʃát-ε Σωt, *p o*
Coutances, Kω-tóṅs, *t* Fr., 8.
Coventry, Kúv-en-tri, *c* Eng., 37; *vs* Vt., R. I., Conn., N-Y., Pa.
Cove of Cork, (now Queenstown,) *s-pt t* Ir., 5.
Covington, Kúv-iŋ-ton, *c* Ky., opposite Cincinnati, 13; *vs* O., Ia. 1½, Ill., Mo., Pa., Va., Ga.
Cowallis, Kω-wól-is, *p o* Oregon.
Cowanesque, Kω-an-ésk, *cr* Pa.
Cowee, Kɤ́-ε, *p o* N. C.
Cowekee, Kɤ-ε-ké, *cr* and *p o* Ala.
Cowelitsk, Kɤ-el-ítsk, Indians, Wash. Ter.
Cowes, Kɤz, *s-pt t* Isle of Wight, 4.
Coweta, Kɤ-é-tα, *co* Ga.
Cowlitz, Kɤ́-lits, *r* Wash. Ter.; — Landing, *t* Wash. Ter.
Coxim, Kω-ʃéṅ, *r* Brazil.
Coxsackie, Kok-sák-ε, *v* N-Y.
Coyle, Kel, *r* Hind., 300 m.
Cozumel, Kω-zω-mél, Island, Yucatan.
Crab Orchard, mineral springs, *v* Ky.
Cracatoa, Krak-a-tώ-α, *i* Malay Arch.
Cracow *or* Krakow, Krá-kω, *c* Poland, 43; the former republic of this name, now included in the grand duchy of Cracow.
Craftsbury, Kráfts-ber-i, *v* Vt.
Craigsville, Krágz-vil, *v* Pa.
Cranberry, Krán-ber-i, *vs* N-J., Pa., O.; *l* N-Y.
Cranborne, Krán-born, *t* Eng.
Cranbrook, Krán-bruk, *t* Eng.
Cranston, Kráns-ton, *v* R. I., 4⅓.
Crawfish, Kré-fiʃ, River, Wis.
Crawford, Kré-ford, numerous *cos* and *vs* U. S.
Crawfordsville, Kré-fordz-vil, *t* Ia., 2½; *vs* Ga., Iowa.
Cree, Krε, *r* Scot. fe
Creek, Krεk, Indians, of Ga. and Ala.
Crefeld, Krá-felt, *t* Rhenish Prussia, 23½.
Crema, Krá-mą, *t* Lombardy, 9¼.
Cremona, Kra-mώ-nα, *ft c* Lom., 28⅓.
Crescent (Krés-ent) City, two *ts* Cal.
Crestline, Krést-lịn, *v* O.
Crete Krεt, (*or* Candia,) *i* Med., belonging to Turkey; 150 by 6 to 35 m.; pop. 158,000.
Creuse, Krez, *dep* and *r* Fr., 175 m.
Creuzot, Le, Lę Kręzώ, *t* Fr., 8.
Creve Cœur, Krev Ker, *p o* Mo.
Crevillente, Kra-vεl-yén-ta, *t* Sp., 7¼.
Crewe, Krω, *t* Eng.
Crewkerne, Krώ-kęrn, *t* Eng., 4½.
Crieff, Krεf, *t* Scot., 4½.
Crimea, Krim-é-α, *pen* S. Rus., on the Black Sea; pop. 190,063.
Crittenden, Krit-en-den, *vs* Ky., Ia.
Crixa *or* Cricha, Kré-ʃą, *r* Brazil; *c* do., 5.
Croatia, Krω-á-ʃi-α, *prov* Aus. Em., area 3398 s. m., pop. 588,204.
Croatia, Turkish, part of anc. Croatia.
Crockett, Krók-et, *v* Texas.
Croghan, Krώ-han, *vs* N-Y., O.
Croia, Croja, Krώ-yą, *t* Turkey in Eu.
Croix-rousse, La, Lą Krwą-rώs, *t* Fr., 19.
Cromarty, Króm-αr-ti, *co* and *t* Scot.
Cromford, Króm-ford, *t* Eng., 1¼.
Cromwell, Króm-wel, *v* Conn.

Cronstadt *or* Kronstadt, Krón-stqt, *s-pt t* Rus., on Kotlin island; pop. in winter, 6; summer, 40.
Crooked, Krúk-ed, Lake, w. N-Y., 18 by 1½ m. [6½.
Crossen *or* Krossen, Krós-en, *t* Prus.,
Cross (*or* La Crosse) Lake, Br. N. Am., origin of the Miss. River.
Crosswicks, Krós-wiks, *v* N-J.
Croton, Kró-ton, *v* N-Y.
Croton River, N-Y.
Crow, Krꝏ, Indians, tribe of Mo. Ter.
Crown Point, Krʊn Pɵnt, *vs* N-Y., Ia.
Crow River, Min. Ter., 100 m.
Crow Wing, *r* and *v* Min. Ter.
Croydon, Krɵ́-don, *t* Eng., 20.
Crozet, Krꝏ-zá, Islands, S. Ind. Oc.
Crozon, Krꝏ-zóṅ, *t* Fr., 9.
Cruces, Krꝏ́-ses, *v* N-Grenada. [6¾.
Cruyshantem, Krɵs-hq́n-tem, *v* Belg.,
Crystal, Krís-tal, Lake, *l* and *v* Ill.
Csaba, Ȼób-o, *v* Hun.
Csacza, Ȼót-so, *t* Hun., 4½.
Csakova, Ȼók-ꝏ-vo, *t* Hun., 4¼.
Csakvar, Ȼqk-vq́r, *v* Hun., 4¾.
Csath, Csat, *or* Csatt, Ȼqt, *t* Hun., 5¾.
Csongrad, Ȼon-grq́d, *t* Hun., 13½.
Cuajiniqualpa, Kwq-*h*ɛ-ni-kwq́l-pq, *t* Guat., 3.
Cuba, Kṻ-bɑ, (Sp. Kꝏ́-bq,) *i* at the mouth of the Gulf of Mexico, largest of the W. Ind., belonging to Spain; 560 by 50 to 60 m.; area 35,757 s. m.; pop. in 1853, 510,988 whites, 176,647 free colored, 330,425 slaves,—total 1,009,060; *vs* N-Y. 1, O., &c.
Cubahatchee, Kṻ-ba-háç-ɛ, *cr* and *p o* Ala. [ezuela, 5.
Cucuisas, Las, Lqs Kꝏ-kwɛ́-sqs, *t* Ven-
Cuddalore, Kud-a-lór, *t* Hind.
Cuenca, Kwén-kq, *c* Sp., 6; *prov* do.
Cuenca, (*or* Rambae,) *c* Ecuador, 20.
Cuero, Kwá-rꝏ, *v* Texas.
Cueva de Vera, Kwá-vq da Vá-rq, *t* Sp., 10¼.
Culebra, Kꝏ-lá-brq, *r* and *s-pt* Costa Rica; *i* W. Ind.
Culiacan, Kꝏ-li-q-kq́n, *t* Mex., 7.
Cullera, Kꝏl-yá-rq, *t* Sp., 7.
Culloden, Kul-ó-den, moory ridge of Scot.; *v* Ga.
Culloma, Kul-ó-mɑ, *t* Cal., 3.
Culna, Kúl-nɑ, *t* Brit. Ind.; 40. [6½.
Cumana, Kꝏ-mq-nq́, *dep* and *c* Ven.,
Cumania *or* Kumania, Kꝏ-má-ni-ɑ, Great and Little, ind. *dis* Hun.
Cumbal, Kꝏm-bq́l, *m p* Andes, N-G., 15,620 ft. high.
Cumberland, Kúm-ber-land, *t* Md., 6; *vs* Me., Ky., O., Ia.
Cumberland Basin, bet. Nova Scotia and N-Brunswick.
Cumberland Island, *is* n. of Ga.; Brit. N. Am.; in the Pacific.
Cumberland Mountains, bet. Va. and Ky., and bet. N. C. and Tenn.
Cumberland River, flows through Ky. and Tenn., 600; nav. 200 to 500.
Cumberl'd University, Lebanon, Tenn.
Cumbola, Kum-bó-lɑ, *v* Pa.
Cumbre, La, Lq Kꝏ́m-brɑ, pass across the Andes, bet. Santiago, in Chili, and Mendoza; elevation, 12,454 ft.
Cumbrian, Kúm-bri-an, Mts., in Eng.
Cumino, Kꝏ-mɛ́-nꝏ, *i* Med., ¾.
Cumming, Kúm-iŋ, *v* Ga.
Cummingsville, Kúm-iŋz-vil, *v* O.
Cunningham's Kún-iŋ-hamz, Island, w. end Lake Erie, 3 by 2½ m.
Cuorgné, Kwɵ́rn-ya, *t* Pied., 5½.
Cupar-Fife, Kṻ-pɑr-Fįf, *t* Scot.
Cupica, Kꝏ-pɛ́-kq, *v* and *b* N-Gran.
Cura, Kꝏ́-rq, *t* Ven., 4.
Curaçoa, Kṻ-ra-sɵ́-ɑ *or* Kṳ-rq-sɵ́, *i* W. Ind., 40 by 6 to 10 m.; pop. 15¼.
Curaray, Kꝏ-rq-rį́, *r* Ecuador.
Curia, Kṻ-ri-ɑ, *v* Ark. [Arab.
Curia Muria, Kꝏ́-ri-q Mꝏ́-ri-q, *is* s. e.
Curico, Kꝏ-rɛ́-kꝏ, *dis* and *t* Chili.
Curitiba, Kꝏ-ri-tɛ́-bq, *r* and *t* Brazil.
Current, Kúr-ent, River, Mo. and Ark., 250 m. [N. C.
Currituck, Kúr-i-tuk, *i* and *sound* n. e.
Curtatone, Kꝏr-tq-tó-na, *v* Milan, 5¼.
Curzola, Kꝏrd-zɵ́-lq, *i* Adriatic, pop. 4¼. [Pa.
Cussawago, Kus-a-wq́-gꝏ, *cr* and *p o*
Cusseta, Kus-ɛ́-tɑ, *v* Ala.
Cutchogue, Kut-çɵ́g, *v* N-Y.
Cuthbert, Kúŧ-bert, *v* Ga.
Cuttack, Kut-ák, *dis* and *c* Br. Ind., 40.
Cuvo, Kꝏ́-vꝏ, *r* Lower Guinea, 400 m.
Cuyaba *or* Cuiaba, Kꝏ-yq́-bq, *r* and *c* Brazil.
Cuyahoga, Kį-a-hɵ́-gɑ, *r* O.
Cuyahoga Falls, *v* O.
Cuyler, Kį-ler, *v* N-Y
Cuyos, Kꝏ́-yꝏs, Is., group of the Phil.
Cuyuni, Kꝏ-yꝏ́-nɛ, *r* Br. Guiana.
Cuzco, Kꝏ́s-kꝏ, *c* Peru, 41¼; *dep* do.
Cwmdu, Kꝏ́m-dɛ, hamlet S. Wales.
Cyclades, Sík-la-dɛz, *is* Grecian Arch., pop. 19.
Cynthiana, Sin-ŧi-án-ɑ, *vs* Ky., O., Ia.
Cypress, Sį́-pres, *vs* Ky., Mo., &c.
Cyprus, Sį́-prus, *i* Turkey in Asia, 148 by 40 m.; pop. 100. [16½.
Czegled, Tsá-gled, large *v* Cen. Hun.,
Czernowitz, Ȼɛ́r-nꝏ-vits, (*or* Tscherno-witz,) *t* Aus. Poland, 12.

# D.

Dacca, Dák-a, *c* Brit. Ind., 200.
Dagöe, Dá-ge-e, *or* Dago, Dá-gō, *i* Rus., Baltic Sea, 34 by 15 m.; pop. 10,000. [Iowa.
Dahlonega, Da-lón-e-ga, *vs* Ga. 1¼,
Dahme, Dá-me, *t* Prus., 3¾.
Dahomey *or* Dahomay, Da-hō-má, *k* W. Af.; pop. 200,000.
Daiman, Dī-mán, *or* Arangua, A-rán-gwa, *r* S. Am., 110 m.
Daimiel, Dī-mi-él, *t* Sp., 9.
Dakhel, El, El Dá-*kel*, w. oasis Upper Egypt, pop, 7,000.
Dakota, Da-kó-ta, *co* and *v* Min.
Dakota Indians, same as Sioux.
Dal-Elf, Dal-élf, *r* Swed., 250 m.
Dalhousie, Dal-hó-ze, *v* Scot.; *t* N-Brunswick.
Dalias, Dá-li-as, *t* Sp., 12.
Dalkeith, Dal-kéth, *t* Scot., 5.
Dallas, Dál-as, *vs* N. C., Tex., Ark., &c.
Dalmatia, Dal-má-ʃi-a, *prov* Aus. Em., comp. anc. Dalmatia, Croatia, Slavonia, and Fiume: pop. 393,715; *v* Pa.
Dalry, Dál-ri, *v* Scot., 9.
Dalton, Dél-ton, *vs* Mass., Ga., O., &c.
Damaran, Da-ma-rán, *i* Malay Arch.
Damariscotta, Dam-a-ris-kót-a, *r* Me.
Damascus, Da-más-kus, *c* Syria, oldest in the world, founded 2000 B. C., 112; *vs* Pa., O., &c.
Dambool, Dam-bōl, *v* Ceylon.
Damietta, Dam-i-ét-a, *t* Low. Eg., 28.
Damme, Dá-me, *i* Malay Arch., 12 m. s.
Dampier, Dám-per, Arch., n. w. coast Australia.
Danbury, Dán-ber-i, *vs* N-H., Conn.
Danby, Dán-bi, *vs* Vt., N-Y.; *p o* Ill.
Dandridge, Dán-drij, *v* Tenn.
Dane, Dan, rel. to Denmark; *co* Wis.
Danemora, Dan-e-mó-ra, *v* O.
Danish, Dán-iʃ, belonging to Den.
Dankali, Dan-ka-lé, *or* Danakil, Da-na-kél, *ind state*, Af., pop. 70,000.
Dannemora, Dan-e-mó-ra, *v* N-Y.
Dan River, Va., and N. C.
Dansville, *v* N-Y., 2½.
Dantzic, *or* Dantzick, *gov* and *ft c* W. Prussia, pop. 58; *gulf* of the same.
Danube, Dán-yūb, *r* Eu., rising in Baden, and falling into the Black sea, 1000 m.; *v* N-Y.
Danvers, Dán-verz, *v* Mass.
Danville, *ts* Pa., 3¼; Va., 3; Ky., 2¼; *vs* Me., Vt., Ia., O., Ill., &c.
Darabgherd, Da-rab-gérd, *t* Per., 20.

D'arbonne, Dar-bón, *bayou* La., nav.
Darby, Dár-bi, *v* Pa. [60 m.
Dardanelle, Dar-da-nél, *v* Ark.
Dardanelles, Dar-da-nélz, (*or* Hellespont,) strait bet. Eu. and As. Tur.; *p o* Or.
Dardenne, Dar-dén, *or* and *v* Mo.
Darfoor, Dar-fōr, *cy* of Af.
Darien, Dá-ri-en, *g* and former *prov* of N-Gran.; *ts* Conn., N-Y., Ga. Wis.
Darling, Dár-liŋ, *r* and *ms* Cen. Aust.
Darlington, Dár-liŋ-ton, *t* Eng., 11½; *vs* Pa., Md., S. C., Ia., &c.
Darmstadt, Dárm-stat, *t* Ger., 27.
Dart, Dart, *r* Eng.; *p o* Ark. [Wis.
Dartford, Dárt-ford, *t* Eng., 6¼; *v*
Dartmouth, Dárt-muth, *s-pt t* Eng. 4½; *vs* Pr. Ed. Is., N. S., Mass.; *r* Mad.
Darmouth College, Hanover, N. H.
Darwar, Dár-war, *dis* and *t* Hind.
Darwen, Over, Dár-wen, Ō'ver, *t* Eng.,
Darwin, Dár-win, *v* Ill. [11⅝.
D'Aubigny, Dō-ben-yé, *v* C. E.
Dauchite, Do-ʃét, *bayou* Ark., La.
Daule, Dá-la, nav. *r* Ec.
Dauphin, Dé-fin, *co* and *v* Pa.
Davenport, Dáv-en-pōrt, *c* Iowa, 5.
Davie, Dá-ve, *co* N. C.
Daviess, Dá-vis, sev. *cos* U. S.
Davis Inlet, *b* e. coast Labrador, 57 m.
Davis's Strait, between Greenland and Brit. N. Am., 750 m.
Dayton, Dá-ton, fourth *c* of O., 17; *vs* Ia., Ala., Ill., Iowa.
Dead Sea, *l* Pal., 41 by 8½ m.
Deal, Del, maritime *t* Eng., 7.
Dean Forest, Eng., 22,000 acres belonging to the crown; pop. 13⅛.
Dearborn's River, Dér-born, Mo., 150 m.
Dearbornville, Dér-born-vil, *v* and U. S. Arsenal, Mich.
Dease River, Des, Brit. N. Am.
Debreczin, *or* Debretzin, Da-brét-sin, free *t* E. Hungary, 63.
Decatur, De-ká-tur, *vs* Ga., Ala., O., Mich., Ia., Ill., Wis.
De Chien Bayou, De-ʃén, w. part Ky.
Deckertown, Dék-er-tūn, *v* N-J.
Decorah, De-kó-ra, *v* Iowa.
Dedham, Déd-ham, *v* Mass.
Dee, De, *r* Wales, 70 m.; two *rs* Scot.
Deegoa, De-gó-a, walled *t* Bornoo, 30.
Deep River, central part N. C., 100 m.
Deerfield, Dér-feld, *r* Vt., numerous *vs* U. S.

Defiance, Dɛ-fį-ans, *co* and *t* O.
De Graff, Dɛ Graf, *v* O.
De Kalb, Dɛ Kalb, *cos* and *vs* U. S.
Dekorra, Dɛ-kór-a, *v* Wis.
Delagoa, Del-a-gó-a, *inlet* Ind. Oc.
De La Palma, De Lą Pál-ma, *p o* O.
Delavan, Dél-a-van, *vs* N-Y., Ill., Wis.
Delaware, Dél-a-wąr, *r*, rises in N-Y. and flows bet. the states of N-Y., and N-J. on one side, and Pa. and Del. on the other; nav. for ships to Philadelphia; whole length 300 m.
Delaware, smallest of the U. S., except R. I.; 2120 s. m., pop. 71,169 whites, 18,073 free blacks, 2,290 slaves,—total, 91,532.
Delaware, *t* O., 2; *b* sep. N-J. and Del., length 60 m.
Delaware City, *v* Del.; settlement in Kansas Ter.
Delaware College, at Newark, Del.
Delawares, tribe of Indians formerly occupying N-Y., Pa., N-J.
Delft, Delft, *t* S. Holland, 17½.
Delhi, Dél-ɛ, *c* Hind., at one time covering 20 s. m., with pop. 2,000,000, now reduced to 250,000; Dél-hį, *vs* N-Y., O., Ill. Iowa, Wis., &c.
Delos, Dé-los, *is* Gr. Arch.
Delphi, Dél-fį, *m* and *t* anc. Gr.; *vs* N-Y., Tenn., Ia., Mo.
Delphos, Dél-fos, *v* O., 1¼.
Delta, Dél-ta, *vs* N-Y., Miss., O.
Delton, Dél-ton, *v* Wis.
Demak, Dem-ąk, *t*, *dis* and *r* Is. Java.
Demavend (Dem-q-vénd,) Mount, *vol* Persia, 14,695 ft.
Dembea, Dém-bɛ-a, *l* Abys.
Dembia, Dém-bi-a, *r* W. Af.
Demer, Dá-mer, *r* Belg.
Demerara, Dem-er-ą-ra, *r* and *dis* Brit. Guiana. [200 m.
Demianka, Da-mi-ąn-ka, *r* Siberia.
Demmin, De-mén, *t* Prus., 6¼.
Demonte, Da-món-ta, *ft t* Pied., 7.
Demopolis, Dɛ-móp-ɷ-lis, *v* Ala.
Demotica, Dɛ-mót-i-ka, *t* Eu. Tur., 8.
Denain, Dę-náṅ, *v* Fr., 8⅔.
Denbigh, Dén-bɛ, *t* N. Wales, 5½.
Dender, Dén-der, *r* Nubia, 250 m.
Dendermonde, Den-der-món-dę, *ft t* Belg., 8½.
Denia, Dá-ni-ą, maritime *t* Sp., 3.
Denmark, Dén-mąrk, *k* N. Eu., having as colonies: Duchies of Sleswick, Holstein, Lauenburg; Faröe Islands; Iceland; Greenland; West India Is. —Santa Cruz, St. Thomas, and San Juan; Nicobar Is. Total area, 62,870; total pop., 2,412,926. The gov. is a hereditary constitutional monarchy; *vs* Tenn., Ill., &c.
Dennis, Dén-is, *v* Mass.
Depauville, Dɛ-pó-vil, *v* N-Y.
Depere, Dɛ-pąr, *or* Dɛ-pér, *v* Wis.
Depeyster, Dɛ-pį-ster, *v* N-Y.
Deptford, Déd-ford, *pt* Eng., 27¾.
Dera Ghazee Khan, Dér-a Gą-zé Kąn, *t* Afg., 25.
Derayeh, El, El Da-rį-e, *t* Ar., 15.
Derbend, Der-bénd, (*or* Derbent,) *t* Rus., 12. [Conn., Ia.
Derby, Dér-bi, *t* Eng., 40⅔; *vs* Vt.,
Derby Centre, *v* Vt.
Derby Line, *v* Vt.
Derry, Dér-i, *v* N-H.
De Ruyter, Dɛ Rį-ter, *v* N-Y.
Derwent, Dér-went, three *rs* Eng., *rs* Van Dieman's Land.
Desaguadero, Des-q-gwą-dá-rɷ, *r* Bol., 180 m. also a *val* in Bol. and Peru, 400 by 30 to 80 m.
Des Allemand's, Daz Al-móṅ, *or* Dez Al-e-mąnz, *l* s. e. of La., 7 m.
Des Arc, Dez Ark, *v* and *bayou* Ark.
Deseret, Dés-er-et, *co* Utah Ter.
Desha, De-ʃá, *co* Ark.
D'Eschambault, Deʃ-ąṅ-bɷ, *v* C. E.
Desirade, Da-zɛ-rąd, *is* Little Antilles, 2½.
Des Moines, De Mɵn, *r* Iowa, 200 m.
Desna, Dés-ną, *r* Rus., 500 m. [Ga.
Desoto, Dɛ-só-tɷ, *co* Miss.; *par* La.; *v*
Des Plaines, Da Plan, *r* Ill., 150 m.
Dessau Dés-ɤ, walled *t* N. Ger., 12.
Detroit, Dɛ-trɵ́t, *c* Mich., 34½.
Detroit River, *str* connecting Lake St. Clair with Lake Erie, 25 m. [7.
Deux-Ponts, Dę-póṅ, *t* Rhenish Bav.,
Deventer, *or* Dewenter, Dév-en-ter, *c* Hol., 14½.
Devereaux, Dév-ɛ-rɷ, *p o* N-Y.
Devizes, Dɛ-vį-zez, *t* Eng., 6½.
Devonshire, Dév-on-ʃɛr, *co* Eng.
Devon, Dév-on, *r* Scot.
Devonport, Dév-on-pɷrt, *ft t* and *naval ars* of Eng., 50¼.
De Witt, Dɛ Wit, *vs* N-Y., Mich., Ill.
Dewsbury, Dų́z-ber-i, *t* Eng., 14.
Dexter, Déks-ter, *vs* Me., N-Y., Mich.
Dezfool, *or* Dezphoul, Dez-fɷ́l, *t* Per., 15.
Dhalak, Dą-ląk, *is* Red Sea.
Dhawalaghiri, Da-wol-a-gér-ɛ, *p* Him. Moun., 28,000 ft.
Diablerets, Dɛ-ąb-lɛ-rá, *m* Swit.
Diamantina, Dɛ-ą-mąn-té-ną, *c* Bra.
Diamante, Dɛ-ą-mąn-ta, *r* La Plata, 170 m.
Diana, Dį-án-a, *v* N-Y.

Diarbekir, Dε-ḁr-bε-kér, c As. Tur., 8000 families.
Dickinson College, Carlisle, Pa.
Dieppe, Dyep, *or* Dε-ép, *s-pt t* Fr., 17⅔.
Diest, Dεst, walled *t* Belg., 7¾.
Diggers, Díg-erz, various tribes degraded Indians in Or. and Cal., who subsist on roots, insects, lizards, &c.
Dijon, Dε-ʒóṅ, *c* Fr., 32¼.
Dilman, Dεl-mḁn, *t* N. Per. 15.
Dinagepoor, Dε-nqj-pǿr, *dis* and *t* Br. Ind., 30.
Dinan, Dε-nóṅ, *t* Fr., 8½. [6¼.
Dinant, Dε-nḁnt, *or* Dε-nóṅ, *t* Belg.,
Dinkelsbühl, Díŋk-elz-bel, *ft t* Bav., 5.
Dinwiddie, Din-wíd-ε, *co* and *v* Va.
Dios Nombre De, Nóm-bra da Dé-ɷs, *t* Mex., 7.
Disco, Dís-kɷ, *i* of Denmark, w. coast of Greenland.
Dismal Swamp, Díz-mal Swomp, Va., N. C., 30 by 10 or 12 m.
District of Columbia, *ter* for the capital of the U. S., ceded to the Gen. Gov. by Md.; 60 s. m., pop. in 1850, whites, 38,027; free blacks, 9,973; slaves, 3,687; total 51,687. The citizens of the District are without any representation in Congress or vote for president.
Ditteah, Dít-ε-q, *t* Hind., 120.
Dixon, Díks-on, *v* Ill., 1.
Djokjokarta, Jok-yɷ-kḁr-tɑ, *dis* Java; *cap* of the dis., pop. 90.
Dnieper, Né-per, *r* Rus., flows s. into Black Sea; length 623 m. including windings, 1230 m.
Dniester, Nés-ter, nav. *r* Aus. and Rus., 400 m.
Doboka, Dɷ-bó-ko, *v* Tran., 67.
Doce, Dó-sa, *r* Bra., 500 m.
Dodgeville, Dój-vil, *v* Wis., 1¼.
Dole, Dɷl, *t* Fr., 10¾.
Dolores, Dɷ-ló-res, *t* Guanajuato.
Dominica, *or* Domenica, Dom-i-né-kɑ, Brit. W. Ind. Is., 29 by 16 m., pop. 22¼, 800 are whites; also one of the Marquesas Is.
Dominick, Dóm-in-ik, *v* Ill.
Don, Don, *r* Eu. Rus., enters the Sea of Azof, 468 m.; *rs* Eng., Scot., Fr.
Donaldson, Dón-ald-son, *v* Pa.
Donaldsonville, *r-pt* La.
Don Benito, Don Ba-né-tɷ, *t* Sp., 15¼.
Doncaster, Dón-kas-ter, *t* Eng. [Pa.
Donegal, Don-ε-gél, *s-pt t* Ir.; three *vs*
Donets, Dɷ-néts, *r* S. Rus., 400 m.
Dong-nai, Doŋ-nį, *r* and *t* Anam.
Dongola, Dóŋ-gɷ-lq, *t* Nubia; *v* Ia.
Doniphan, Dón-i-fan, *v* Mo.; — City, *t* Kanzas.
Donnybrook, Dón-i-brɷk, *par* and *v* Ir.
Doon, Dɷn, *r* and *loch* Scot., 18 m.
Dor, D'or, *or* Dore, (Mont,) Móṅ-dor, *ms* Fr.
Dora Baltea, Dɷ-rq Bql-tá-q, *r* Pied.
Dorchester, Dér-ϛes-ter, *t* Eng., 6¼; *ts* Mass., 8; N-B., S. C., &c.
Dordogne, Dor-dóṅ, *r* Fr., 220 m.
Dorogoboozh, Dɷ-rɷ-gɷ-bɷ́ʒ, *t* Rus., 5.
Dorpat, Dór-pqt, *t* Rus. 12.
Dort, Dort, *t* S. Hol., 21.
Douai, *or* Douay, Dɷ-á, *ft t* Fr., 20½.
Doubs, Dɷbz, *r* Fr., 263 m.
Douglas, Dúg-las, *s-pt* Isle of Man, 9¾; *vs* Scot., Mass., Pa., Kansas, &c.
Doune, Dɷn, *v* Scot., 1½.
Douro, Dɷ́-rɷ, *r* Sp. and Port., 400 m.
Douw, Dɤv, *or* Dɤ, *i* Malay Arch., 5.
Dover, Dó-ver, *t* Eng., 22¼; *t* N-H., 8¼; *vs* Me., Mass., N-Y., N-J., Del., O., &c.
Dover, Strait of, sep. Eng. and Fr.
Dovrefield, Dó-vre-fε-éld, *m* range Nor.
Dowagiac, Dɷ-wá-ji-ak, *r* and *v* Mich.
Downs, The, portion, N. Sea, s. e. of Eng.
Dracut, Drá-kut, *v* Mass.
Draguignan, Drq-gεn-yóṅ, *t* Fr., 9.
Drammen, Drḁ-men, *s-pt t* Nor., 8.
Drave, Drav, *r* S. E. Eu., 360 m.
Drennon Springs, Drén-on, watering place, near Louisville, Ky.
Dresden, Dréz-den, *c* and *cap* Saxony, 94; *vs* Me., O., Ill.
Drin, Drεn, two *rs* Eu. Tur.
Drogheda, Dró-*hε*-dɑ, *s-pt t* Ir., 16¾.
Droitwich, Dró-t-iq, *t* Eng.
Drummond's Island, Drúm-ondz, Lake Huron.
Druses, Drɷ́-sez, people inhabiting the chain of Lebanon, in Syria.
Dublin, Dúb-lin, *cap c* Ir., 254¾; *vs* N-H., Ia., Ga., &c.
Dubois, Dq-bó, *co* Ia.
Dubuque, Dq-bḁk, *c* of Iowa, 9.
Duck River, Middle Tenn., 250 m.
Duddeston, Dúd-es-ton, *t* Eng., 20.
Dudley, Dúd-li, *t* Eng., 38; *v* Mass.
Dugdemona, Dug-dε-mó-nɑ, *vs* La., Iowa.
Duida, Dwé-dq, *m* Ven., 8500 ft.
Duisburg, Dɷ́-is-búrh, *t* Rhenish Prussia, 7¾.
Dulce, Dɷ́l-sa, *l* Gua., 25 by 10.
Dulce Rio, Ré-ɷ Dɷ́l-sa, *r* La Plata.
Dulcigno, Dɷl-ϛén-yɷ, *s-pt t* Eu. Tur., 8.

Dumbarton, Dum-bqr-ton, *s-pt t* Scot., 4½.
Dumfries, Dum-frés, *r-pt* Scot., 11¼.
Dummodah, Dum-ó-da, *r* Brit. Ind., 300 m.
Düna, Dé-nq, *or* Dwina, Dwé-nq, *r* of Rus., nav. 400 m. [6⅓.
Dünaburg, Dé-nq-bœrg, *ft t* Rus. Pol.,
Dunbar, Dun-bqr, *s-pt t* Scot.
Dundalk, Dun-dék, *s-pt t* Ir., 10¾.
Dundas, Dún-das, *t* C. W. 3.
Dundee, Dun-dé, *s-pt* Scot., 78¾; *vs* N-Y., 1⅓; Mich., Ill.
Dunfermline, Dum-fér-lin, *t* Scot., 8½.
Dungannon, Dun-gán-non, *t* Ir., *v* O.,
Dungarvan, Dun-gqr-van, *s-pt t* Ir., 8¾.
Dunkirk, Dún-kerk, *ft s-pt t* Fr., 29; *t* N-Y., 4⅓; *v* Wis.
Dunmore, Dun-mór, *vs* Ir., Pa.
Dunse, Duns, *t* Scot., 2¾.
Dunstable, Dún-sta-bl, *t* Eng., 3½.
Duntocher, Dun-tóh-er, *v* Scot., 3¾.
Dunville, Dún-vil, *v* C. W., 1.
Du Page, Dq Paj, *co* and *v* Ill.
Duquesne, Dq-kán, a *ft* formerly on the site of Pittsburg; *v* two miles off.
Duquoin, Dq-kwán, *v* Ill.
Durango, Dœ-rán-gœ, *st* Mex.; area 48,489 s. m., pop. 137½; *cap* same, 22.
Düren, Dé-ren, *t* Rhen. Prus., 8.
Durham, Dúr-ham, *c* Eng., 13.
Dusseldorf, Dús-el-dorf, *gov* and Rhen. Prus., 23½.
Duxbury, Dúks-ber-i, *v* Mass.
Dwina, Dwí-na *or* Dwé-nq, *r* Rus., 330 m.
Dysart, Dí-zart, *s-pt t* Scot.

# E.

Eagle Harbor, E'gl Hqr-bor, *v* Mich.
Eagle Pass, *v* Texas.
East Aurora, Est Θ-ró-ra, *v* N-Y., 2.
East Greenwich, Grén-wiq, *v* R. I., 2⅓.
East Haddam Landing, *v* Conn. [Y.
East Hampton, Hámp-ton, *vs* Mass., N-
East Hartford, Hqrt-ford, *v* Conn.
East Haven, Há-ven, *v* Conn.
East Indies, In'dez, applied to Hin., Farther India, Malay Arch.
East Liverpool, Lív-er-pœl, *v* O.
East-Main *or* Slade River, Lab., 400 m.
Easton, Es'ton, *t* Pa., 7¼; *vs* N-Y., Md., Mass., Kansas.
Eastport, Est'port, *vs* Me., Miss.
East Randolph, Rán-dolf, *vs* Vt., Mass., N-Y.
East River, con. Long Island Sound with N-Y. Bay, 20 m.
East Saginaw, Ság-i-ne, *v* Mich.
East Salisbury, Sálz-ber-i, *v* Mass.
East Schuyler, Skí-ler, *p o* N-Y.
East Stoughton, Stó-ton, *v* Mass.
Eastville, *co t* Va.
East Weare, Wqr, *v* N-H.
East Windsor, Wind-sor, *vs* Mass., Conn.
East Woburn, Wó-burn, *v* Mass.
Eaton, E'ton, *vs* N-H., N-Y., Pa., Tenn.; *co t* O.
Eaton Rapids, *v* Mich.
Eatonton, E'ton-ton, *co t* Ga.
Ebenezer, Eb-en-é-zer, *vs* Pa., Miss.
Ebersbach, A'berz-bqh, *v* Saxony, 5½.
Ebro, A'brœ, *r* Sp., 340 m.
Eccleshall, Ek'lz-hel, *t* Eng., 4¾.
Echmiedzin, Eq-mi-ed-zén, *t* Armenia.
Ecija, A'ti-hq, *t* Sp., 28½.
Eckford, Ek'ford, *v* Mich.
Eckhung Choo, Ek-úŋ Cœ, *r* Thibet.
Eckmansville, Ek'manz-vil, *v* O.
Economy, E-kón-œ-mi, *vs* Pa., O., Ia.
Ecorce, A-kórs, *v* Mich.
Ecuador, Ek-wq-dór, (*i. e.* "Equator;") a republic of S. Am.; area 240,000 s. m., pop. 500,000.
Eddystone (Ed'i-stœn) Island, S. Pac.; — Light-House, Eng. Channel.
Eddyville, *vs* N-Y., Ky., Iowa.
Eden, E'den, *rs* Eng., Scot.; *vs* U. S.
Edenkoben, A'den-kœ-ben, *t* Rhenish Bavaria, 5. [O.
Edenton, E'den-ton, *co t* N. C.; *vs* N-Y.,
Edgartown, Ed'gar-tun, *co t* Mass.
Edgecomb, Ej'kœm, *v* Me.
Edgefield, *v* Tenn.; *co t* S. C.
Edgington, Ej'iŋ-ton, *v* Ill.
Edin, E'din, *v* O.
Edina, E-dí-na, *co t* Mo.
Edinborough, Ed'in-bur-œ, *v* Pa.
Edinburg, Ed'in-burg, *vs* U. S.
Edinburgh, Ed'in-bur-u, metropolis of Scot., 158.
Edinburgh, New, *s-pt* S. Am.
Edisto, Ed'is-tœ, *r* S. C.
Edmonton, Ed'mon-ton, *vs* Eng., Brit. N. Am., Ky.
Eelee, Ele, Ili, E'le, *r* and *c* Chi., 75.
Eel River, two *rs* Ia.
Eels, Elz, Eeleeyats *or* Iliyats, E-le-yqts, wandering tribes of Persia.

Eem, Ɑm, *r* Holland.
Eessah Somaulee, Ɛ'sa Sɷ-mó-lɛ, tribe in E. Af.
Efbe, Ef'ba, *i* Malay Arch.
Effingham, Ef'iŋ-ham, *vs* N-H., S. C.
Eger, Eg'er *or* Ɑ'ger, *r* E. Ger.; *t* Bohemia, 10½.
Egerdir, Eg-er-dér, *l* and *t* Asia Minor.
Egga, Eg'a, large *t* Guinea.
Eggebee, Eg'ä-bɛ, *t* W. Af., 14.
Egg Is. Point, s. ex. Egg Is., Del. Bay.
Egmont, Eg'mont, (*or* Six Islands,) Ind. Oc.; *i* Santa Cruz Arch.; *vol* N-Zealand.
Egypt, *cy* in n. e. Af.; area 11,000 s. m., pop. 2,500,000; *vs* N-Y., Pa., &c.
Ehen, Ɛ'hen, *r* Eng.
Ehrenbreitstein, Ɑ'ren-brȋt-stȋn, *ft t* Rren. Prus., 2.
Eichstädt *or* Aichstadt, Ɨk'stet, *t* Bav., 7⅓.
Eider, Ɨ'der *or* Id'er, *r* Den., nav. 70 m.
Eig, Eigg, Ɛg, *or* Egg Is., Heb. of Scot.
Eiger, Ɨ'ger, *m* Swit., 13,045 ft. high.
Eijerland *or* Eierland, Ɨ'er-lqnt, n. part island of Texel. [8¾.
Eilenburg, Ɨ'len-burh, *t* Prus. Saxony,
Eil, Loch, Lo*h* Ɛl, *l* Scot.
Eimbeck, Ɨm'bek, *t* Han., 5¾.
Eimeo, Ɨ'mɛ-ɷ, one of the Society Islands, Pac. Oc., 1¼.
Einsiedeln, Ɨn'sɛ-deln, *t* Swit., 3.
Eisenach, Ɨ'zen-q*h*, *t* Cen. Ger., 9½.
Eisenstadt, Ɨ'zen-stqt, *t* Hun., 9¾.
Eisleben, Ɨs'la-ben, *t* Prus. Sax., 8⅓.
Ekhe, Ek'e, *or* Iga, Ig'a, *r* Mongolia, 170 m.
Elba, El'ba; *i* of Tuscany, Med., 18½; *vs* N-Y., Va., &c.
Elbe, Elb, (Ger. El'be,) *r* Ger., 550 m.
Elberfeld, El'ber-felt, *t* Rhen. Prus., 35.
Elbeuf *or* Elbœuf, El-bęf, *t* Fr., 17½.
Elbing, El'biŋ, *t* e. Prus., 20.
Elbingerode, El'biŋ-*h*a-ró-de, *t* Han., 3.
Elbogen *or* Ellbogen, El-bó-*h*en, *t* Bohemia, 2.
Elbridge, El'brij, *vs* N-Y. 1, Ill.
Elbrooz, El-bróz, range of mountains, Cen. Asia, breadth 200 m.
Elburg, El'bur*h*, *t* Hol., 2.
Elche, El'ça, *t* Sp., 18.
Elde, El'de, *r* Meck.-Schwerin, 94 m.
El Dorado, El Dɷ-rq́-đɷ, part of S. A.; *co* Cal., area 2,000 s. m., pop. 40; *vs* Ark. ½, Ky., Mo.
Elek, Ɑ-lék, *v* Hun., 2⅓.
Elemer, Ɑ-la-mq́*r*, *v* Hun., 2¾.
Eleuthera (Ɛ-lq́-đɛ-ra) Island and Keys, Bahama Islands, 2½.
Elfeld, El'felt, *t* Cen. Ger., 2¼.
Elgg, Elk, *v* Swit., 3.
Elgin, El'gin, *t* Scot., 6⅓; *vs* N-Y., Ill. 2⅓, &c.
Elisabethstadt, Ɑ-lé-zq-bet-stqt, *t* Transylvania, 4.
Elisavetopol, Ɑ-lɛ-zq-va-tó-pol, *t* Ga. in Eu., 12.
Elizabeth, *vs* Pa. 2½, Ark., &c.
Elizabeth City, *co* Va.; *t* N. C., 2.
Elizabeth Islands, coast of Mass., and likewise the names of other small islands in the At. and Pac. Oceans.
Elizabeth Port, *v* N-J., 1.
Elizabethtown, *vs* N-J. 4, Pa., Va., &c.
El Kader, El Kq́-der, *v* Iowa.
El-Kasr *or* El-Kasar, El-kqs-r', *cap* of Dakhel, in Upper Egypt.
El-Khargeh, El-kq́*r*-ge, *t* Up. Eg., 6.
Elkhart (Elk'hqrt) River, Ia., 100 m.
Elk Mountain, *m* Pa.
El-Kos, El-kós, *r* Morocco.
Elk River, *rs* Pa., Va., Tenn. and Ala.
Ellé, El-á, *r* Fr.
Ellezelles, El-zél, *t* Belg., 6¼.
Ellice (El'is) Islands, group of islets in the Pacific, ¼.
Ellichpoor, El-ik-pɷ́r, *c* India.
Ellicotville, El'i-kot-vil, *v* N-Y., 1¼.
Ellsworth, Elz'wurđ, *t* and *pt* Me., 5.
Ellwangen, El'wqŋ-en, *t* Würt., 3.
Elmina, El-mé-nq, (*or* St. George del Mina,) *t* and *ft*, cap. Dutch posses. on the Guinea coast, Af.; 10 blacks.
Elmira, El-mȋ-ra, *vs* N-Y. 10, O., Ill.
Elmshorn, Elms'hɘrn, *t* Denmark, 5½.
El Paso del Norte, El Pq́-sɷ del Nér-ta, (often written El Passo,) a line of settlements on the right bank of the Rio Grand, Mex., 5.
El Rosario, El Rɷ-sq́-ri-ɷ, *t* Mex., 5.
Elsinore, El-si-nór, *or* Elsineur, El-si-nq́r, *s-pt t* Den., noted as the place where the Sound dues are levied on vessels entering or clearing the Baltic; pop. 8.
Elster, El'ster, White, *r* Ger., 110 m.
Elster, Black, *r* Ger., 105 m.
El Tyh, Wady, Wq́-di el Tɛ, ("Valley of the Wandering,") Middle Egypt.
Elvas, El'vqs, *ft c* Port., 16½.
Elven, El-vóñ, *t* Fr., 3½.
Ely, Ɛ'lɛ, Isle of, *dis* Eng., *co* of Cambridge; area 225,150 acres.
Elyria, Ɛ-lir-i-a, *v* O., 2⅓.
Elza, El'zq, *r* Tuscany.
Elze, Elt'sɛ, *t* Hanover, 2.
Emba, Em'bq, (Jem *or* Djem, Jem,) *r* Cen. Asia, 250 m.
Embach, Em'bq*h*, Great and Little, *r* Russia.

Embrun, Em'brun *or* Oṅ-brúṅ, *t* Fr., 4¾.
Emden *or* Embden, Em'den, *s-pt t* Hanover, 12.
Emenabad, Em-en-q-bq́d, *or* Aminabad, A-min-q-bq́d, *t* of the Punjab.
Emerina, Em-e-ré-nq, *dis* island of Madagascar.
Emmerich, Em'e-ri*h*, *or* Emrich, Em'ri*k*, walled *t* Rhen. Prus., 6⅓.
Empoli, Em'pω-lε, *t* Tuscany, 5½.
Ems, *r* n. w. Ger.
Ems Höhen, Ems Hę-en, *t* Aus.
Enara, Ɛ-nq́-rq, *l* Rus. Lapland. [3½.
Encina-Sola, En-ŧé-nq-Só-lq, *t* Sp.,
Encruzilhada, En-krω-zεl-yq́-dq, *v* and *har* Brazil, 2.
Endava, En-dq́-vq, *r* S. Am.
Ende, En'da, *s-pt t* Malay Arch.
Endingen, En'diŋ-en, *t* Baden, 3.
Enfield, En'fεld, *v* N-H., Conn.
Engano, En-gq́-nω, *is* Malay Arch., northern coast of Papua.
Engedi, Eŋ'gε-dį, *or* Ainjidy, Ɛn-jíd-ε, anc. *t* Palestine.
Engelberg, Eŋ'el-bęr*h*, *v* Swit.
Engelhardszell, Eŋ'el-hq*r*t-sel, *t* Upper Aus., 1.
Engelholm, Eŋ'gel-hωm, *s-pt t* Swed.
Engelsberg, Eŋ'gels-bęr*h*, *t* Austrian Silesia, 2¼.
Engenho-do-Matto, En-ʒén-yω-dω-mq́-tω, *v* Brazil, 3.
Enghien, Oṅ-gi-áṅ, *t* Belg., 3¾.
England, Iŋ'gland, a famous *cy* of Europe, forming, with Wales, the southern part of the island of Great Britain. Area, 57,812 s. m., of which 50,377 are in England, and 7,425 in Wales; pop. of Eng., in 1851, was 16,921,888, Wales, 1,050,721.
Engua-Guaçu, (*or* Guazu,) Eŋ'gwq-gwq-sǿ, *i* of Brazil.
Enguera, En-gwá-rq, *t* Sp., 5¾.
Enkhuysen, Eŋk-hǿ-sen, Enkhuizen, Enchusa, En-kǿ-sq, *s-pt t* Neth., 5.
Enkirch, En'kεr*h*, *v* Rhen. Prus., 2.
Enkjöping, Enköping, En'çę-piŋ, *t* Sweden, 1¼.
Ennaska, En-q́s-kq, *i* N. Pac. Oc.
Enneda, En-á-dq, *v* Swit., 2.
Ennel, En'el, *l* Ir.
Ennis, En'is, *t* Ir., 9⅓.
Enniscorthy, En-is-kór-ŧi, *t* Ir., 7.
Enniskillen, En-is-kil-en, *t* Ir., 5¾.
Enns *or* Ens, *r* and *t* Aus., 3½.
Enos, Ɛ'nos, *s-pt t* Eu. Tur., 7.
Enosburg, Ɛ'nos-burg, *v* Vt., 2.
Enotaevsk, Ɛ-nω-tq-évsk, *t* Rus., 3.
Enschede, En-ská-de, *t* Netherlands, 5.
Ensenada de Barragon, En-sa-nq́-dq da Ba*r*-q-gón, *b* and *v* Argentine Republic.
Ensisheim, En'sis-hįm, *or* Ensheim, Ens'hįm, *t* Fr., 4.
Entrague, Oṅ-trq́g, *v* Sard. States, 3.
Entrecasteaux, Oṅ-tr-kqs-tó, *t* Fr., 2.
Entre Rios, En'tra Ré-ωs, *prov* Argentine Republic, 30.
Entry (En'trε) Island, Kapito, Kq́-pε-tω, *i* of N-Zealand.
Envie, Oṅ-vé, *v* Pied., 2½.
Enzweihingen, Ents-vį-hiŋ-en, *v* Würt.
Eoa, Ɛ-ó-q, *or* Eooa, Ɛ-ǿ-q, *i* Pac. Oc.
Epaignes, E-pán, *v* Fr., 2⅓.
Epe, Ɛ'pe, *or* Eep, Ɛp, *v* Hol., 3⅓.
Eperies, Ɛ-pa-ri-éʃ, *or* Heperjes, Haper-yéʃ, *t* Hun., 8½.
Epernay, Ɛ-pe*r*-ná, *t* Fr., 6.
Ephratah, Ɛ-frá-tα, *v* N-Y., 2.
Epila, Ɛ-pé-lq, *t* Sp., 3.
Epinal, Ɛ-pε-nq́l, *t* Fr., 11.
Epsom, Ep'som, *t* Eng., 3½.
Epte, Ept, *r* Fr.
Erbach, E*r*'bq*h*, *vs* Hesse-Darmstadt, Nassau, and Würt.; *r* Rhen. Bavaria.
Ercsi, E*r*-çé, *or* Ercseny, E*r*-çény, *v* Hun., 3¼.
Erdeven, E*r*d-vóṅ, *v* Fr., 3.
Erfurt *or* Erfurth, E*r*'fu*r*t, *t* Prussian Saxony, 24½.
Ericeira, Ɛ-ri-sá-i-rq, *mar t* Port., 2½.
Ericht, Loch, Lo*h* Er'i*h*t, *l* Scot.
Ericht, *r* Scot.
Erie, Ɛ-ri, *l* n. U. S., one of the five drained by the St. Lawrence River; *ts* Pa., Mich., &c.
Erivan, Er-i-vq́n, *ft t* Rus. Arm., 11¼.
Erlangen, E*r*'lqŋ-en, *t* Bavaria, 11¾.
Erlau, E*r*'lɤ, *ft t* Hun., 19¾.
Erne, Ern, *r* and two *ls* Ir.
Ernée, E*r*-ná, *t* Fr., 5½.
Ernsthal, E*r*ns'tql, *t* Sax. [6¾.
Ersek-Ujvar, E*r*-ʃék-ω-i-vq́*r*, *t* Hun.,
Erstein, E*r*'stįn, *t* Fr., 3½.
Ertvaag-Oe, E*r*'vog-ę-e, *i* of Norway.
Ertvelde, E*r*t-vél-de, *v* Belg., 3.
Erzberg, E*r*ts'bę*rh*, *m* Styria.
Erzengan, Er-zen-gq́n, *t* As. Tur.
Erz-Gebirge, E*r*ts-ga-bí*r*-gα, *m* s. Ger.
Erzroom, Erzroum *or* Erzrum, Erz-rǿm, *c* Armenia, 50.
Erzroom, Pashalic of, one of the subdivisions of As. Tur.
Escalaplano, Es-kq-lq-plq́-nω, *or* Scalaplano, Skq-lq-plq́-nω, *v* island of Sardinia, 1¼.
Escalonilla, Es-kq-lω-nél-yq, *v* Sp., 2.
Escambia, Es-kám-bi-α, *r* Ala.; *co* Fa.
Escholzmatt, Eʃ'olts-mqt, *v* Swit., 3.

Eschwege, Eʃ'va-ge, *t* Hesse-Cassel, 6.
Eschweiler, Eʃ'vi-ler, *t* Rhen. Prus., 8.
Escudo de Veragua, Es-kú-do da Va-rá-gwa, *r* S. Am.
Escuintla, Es-kwént-la, *t* Cen. Am., 2½.
Eskee-Sara, Es'ke-sá-ra, *or* Eski-Sagra, Es'ke-sá-gra, *t* Eu. Tur., 20.
Esla, Es'la, *r* Sp.
Eslingen, Es'liŋ-en, *t* Würt., 6¾.
Esmeralda, Es-ma-rál-da, *r* S. Am.; *m* Brazil. [2½.
Esparraguera, Es-par-a-gá-ra, *t* Sp.,
Espejo, Es-pá-*h*o, *t* Sp., 5¼.
Espinhaço, Serra do, Sér-a do Es-pen-yá-so, *ms* Brazil.
Espiritu Santo, Es-pír-i-to Sán-to, *is* Pac. Oc., Gulf of Cal., one of the Bahama Is.; *t* Cuba; sev. *vs* and *cas.*
Espita, Es-pé-ta, *t* Cen. Am., 3.
Espluga de Francoli, Es-plú-ga da Fran-ko-lé, *t* Sp., 2¾.
Esquimaux, Es'ki-mo, *or* -moz, the inhabitants of Greenland and the extreme north of America.
Esquimaux, *i* and *har* N. Am.
Essarts, Les, Laz Es-ár, *t* Fr., 2¾.
Essen, Es'en, *t* Prus. Westphalia, 7¼.
Essequibo, Es-e-ké-bo, *r* Br. Guiana.
Essex, Es'eks, *cos* and *vs* U. S.
Este, Es'ta, *t* Lombardy, 8.
Estella, Es-tél-ya, *t* Sp., 6.
Estepona, Es-ta-pó-na, *t* Sp., 9¼.
Estrella, Serra da, Sér-a da Es-trél-a, *ms* Brazil and Port. [Port., 748½.
Estremadura, Es-tra-ma-dú-ra, *prov*

Eszek, Esseck, Es'ek, *or* Essegg, Es'eg, *cap* Aus. Slavonia, 12¼.
Etampes, A-tóŋp, *t* Fr., 8.
Ethiopia, E-thi-ó-pi-a, *cy* S. Egypt.
Etna, Et'na, *vol* n. e. Sicily.
Eton, E'ton, *t* Eng., 3⅔.
Etowah, Et'o-wa, *or* Hi-to-wa, *r* Ga.
Ettrick, Et'rik, *r* and *par* Scot.
Eubœa, Ya-bé-a, *or* Negropont, the largest island of the kingdom of Gr.
Euclid, Yú-klid, *vs* N-Y., O.
Eupen, O'pen, *t* Rhen. Prus., 11.
Euphrates, Ya-frá-tez, called also by the natives, Moorad, *r* Egypt.
Eure-et-Loir, Er-a-Lwar, *prov* Fr., 295.
Europe, Yú-rop, the least of the great divisions of the earth, Australia excepted, yet a quarter in which civilization has progressed most extensively. Area, 3,830,130 s. m.; pop., 264,209,000.
Eutaw, Yú-ta, *v* Ala., 2.
Evansville, Iv'anz-vil, *t* Ia. 9; *vs* Va., &c.
Everghem, A'ver-*h*em, *v* Belg., 7¾.
Evora, Ev'o-ra, *c* Port., 15.
Evreux, Ev-rê, *c* Fr., 13.
Ewington, Yú-iŋ-ton, *co t* Ill.
Exe, Eks, *r* Eng.
Exeter, Eks'e-ter, *c* Eng., 33; *vs* Me., N-H., and other States.
Exmouth, Eks'muth, *t* Eng., 5.
Eyafialla-Yokul, I-a-fi-á-la-Yó-kul *vol* Iceland. [*s-pt t* Eng.
Eye, I, *bor* and *t* Eng., 7½; -mouth,
Eynesford, Anz'ford, *par* Eng.

# F.

Faaberg, Fó-berg, *ts* Nor. 4¾., Den.
Fabbriano, Fab-ri-á-no, *c* Cen. It., 6½.
Facone, Fa-kó-na, *l* Japan.
Fadievskoi, Fa-di-év-sko, *i* Arc. Oc.
Fæmund *or* Famund, Fá-mond, *l* Nor.
Faenza, Fa-én-za, *c* Cen. It., 19¾.
Fairfax, Fár-faks, *co t* Va.; *vs* Vt., O.
Fairfield, Fár-feld, *v* port of entry, Conn.; *vs* N-Y., O., Ia., Ill., Iowa.
Fairhaven, Far-há-ven, *v* Mass., 5; *vs* N-Y., Conn., O., Ill.
Fairmont, Fár-mont, *co t* Va.
Fairweather, Far-wéth-er, *m* Rus. Am., 14,900 ft. high. [Conn.
Fairweather's Is., Black Rock Harbor,
Falaba, Fa-lá-ba, *t* W. Af., 6.
Falaise, Fa-láz, *t* Fr., 9.
Falalu, Fa-la-lú, *i* Pac. Oc.
Falkirk, Fol-kérk, *t* Scot., 9.
Falkland, Fók-land, Islands, S. At. Oc.

Fall River, *ts* Mass. 11½, Wis.
Falmouth, Fál-muth, *s-pt t* Eng., 5; *vs* Me., Mass., &c.
Falster, Fál-ster, *i* in the Baltic, 23¼.
Fano, Fá-no, *s-pt t* Cen. It., 10.
Farallones de los Frayles, Fa-ral-yó-nes da los Fri-les, *is* coast of Cal.
Fareham, Fár-ham, *t* Eng., 3½.
Farmington, Fárm-iŋ-ton, *vs* Me., N-H., Conn., N-Y., &c. [Eng.
Farne (Farn) *or* Fern Is., off coast of
Farnham, Fárn-ham, *t* Eng., 3½; *v* Va.
Faro, Fá-ro, *s-pt c* Port., 8½. a
Färöe, Fá-ro *or* Fá-re-e, *i* N. At. Oc.
Farsan, Far-sán, Islands, Red Sea.
Fasano, Fa-sá-no, *c* Nap., 9.
Fatsizio, Fat-sé-zi-o, *i* of Japan.
Fauquier, Fé-ker, *co* Va.
Fausse (Fos) Point, *p o* La.
Fausse Rivière, Fos Re-vi-ár, *v* La.

Faversham, Fáv-er-ʃam, *s-pt t* Eng.
Favignana, Fq-ven-yq-nq, *i* Med.
Faxardo *or* Fajardo, Fq-*hq́r*-dœ, *t* and *i* Porto Rico, 3.
Fayal, Fị-q́l, *i* Azores, N. At. Oc., 26.
Fayette, Fa-ét, *vs* N-Y., Pa., Miss., &c.
Fayetteville, Fa-ét-vil, *t* N. C., 7; *vs.*
Fayoom *or* Faioum, Fị-œ́m, *prov* Eg.
Feather (Féđ-er) River, Cal.
Fécamp, Fa-kóṅ, *s-pt t* Fr., 11½.
Feejee, Fidji, Fiji, Fé-jɛ, *or* Viti, Vé-tɛ, Islands, group in the S. Pac. Oc.
Feia, Fa-é-q, *l* Brazil.
Felaniche, Fa-lq-néq, *t* Sp., 9¾.
Felegyhaza, Fa-lej-hq́-zo, *t* Hun., 17.
Feliciana, Fɛ-liʃ-i-án-a, *par* La.; *v* Ky.
Felicity, Fɛ-lís-i-ti, *v* O.
Femern, Fa-mẹrn, *i* Den., 9.
Fermoy, Fer-mœ́, *t* Ir., 5¾.
Fernando de Noronha, Fe*r*-nq́n-dœ da Nœ-rœ́n-yq, *i* S. At. Oc.
Fernando Po, Fer-nq́n-dœ Pœ, *i* W. Af.
Fernan Nunez, Fe*r*-nq́n Nœ́n-yeŧ, *t* Sp., 5⅔.
Ferrara, Fe*r*-q́-rq, *c* Papal States, 31.
Ferret, Col de, Kol dẹ Fe*r*-á, *pass* in Pennine Alps.
Ferro, Fér-œ, one of Canary Is., 4⅓.
Ferrol, Fer-œ́l, *s-pt t* Sp., 16½.
Fesa, Fés-q *or* Fá-sq, *t* Per., 18.
Fez, Fez, *k* Morocco; *c* do., 90.
Fezarah, Fa-zq́-rq, *l* Algeria.
Fezzan, Fez-q́n, *k* N. Af.
Fichtelberg, Fi*h*-tel-bẹ*rh*, *or* Fichtelgebirge, Fi*h*-tel-ga-bé*r*-*h*a, *ms* Bav.
Figueira, Fɛ-gá-i-rq, *t* Port., 6.
Figueras, Fɛ-gá-rqs, *t* Sp., 8.
Fillmore, Fil-mœr, *vs* U. S.; — City, *t* Utah.
Finale, Fɛ-nq́-la, *ts* It., 5 and 8.
Finana, Fɛn-yq́-nq, *t* Sp., 3¼.
Fincastle, Fin-kas-l, *vs* Va., O., Ill., &c.
Findlay, Find-la, *v* O., 3.
Finesville, Fịnz-vil, *v* N-J.
Fingal, Fin-gél, *dis* Ir.; *v* C. W.
Fingoes, Fiŋ-gœz, *race* S. Africans.
Finland, Fin-land, Grand Duchy of, a *gov* N. W. Russia, 1,637.
Finland, Gulf of, arm of Baltic Sea.
Finmark, Fin-mqrk, *prov* of Nor., 44.
Finster-Aarhorn, Fin-ster-Ar*'*he*r*n, *m* Swit., 14,026 ft. high.
Fishkill, Fiʃ-kil, *v* N-Y., 9¼.
Fitchburg, Fiq-burg, *t* Mass., 7.
Fiume, Fi-œ́-ma, *s-pt t* Aus., 11.
Flanders, Flán-derz, former *dis* Eu., now included in Hol., Belg. and Fr.
Fleetwood, Flét-wud, *s-pt* Eng.
Flemingsburg, Flém-iŋz-burg, *t* Ky., ¾.
Flemington, *vs* N-J. 1, Pa., N. C.

Flensborg, Flénz-bo*rh*, *t* Den., 16½.
Flint, Flint, *s-pt* N. Wales; *vs* Mich., Ia.
Flint River, *rs* Ga., 300 m.; Mich.
Florence, Flór-ens, *c* It., 102¼; *vs* U. S.
Flores, Flœ́-res, *is* Malay Arch., Azores 9, Plata estuary, N. Pac. Oc.; *t* Brazil.
Florida, Flór-i-da, most southern U. S.; area, 59,268 s. m.; pop. 47,203 whites, 932 free blacks, 39,310 slaves—total, 87,445; *vs* U. S.
Floridia, Flœ-ré-di-q, *t* Sic., 4¾.
Flushing, Flúʃ-iŋ, *s-pt t* Neth., 7¾; *v* N-Y., 2½.
Fogaras, Fœ́-go-róʃ, *t* Transylvania, 5.
Foggia, Fód-jq, *c* Nap., 24.
Fogo, Fœ́-gœ, *or* Fuego, Fœ-á-gœ, one of the Cape Verd Is., 7.
Föhr, Fẹr, *i* of Den., 4¾.
Földvar, Fẹld-vq́r, *t* Hun., 10½.
Folgefonden-Field, Fól-ge-fon-den-Fi-éld, *ms* Nor.
Foligno, Fœ-lén-yœ, *t* Cen. It., 15½.
Folkestone, Fœ́k-stœn, *s-pt t* Eng., 7½.
Fond-des-Negres, Fœṅ-da-Ná-gr, *t* Hayti.
Fon du Lac, Fon dq Lak, *t* Wis., 5.
Fong-Tsiang, Foŋ-Tsi-q́ŋ, *c* China.
Fontainebleau, Fœṅ-ten-blœ́, *t* Fr., 10⅓.
Foochoo, Fœ-çœ́, Foo-Choo-Foo, Fœ-Çœ-Fœ́, *or* Foo-Tchow-Foo, Fœ-Çɤ-Fœ, *c* China, 500.
Foolahs *or* Fulahs, Fœ́-lqz, sing. *race* W. Af.
Foosee, Fousi *or* Fusi, Fœ-sé, *m* Japan.
Foo-Shan *or* Fou-Schan, Fœ-Σq́n, *c* China, 200.
Foota-Jallon, Fœ́-tq-Jq-lón, *dis* W. Af.
Forcados, Rio dos, Ré-œ dœs Fo*r*-kq́-dœs, *r* W. Af.
Fordoche, For-dœ́ʃ, *bayou* La.
Forestville, Fór-est-vil, *vs* Conn., N-Y., &c.
Forfar, Fér-far *t* Scot., 11.
Forli, Fo*r*-lé, *c* Cen. It., 16.
Formentera, Fe*r*-men-tá-rq, *i* Med.
Formosa, Fo*r*-mœ́-sq, *is* China Sea, 2,500,000; *i* off W. coast Af. — Mount *and* River, Malay Peninsula.
Forsyth, For-sịđ, *vs* Ga., Mo.
Fort Anne, Fœrt An, *v* N-Y.
Fort Beversede, Bá-ver-sa-de, Pa.
Fort Boisé, Bwq-zá, Oregon.
Fort Des Moines, De Mœ́n, *t* cap. Iowa.
Forteau (For-tœ́) Bay *islet* s. e. Lab.
Fort Edward, *v* N-Y., ¾.
Fort Gaines, Ganz, *v* Ga.
Fort Gibson, *v* and *mil sta* Ind. Ter.
Forth, Fœrŧ, *r* Scot.
Fort Hamilton, *v* and *ft* defending N-Y. Harbor.
Fort Howard, *v* Wis., ½.

Fort Isle Aux Noix, El Ꝏ Nwq, *ft* C. E.
Fort Kearny, Kẹr-ni, Neb., on Or. route.
Fort Laramie, Lár-a-mɛ, *mil post* Platte River, Ind. Ter.
Fort Leavenworth, Lév-en-wurϑ, *mil post*, Kansas.
Fort Liberté, Lɛ-ber-tá, *s-pt t* Hayti.
Fort Madison, Mád-i-son, *t* Iowa, 3.
Fort Plain, *v* N-Y., 1½.
Fort Ridgely, Rij-li, Min. Ter.
Fort Riley, Rị-li, Kansas Ter.
Fort Royal, Rő-al, *ft t* Fr. W. Ind.
Fort Smith, *t* Ark., 1½.
Fort Snelling, *mil post* and *v* Min.
Fortune, Fért-yꝗn, Bay, *inlet* s. N-Fd.
Fort Union, U. S. *ft* bet. Independence and Santa-Fé.
Fort Valley, *t* Ga., 1. [Ter.
Fort Wallawalla, Wól-a-wol-ɑ, Wash.
Fort Washita, Wóʃ-i-tɑ, Ind. Ter.
Fort Wayne, Wan, *t* Ia., 6½.
Fort Yuma, Yꝏ́-mɑ, Cal.
Fossano, Fos-q̇-nꝏ, *t* Pied., 16.
Foster, Fós-ter, *ts* R. I. 2, Ky., &c.
Fourche a Reynault, Fꝏrʃ q Ra-nó, *v* Mo.
Fowey, Fő, *r* Eng.
Fowla *or* Foula, Fȣ́-lq, one of Shet. Is.
Fox River, *rs* Wis., Iowa, Mo., Canada.
Framingham, Frá-miŋ-ham, *v* Mass., 4½.
France, Frɑns, one of the mightiest empires in the world, w. part of Eu., embracing the following islands and colonies: Corsica; Algeria; Senegal in W. Af.; Bourbon, Ind. Oc.; St. Marie; W. Ind.,—Martinique, Guadeloupe, n. part of St. Martin, Marie Galante, Desirade, and the Saintes Group; French Guiana, St. Pierre and Miquelon Is., coast of N. Am.; Marquesas Is., Taiti and Akarno; and New Caledonia. Area, 321,016 s. m.; pop. 38,489,979.
Francestown, Frán-ses-tȣn, *t* N-H., 1¼.
Franconia, Fran-kó-ni-ɑ, *ts* N-H., Pa.
Frankfort (Fráŋk-fort,) on the Main, *c* of Ger., seat of the Germanic Diet, pop. 62¼.
Frankfort, (Fráŋk-fort,) on the Oder, *c* Prus., 30½. [O., Ia.
Frankfort, *t*, *cap* Ky., 5; *vs* Me., N-Y.,
Franklin, Fráŋk-lin, 20 *cos*; 33 *vs*; 60 *ts*, U. S. [4¾.
Frederica, Fred-er-íʃ-i-q, *s-pt t* Den.,
Frederick, Fréd-er-ik, *cos* in Md., Va.; *ts* in Pa., O., &c.; — City, Md., 6.
Fredericksburg, *t* Va., 4; *vs* O., Tex.
Fredericksville, *v* Ill.
Fredericktown, *vs* Ky., O., 1, Mo.
Fredericton, Fréd-er-ik-ton, *c* N-Brun., 4½. [Den.
Frederikshavn, Fréd-er-iks-hȣn, *s-pt t*
Fredonia, Frɛ-dó-ni-ɑ, *v* N-Y., 1¼; *vs* Ala., Ky., O., Ill., &c. [O., Ia., Ill.
Freedom, Fré-dom, *vs* Me., N-H., Pa.,
Freehold, Fré-hold, *v* N-J.
Freeport, Fré-pꝏrt, *vs* Ill., Me., Pa., &c.
Free-town, *or* St. George, *cap* Sierra Leone, 18. [Sax., 14¼.
Freigburg, *or* Freyberg, Frị-bẹrg, *t*
Freiberg, *or* Freyburg, Frị-bꝏrg, *c* grand duchy of Baden, 15⅓.
Fremont, Fré-mont, formerly Lower Sandusky, *v* O., 1¾; numerous *vs* and *cos* U. S. [200 m.
French Broad River, N. C. and Tenn.,
Frenchman's Bay, on coast Me.
Frenchman's Cap, *m* Van Diemen's Land, 5000 ft.
Frenchtown, *vs* N-J., Pa., Md., &c.
Freneuse, Frẹ-nṳ́z, *l* N-Brun.
Fresnillo, Fres-nél-yꝏ, mining *t* Mex., 8.
Freyburg, Frị-bꝏrg, *canton* and *t* Swit., 9.
Freycinet (Frị-si-net) Island, in Pac.
Frey-Oe, Frị-ẹ-e, *i* w. coast of Nor.
Friendly, Frénd-li, (*or* Tonga, Tón-gq,) *is*, upwards of 150 islands, Pa. Oc.
Friendship, *vs* N-Y., ¾, Md., N-C.
Friesland, Fréz-land, *prov* of the Neth.
Frignano, Frɛn-yq̇-nꝏ, *vs* Nap., 2⅓.
Frodsham, Fród-ʃam, *t* Eng., 6⅓.
Frome, *or* Frome Selwood, Frꝏm Sél-wꝏd, *t* Eng., 10¼.
Fronton, Fron-tón, *v* Tex.
Front Royal, *v* Va., ½.
Frosinone, Frꝏ-sɛ-nó-nɑ, *t* It., 7⅔.
Fronton, Fron-tón, *c* Tex.
Fryeburg, Frị-burg, *v* Me., 1½.
Fuca, *or* Juan De Fuca, (Sp. pron. *H*ꝏ-q̇ŋ Da Fó-kq,) *str* N. Am., in Or. Ter.
Fucino, Lago, Lq̇-gꝏ Fꝏ-çé-nꝏ, *l* Nap., 11 by 5 m. [Phil. Is.
Fuegos, Fwá-gꝏs, *or* Fꝏ-á-gꝏs, one of
Fuego, Volcano de, Vol-kq̇-nꝏ da Fwá-gꝏ, (Fꝏ-á-gꝏ,) *m* Cen. Am.
Fuen-Ho, Fwen-Hó, *r* China, 300 m.
Fuerte de San Jose, Fwér-ta dá Sqn *H*ꝏ-sá, *t* of the Argentine Republic.
Fuerteventura, Fwér-tq-ven-tó-rq, one of the Can. Is. [9⅔.
Fulda, Fúl-dq, *r* Ger.; *t* Hesse-Cassel,
Fulton, Fúl-ton, *cos* N-Y., Pa., Ky.; *vs* N-Y., 2, Miss., O., Ill., Mo.
Funchal, Fꝏn-ʃq̇l, *cap* of the Island Maderia, 18.
Fundy, Bay of, inlet of the Atlantic separating Nova Scotia from N-B.

Fünfkirchen, Fęnf-kęrh-en, *t* S. Hun., 14½.
Furca, La, Lq Fór-kq, *m* Swit.
Furneaux, Fur-nó, *is* of Australasia.
Furruckabad, Fur-uk-q-bq́d, *t* Brit. [Ind., 66.
Furth, Fęrt, *t* Bav., 15.
Fusagasuga, Fœ-sq-gq-só-gq, *r* N-Gran. [12,000 ft.
Futi-Panjal, Fó-tɛ-Pqn-jq́l, *m* Cash.,
Futtoolah-Killa, Fu-tó-lq-Kíl-q, *v* Af.
Fuur, Fœr, *or* Fuurland, Fór-lqnd, *i* [Den., 1.
Fyzabad, Fį-zq-bq́d, *t* of Ind.

# G.

Gaddada, Gqd-dq́-dq, (*or* Tchin-Tchoo,) *r* Hind., 150 m.
Gadjatsch, Gqd-yáq, *or* Gaditch, Gq-díq, *t* S. Rus., 3½.
Gaeta, Gq-á-tq, *s-pt c* Naples, 3.
Gagy, Gq́-gɛ, *or* Gaga, Gq́-gq, *i* Malay Arch.
Gaillac, Ga-yq́k, *or* Gql-yq́k, *t* Fr. 8¼.
Gainesville, Gánz-vil, *vs* N-Y., Ga., Ala., &c.
Gainsborough, Gánz-bur-œ, *s-pt t* Eng., 7½; *v* in Va. [Far. Ind.
Galadzet, (Gq-lqd-zét,) Hills, range in
Galapagos, Gq-lq́-pq-gœs, *is* Pac. Oc.
Galashiels, Gal-a-ʃélz, *t* Scot., 6.
Galatz, Gq́-lqts, *t* Moldavia, 36.
Galena, Ga-lé-na, *c* Ill., 8; name of *vs* O., Ia., Mo.
Galesburg, Gálz-burg, *vs* Ill., 1, Mich.
Galiano, (Gq-li-q́-nœ,) Island, of Brit. N. Am., in Queen Charlotte's Sound.
Galicia, Gal-iʃ-i-a, *prov* Aus., 4,702,383.
Galilee, Gál-i-lɛ, *prov* ancient Judea, w. of the Jordan. [i-on, *v* O.
Galion, Gq́-li-on, *i* n. e. of Java; Gál-
Gallas, Gq́-lqz, powerful race E. Af.
Gallatin, Gál-a-tin, *vs* Miss., Tenn.
Gallego, Gql-yá-gœ, *r* Sp.
Gallegos, Gql-yá-gœs, *r* Patagonia.
Gallia, Gál-i-a, (Latin for Fr.,) *co* O.
Gallipoli, Gq-líp-œ-lɛ, *ts* Tur., Nap.; and peninsular bet. Ægean Sea and Hellespont.
Gallipolis, Gal-i-pœ-lés, *t* O.
Galloway, Gál-œ-wa, *v* Ill.
Galoengong, Gq-lœn-góŋ, *vol* Java.
Galt, Gɵlt, *t* C. W., 2⅓.
Galveston, Gál-ves-ton, *pt* of entry, *c* Tex., 8.
Galway, Gɵ́l-wa, *co* and *t* Ir., 24¾; *b* Ir.
Gambia, Gq́m-bi-a, *r* W. Af.; Brit. colony of W. Af.
Gambier (Gám-bɛr) Is. Pa. Oc.; *t* O.
Gamla Karleby, Gq́m-lq Kq́r-le-bę, *t* Finland., 2.
Gananoque, Gq-nq-nók, *v* C. W.
Ganci, Gq́n-ςɛ, *t* Sic., 9⅓.
Ganges, Gán-jɛz, *r* Hind., 196 m.; *v* O.
Ganges, Góŋʒ, *t* Fr.
Gangpoor, Gqŋ-pór, *t* Brit. Ind.
Gannet (Gán-et) Islands, S. Pa. Oc., Brit. N. Am., on coast of Labrador.
Gantheaume (Gan-tóm) Bay, Aus.
Gap, Gqp, *t* Fr., 8¾; Gap, *v* Pa.
Garda (Gq́r-da) Lake of, N. It., 35 by 2 to 10 m.
Gardaia, Gqr-dį-q, *t* Algeria.
Gardiner, Gq́r-din-er, *c* Me., 6½.
Gardner, Gq́rd-ner, *v* Mass., 1½.
Gargano, Gqr-gq́-nœ, *m* Nap.
Garigliano, Gq-rɛl-yq́-nœ, *r* Nap.
Garlasco, Gqr-lq́s-kœ, *t* Pied., 5½.
Garnavillo, Gqr-na-víl-œ, *v* Iowa.
Garonne, Gq-rón, *r* Fr., 384 m.
Garrard, Gár-ard, *co* Ky.
Garrabillas, Gqr-œ-bél-yqs, *t* Sp., 4½.
Garrote, Gqr-ó-ta, *p o* Cal.
Garstang, Gq́rs-taŋ, *t* Eng., 7½.
Gartempe, Gqr-tóṅp, *or* Gardempe, Gqr-dóṅp, *r* Fr.
Gasconade, Gas-kœ-nád, *r*, *co* and *v* Mo.
Gaspe, Gás-pa, *t* C. E.
Gas Port, *v* N-Y.
Gaston, Gás-ton, *v* N. C.
Gatehouse, Gát-hʊs, *t* Scot., 1¾.
Gatesbead, *par* and *t* Eng., 24.
Gatineau, Gq-tɛ-nó, *r* C. E., 300 m.
Gatshina, Gqt-ʃé-nq, *t* Rus., 7.
Gatun, Gq-tón, *r* Isthmus of Panama; *t* N-Gran.
Gauir, Gʊ́-er, *r* Scot.
Gauley (Gɵ́-lɛ) Bridge, *v* Va.; *r* ditto.
Gavia, Gq́-vi-q, *m* Brazil.
Gavilan, Sierra De, Sɛ-ér-q Da Gq-vi-lq́n, *m* Cuba.
Gaya *or* Gayah, Gį-q, *c* Brit. Ind., 36.
Gaya (Gį-q) Islands, Ind. Arch.
Gaza, Gá-zq, *c* Pal., 15.
Gazuolo, Gqd-zœ-ó-lœ, *v* Lom., 2.
Gazzo, Gq́t-sœ, *v* N. It., 1¾.
Geant, Ʒa-óṅ, summit Pennine Alps.
Geauga, Jɛ-ɵ́-ga, *co* O.
Geddes, Géd-ez, *v* N-Y.
Gedeh, Gá-de, *m* Java.
Geelong, Gɛ-lóŋ, *t* Aus.
Gefle, Yév-la, *s-pt t* and *prov* Swed.

Geish, Gaʃ, *m* Abys.
Genesee, Jen-e-sé, *r* and *co* N-Y.; *co* Mich., &c.
Genesee Falls, *v* N-Y., 1.
Geneseo, Gen-e-sé-ɷ, *vs* N-Y., 1½, Ill.
Geneva, Jen-é-vɑ, *c* Swit., 30; *vs* N-Y., 5; O., 1⅓; Ill., 1; Wis. [of Wis.
Geneva, Lake of, s. of Swit.; *l* s. part
Genevieve, Jen-e-vév, *tp* Mo., 1⅓.
Genèvre Mont, Mɷñ Ꝁe-náv-r, Cottian Alps.
Genoa, Jén-ɷ-ɑ, *s-pt c* N. It., 125⅓.
Genoa, Jɛ-nó-ɑ, *v* N-Y., 2½; *vs* O., Mich., Ill.
Gentilly, Ꝁoñ-tɛ-yé, *v* Fr., 13¾; *v* C. E.
George, Lake, (*or* Hóricon,) *l* N-Y.
Georgetown, *c* Dis. of Col., 8⅓; *co ts* Del., S. C., Ky. O.
Georgetown, (Dutch Stabrock, Stɑ̈-brɯk,) *cap* Brit. Guiana, 25½.
Georgia, Jór-ji-ɑ, *or* Grusia, Grɷ́-si-ɑ, *cy* Asia, pop. 300,000.
Georgia, one of the original states of the U. S.; pop. 521,572 whites, 2,931 free blacks, 381,682 slaves, total 906,185.
Gera, Gá-rɑ, *t* Cen. Ger., 11¼.
Gerard-de-Rys, Ꝁa-rɑ́r-de-Res, *i* Pac. Oc., inhabited by Papuan Negroes.
Gerasa, Jɛ-rɑ́-sɑ, *or* Jerash, Jɛ-rɑ́ʃ, ruined city of Syria. [Port.
Gerez, Serra de, Sér-ɑ da Ꝁá-rez, *m*
Germantown, Jẹ́r-man-tɤn, *vs* N-Y., 1; Pa., Va., Tenn., Ky., O., Ia., &c.
Germany, Jẹ́r-man-i, a large portion of Central Europe, composed of numerous sovereign states, bound together by a common league, called the Germanic Confederation, namely: Anhalt-Bernburg, — Dessau, — Kothen, Austria, Baden, Bavaria, Bremen, Brunswick, Frankfort, Hamburg, Hanover, Hesse-Cassel, — Darmstadt, — Homburg, Hohenzollern-Hechingen, — Sigmaringen, Holstein and Lauenburg, Liechtenstein, Lippe-Detmold, — Schaumburg, Lubeck, Luxemburg with Limburg, Mecklenburg-Schwerin, — Strelitz, Nassau, Oldenburg and Kniphausen, Prussia, Reuss (old line,) — (young line,) Saxony, Saxe-Altenburg, — Coburg-Gotha, — Meiningen, — Weimar-Eisenach, Schwarzburg-Rudolstadt, — Sondershausen, Waldeck, Wurtemburg; Area, 235,029; pop. 41,187,000.
Gerona, Jerona, *or* Xerona, *Ha*-ró-nɑ, *c* Sp.
Gettysburg, Gét-iz-burg, *bor* Pa., 3½.
Ghara, *or* Garra, Gɑ́r-ɑ, name of Sutlej River, for 260 m., Brit. Ind.
Ghauts, Gɑts, *m* Hind.
Gheel, *or* Geel, Gal, *t* Belg., 7.
Gheezeh, Ghizeh, Gé-ze, *t* Egypt, near the great Pyramids.
Ghent, Gent, *c* Belg., 112½; *vs* N-Y., 2¼, Ky.
Ghio, Gé-ɷ, *or* Ghemlek, Gem-lék *s-pt t* As. Minor.
Gholson, Gól-son, *v* Miss.
Ghuznee, Ghuzni, Gúz-nɛ, *r* and *ft c* Afg., est. 3 to 10. [N. Ir.
Giant's Causeway, basaltic formation,
Giant's Mountain, Asia Minor.
Gibraltar, Ji-brɑ́l-tɑr, *c* and *ft rock* S. Sp., 13¼; *vs* Mich., Wis.; — Bay and Strait, same location.
Giessen, Gés-en, *t* Ger., 10.
Gijon, Jijon, *or* Xixon, *Hɛ*-hón, *ft s-pt t* Sp., 6½.
Gila, *or* Jila, *Hél*-ɑ, *r* N-Am. [60.
Gilbert (Gil-bert) Islands, Pac. Oc.,
Gilboa, Gil-bó-ɑ, *vs* N-Y., Va., O.
Gilead, Gil-ɛ-ad, *vs* Me., O., Ill., &c.; — Mount, in Syria.
Giles Jilz, *cos* Va., Tenn.
Gilge, Gil-ge, *r* Prus.
Gillespie, Gil-és-pɛ, *co* Tex; *p o* Mo.
Gilly Ꝁɛl-yé, *v* Belg., 5⅔.
Gilmer, Gil-mer, *vs* Tex., Ill.
Gilolo, Jɛ-ló-lɷ, *is* Malay Arch.
Gilopolis, Gil-óp-ɷ-lis, *p o* N. C.
Gilroy, Gil-rɤ́, *p os* Mo., Cal.
Gimone, Ꝁɛ-món, *r* Fr. [Ind.
Gingee, *or* Jhinji, Jin-jɛ, *ft t* Brit.
Girard, Ji-rɑ́rd, *vs* Pa., Ala., O.
Girgenti, Jir-jén-tɛ, *c* Sicily, 18⅗.
Givet, Ꝁɛ-vá, *ft t* Fr., 5⅔.
Givors, Ꝁɛ-vór, *t* Fr., 9¼.
Gladova, Glɑ-dó-vɑ, t Servia.
Glasgow, Glás-gɷ, large com. *c* Scot., 347; also *vs* in Mo., Ky., &c.
Glassborough, Glás-bur-ɷ, *v* N-J., 1½.
Glastenbury, Glás-ten-ber-i, *v* Conn.
Glatz, Glɑts, *ft t* Prus. Silesia, 7¾.
Glauchau, Glɤ́-*hɤ*, *t* Saxony, 8¼.
Gleiwitz, Glʃ-vits, *t* Prus. Silesia, 7½.
Glendale, Glén-dal, *vs* O., Mass., N-J.,
Glenn's Falls, *v* N-Y., 2½.
Glogau, Gló-gɤ, *ft t* Prus. Silesia, 14⅗.
Glommen, Glóm-en, *r* Norway.
Glookhov, *or* Gluchow, Glɷ-kóv, *t* Rus., 7.
Glossop, Glós-op, *t* and *par* Eng., 22¾.
Gloucester, Glós-ter, *c* Eng., 18.
Gloucester, *ts* N-J., Mass., 8.
Gluckstadt, Glẹ́k-stɑt, *t* Den., 6.
Gnesen, Gá-zen, *t* Prus., 7¼.
Godavery, Gɷ-dɑ́-ver-i, *r* Ind., 700 m.

Goentoer, Gœn-tœ́r, *vol* Island of Java.
Goes, *Hœs*, *t* Neth., 5½.
Goggra, Góg-rq, *r* N. Hind., 400 m.
Golconda, Gol-kón-dq, *t* Hind.; *v* Ill.
Goldberg, Gólt-ber*g*, *t* Prus. Sil., 7⅓.
Gold Coast, *cy* Guinea, W. Africa.
Goldsborough, Góldz-bur-o, *vs* Pa., N. C. [Oc.
Golfe, Isles Du, Ɛl dȩ Golf, *is* S. Pac.
Goliad, Go-li-ád, *co* and *v* Tex.
Gomera, Go-má-rq, *i* Canaries, 11¾.
Gondar, Gón-dqr, *cap c* Abys., 50.
Gonzales, Gon-zq́-lez, *co* and *v* Tex.
Good Hope, *ter* Gr. Brit., S. Af.; *vs* O., Wis., &c.
Gookeka, Gœ́-kɛ-kq, *l* and *v* Eu. Ga.
Goole, Gœl, *r-pt* and *t* Eng., 5.
Goolkoo, Gœl-kœ́, *m* Afg., 13,000 ft.
Goomree, Gœ́m-rɛ, ruined *t* Rus. Ar., now the city of Alexandropol, 10.
Goomty, *or* Goomtee, Gœ́m-tɛ, *r* Brit. Ind. [5.
Göppingen, Gȩ́p-iŋ-en, *t* Würtemburg.,
Gordon, Gór-don, *vs* Ga., O.
Gorgona, Gor-gó-nq, *is* Med., Bay of Chocho; *v* N- Gran.
Gorham, Gó-ram, *v* Me., N-H., N-Y.
Goritz, Gȩ́-rits, *t* Illyria, 12¼.
Gorkum, Gór-kum, *ft t* Neth., 8¼.
Görlitz, Gȩ́r-lits, *t* Prus. Silesia, 15⅓.
Goroguea, Go-ro-gá-q, *r* Brazil.
Gort, Gort, *t* Ir., 3. [&c.
Goshen, Gó-ʃen, *vs* N-Y., 3¼; Ia.,
Goslar, Gós-lqr, *t* Hanover, 7¼.
Gosport, Gós-pœrt, *ft s-pt t* Eng., 7½; *vs* Ala., Ia.
Gotha, Gó-tq, *t* Cen. Ger., 13¾.
Götha (Gȩ́-tq) Canal, Sweden.
Gothenburg, *or* Gottenburg, Gót-en-burg, *s-pt c* Sweden, 28¾.
Göttingen, Gȩ́-tiŋ-en, *t* Han. 10⅔.
Gottland, Gót-land, *is* Baltic, 41½.
Gouda, Gɤ́-dq, *t* Neth. 14½.
Gouffre, Gœ́f-r, *r* C. E. [1½.
Gouldsborough, Gœ́ldz-bur-o, *v* Me.,
Gourdon, Gœr-dœ́ṅ, *t* Fr., 5.
Gouverneur, Gœv-er-nœ́r, (often pronounced, Guv-er-nér,) *v* N-Y., 1.
Governador, Go-ver-nq-dór, *i* Brazil.
Governor's Island, N-Y Harbor.
Gowanda, Go-wón-dq, *v* N-Y.
Gowanus, Go-wé-nus, *v* N-Y.
Gower (Gɤ́-er) Island, Solomon group.
Goyanna, Go-yq́n-q, *c* Brazil, 5.
Goyaz, Go-yq́z, *c* Bra., 8.
Gozo, *or* Gozzo, Gót-zo, *is* Med., 16.
Graciosa, Grq-sɛ-ó-sq, *is* Atlantic.
Gräfenberg, Grá-fen-bȩr*h*, *t* Bavaria.
Grafton, Gráf-ton, *vs* Mass., Vt., O., Ill., C. W., &c.

Graham, Grá-ham, *vs* N-C., Ia., Mo.
Grajehu, Grq-ʒa-hœ́, *r* Bra.
Grammichele, Grqm-i-ká-lɛ, *t* Sic., 8.
Grammont, Grq-móṅ, *t* Belg., 7⅓.
Grampians, Grám-pi-anz, *ms* Scot., do.
Gran, Grqn, *c* of Hun., 12. [Aust.
Granada, Grq-nq́-dq, *c* Sp., 61¾; *c* Nicaragua, 10.
Grand Caillou, Ka-yœ́, *bayou* La.
Grand Coteau, Ko-tó, *v* La.
Grand Cote Prairie, *H*ot Prá-rɛ, *v* Ill.
Grand Detour, Da-tœ́r, *v* Ill.
Grand Ecore, Ɛ-kór, *p o* La.
Grand Gulf, *v* Miss.
Grand Haven, Há-ven, *t* Mich.
Grand Island, in the Niagara River.
Grand Isle, *co* Vt., consisting of *is* Lake Champlain; *i* Lake Superior.
Grand Rapids, *c* Mich. 5; *v* Wis.
Grand River, Mich., 220 m.; *rs* La., O., Mo. [Mich.
Grand Traverse, Tráv-ers, *b* and *p o*
Grandville, Gránd-vil, *vs* Mich., Ill.
Grangemouth, Gránj-muƀ, *s-pt t* Scot.
Granger, Grán-jer, *co* Tenn.; *vs* N-Y., O.
Granicus, Gra-nį-kus, *r* As. Minor.
Granville, Groṅ-vél, *ft s-pt t* Fr., 10; *vs* N-Y., Va., O., 2¼; Ia., Ill., &c.
Grasse, Grqs, *t* Fr., 11¾.
Grass Lake, *v* Mich., ½; — River, N-Y.
Grasville, Graville, Grq-vél, *v* Fr., 12¾.
Gratiot, Gráʃ-i-ot, *cos* and *vs* Mich., O., and Wis.
Grätz, Grets, *cap c* Styria, 50.
Graudenz, Grɤ́-dents, *ft t* Prus., 6¾.
Grave Creek, *v* Va., 1¼.
Gravelines, Grqv-lén, *ft s-pt t* Fr., 5¾.
Gravesend, Grávz-end, *t* Eng., 6¾.
Gravina, Grq-vé-nq, *c* Naples, 8.
Gray, Grá, *t* Fr., 7¼.
Graysville, Gráz-vil, *vs* Pa., O., Ill.
Great Barrington, Bár-iŋ-ton, *v* Mass., 3¼.
Great (*or* Fremont) Basin, a singular region in the w. part of Utah Ter.
Great Bend, *vs* N-Y., Pa., 1¼, Ia.
Great Britain, Brit-en, largest and most important island of Eu., composed of the united territories of Eng., Wales, and Scot.; area, 87,903 s. m., pop 20,816,351. [*l* Wis.
Great Butte des Morts, Bqt dq Mor,
Great Egg Harbor River, N-J., 60 m.
Great Falls, *v* N-H., 4½.
Great Fish River, S. Af., 230 m.; *r* Br. N. Am. [N-H.
Great Island, in Portsmouth Harbor,
Great Kanawa, Ka-nó-wq, *r* N-C., and Va.
Great Salt Lake, Utah Ter.

Great Slave Lake, Brit. N. Am.
Great Slave River, Brit. N. Am., 300 m.
Greece, Grεs, *k* S. E. Eu., consisting of two peninsulas of main land, and various contiguous islands; pop. in 1852, 1,002,112.
Green Bay, arm of Lake Mich., 100 by 15 to 35 m.; *co t* Wis., 2½.
Greenbush, Grén-bʊʃ, *v* N-Y. [1⅓.
Greencastle, Grén-kas-l, *ts* Pa. 1¼, Ia.
Greene, Grεn, num. *ts* and *cos* U. S.
Greenfield, Grén-fεld, *vs* Mass. 2½, Pa., O. 1, Ia., Ill., Wis.
Greenland, large *i* of Den., n. e. N. A., 9½, Esquimaux. [E.
Green Mountains, Conn., Mass., Vt., C.
Greenock, Grén-ok, *s-pt t* Scot., 36⅔.
Green Point, *v* N-Y., 3.
Greenport, *v* and *pt of entry* N-Y., 1¼.
Green River, *rs* Ky., Ill., Or., etc.; *vs.*
Greensborough, Grénz-bur-ɷ, *vs* N. C., Ga., Pa. [¾.
Greensburg, *vs* Pa. 1½, La., Ky., Ia.,
Greenupsburg, Grén-ups-burg, *co t* Ky.
Greenville, *vs* O. 1⅓, R. I., Conn., Pa., N. C., S. C., Ga., Ala., Tex., Tenn., Ky.
Greenwich, Grín-ij, *par* Eng., 105¾.
Greenwich, Grén-wiç, *vs* Mass., Conn., N-Y., N-J.
Greenwood, Grén-wʊd, *vs* Miss., La., Ia.
Greiffenhagen, Grȷf-en-hq-gen, *t* Prus.
Greifswalde, Grȷfs-vq́l-de, *t* Prus., 11⅓.
Grenada, Gren-á-da, *i* Brit. W. Ind., 32½; *v* Miss.
Grenadines, Gren-q-dénz, *is* W. Ind.
Grenelle, Gre-nél, *v* Fr., 8.
Grenoble, Gren-ɷ-bl', *c* Fr., 31⅓.
Gretna (Grét-na) Green, *v* on the line bet. Scot. and Eng.
Grey Town, *or* San Juan de Nicaragua, San Hɷ-q́n da Nε-kq-rq́-gwq, *s-pt t* Cen. Am.
Griffin, Gríf-in, *t* Ga., 3½.
Griggsville, Grígs-vil, *v* Ill., 1.
Grimes, Grȷmz, *co* Tex. [12½.
Grimsby, (Grímz-bi,) Great, *s-pt t* Eng.,
Grinnell (Grin-él) Land, in Arc. Oc.
Grodno, Gród-nɷ, *gov* Rus., 795½; *t* do., 16.
Groningen, Grón-iŋ-en, *t* Neth.
Grossenhain, Grɷ́s-en-hȷn, *t* Sax., 6⅓.
Grossetete, Grɷs-tát, *p o* La.
Grossetete Bayou, — Bȷ-ɷ, La.
Grosswardein, Grɷs-wér-dȷn, *c* Hun., 18¼.
Groton, Gró-ton, *vs* Mass., N-Y.
Grottaglie, Gro-tq́l-ya, *t* Nap., 5.
Grünstadt, Grẹn-stqt, *t* Rhen. Bav., 3½.
Guacara, Gwq-kq́-rq, *t* Ven., 4.
Guachinango, Gwq-çi-nq́n-gɷ, *t* Mex., 6.
Guachipe, Gwq-çé-pa, *or* Guachipas, Gwq-çé-pqs, *r* La Plata.
Guacuba, Gwq-kɷ́-bq, *r* N-Gran.
Guadalajara *or* Guadalaxara, Gwq-dq-lq-*h*q́-rq, *c* Mex., 70.
Guadalaviar, Gwq-dq-lq-vi-q́r, *r* Sp.
Guadalquivir, Ge-dal-kwív-er, *r* Sp.
Guadalupe, Gwq-dq-lɷ́-pa, *ms*, *r* and *t* Sp., 3¾.
Guadalupe, Ge-da-lɷ́p, *r* and *co* Tex.
Guadalupe Hidalgo, Gwq-dq-lɷ́-pa Hε-dq́l-gɷ, *t* Mex.
Guadalupe-y-Calvo, Gwq-dq-lɷ́-pa-i-Kq́l-vɷ, *t* Mex., 10.
Guadeloupe, Ge-de-lɷ́p *or* Gq-de-lɷ́p, *i* W. Ind.
Guadiana, Gwq-di-q́-nq, *r* Sp., Port.
Guaduas, Gwq́-dwqs, *t* N-Gran.
Guahan, Gwq-hq́n, *i* Pac. Oc.
Guaianeco, Gwȷ-q-ná-kɷ, *i gr* w. Pat.
Gualan, Gwq-lq́n, *t* Cen. Am., 2.
Gualateiri, Gwq-lq-ta-i-ré, *m p* Andes.
Gualillas, Gwq-lél-yqs, *m pass* Peruvian Andes, 14,750 ft. high. [16½.
Guanabacoa, Gwq-nq-bq-kɷ́-q, *t* Cuba,
Guanajuato *or* Guanaxuato, Gwq-nq-*h*wq́-tɷ, *st* Mex.; *c* same, 63.
Guanaparo, Gwq-nq-pq́-rɷ, *r* Ven.
Guanare, Gwq-nq́-ra, *t* Ven., 12.
Guano (Gwq́-nɷ) Islands, coast S. Am. and Af., some of which are the Seal and Chincha Islands. [Cuba.
Guantanamo, Gwqn-tq-nq́-mɷ, *har* s.
Guapai, Gwq-pȷ́, *r* Bol.
Guarambari, Gwq-rqm-bq-ré, *r* Par.
Guarapari, Gwq-rq-pq-ré, *r*, *m* and *t* Brazil.
Guarapiche, Gwq-rq-pé-ça, *r* Ven.
Guaratiba, Gwq-rq-té-bq, *s-pt v* Bra., 4.
Guarico, Gwq-ré-kɷ, *r* Ven., 200 m.
Guaruapo, Gwq-rɷ-q́-pɷ, two *rs* Ven.
Guatavita, Gwq-tq-vé-tq. *v* and *l* N-Granada.
Guatemala, Gwq-ta-mq́-lq, *st* Cen. Am. Area, 44,500 s. m.; pop. 1,000,000. — New, *cap* above state, 50. — Old, *c* 12.
Guaviare *or* Guabiare, Gwq-vi-q́-ra, *r* N-Gran., 450 m.
Guayama, Gwȷ-q́-mq, *s-pt t* Porto Ri., 5.
Guayaquil, Gwȷ-q-kél, *c* Ecuador, 20. — Gulf of, ditto.
Guaytara, Gwȷ-tq́-rq, *r* Ecuador, 75 m.
Gubbio, Gɷ́-bi-ɷ, *c* Cen. It., 17.
Guben, Gɷ́-ben, *t* Prus., 9¾.
Guelph, Gwelf, *t* C. W., 2.
Guerande, Ga-rónd, *t* Fr., 8⅔.
Guerara, Ga-rq́-rq, *t* Algeria.
Guéret, Ga-rá, *t* Fr., 5. [*co* O.
Guernsey, Gẹrn-zε, one of Channel Is.;

Guerrero, Ger-á-rɷ, *st* Mex., 270.
Güglingen, Gę́g-liŋ-en, *t* Würt., 14¼.
Guiana *or* Guyana, Gɛ-ą́-nq, *ter* S. Am.
Guicowar's, Gwik-ɷ-warz, *st* Hind.
Guijar *or* Guixar, Gɛ-*hą́r*, *l* San Salv.
Guilford, Gil-ford, *vs* Me., Vt., Conn., N-Y., &c. [30.
Guillotiere, La, Lq Gɛ-yɷ-ti-ą́r, *t* Fr.,
Guiloom, Gɛ-lɷ́m, *r* Senegambia.
Guinea, Gin-ɛ, a geographical division of Af. [Cuba, 4.
Güines, Gwé-nes, (almost Wé-nes,) *t*
Guingamp, Gɛn-gón, *t* Fr., 7¼.
Guionsville, Gį-onz-vil, *p o* Ia.
☞ For gulfs not mentioned below, see proper name.
Gulf of Guinea, At. Oc., coast N. Gui.
Gulf of Lyons, Lį-onz *or* Lɛ-ón, Med., s. Fr.
Gulf of Mexico, s. coast of the U. S.
Gulf of Panama, Pq-nq-mą́, Pac. Oc., N-Gran.
Gulf of Paria, Pą́-ri-q, Carib. Sea, Ven.
Gulf of St. Lawrence, Lé-rens, At. Oc., lying bet. C. E. and Newfoundland.
Gulf of Tehuantepec, Ta-wqn-ta-pék, Pac. Oc., Cen. Am.
Gulf Stream, a singular current in the At. Oc., having its origin in the Gulf of Mexico.
Gumoorjeena, Gum-ɷr-jé-nq, *t* Eu. Tur., 8.
Güns, Gęns, *fr t* Hun., 8.
Gurupatuba, Gɷ-rɷ-pq-tɷ́-bq, *r* Brazil.
Gurupi, Gɷ-rɷ-pé, *r* and *t* Brazil.
Gurutuba, Gɷ-rɷ-tɷ́-bq, *r* Brazil.
Gustavia, Gɷs-tą́-vi-q, *cap* island St. Bartholomew, 10.
Güstrow, Gę́s-trov, *t* N. Ger., 9.
Guyandotte, Gį-an-dót, *r* and *v* Va.
Gwalior, Gwą́-li-or, *c* Hind.
Gwinnett, Gwin-ét, *co* Ga.
Gyöngyös, Dyęn-dyęʃ, *t* Hun., 14⅝.
Gyula, Dyɷ́-lo, *t* Hun., 13¾.

# H.

Haarlem *or* Harlem, Hą́r-lem, *c* Neth., 25¾.
Habersham, Háb-er-ʃam, *co* Ga.
Haddam, Hád-am, *v* Conn., 2¼.
Haddington, Hád-iŋ-ton, *burgh* Scot., 4.
Haddonfield, Hád-on-fɛld, *v* N-J.
Hadersleben, Hą́-ders-la-ben, *s-pt t* Den., 6.
Hadleigh, Hád-li, *t* Eng., 3⅓.
Hadley, Hád-li, *vs* Mass., Mich., Ill.
Hagerstown, Há-gerz-tɤn, *t* Md., 4; *vs* Ia., O.
Hague, Hag, The, *t* Neth., 72½.
Haguenau, Hqg-nó *or* Ag-nó, *t* Fr., 11⅓.
Haina, Hį-nq, *r* and *b* Hayti.
Hainan, Hį-nąn, *i* of China, 1,000,000.
Hainaut *or* Hainault, Ha-nó, *prov* Belg.
Hainichen, Hį-ni*h*-en, *t* Sax., 5½.
Hala (Hą́-lq) Mountains, Beloochistan.
Halberstadt, Hą́l-ber-stqt, *t* Prus. Sax., 18⅓.
Halcyon, Hál-si-on, *p o* Pa.
Halesowen, Halz-ó-en, *t* Eng., 2½.
Halfmoon, Hqf-mɷn, *t* N-Y., 2¾.
Halibut, Hól-i-but, Island, N. Pac.
Halifax, Hál-i-faks, *t* Eng., 33⅙; *c* Nova Scotia, 27; *vs* U. S.
Halle, Hą́-le, *c* Prus. Sax., 29¾.
Hallettsville, Hál-ets-vil, *co t* Texas.
Hallowell, Hál-ɷ-el, *t* Me., 3.
Hall's Landing, *v* Ill.
Halstead, Hál-sted, *t* Eng., 5⅜.
Hamadan, Hq-mq-dą́n, *c* Persia, 30.
Hamah, Hą́-mq, *c* Syria, 44.
Hamburg, Hám-burg, (Ger. Hą́m-bur*h*,) *c* Ger., 161⅓; *ts* N-Y., N-J., Pa., S. C., Ill., &c.
Hameln, Hą́-meln, *t* Han., 6¼.
Hamilton., Hám-il-ton, *t* Scot., 9⅙; *cs* O., 8; C. W., 18; *vs* N-Y., N. C., Ga., &c.
Hamm, Hqm, *t* Westphalia, 7.
Hammersmith, Hám-er-smiþ, *t* Eng., 13½.
Hammond, Hám-ond, *v* N-Y.
Hammondsport, *v* N-Y., ¾. [Va.
Hampstead, Hámp-sted, *vs* Eng., Md.,
Hampton, Hámp-ton, *vs* N-H., Va., N-Y., Conn.; *t* Eng., 5.
Hampton Roads, arm of Chesapeake *b*.
Hanau, Hą́-nɤ, *t* Ger., 15¼.
Hancock, Hán-kok, num, *cos* U. S.
Hang-Chow-Foo, Hqŋ-Ɛɤ-Fɷ́, *c* China.
Hanging Rock, *v* O., 1.
Han-Kiang, Hqn-Ki-ą́ŋ, two *rs* China, 600 and 200 m.
Hannibal, Hán-i-bal, *t* Mo., 4.
Hanover, Hán-ɷ-ver, *c, k &c.*, N. Ger.; *vs* N-H., seat of Dartmouth College; O., Ill.; *t* Pa., 1½.
Hanover Court-House, *co t* Va.
Hanse (Hans) Towns, *or* Hanseatic (Han-sɛ-át-ik) League, an association of towns for mutual support, Germany.

Han-Yang *or* Han-Yang-Foo, Hqn-Yqŋ-Fœ, *c* China.
Hapai, Hq-pį, *i gr* S. Pac. Oc.
Harburg *or* Haarburg, Hqr-burh, *t* Ger., 5. [5½.
Harderwick, Hqr-der-vik, *s-pt t* Neth.,
Hardin, Hqr-din, *vs* O., Ill., Iowa.
Hardinsburg, Hqr-dinz-burg, *v* Ky., 1.
Harlem, Hqr-lem, *sub* N-Y. City, 5; *vs* O., Ill., &c.
Harlingen, Hqr-liŋ-en, *ft t* Neth., 8½.
Harmar, Hqr-mqr; *v* O., 1¾.
Harmony, Hqr-mœ-ni, *vs* N-J., Pa., &c.
Haro, Ä'rœ, *t* Sp., 6.
Harper's Ferry, Hqr-perz Fér-i, *v* and *U. S. armory*, Va.
Harpeth, Hqr-peŧ, *r* Tenn., 100 m.
Harricanaw, Har-i-kán-e, *r* Br. N. Am.
Harrisburg, Hár-is-burg, *cap* Pa., 10; *vs* Texas, O., Ia., Mo., Iowa.
Harrison, Hár-i-son, *vs* Tenn., ½; O., 1¼; Ia., Ill, &c.
Harrisonburg, *vs* Va., 1⅓; La.
Harrisonville, *vs* N-J., Pa., Ky., O., &c.
Harrisville, Hár-is-vil, *v* Pa., Va., O.
Harrodsburg, Hár-odz-burg, *co t* Ky., 3; *vs* Ia., Mo.
Harrowgate, Hár-œ-gat, watering-place of Eng., 3¾.
Hartford, Hqrt-ford, *c, semi cap* Conn., 20; *ts* Me., N-Y., Pa., Miss., Ky., &c.
Hartland, *t* Eng.; *vs* Mich., Wis.
Hartlepool, Hqr-tl-pœl, *s-pt t* Eng., 9½.
Hartsgrove, Hqrts-grœv, *v* O., ¾.
Hartsville, *vs* N-Y., Mass., Pa., Ia., &c.
Hartwick, Hqrt-wik, *v* N-Y., ½.
Harvard University, Cambridge, Mass.
Harveysburg, Hqr-viz-burg, *v* O.
Harwich, Hár-ij, *s-pt t* Eng., 4½.
Harwich, Hqr-wiq, *t* Mass.
Harwington, Hqr-wiŋ-ton, *v* Conn.
Haslingden, Hás-liŋ-den, *t* Eng., 9.
Hasselt, Hás-elt, *t* Belg., 8¾.
Hassloch, Hás-loh, *v* Rhen. Bav., 4¾.
Hastings, Hás-tiŋz, *t* Eng.; *vs* N-Y., Mich.; *r* Australia.
Hatborough, Hát-bur-œ, *v* Pa.
Hatchie *or* Hatchy, Háq-i, *r* Tenn., nav. 150 m.
Hatfield, *t* Eng., 6¼; *vs* Mass., Pa.
Haukivesi, Hɤ-ki-vá-sɛ, *l* Finland.
Havana, Ha-ván-q, *cap* Cuba, 134¼; *vs* N-Y., Ill., &c.
Havel, Hq-vel, *r* Ger., 180 m.
Haverford, Háv-er-ford, *t* Pa. —West, *r-pt* S. Wales.
Haverhill, Háv-er-il, *t* Eng. [O.
Haverhill, Há-ver-il, *vs* Mass. 4, N-H.,
Haverstraw, Háv-er-stre, *v* N-Y.
Havré, Hq-vrá, *v* Belg., 2.
Havre, Le, Lę Hqv-r, *s-pt c* Fr., 30.
Havre de Grace, Háv-er dę Grqs, *v* Md., 1¾.
Hawaii, Hq-wį-ɛ, (*or* Owhyhee,) largest of Sandwich Islands, 24¼.
Hawash, Hq-wqʃ, *r* Abys., 460 m.
Hawes, Hez, *t* Eng., 1¾.
Hawesville, Héz-vil, *v* Ky.
Hawick, Hé-wik, *t* Scot., 6¾.
Hawkeshead, Héks-hed, *t* Eng.
Hawley, Hé-li, *v* Pa., 3.
Haw River, N. C.
Hayes (Haz) River, Brit. N. Am.
Hayneville, Hán-vil, *v* Ala., ¾.
Haysville,Ház-vil, *vs* Pa., O., Ia.
Hayti *or* Haiti, Há-tɛ, *i* second in size W. Ind., 943.
Hazebrouck, Hqz-brœk, *t* Fr., 8.
Heathsville, Héŧs-vil, *co t* Va. [115.
Hebrides, Héb-ri-dɛz, 160 *is* w. Scot.,
Hebron, Hé-bron, *t* Palestine, 10; *vs* Conn., N-Y., O., Ill.
Hechingen, Héh-iŋ-en, *t* Ger., 3⅓.
Hecla, (Hék-lq,) Mount, *vol* Iceland.
Hee-Ho *or* Hi-Ho, Hɛ-Hœ, *r* Corea.
Heidelberg, Hį-del-bęrh, *c* W. Ger., 12.
Heilbronn, Hįl-brón, *t* Würt., 8½.
Heiligenstadt, Hį-li-gen-stqt, *t* Prus., 4¾. [Wis.
Helena, Hel-é-nq, *vs* N-Y., Ark., Ky.,
Helgoland, Hél-gœ-lqnd, *i* of Great Britain, North Sea, 2¼.
Helicon, (Hél-i-kon,) Mount, *m* Greece.
Hell Gate *or* Hurl Gate, rocky *pass* East River, near New-York.
Helmsley, Hélmz-li, *t* Eng., 3½.
Helmstädt, Hélm-stet, *t* Ger., 5¼.
Helmund, Hel-múnd, *r* Afg., 650 m.
Helsingfors, Hél-siŋ-fers, *s-pt t* Rus., *cap* Finland, 16.
Helstone, Hél-stœn, *bor* and *t* Eng.
Helvetia, Hel-vé-ʃi-q, anc. name of Switzerland; *v* Ill.
Helvoetsluis, Hel-vœt-slés, *ft s-pt t* Neth., 2¾.
Hemel-Hempstead, Hém-el-Hémp-sted, *t* and *par* Eng., 7¼.
Hempstead, *v* N-Y., 1½.
Henderson, Hén-der-son, *vs* Ky. 1¾, N-Y., N. C., Ill., Tex., Min.
Heng-Choo-Foo, Heŋ-Cœ-Fœ, *c* China.
Heng-Kiang, Heŋ-Ki-qŋ, *r* China.
Henley-on-Thames, Hén-li-on-Témz, *t* Eng., 3¾.
Hennepin, Hén-ɛ-pin, *co t* Ill.
Henrico, Hen-rį-kœ, *co* Va.
Henrietta, Hen-ri-ét-q, *v* N-Y.
Henry, Hén-ri, *v* Ill., 1½.
Henryville, Hén-ri-vil, *vs* C. E. 1¼, Ia.
Herat, Her-qt, *ft c* W. Afg., 40.

Hereford, Hér-ɛ-ford, *co* and *c* Eng., 12.
Herford, Hér-fort, *t* Wesphalia, 5½.
Herkimer, Hér-ki-mer, *v* N-Y., 1¼.
Hermann, Hér-man, *v* Mo., 1.
Hermannstadt, Hér-mqn-stqt, *t* Aus., 21½.
Hermitage, Hér-mit-aj, *vs* N-Y., Ga., Ill.
Hermon, Hér-mon, *v* N-Y.
Hertford, Hqr-ford, *bor* and *t* Eng., 6½.
Hertford, Hért-ford, *co* and *v* N. C.
Hesse-Cassel, Hes-Kás-el, Ger. *principality*, pop. 759,751.
Hesse - Darmstadt, Hes - Dqrm - stqt, Grand Duchy, ind. Ger. *st*, pop. 854,319.
Hesse-Homburg, Hes-Hóm-burg, *div* W. Ger., pop. 24,921.
Heuvelton, Hq-vel-ton, *v* N-Y.
Hexham, Héks-ham, *t* Eng., 4⅜.
Hiang-Ho-Vou, Hi-qŋ-Hω-Vó, *c* China.
Hibernia, Hi-bér-ni-a, a name of Ireland; *v* Mo.
Hickman, Hík-man, *co t* Ky., 2.
Hickory, Hík-ω-ri, *vs* Pa., O., Ill.
Hicksford, Híks-ford, *co t* Va.
Hierapolis, Hi-er-áp-ω-lis, anc. ruined *c* As. Tur.
Higginsport, Híg-inz-pωrt, *v* O., ⅔.
Highland, Hi-land, *vs* Pa., O., Ia., &c.
Highlands, Hi-landz, *div* N. and N. W. Scotland.
Hightstown, Hits-tɤn, *v* N-J.
Highworth, Hi-wurθ, *bor* and *t* Eng., 4.
Hildesheim, Hil-des-him, *t* Han., 14¾.
Hillah *or* Hilla, Hil-a, *t* As. Tur., 10.
Hillsborough, Hilz-bur-ω, *ts* Ir. 3½, N-H., Va., N. C., O., Ia., Ill., Mo.
Hillsdale, Hilz-dal, *vs* N-Y., Mich.
Himalaya, Him-a-li-a, *or* Himmaleh, Him-q-la, Mountains, Hind.
Hinckley, Híŋk-li, *t* Eng., 6¼; *v* O.
Hindoo-Koosh, Hin-dω-Kωʃ, *or* Ghoor Mountains, Cen. Asia.
Hindostan, Hin-dω-stán, extensive region, S. Asia; pop. 150,000,000.
Hinds, Hindz, *co* Miss.
Hinesburg, Hinz-burg, *v* Vt.
Hingham, Híŋ-ham, *v* Mass., 4.
Hinsdale, Hínz-dal, *vs* N-H., Mass., N-Y.
Hiram, Hi-ram, *vs* Me., O.
Hirschberg, Hérʃ-berh, *ft t* Prus. Silesia, 7⅓.
Hivaoa, Ɛ-vq-ó-q, *i* S. Pac. Oc., 6½.
Hjelmar *or* Hielmar, Hyél-mar, *l* Swed.
Hoai-Ho, Hω-i-Hó, *r* China, 400 m.
Hoai-Khing, Hω-i-*Hí*ŋ, *c* China.
Hoang-Ho, Hω-aŋ-Hó, *r* Chinese Em.
Hobart, Hó-bart, *vs* N-Y., Ia. [25.
Hobart Town, *cap* Van Diemen's Land,
Hoboken, Hó-bω-ken, *c* N-J., 6; *t* Cal.

Hochstadt, Hóh-stqt, *t* Bav., 2½.
Hocking, Hók-iŋ, *r* and *co* O.
Hodgdon, Hój-don, *v* Me.
Hoei-Ho, Hω-á-Hó, *r* China, 400 m.
Hoei-Ngan, Hω-a-ngqn, *c* Chinese Em.
Hoei-Tong, Hω-a-Tóŋ, *c* China, 44.
Hoeksche-Waard, De, De Húk-she-Vqrd, *i* of Hol., 22.
Hof, Hof, *t* Bav., 8.
Hogansburg, Hó-ganz-burg, *v* N-Y.
Hohenzollern-Hechingen, Hω-en-tsól-ern-Héh-iŋ-en, *prin.* Ger., 20¼.
Hohenzollern-Sigmaringen, —Síg-mq-riŋ-en, *prin.* Ger., 45½.
Holbeach, Hól-bɛq, *t* and *par* Eng., 2¼.
Holland, Hól-and, (North *and* South,) *k* Neth., composed of peninsulas and islands; pop. 1,106,248: *vs* N-Y., Mich.
Holley, Hól-i, *v* N-Y., 1¼. [2½.
Hollidaysburg, Hól-i-daz-burg, *t* Pa.,
Holliston, Hól-is-ton, *v* Mass., 2½.
Holly (Hól-i) Springs, *v* Miss., 4.
Hollywood, *v* Ir., 1½.
Holmes' (Hómz-ez) Hole, *v* Mass.
Holmesville, Hómz-vil, *vs* O., Ia., Miss.
Holstein, (Hól-stin,) Duchy of, belonging to Den.; pop. in 1850, 482,364.
Holston, Hól-ston, *r* Tenn., 200 m.
Holt, Hωlt, *t* Eng.; *co* Mo.
Holyhead, Hól-i-hed, *i* and *s-pt t* of N. Wales, 5¾.
Holyoke, Hól-yωk, *v* Mass., 3¼.
Holywell, Hól-i-wel, *t* N. Wales, 5¾.
Homburg, Hóm-burh, *ft t* Rhen. Bav. 3.
Home City, *v* O.
Homer, Hó-mer, *vs* N-Y. 1½, La., O.
Homs, Hωms, *or* Hums, *t* Syria, 30.
Honda, Hón-da, (Sp. Ɯn'dq,) *t* New Granada, 5.
Honduras, Hon-dó-rqs, *st* and *b* Cen. A.
Honeoye, Hω-nɛ-ó, *v* N-Y.; — Falls, *v* N-Y., 1½.
Honesdale, Hónz-dal, *co t* Pa., 5.
Hong-Kiang, Hoŋ-Kɛ-qŋ, nav. *r* China, 800 m.
Hong-Kong, Br. *i* s. e. China, 37.
Honiton, Hún-i-ton, *t* Eng., 3½.
Honolulu, Hon-ω-ló-lω, *t* and *s-pt* Sandwich Islands, 6.
Hoobly, Hó-bli, *t* Br. Ind., 15.
Hoogly *or* Hooghly, Hóg-lɛ, *t* and *r* Br. Ind.
Hoorn, Hωrn, *ft t* N. Hol., 8¾.
Hoosick (Hó-sik) Falls *and* Tunnel, near Troy, N-Y.
Hopedale, Hóp-dal, *v* Mass.; *v* O., and seat of McNeely Normal School.
Hopkinsville, Hóp-kinz-vil, *co t* Ky., 3½; *v* O.
Horicon, Hór-i-kon, *vs* N-Y., Wis.

Horncastle, Hérn-kas-l, *t* and *par* Eng. 5.
Hornellsville, Hér-nelz-vil, *v* N-Y., 1¼.
Horsham, Hérs-am, *bor* and *t* Eng., 6; *v* Pa.
Horton, Hér-ton, *s-pt* Nova Scotia.
Hot Springs, *vs* Va., Ark.
Hottentots, Hót-en-tots, an Af. *race*, Cape of Good Hope.
Houghton, Hó-ton, *co* and *p o* Mich.
Houghton-le-Spring, *t* and *par* Eng., [3¼.
Houlton, Hól-ton, *v* Me.
Houma, Hó-mq, *v* La.
Hounslow, Hȣnz-lꝏ, *t* Eng., 3½.
Housatonic, Hꝏ-sa-tón-ik, River, Mass., 150 m.
Houston, Hꝏs-ton, *co ts* Miss., Texas 6; *t* Kansas Ter.
Howden, Hȣ-den, *t* and *par* Eng., 2⅓.
Howell, Hȣ-el, *co t* Mich., ¾.
Hoy, Hơ, *i* and *par* Eng., 1½.
Huaheine, Hꝏ-q-hé-na, Society Is., 2.
Huallaga, Wql-yq́-gq *or* Hwql-yq́-gq, *r* Peru, 500.
Huamanga, Wq-mq́ŋ-gq, *or* Guamanga, Gwq-mq́ŋ-gq, *c* Peru, 20.
Huamantla, Wq́-mq́nt-lq, *t* and battle field, Mex.
Huancavelica, Wqn-kq-va-lé-kq, *t* Peru, 8.
Huaraz, Wq-rq́s, *t* Peru, 5.
Huaura, Wȣ-rq, *s-pt t* Peru.
Huddersfield, Húd-erz-feld, *bor* and *t* Eng., 25.
Hudson, Húd-son, *or* North River, N-Y., the finest in the U. S., 300 m.; nav. for the largest ships to Hudson, 117 m.; *c* N-Y., 7; *vs* O. 1⅓, Mich.; *co t* Wis.
Hudson's Bay, inland sea of Br. Am., 850 by 600 m.
Hudson's Bay Territory, the whole of Br. N. Am., excepting the Canadas, N-Brunswick, Nova Scotia and Newfoundland, over which Hudson's Bay Company have a charter for its use as hunting ground for furs.
Hué, Hwa *or* Hꝏ-á, *r* Anam.
Hué, *or* Thua-Thien, T-hwq-Ti-én, *cap* empire of Anam.
Huesca, Wés-kq *or* Hwés-kq, *c* Sp., 9.
Hughesville, Hq́z-vil, *vs* N-J., Pa., Va.
Hull, Hul, *r-pt* and *bor* Eng., 83.
Hulmesville, Hómz-vil, *v* Pa.
Humber, Húm-ber, *r* Newfoundland, 150 m.; *est.* Eng.
Humboldt, Húm-bolt, *v* Wis.; *b* and *r* Cal., 350 m.
Humphreys, Um'friz, *co* Tenn.
Humphreysville, *vs* Conn., O.
Hungary, Húŋ-ga-ri, *cy* S. E. Europe, forming a part of the Austrian Empire; ar. 69,170 s. m., pop. 11,000,000.
Hungerford, Húŋ-ger-ford, *t* and *par* Eng., 2¾.
Hunslet, Hún-slet, *chapelry* Eng., 20.
Huntersville, Hún-terz-vil, *co t* Va.
Huntingdon, Húnt-iŋ-don, *bor* and *t* Eng., 6¼; *co ts* Pa. 1¾, Tenn.
Huntington, Húnt-iŋ-ton, *vs* N-Y., Vt., S. C.; *co t* Ia.
Huntly, Húnt-li, *t* and *par* Scot.
Huntsville, Húnts-vil, *co ts* Ala. 4, Mo., Tex. 1¼; *vs* O., Ia., Ill.
Hurdwar, Hurd-wér, *t* famous for its annual fairs, N. Hind.
Huron, (Hq́-ron,) Lake, third in size of N. Am.; *vs* N-Y., O.
Hurst Monceaux, (Mon-só,) *par* Eng.
Husum, Hó-sum, *s-pt t* Den., 4.
Huy, Hơ, *t* Belg., 8¼.
Huyton, Hị-ton, *par* Eng.
Hyannis, Hị-án-is, *v* and *s-pt* Mass.
Hydepark, Hịd-pqrk, *co t* Vt.; *vs* N-Y., Pa. 1⅓.
Hyderabad, Hị-der-a-bq́d, *c* India, 200; *t* and *ft* Hind., 20.
Hydra, Hé-drq, *or* Idra, Ɛ'drq, *i* of Greece, 20.
Hyères *or* Hières, Hɛ-ą́r, *t* Fr., 10.
Hythe, Hịd, *bor* and *t* Eng., 2¼.

# I.

☞ In order to agree with Lippincott's Gazetteer, "names in Eastern Europe and Asia, beginning with I, followed immediately by a vowel, will generally be found under Y; thus, for Iakoutsk, see Yakootsk; Iana, see Yana, &c.

Ibague, Ɛ-bq́-ga, *t* N-Gran., 5.
Ibarra, Ɛ-bq́r-q, *t* Ecuador, 11.
Iberia, Ɨ-bé-ri-a, *vs* O., Mo.
Iberville, Ɨ'ber-vil, *par* and *co t* La.
Ibicui, Ɛ-bi-kwé, *r* S. Am., 400 m.
Iceland, Ɨs'land, *i* of Den., bet. N. At. and Arc. Oceans, 60.
Ico *or* Icco, Ɛ'kꝏ, *t* Brazil, 7.
Icod, Ɛ-kód, *t* island of Teneriffe, 5½.
Ida, Ɨ'da, *co* Iowa; *p o* Mich.
Idjeng, Id-jéŋ, active *vol* is. of Java.

Idle, Ī'dl, *r* Eng.
Idria, Id'ri-a *or* Ē'dri-q, *t* Illyria, 4½.
Idumæa, Id-yq-mé-a, anc. *cy* W. Asia.
Iesi, Ē-á-se, *t* It., 9.
Igatimi, Ē-gq-ti-mé, *r* S. Am., 200 m.
Iglau, Ig'lȣ, *t* Moravia, 16½.
Iglesias, Ē-glá-si-qs, *t* Sardinia, 12½.
Iglo, Ig'lo, *t* N. Hun., 6.
Iguaçu, Ē-gwq-sū, *t* and *r* Brazil.
Igualada, Ē-gwq-lq-dq, *t* Sp., 10.
Igualapa, Ē-gwq-lq-pq, *t* Mex., 3.
Iguape, Ē-gwq-pa, *r* Brazil, 150 m.
Ikropa, Ē-kró-pq, *r* Madagascar, 270 m.
Ilfracombe, Il'fra-kom, *s-pt t* Eng., 3.
Ilha Grande, Ēl'yq Grqn-da, *i* of Brazil, 2.
Iliniça, Ē-li-né-sq, *m p* Andes, Ec., 17,380 ft.
Ilkeston, Il'kes-ton, *t* and *par* Eng., 6¼.
Ill, Ēl, *r* Fr., 100 m.
Iller, Il'er, *r* S. Ger., 85 m.
Illimani, Ēl-yq-mq-ni, *m* Bol. Andes, 21,149 ft.
Illinois, Il-i-nó, one of the w. U. S.; area 55,409 s. m., pop. 857,470; *r* Ill.
Illinois College, Jacksonville, Ill.
Illyria, Il-ír-i-a, *ter* forming the s. w. part of Austria; area 10,996 s. m., pop. 1,284,947, of whom ¾ are slaves.
Ilminster, Il'min-ster, *t* and *par* Eng., 3⅓.
Iloilo, Ē-ló-lo, *prov* of Panay, 259¾.
Imbros, Im'bros, *or* Imbro, Im'bro, *i* Gr. Arch., 4.
Imola, Ē'mo-lq, *t* Cen. It., 9¾.
Inagua, Ē-nq-gwq, one of Bahama Is.
Independence, *c* Mo., 3; *co ts* Ky., Io.; *vs* Tex., O., Ia., &c.
India, In'di-a, region of *cy* S. Asia; divided into India beyond the Ganges, and Brit. Ind.; area of the latter 1,427,547 s. m.; pop. 170,813,668. "The gov. is vested in the East Ind. Company as trustees for the crown, consisting of the Governer-General, and a council of five members."
Indiana, In-di-án-a, one of the w. U. S.; area, 33,809 s. m., pop. 988,342.
Indiana, *co t* Pa., 1; *v* C. W.
Indianapolis, In-di-an-áp-o-lis, *c cap* of Ia., 18; *v* Iowa. [coast.
Indian Ocean, a vast sea off the Af.
Indianola, In-di-an-ó-la, *vs* Tex., Iowa, Kansas.
Indian River, Fa., 100 m.
Indian Territory, w. Ark., set apart by gov. of U. S. for the exclusive occupation of the Indian tribes of the West. [750 m.
Indighirka, In-di-gír-kq, *r* E. Siberia,
Indragiri, In-drq-gér-e, nav. *r* Sumatra.
Indre, Ańd'r, *r* Fr.
Indus, In'dus, *r* S. As., 1650 m.
Industry, In'dus-tri, *vs* Pa., O., Ill. C. E. [9¼.
Ingolstadt, Iŋ'ol-stqt, *ft t* Upper Bav.,
Ingoolets, In-goo-léts, *r* Rus., 220 m.
Inkerman, Iŋk-er-mqn, *v s-pt* of S. Rus. in the Crimea.
Inn, *r* Swit. and Bav., 250 m.
Innspruck, Ins'pruk, *cap* Tyrol, 12¾.
Insterburg, Ins'ter-burh, *t* E. Prussia, 9¾.
Inverness, In-ver-nés, *s-pt t* Scot., 12¾; *v* Mich. [Ter.
Inyan Reakah, In'yqn Re-q-kq, *r* Min.
Inyan Yankey (Yáŋ-ki) River, Iowa.
Iona, Ē-ó-na, *i* Hebrides, Scot., 1.
Ionia, Ī-ó-ni-a, *vs* Mich., Ill., Mo.
Ionian (Ī-ó-ni-an) Islands, Med., w. of Gr.; bel. to Gr. Br.; pop. 219¾; *sea*, part of Med.
Iowa, Ī'o-wa, one of U. S.; area 50,914 s. m., pop. 330; *r* Iowa, 300 m.
Iowa City, *cap* Iowa, 4.
Ipswich, Ips'wiç, *bor* and *t* of Eng., 33; *t* Mass., 3⅓.
Iquique, Ē-ké-ka, *s-pt t* S. Peru.
Iraja, Ē-rq-ʒq, *v* Brazil, 5.
Irasburg, Ī'ras-burg, *v* Vt.
Irasu, Ē-rq-sū, *vol* Costa-Rica, 11,478 ft.
Iren, Ē-rén, *or* Ē-rán, *r* Rus., 150 m.
Iredell, Īr'del, *co* N. C.
Ireland, Īr'land, western *is* of the Kingdom of Gr. Brit.; area 32,513, pop. 6,553,163.
Irish Sea, Ī'riʃ, portion At. Oc., bet. Ir. and Eng.
Irkootsk, Ir-kótsk, *c* Siberia, 120.
Iroquois, Ir-o-kwó, *r* Ia., Ill.; *v* Ill.
Iroquois, *or* Six Nations, Fr. name of the united Mohawk, Oneida, Onondaga, Cayuga, Seneca, and Tuscaroras Indians. [1200 m.
Irrawaddy, Ir-a-wód-i, *r* S. E. Asia,
Irtish, Ir'tiʃ, *r* N. As., 1700 m.
Irvine, Er'vin, *s-pt t* Scot., 4¾; *vs* Pa., Ky.
Isar, Ē'zar, *or* Iser, Ē'zer, *r* Ger., 165 m.
Ischia, Is'ki-q, *i* in Med., 24.
Iseghem, Ē'se-hem, *t* Belg., 8¾.
Iserlohn, Ē-zer-lón, *t* Prus., 10¾.
Isernia, Ē-sér-ni-q, *t* Nap., 5¼.
Iset, Ē-sét, *r* Siberia, 250 m.
Ishim, *or* Ischim, Iʃ'im, *r* Sib., 700 m.
Isla de Leon, Ēs'lq da La-ón, *c* Sp., 9¾.
Isla de Negros, Ēs'lq da Ná-gros, *is* in the Malay Arch., 35¾. [12.
Islamabad, Is-lqm-a-bqd, *t* Brit. Ind.,

Island Pond, *v* Vt.
Islay, Ī'la, *is* Hebrides in Scot., 16.
Isle, Ēl, *r* Fr., 100 m.
Isle Au Bois, Ēl ō Bwq, *p o* Mo.
Isle Au Haut, Ēl ō Hō, an entrance of Penobscot Bay.
Isle-aux-Coudres, Ēl-ō-Kōd-r, *i* C. E.
Isle-Dieu, Ēl-Dε-é, *ft i* Fr., 2¾.
Isle of Pines, *i* Pac. Oc., 2½; *i* W. Ind. Arch., 1½. [50⅓.
Isle of Wight, Īl ov Wīt, *i* Eng. Chan.,
Isle Royale, Īl Rō'-al, *i* Lake Superior.
Islington, Is'liŋ-ton, *par* Eng., 95⅓.
Islip, Is'lip, *v* N-Y.
Ismail, Is-mq-ēl, *ft t* Rus., 21¾.
Isola, Ē'sō-lq, *t* Illyria, 3½.
Isola Grossa, Ē'sō-lq Grós-q, *i* Adriatic Sea, 12.
Ispahan, Is-pa-hqn, *or* Spahawn, Spq-hón, *c* Persia, 150.
Issaquena, Is-a-kwé-na, *co* Miss.
Issoire, Ēs-wqr, *t* Fr., 5¾.
Issoudun, Ē-sō-dúṅ, *t* Fr., 13⅓.
Istip, Is'tip, *t* Eu. Tur., 8.
Italy, It'a-li, (It. I-tq-li-q,) *cy* in S. Eu. consisting of divisions, kingdoms, dutchies, &c., formed of the peninsula, and adjacent islands; area 118,356 s. m., pop. 24,733,385.
Itamaraca, Ē-tq-mq-rq-kq, *i* Bra., 8.
Itapicuru-Grande, Ē-tq-pi-kō-rō-Grqn-da, *r* Brazil, 410 m.
Itasca Lake, It-ás-ka, the head of the Mississippi. [Chili.
Itata, Ē-tq-tq, *or* Chillan, Ēεl-yqn, *r*
Itawamba, It-a-wóm-ba, *co* Miss.
Ithaca, Ith'a-ka, Ionian Is., 9¾; *co t* N-Y., 7; *v* O. [Oc.
Itooroop, Ē-tō-rōp, Koorile Is., N. Pac.
Itu, Hitu, *or* Ytu, Ē-tō, *t* Bra., 10.
Itzehoe, It'se-hō-e, *t* Den., 6. [Bra.
Ivahi, Ē-vq-hé, *or* Ubahi, Ō-bq-hé, *r*
Iviça, Iviza, Ē-vé-sq, *i* Sp., 11.
Ivinghoe, Iv'iŋ-hō, *t* Eng., 2.
Ivrea, Ē-vrá-q, *t* Pied., 7. [8½.
Ivry-sur-Seine, Ē-vré-sẹr-San, *v* Fr.,
Izard, Iz'ard, *co* Ark. [15,705 ft.
Iztaccihuatl, Ēs-tqk-si-hwq-tl', *vol* Mex.,

# J.

☞ To agree with Lippincott, "Names beginning with J, in Eastern Europe and Asia, will generally be found under Y, thus: for Jablonoi, see Yablonoi; Jassy, see Yassy, &c."
Jabary, Xabary, *Hq*-bq-ré, *or* Yavary, Yq-vq-ré, *r* S. Am., 450 m.
Jaca, *or* Xaca, *Hq*-kq, *t* Sp., 3.
Jacarehi, Zq-kq-ra-hé, *t* Bra., 7.
Jacinto, Ja-sin-tō, *v* Miss.
Jackson, Ják-son, *vs* La., Tenn., Ky., O., Mich., Mo., &c.
Jacksonville, *co t* Ill., also of Va., Ga., Fa., Ala.
Jacuhy, Zq-kō-é, *r* Bra., 250 m.
Jaen, *or* Xaen, *Hq*-én, *c* Sp., 17⅓.
Jaen de Bracamoros, *Hq*-én da Brq-kq-mó-rōs, *t* Ec., 2.
Jaffa, Jáf-a, *or* Yqf-q, *t* Pal., 5.
Jaffnapatam, Jqf-nq-pq-tqm, *s-pt t* Ceylon, 8. [120 m.
Jagua, *or* Xagua, *Hq*-gwq, *r* Hon.,
Jaguaribe, Zq-gwq-ré-ba, *r* Bra., 460 m.
Jalapa, *or* Xalapa, *Hq*-lq-pq, *c* Mex., 10; Ja-lq-pa, *vs* Tenn., Ia., Ill.
Jallore, Jq-lór, *t* Hind., 15. [m.
Jalomnitza, Yq-lom-nít-sq, *r* Wal., 140
Jaloun, Jq-lón, *t* Hind., 180.
Jamaica, Ja-má-ka, largest of the Brit. W. Ind. Is., Caribbean Sea; pop. 377,433; *v* in N-Y., 4⅓.
Jamaica Plain, *v* Mass.
Jamesburg, *v* N-J.
James River, Va., 450 m.
James's (Jámz-ez) Bay, *g* Brit. Am.
James Town, *cap* of *is* St. Helena; *co ts* Tenn., Ky.; *v* N-Y., 2¼; Va., O., Ia.
Janesville, Jánz-vil, *c* Wis., 6.
Japan, Jq-pán, (called Niphon, Nip-hón, by the Japanese,) an empire in the N. Pac., composed of three large and several small islands area 116,-405 s. m.; pop. 35,000,000.
Japura, *Hq*-pō-rq, *r* S. Am., 1000 m.
Jarrow, Jár-ō, *par* and *v* Eng., 42½.
Jasper, Jás-per, *co ts* Ala., Tex., Ark., Tenn., Ia. 8¾.
Jasz-Apathi, Yqs-O-pó-tε, *t* Cen. Hun.,
Jasz-Bereny, Yqs-Ba-rány, *t* Hun., 17.
Jauer, Yŏ-er, *t* Prus. Silesia, 6½.
Jauja, *Hŏ-hq*, *or* Atanjauja, Ā-tqn-*hŏ-hq*, *r* 400 m.
Jauru, Zŏ-rō, *r* Brazil, 220 m.
Java, Jq-vq, an *i* Malay Arch.; area 49,730 s. m., pop. 9,600,000; Já-va, *v* N-Y.
Javana, Jq-vq-nq, *t* Java, 10.
Jawahir, Jq-wq-hεr, peaks of Himalaya Mountains, 25,670 ft.
Jaxartes, Jaks-qr-tεz, *r* Ind. Toorkistan, 900 m.

Jedburgh, Jéd-bur-u, *t* Scot., 2¾.
Jefferson, Jéf-er-son, *v* N-Y., 1½; *co.ts* N. C., Ga., Ala., Tex., O., Wis., 1¼; *v* Ia.
Jefferson City, *cap* Mo., 3.
Jeffersonville, *t* Ia., location state penitentiary, pop. 3; *co t* Va.
Jehoshaphat, Jɛ-hóʃ-a-fat, Valley of, [Pal.
Jemmapes, Ƶa-mɑ́p, *v* Belg., 4¾.
Jena, Jén-a, *or* Yá-nq, *t* Cen. Ger., 6¼.
Jenne, Jén-e, *t* W. Af., 9.
Jequitinhonha, Ƶa-kɛ-tɛn-yɑ́n-yq, *r* [Bra.
Jerez de La Frontera, *Ha*-réð da lq Fron-tá-rq, *t* Sp.
Jerez-de-Los-Caballeros, Ha-réð-da-Lɷs-Kq-bq-lá-rɷs, *c* Sp., 6¼.
Jericho, Jér-i-kɷ, anc. *c* Pal.; *vs* Vt., [N-Y., Ala.
Jerome, Jɛ-rɷ́m, *v* Ia.
Jersey, Jẹr-zi, the largest of the Is. of Gr. Brit. in the Eng. Chan.; area 39,000 acres, pop. 57¼.
Jersey City, N-J., 22.
Jersey Shore, *v* Pa., ¾.
Jerseyville, Jẹr-zi-vil, *co t* Ill., ¾.
Jerusalem, Jɛ-rɷ́-sa-lem, a revered *c* Pal., 10; *vs* N-Y., Va.
Jessulmeer, Jes-ul-mér, *t* Hind., 20.
Jeypoor, *or* Jypoor, Jị-pɷ́r, *st* and *c* Hind., 60.
Jhylum, *or* Jilum, Jị-lum, *r* Punjab.
Jiddah, *or* Djiddah, Jíd-q, *s-pt t* Ar., 22.
Johnson, Jón-son, *vs* Vt., Ga., Ill.
Johnson, Jón-ston, *v* Scot., 5¾.
Johnstown, *co t* N-Y., 1⅔; *v* Pa., 2.
Joigny, Ƶwqn-yé, *t* Fr., 6½.
Joliet, Jól-i-et, *co t* Ill., 4.
Jonesborough, Jɷ́nz-bur-ɷ, *co ts* Tenn., Ill.; *vs* Ga., Ala., Ia., Mo.
Jonesville, *co t* Va.; *v* Mich., 1.
Joodpoor, Jɷd-pɷ́r, *st* and *t* Hind., 60.
Jordan, Jór-dan, *r* As. Tur., 120 m.; *v* N-Y.
Jorullo, Xurullo, *H*ɷ-rɷ́l-yɷ, *vol* Mex.
Josephine, Jɷ-ze-fén, *v* Ill.
Jouna, Jɷ́-nq, *r* Rus. Am., 300 m.
Juan Fernandez, Jɥ́-an Fer-nán-dez, *i* Pac. Oc., 18 by 6 m.
Judea, Jɥ-dé-a, anc. *k* of Pal.
Juggernaut, Juggernauth, Jug-er-nét, *t* and *temple* of Ind.; pop *t* 30.
Jujuy, *H*ɷ-*h*wé, *r* La Plata, 300 m.
Jumna, Júm-nq, *r* Ind., 680 m.
Juneau, Jɥ-nɷ́, *v* Wis.
Jungfrau, Yúŋ-frɤ, *m* Swiss Alps., 13- [671 ft.
Juniata, Jɥ-ni-ɑ́-ta, *r* and *co* Pa.
Jura, Jɥ́-ra, *i* Inner Hebrides Scot., *ms* separating Fr. from Swit.
Jutland, Jút-land, *pen* and *prov* Den.

# K.

Kaffa, Caffa, Kɑ́f-q, *t* Rus., 7¼.
Kaffraria, Caffraria, Kq-frɑ́-ri-q, region of S. E. Af.; pop., 345,000.
Kafiristan, Kq-fɛ-ris-tɑ́n, *cy* Cen. As.
Kairwan, *or* Cairwan, Kị́r-wɑ́n, *c* N. Af., 50. [8000 h.
Kaisareeyeh, Kị-zar-é-e, *c* As. Min.,
Kalafat, Kq-lq-fɑ́t, *t* Eu. Tur. 2000 h.
Kalamazoo, Kal-a-ma-zɷ́, *r* and *co t* Mich., 5.
Kalantan *or* Calantan, Kq-lqn-tɑ́n, *st* Malay Pen., 50.
Kalida, Ka-lị-da, *co t* O.
Kalimno, Kq-lím-nɷ, *or* Calamo, Kɑ́-lɑ́-mɷ, *is* s. w. coast As. Min.
Kalisz *or* Kalisch, Kɑ́-liʃ, *c* Pol., 12.
Kallo, Nagy, Noj Kq-lɷ́, *t* Hun., 5⅓.
Kallsiöen, Kɑ́l-si-ẹ-en, *l* Swed.
Kalmar, Kɑ́l-mar, two *cs* of Swed.
Kalocsa, Ko-lóç-o, *t* Hun., 6. [½.
Kalooga, Kq-lɷ́-gq, *gov* and *t* Rus., 29-
Kalwarya, Kql-vɑ́-ri-q, *t* Pol., 1.
Kama, Kɑ́-mq, *r* Rus., 1400 m. [15.
Kamieniec, Kqm-yén-yets, *t* Rus. Pol.,
Kampen, Kɑ́m-pen, *t* Neth., 10¾.
Kamtchatka *or* Kamtschatka, Kqm-çɑ́t-ka, *pen* forming a part of the Siberian Gov., n. e. of Asia, 6.
Kanawha, Ka-nó-wa, *co* and *r* Va.
Kanayawa, Kq-nị-ɑ́-wq, *c* Japan, 200.
Kan-choo *or* Kan-Tchou, Kqn-çɷ́, *ft c* China. [jee Is., 10.
Kandaboo, Kqn-dɑ-bɷ́, one of the Fee-
Kandy *or* Candy, Kɑ́n-dɛ, *t* Ceylon, 7.
Kane, Kan, *v* and *co* Ill.
Kangaroo, Kaŋ-ga-rɷ́, *is* S. Aust. [¾.
Kanisa, Nagy, Noj Kó-nɛ-ʃo, *t* Hun., 8-
Kankakee, Kan-ké-kɛ, *r* Ia. and Ill.; *v* Ill.; — City, *co t* Ill.
Kankaree, Kɑ́n-kq-rɛ, *t* As. Tur., 18.
Kan-Kiang, Kqn-Ki-ɑ́ŋ, *r* Chi., 350 m.
Kanona, Ka-nɷ́-na, *v* N-Y.
Kanum, Kq-nɷ́m, *c* Little Thibet.
Kanzas, *or* Kansas, west. Ter. U. S., the "bone of contention" between the free and slave states, commencing with the repeal of the "Missouri Compromise," in 1854; area 114,798 s. m.; *r* of the ter., 120 m; *v* Mo., ¾; *tr* Indians.

Kara, Kq́-rq, *r* Rus., 125 m.
Karakool *or* Karakoul, Kq-rq-kǿl, *t* Bokhara, 30.
Karaman, Kq-rq-mq́n, *t* As. Min., 12.
Karang-Assam, Kq-rq́ŋ-A-sq́m, *st* Malay Arch., pop. 250,000.
Kara Soo, Kara Sou, *or* Kara Su, Kq-rq́ Sœ, *rs* As. Min., Per., As. Tur., Eu. Tur. [S. Rus., 15.
Kara-Soo-Bazar, Kq-rq́-Sœ-Bq-zq́r, *t*
Kardzag, Kord-sóg, *t* E. Hun., 11½.
Karikal, Kq-ri-kq́l, *t* Ind., 15.
Karlsburg, *or* Carlsburg, Kq́rls-burh, *t* Tran., 12⅓.
Karlstadt, *or* Carlstadt, Kq́rl-stqt, free *t* Aus. Croatia, 4½; *t* Bav., 2¼.
Kars *or* Khars, Kqrs, *c* As. Tur., 12.
Kasanlik, Kqz-qn-lík, *t* Eu. Tur., 10.
Kaschau, Kq́-ʃɤ, *or* Kositze, Kœ-sít-sa, *c* Hun., 15¾.
Kashan, *or* Cashan, Kq-ʃq́n, *t* Per., 30.
Kashgar, *or* Cashgar, Kqʃ-gq́r, *c* Chi. Toork., 16. [7⅓.
Kasimov, Kasimow, Kq-si-móv, *t* Rus.,
Kaskaskia, Kas-kás-ki-a, *r* Ill., 300 m.; *v* Ill.
Kassaca, Kq-sq́-kq, *c* Japan, 150.
Kastamoonee, *or* Kastamouni, Kqs-tq-mǿ-nɛ, *t* As. Min., 48.
Katonah, Ka-tó-na, *v* N-Y.
Katrine, Ká-trin, *or* Kát-rin, *l* Scot.
Kaufman, Kéf-man, *co* Tex.
Kaukauna, Ke-ké-na, *v* Wis.
Kavala, Kq-vq́-lq, *s-pt t* Tur., 4. [10.
Kavaya, Kavaja, Kq-vį-q, *t* Eu. Tur.,
Kazan, Kasan, Kq-zq́n, *gov* and *c* Rus., 41⅓.
Kecskemet, Kéq-kem-át, *t* Hun., 42.
Kediri, Ka-dé-rɛ, *prov*, *t* and *r* Is. of Java.
Kedron, Ké-dron, *brook* of Pal., in the Valley of Jehoshaphat.
Keea-Hing-Foo, Ká-q-Hiŋ-Fœ, *ft c* China, 270.
Keene, Kɛn, *co t* N-H., 2¾; *v* Ky.
Keeseville, Kéz-vil, *v* N-Y., 2.
Keighley, Két-li, *t* Eng., 13.
Keith, Kɛt, *t* and *par* Scot., 5.
Keithsburg, Kéts-burg, *co t* Ill., ½.
Kelat, *or* Khelat, Kɛ-lq́t, *t* Belg., 12.
Kelso, Kél-sœ, *t* and *par* Scot., 4¾; *v* Ia.
Kemijoki, Ká-mi-yó-kɛ, *or* Kemi, Ká-mɛ, *r* Rus., 300 m.
Kempten, Kémp-ten, *t* Bavaria, 7¾.
Kemptville, Kémt-vil, *v* C. W., 1¼.
Ken, *or* Kent, *r* Eng.; Ken, *r* Scot.
Kenansville, Kén-anz-vil, *co t* N. C.
Kendal, Kén-dal, *t* and *par* Eng., 10⅓.
Kenduskeag, Ken-dus-kág, *v* Me.

Kenesaw, Ken-ɛ-sé, *p o* Ga.
Kenilworth, Kén-il-wurt, *t* and *par* Eng., 3½.
Kenjua, Kén-jq-a, *v* Pa.
Kenmare, Ken-mq́r, *r* and *t* Ir., 1⅓.
Kennebec, Ken-ɛ-bék, *r* Me., 150 m.
Kennebunk, Ken-ɛ-búŋk, *r* and *v* Me.
Kennedysville, Kén-ɛ-diz-vil, *v* N-Y.
Kennet, Kén-et, *r* Eng.
Kenosha, Ken-ó-ʃa, *t* Wis., 5½.
Kensico, Kén-si-kœ, *v* N-Y.
Kensington, Kén-siŋ-ton, *t* and *par* Eng., 44; *sub* Philadelphia, 48.
Kent, *vs* Conn., Ia.
Kenton, Kén-ton, *co t* O.
Kent's Hill, *v* Me.
Kentucky, Ken-túk-i, one of the w. U. S.; area 37,680 s. m., pop. 761,449 whites, 10,011 free blacks, 210,981 slaves,—total, 982,405; *r* Ky.
Keokuk, Ké-œ-kuk, *co* and *t* Iowa, 5.
Keosauque, Ké-œ-se-kwɛ, *co t* Iowa.
Kerah, Ká-rq, *r* Per., 350 m.
Kerman, Ker-mq́n, *ft c* Per., 30.
Kermanshah, Ker-mqn-ʃq́, *t* Per., 35.
Kern Lake, Cal.
Kertch, Kerq, *t* Rus., 10. [2⅔.
Keswick, Kéz-wik, *or* Kéz-ik, *t* Eng.,
Keszthely, Kest-hély, *t* W. Hun., 7½.
Ket, Ket, *r* As. Rus., 500 m.
Keta, Ká-tq, *r* As. Rus. 300 m.
Ketcho, Kéq-œ, *or* Cachao, Kaq-q́-œ, *c* of Anam, in S. E. As., 100.
Kettering, Két-er-iŋ, *t* and *par* Eng., 5¼.
Kew, Kq, *v* Eng., palace of George III.
Kewaunee, Kɛ-wé-nɛ, *r* and *co* Mich.
Keweenaw (Kɛ-wé-ne) Bay, Lake Superior; — Point, n. part Mich.
Key, *or* Ki, Kį, *is* Malay Arch.
Keyport, Ké-pœrt, *v* N-J.
Keysport, Kéz-pœrt, *v* Ill.
Keys, Kɛz, (*or* Cays,) islets on the shores of Honduras.
Keytesville, Kéts-vil, *co t* Mo.
Key West City, *co t* Fa., 3.
Khania, *H*q-né-a, (*or* Canea,) *s-pt t* Crete, 8.
Khanpoor, *H*qn-pǿr, *t* Hind., 20.
Kharkov, *H*qr-kóv, (*or* Slobodisch Ukraine, Slǿ-bœ-diʃ Ꝏ'kran,) *gov* s. Eu. Rus., area 20,931 s. m., pop. 1,366,188.
Kharkov, *or* Charkow, *c*, *cap* of the above, 35.
Khartoom, *H*qr-tǿm, *cap* Nubia, 20.
Khatanga, *H*q-tq́ŋ-gq, *r* As. Rus., 700 m.
Khatmandoo, Kqt-mqn-dǿ, (*or* Kath maro, Kqt-h-mq-rǿ,) *cap* of Nepaul.

Kherson, *or* Cherson, *H*er-són, *gov* and *ft t* S. Rus., 24⅓.
Khilok, *H*ɛ-lók, *r* As. Rus., 430 m.
Khiva, Kέ-vα, *cy* and *cap* in Ind. Toork., 10.
Khoi, *H*ơ, *t* N. Per., 30.
Khonsar, *H*on-sq̈r, *t* Per., 13.
Khooloom, *H*ꞷ-lꞷm, *t* Afg., 10.
Khyen-Dwem, Kį-en-Dwém, *r* Far. Ind., 400 m.
Khyerpoor, Kį-er-pꞷr, *t* Sinde, 15.
Kiakhta *or* Kiachta, Kɛ-q̈*h*-tq, *t* Sib., 5.
Kickapoo (Kik-a-pꞷ) Indians, Kansas Ter.; *r* Wis.
Kidderminster, Kid-er-min-ster, *bor* and *t* Eng., 23¾.
Kiel, Kɛl, *s-pt t* Den., 15.
Kielce, Kɛ-élt-sa, *c* Pol., 5¼.
Kiev, Kiew, Kɛ-év, (*or* Kief, Kɛ-éf;) *gov* Eu. Rus.; area 1942 s. m., pop. 1,636,339; *c* do., 47½.
Kilbarchan, Kil-bq̈r-*h*an, *t* and *par* Scot., 5½.
Kilbeggan, Kil-bég-an, *par* and *t* Ir., 2.
Kilbirnie, Kil-bẹ́r-nɛ, *v* and *par* Scot., 3⅓.
Kildare, Kil-dą́r, *co* and *t* Ir.
Kilia, Kέ-li-q, *ft t* Bessarabia, 7.
Kilkenny, Kil-kén-i, *co, c* and *bor* Ir., pop of *c* 20¼.
Killaloe, Kil-a-lꞷ́, *t* Ir., 2¾.
Killarney, Kil-q̈r-ni, *t* and *par* Ir., 6; three *ls*, do.
Killiecrankie, Kil-ɛ-kráŋ-kɛ, *pass* in Grampian Mountains, Scot.
Killough, Kíl-o, *s-pt t* Ir., 1.
Killucan, Kil-ꞷ́-kan, *par* Ir.
Killyleagh, Kil-i-lá, *s-pt t* Ir., 1.
Kilmacduagh, Kil-mak-dꞷ́-α, *par* Ir.
Kilmalie, Kil-má-lɛ, *par* Scot.
Kilmalloch, Kil-mál-o*h*, *t* Ir., 1½.
Kilmarnock, Kil-mq̈r-nok, *t* Scot., 21½; *v* Va.
Kilmuir, Kil-mẹ́r, *par* Scot.
Kilmun, Kil-mún, sea-bathing *v* Scot.
Kilrea, Kil-rá, *t* and *par* Ir., 1¼.
Kilrenny, Kil-rén-i, *s-pt* and *par* Scot., 2¼.
Kilrush, Kil-rú∫, *s-pt* and *t* Ir., 4½.
Kilsyth, Kil-sįd, *t* and *par* Scot., 4.
Kilwinning, Kil-win-iŋ, *t* and *par* Scot., 3¼.
Kinboorn, Kin-bꞷrn, *ft* Rus., at the mouth of the Dnieper.
Kincardine, Kiŋ-kq̈r-din, *s-pt t* Scot.
Kinderhook, Kin-der-húk, *vs* N-Y. 4, Ark., Ia., Ill.
King-Ki-Tao, Kiŋ-Ki-Tq̈-ꞷ, *cap* Corea.
King-and-Queen Court-House, *co t* Va.
Kingsbury, Kiŋz-ber-i, *vs* N-Y. 3, Ia.
Kingston, *cs* C. W. 14; Jamaica 35; *cap* island St. Vincent, 5; *co t* R. I; *vs* N-Y., Pa., Ga.
Kingston-upon-Thames, (— Temz,) *t* and *par* Eng., 12¼.
Kingstown, Kiŋz-tɤn, *s-pt t* Ir., 10½.
Kingsville, *vs* O., Md., S. C.
King-Te-Tchiang, Kiŋ-Ta-Ꞓi-q̈ŋ, *t* Ch.
Kington, Kiŋ-ton, *t* and *par* Eng., 3¼.
King William Court-House, *co t* Va.
Kingwood, *co t* Va.
Kinsale, Kin-sál, *bor* and *s-pt t* Ir., 5½.
Kiong-Choo, Kɛ-oŋ-Ꞓꞷ́, *c* China, 100.
Kirengha, Kɛ-rén-gq, *r* Siberia, 300 m.
Kirgheez, Kẹr-gέz, Mongol *race* of Cen. As., num. 2,260,000, sub. to Rus.
Kirkcaldy, Kẹr-kól-di, *s-pt, t* and *par* Scot., 10½. [Scot., 2¾.
Kirkcudbright, Kẹr-kꞷ́-brɛ, *t* and *par*
Kirkintilloch, Kẹrk-in-tíl-o*h*, *t* and *par* Scot., 6½. [N. C.
Kirkland, Kẹ́rk-land, *vs* Scot., N-Y.,
Kirkwall, Kẹrk-wól, *s-pt t* and *par* Scot., 3½.
Kirriemuir, Kẹ́r-i-mẹr, *or* Killamuir, Kíl-a-mẹr, *t* and *par* Scot., 3½.
Kirtland, Kẹ́rt-land, *v* O.
Kishenev, Ki∫-ɛ-név, *t* Rus., 43.
Kishm, Ki∫m, *i* Persian Gulf, 5, Arabs.
Kistnah, Kist-nα, *r* India, 600 m.
Kittanning, Kit-án-iŋ, *v* Pa.
Kittatinny, Kit-a-tín-i, *or* Blue Mountains, running through N-Y., N-J., Pa., Va., N. C., Tenn., Ala.
Kizil-Irmak, Kíz-il-Er′mqk, *r* Asia Minor, 520 m.
Kizliar, Kiz-li-q̈r, *ft t* Rus., 12.
Kjöge, Kɛ-ẹ́-ge, *t* Den., 2⅓. [14¼.
Klagenfurth, Klq̈-gen-fꞷrt, *t* Illyria,
Klamath, Klq̈-mat *or* Klq̈-mat-h, written also Tlamath, *r* and *t* Oregon.
Klattau, Klq̈-tɤ, *t* Bohemia, 6½.
Klausenburg, Klɤ-zen-bꞷr*h*, *cap c* Transylvania, 25½. [Eng., 10¼.
Knaresborough, Nq̈rz-bur-ꞷ, *t* and *par*
Knightstown, Nįts-tɤn, *v* Ia., 1⅔.
Knottingley, Nót-iŋ-li, *v* Eng., 4½.
Knowlesville, Nꞷ́lz-vil, *v* N-Y.
Knoxville, Nóks-vil, *c* Tenn., 5; *co ts* Ga., Ill., Iowa. [4½.
Knutsford, Núts-ford, *t* and *par* Eng.,
Koisoo, Kơ-sꞷ́, *r* Rus., 1200 m.
Kokomo, Kꞷ́-kꞷ-mꞷ, *v* Ia.
Kokoora, Kꞷ-kꞷ́-rq, *t* Japan, 16.
Kolin, *or* Neu Kolin, Nơ Kꞷ-lén, *t* Bohemia, 5¾.
Kolomea, Kꞷ-lꞷ-má-q, *t* Aus. Galicia, 7.
Kolomna, Kꞷ-lóm-nq, *t* Rus., 13.
Kolyma *or* Kolima, Kꞷ[illegible]-mq̈ *or* Kꞷ-lé-mq, *r* Siberia, 700 m.

Konieh, Kó-ni-e, *c* Asia Minor, 40.
Königgrätz, Kẹ-ni*h*-grets, *t* Aus., 8½.
Königsberg, Kén-igz-bẹrg, *c* Prus., 75.
Kooban, Kœ-bq̇n, *r* S. Russia, 380 m.
Koordistan *or* Kourdistan, Kœr-dis-tán, *cy* of W. Asia, divided bet. Turkey and Persia; area 500,000 s. m., pop. 3,000,000.
Koorile (Kœ́-ril) Islands, N. Pac., pop. small.
Koorsk, Kœ*r*sk, *div* Eu. Rus.; area 17,382 s. m., pop. 1,665,215; *cap* of same, 30½.
Kordofan, Kɛr-dœ-fq̇n, *cy* Cen. Af., 400.
Körös, Nagy, Noj Kẹ-rẹʃ, *t* Hun., 18½.
Kosciusko, (Kos-i-ús-kœ) Mount, Australia; *co t* Miss.; *co* Ia.
Koslov, Kos-lóv, *t* Rus., 8.
Kossuth, Ko-ʃœ́t, *co* Iowa; *v* Ill.
Kostroma, Kos-tró-mq, *r*, *gov* and *c* Rus., 14.
Kovno, Kóv-nœ, *t* Rus. Poland, 7.
Krajova, Krq-yó-vq, *cap* Lit. Wal., 8.
Krementchoog, Krem-ent-ʃœ́g, *t* Rus., 17.
Kremnitz, Krém-nits, *t* Hun., 6⅓.
Kreutznach, Krœ́ts-nq*h*, *t* Rhen. Prus., 9⅓.
Kronstädt, Krón-stqt, *t* Aus., 36.
Kuenlun, Kwen-lœ́n, *ms* Cen. Asia, [22,000 ft.
Kumo, Kó-mœ, *r* Rus.
Kurrachee, Kur-a-çé, *s-pt t* Sinde, 15.
Kurrichane, Kur-i-kq́-na, *t* S. Af., 16.
Kussnacht, Kœ́s-nq*h*t, *v* Swit., the scene of William Tell's trial.
Kutaieh *or* Kutaiah, Kœ-tị-ye, *t* Asia Minor. [2½.
Kyparissia, Kɛ-pq-ris-é-q, *t* Greece,

# L.

Laaland, Lé-land, *or* Lolland, Lól-qnd, *i* of Den., 55¾.
La Baie du Febore, Lq Ba dẹ Fe-bé*r*, *v* C. E.
Labansville, Lá-banz-vil, *v* Pa., ½.
La Bathie, Lq Bq-té, *v* Sard. States, 1.
Labooan, Lq-bœ-q́n, *i* Malay Arch.
Labrador, Lab-ra-dœ́r, *pen* e. coast Br. N. Am., as yet very little known in the interior; area 450,000 s. m., pop. 5,000. [210 m.
Lacantuu, Lq-kqn-tœ́n, *r* Cen. Am.,
Laccadive (Lq́k-a-dịv) Isles, group in Ind. Oc., 10. [cian *st.*
Lacedæmon, Las-ɛ-dé-mon, anc. Gre-
Lachine, Lq-ʃén, *v* C. E.
Lachlan, Lq́k-lqn, *r* Australia, 400 m.
Lackawanna, Lak-a-wán-a, *or* Lackawannock, Lak-a-wán-ok, *r* Pa.
Lackawannock Mountain, Pa. [Pa.
Lackawaxen, Lak-a-wáks-en, *r* and *v*
La Clair, La Klq*r*, *v* Ill.
La Clede, La Klad *or* La Klɛd, *co* Mo.
Lac Maskinongé, Lqk Mqs-kɛ-nœṅ-ʒá, *v* C. E., 2.
Lacon, Lá-kon, *co t* Ill.
Laconia, Lq-kó-ni-q, *gov* Greece; *v* Ia.
La Cote St. Marie, Lq Kœt Sent Má-rɛ, *p o* Wis.
Lac Qui Parle, Lqk Kɛ Pq*r*l, *v* Min.
La Crosse, La Krós, *r*, *co* and *co t* Wis.
Ladakh, Lq-dq́k, *prov* Cen. Asia; area 30,000 s. m., pop. supposed to be 500,000. [Eu.; *v* Ia.
Ladoga, Lq-dó-gq, *l* Rus., largest in
Ladrones, Lq-drónz, *or* Mariana, Mq-ri-q́-nq, Islands, of Sp., group N. Pac., 10.
Lafayette, Lq-fa-ét, *c* Ia., 9; *par* La., and *sub* N-Orleans, 7; *co ts* Ga., Tenn.; *vs* N-Y., N-J., Pa., Va., Ky., O., Ia., Iowa, Or. [100 m.
La Fourche, Lq Fœ́rʃ, *bayou* La., nav.
Lagan, Lá-gan, *r* Ir.
Lago Maggiore, Lq́-gœ Mqd-jó-ra, *or* Lake of Locarno, Lœ-kq́*r*-nœ, *l* N. It., 40 by 2 m.
Lagos, Lq́-gœs, *ft s-pt t* Port., 7; *t* Mex.; *t* Guinea, 5; *g* and *t* Eu. Tur.
La Grange, La Gránj, *co* Ia.; *co ts* Ga., Tex., Ky., Ia.; *vs* Ala., Tenn., &c.
Lagro, Lá-grœ, *v* Ia. [8.
La Guayra, Lq Gwị-rq, *t* and *s-pt* Ven.,
Laguemba, Lq-gém-bq, Feejee *i.*
Laguna del Madre, Lq-gœ́-nq del Mq́d-ra, *lagoon* or *bayou* Tex., 110 by 14 m.
Laguna Seca, Lq-gœ́-nq Sá-kq, *p o* Cal.
Lahajan, Lq-hq-jq́n, *t* Persia, 15.
La Harpe, La Hqrp, *v* Ill.
Lahaska, La-hás-ka, *p o* Pa.
Lahore, Lq-hór, *cap* of the Punjab, Br. Ind., 100.
La Hoya, Lq Hó-yq, *v* Mex.
Lahsa, Lq́*h*-sq, fertile *dis* E. Arabia, 50.
Lake Kattakittekon, Kat-a-kít-ɛ-kon, head of Wisconsin River.
Lake Mills, *v* Wis.
Lake of the Woods, *l* Br. N. Am.
Lake Pleasant, Pléz-ant, *co t* N-Y.
Lake Prairie, Prá-rɛ, *v* Iowa.

Lake Providence, Próv-i-dens, *v* La.
Lake Village, *v* N-H.
Lakeville, Lák-vil, *vs* Conn., N-Y., &c.
Lake Zurich, Zụ́-rik, *v* Ill.
Lalita-Patan, Lq-lé-tq-Pq-tq́n, *t* N. Hind., 24.
Lamar, La-mq́r, *co* Tex.; *v* Miss.
Lamartine, Lam-ar-tén, *p os* Pa., Ala., Ark., Tenn., O.; *v* Wis.
Lambayeque, Lqm-bj-á-ka, *t* Peru, 8.
Lambertville, Lám-bert-vil, *t* N-J., 2.
Lambourn, Chipping, Cip-iŋ Lám-burn, *t* and *par* Eng., 2¾.
Lamego, Lq-má-gω, *c* Port., 9.
La Mine, La Mεn, *r* and *v* Mo.
Lamoille, La-moil, *r* and *co* Vt.; *v* Ill.
La Motte, La Mót, *i* Lake Champ., ½; *v* Iowa.
Lanark, Lán-ark, *co* and *t* Scot.
Lancaster, Láŋ-kas-ter, *co* and *s-pt t* Eng., 16¼; *c* Pa., 15; *co ts* N-H., Ky., O., Mo., Iowa, Wis.; *vs* Mass., N-Y., Ia.
Lancaster Court-House, *co ts* Va., S. C.
Lancaster Sound, bet. Baffin's Bay and Barrow's Strait.
Lanchang, Lqn-çq́ŋ, *cap* Laos country.
Lanciano, Lqn-çi-q́-nω, *t* Nap., 13.
Landau, Lq́n-dɤ, *ft t* Rhen. Bav., 6; *ts* Germany.
Landerneau, Loṅ-der-nó, *s-pt t* and *r* Fr.
Landsberg, Lq́nts-bęrh, *t* Prus., 11⅔.
Land's End, *headland* w. Eng.
Landshut, Lq́ndz-hωt, *t* Low. Bav., 9⅓.
Lane End, *t* Eng., 12⅓.
Lanesborough, Lánz-bur-ω, *vs* Mass.,Pa.
Lanesville, *vs* Ia., Ky., Va.
Langeland, Lq́ŋ-ε-lqnd, *i* of Den., 17⅓.
Langensalza, Lq́ŋ-en-sqlt-sq, *t* Prus. Sax., 7⅔.
Langholm, Láŋ-um, *bor* and *t* Scot., 3.
Langres, Loṅ-gr, *ft t* Fr., 11⅓.
Lanho, Lqn-hó, *r* China, 300 m.
Lanier, La-nér, *co t* Ga.
Lannion, Lqn-i-óṅ, *t* Fr., 6¼.
Lansing, Lán-siŋ, *cap* Mich., 3.
Lansingburg, Lán-siŋ-burg, *v* N-Y., 5.
Lanzarote, Lqn-sq-ró-ta, Canary *i*, 18.
Laon, Lq-óṅ, *c* Fr., 10.
Laona, La-ó-na, *vs* N-Y., Ill.
Laos, Lq́-ωs, *cy* S.-E. Asia; area unknown, pop. supposed to be 1,000,000.
La Paz, Lq Pqz, *dep* and *t* Bol., 20; *cap* Lower California.
Lapeer, La-pér, *co* and *v* Mich.
Lapland, Láp-land, *ter* N. Eu., inhabited by a people noted for their singular physical appearance, ethnographers being unable to say whether they belong more to the Mongolian or Caucasian race; area 130,000 s. m., pop. 20,000.
La Pointe, La Point, *co* and *v* Wis.
Laporte, La-pórt, *co ts* Pa., Ia. 2½.
La Prairie, Lq Prá-rε, *v* C. E., 1¾.
La Purissima, Lq Pω-rés-i-mq, *v* Cal.
Lar *or* Laar, Lqr, *t* Persia, 12.
Laredo, La-rá-dω, *co t* Tex.
Largs, Lqrgz, *s-pt* and *par* Scot., 3.
Larissa, Lq-ris-q, *t* Eu. Tur., 20.
Larissa, La-ris-a, *v* Texas.
Larkhana, Lqr-kq́-nq, *ft t* Sinde, 12.
La Rue, Lq Rω, *p o* O.; *co* Ky.
Lasalle, Lq-sq́l, *v* Fr., 2½.
La Salle, La Sal, *co* and *v* Ill., 3¼; *p o* N-Y.; *v* Texas.
Las Palmas, Lqs Pq́l-mqs, *c* island of Gran Canaria, 17⅓. [50.
Lassa *or* H'lassa, H-lq́s-q, *cap* Thibet,
L'Assomption, Lqs-ωṅ-si-óṅ, *v* C. E.
Latakeea, Lq-ta-ké-a, *s-pt t* Syria, 10.
Lauderdale, Ló-der-dal, *cos* Ala., Miss., Tenn. [Den.; *t* Prus.
Lauenburg, Lɤ́-en-burg, *duchy* and *c*
Launceston, Lq́ns-ton, *bor* and *t* Eng., 6; *t* Van Diemen's Land, 5.
Laureana, Lɤ-ra-q́-nq, *t* Naples.
Laurel, Ló-rel, *vs* Del. 1¼, O., Ia. ¾.
Laurel Factory, *v* Md., 1. [Pa.; *v* Ill.
Laurel Hill, *cemetery* Philadelphia; *ms*
Laurens, Ló-rens, *dis* S. C.; *co* Ga.
Laurens Court-House, *co t* S. C.
Lauria, Lɤ́-ri-q, *t* Nap., 6¾.
Lauricocha, Lɤ-ri-kó-çq, *l* Peru.
Lausanna, Lω-zq́n, *c* Swit., on the Jura Mountains, 450 feet above lake Geneva, 20. Here Voltaire, Haller, Tissot, Gibbon and Byron once resided.
Lausanne, Lə-sán, *v* Pa.
Lauven, Lɤ́-ven, *r* Nor.
Lavacca, La-vák-a, *r* and *co* Tex.
Laval, Lq-vq́l, *t* Fr., 19¼.
Lavaur, Lq-vór, *t* Fr., 7⅓. [Bra., 12.
Lavras-de-Funil, Lq́-vrqs-da-Fω-nél, *t*
Lawrence, Ló-rens, *c* Mass., 15; a rapidly growing *c* Kanzas Ter.; also numerous *cos* in the states. [*v* Pa.
Lawrenceburg, *t* Ia., 5; *co ts* Ky., Tenn.;
Lawrenceville, *v* and *U. S. arsenal*, Pa.; *co ts* Va., Ill.; *vs* Ia., &c.
Laybach, Lj-bqh, *r* and *t* Aus., 17½.
Leakesville, Léks-vil, *v* N. C.; *co t* Miss.
Leamington, Lém-iŋ-ton, *t* Eng., 15¾.
Leavenworth, Lév-en-wurþ, *c* Kanzas Ter., 1.
Lebanon, Léb-a-non, *ms* Syria, celebrated for their ancient and historic associations; *co ts* Pa. 3, Va., Ala., Tenn., Ky., O. 3½, Ia.; *vs* N-H., Ill., Conn., &c.

Lebrija *or* Lebrixa, La-bré-*h*q, *t* Sp., 7¾; *r* N-Gran.
Lecce, Lét-ça, *c* Nap., 19½.
Le Claire, Le Klar, *v* Iowa. [Ter.
Lecompton, Le-kómp-ton, *cap* Kansas
Lectoure, Lek-tór, *t* Fr., 6¾.
Ledbury, Léd-ber-i, *t* and *par* Eng. 4¾.
Ledyard, Léd-yard, *vs* Conn., N-Y.
Leeds, Ledz, *c* or *bor* Eng., 152.
Leedsville, Lédz-vil, *vs* N-Y., N-J., Va.
Leek, Lek, *t* and *par* Eng., 13¼.
Leesburg, Léz-burg, *co t* Va., 2; *vs* O., Ia., Ky., Tenn., Ala.
Leesport, *v* Pa.
Leesville, *vs* N-Y., Va., Ky., O., Ia., Ill.
Leeuwarden, Lé-wer-den *or* Lé-u-var-den, *t* Hol., 24½. [Ind.
Leeward (Lé-ward) Is., applied to W.
Lefkosia, Lef-ko-zé-q, (*or* Nicosia,) *cap* island of Cyprus, 18.
Leflore, Le-flór, *v* Miss.
Leghorn, Lég-horn *or* Leg-hórn, *s-pt t* Tuscany, 78. [*t* Aus. It.
Legnago, Len-yá-go, *ft t* Lombardy, 6;
Leh, La, *or* Lei, Lá-e, *c* Cen. Asia, 8.
Lehi (Lé-hi) City, *v* Utah Ter.
Lehigh, Lé-hi, *r* and *co* Pa.
Lehighton, Le-hi-ton, *v* Pa. [*v* Mass.
Leicester, Lés-ter, *co* Eng.; *t* do., 60½;
Leigh, Le, *t* and *par* Eng., 5¼.
Leighton-Buzzard, Lé-ton-Búz-ard, *t* and *par* Eng., 7.
Leipsic, Lip-sik, *prov* and *c* Saxony, noted for its fairs, 70.
Leipsic, Lép-sik, *v* Del.; *p os* O., Ia.
Leisnig, Lis-ni*h*, *t* Sax., 5¼.
Leith, Leth, *s-pt t* Scot., 31.
Leitmeritz, Lit-mer-its, *ft t* Boh., 4⅓.
Leitomischel, Li-to-mis-el, *t* Boh., 6⅓.
Leixlip, Lás-lip, *t* and *par* Ir.
Lema (Lá-mq) Islands, Chinese Sea.
Le Maire, Le Mar, *str* S. Am.
Lemberg, Lém-berg, (*or* Leopold) *t* Aus., 71. [m.
Lena, Lé-na, (Rus. La-ná,) *r* As., 2400
Lenawee, Lén-a-we, *co* Mich. [5½.
Lendinara, Len-di-ná-rq, *ft t* Aus. It.,
Lennox Town, Lén-oks Tsn, *v* Scot., 3.
Lenoir, Le-nór, *co* and *co t* N. C.
Lenox, Lén-oks, *co t* Mass., ¾.
Lenoxville, Lén-oks-vil, *v* C. E.
Lens, Lon, *t* Fr., 9¾.
Lentini, Len-té-ni, *t* Sicily, 5.
Leominster, Lém-in-ster, *t* and *par* Eng., 4¼; *v* Mass.
Leon, Lé-on, *c* Sp., 7; *t* Nicaragua, 30; *vs* Va., O.; *r* Tex.
Leon, La-ón, *t* Guanajuato, 6.
Leon, *or* Managua, Mq-ná-gwq, *l* Nic.
Leona, Le-ó-na, *co t* Tex.
Leonardstown, Lén-ardz-tsn, *co t* Md.
Leonardsville, Lén-ardz-vil, *v* N-Y.
Leonforte, Lá-on-fór-ta, *t* Sic., 10¾.
Leoni, Le-ó-ni, *v* Mich., ¾.
Leonidas, Le-ón-i-das, *v* Mich., ¼.
Leopold, Lé-o-pold, *v* Ia. [Hun., 1¾.
Leopoldstadt, La-ó-pold-stqt, *ft t* Cen.
Lepanto, Le-pán-to, *s-pt t* Greece, 2.
Lerchenfeld, Lér*h*-en-felt, *v* Aus., 7¾.
Lerici, Lér-i-çe, *t* It., 5¼.
Lerida, Lér-i-dq, *t* Sp., 12¼.
Lerins (Le-rán) Isles, Med., bel. to Fr.
Le Roy, Le Ró, *vs* N-Y. 2, Mich., &c.
Lesina, Lés-i-nq, *i* of Dalmatia, 12½.
Le Sueur, Le Só-er, *co* and *v* Min.
Leutschau, Lót-ʃs, *fr t* Hun., 5⅓.
Levanna, Le-ván-a, *vs* N-Y., O.
Levant, Le-vánt, e. coasts Med. Sea; *vs* Me., N-Y.
Levanto, La-ván-to, *t* Sard., 4½.
Leven, Lé-ven, *rs* Eng., Scot.
Leven, Loch, Lo*h* Lév-en, *l* Scot.
Levenworth, Lév-en-wurth, *co t* Ia., ¾.
Levering, Lév-er-iŋ, *v* O.
Lewes, Lú-is, *bor* and *t* Eng., 9⅓.
Lewis, Lú-is, *i* of the Outer Hebrides; *cos* N-Y., Va., &c.
Lewisburg, Lú-is-burg, *t* Pa.; *co ts* Va., Tenn.; *vs* Ky., O., Ia.
Lewis *or* Snake River, largest tributary of Columbia River. [2.
Lewiston, Lú-is-ton, *t* Me., 7; *co t* N-Y.,
Lewistown, Lú-is-tsn, *co ts* Pa. 3, Ill.; *v* O. [Ark.
Lewisville, Lú-is-vil, *vs* Pa., O., Ia.; *co t*
Lexington, Léks-iŋ-ton, *c* Ky., 12; *co ts* Va., N. C., Ga., Miss., Tenn., Mo., S. C.; *v* Mass.
Leyden *or* Leiden, Li-den, *c* Neth., 36.
Leyland, Lé-land, *t* and *par* Eng., 13¾.
Leyte, Lá-i-ta, Philippine *i*, 92¼.
Leytha, Li-tq, *r* Aus., 90 m.
Leyton, Lá-ton, *v* and *par* Eng., 3¼.
Libau, Lé-bs, *s-pt t* Rus., 10¼.
Liberia, Li-bé-ri-a, *rep* of Af.; it was founded in 1820, by the American Colonization Society, for the occupation of the free American blacks; the enterprise cannot be said to have proved, as yet, very successful; 250.
Liberty, Lib-er-ti, *co ts* Va., Miss., Tex., Ky., Ia., Mo.; *vs* N-Y., Pa.
Liberty Falls, *v* N-Y.
Libertyville, *vs* Ill., Iowa.
Libourne, Le-bórn, *t* Fr., 12⅔.
Libyan Desert, Líb-i-an Déz-ert, part of Sahara.
Lichfield, Líç-feld, *c* Eng., 7. [5⅔.
Lichtervelde, Lí*h*-ter-vél-de, *l* Belg.,
Licking, Lík-iŋ, River, *rs* Ky. 200 m.; O.

Licordia, Li-kór-di-a, *t* Sicily, 7.
Liddel, Líd-el, *r* Scot. [Con., 7⅓.
Liechtenstein, Léh-ten-stin, *prin* Ger.
Liege, Lej, *c* Belg., 60.
Liegnitz, Lég-nits, *t* Prus. Silesia, 14.
Lierre, Le-ár, *t* Belg., 13½.
Lifu, Le-fú, *i* Pac. Oc.
Lignières, Len-ye-ár, *t* Fr., 2⅓.
Ligny, Len-yé, *v* Belg.
Ligonier, Lig-o-nér, *bor* and *t* Pa.
Lika, Lé-ka, *r* Aus. Croatia. [Fr., 76.
Lille *or* Lisle, Lel, a manufacturing *c*
Lillebonne, Lel-bón, *t* Fr., 5¼. [100.
Lima, Lé-ma, *prov* Peru, 125; *cap* do.,
Lima, Lí-ma, *vs* N-Y., Mich., Ia., Wis.; *co t* O. [prus.
Limasol, Le-ma-sól, *s-pt t* is. of Cy-
Limburg, Lím-burg, *t* Ger., 3¼.
Limerick, Lím-er-ik, *co* and *c* Ir., 55¼; *vs* Me., Pa., &c.
Limestone (Lím-ston) Springs, *v* S. C.
Limington, Lím-ing-ton, *v* Me.
Limoges, Le-móz, *c* Fr., 27.
Limoux, Le-mú, *t* Fr., 7⅔.
Linares, Le-ná-res, *t* Sp., 6½.
Lincoln, Líng-kon, *co* Eng.; *c* do., 14; *vs* Me., N-H., Mass., O.
Lincoln Centre, *v* Me.
Lincolnton, Líng-kon-ton, *co ts* N. C., Ga.
Linden, Lin-den, *vs* N-Y., Pa., Wis.; *co ts* Ala., Tenn.
Lindenville, *vs* O., Wis.
Lindville, Lind-vil, *v* Iowa. [20 m.
Lingen, Líng-gen, *i* Malay Arch., 40 by
Linköping, Lin-ce-ping, *t* Swed., 4¾.
Linlithgow, Lin-lith-go, *co* Scot.; *t* do.,
Linn, Lin, *co t* Mo. [4¼.
Lintz, Lints, *cap* Upper Aus., 31.
Lipan, Le-pán, *Ind tr* of Tex., Mex.
Lipari (Líp-a-ri) Islands, *vol is* Med., 22; *t* same, 12½. [Ger., 106½.
Lippe-Detmold, Líp-e-Dét-molt, *prin*
Lippstadt, Líp-stat, *ft t* Prus. Westp.
Liria, Lé-ri-a, *t* Sp., 8½. [⅓.
Lisbon, Líz-bon, *cap* Port., 280; *v* Ill.,
Lisburn, Líz-burn, *t* Ir., 7; *v* Pa.
Lisieux, Le-zi-é, *t* Fr., 11⅓.
Liskeard, Lis-kárd, *t* and *par* Eng., 3.
Lisle, Lil, *v* Mo.
L'Islet, Le-lá, *co* and *v* C. E.
Lismore, Liz-mór, *i* w. Scot., 1⅓; *c* and *par* Ir., 3. [8¾.
Lissa, Lís-a, *i* Adriatic, 3; *t* Prus. Pol.,
Litchfield, Líc-feld, *co ts* Conn., Ky.; *vs* O., Mich.
Lithonia, Lith-ó-ni-a, *v* Ga., ¼.
Lithopolis, Lith-óp-o-lis, *v* O.
Lithuania, Lith-yu-á-ni-a, anc. *ter* Eu.,
Litiz, Lít-its, *v* Pa. [bel. to Rus.
Little Chute, Shot, *v* Wis.
Little Egg Harbor River, N-J.
Little Falls, *vs* N-Y., 4; N-J.
Littlehampton, Lit-l-hámp-ton, *t* and *watering place* Eng., 2½. [150 m.
Little Kanawha, Ka-né-wa, *r* Va.,
Little Miami (Mi-ám-i) River, cen. O.
Little Missouri, Mi-zó-ri, *rs* Ark., Mo. Ter. [foundland.
Little Placentia, Pla-sén-shi-a, *s-pt* New-
Little Red River, Ark., 150 m.
Little River, La., nav. 150 m.; various other streams. [S. arsenal; 3.
Little Rock, *cap* Ark., and seat of U.
Littleton, Lít-l-ton, *v* N-H.
Livadia, Liv-a-dé-a, (*or* Libadia,) *div* Gr., 332¾; *cap* same, 9.
Liverpool, Lív-er-pool, *c* Eng., and second in commercial importance, 376; *s-pt ts* Nova Scotia, N-Brunswick; *vs* Pa., O., Ia., Ill.
Livingston, Lív-ing-ton, *co ts* Ala., Tex., Tenn.; *vs* Mich., Ill.
Livonia, Li-vó-ni-a, maritime *gov* Rus.; area 20,450 s. m., pop. 821,457; *v* Ia.
Ljusne *or* Liusne, Lyús-na, *r* Swed., 220 m.
Llanbedr, Lán-bed-er, *bor* S. Wales.
Llanberris, Lan-bér-is, *par* N. Wales, containing scenery among the most magnificent to be found in N. Eu.
Llandeilo-Vawr *or* Fawr, *or* Llandilo, Lan-dí-lo-Vor, *t* S. Wales, 1⅓. Here is Grongar Hill, where, in 1282, the last effort was made for the independence of Wales. [2.
Llandovery, Lan-dó-ver-i, *t* S. Wales,
Llanelly, Lan-é-le, *s-pt t* S. Wales, 8¾.
Llangollen, Lan-go-len, *t* N. Wales, 5.
Llanidloes, Lán-id-les, *bor* and *t* N. Wales, 3.
Llanrwst, Lán-roost, *t* N. Wales, 3½.
Llantrissent, Lan-trís-ent, *t* S. Wales, 1.
Llewellyn, Lu-él-in, *v* Pa.
Lloughor, Ló-gor, *r* and *t* S. Wales, 1.
Llumayor, Lyoo-mi-ór, *t* is. of Majorca,
Loa, Ló-a, *s-pt t* and *r* Peru. [7.
Locarno, Lo-kár-no, *t* Swit., 2¾.
Lochaber, Loh-á-ber, moun. *dis* Scot.
Lochapoka, Lo-ka-pó-ka, *v* Ala.
Loches, Losh, *t* Fr., 5¼.
Lochgilp-Head, Loh-gilp-Hed, *v* Scot. 3.
Lochinvar, Loh-ín-var, *l* Scot.
Lochmaben, Loh-má-ben, *bor* and *par* Scot., 1.
Lochwinnoch, Loh-win-oh, *par* Scot.
Lockhart, Lók-hart, *co t* Tex.
Lock Haven, Lok Há-ven, *v* Pa., 1.
Lock-Hoi, Lok-Hó, *s-pt t* China, 90.
Lockland, Lók-land, *v* O.

Lockport, Lók-pɷrt, *vs* N-Y. 12⅓, Ill. 2, Pa., O., La., &c.
Locle, Le, Lẹ Lok-l', *v* Swit., 8½.
Lodève, Lɷ-dáv, *t* Fr., 10⅓.
Lodi, Ló-dɛ, *c* Lom., 15¾; Lɷ-dį, *vs* N-Y., O., Ia., Wis.
Loffoden, Lo-fó-den, *is* n. w. Nor., 4.
Lofo, Ló-fẹ, *i* Gulf of Bothnia.
Logan, Ló-gan, *v* O., 1¼.
Logansport, Ló-ganz-pɷrt, *c* Ia., 3½.
Logazohy, Lɷ-gą-zɷ-hé, *t* W. Af., 9.
Loggun, Lo-gɷ́n, *cy* Af. [7¼.
Logrono, Lɷ-grɷ́n-yɷ, *prov* and *t* Sp.,
Loir, Lwąr, *r* Fr., 150 m.
Loire, Lwąr, largest *r* in Fr., 645 m.
Loja *or* Loxa, Ló-*h*ą, *c* Sp., 15; *t* Ec., 10.
Lokeren, Ló-ker-en, *t* Belg., 16¼.
Lombardo-Venetian, Lom-bąr-dɷ-Ven-é-ʃan, *k* Austrian dominions; area 17,511 s. m., pop. 5,000,000.
Lombardy, Lóm-bɑr-di, former *div* It.
Lomblem, Lom-blém, *i* Malay Arch.
Lombok, Lom-bók, *i* Malay Arch.; area 1,480 s. m., pop. 250,000.
Lomond, Loch, Lo*h* Ló-mond, *l*, largest in Scot., 40 s. m.
Lonato, Lɷ-ną-tɷ, *t* Lom., 5½.
London, Lún-don, *cap* Gr. Brit., and largest city in the world; circumference estimated at 30 m.; pop. 2,362,236; *c* C. W., 7; *co ts* Ky., O.
Londonderry, Lún-don-der-i, *c* Ir., 20; *vs* N-H., O., &c.; *s-pt t* Nova Scotia.
Long Branch, watering-place, N-J.
Longford, Lóŋ-ford, *t* Ir., 4¼.
Long Island, portion of N-Y., separated from the state by a strait; *is* Hebrides.
Long Island Sound, separates Long Island from N-Y. and Conn.
Longueil, Lɷŋ-gẹly, *v* C. E., 4½.
Longwy, Lɷń-vé, *ft t* Fr., 3⅓. [Fr., 8½.
Lons-le-Saulnier, Lɷń-lẹ-Sɷ-ni-á, *t*
Loo Choo, Lɷ Ƈɷ́, *is* Pac. Oc. [20.
Loodianah, Lɷ-di-ą-ną, *ft t* N. W. Hin.,
Lorain, Lɷ-rán, *co* and *v* O.
Lorca, Lór-ką, *c* Sp., 48¼.
Loreto, Lɷ-rá-tɷ, *or* Loretto, Lɷ-rét-ɷ, *c* Cen. It., 8.
Loretto, Lɷ-rét-ɷ, *v* Pa. [Fr., 25¾.
Lorient *or* L'Orient, Lɷ-ri-óń, *s-pt t*
L'Orignal, Lɷ-rɛn-yąl, *v* C. W., ¾.
Los Angeles, Lɷs An'je-lez, *co* Cal.
Lossini, Los-é-nɛ, *i* of Illyria, 6¼.
Lothians, Ló-ŧi-anz, *divs* Scot.
Loudon, Lȣ́-don, *co* Va.; *vs* N-H., Pa.
Loudonville, Lȣ́-don-vil, *v* O.
Loudoun, Lɷ́-dɷn, *v* Scot., 4½.
Lougen, Lɷ́-gan, *r* Nor., 200 m.
Loughborough, Lúf-bur-ɷ, *t* Eng., 11.
Loughrea, Lo*h*-rá, *t* Ir., 5½.

Louisa, Lɷ-é-zą, *co ts* Ky., Va. [C.
Louisburg, Lɷ́-is-burg, *t* Fr.; *vs* Pa., N.
Louisiade (Lɷ-ɛ-zi-ąd) Archipelago, *is* S. Pac. Oc.
Louisiana, Lɷ-ɛ-zi-á-nɑ, one of the s. U. S., on the Gulf of Mexico; area 41,225 s. m.; pop. 255,451 whites, 17,462 free blacks, 244,809 slaves—total, 517,762.
Louis-Philippe (Lɷ-é-Fil-ép) Land, a tract in the Ant. Oc., off S. Shetland.
Louisville, Lɷ́-is-vil *or* Lɷ́-i-vil, *c* Ky., 51¾; *co ts* Ga., Miss.; *vs* O., Ia., &c.
Loule, Lɷ́-la, *ft t* Port., 8¼.
Lourdes, Lɷrd, *t* Fr., 4½.
Louth, Lȣŧ, *t* Eng., 10½.
Loutre (Lɷ́t-er) River, Mo.
Louvain, Lɷ-ván, *c* Belg., 24¾.
Louviers, Lɷ-vi-á, *t* Fr., 10.
Lovat, Lɷ-vąt, *r* Rus., 175 m.
Loveland, Lúv-land, *v* O.
Lovettsville, Lúv-ets-vil, *v* Va.
Lovingston, Lúv-iŋ-ston, *co t* Va.
Low Archipelago, (Ar-ki-pél-a-gɷ,) *is* Pac. Oc.
Lowell, Ló-el, manufacturing *c* Mass., 37; *vs* Ga., O., Mich., Iowa, Wis.
Lower Blue Lick, watering-place, Ky.
Lower Saginaw, Ló-er Ság-i-nɐ, *v* Mich., 1⅓.
Lowestoft, Lȣ́-es-toft, *s-pt t* Eng., 1¾.
Lowndes, Lȣndz, *cos* Ga., Ala., Miss.
Lowville, Ló-vil, *vs* N-Y. 1, Pa.
Loyalty (Lɷ́-al-ti) Islands, Pac. Oc., 3.
Loyola, Lɷ-yó-lą, *v* Sp.
Lübeck, Lẹ́-bek, *prin* Ger., 22¼; *cap* same, 27; Lų́-bek, *v* Me.
Lublin, Lɷ́-blin, *c* Pol., 16.
Lucas, Lų́-kas, *co* and *v* Iowa.
Lucca, Lúk-ɑ, *ter* and *c* Cen. It., 22¾.
Lucena, Lų-sé-nɑ *or* Lɷ-ŧá-ną, *c* Sp., 16¾.
Lucera, Lɷ-çá-rą, *t* Nap., 11.
Lucerne, Lų-sérn, *c*, *canton* and *l* Swit.; pop. of *c* 10.
Lucknow, Lúk-nȣ, *c* Hin., 200.
Ludlow, Lúd-lɷ, *t* Eng., 5⅓: *v* Vt.
Ludlowville, Lúd-lɷ-vil, *v* N-Y. [6¼.
Ludwigsburg, Lɷ́d-wigz-burg, *c* Würt.,
Lugano, Lɷ-gą́-nɷ, *l* and *t* Swit., 5¼.
Lugo, Lɷ́-gɷ, *c* Sp., 7¼; *t* It., 7¼.
Lumberton, Lúm-ber-ton, *v* N-J.; *co t*
Lumpkin, Lúmp-kin, *co t* Ga. [N. C.
Lund, Lɷnd, *c* Swed., 5¼.
Lüneburg, Lẹ́-ne-burg, *t* Ger., 11¾.
Lunenburg, Lų́-nen-burg, *v* Vt., 1¼; *s-pt* Nova Scotia.
Lunéville, Lẹ-na-vél, *t* Fr., 12¼.
Luray, Lų-rá, *co t* Va.; *vs* O., Ia.
Lurgan, Lúr-gan, *t* Ir., 4¾.

Luton, Lų-ton, *t* Eng., 10¾.
Luxemburg, Lúks-em-burg, *ter* and *t* Hol., 11.
Luzerne, Lų-zérn, *co* Pa.
Luzon, Lɷ-zón, *i* Malay Arch., 2,176,900.
Lycoming, Lį-kóm-iŋ, *co* Pa.
Lykens, Lį-kenz, *v* Pa.
Lyman, Lį-man, *v* N-H.
Lyme, Lįm, *vs* N-H., Conn.
Lyme-Regis, Lįm-Ré-jis, *s-pt t* and *par* Eng., 3½.
Lymington, Lím-iŋ-ton, *s-pt t* and *par* Eng., 5¼.
Lynchburg, Línq-burg, *t* Va., 10; *vs* S. C., Tex., Ky., O.
Lyndon Corner, Lín-don Kór-ner, *v* Vt., 1½.
Lyndhurst, Línd-hurst, *v* Eng., 1⅓.
Lynn, Lin, *c* Mass., 14¼.
Lynn-Regis, Lin-Ré-jis, *t* Eng., 19⅓.
Lyons, Lį-onz, second *c* Fr., 156¼; *vs* N-Y., Mich.

# M.

Maad, Mqd, *t* N. Hun., 5¾.
Maassluis, Mqs-lɷs, *t* Neth., 4.
Macao, Mq-kɤ, *s-pt t* China, 30.
Macapa, Mq-kq-pq, *t* Brazil, 6.
MacArthur, Mak-Ar'tur, *v* O.
Macassar, Mq-kqs-ar, *gov* and *t* Is. Celebes, 20; — Strait, separating Is. Borneo and Celebes.
Maçayo, Mq-sį-ɷ, *t* Brazil, 5.
Macclesfield, Mák-lz-fɛld, *t* Eng., 39.
MacConnellsburg, Ma-Kón-elz-burg, *co t* Pa.
MacConnellsville, *v* O.
MacDonough, Mak-Dón-ɷ, *co* Ill.; *co t* Ga.; *v* N-Y.
Macedon, Más-ɛ-don, *v* O.
Macedonia, Mas-ɛ-dó-ni-a, *anc cy* Eu., now in Tur.; *vs* Tenn., Iowa.
Macerata, Mq-ça-rq-tq, *t* Papal Sts., 16.
MacEwensville, Mak-Yų-enz-vil, *v* Pa.
MacGillivray's, Kootanie, Mak-Gil-iv-raz, Kɷ-tq-nį, *or* Flat Bow River, W. Brit. Am., 400 m.
MacGrawville, Mak-Gré-vil, *v* N-Y.
Machias, Ma-çį-as, *co t* Me.; *v* N-Y.
Machias Port, *v* Me.
Machynlleth, Mq-húnt-let, *t* and *par* N. Wales, 1¾.
MacKenzie, Ma-Kén-zɛ, *r* Brit. N. Am., 2500 m.
Mackinac, Mák-in-ɵ, *vs* Mich., 1¼; Ill.
MacKinney, Ma-Kín-i, *co t* Tex.
Macksville, Máks-vil, *vs* Ia., Ky.
MacLaughlinsville, Mak-Lóh-linz-vil, *v* Pa.
MacLean, Mak-Lán, *v* N-Y.
MacLeansborough, Mak-Lánz-bur-ɷ, *co t* Ill.
MacLemoresville, Mak-Lém-orz-vil, *v* Tenn.
Macomb, Ma-kɷm, *co* Mich.; *v* Ill., 1½.
Macon, Ma-kóń, *t* Fr., 12¾.
Macon, Má-kon, *c* Ga., 7; *co t* Miss.; *bayou* La., *r* Mich.
Macoupin, Ma-kɷ-pin, *co* and *cr* Ill.
MacQuarie, Ma-Kwór-ɛ, *rs* E. Aust., 280 m.; Van Diemen's; *s-pt t* N-S. Wales., &c.
Macroom, Ma-krɷm, *t* Ir., 5.
Mactan, Mqk-tqn, *i* Philippines.
MacVeytown, Mak-Vá-tɤn, *v* Pa., 1.
Madagascar, Mad-a-gás-kar, *i* Ind Oc., area 240,000 s. m., pop. 4,700,000.
Madawaska, Mad-a-wás-ka, *p o* Me.
Maddalena, La, Lq Mq-dq-lá-nq, *i* of Sardinia, 12.
Maddaloni, Mq-dq-ló-nɛ, *c* Nap., 11¾.
Madeira, Mq-dé-ra, *i* of Port., in At. Oc., area 300 s. m., pop. 110,000.
Madeira, *or* Madera, Mq-dá-rq, (*or* Cayari, Kį-q-ré,) *r* S. Am., 1500 m.
Madeley, Mád-li, *t* and *par* Eng., 8¼.
Madison, Mád-i-son, *c* Ia., 13; *cap* Wis., 7; *co t* Ga; *vs* Conn., N-Y., N-J.
Madison, Court House, *co ts* Va., Fa.
Madison Springs, *v* Ga.
Madisonville, Mád-i-son-vil, *co ts* Tenn., Ky.
Madjicosima (Mq-ji-kɷ-sé-mq) Islands, *arch* Pac. Oc., 11¼.
Madras, Ma-drás, *c* and *ter div* Br. Ind.; pop. of *c* 720,000, of *ter* 19,901,808.
Madre-de-Dios, (Mq-dra-da-Dé-ɷs,) Archipelago, off s. w. coast Pat.
Madrid, Mád-rid, (Sp. Mq-dréd,) *cap c* Sp., 260.
Mad River, *streams* N-H., Vt., Conn., O.
Madura, Mq-dɷ-ra, *i* Malay Arch., 263; *ft c* Hind., 20.
Mælar, Má-lar, *l* E. Swed., containing 1300 islands.
Maelström, *or* Malstrom, Mál-strem, a whirlpool near Norway.
Maestricht, Mqs-trikt, *t* Hol., 25¼.
Mafra, Mq-frq, *t* Port., 3¼.
Magdalen, Mág-da-len, *sound* s. Pat.
Magdalena, Mag-da-lé-na, *r* S. Am.; *dep* N-Gran.; *r* Bol., called also Ubahy, Ɵ-bq-hé, *t* Mex.
Magdalen Islands, Gulf St. Lawrence.
Magdeburg, Mág-de-burg, *gov* and *c* Prus., 56¼.
Magellan, Mq-jél-an, *strait* bet. Terra del Fuego and Patagonia.

Mageröe, Mág-er-ɷ, *i* Arctic Oc.
Magnolia, Mag-nó-li-ɑ, *v* N-Y., Ill., Wis.
Mahanuddy, Mɑ-ha-núd-i, *r* Ind., 500 m.
Mahaska, Ma-hás-kɑ, *co* Iowa.
Mahavillygunga, Mɑ-hɑ-vil-i-gún-gɑ, *r* Ceylon.
Mahoning, Ma-hón-iŋ, *r* and *co* O.
Mahratta (Mɑ-rɑ́-tɑ) States, Hind.
Maidenhead, Mád-en-hed, *bor* and *t* Eng., 3⅔. [20¾.
Maidstone, Mád-ston, *par* and *t* Eng.,
Main, Man, *r* Ir.; Mịn, *r* Sib., 180 m.
Main, Mayne, *or* Maine, Man, (Ger. Mịn,) nav. *r* Ger., 280 m.
Maine, Man, n. e. N-Eng. St., U. S., area 31,766 s. m., pop. 590,000.
Majorca, Ma-jér-kɑ, *i* Sp. in Med., pop. 179,753.
Makallah, Mɑ-kɑ́-lɑ, *s-pt t* Ar., 4½.
Mako, Mo-kó, *or* Makovia, Mɑ-kó-vi-ɑ, *t* Hun., 21.
Makoqueta, Ma-kó-ke-tɑ, *r* and *v* Io.
Makree *or* Makri, Mɑ́-krɛ, *s-pt t* Tur., 3.
Malabar, Mal-a-bɑ́r, *dis* Br. Ind.; area 6060 s. m., pop. 1,514,909.
Malacca, Mɑ-lák-ɑ, *dis* Malay Pen.; *cap* of the same, pop. 12¼; — Strait, bet. Malay Pen. and Is. Sumatra.
Malaga, Mál-a-gɑ, *s-pt c* and *prov* Sp., pop. of *c* 68,577; of *prov* 438,000.
Malay Archipelago, Ma-lá Ar-ki-pél-a-gɷ, largest group *is* on the globe, s. e. of Asia.
Malay Peninsula, s. part of As.; area 45,000 s. m., pop. 375,000.
Malden, Mél-den, *vs* Mass., 2; N-Y.
Maldive (Mál-dịv) Islands, Ind. Oc.; pop. 175,000.
Maldon, Mél-don, *t* Eng., 5¾.
Maldonado, Mɑl-dɷ-nɑ́-dɷ, *s-pt t* Ur.
Mallicollo, Mɑ-li-kól-ɷ, *is* Pac. Oc.
Mallow, Mál-ɷ, *t* and *watering-place* Ir., 9¼.
Malmaison, Mɑl-ma-sóṅ, chateau in Fr., residence of Empress Josephine.
Malmesburg, Mɑ́mz-ber-i, *t* and *par* Eng., 7.
Malmo, Mál-mẹ, *s-pt t* Swed., 10¼.
Malone, Ma-lón, *v* N-Y., 4½.
Malpas, Mál-pas, *t* and *par* Eng., 5¾.
Malta, Mél-tɑ, *is* Br. in Med.; area 98 s. m., pop. 100,000; *v* O., ¾.
Malton, Mél-ton, *t* Eng., 7⅔.
Malvern, Mé-vern, watering-place Eng., 3¾; Mél-vern, *v* O.
Mamanguape, Mɑ-mɑn-gwɑ́-pa, *r* and *t* Brazil.
Mamaroneck, Mɑ-már-ɷ-nek, *v* N-Y.
Mamers, Mɑ-mɑ́r, *t* Fr., 6.
Mammoth Cave, Edmonson co., Ky.

Mamore, Mɑ-mɷ-rá, *r* Bol., 500 m.
Man, Isle of, *i* Irish Sea, 52¼.
Mana, Mɑ-nɑ́, *r* Fr. Gui., 157 m.
Manacor, Mɑ-nɑ-kór, *t is* Majorca, 10½.
Manahocking, Man-a-hók-iŋ, *v* N-J.
Manasarowar, Mɑ-nɑ-sɑ-rɷ-wɑ́r, *l* Thibet.
Manasquan (Man-ás-kwon) River, N-J.
Manatawny, Man-a-té-ni, *p o* and *cr* Pa.
Manawatu, Mɑ-nɑ-wɑ-tɷ́, *r* N-Zeal.
Manayunk, Man-a-yúŋk, *t* Pa., 7.
Manchester, Mán-çes-ter, manufacturing *c* Eng., 401⅓; *c* N-H., 22; *vs* Vt., Mass., Conn., N-Y., Pa.; *co ts* Tenn., Ky. [50.
Mandavee, Mán-da-vɛ, *s-pt t* Hind.,
Mandingos, Man-díŋ-gɷs, *tr* W. Af., remarkable for advance in civilization.
Maneesa, Mɑ-né-sɑ, *t* As. Minor, 25.
Manfredonia, Man-frɛ-dó-ni-ɑ, *s-pt t* Naples, 5.
Mangaia, Mɑn-gị-ɑ, *i* S. Pac. Oc., 2.
Mangalore, Maŋ-ga-lór, *s-pt t* Br. Ind., 30.
Mangola, Mɑn-gó-lɑ, *is* Malay Arch.
Mangueira, Mɑn-gá-i-rɑ, *l* Brazil.
Manhattan, Man-hát-an, *vs* O., Ia.
Manhattan Island, s. e. part N-Y.
Manheigan (Man-hé-gan) Island, off the coast Me.
Manheim, Mán-hịm, *v* Pa.
Manicouagan, Man-i-kwɑ́-gan, *r*, *l* and *b* C. E.
Manidowish, Man-i-dɷ-íʃ, *r* Wis.
Manila, Mɑ-né-lɑ, *cap c* Is. Luzon, 15.
Manilla, Man-íl-ɑ, *v* Ia.
Manitch, Mɑ-néç, *r* Rus., 300 m.
Manitoba (Man-i-tó-bɑ) Lake, Br. N. Am. [Wis., 2½.
Manitoowoc, Man-i-tɷ-wók, *r* and *co t*
Manitou (Mán-i-tɷ) River, Wis.
Manitoulin, Man-i-tó-lin, *is* Br. Am.
Manlius, Mán-li-us, *v* N-Y., 1½
Mannheim, Mɑ́n-hịm, *t* Baden, 23¼.
Manoel-Alves-Septentrional, Mɑ-nɷ-él-Al′ves-Sep-ten-tri-ɷ-nɑ́l, *r* Brazil, 400 m.
Manona, Ma-nó-nɑ, *co* and *v* Iowa.
Manresa, Mɑn-rá-sɑ, *t* Sp., 13⅓.
Mans, Le, Lẹ-Moṅ, *t* Fr., 22¾.
Mansfield, Mánz-fɛld, *t* and *par* Eng., 10; *co ts* O., 4; La.; *vs* Mass., Conn., N-Y., &c.
Mantchooria, Man-çó-ri-ɑ, *div* China; area 700,000 s. m., pop. 2,500,000.
Mantiqueira, Mɑn-ti-ká-rɑ, *ms* Brazil.
Mantua, Mán-tɑ-ɑ, *c* Aus. It., 30¾.
Manua, Mɑ-nó-ɑ, *is* S. Pac. Oc.
Manzanares, Mɑn-ŧɑ-nɑ́-res, *t* Sp., 8⅔.
Manzanilla, Mɑn-sɑ-nél-yɑ, *b* Mex.

Maracaybo, Mq-rq-kị-bω, *s-pt c* Ven., 8½; *l* and *g* of same.
Maragha, Mq́-rq-gq, *c* Per., 15.
Marajo, Mq-rq-ʒώ, *i* At. Oc., 20.
Maranhao, Mq-rqn-yɤ́n, *c* Brazil, 30; — Island, Brazil, 40.
Marburg, Mq́r-burg, *t* Hesse-Cassel, 8.
Marcellus, Mqr-sél-us, *v* N-Y.
Marchena, Mqr-çá-nq, *t* Sp., 11¾.
Maree, Loch, Loh Mq-ré, *l* Scot.
Marengo, Ma-rén-gω, *vs* N-Y., Ill., Io.
Margarita, Mqr-ga-ré-ta, *i* Caribbean Sea, 15.
Margate, Mq́r-get, *s-pt* Eng., 9¼.
Mariana, Mq-ri-q́-nq, *c* Brazil, 5¼.
Marianna, Ma-ri-án-a, *co t* Fa.
Marias, Las Tres, Lqs Tres Mq-ré-qs, *is* Pac. Oc.
Maria's (Ma-rị-az) River, Nebraska Ter., 300 m.
Marica, Mq-ré-kq, *t* Brazil, 6.
Marie Galante, Mq-ré Gq-lóńt, one of the W. Ind. Is., 12¾.
Marienwerder, Mq-ré-en-ver-der, *c* W. Prus., 7⅔.
Marienzell, Mq-rε-en-tsél, *t* Styria.
Marietta, Ma-ri-ét-a, *t* O., 5; *co t* Ga.; *vs* Pa., Ia.
Marin, Mq-rén, *co* Cal.
Marinduque, Mq-rεn-dώ-ka, *i* Malay Arch.
Marinilla, Mq-ri-nél-yq, *t* N-Gran., 5.
Marion, Má-ri-on, *co ts* Va., N. C., Ga., Ala., Miss., Tex., Ark., Ky., O., Ia., Ill., Io., S. C., &c.
Mariposa, Mar-i-pó-sa, *r*, *co* and *v* Cal.
Marlborough, Mq́rl-bur-ω, *or* Mél-brω, *t* Eng., 5¼; Mq́rl-bur-ω, *vs* N-H., Vt., Mass., N-Y., O.
Marlow, Great, *t* and *par* Eng., 6½.
Marlton, Mq́rl-ton, *v* N-J.
Marmande, Mqr-móńd, *t* Fr., 8⅓.
Marmora, Mq́r-mω-ra, *sea* bet. Eu. and Asia.
Marne, Mqrn, *r* Fr., 210 m.
Maros, Mor-óʃ, *r* Tran., 400 m.
Maros-Vasarhely, Mo-róʃ-Va-ʃqr-hély, *t* Tran., 10.
Marowyne, Mq́-rω-wịn, *r* S. Am., 400 m.
Marquesas, Mqr-ká-sqs, *is* Pac. Oc., 20.
Marquette, Mqr-két, *co* and *co t* Wis.
Marsala, Mqr-sq́-lq, *s-pt c* Sicily, 21.
Marseilles, Mqr-sálz, (Fr. Marseille, Mqr-sály,) *c* Fr., 195; *vs* O., Ia., Ill.
Marshall, Mq́r-ʃal, *co t* N. C., Tex., Mich., 2½; Mo.
Martha's Vineyard, Mq́r-ƫaz Vin-yard, *i* s. e. of Mass.
Martigues, Mqr-tég, *t* Fr., 8½. [121.
Martinique, Mqr-tin-ék, W. Ind. Is.,
Martinsburg, Mq́r-tinz-burg, *co ts* N-Y., ¾; Va., 2½.
Martinsville, Mq́r-tinz-vil, *vs* N-Y., ⅔. Pa., Va.; *co t* Ia., 1.
Martirios, Mqr-té-ri-ωs, *v* Brazil, 7.
Martos, Mq́r-tωs, *t* Sp., 11.
Maryland, Má-ri-land, one of the original U. S.; area, 9,356 s. m., pop. 417,943 whites, 74,723 free blacks, 90,368 slaves,—total, 583,034.
Maryport, Má-ri-pωrt, *s-pt t* Eng., 5¾.
Marysville, *c* Cal., 10; *co ts* Va., Tenn., Mo.; *v* O., ¾.
Masbate, Mqs-bq́-ta, Phil. Is.
Maskegon, Mas-ké-gon, *r* Mich. 300 m.
Mason, Má-son, *co t* Mich., ¾; *v* O., ½.
Massachusetts, Mas-a-çq́-sets, one of the original U. S.; area 7800 s. m., pop. 996,000.
Massa Ducale, Mq́-sq Dω-kq́-la, *c* It., [9¾.
Massapeag, Mas-a-pég, R. R. station Conn.
Massaroony, Mq-sq-rώ-nε, *r* Brit. Gui., [400 m.
Massena, Ma-sé-na, *v* N-Y.
Massillon, Más-i-lon, *t* O., 4; *v* Io.
Massowah, Mq́-sω-wq, *s-pt t* Abys., 4.
Matagorda, Mat-a-gér-da, *b* and *co t* Tex., 1¼.
Matamora, Mat-a-mώ-ra, *v* Tenn.
Matamoras, Mat-a-mώ-ras, *t* Mex., 20; *vs* Pa., Ia.
Matanzas, Mq-tán-zas, *s-pt t* Cuba, 26.
Matareeyeh, Mq-tq-ré-ye, *v* Lower Eg.
Mataro, Mq-tq-rώ, *c* Sp., 13.
Matawamkeag, Mat-a-wóm-keg, *r* and *p o* Me.
Matelica, Mq-tél-i-kq, *t* Cen. It., 7¼.
Matera, Mq-tá-rq, *t* Nap., 11¼.
Mathura, Mút-ra, *t* Brit. Ind., 60.
Matina, Mq-té-nq, *r* and *v* Costa-Rica.
Matlock, Mát-lok, watering-place Eng., 3¾.
Matsmai, Mqts-mị, *c* Japan; *i* Yesso, [50.
Mattapoisett, Mat-a-pé-set, *v* Mass.
Mattawan, Mat-a-wón, *v* Mich.
Mattewan, Mat-ε-wón, *v* N-Y.
Matto-Grosso, Mq́-tω-Grós-ω, *prov* and *c* Brazil, 180.
Maubeuge, Mω-béʒ, *ft t* Fr. 7¾.
Mauch Chunk, Mɐk Çuŋk, *t* Pa., 3½.
Maui, Mɤ́-ε, Sandwich Island, 17⅓.
Maule, Mɤ́-la, *r* Chili, 180 m.
Maulmain, Mɐl-mịn, *s-pt t* Fur. Ind., 10.
Maumee, Mɐ-mé, *r* Ia.; *t* O.
Maurepas, Mώ-rε-pq, *l* e. part La.
Maurice (Mé-ris) River, N-J.
Mauritius, Mɐ-riʃ-i-us, (*or* Isle of Fr. *i* Ind. Oc., 162.
Mauvaise (Mω-váz) River, Wis.
Maxey, Máks-i, *v* Ga.
Maxville, Máks-vil, *vs* Ky., Ia.
Mayari, Mị-q-ré, *s-pt t* Cuba, 3.

Mayenne, Mq-yén, *t* Fr., 10.
Maynooth, Má-noꝺ, *t* Ir., 2¼.
Mayo, Má-ꝏ, *r* Va., N. C.; Mį-ꝏ, Cape Verd Is.; *r* Sonora.
Maypu, Mį-pꝏ́, *r* Chili, 130 m.; *m peak* Andes, 15,000 ft.
May's Landing, *co t* N-J.
Maysville, Máz-vil, *c* Ky., 7; *co ts* N-Y., Va., Ill.; *v* Ia.
Mayville, Má-vil, *v* Wis., ¾.
Mazamet, Mq-zq-má, *t* Fr., 9¾. [12.
Mazatlan, Mqz-at-lq́n, *t* Cinaloa, Mex.,
Mazzara, Mqt-sq́-rq, *t* Sic., 8½.
Mazzarino, Mqt-sq-ré-nꝏ, *t* Sicily, 11½.
Meade, Mɛd, *co* Ky. [*v* Va.
Meadville, Méd-vil, *co ts* Pa., 2⅜; Miss.;
Meaux, Mꝏ, *t* Fr., 10.
Mecca, Mék-ɑ, *c* Arabia, visited annually by 100,000 Mohammedan pilgrims; pop. 28,000.
Mechanicsburg, Mɛ-kán-iks-burg, *vs* O., 1¼; Pa., Ia., &c.
Mechlin, Mék-lin, *c* Belg., 27¼.
Mecklenburg-Schwerin, Mék-len-bɯrh-Σwa-rén, *st* of the German Confederation; pop., 541,449.
Mecklenburg-Strelitz, Mek-len-bɯrh-Strá-lits, *st* German Confederation; pop., 100,000; *cos* Va., N. C.
Medellin, Ma-del-yén, *c* N-Gràn., 14.
Medford, Méd-ford, *v* Mass.
Media, Mé-di-ɑ, *cy* Per.; *co t* Pa., ½.
Medina, Ma-dé-nq, *c* Arabia, 18.
Medina, Mɛ-dį-nɑ, *rs* Eng., Tex.; *v* N-Y.; *co t* O.
Medina-Sidonia, Ma-ꝺé-nq-Sɛ-dó-ni-q, *c* Sp., 10½.
Mediterranean Med-i-ter-á-nɛ-an Sea, Eu., connecting with the Atlantic and the Strait of Gibralter.
Medvieditza, Med-vi-a-dit-sq, *r* Rus.
Meerpoor, Mɛr-pꝏ́r, *t* Sinde, 10.
Meerut, Mɛ-rút, *dis* and *t* Br. Ind.
Meherrin, Mɛ-hér-in, *r* Va., 150 m.
Meigs, Megz, *cos* Tenn., O.
Meigsville, Mégz-vil, *v* Cal.
Meiningen, Mį-niŋ-en, *ft t* Ger., 6¼.
Meissen, Mį-sen, *t* Sax., 9.
Meklong, Ma-klóŋ, *t* Siam, 13.
Me-Kong, Ma-Kóŋ, *rs* As.
Melbourne, Mél-burn, *c* Aust., 50; *i* Pac. Oc.
Melegnano, Ma-len-yq́-nꝏ, *t* Aus. It., 7.
Melfi, Mél-fɛ, *t* Naples, 8½.
Melford, Mél-ford, *v* and *par* Eng., 2½.
Melksham, Mélks-ham, *t* and *par* Eng., 2¾.
Melrose, Mel-rꝏ́z, *burgh* and *par* Scot., 7½; *v* Mass., Tex., Ill.
Meltham, Mél-ꝺam, *vs* Eng. 3¼.
Melton-Mowbray, Mó-brɛ, *t* Eng., 4⅓.
Melun, Me-lúñ, *t* Fr., 7½.
Melville (Mél-vil) Island; off N. Aust., also in the Artic and S. Pac. Ocs.
Memel, Mém-el, *or* Má-mel, *t* Pru., 10.
Memingen, Mém-iŋ-en, *t* Bav., 6¾.
Memphis, Mém-fis, *c* Tenn., 12; *co t* Mo.; anc. *c* Lower Eg.
Memphremagog, ( Mem-frɛ-má-gog ) Lake, Vt.
Menai (Mén-į) Strait, N. Wales.
Menam, Ma-nq́m, *r* S. As., 800 m.
Menard, Men-q́rd, *co* Ill.
Menasha, Men-áʃ-ɑ, *v* Wis., 1¼.
Mende, Moñd, *t* Fr., 6.
Mendham, Ménd-ham, *v* N-J., ½.
Mendocino, Men-dꝏ-sé-nꝏ, *co* Cal.
Mendon, Mén-don, *vs* Mass., N-Y., Mich., Ill., Iowa.
Mendota, Men-dó-tɑ, *v* Ill.; *co t* Min.
Mendoza, Men-dó-zɑ, *r* and *c* La Plata,
Menin, Me-nàñ, *ft t* Belg., 8. [12.
Menomonee, Mɛ-nóm-ꝏ-nɛ, *r* Wis.; — Falls, *v* Wis.
Mentz, Mentz, *c* Hesse-Darmstadt, 32.
Mequanigo, Mɛ-kwán-i-gꝏ, *v* Wis., ½.
Mequinez, Mék-i-nez, *c* Morocco, 60.
Mequon, Mɛ-kwón, *v* Wis.
Mercede, Mer-sád, *r* Cal.; — City, *t* Cal.
Mercer, Mę́r-ser, *co t* Pa., 1.
Mercersburg, Mę́r-serz-burg, *t* Pa., 1¼.
Meredith (Mér-ɛ-diꝺ) Bridge, *co t* N-H.
Meredosia, Mer-ɛ-dó-ʃi-ɑ, *v* Ill. [8.
Mergui *or* Merghi, Mer-gé, *t* Br. Ind.,
Merida, Mér-i-ꝺq, *c* Sp., 6.
Merida, Mér-i-dq, *cap c* Yucatan, 23; *t* Ven., 4.
Meriden, Mér-i-den, *v* Conn.
Merrimack, Mér-i-mak, *r* N-Eng., 110 m.
Merseburg, Mę́r-se-bɯrh, *t* Prus. Sax.,
Mersey, Mę́r-zɛ, *r* Eng., 60 m. [11½.
Merthyr-Tydvil, Mę́r-ꝺer-Tíd-vil, *t* and *par* S. Wales, 63.
Meshed, Méʃ-ed, *c* Per., 45.
Mesilla (Ma-sél-yq) Valley, tract land s. part N-Mex. [*cy* As.
Mesopotamia, Mes-ꝏ-pꝏ-tá-mi-ɑ, anc.
Messina, Me-sé-nq, *c* Sicily, 97. — Strait, separating Sicily from Italy.
Mestre, Més-tra, *t* Aus. It., 6.
Meta, Má-tq, *r* S. Am., 500 m.
Metamora, Met-a-mó-rɑ, *co t* Ill.
Metapa, Ma-tq́-pq, *t* Guat., 8.
Metetecunk, Mɛ-té-tɛ-kuŋk, *r* N-J.
Methuen, Méꝺ-yq-en, *v* Mass.
Metomen, Mɛ-tó-men, *v* Wis. [Ill., ⅜.
Metropolis (Mɛ-tróp-ꝏ-lis) City, *co t*
Metz, Mets, *ft c* Fr., 43½.
Meuse, Mqz, *r* rising in Fr., courses through Belg., Hol 434 m.

Mexico, Méks-i-kω, Sp. *rep* s. N. Am., having the following states and territories: Aguascalientes, Chihuahua, Chiapa, Cinaloa, Cohahuila, Durango, Guanajuato, Guerrero, Jalisco, Mexico, Michoacan, New Leon, Oajaca, Puebla, Queretaro, San Luis Potosi, Sonora, Tabasco, Tamaulipas, Vera Cruz, Yucatan, Zacatecas, Tlaxcala, Colima, Tehuantepec, Lower California, Isla de Carmen; area 834,140 s. m., pop. 7,852,394.
Mexico, *cap* of the Republic, 200; *vs* N-Y. ¾, Pa., O., Ia.; *co t* Mo.
Mezen, Mez-án, *v* and *r* Rus., 450 m.
Mézières, Ma-zi-ą̂r, *ft t* Fr., 4.
Miako *or* Meaco, Mε-ą̂-kω, *c* Japan, 500.
Miami, Mį-ám-i, *v* Fa.
Miami River, (Little and Big,) O.
Miamisburg, Mį-ám-iz-burg, *v* O.
Miamisville, *v* O.
Miamitown, Mį-ám-i-tʊn, *v* O.
Miami University, Oxford, O.
Miarim, Mε-q-réṅ, *r* Brazil, 350 m.
Miava, Mε-ó-vo, *t* Hun., 10.
Michigan, Miʃ-i-gan, n. w. of U. S.; area 56,243 s. m., pop. 525,000; *l* within and w. of the state.
Michigan City, *v* Ia., 3.
Michigantown, Miʃ-i-gan-tʊn, *v* Ia.
Michigan University, Ann Arbor, Mich.
Michilimackinac, Miʃ-il-i-mák-in-ɵ, *co* Mich. [Superior.
Michipicoton, Miʃ-i-pi-kó-ton, *b* Lake
Michoacan, Mi-çω-q-kq̂n, *st* Mex.; area 22,993 s. m., pop. 491,679.
Micmac, Mik-mak, *tr Ind* Br. Am.
Middelburg, Mid-el-burg, *t* Hol., 16.
Middleborough, Mid-l-bur-ω, *v* Mass., 5⅓. [O.
Middlebourne, Mid-l-bωrn, *co t* Va.; *v*
Middleburg, Mid-l-burg, *vs* N-Y., Pa., O., Va., &c. [O., &c.
Middlebury, Mid-l-ber-i, *vs* Vt., Conn.,
Middleport, Mid-l-pωrt, *vs* N-Y. 1, O.; *co t* Ill. [*par* Eng., 7½.
Middlesborough, Mid-lz-bur-ω, *r-pt* and
Middlesex, Mid-l-seks, *vs* Pa.
Middleton, Mid-l-ton, *t* and *par* Eng., 5¾; *t* Ir., 6.
Middletown, Mid-l-tʊn, *c* Conn., 4¼; *vs* O. 1½, Pa., N-Y., Del.
Middletown Point, *v* N-J.
Middleway, Mid-l-wa, *v* Va., ½. [4½.
Middlewich, Mid-l-wiç, *t* and *par* Eng.,
Middle Yuba, Yų̂-bα, *r* Cal.
Midhurst, Mid-hurst, *t* and *par* Eng., 7.
Midnapoor, Mid-na-pώr, *dis* and *t* Br. India.
Midway, Mid-wa, *vs* Ga., Ky., Pa., S. C.
Mifflinsburg, Mif-linz-burg, *v* Pa.
Mifflintown, Mif-lin-tʊn, *co t* Pa.
Milam, Mį-lam, *co ts* Tex.
Milan, Mil-an, *prov* and *c* Aus. It., 160
Milan, Mį-lan, *vs* O. 3, Ia., Ill., &c.
Milazzo, Mε-lq̂t-sω, *s-pt t* Sic., 7.
Milbourn, Mil-burn, *v* Ky. [Eng., 4⅓.
Mildenhall, Mil-den-hɵl, *t* and *par*
Miletus, Mį-lé-tus, ruined *c* As. Minor.
Milford, Mil-ford, *s-pt t* S. Wales, 3; *vs* Eng. 1, N-H., Mass., Conn., N-Y., N-J., Del., Va., O., Ia., &c.; *co t* Pa.
Milford Centre, *vs* N-Y., O.
Military Frontier, Mil-i-ta-ri Frún-tεr; *cy* Aus.; area 12,922 s. m., pop., [1,747,733.
Millau, Mε-ló, *t* Fr., 10.
Millbrook, Mil-brʊk, *v* O.
Millburn, Mil-burn, *v* Ill.
Millbury, Mil-ber-i, *v* Mass. [*v* Ill.
Milledgeville, Mil-ej-vil, *cap* Ga., 3½;
Millersburg, Mil-erz-burg, *co t* O.; *vs* Pa., Ky., O., Ia., Ill.
Millerstown, Mil-erz-tʊn, *vs* Pa., 1.
Millersville, Mil-erz-vil, *vs* Pa., Md., O., Ia.
Millerville, Mil-er-vil, *v* N-Y.
Milleville, Mil-vil, *v* N-Y.
Mill Grove, *vs* O., Ia.
Mill Hall, *v* Pa.
Millheim, Mil-hįm, *v* Pa.
Millport, Mil-pωrt, *vs* N-Y., Pa.
Millville, Mil-vil, *vs* Mass., N-J. 1½, Mo., Iowa, &c.
Millwood, Mil-wʊd, *v* O., ½.
Milo, Mé-lω, *i* Grecian Arch., 4.
Milo, Mį-lω, *v* Me., ¾.
Milton, Mil-ton, *vs* N-H., Mass., Pa. 2, N. C. 1¼, Miss., Ia.; *co t* Fa.
Miltonsburg, Mil-tonz-burg, *v* O.
Miltonville, Mil-ton-vil, *v* O. [do.
Milwaukee, Mil-wé-kε, *c* Wis., 35; *r*
Minchinhampton, Min-çin-hámp-ton, *t* and *par* Eng., 4½. [74.
Mindanao, Min-dq-nq̂-ω, *i* Malay Arch.,
Minden, Min-den, *ft t* Prus., 12¾; *v* La., 1.
Mindoro, Min-dó-rω, Philippine *i*, 29¾.
Mineral Point, *co t* Wis., 3.
Minersville, Mį-nerz-vil, *t* Pa., 4
Minerva, Mi-nér-vα, *vs* Ky., O.
Minho, Mén-yω, *prov* and *r* Port.
Minisink, Min-i-siŋk, *v* N-Y. [½.
Minneapolis, Min-ε-áp-ω-lis, *co t* Min.,
Minnesota, Min-ε-só-tα, *ter* n. w. U. S., area 166,025 s. m., pop. from 10,000 [to 15,000.
Minnesota City, *co t* Min.
Minnetonka, Min-ε-tóŋ-kα, *l* Min., 28 m.
Minni Wakan, Min-ε Wɵ-kq̂n, *l* Min. Ter., 40 by 12 m.
Minorca, Min-ór-kα, *i* of Sp., Med., 40.

Minot, Mi-nót, *v* Me.
Minsk, Minsk, *gov* and *t* Rus., 23.
Miösen, Mɛ-ę́-zen, *l* Nor., 55 m.
Miquelon, Mɛ-ke-lóṅ, *is* off coast Newfoundland; area 85 s. m., pop. 510.
Miramichi, Mir-a-mi-ʃé, *b, r* and *pt* N-Brunswick.
Miranda, Mi-rán-dɑ, *v* N-C.
Mirandola, Mɛ-rq̇n-dɷ-lq, *ft t* It., 6.
Mirim, Mɛ-réṅ, *l* S. Am.
Mirzapoor, Mẹr-za-pɷ́r, *t* Hin., 100.
Mishawaka, Miʃ-a-wé-kɑ, *v* Ia., 2½.
Miskolcz, Miʃ-kólts, *t* Hun., 30.
Missisque, Mi-sís-kwɛ, *r* Vt.
Mississinewa, Mis-i-sín-ɛ-wɑ, *r* Ia.
Mississippi, Mis-i-síp-i, *r* N. Am.; with the Missouri, its principal tributary, the longest river in the world; 4350 m., including the Missouri.
Mississippi, one of the s. U. S.; area 47,156 s. m; pop. 295,718 whites, 930 free blacks, 309,300 slaves,—total, 605,948.
Missouri, Mi-zɷ́-ri, one of the s. w. U. S.; area 67,380 s. m.; pop. 592,004 whites, 2,618 free blacks, 87,422 slaves,—total, 682,044.
Missouri Territory, now divided into Kanzas and Nebraska.
Missouri University, Columbia, Mo.
Mitau, Mé-tɤ, *t* Rus., 28.
Mittineague, Mit-i-nég, *p o* Mass.
Mitylene, Mit-i-lé-nɛ, *i* Gr. Arch., 40.
Mobile, Mɷ-bél, *r* and *c* Ala., 20½; — Bay, s. w. Ala.
Mocha, Mó-ɡq, *i* of Chili; *t* Arabia.
Modena, Mód-en-q, *st* It.; area 2,073 s. m.; pop. 586,458; *c* do., 27½.
Modica, Mód-i-kq, *t* Sicily, 17½.
Möen, Mę́-en, *i* of Den., 13¾.
Moffat, Móf-at, *t* and *par* Scot., 2⅓.
Mogadore, Mog-a-dɷ́r, *ft c* Morocco, 17; *v* O. [Brazil.
Mogi-das-Cruzes, Mó-ʒɛ-dqs-Krɷ́-zes, *t*
Moguer, Mɷ-gq̇r, *t* Sp., 6½.
Mogul, Mɷ-gúl, *empire*, Hin.
Mohacs, Mɷ-hq̇ç, *t* S. Hun., 10. [Y.
Mohawk, Mó-hɵk, *r* N-Y., 160 m.; *v* N-
Moheelev, Mɷ-*h*é-lev, *t* Rus., 16.
Mohiccanville, Mɷ-hik-an-vil, *v* O.
Moissac, Mwq-sq̇k, *t* Fr., 10⅔.
Moldau, Mól-dɤ, *r* Boh., 200 m.
Moldavia, (Mol-dá-vi-ɑ,) Principality of, *st* S. Eu.; area 18,000 s. m., pop. 1,419,105.
Molfetta, Mol-fét-q, *s-pt t* Nap., 13.
Moline, Mɷ-lén, *v* Ill.
Molino del Rey, Mɷ-lé-nɷ del Ra, range of stone buildings near city of Mexico; *p o* Ark.

Molton, (Mɷl-ton,) South, *t* and *par* Eng., 4½.
Molua, Mɷ-lɷ́-q, *nation* in int. Af.
Moluccas, Mɷ-lúk-az, *or* Spice Islands, group in the Malay Arch.
Mombas, Mom-bq̇s, *i* and *t* Af., 6.
Mompox, Mom-pó*h*, *t* N-Gran., 10.
Monastir, Mɷ-nqs-tér, *s-pt t* N-Af., 12; *c* Eu. Tur., 15.
Moncalieri, Mon-kq-li-á-rɛ, *t* Pied., 8.
Mondego, Mon-dá-gɷ, nav. *r* Bra., 180 m.
Mondovi, Mon-dɷ-vé, *t* Pied., 16.
Monee, Mɷ-né, *v* Ill. [Ind., 30.
Monghir *or* Mungeer, Muŋ-gẹ́r, *t* Br.
Mongolia, Mon-gó-li-ɑ, *reg* Asia; area 1,400,000 s. m., pop. 2,000,000.
Moniteau, Mon-i-tó, *co* and *v* Mo.
Monmouth, Món-muŧ, *t* and *par* Eng., 6; *v* Me.; *co t* Ill.
Monomoezi, Mɷ-nɷ-mɷ-á-zɛ, *em* Af.
Monomotapa, Mɷ-nɷ-mɷ-tq̇-pq, *em* Af.
Monongahela, Mɷ-non-ga-hé-lɑ, *r* Pa., 150 m. — City, opp. Pittsburg, Pa., 1½.
Monongalia, Mɷ-non-gá-li-ɑ, *co* Va.
Monopoli, Mɷ-nóp-ɷ-lɛ, *t* Nap., 16.
Monreale, Mon-ra-q̇-la, *t* Sic., 13.
Monroe, Mon-rɷ́, *co ts* Mich. 4, Wis., La., Ga., N. C.; *vs* N-Y., Tenn.
Monroeville, Mon-rɷ́-vil, *vs* O.; *co t* Cal.
Mons, Mɷṅs, *ft t* Belg., 23¼.
Monserrat, Mon-ser-q̇t, *m* Sp.
Monson, Món-son, *v* Mass.
Montague, Món-ta-gq, *vs* Mass. 1½, Va.; *i* Pac. Oc.
Montauban, Mɷṅ-tɷ-bóṅ, *t* Fr., 24¾.
Montauk (Mon-tɵ́k) Point, *prom* L. I.
Montbéliard, Mɷṅ-ba-li-q̇r, *t* Fr., 6¼.
Mont Blanc, Mɷṅ Blóṅ, highest *m* in Eu., 15,810 ft. high.
Montbrison, Mɷṅ-brɛ-zɷ́ṅ, *t* Fr., 6.
Montcalm, Mont-kq̇m, *co* and *co t* Mich.
Monte-Christi, Mon-ta-Krís-tɛ, *t* Hayti, 3. [maica, 4.
Montego (Mon-té-gɷ) Bay, *s-pt t* Ja-
Montélimart, Mɷṅ-ta-lɛ-mq̇r, *c* Fr., 10.
Montello, Mon-tél-ɷ, *v* Wis., ¼.
Montenegro, Mon-ta-ná-grɷ, *ind* Eu. Tur., 100.
Mentereau, Mɷṅ-te-rɷ́, *t* Fr., 6½.
Monterey, Mon-ta-rá, *c* Mex., 12; *co* and *c* Cal., 2. [Alps.
Monte-Rosa, Mon-ta-Rɷ́-sq, *m* Pennine
Monte San Giuliano, Món-ta Sqn Jɷ-li-q̇-nɷ, *t* Sic., 7½.
Montevallo, Mon-tɛ-vál-ɷ, *v* Ala.
Montevideo, Mon-tɛ-víd-i-ɷ, *s-pt c, cap* Uruguay, S. Am., 12.
Montezuma, Mon-tɛ-zq̇-mɑ, *vs* N-Y., Ga., Ia., &c.

Montgomery, Mont-gúm-er-i, *cap* Ala., 7; *co t* Tex.; *vs* N-Y. 1¼, O.
Monticello, Mon-ti-sél-ɷ, residence of Thomas Jefferson, Va.; *v* N-Y., 1¼; *co ts* Ga., Fa., Miss., Ark., Tenn., Ky., Ia., Ill.
Montilla, Mon-tél-yq, *t* Sp., 13¼.
Montluçon, Mɷṅ-lę-sóṅ, *t* Fr., 9.
Montmartre, Mɷṅ-mqrt-r', *t* Fr., 23¼.
Montmorency, Mɷṅ-mɷ-roṅ-sé, *v* Fr., 2¼; Mont-mɷ-rén-si, *co* Mich.; *r* C. E.
Montoro, Mon-tó-rɷ, *c* Sp., 10¾.
Montour, Mon-tɷ́r, *co* Pa.
Montoursville, Mon-tɷ́rz-vil, *v* Pa., ⅓.
Montpelier, Mont-pél-yer, *cap* Vt., 2⅓; *vs* Ga., Ia.
Montpellier, Mont-pél-i-er, *c* Fr., 37⅝.
Montreal, Mon-trɛ-él, *c* C. E., 58. Island, on which the city is built, is 32 by 10 m. — River, Wis.
Montrose, Mont-róz, *s-pt t* Scot., 15¼; *co t* Pa., 1½; *v* Iowa, ¾.
Montrouge, Mɷṅ-rɷ́ʒ, *v* Fr., 9¼. [8.
Montserrat, Mont-ser-át, Br. W. Ind. *i*,
Monza, Món-zq, *c* Aus., 18¼.
Mooltan, Mɷl-tq́n, old *c* of Punjab, 80.
Moorefield, Mɷ́r-fɛld, *co t* Va.; *v* O.
Mooreshill, Mɷ́rz-hil, *v* Ia., ¼.
Moorestown, Mɷ́rz-tɤn, *v* N-J., 1.
Mooresville, Mɷ́rz-vil, *v* Ia., ½.
Moorshedabad, Mɷr-ʃɛ-da-bq́d, *c* Br. Ind., 165.
Moose, Mɷs, *r* Br. N. Am., 250.
Moosehead (Mɷs-héd) Lake, Me., 35 by 10 m.
Moquehua, Mɷ-ká-wq, *c* Peru, 32½.
Moquelumne, Mɷ-kál-um-nɛ, *r* Cal.
Moradabad, Mɷ-rq-dq-bq́d, *t* Br. Ind.,
Morano, Mɷ-rq́-nɷ, *t* Nap., 8. [32⅗.
Morant, Mɷ-ránt, *t* Jamaica, 7.
Moratalla, Mɷ-rq-tq́-lq, *t* Sp., 8.
Morava, Mɷ-rq́-vɑ, *r* Servia, 130 m.
Moravia, Mɷ-rá-vi-ɑ, *prov* Aus.; area 10,239, pop. 2,238,424; *v* N-Y.; *p o* Io.
Morea, Mɷ-ré-ɑ, *or* Peloponnesus, Pel-ɷ-pon-é-sus, *pen* Greece.
Moreau, Mɷ-ró, *p o* N-Y. [Tenn.
Morgan (Mér-gan) Court-House, *co t*
Morganfield, Mér-gan-fɛld, *co t* Ky.
Morgantown, *co ts* Va. 1, N. C., Ky.; *v*
Moriah, Mɷ-rį-ɑ, *v* N-Y., 1. [Ia.
Morlaix, Mɘr-lá, *t* Fr., 12⅓.
Morocco, Mɷ-rók-ɷ, *c* and *em* Af.; area 222,560 s. m., pop. 8,000,000.
Moron, Mɷ-rón, *t* Sp., 10¼.
Morpeth, Mér-peŧ, *t* and *par* Eng., 10.
Morris, Mór-is, *co t* Ill., 1.
Morrisiana, Mor-is-i-á-nɑ, *v* N-Y.
Morristown, Mór-is-tɤn, *vs* Vt., N-Y., Tenn., O., Ia., &c.; *co t* N-J.
Morrisville, *v* Vt. ⅓, Pa., Ia.; *co t* N-Y.
Morrow, Mór-ɷ, *v* O., 1.
Mors, Mɘrs, *i* of Den., 6.
Mortara, Mɘr-tq́-rq, *t* Pied., 5⅓.
Mortimer, Mér-ti-mer, *v* Ill.
Mortonsville, Mér-tonz-vil, *v* Ky., ⅓.
Moscow, Mós-kɷ, *gov* Rus.; area 12,609 s. m., pop. 1,349,000; *cap c* 350; *vs* N-Y., Ky., Tenn., O., Mich., Ia., &c.
Moselle, Mɷ-zél, *r* Fr. and Ger., 328 m.;
Mosiertown, Mó-ʒer-tɤn, *v* Pa. [*v* Ill.
Moskva, Mósk-vq, *r* Moscow, 200 m.
Mosquito (Mos-ké-tɷ) Territory, *cy* Cen. Am.; area 34,000 s. m.
Mosul *or* Mosel, Mó-sul *or* Mó-sul, *t* As. Tur., 40.
Motagua, Mɷ-tq́-gwq, *r* Cen. Am.
Motril, Mɷ-trél, *c* Sp., 10¼.
Mottville, Mót-vil, *v* Mich., ½.
Moulins, Mɷ-láṅ, *t* Fr., 14¾.
Moulton, Mól-ton, *co t* Ala.
Mount Auburn, Mɤnt Θ'burn, *cemetery*, Cambridge, Mass.; *vs* Ia., Ill.
Mount Carmel, Kq́r-mel, *vs* Ky., Ia.; *co t* Ill., 1½.
Mount Carroll, Kár-ol, *co t* Ill., ¾.
Mount Clemens, Klém-ens, *co t* Mich., 2½.
Mount Desert, Déz-ert, *i* coast Me., ¾.
Mount Etna, Et'nɑ, *v* Ia.
Mount Gilead, Gíl-ɛ-ad, *vs* Va., Ky., O.
Mount Healthy, Hél-ŧi, *vs* O., Ia.
Mount Holly, Hól-i, *co t* N-J., 2; *v* O.
Mount Holyoke, Hó-li-ɷk *or* Hól-yok, *mt* Mass.
Mount Hope, *vs* N-Y., Pa.
Mount Ida, Ɨ'dɑ, *co t* Ark.
Mount Jackson, Ják-son, *vs* Pa., Va.
Mount Joy, Jɘ, *v* Pa.
Mount Morris, Mór-is, *vs* N-Y., Ill.
Mount Pleasant, Pléz-ant, *co ts* Tex., Ky., Iowa; *vs* Pa. ½, Tenn., O., Ia.
Mount Sidney, Síd-ni, *v* Va.
Mount St. Elias, Ɛ-lį-as, *vol m* N. Am., 17,900 ft.; var. *ms* Eu. [*v* O.
Mount Sterling, Stér-liŋ, *co ts* Ky., Ill.;
Mount Tahawus, Ta-hé-wus, *peak* of Adirondack Mts., N-Y.
Mount Union, Yq́n-yon, *vs* Pa., O.
Mount Vernon, Vér-non, residence of George Washington, Va.; *t* O., 5.; *co ts* Ga., Ky., Ia., Ill., Mo.; *vs* N-Y., Wis.
Mount Washington, Wóʃ-iŋ-ton, *peak* White Mts., N-H.; *vs* Pa., Ky., O.
Mount Zion, Zį-on, *v* Ga., ½.
Moyamensing, Mɘ-a-mén-siŋ, *sub* Philadelphia, Pa., 27.
Mozambique, Mɷ-zam-bék, *c* Af., 6. — Channel, *str* Ind. Oc. [250 m.
Msta, M-stq, *or* Masta, Mq-stq́, *r* Rus.,

Muhalitch, Mu-q-léç, *t* As. Minor, 11.
Muhlenburg, Mų-len-burg, *co* Ky.
Mühlhausen, Mel-hʊ-zen, *t* Prus., 13¾.
Mülhausen, Mél-hʊ-zen, *t* Fr., 29¾.
Mülheim-am-Ruhr, Mél-him-qm-Rœr, *t* Prus., 10¼.
Mull, Mul, Hebrides *i*, 15¼. [4¾.
Mullingar, Mul-iŋ-gár, *t* and *par* Ir.,
Mulweeya *or* Muluia, Mul-wé-yq, *r* Morocco, 350 m. [Ia., 1½.
Muncie, Mún-se, *or* Muncietown, *co t*
Muncy, Mún-si, *v* Pa., 1. [½.
Munfordsville, Mún-fordz-vil, *co t* Ky.,
Munich, Mų-nik, *cap c* Bav., 95½.
Munster, Mún-ster, *prov* Ir.
Münster, Mén-ster, *cap c* Westphalia, 25.
Murcia, Múr-ʃi-a, *c* Sp., 55.
Murfreesborough, Múr-frez-bur-œ, *v* N. C.; *co ts* Ark., Tenn.
Murphy, Múr-fi, *co t* N. C.
Murphysborough, Múr-fiz-bur-œ, *co t* Ill.
Murray, Múr-a, *r* Australia; *co t* Ky.
Murrumbidgee, Múr-um-bíj-e, *r* Australia, 400 m.
Murviedro, Mœr-vi-á-drœ, *ft t* Sp., 7½.
Muscat, Mus-kát, *st* and *c* Arabia.
Muscatine, Mus-ka-tén, *co t* Iowa, 6.
Muscoda, Mus-kó-da, *v* Wis.
Muscogee, Mus-kó-ge, *co* Ga.
Musconetcong, Mus-kœ-nét-koŋ, *r* N-J.
Muscovy, Mús-kœ-vi, applied to Russia.
Muskingum, Mus-kíŋ-gum, *r* O., 110 m.
Musselburgh, Mús-el-bur-œ, *s-pt t* Scot., 7. [6.
Myconus, Mík-œ-nus, *i* Grecian Arch.,
Myerstown, Mį-erz-tʊn, *v* Pa., 1.
Mystic, Mis-tik, *r* and *v* Conn.

# N.

Nabloos, Nq-blós, *c* Pal., 8. [Tex.
Nacogdoches, Nak-œ-dó-çez, *co* and *v*
Nacoochee, Na-kó-çe, *v* Ga.
Nadudvar, No-dœd-vár, *t* Hun., 6¼.
Nagaranu, Nq-gq-rq-nó, *t* Hin., 6.
Nagasaki, Nq-ga-sá-ke, *c* Japan, 65.
Nagore, Nq-gór, *ts* Br. Ind., 40.
Nagpoor, Nqg-pór, *ter* India; area 76,-432 s. m., pop. 4,650,000; *c* do., 115.
Nahant, Na-hánt, *v* Mass.
Nailsea, Nál-se, *v* Eng., 2½.
Nain, Nįn, *t* Hin., 10.
Nairai, Nį-rį, Feejee *i*, Pac. Oc.
Nairn, Nqrn, *co* and *t* Scot., 3½.
Nakhitchevan, Nq-ket-ʃe-ván, *t* Rus, 10.
Namalouk, Nq-mq-lók, Islands, Pac. Oc.
Namur, Ná-mur, *prov* and *c* Belg., 24⅓.
Nanas, No-nóʃ, *t* Hun., 7¾.
Nanche, Nqn-çá, *c* China, 200.
Nancy, Nán-si, (Fr. Noñ-sé,) *c* Fr., 45.
Nanking, Nqn-kíŋ, *or* Nankin, Nqn-kin, *c* China, 400.
Nan-Ling, Nqn-Líŋ, *ms* China.
Nantasket, Nan-tás-ket, *pen* Mass.
Nantes, Nants, *c* Fr., built partly on islands in the Loire, 96½.
Nanticoke, Nán-ti-kœk, *v* Pa.
Nantucket, Nan-túk-et, *co t* Mass., 8.
Nantwich, Nánt-iç, *t* Eng., 5½.
Napa, Ná-pa, *r*, *co* and *t* Cal.
Napanee, Nap-a-né, *v* C. W. [C. E., 1.
Napierville, Ná-per-vil, *co t* Ill., 2½; *v*
Naples, Ná-plz, *k*, *c* and *b* It.; area of *k* 32,571 s. m., pop. 6,610,873; pop. *c*, 400; *vs* Me., N-Y., I
Napo, Ná-pœ, *r* S. Am., 500 m.
Napoleon, Na-pó-le-on, *vs* Ark. 1, O., Ia. ⅔.
Napoleonville, Na-pó-le-on-vil, *v* La.
Naponock, Náp-œ-nok, *v* N-Y.
Naraul, Nq-rél, *t* Hin., 6.
Narberth, Nár-berθ, *bor* S. Wales, 1½.
Narbonne, Nqr-bón, *c* Fr., 13.
Narborough, Nár-bur-œ, Islands, S. Pac.
Nardo, Nár-dœ, *t* Nap., 8.
Narew, Ná-rev, *r* Rus., 200 m.
Naro, Ná-rœ, *t* Sic., 10.
Narraganset, Nar-a-gán-set, Bay, R. I.
Narraingunge, Nar-įn-gúnj, *t* Br. Ind.,
Narva, Nár-vq, *ft t* Rus., 3. [15.
Nashport, Náʃ-pœrt, *v* O.
Nashua, Náʃ-yų-a, *r* and *t* N-H., 5¾.
Nashville, Náʃ-vil, *cap c* Tenn., 20; *co ts* Ia., Ill.; *vs* N. C., Tex., O.
Nassau, Nás-e, *st* Ger., pop. 429,341; *vs* N-Y., Pa., Iowa; *c* Bahama Islands, 7.
Nassuck, Nq-súk, *c* Br. Ind., 30.
Natal, Nq-tál, *cy* Af., bel. to. Gr. Br.; area 18,000 s. m., pop. 121,000; *ts* Brazil 10, Sumatra.
Natchez, Náç-ez, *c* Miss., 6; *vs* O., Ia.
Natchitoches, Naç-i-tóç-ez, *par* and *co*
Natick, Ná-tik, *v* Mass., 2¾. [*t* La.
Naugatuck, Ne-ga-túk, *v* Conn.
Naumburg, Nʊm-burh, *t* Ger., 12¾.
Nauplia, Né-pli-a, *ft s-pt t* Gr., 15; *g* Ægean Sea.
Nauvoo (Ne-vó) City, Ill., 2.
Navarre, Na-vár, *prov* Sp.; area 4,069 s. m., pop. 280,000.

Navaza, Nq-vq́-sq, *i* Caribbean Sea.
Navigator's, Náv-i-ga-torz, *or* Samoan, Sa-mó-an, Islands, populous *is*, Pac.
Naxos, Náks-os, *i* Grecian Arch., 20.
Nayoe *or* Nayoo, Nį-ó, *is* Malay Arch.
Nazareth, Náz-a-reŧ, *ts* Pal., Pa. ½.
Nazareth, Nq-zq-rét, *ts* Belg. 5⅓, Bra.
Naze, Nq́-ze, *cape* Nor.; *headland* Eng.
Ne, Na, *v* Sard. States, 3½.
Neagh, Lough, Lo*h* Na, *l* Ir.
Neath, Nɛŧ, *r* and *bor* S. Wales, 6.
Nebraska, Nɛ-brás-ka, *ter* U. S., organized in 1854; area 335,882 s. m.; *v* Io.
Neches, Néç-ez, *r* Tex., 100 m.
Nechow, Na-çŏ, *t* China, 30.
Neckalofa, Nek-q-ló-fq, *t* island of Tonga, Friendly Islands, 2.
Neckar, Nék-ar, *r* Ger., 210 m.
Necosta, Nɛ-kós-ta, *co* Mich. [3¾.
Nederbrakel, Ná-der-brq-kel, *t* Belg.,
Nedjed, Néj-ed, interior portion of Arabia. [Brunswick.
Negowac, Neg-ɷ-wák, Indian *v* New
Negros, Ná-grɷs, Philippine *i*.
Neilgherry, Nɛl-gér-ɛ, Mts., S. India.
Neisse, Nį-se, *t* Prus. Silesia, 17⅓.
Neiva *or* Neva, Ná-vq, *r* Rus., 300 m.
Nekimi, Nék-i-mį, *v* Wis.
Nellore, Nel-ór, *t* Br. Ind.
Nelson, Nél-son, *vs* N-Y., O., N-Brun.
Nelsonville, Nél-son-vil, *v* O.
Nemi, Ná-mɛ, *l* and *v* Cen. It.
Nenagh, Ná-na, *t* Ir., 9½.
Nene, Nen, *r* Eng. [*v* Wis.
Neosho, Nɛ-ó-ʃɷ, *r* Kanzas; *co t* Mo.;
Neosho City, a vegetarian settlement, Kanzas.
Nepaul, Nɛ-pól, *ind cy* Hin.; area 53,000 s. m., pop. 2,000,000.
Nepenski, Nɛ-pén-skį, *v* Wis.
Nephi (Né-fį) City, *v* Utah.
Neponset (Nɛ-pón-set) Village, Mass.
Nérac, Na-rq́k, *t* Fr., 7¼.
Nerbudda, Ner-búd-a, *r* India, 620 m.
Nescopeck, Nés-kɷ-pek, *m* and *v* Pa.
Nesochaque, Nes-ɷ-çá-kwɛ, River, N-J.
Nesqually, Nes-kwól-i, *r* Wash. Ter.
Nèthe, Ná-te, *r* Belg.
Netherlands, Néđ-er-landz, called also Kingdom of Holland, *cy* in the western part of Eu., embracing the following provinces: North Brabant, Gelderland, South Holland, North Holland, Zealand, Utrecht, Friesland, Overyssel, Groningen, Drenthe, Limburg; area 12,662 s. m., pop. 3,767,671.
Nethou, Pic, Pɛk Ne-tó, highest *peak* of the Pyrenees, 11,168 ft.
Neu-Brandenburg, Nɷ-Brq́n-den-bɷr*h*, *t* Meck.-Strelitz, 6.
Neuburg, Nɷ́-bɷr*h*, *t* Bav., 6⅓.
Neufchatel, Nęʃ-q-tél, *l*, *canton* and *t* Swit., 7¾.
Neuhausel, Nɷ́-hɷ-sel, *t* Hun., 6¾.
Neuilly-sur-Seine, Nę-yɛ́-sęr-San, *t* Fr., 16.
Neurode, Nɷ́-rɷ-de, *t* Prus. Silesia, 5⅓.
Neusatz, Nɷ́-sqts, *t* Hun., 17½.
Neuse, Nųs, *r* N. C., 300 m.
Neú-Shehr, Na-ɷ-ʃe-r', *t* As. Tur., 15.
Neusiedl, Nɷ́-sɛd-l, *l* Hun.
Neuss, Nɷs, *t* Rhen. Prus., 9.
Neustadt, Nɷ́-stqt, *ts* Prus., 6¾; Aus., 9⅓; Prus. Saxony, 6¾.
Neustadt-an-der-Hardt, Nɷ́-stqt-qn-dęr-Hqrt, *t* Rhen. Bav., 6.
Neustadt-Eberswalde, Nɷ́-stqt-Ɑ'bers-vql-de, *t* Prus., 5⅓.
Neustädtl-an-der-Waag, Nɷ́-stet-l-qn-dęr-Vqg, *t* Hun., 5½.
Neu-Strelitz, Nɷ-Strá-lits, *t* Ger., 6½.
Neutitschein, Nɷ́-tit-ʃįn, *t* Moravia, 9.
Neuwied, Nɷ́-vɛt, *t* Rhen. Prus., 6¼.
Neva, Na-vq́, *r* or *str* Rus.
Nevada, Na-vq́-dq, *co* Cal. — City, *co t* Cal., 5.
Nevers, Ne-vąr, *c* Fr., 17.
Neville, Név-il, *v* O.
Nevis, Név-is, W. Ind. *i*, 10¼.
New Albany, Nų Θl'ba-ni, *c* Ia., 15.
Newark, Nų́-ark, *c* N-J., 50; *co t* O., 5; *vs* Del., Ia., Ill., &c.; *bor* Eng., 11⅓.
New Bedford, Nų Béd-ford, *c* Mass., 18.
New Berlin, Bęr-lin, *v* N-Y.; *co t* Pa.
Newbern, Nų́-bern, *co t* Va.; *t* N. C., 4½; *v* Ia. [Ia.
Newberry, Nų́-ber-i, *co t* S. C.; *vs* Pa.,
New Boston, Nų Bós-ton, *vs* Ill. ¾, N-H.
New Brighton, Brį-ton, *vs* N-Y., Pa.
New Britain, Brit-en, *v* Conn., 3; *arch* Pac. Oc.
New Brunswick, Brúnz-wik, Br. *ter* N. Am.; area 27,700 s. m., pop. 194,000; *c* N-J., 13½.
New Buda, Bų́-da, *v* Iowa.
New Buffalo, Búf-a-lɷ, *vs* Pa., Mich.
Newburg, Nų́-burg, *co ts* N-Y., Tenn.; *vs* Pa., O., Ia., Wis., Ala.
Newbury, Nų́-ber-i, *t* and *par* Eng., 6½; *vs* Vt., Mass. [13½.
Newburyport, Nų́-ber-i-pɷrt, *c* Mass.,
New Caledonia, Kal-ɛ-dó-ni-a, *i* S. Pac. Oc.; area 6600 s. m.
New Carlisle, Kar-lįl, *v* O., 1.
New Castle, Nų́ Kas-l, *co ts* Pa. 1¾, Del., Va., Ky.
Newcastle, Nų́-kas-l, *co t* Ia.
Newcastle (Nų-kás-l) upon-Tyne, *c* Eng., 87¾. [10¾.
Newcastle-under-Lyme, *bor* and *t* Eng.,

New Cumberland, Kúm-ber-land, *vs* Pa., Va., Ia.
New Diggings, Díg-iŋz, *v* Ill., ¾.
New England, Iŋ'gland, embraces Me., N-H., Vt., Mass, R. I., Conn.
Newfoundland, Nų́-fund-lánd, *i* Br. N. Am., At. Oc., bel. to Gr. Br.; area 57,000 s. m., pop. 102,000.
New Granada, Nų Grq-nq́-dq, *rep* S. Am.; area 480,000 s.m., pop. 2,364,000.
New Hampshire, Hámp-ʃɛr, one of the original U. S.; area 9280 s. m., pop. 318,000.
New Hampton, Hámp-ton, *vs* N-Y., N-J.
New Harmony, Hq́r-mɷ-ni, *v* Ia.
New Hartford, Hq́rt-ford, *vs* Conn., N-Y.
New Haven, Há-ven, *c, semi-cap* Conn., noted for its beauty, and being the seat of Yale College; *vs* N-Y., Pa., Ky., O., Ill.
New Hebrides, Héb-ri-dɛz, *is* Pac. Oc.
New Holland, Hól-and, *v* Pa.
New Hope, *vs* Pa. 1¼, O.
New Ipswich, Ips'wiq, *v* N-H.
New Ireland, Ir'land, *i* S. Pac. Oc.
New Jersey, Jér-zi, one of the original U. S.; area 8320 s. m., pop. 489,555.
New Leon, Lé-on, *st* Mex.; area 16,687 s. m., pop. 133,361.
New Lisbon, Líz-bon, *co t* O., 2½; *vs* Ia.
New London, *c* Conn., 10; *vs* O., Ia., Mo.,
New Madrid, Mád-rid, *co t* Mo. [&c.
New Market, Mq́r-ket, *vs* N-H., N-J.
New Mexico, Méks-i-kɷ, *ter* of the U. S.; area 207,007; pop. is of a mixed character, 61,547 being Mexicans and Americans, and 45,000 Indians.
New Milford, Mil-ford, *vs* Conn., Ill.
Newnan, Nų́-nan, *co t* Ga.
New Orkney, Ɵrk'ni, *is* S. At. Oc.
New Orleans, Ɵr'lɛ-anz, *c* La., built on deposit made by the Mississippi river, which is about 5 feet lower than the river level; 126⅓. [2.
New Philadelphia, Fil-a-dél-fi-ɑ, *v* O.,
Newport, Nų́-pɷrt, two important *bors* Eng.; *s-pt t* S. Wales, 1¾; *t* Eng., 2½; *c, semi-cap* R. I., 9½; *c* Ky., 9; *co ts* N-H., Ia.; *vs* N-Y., Pa., O., Mich.
Newport-Pagnell, Nų́-pɷrt-Pág-nel, *t* Eng., 3⅓. [*i*; *v* Tenn.
New Providence, Próv-i-dens, Bahama
New Richmond, Ríq-mond, *v* O., 2½.
New Rochelle, Rɷ-ʃél, *v* N-Y., 1¾.
Newry, Nų́-ri, *bor* Ir., 25.
New Sharon, Σá-ron, *v* Me.
New Siberia, Sị-bé-ri-ɑ, *is* Arc. Oc. a
New South Wales, Nų Sɤð Walz, extensive *cy* Australia; area 350,000 s. m., pop. 208,254.
Newton, Nų́-ton, *co ts* N-J., N. C., Ga., Ala., Ill., Iowa; *v* O., ½.
Newton-Abbot (Ab'ot) with Newton-Bushell, (Búʃ-el,) *t* Eng., 3¼.
Newton-upon-Ayr, (Ar,) *burgh* Scot., 5.
Newton Falls, *v* O., ¾.
Newton-Stewart, Stų́-ɑrt, *t* Scot., 2⅔.
Newtown, Nų́-tɤn, *bor* N. Wales, 3¼; *vs* Mass., Conn., N-Y., Pa., Va., Ky., Md., O., Ia. [Ir., 10¾.
Newtown-Ardes, Ardz, *bor* and *s-pt t*
Newtown-Limavaddy, Lim-a-vád-i, *bor* and *t* Ir., 3¼.
New York, Nų Yɵrk, the most populous of the U. S., and pre-eminent in internal improvements and commercial importance; area 47,000 s. m.; pop., in 1850, 3,097,394: 3,048,325 whites, 49,069 colored; in 1856, 3,345,840.
New York, *c* of the above state, the most important in the New World, and the third, only, in point of wealth and population on the globe; pop. 625; *vs* Tenn., Ia., Ill., Wash. Ter.
New Zealand, Zé-land, *is* of Gr. Brit., in S. Pac. Oc., area, 105,115 s. m. pop. 26,656.
New Ulster, and New Munster, principal *is* of New Zealand.
Neyva, *or* Neiva, Ná-i-vq, *t* N-Gran.
Nezheen, Na-ʒén, *t* Rus., 16.
Nez Percé (Na-Per-sá) Indians, *tr* Or.
Ngami, N-gq́-mɛ, *l* S. Af.
Niagara, Nị-ág-a-rɑ, *r* N. Am., forming between lakes Erie and Ontario the celebrated "Falls of Niagara."
Niagara, *co t* C. W., 3.
Niagara Falls, *v* N-Y., 1½.
Nias, Nị-as, *i* of Malay Arch.
Nicaragua, Nik-ar-q́-gwq, *st* Cen. Am., area, 36,000 s. m., pop. 235,000; *t* Nicaragua, 8; *l* ditto, 90 by 30 m.
Nicaria, Nɛ-kq-ré-q, *i* Gr. Arch., 1.
Nicastro, Nɛ-kq́s-trɷ, *t* Naples, 10.
Nice, Nɛs, *c* It., 25.
Nicholas, Ník-ɷ-las, *t* Cal.
Nicholasville, Ník-ɷ-las-vil, *co t* Ky., 1.
Nicobar (Ník-ɷ-bɑr) Islands, *is* Ind. Oc.
Nicolet, Nɛ-kɷ-lá, *co* and *v* C. E.
Niccollet, Nik-ɷ-lá, *co* and *l* Min.
Nicopolis, Nɛ-kóp-ɷ-lis, *t* Eu. Tur., 10.
Nicosia, Nɛ-kɷ-sé-q, *c* Sicily, 13.
Nicoya, Nɛ-kó-yq, *pen, b, r* and *ts* Costa Rica.
Nicuman, Nɛ-kɷ-mq́n, *r* China, 220 m.
Nieder-Hessen, Né-der-Hés-en, *prov* Hesse-Cassel, pop. 366,663.
Niemen, Né-men, *r* Rus. Pol., 400 m.
Nièvre, Nɛ-ávr, *dep* Fr., area, 2595 s. m., pop. 327,161.

Nigdeh, Níg-de, *t* As. Min., 5.
Niger, Nį-jer, *r* W. Af., 2000 m.
Nikolaiev, Nε-kɷ-lį-év, (*or* Nikolaief,) *ft t* Rus., 12.
Nikolsburg, Ník-olz-burg, *t* Moravia, 8.
Nile, Nįl, *r* E. Af., 700 m.
Niles, *vs* O., ¾; Mich., 2½.
Nimar, Nε-mq́r, *dis* Ind., area, 7000 s. m., pop., 250,000.
Nimes, Nεm, *i* Fr., 53⅝.
Nineveh, Nín-ε-ve, *anc c* and *cap* of the Assyrian Empire, now in ruins.
Ning-Po, Niŋ-Pɷ, *c* China, 250.
Ninove, Nε-nɷ́-va, *t* Belg., 4½.
Nio, Né-ɷ, *is* Gr. Arch., 3¾.
Niort, Nε-ór, *t* Fr., 18¾.
Nipe (Né-pa) Bay, Cuba.
Niphates, Nε-fq́-tεz, *m* Armenia.
Niphon, Nif-ón, (*or* Nipon, Nip-ón,) largest *is* Japan, area, 200,000 s. m.
Nipissing (Níp-is-iŋ) Lake, C. W., 50 by 35.
Nisari, Nε-sq́-rε, *i* Gr. Arch.
Nishapoor, Niʃ-q-pɷ́r, *c* Per., 8.
Nisita, Né-si-tq, *i* Naples.
Nitinat, Nit-i-nát, *or* Berkeley (Bérk-li) Sound, N. Am., w. Vancouver's Is.
Nivelles, Nε-vél, *t* Belg., 8.
Nixdorf, Níks-dorf, (Groce and Klein, Grɷs and Klįn,) *vs* Bohemia.
Nizhnee-Lomov, Níʒ-nε-Lɷ-móv, *t* Rus., 7
Nizhnee Novgorod, Níʒ-nε-Nov-gɷ-ród, *t* Rus., 32.
Nizhnee-Taghilsk, *or* Nijnii-Taghilsk, Níʒ-nε Tq-gílsk, *t* Rus., 22.
Noblesville, Nɷ́-blz-vil, *v* Ia., 1⅓.
Nobosque (Nɷ-bósk) Point, Buzzard's Bay, Mass.
Nocera Dei Pagani, Nɷ-çá-rq Dá-ε Pq-gq́-nε, *anc t* Naples, 7½.
Noceto, Nɷ-çá-tɷ, *t* It., 5¾.
Noci, Nɷ́-çε, *t* Naples, 6.
Noessa-Laut, Nɷ-és-q-Lɷt, *is* Malay Arch.
Nogent, Nɷ-ʒóń, *t* Fr., 3.
Nogent-le-Ber-nard, Nɷ-ʒóń-lə-Ber-nq́r, *t* Fr., 3.
Nogent-le-Rotrou, Nɷ-ʒóń-lə-Rɷ-trɷ́, *t* Fr., 7.
Nogent-sur-Seine, Nɷ-ʒóŋ-sur-San, *t* Fr., 3½. [6.
Nohcacab, Nɷ-kq-kq́b, *v* Yucatan, Mex.,
Noir, Nwqr, *i* S. Am.
Noirmoutiers, Nwqr-mɷ-ti-á, *i* w. of Fr., 8¼.
Noja, Nɷ́-yq, *t* Naples, 5½.
Nola, Nɷ́-lq, *c* Naples, 5½.
Nombre-de-Dios, Nóm-bra-da-Dé-ɷs, *t* Mex., 6¾; *pt* N-Gran.
Nookaheeva, Nɷ-kq-hé-vq, one of the Marquesas Isles, Pac. Oc., 18.

Noon, Nɷn, *r* Mantchooria, 500 m.
Noonivak, Nɷ-ni-vq́k, *i* Rus. Am.
Nootka-Sound, Nɷ́t-ka-Sɤnd, *inlet* w. of Vancouver Is.
Nord, Nor, *dep* Fr., area 2170 s. m., pop. 1,158,285.
Norden, Nór-den, *t* Hanover, 5¾.
Norderney, Nór-der-nį, *i* N. Sea, ¾.
Nordhausen, Nórt-hɤ-zen, *t* Prus. Sax., 13.
Nordland, Nórd-lqnd, *div* Norway; area, 14,337 s. m., pop. 65,512.
Nördlingen, Nért-liŋ-en, *ft t* Bav., 6½.
Nordstrand, Nórt-strqnd, *i* Den., 3.
Norfolk, Nór-fok, *c* Va., 16; *cos* Eng., Mass., Va.; — Bay, Van Die. Land; — Island, Pac. Oc.; — New, *dis* Van Dieman's Land.; —Sound, Rus. Am.
Norman, Nór-man, *is* W. Ind.
Normandy, Nór-man-di, anc. *prov* Fr., area, 10,534 s. m.
Norman Isles, comprise Channel Is., Jersey, Guernsey, &c.
Norridgewock, Nór-ij-wok, *v* Me., 1¾.
Norristown, Nór-is-tɤn, *t* Pa., 6; *vs* Ark., O.
Norrkjöping, Nór-çə-piŋ, *t* Swed., 11½.
Norrska Fiellen, Nórs-kq Fyél-en, *ms* Norway.
North Adams, Ad'amz, *v* Mass., 3.
Northallerton, Norθ-ál-er-ton, *bor* and *t* Eng., 5.
Northampton, Norθ-ámp-ton, *bor* and *t* Eng., 26¾; *v* Mass., 4.
North Bellerica, Bél-er-i-ka, *v* Mass., ⅓.
North Bend, country residence of Gen. W. H. Harrison, near Cincinnati.
North Bridgewater, Brij-we-ter, *v* Mass., 4.
North Carolina, Kar-ɷ-lį-na, one of the original U. S.; area 50,704 s. m., pop. 553,028 whites, 27,563 fr. blacks, 288,548 slaves,—total 868,903.
North Clarendon, Klár-en-don, *v* Vt.
North Danvers, Dán-verz, *v* Mass.
North-East, *vs* Pa., Md., &c.
North-East Pass, *or* Balize, Ba-léz, *v* La.; at the mouth of Mississippi.
Northern Circars, Sər-kq́rs, *prov* Br. Ind.; area 17,000 s. m., pop 2,995,500.
North Ferrisburg, Fér-is-burg, *v* Vt.
Northfield, Nórθ-fεld, *vs* Vt., 3; Mass., 1¾; N-J., O., Ia.
North Granville, Grán-vil, *v* N-Y.
North Hadley, Hád-li, *v* Mass.
North Haven, Há-ven, *v* Conn., 1⅓.
North Hero, Hé-rɷ, *co t* Vt., ¾.
North Lawrence, Ló-rens, *v* N-Y.
North Lebanon, Léb-an-on, *v* Pa., ⅕.
North Madison, Mád-i-son, *v* Ia., ¾.

North Scituate, Sit-yu-at, *vs* Mass., R. I.
North Sea, *or* German Ocean, an arm At. Oc., between the Brit. Is. and German States.
Northumberland, Nor-thúm-ber-land, *t* Pa., 1¼; *v* N-H.
North Vernon, Vér-non, *v* Ia.
Northville, Nórth-vil, *vs* Mass., Mich., Ill.
Northwich, Nórth-wic, *t* Eng., 1⅓.
Norton, Nór-ton, *vs* Eng., 2; Mass., 2; O.
Norton-Chipping, Cip-in, *bor* Eng., 3.
Norton Sound, *inlet* Behring Sea, Rus. Am. [1¾.
Norwalk, Nór-wok, *t* Conn., 4⅔; *v* O.,
Norway, Nór-wa, *cy* of Eu., forming the extreme n. w. part; provinces, Aggershuus or Christiania, Christiansand, Bergen, Trondhjem, Tromsoe; area 123,386 s. m., pop. 1,330,000; *vs* Me., 2; N-Y., 1; Ia.
Norwich, Nór-ij, *c* Eng., 12½; Nór-wic, *vs* N-Y., ¼; Pa., O.
Norwood, Upper and Lower, two *vs* Eng., United pop. 6046.
Nos-Beh, Nós-Ba, *i* of Fr., coast of Madagascar, 15¼.
Noss-Island, one of Shetland Is.
Noto, Nó-to, *c* Sicily 10¾.
Notre Dame, Nót-r Dqm, *p o* Ia.; — Bay, Newfoundland.
Notre Dame de Cenilly, Nót-r Dqm de Se-ne-yé, *v* Fr., 2.
Notteröe, Nót-e-re-e, *i* Norway.
Nottingham, Nót-in-am, *bor* and *t* Eng., pop., 57,407.
Nottoway, Nót-o-wa, *r* and *co t* Va.
Novara, No-vq-rq, *c* It. 18½.
Nova Scotia, Nó-va Skó-ʃi-a, *prov* Br. N. Am.; area 15,627 s. m., pop. 276,119.
Nova Zembla, Nó-va Zém-bla, two *is* Arctic Oc., area, about 61,967 s. m., has no permanent inhabitants.
Novelda, No-vél-dq, *t* Sp., 8.
Novellara, No-vel-q-rq, *t* It., 4.
Novgorod, Nov-go-ród, *gov* Rus., *c* do., pop. 15,000.
Novgorod-Severskoie, Nov-go-ród-Sa-ver-skó-ya, *t* Rus., 8.
Novi, Nó-ve, *t* It., 10¼.
Novi-Bazar, Nó-ve-Bq-zqr, *t* Bosnia, 8.
Novoi-Oskol, No-vé-Os-kól, *t* Rus., 5.
Novomoskovsk, No-vo-mos-kóvsk, *ft t* Rus., 7⅓. [Rus., 17¾.
Novo-Tcherkask, Nó-vo-Cer-kqsk, *t*
Now-Chow, Nɤ-Cɤ, *i* China.
Noxubee, Nóks-yu-be, *r* and *co* Miss.
Noyon, No-yóṅ, *t* Fr., 6⅓.
Nubia, Nú-bi-a, *cy* E. Af.; area 35,000 s. m., pop. 400,000.
Nublada, No-blq-dq, *i* N. Pac.
Nueces, Nwá-ses, *r* Tex., 350 m.
Nuevitas, Las, Lqs Nwa-vé-tqs, *t* Cuba.
Nuits, Nwe, *t* Fr., 3⅓.
Nuko, Nó-ko, *i* Rus., Gulf of Fin., ⅙.
Numa, Nú-ma, *v* Ia.
Numidia, Nu-míd-i-a, *anc cy* N. Af.
Nunda, Nun-dá, *v* N-Y., 2.
Nuneaton, Nún-e-ton, *t* Eng., 4¾.
Nunez, No-néz, *r* W. Af.
Nuremberg, Nú-rem-berg, important *c* Bavaria, pop. 46,000.
Nurpur, Nur-púr, *t* Punjab, 6.
Nyack, Nj-ak, *v* N-Y., ¾.
Nyassi, Ne-qs-e, *l* S. E. Af.
Nyborg, Né-borg, *ft t* Den., 3. [15¾.
Nyireghyhaza, Nye-rej-hq-zo, *t* Hun.,
Nyköping, Né-ce-pin, *dis* Swed.; area 2516 s. m., pop. 120,113; *t* Swed., 3½.
Nymwegen, Nim-wa-gen, *ft t* Neth. 21¼.

# O.

Oahu *or* Wahoo, Wq-ho, one of the Sandwich Islands, 19¼.
Oajaca *or* Oaxaca, Wq-hq-kq, *st* of Mex.; area, 31,822 s. m., pop. 525,101; *c* Mex., 25.
Oakham, Ok'am, *t* Eng., 3. [Ill.
Oakland, Ok'land, *c* Cal., 2½; *vs* O.,
Oakville, *vs* N. Y., Mich., C. W.
Oban, O'ban, *bor* and *spt t* Scot., 1¾.
Obeid, O-bád, *cap t* Kordofan, Af., 30.
Oberlin, O'ber-lin, *v* O., noted for its College, free to people of color, 2.
Obernai, O-ber-ná, *t* Fr., 5. [7½.
O-Bessenova, O-beʃ-a-nó-vo, *t* Hun.,
Obi, Oby, *or* Obe, O'be, *r* Sib., 2000 m.
Obidos, O-bé-dos, *t* Brazil, 6.
Obies, O'bez, *r* Tenn.
Obion, O'bi-on, *r* Tenn., 150 m.
Oboyan, O-bo-yqn, *t* Rus., 5½.
Ocana, O-kón-yq, *ts* Sp. 5; N-Gran., 5.
Occoquan, Ok'o-kwon, *r* and *v* Va.
Ocean, *or* Curè, Kó-ra, *i* Pac. Oc.
Ocean, *or* Paanopa, Pq-no-pq, *i* Pac. Oc., ½.
Oceania, O-ʃe-q-ni-a, *or* Oceanica, O-ʃe-án-i-ka, fifth division of the globe, consisting of Malaisia, Australia, and Polynesia.

Ochil (Ō'*h*il,) Hills, *ms* Scot.
Ocmulgee, Ok-múl-gɛ, *r* Ga., 300 m.
Oconee, Ō-kō-nɛ, *r* Ga., 300 m., *vs* Ga., S. C. [*v* Wis.
Oconomewoc, Ok-ω-nōm-ɛ-wok, *cr* and
Ocrakoke, Ō'kra-kωk, *v* N. C.
Odense, Ō'den-sa, *t* Den., 11¼.
Odense-Fiord, Fɛ-ērd, *b* is. of Funen.
Odenwald, Ō'den-vqlt, *m* Ger.
Oder, Ō'der, *r* Ger., 550 m.
Odessa, Ō-dés-a, *c* Rus., 71⅓.
Odowara, Ō-dω-wq́-rq, *t* is. of Niphon, Japan, 5. [4½.
Oedenburg, E'den-bω*rh*, *t* W. Hun.,
Oederan, E'da-rqn, *t* Saxony, 4½.
Oeiras, Ō-á-ɛ-rqs, *c* Brazil, 5.
Oels, Els, *t* Prus. Silesia, 6. [40.
Oesel, E'sel, *i* Rus., area, 1200 s. m.,
Offenbach, Of'en-bq*h*, *t* Hesse-Darmstadt, 9½.
Ogdensburgh, Og'denz-burg, *t* N-Y., 8.
Ogeechee, Ō-gḗ-çɛ, *r* Ga., 250 m.
Ogle, Ō'gl, *co* and *v* Ill.
Oglethorpe, Ō'gl-ŧerp, *c* Ga., 2½.
Ogono, Ō-gōn-yω, *cape* Sp.
Oheteroa, Ō-ha-ta-rō-a, *i* S. Pac. Oc.
Ohio, Ō-hį-ω, one of the U. S., third in population and commercial importance. Area, 39,964 s. m., pop. in 1850, 1,980,329; whites, 1,955,050, colored, 25,279. In 1856, 2,138,754; *r* U. S., 950 m.
Ohomura, Ō-hω-mō-rq, *t* Japan, 20.
Oich, Loch, Lo*h* Ɵ*h*, *l* Scot.
Oignies, Wan-yḗ, *v* Belgium, 1¼.
Oise, Wqz, *r* and *dep* Fr.
Oits Mitsoo, Ɵts Mít-sώ, *l* Japan.
Ojalava, Ō-yq-lq́-vq, one of Nav. Is., Pac. Oc. [beria, 500 m.
Oka, Ō'kq, *rs* Cen. Rus., 650 m.; Si-
Okanagon, Ō-kan-ág-on, *r* N. Amer., 200 m.
Okau *or* Okaw, Ō'ke, *v* Ill.
Okauchee, Ō-ké-çɛ, *v* Wis.
Okhota, Ō-*h*ō-tq, *r* Siberia, 200 m.
Okhotsk, Ō-*h*ótsk, Sea of, inlet of Pac. Oc.
Okladnikovo, Ok-lqd-ni-kō-vω, *l* Rus.
Okolona, Ok-ω-lō-na, *v* Miss.
Oktibbeha, Ok-tíb-ɛ-he, *r* and *co* Miss.
Oland, E'lqnt, *i* Sweden, 31.
Olcott, Ol'kot, *v* N-Y.
Oldburg, Ōld'burg, *t* Eng., 5¼.
Oldenburg, Ol'den-burg, grand-duchy, Ger., 252,699; *t* Ger., 8; *v* Ia.
Oldham, Ōld'am, *bor* and *t* Eng., 72⅓.
Old Point Comfort, *v* Va.
Old Providence, *i* Carribbean Sea, ⅓.
Oldtown, *v* Me., 3.
Olean, Ō-lɛ-án, *v* N-Y.; *p o* Ind.
Oleggio, Ō-léd-jω, *t* It., 7½.
Olekma, Ō-lék-mq, *r* Siberia, 400 m.
Olenek, Ō-la-nék, *r* Siberia, 800 m.
Olentangy, Ol-en-tán-ji, *r* O.
Oléron, Ō-la-rōṅ, *i* coast of France, 17.
Olhao, Ol-yɤ̇n, *t* Portugal, 6.
Olinda, Ō-lín-da, *c* Brazil, 8.
Oliva, Ō-lḗ-vq, *t* Sp., 5½.
Olivenza, Ō-lɛ-vén-sq, *t* Sp., 7½.
Olkhon, Ol'*h*on, *i* Lake Baikal, Siberia.
Olmutz, Ol'muts, *c* Moravia, 12½.
Olney, Ol'ni, *t* Eng., 2⅓; *vs* Penn., Ill.
Oloron, Ō-lω-rōṅ, *t* Fr., 6⅓.
Olot, Ō-lót, *t* Sp., 12.
Olvera, Ol-vá-rq, *t* Sp., 6¼.
Olympia, Ō-lím-pi-a, *cap* Wash. Ter.
Olympus, Ō-lím-pus, *m* Thessaly.
Om, *r* As. Rus., 330 m.
Omaha City, Ō-mq́-hq Sít-i, *cap* Neb.
Ombay, Om-bį, *i* Malay Arch.
Ometepe, Ō-ma-ta-pá, *vol i* Cen. Am.
Omsk, Omsk, *ft t* As. Rus., 11⅓.
Omun, Ō-mōn, *t* Guinea, 5.
Ona, Ō'nq, *r* Siberia, 280 m.
Oneco, Ō-nḗ-kω, *v* Ill. [Rus.
Onega, Ō-nḗ-ga, *r* Rus., 250 m.; *l*
Oneglia, Ō-nél-yq, *t* Sard. States, 5½.
Oneida, Ō-nį-da, *l* and *co* N-Y.
Onekotan, Ō-na-kω-tq́n, Koorile Is.
Oneonta, Ō-nɛ-ōn-ta, *v* N-Y.
Onghin, On-gén, *r* Mongolia, 200 m.
Onion, Un'yon, *rs* Vt., Wis. [N-Y.
Onondaga, On-on-dé-ga, *l*, *co* and *v*
Onondaga Valley, *v* N-Y., 1.
Onslow, Onz'lω, *s-pt t* Nova Scotia; *b* and *co* N. C.
Ontario, On-tá-ri-ω, one of the five great lakes, U. S.; *co* N-Y.; *co* C. W.
Onteniente, On-ta-nɛ-én-ta, *t* Sp., 9½.
Ontonagon, On-ton-ág-on, *r* and *v* Mich.
Oobsa, Ɵb'sq, *l* Chinese Empire.
Ooch, Ɵq, *t* N. W. Hindostan, 20.
Ooda, *or* Ouda, Ɵ'dq, *r* Siberia, 200 m.
Oofa, Ɵ'fq, *t* Rus., 6.
Ooglitch, Ɵg-liç, *t* Rus., 8. [ak.
Oojak, Ɵ-jq́k, *b* N. Pac. Oc., is. Kodi-
Oojein, Ɵ-ján, *ft c* Hindostan.
Oo-Kiang, Ɵ-kɛ-q́ŋ, *r* China, 500 m.
Oonalaska, Ɵ-na-lq́ʃ-ka, Fox Island, N. Pac. Oc.
Oonimak, Ɵ-nɛ-mq́k, Fox Island.
Ooralsk, Ɵ-rq́lsk, *t* Rus., 13.
Oorfa, Ɵr'fq, *t* As. Tur., 30.
Oorga, Ɵr'gq, *c* Mongolia, 7.
Ooroomeeyah, Ɵ-rω-mé-yq, *ft t* North Persia, 25.
Ooroomtsee, Ɵ-rōmt-sɛ, *c* China.
Ooroop, Ɵ-rōp, one of Koorile Is. [m.
Oosooree, Ɵ-sω-ré, *r* Mantchooria, 340
Oostacker, Ōs'tqk-er, *v* Bel., 5¼.

Oostioog, Ꝏs-ti-óg, *t* Rus. 13.
Oozen, *or* Ouzen, Ꝏ-zén, *two rs* Rus., 250 m.
Opelousas, Op-ɛ-ló-sas, *v* La.
Ophir, Ꝍ'fer, Mount, *ms* Malay Pen., and Sumatra.
Oporto, Ꝍ-pór-tꝍ, *c* Port., 80.
Oppeln, Op'eln, *t* Prus. Silesia, 7½.
Opwyck, *or* Opwijk, Op'wįk, *v* Belg., 3½.
Oquaka, Ꝍ-kwá-ka, *v* Ill., 1.
Oran, Ꝍ-rán, *ft c* Algeria, 25; *v* N-Y.
Orange, Or'anj, *r* S. Africa; *t* Fr., 10; *vs* Mass., N-J.; *b* Terra del Fuego.
Orange Court House, *co t* Va., ½.
Orange River, Republic of, div. S. Af., area, 50,000 s. m.
Orbey, Ꝋr-bá, *t* Fr., 5½.
Oregon, O'rɛ-gon, most western of the territories, U. S.; area, 185,030 s. m., pop. 13,294.
Oregon City, *v* Ill.; *t* Oregon, 1.
Orel, Ꝍ-rél, *t* Rus., 25¾.
Orenboorg, Ꝍ'ren-bŭrh, *c* Rus. 6.
Orense, Ꝍ-rén-sa, *t* Sp., 5.
Orgaos, Serra Dos, Sér-q dꝍs Ꝋr-gá-ꝍns, *ms* Brazil.
Oria, Ꝍ'ri-q, *t* Sp., 5¾; *t* Naples, 4¼.
Orihuela, Ꝍ-rɛ-wá-lq, *c* Sp., 17½.
Orinoco, Ꝍ-ri-nó-kꝍ, large *r* S. Am., 1600 m.
Oriskany, Ꝍ-rís-kan-i, *v* N-Y.
Oristano, Ꝍ-ris-tá-nꝍ, *t* is. Sardinia, 10; *g* is. of Sardinia.
Orizaba, Ꝍ-ri-sá-bq, *t* Mex., 15.
Orkhon, Ꝋr-hón, *r* Mongolia, 380 m.
Orkney Ꝋrk'ni, Islands, *arch* N. of Scot.
Orland, Ꝋr'land, *v* Me.
Orleans, Ꝋr'lɛ-anz, *c* Fr., 47½.
Ormus, Ꝋr'mus, *i* Persian Gulf.
Orontes, Ꝍ-rón-tɛz, *r* N. Syria, 240 m.
Oroshaza, Ꝍ-roʃ-á-zo, *v* Hun., 9½.
Orotava, Ꝍ-rꝍ-tá-vq, *t* Canary Is., 8⅓.
Orphano, Ꝋr'fq-nꝍ, *g* of Gr. Arch.
Orphan's Island, Penobscot river.
Orthez, Ꝋr-tá, *t* Fr., 10.
Ortler, Ꝋrt-ler, *m* Austria.
Ortona, Ꝋr-tó-na, *t* Naples, 7.
Oruro, Ꝍ-ró-rꝍ, *t* Bolivia, 5.
Orust, Ꝍ'rꝍst, *i* Sweden.
Orvieto, Ꝋr-vɛ-á-tꝍ, *c* Cen. It., 6¼.
Orwigsburg, Ꝋr'wigz-burg, *bor* Pa., 1.
Osage, Ꝍ-sáj, *r* Ind. Ter., U. S., 500 m.
Osaka, Ꝍ-sá-kq, *s-pt t* Japan.
Osceola, Os-ɛ-ó-la, *cos* Mich., Iowa; *p os* in many of U. S.
Oschatz, Ꝍ-ʃáts, *t* Sax., 5⅓.
Oshkosh, Oʃ'koʃ, *v* Wis., 3.
Oshmooneyn, Oʃ-mꝏ-nán, *v* Egypt.
Oskaloosa, Os-ka-ló-sa, *v* Iowa, 1½.
Osnaburg, Os'na-burg, *t* Han., 11¾.
Ostashkov, Os-taʃ-kóv, *t* Rus., 9.
Ostend, Os-ténd, *ft spt t* Belg., 14½.
Osterode, Os'ta-rꝍ-da, *t* Han., 5¼.
Ostrog, Os-tróg, *t* Rus. Poland, 6½.
Osuna, Ꝍ-só-nq, *t* Sp., 17½.
Oswegatchie, Os-wɛ-gáq-ɛ, *r* N-Y., 120 m.
Oswego, Os-wé-gꝍ, *c* N-Y., 16; *co* and *r* N-Y.; *vs* Ia. and Ill.
Oswestry, Oz'es-tri, *bor* Eng., 5.
Otago, Ꝍ-tá-gꝍ, settlement of N-Zeal., 1¾.
Otisville, Ꝍ'tis-vil, *v* N-Y.
Otranto, Ꝍ-trán-tꝍ, *t* Naples, 4½; *str* connecting Adr. and Med. Sea.
Otsego, (Ot-sé-gꝍ,) Lake, N-Y.
Ottawa, Ot'a-wa, *t* Ill., 3½; *r* Canada; *cos* O., Mich., and Canada.
Ottery St. Mary, Ot'er-i Sant Má-ri, *t* Eng., 2½.
Ottumwa, Ot'um-wɵ, *v* Iowa.
Ouachita, (Woʃ-i-tó,) City, *v* La. 1.
Oualan, Ꝏ-q-lán, *i* Pac. Oc., Carolines,
Oude, Ꝏd, *k* Hindostan; area, 23,738 s. m., pop. 2,970,000; *c* of the above.
Oughter, Loch, Loh Oh'ter, *l* Ir.
Oundle, Un'del, *t* Eng., 3.
Ouro Preto, Ꝏ'rꝍ Prá-tꝍ, *c* Brazil, 8.
Ouse, Ꝏz, *r* Eng.
Outagamie, Ꝏ-ta-ga-mé, *co* Wis.
Ovada, Ꝍ-vá-dq, *t* Piedmont, 6¼.
Ovar, Ꝍ-vár, *t* Portugal, 5.
Ovari, Ꝍ-vá-rɛ, Bay of, inlet on is. Niphon.
Overflakkee, Ꝍ'ver-flqk-a, *i* Neth.
Overyssel, Ꝍ'ver-į-sel, *prov* Neth.; area, 1,312 s. m., pop. 227,683.
Ovid, Ꝍ'vid, *v* N-Y., 1.
Oviedo, Ꝍ-vi-á-đꝍ, *c* Sp., 9⅓.
Owasco, (Ꝍ-wós-kꝍ,) Lake, N-Y.
Owego, Ꝍ-wé-gꝍ, *co t* N-Y., 4.
Owenborough, Ꝍ'en-bur-ꝍ, *v* Ky., 1½.
Owen's Lake, Cal.
Owenton, Ꝍ'en-ton, *co t* Ky.
Owingsville, Ꝍ'iŋz-vil, *co t* Ky.
Oxford, Oks'ford, *c* Eng., 28; *co ts* N. C., Miss., Ind.; *vs* Mass., N-Y., Md., Ga., O.
Oxus *or* Amoo, *rs* Cen. Asia, 1300.
Oyapok, Ꝍ-yq-pók, *r* S. Am., 180 m.
Oyonnax, Ꝍ-yo-ná, *t* Fr., 3¼.
Oyster Bay, Ꝋs'ter Ba, *v* N-Y., 7.
Ozark, Ꝍ-zárk, *co t* Ark.; *v* Mo.; *ms* Ark., and Mo.
Ozaukee, Ꝍ-zó-kɛ, *co* and *co t* Wis.
Ozieri, Ꝍ-zi-á-rɛ, *t* is. of Sardinia, 8.
Ozorkow, Ꝍ-zór-kov, *t* Poland, 5.

# P.

Pabba, Páb-a, *i* Hebrides, ⅓.
Pacaja, Pq-kq-zq, *r* Brazil, 150 m.
Pacajes, Pq-kq-hes, *r* and *m* Bolivia.
Pachacama, Pq-çq-kq-mq, *v* Peru.
Pacheco, Pq-çá-kω, *t* Sp., 5.
Pachitea, Pq-çi-tá-q, *r* Peru, 200 m.
Pachucaca, Pq-çω-kq-kq, *r* Peru, 130 m.
Pacific Ocean, Pa-sif-ik Ω'ʃan, the largest division of water on the globe.
Paco, Pq-kω, *v* is. Luzon, 6½.
Pacora, Pq-kω-rq, *r* Isthmus Panama.
Paddock-with-Marsh, *hamlet* Eng., 3½.
Paderborn, Pq-der-bωrn, *t* Prus., 8¾.
Padron, Pq-drón, *t* Sp., 6.
Padstow, Pád-stω, *s-pt t* Eng., 2¼.
Padua, Pád-yq-a, *ft c* Aus. It., 60.
Paducah, Pa-dq-ka, *co t* Ky., 3.
Padula, Pq-dó-lq, *t* Naples, 8.
Pæjæne, Pa-yá-na, *l* Finland, 90 by 20.
Paete, Pq-á-ta, *v* Philippines, 3½.
Pago, Pq-gω, *i* Dalmatia, Adriatic, 5.
Pagsanjan, Pqg-sqn-jqn, *t* Phil. Is., 4¾.
Pahang, Pq-hqŋ, *st* Malay Pen., 40.
Pah Utah, Pq Yó-tq, *ind tr* Ter. Utah.
Paimbœuf, Pań-bęf, *t* Fr., 4¼.
Painesville, Pánz-vil, *co t* O., 3¼.
Painswick, Pánz-wik, *t* and *par* Eng., 3½.
Painted Post, *v* N-Y., 1½.
Paintville, *co t* Ky.
Paisley, Páz-li, *burg* and *t* Scot., 48.
Paks, Pokʃ, *t* Hun., 8¾.
Palanpore, Pql-an-pór, *t* Hind., 30.
Palatine, Pál-a-tin, *v* Va.
Palawan, Pq-lq-wqn, *i* Malay Arch.
Palazzuolo, Pq-lqt-sω-ó-lω, *t* Sic., 8½.
Palembang, Pq-lem-bqŋ, *t* Sumatra, 25.
Palencia, Pq-lén-tε-q, *c* Sp., 11½.
Palermo, Pq-lęr-mω, *ft c* Sicily, 167¼.
Palestine, Pál-es-tin, anc. *cy* in s. w. Asia; area, 11,000 s. m.; *co ts* Tex., Ill.; *vs* O., Ind.
Palestrina, Pq-les-tré-nq, *c* Italy, 4¾.
Palhanpoor, Pql-hqn-pór, *ft t* Hind., 30.
Palk's (Peks,) Strait, bet. Ceylon and Hind.
Palma, Pql-mq, *ft t* of the Balearic Is., 40½.; *ts* Sicily, 8; Naples, 6; Sp., 3¾; *i* Canary Islands, 33. [5½.
Palma del Rio, Pql-mq del Ré-ω, *t* Sp.,
Palmar, Pql-mqr, *t* Sp., 6.
Palme, Pqlm, *lagoon* of Fr.
Palmer, Pqm-er, *v* Mass., 4.
Palmer Depot, Dé-pω, *v* Mass.
Palmetto, Pal-mét-ω, *r* and *v* Ga.
Palmi, Pql-mε, *c* Nap., 6¼.
Palmyra, Pal-mi-ra, anc. *c* of Syrian Desert; *co ts* Va., Mo., 2; *vs* N-Y., 3; O., Mich., Wis.
Palo Alto, Pq-lω Al'tω, battle-field, Mex.; *co* Iowa; *vs* Ga., Miss., Iowa.
Palte, Pql-ta, *l* East Thibet.
Pamiers, Pq-mε-á, *t* Fr., 7¾.
Pamlico, Pám-li-kω, *r* N. C.
Pamlico Sound, e. coast of N. Carolina.
Pampas, Pqm-pqs, *plains* S. Am.; area, 1,620,000 s. m.
Pampas del Sacramento, Sq-krq-mén-tω, *plains* of Peru; area, 60,000 s. m.
Pamplona, Pqm-pló-nq, *ft t* Sp., 11; *t* New Granada, 3¼.
Panama, Pan-a-mq, *s-pt c* N-Gran., 6; Isthmus of, connecting land bet. N. and S. America.
Panaon, Pq-nq-ón, Philippine Is.
Panay, Pq-ni, Philippine Is.
Pancsova, Pqn-çω-vo, *ft t* Hun., 11¾.
Pandacan, Pqn-dq-kqn, *v* Phil., 4⅔.
Pangansane, Pqŋ-gqn-sán, *i* Mal. Arch.
Panola, Pa-nó-la, *co t* Miss., ½.
Pantar, Pqn-tqr, *i* Malay Arch.
Pantellaria, Pqn-tel-q-ré-q, *i* Nap., 5.
Paola, Pq-ω-lq, *c* Naples, 5.
Paoli, Pa-ó-li, *v* Pa.; *co t* Ind.
Paoo, Pq-ω, Fejee island, Pac. Oc.
Papa, Pq-po, *t* Hun., 16½. [Am.
Papagayo, Pq-pq-gi-ω, *g* and *vol* Cen.
Papandayang, Pq-pqn-dq-yqŋ, *vol* Java.
Papa-Stour, Pá-pa-Stωr, Shetland *i*, ½.
Papinsville, Pá-pinz-vil, *co t* Mo.
Papua, Páp-ω-a, *or* New Guinea, *i* bet. Asiatic Seas and Pac. Oc.; area 250,-000 s. m., inhabited by Malays and Papuans. [Brazil, 10.
Pará, Pq-rq, *r* S. Am., 200 m.; *s-pt c*
Paraçatu, Pq-rq-sq-tó, *r* and *c* Brazil.
Paradise, Pár-a-dis, *v* Pa., 2.
Paragau, Pq-rq-gŏ, *rs* Bol., Ven.
Paraguaçu, Pq-rq-gwq-só, *r* Bra., 260 m.
Paraguana, Pq-rq-gwq-nq, *pen* S. Am.
Paraguay, Pq-rq-gwá, *st* S. Am.; area 84,000 s. m., pop. 1,000,000; *r* do., 1600 m.
Parahiba, Pq-rq-é-bq, *c* Bra., 15.
Parahiba-do-Sul, Pq-rq-é-bq-dω-Sωl, *r* Bra., 500 m.
Parahitinga, Pq-rq-ε-tín-gq, *t* Bra., 4.
Paramaribo, Par-a-már-i-bω, *cap t* D. Guiana, 20. [4½.
Paramatta, Par-a-mát-a, *t* N-S. Wales,
Paramoosheer, Pq-rq-mω-ʃér, Koorile *i*, area 120 s. m.

Paramythia, Pq-rq-mi-tē-q, *t* Eu. Tur., 5.
Paraná, Pq-rq-nq́, *r* S. Am., 2000 m.
Paranagua, Pq-rq-nq-gwq́, *t* Bra., 7.
Parana-Iba, Pq-rq-nq-ē'bq, *r* Bra. 500 m.
Paranpeba, Pq-rqn-pá-bq, *r* Bra., 250 m.
Parati, Pq-rq-té, *s-pt t* Bra., 10.
Parchim, Pq́*rh*-im, *t* Ger., 6½.
Parcipany, Par-sip-a-ni, *v* N-J., ⅓.
Pardo, Pq́*r*-dō, *r* Bra., 280 m.
Paredon, Pq-ra-dón, *i* W. Ind. [Ven.
Parima, Sierra, Sε-ér-q Pq-ré-mq, *ms*
Parinacochas, Pq-ri-nq-kó-çqs, *l* Peru.
Paris, Pár-is, (Fr. Pq-ré,) metropolis and *cap* of France; pop. 1,053,262; *co ts* Me. 3, Ky. 2½, Tenn., Tex., Ill., Mo.; *v* C. W., 2½.
Parisburg, Pár-is-burg, *co t* Va.
Parita, Pq-ré-tq, *g* Cen. Am.; *t* N-Gran.
Parkersburg, Pq́rk-erz-burg, *co t* Va.,
Parkesburg, Pq́rks-burg, *v* Pa., ½. [3½.
Parkman, Pq́rk-man, *v* O., 1⅓.
Parkville, Pq́rk-vil, *t* Mo., 1. [Mich.
Parma, Pq́r-ma, *c* It., 41; *vs* N-Y. 3,
Parnahiba, Pq*r*-nq-é-bq, *r* Bra., 750 m.
Parnassus, Pqr-nás-us, cel. *m* Greece.
Paropamisan, Pq-rō-pq-mi-sq́n, *ms* Afg.
Paros, Pá-ros, *i* Grecian Arch., 6.
Partenico, Pq*r*-tén-i-kō, *c* Sic., 11.
Parthenay, Pq*r*-te-ná, *t* Fr., 5.
Partick, Pq́r-tik, *v* Scot., 2¾.
Paru, Pq-ró, *r* Bra., 350 m.
Paruro, Pq-ró-rō, *t* Peru.
Pascagoula, Pas-ka-gó-la, *r* and *b* Miss.
Pasco, Pq́s-kō, *t* Peru, 12.
Pascoag, Pás-kō-ag, *v* R. I., 1½.
Pascuaro, Pqs-kwq́-rō, *t* Mex., 6.
Pas-de-Calais, Pq-dę-Kq-lá, *dep* Fr.
Pasewalk, Pq́-ze-vqlk, *t* Prus., 5¾.
Pasman, Pqs-mq́n, *i* of Dalmatia.
Paspaya, Pqs-pí-q, *r* Bol., 200 m.
Pasquotank, Pás-kō-taŋk, *r* N. C.
Passaic, Pa-sá-ik, *r* N-J., 100 m.
Passamaquoddy (Pas-a-ma-kwód-i) Bay, s. e. Me.
Passau, Pq́s-ɤ, *ft t* Bav., 10¼.
Passoeroean, Pq-sō-rō-q́n, *prov* Java; pop. 310,000.
Passy, Pq-sé, *t* Fr., 11¼.
Pastaza, Pqs-tq́-sq, *r* S. Am., 400 m.
Pasto, Pq́s-tō, *t* S. Am., 7.
Patagonia, Pq-tq-gó-ni-a, *div* S. Am.; area 350,000 s. m., inhabited only by Indians.
Patak, Pó-tok, *t* Hun., 5.
Patapsco, Pa-táps-kō, *r* Md., 80 m.
Patchogue, Pat-çóg, *v* N-Y.
Paterno, Pq-te*r*-nó, *c* Sic., 11.
Paterson, Pát-er-son, *c* N-J., 17½.
Path-Head, Páŧ-Hed, *t* Scot., 4.
Patia, Pq́-ti-q, *r* N-Gran., 200 m.
Patmos, Pát-mos, *i* As. Minor, 4.
Patna, Pát-na, *c* Hin., 285.
Patoka, Pa-tó-ka, *creek* and *v* Ia.
Patos, Pq́-tōs, *l* Bra.
Patras, Pq-trq́s, *s-pt t* Greece, 8.
Patterson, Pát-er-son, *vs* N-Y., Pa., O.
Pattersonville, Pát-er-son-vil, *v* La., ¾.
Patti, Pq́-tε, *c* Sic., 5.
Paturages, Pq-tę-rq́ʒ, *t* Belg., 6¼.
Patuxent, Pa-túks-ent, *r* Md., 90 m.
Patzum, Pqt-sóm, *t* Guat., 5⅓.
Pau, Pō, *t* Fr., 16¼.
Paucartambo, Pɤ-kq*r*-tq́m-bō, *t* Peru, 17; *r* do., 300 m.
Paulding, Pól-diŋ, *co t* Miss.
Paulina, Pɵ-lé-na, *v* N-Y.
Pavia, Pq-vé-q, *c* Aus. It., 28¼.
Pavlovo, Pqv-ló-vō, *t* Rus., 8.
Pawcatuck, Pɵ-ka-túk, *r* and *v* R. I.
Paweea, Pq-wé-a, *t* Guinea, 16.
Pawlet, Pó-let, *v* Vt., 2.
Pawpaw, Pó-pɵ, *r* and *v* Mich., 1½.
Pawtucket, Pɵ-túk-et, *t* R. I. and Mass., 10; *r* N-Eng. [1¾.
Pawtuxet, Pɵ-túks-et, *r* and *v* R. I.
Paxo, Páks-ō, Ionian *i*, 5¼.
Paxton, Páks-ton, *v* Mass., ¾.
Payta, Pí-tq, *s-pt t* Peru, 5.
Peabody (Pé-bod-i) Bay, Greenland.
Peace (Pεs) River, Br. N. Am., 1100 m.
Pearl (Pęrl) Islands, of N-Gran.
Pearl River, Miss., 250 m.
Pe-Chee-Lee, Pa-Ȼε-lé, *inlet* Yel. Sea.
Peckham, Pék-am, *v* Eng., 19½.
Pecos, Pá-kōs, *r* N-Mex., 700 m.
Pedee, Pε-dé, (Great *and* Little,) *rs* S. C.
Pedraza, Pa-drq́-sq, *t* Ven., 3¼.
Peebles, Pé-blz, *t* Scot., 2⅔.
Peekskill, Péks-kil, *v* N-Y., 2½.
Peel, Pεl, *s-pt t* Isle of Man, 2⅓.
Peel River, Br. N. Am.
Pegau, Pá-gɤ, *t* Sax., 3½.
Pego, Pá-gō, *t* Sp., 5½.
Pegu, Pε-gó, *cy* India, 70; *c* do.
Peipus *or* Peipous, Pá-ε-pōs, *l* Rus.
Pekatonica, Pek-a-tón-i-ka, *r* Wis. and Ill.; *p o* Ill.
Pekin, Pé-kin, *vs* N-Y., Ill. 2.
Peking, Pε-kíŋ, *or* Pekin, Pε-kín, *cap c* China, pop. 2,000,000. [4.
Pelestrina, Pa-les-tré-nq, *i* and *t* N. It.,
Pelew (Pε-lq́) Islands, Caroline *is*, N. Pac. Oc.
Pelham, Pél-ham, *vs* N-H., N-Y.
Pellew (Pél-q) Islands, of Australia.
Pelworm, Pél-vo*r*m, *i* of Den., 2.
Pemadumcook, Pem-a-dúm-kuk, *l* Me.
Pemba, Pém-ba, *i* of Af.
Pemberton, Pém-ber-ton, *vs* N-J. ¾, O.

Pembina, Pém-bi-nɑ, *l* and *co* Min.
Pembroke, Pém-bruk, *s-pt t* S. Wales; *vs* N-H., Mass.
Pemigewasset, Pem-i-jɛ-wós-et, *r* N-H.
Pemiscot, Pém-i-skot, *l* Mo.
Penang, Pɛ-náŋ, *or* Prince of Wales' Island, on Strait of Malacca, 43¼.
Penchant, Pen-ʃɑ́nt, *bayou* La.
Pendleton, Pén-dl-ton, *vs* Eng. 14¼, Ia.
Penedo, Pa-ná-dɷ, *c* Bra., 14.
Penha, Pén-yɑ, *v* Bra., 1.
Penicuick, Pen-i-kẹ́k, *burgh* Scot., 3.
Penjinsk, Pen-jínsk, *g* Siberia.
Penkridge, Pén-krij, *t* Eng., 3¼.
Pennar, Pen-ɑ́r, *r* India, 270 m.
Pennington, Pén-iŋ-ton, *v* N-J., ½.
Penniston, Pén-is-ton, *t* Eng., 6⅓.
Penn's Cove, Penz Kɷv, *co t* Wash. Ter.
Pennsgrove, Pénz-grɷv, *v* N-J.
Pennsylvania, Pen-sil-vá-ni-ɑ, one of the original U. S., second in population; area 46,000 s. m.; pop., in 1850, 2,311,786: 2,258,160 whites, 53,626 colored; in 1856, 2,496,728.
Penn Yan, Pen Yan, *v* N-Y., 2¼.
Penobscot, Pɛ-nób-skot, *r* Me., 300 m.
Penrhyn (Pén-rin) Islands, Pac. Oc.
Penrith, Pén-riŧ, (often Pé-riŧ,) *t* and *par* Eng., 6¾.
Penryn, Pen-rín, *bor* and *t* Eng., 4.
Pensacola, Pen-sa-kó-lɑ, *co t* Fa., 2¼; [*b* Fa.
Pensaukee, Pen-sé-kɛ, *r* Wis.
Pensnett, Péns-net, *v* Eng., 5.
Pentland Frith, Pént-land Friŧ, *sound* bet. Scot. and Orkney Islands.
Penza, Pén-zɑ, *gov* Rus.; area 14,768 s. m., pop. 1,058,444; *c* of same, 10¼.
Penzance, Pen-záns, *bor* and *s-pt t* [Eng., 9¼.
Peoria, Pɛ-ó-ri-ɑ, *c* Ill., 8.
Pepperell, Pép-er-el, *v* Mass., 1¾.
Pequot, Pé-kwot, *vs* Conn., Wis.
Perekop, Pa-ra-kóp, *ist* Rus. Crimea.
Pereslavl, Per-a-slɑ́v-l, *t* Rus., 7.
Périgueux, Pa-rɛ-gẹ́, *t* Fr., 13½.
Perleberg, Pẹ́r-la-bẹrh, *t* Prus., 6¼.
Perm, Pẹrm, *t* Rus., 10.
Pernagoa, Pẹr-nɑ́-gɷ-ɑ, *t* Bra., 4.
Pernau, Pẹ́r-nɤ, *s-pt t* Rus., 9.
Peros Banhos, Pá-rɷs Bɑ́n-yɷs, *is* Chagos Arch., Ind. Oc.
Perote, Pa-ró-ta, *t* Mex.
Perpignan, Pẹr-pɛn-yóñ, *t* Fr., 21¾.
Perry, Pér-i, *co t* Ga., 1¼; *vs* N-Y. 3, Ill. ½, Pa.
Perryopolis, Per-i-óp-ɷ-lis, *v* Pa.
Perrysburg, Pér-iz-burg, *v* O., 1⅜.
Perrysville, Pér-iz-vil, *vs* Pa., O.
Perryville, Pér-i-vil, *co ts* Miss., Ark.; *vs* N-J., Pa., Ia. 1. [*cap* Persia.
Persepolis, Pẹr-sép-ɷ-lis, anc. ruined
Pershore, Pẹ́r-ʃɷr, *t* Eng., 2¾.
Persia, Pẹ́r-ʃi-ɑ, *cy* Asia; area 450,000 s. m., pop. 11,299,500.
Persian (Pẹ́r-ʃan) Gulf, arm Ind. Oc.
Perth, Pẹrŧ, *c* Scot., 22¼; *t* C. W., 2; *dis* and *cap* W. Australia.
Perth Amboy, Pẹrŧ Am-bɵ́, *v* N-J., 2.
Peru, Pɛ-rɷ́, *rep* S. Am., comprising eleven departments; area 370,000 s. m., pop. 2,279,085; *co t* Ia., 1¾; *vs* Ill. 3, N-Y., O., &c.
Perugia, Pa-rɷ́-jɑ, *l* and *c* Cen. It., 18⅓.
Peruwels, Pá-rẹ-vels, *t* Belg., 7½.
Pesaro, Pés-a-rɷ, *t* Cen. It., 12.
Pescadores, Pes-kɑ-dɷ́-res, *is* of Peru; N. Pac. Oc.
Peshawer, Peʃ-ɤ́-er, *c* Afg., 50.
Pesth, Pest, *fr c* Hun., 100.
Petchenegue, Peɥ-nég, *t* Rus., 7.
Petchora, Péɥ-ɷ-rɑ, *r* Rus., 900 m.
Peten, Pa-tén, *l* and *i* Guatemala.
Peterborough, Pé-ter-bur-ɷ, *c* Eng., 8⅜; *co t* C. W., 2½; *v* N-H., 2¼.
Peterhead, Pé-ter-hed, *s-pt t* Scot., 5.
Petersburg, Pé-terz-burg, *ts* Va. 15, Pa. 1; *co ts* Ia., Ill.; *v* Ky., ½.
Petersfield, Pé-terz-fɛld, *bor* Eng., 5½.
Peterwardein, Pé-ter-wér-dịn, *cap t* Slavonia, 4.
Petit-Canal, Pe-té-Kɑ-nɑ́l, *t* island of Guadeloupe, 7¾.
Petra, Pé-trɑ, anc. *c* Arabia Petræa.
Petropaulovski, Pa-trɷ-pɤ-lóv-skɛ, *cap t* Kamtchatka, 1.
Petrovacz, Pa-trɷ-vɑ́ts, *v* Hun., 5¼.
Petrovoszelo, Pa-trɷ-vo-sá-lɷ, *v* Hun., [5½.
Petrovsk, Pa-tróvsk, *t* Rus., 7.
Petrozavodsk, Pa-trɷ-zɑ-vódsk, *ft t* Rus., 8.
Petsh, Peɥ, *t* Eu. Tur., 12.
Petworth, Pét-wurŧ, *t* Eng., 2½.
Petzka, Péts-*h*ɑ, *t* Hun., 13½.
Peveragno, Pa-va-rɑ́n-yɷ, *t* It., 6.
Pewaukee, Pɛ-wé-kɛ, *v* and *l* Wis.
Peyster, Pị-ster, *i* Pac. Oc.
Pézénas, Pa-za-nɑ́, *t* Fr.; 7⅓. [7¼.
Pforzheim, Pfórts-hịm, anc. *c* Baden,
Phatuka, Fɑ-tɷ́-kɑ, *t* Br. Ind., 12.
Pheng-Hoo, Feŋ-Hɷ, *i* China Sea.
Philadelphia, Fil-a-dél-fi-ɑ, *c* Pa., and second in the U. S., 408¾; *co t* Miss.; *vs* N-Y., Ia., &c. [3¾, Belg.
Philippeville, Fɛ-lɛp-vɛ́l, *ft ts* Algeria
Philippi, Fi-líp-ị, *t* in ruins, Eu. Tur.; *co t* Va.
Philippine (Fíl-ip-ɛn) Islands, a group in the N. Malay Arch., comprising 1200 islands, of which Luzon, Mindanao and Palawan are the principal; area 120,000 s. m., pop. 5,000,000.

Philipsburg, Fíl-ips-burg, *vs* N-J., Pa.,
Philipsville, Fíl-ips-vil, *v* N-Y., 1. [O.
Phocæa, Fɷ-sé-ɑ, *s-pt t* As. Minor, 4.
Phœnix, Fé-niks, *v* N-Y.
Phœnixville, Fé-niks-vil, *v* Pa., 3.
Phookok, Fɷ-kók, *i* Gulf of Siam.
Piacenza, Pɛ-ɑ-ɕén-zɑ, *ft c* N. It., 30.
Piana, Pɛ-ɑ́-nɑ, *t* Sic., 5.
Piasina, Pɛ-ɑ-sé-nɑ, *l* and *r* Sib., 250 m.
Piauhi, Pɛ-ɤ-é, *r* Bra., 300 m.
Piavozero, Pɛ-ɑ́-vɷ-zá-rɷ, *l* Rus.
Piazza, Pɛ-ɑ́t-sɑ, *c* Sic., 16¼.
Pichincha, Pɛ-ɕin-ɕɑ, *vol* S. Am.
Pickaway, Pík-a-wa, *co* O. [C.
Pickens (Pík-enz) Court-House, *co t* S.
Pickering, Pík-er-iŋ, *t* Eng., 2½.
Pico, Pé-kɷ, Azores *i* At. Oc., 36.
Picton, Pík-ton, *c t* C. W., 1¾.
Pictou, Pik-tɷ́, *s-pt t* Nova Scotia.
Piedimonte, Pɛ-a-di-món-ta, *t* Nap., 5¾.
Piedmont (Péd-mont) Principality, *cy* Eu.; area 11,913 s. m., pop. 2,134,152;
Pielis, Pɛ-á-lis, *l* Finland. [*v* Va.
Piermont, Pér-mont, *v* N-Y., 1¼.
Pierpont, Pér-pont, *v* O.
Pierre Bayou, Pɛ-ɑ́r Bį-ɷ, *stream*, Miss.
Pierrepont Manor, Pér-pont Mán-or, *v* N-Y. [8½.
Pietraperzia, Pɛ-a-trɑ-pérd-zɛ-ɑ, *t* Sic.,
Pietro-in-Calatina, Pɛ-á-trɷ-in-Kɑ-lɑ-té-nɑ, *t* Nap., 7¾.
Pig Island, *i* S. Pac. Oc. [ft.
Pike's (Pįks) Peak, Rocky Mts., 11,497
Piketon, Pįk-ton, *co t* O., ¾; *v* Ia.
Pikeville, Pįk-vil, *co ts* Ky., Tenn., Ala.
Pilao Arcado, Pɛ-lɤ́n Ar-kɑ́-dɷ, *t* Bra.,
Pilatka, Pi-lát-kɑ, *co t* Fa. [5.
Pilaya, Pɛ-lį-ɑ, *r* S. Am., 300 m. [m.
Pilcomayo, Pil-kɷ-mį-ɷ, *r* S. Am., 1000
Pilsen, Píl-sen, *t* Boh., 9¾.
Pinckney, Píŋk-ni, *v* Mich., ½.
Pinckneyville, Píŋk-ni-vil, *co t* Ill.
Pine Bluff, Pįn Bluf, *co t* Ark., ½.
Pinega, Pɛ-ná-ɡɑ, *r* Rus., 290 m.
Pine Plains, *v* N-Y.
Pinerolo, Pɛ-na-ról-ɷ, *t* Sard. S., 13½.
Pinos, Pé-nɷs, *i* Caribbean Sea.
Pinsk, Pinsk, *t* Rus., 5⅓.
Piqua, Pík-wa, *t* O., 4.
Pirahi, Pɛ-rɑ-hé, *t* Bra., 3.
Pirano, Pɛ-rɑ́-nɷ, *s-pt t* Istria, 6¼.
Pirate (Pį-rat) Islands, Gulf of Tonquin.
Piratinim, Pɛ-rɑ-tɛ-nén, *t* Bra., 3¾.
Pirmasens, Pír-mɑ-sents, *t* Rhen. Bav.,
Pirna, Pír-nɑ, *ft t* Sax., 6. [5⅔.
Piron, Pɛ-rón, *i* Louisiada Arch.
Pir-Panjal, Pɛr-Pɑn-jɑ́l, *ms* bet. Cashmere and Punjab.
Pisa, Pé-zɑ, *c* Tus., 22.

Piscataqua, Pis-kát-a-kwɑ, River, N-H.
Piscataquis, Pis-kát-a-kwis, *r* and *co* Me,
Piscataway, Pis-kát-a-wa, *vs* N-J., Md.
Pisek, Pé-sek, *t* Boh., 5½.
Pisgah, Píz-gɑ, anc. *m* Pal.; *v* Iowa.
Pisticci, Pis-té-ɕɛ, *t* Nap., 6¼.
Pistoja, Pis-tɷ́-yɑ, *t* Tus., 12⅓.
Pitcairn (Pit-kɑ́rn) Island, Pac. Oc., ⅙.
Pitcher, Píɕ-er, *v* N-Y., 1½.
Pitic, Pɛ-tík, *t* Mex., 5.
Pitt's Archipelago, Pac. Oc.
Pittsborough, Píts-bur-ɷ, *co t* N. C.
Pittsburg, Píts-burg, *c* Pa., 46⅔; *vs* Ia., Mo., Iowa.
Pittsfield, Píts-fɛld, *t* Mass., 6½; *co t* Ill.; *v* Pa.
Pittsford, Píts-ford, *vs* Vt., N-Y.
Pittston, Píts-ton, *vs* Me. 3, Pa. 2.
Pizzo, Pít-sɷ, *c* Nap., 5¾.
Placentia, Pla-sén-ʃi-ɑ, *s-pt t* Newfoundland; — Bay, inlet, do.
Placer, Plɑ-sɑ́r *or* Plá-ser, *co* Cal.
Placerville, Plá-ser-vil, *v* Cal., 5⅔.
Plainfield, Plán-fɛld, *vs* Vt. ¾, Conn., N-J. 2, Ia.
Plainville, Plán-vil, *vs* R. I., Conn., O.
Plaquemine, Plak-mén, *bayou*, *par* and *v* La.
Plasencia, Plɑ-sén-θi-ɑ, *c* Sp., 6¾.
Plata, La, Lɑ Plɑ́-tɑ, (*or* the Argentine Republic,) *rep* S. Am., consisting of the provinces of Buenos Ayres, Santa Fé, Entre Rios, Corrientes, Cordova, La Rioja, Santiago del Estero, Tucuman, Catamarca, Salta and Jujuy, San Luis, Mendoza, San Juan; area 820,000 s. m., pop. 820,000.
Platte, Plat, *r* tributary to Mo. River, 1200 m.; also *rs* Iowa, Wis.
Platte City, *co t* Mo., ⅔.
Platteville, Plát-vil, *v* Wis., 1¼. [Mo.
Plattsburg, Pláts-burg, *co ts* N-Y. 5⅔,
Plauen, Plɤ́-en, *t* Sax., 10⅔. [2¼.
Pleasant Valley, Pléz-ant Vál-i, *v* N-Y.,
Pleasant View, Vɥ, *v* Ia.
Pleschen, Pléʃ-en, *t* Prus., 5.
Plesse, Plés-e, *t* Prus. Silesia, 3½.
Plock, Plotsk, *c* Poland, 6.
Ploërmel, Plɷ-ér-mél, *t* Fr., 8½.
Ploeuc, Plɷ-ék, *v* Fr., 6.
Plouaret, Plɷ-ɑ-rá, *v* Fr., 5⅓.
Plover, Plúv-er, *v* Wis., ½.
Plumb (Plum) Island, coast of Mass.; also in Long Island Sound.
Plymouth, Plím-uθ, *bor* and *s-pt t* Eng., 52¼; *co ts* Mass. 6½, N. C., Ia.; *vs* Pa. 1½, O., Mich., Wis.; — Sound, inlet of Eng. Channel.
Po, Pɷ, *r* It., 340 m. [*v* Ill.
Pocahontas, Pɷ-ka-hón-tas, *co t* Ark.;

Pocklington, Pók-liŋ-ton, *t* and *par* Eng., 2¾.
Pocomoke, Pó-kœ-mœk, *r* and *b* Md.
Podgoritza, Pod-gœ-rít-sq, *t* Eu. Tur., 6.
Point-a-Pitre, La, Lq Pwaṅt-q-Pét-r, *t* island of Guadeloupe, 12¼.
Point Commerce, Pønt Kóm-ęrs, *v* Ia.
Pointe Coupée, Pønt Kœ-pé, *par* and *v* La.
Point Isabel, Iz'a-bel, *vs* Tex., Ky.
Point Pleasant, *co t* Va.; *vs* O., Mo.
Poirino, Pø-ré-nœ, *t* It., 5⅔.
Poitiers, Pø-térz, *t* Fr., 29¼.
Poland, Pó-land, a former *k* of Cen. Eu., now divided between Rus., Aus. and Prus.; area 284,000 s. m., pop. 11,000,000; *vs* N-Y., O. 1¼.
Polar Regions, Pó-lar Ré-jonz, *ter* about the n. and s. poles.
Polar Sea, (Northern,) Arctic Ocean; (Southern,) Antarctic Ocean.
Policandro, Pol-i-kq́n-drœ, *i* Grecian Arch., ¼.
Policastro, Pœ-li-kq́s-trœ, *t* Nap., 7.
Poligny, Pœ-lɛn-yé, *t* Fr., 5¾. [m.
Polillo, Pœ-lil-œ, Philippine *i*, 30 by 20
Polk, Pœk, *cos* U. S.
Pollenza, Pol-én-zq, *t* is. Majorca, 6½.
Pollockshaws, Pol-ok-ʃéz, *t* Scot., 6.
Polochic, Pœ-lœ-çék, *r* Guat., 120 m.
Polotzk, Pœ-lótsk, *t* Rus. Poland, 9.
Poltava, Pol-tq́-va, *c* Rus., 20.
Polynesia, Pol-i-né-ʃi-a, numerous *is* Pac. Oc.; united pop. 1,500,000.
Pomerania, Pom-ɛ-rá-ni-a, *prov* Prus.; area 12,304 s. m., pop. 1,197,701.
Pomeroy, Púm-rø, *co t* O., 4.
Pomfret, Póm-fret, *v* Conn., 2.
Pomigliano D'Arco, Pœ-mɛl-yq́-nœ-Dq́r-kœ, *t* Nap., 6. [Mo.
Pomme de Terre (Pom dę Tąr) River,
Pomona, Pœ-mó-na, Orkney *i*, 16¼.
Pompeii, Pom-pé-yį *or* Pom-pá-yɛ, anc. ruined *c* It.
Pondicherry, Pon-di-ʃér-ɛ, *cap* French settlements in India, 40.
Ponta Delgada, Pón-tq Del-gq́-dq, *t* Azores Islands, 22. [7¾.
Pont-a-Mousson, Pœṅt-q-Mœ-sóṅ, *v* Fr.,
Pont-Audemer, Pœṅ-Ꭷ-dę-mą́r, *t* Fr.
Pontchartrain (Pon-ʃar-trán) Lake, La., 40 by 24 m.
Pontecorvo, Pon-ta-kér-vœ, *t* It., 5¼.
Pontefract, Póm-fret, *bor* and *t* Eng., 11½.
Pontevedra, Pon-ta-vá-drq, *t* Sp., 4½.
Pontevico, Pon-ta-vé-kœ, *t* Lom., 5.
Pontiac, Pón-ti-ak, *co ts* Mich., 2½; Ill.
Pontianak, Pon-ti-q-nq́k, Dutch *c* of Borneo, 19¼.
Pontifical (Pon-tíf-i-kal) *or* **Papal** States, central portion Italian Peninsula, of twenty divisions; area 17,-210, pop. 3,006,771.
Pontivy, Pœṅ-tɛ-vé, *t* Fr., 5.
Pontoise, Pœṅ-twq́z, *t* Fr., 5⅔.
Pontoosuck, Pon-tó-suk, *vs* Mass., Ill.
Pontotoc, Pon-tœ-tók, *co* and *co t* Miss.
Pont-Saint-Esprit, Pœṅ-Saṅt-Es-pré, *t* Fr., 5½.
Pontypool, Pón-ti-pœl, *t* Eng., 3¾.
Ponza, Pón-zq, *is* Med. Sea, 1½. [10.
Pooching-Hien, Pœ-çiŋ-Hɛ-én, *t* Chi.,
Poole, Pœl, *bor* and *t* Eng., 9¼.
Poona, Pó-na, *c* Br. Ind., 86.
Poor *or* Pur, Pœr, *r* Sib., 200 m.
Poorbunder, Pœr-bún-der, *t* Hind.
Pootivl, Pœ-tɛv-l', *t* Rus., 9.
Pooto, Pó-tœ, pop. *i* coast of China.
Popayan, Pœ-pq-yq́n, *c* S. Am., 20.
Poperinghe, Pœ-per-áṅh, *t* Belg., 10½.
Poplar Plains, *v* Ky., ⅓.
Popocatepetl, Pœ-pœ-kq-ta-pét-l, *vol* Mex., 17,720 ft.
Popo Great, Pó-pœ Grat, *t* Guinea, 5.
Popo Isles, Malay Arch.
Poppi, Póp-ɛ, *t* Tus., 5⅔.
Porcuna, Pør-kó-nq, *t* Sp., 5¼.
Pordenone, Pør-da-nó-na, *t* Aus. It., 5.
Poros, Pó-ros, pop. *i* Gr.
Port Adelaide, Ad'ɛ-lad, *t* S. Aust., 10.
Port Adown, Pœrt A-dšn, *t* Ir. 3.
Portaferry, Pœrt-a-fér-i, *s-pt t* Ir., 2.
Portage, Pórt-ag, *v* Ia., 1¼.
Portage City, *co t* Wis., 2.
Portalegre, Pœr-tq-lá-gra, *t* Port., 5¾.
Portarlington, Pœrt-q́r-liŋ-ton, *t* Ir., 2¾.
Port Au Prince, Pœrt-œ-Prins, *cap c* Hayti, 20.
Port Byron, Bį-ron, *v* N-Y., 1½.
Port Carbon, Kq́r-bon, *bor* Pa., 3.
Port Chester, Ͼés-ter, *v* N-Y.
Port Clinton, Klín-ton, *co t* O.
Port Dalhoozee, Dal-hó-zɛ, *v* C. W.
Port Deposit, Dɛ-póz-it, *v* Md.
Port Discovery, *co t* Washington Ter.
Port Elizabeth, *s-pt t* S. Af., 4; *v* N-J., 1.
Port Gibson, *v* Miss., 1. [Scot., 7.
Port Glasgow, Glás-gœ, *burgh* and *t*
Port Hope, *t* Upper Canada, 2½.
Port Hudson, Húd-son, *v* La., ⅓.
Port Huron, Hq́-ron, *v* Mich., 4.
Portici, Pór-tɛ-çɛ, *t* Nap., 5.
Port Jefferson, Jéf-er-son, *v* O., ½.
Port Jervis, Jęr-vis, *v* N-Y.
Port Kennedy, Kén-ɛ-di, *v* Pa., ⅓.
Portland (Pórt-land) Isle of, *pen* and *par* Eng., 5¼; *c* Me., 22½; *c* Or., 6-½; *co t* Ia.; *vs* Conn., Ala., Ky., Mich., Mo.

Portlaw, Pωrt-ló, *t* Ir., 3⅔.
Port Leon, Lé-on, *pt entry* Fa.
Port Louis, Lώ-is, *cap t* Is. Mauritius, 35; *t* Guadeloupe, 4¾.
Port Mahon, Mq-hώn, *ft t* Sp., 13¼.
Portneuf, Pωrt-nẹ́f, *co* and *v* C. E.
Porto Alegrẹ, Pόr-tω Ꭿ-lá-gra, *c* Bra., 12; *t* do. 4. [*har* S. Am.
Porto Atacames, Pόr-tω Ꭿ-tq-kq́-mes,
Porto Bello, Pόr-tω Bél-ω, *s-pt t* Scot., 3½; *t* N-Gran.; *t* Bra.
Porto Ferrago, Pόr-tω Fer-q́-yω, *cap t* Elba, Tuscany, 4½.
Port-of-Spain, *t* W. Ind., *cap* Is. Trinidad, 11⅔. [Verd Is.
Porto Praya, Pόr-tω Prʝ-q, *t* Cape
Porto Rico, Pόr-tω Ré-kω, W. Ind. Is., area 2580 s. m.; pop. 500,000, 50,000 being slaves. [Is., 6.
Porto Santo, Pόr-tω Sq́n-tω, Madeira
Port Philip, Fíl-ip, *b* Aust.
Port Royal, Rό-al, *ft t* Jam.; *v* Va., ⅔.
Portsea (Pόrt-sε) Island, coast of Eng., pop. 72,126.
Portsmouth, Pόrts-muθ, *bor* and *s-pt t* Eng., 72; *c* N-H., 11; *s-pt* and *naval depot* Va., 8⅔; *co t* O., 5; *v* Mich.
Portsoy, Pόrt-sσ, *s-pt t* Scot., 2.
Port Tobacco, Tω-bák-ω, *co t* Md.
Portugal, Pόr-tq-gal, *k* Eu., area 35,-268 s. m.; pop. 3,471,203. [m.
Portuguesa, Pωr-tω-gá-sq, *r* Ven., 200
Port Washington, *v* O., ½; *co t* Wis.,
Port William, *v* Scot., ¾. [2½.
Posega, Pω-ʃá-gq, *t* Aus., 6¾. ȼ
Posen, Pό-zen, *c* Prus., 32; — Grand Duchy, polish *prov* Prus.; area 12,248, s. m., pop. 1,352,014.
Pössneck, Pẹ́s-nek, *t* Cen. Ger., 3¾.
Potawatamies, Pot-a-wót-a-miz, *tr* Indians, n. Ia.
Poteau (Pω-tό) River, Ark.
Potenci, Pω-ten-ʒé, *r* Bra.
Potenza, Pω-tén-zq, *t* Naples, 12⅓.
Poti, Pω-té, *r* Brazil, 200 m.
Potomac, Pω-tό-mak, *r* Va., 350 m.
Potosi, Pω-tω-sé, *dep* Bol.; *c* do. 16¾.
Potosi, Pω-tό-si, *co t* Mo.; *t* Wis.; 2½.
Potsdam, Póts-dqm, *gov* and *c* Prus., 38; Póts-dam, *v* N-Y., 2¼.
Pottstown, Póts-tʊn, *bor* Pa., 2.
Pottsville, Póts-vil, *t* Pa., 10.
Poughkeepsie, Pω-kíp-sε, *c* N-Y., 15; *v* Ia.
Pouinipete, Pwε-ni-pét, *i* Pac. Oc., 2.
Poultney, Pólt-ni, *v* Vt. 2⅓.
Poulton, Pól-ton, *t* Eng., 7¼.
Poviglio, Pω-vél-yω, *t* It., 1⅓.
Povoa de Meadas, Pω-vό-q da Ma-q́-dqs, *t* Port., 7¾.
Povoa de Varzim, Pω-vό-q da Vqr-zéñ, *t* Port., 6¼.
Poweshiek, Pʊ́-ε-ʃεk, *co* Iowa.
Powhatan, Pω-ha-tán, *co* Va.; *v* Ark.
Poxim, Pω-ʃéñ, *t* Bra., 3. [Ter.
Poyais, Pwq-yá, *r* and *dis* Mosquito
Poyang, Pω-yq́ŋ, *l* China, 80 by 40 m.
Pozoblanco, Pω-tω-blq́n-kω, *t* Sp., 6½.
Pozzuoli, Pot-sω-ό-lε, *t* Nap., 8½.
Prado, Prq́-dω, *t* Port., 7.
Praga, Prq́-gq, *t* Poland, 4.
Prague, Prag, important *c* Bohemia, Eu., 68¾. [Wis.
Prairie du Chien, Prá-ri dẹ Σεn, *co t*
Prairie du Rocher, Rό-ʃer, *v* Ill.
Prairie du Sac, Sqk, *v* Wis., ¾.
Prairie mer Rough, Prá-ri mąr Rωʒ, *p o* La.
Prairie Ronde, Rωnd, *v* Mich., ¾.
Prairieton, Prá-ri-ton, *v* Ia.
Prairieville, *vs* Ia., Mo., Mich.
Praslin, Prqs-lén, *is* Ind. Oc. [3¼.
Prats de Mollo, Prq dẹ Mo-ló, *ft t* Fr.,
Prattsville, Práts-vil, *v* N-Y., 1¾; *v* Ala., 6. [Java, 700,000.
Preanger, Pra-q́ŋ-her, Dutch residency,
Preble, Préb-l, *co* O.; *v* N-Y.
Pregel, Prá-gel, *r* Prus., 120 m.
Prenzlow, Prénts-lov, *t* Prus., 12¾.
Presburg, Prés-burg, *c*, *cap* Hun., 38.
Prescot, Prés-kot, *t* and *par* Eng., 7⅓; *co t* Wis.; *t* C. W., 2⅓.
Presque Isle, Presk él, *co* Mich. [¾.
Presteigne, Pres-tán, *bor* and *t* Eng., 1-
Preston, Prés-ton, *bor* and *t* Eng., 69½; *vs* Tex., Ky.; *t* C. E., 1¼.
Prestonburg, Prés-ton-burg, *co t* Ky.
Prestonpans, Pres-ton-pánz, *s-pt t* and *par* Scot., 1⅔.
Preto, Prá-tω, *rs* Brazil, 150 m.
Prevesa, Prá-va-sq, *ft t* Eu. Tur., 4.
Pribylov, Prε-bi-lóv, *is* Behring Sea.
Priego, Prε-á-gω, *t* Sp., 13½.
Prince Edward Island, Br. Am., area 1950 s. m., pop. 90,000; *i* Upper C.
Prince of Wales Archipelago, Rus. Am.
Prince of Wales Island, Pac. Oc.; Malay Arch.; *is* Torres Strait.
Prince's Island, Gulf of Guinea.
Princes' Islands, Sea of Marmora.
Princess Anne, *co t* Md.
Princess Charlotte (Σq́r-lot) Bay, Aust.
Princeton, Príns-ton, *bor* N-J., 2½; *co ts* Va., Miss., Ark., Ky., 1½; *vs* Ia., 1; Ill., &c.
Princeville, Príns-vil, *v* Ill., ½. [Oc.
Prince William Island, Feejee Is., Pac.
Prince William Sound, Rus. Am.
Pripets, Príp-ets, *r* Rus. Pol., 350 m.
Prisrend, Pris-rénd, *t* Eu. Tur., 20.

Pristina, Pris-té-nq, *t* Eu. Tur., 12.
Pritzwalk, Príts-vok, *t* Prus., 4.
Privas, Prε-vq̧s, *t* Fr., 5¼.
Prizzi, Prit-sε, *t* Sic., 7½.
Procida, Pró-çi-dq, *i* Bay of Naples, 13.
Proctor, Prók-tor, *v* Ky.
Proctorsville, *vs* Vt., Ia.
Prolog, Prɷ-lóg, *ms* Dalmatia.
Prome, Prɷm, *t* Burmese dominions.
Pronsk, Pronsk, *t* Rus., 6¾.
Prossnitz, Prós-nits, *t* Moravia, 8.
Providence, Próv-i-dens, *c* R. I., 47½; *co t* La.; *v* O.; *i* Carribean Sea; — Lake, La.
Province Wellesley, Wélz-lε, British settlement Malay Peninsula, 47½.
Provins, Prɷ-váṅ, *t* Fr., 7.
Prussia, Pró-ʃi-ɑ, extensive *k* Eu., consisting of Prussia, Posen, Brandenburg, Pomerania, Silesia, Saxony, Westphalia, Rhine. Prussia, has adopted the most complete system of education in the world; area 109,314, pop. 16,935,420.
Prussian Poland, Pró-ʃan Pó-land, e. Prus., formerly part of Poland.
Pruth, Prɷt, *r* E. Eu., 360 m.
Psilorati (Psε-lɷ-rq̧-tε) Mount, is. Crete.
Pskov, Pskov, *gov* Rus., 657¼; *c* do. 9.
Puebla La, Lq Pwéb-lq, *st* Mex.; area 12,042 s. m., pop. 580,000; *c*, *cap* of the above state, pop. 50,000.
Pueblo Viejo, Pwéb-lɷ Vε-á-*h*ɷ, *t* Vera Cruz, 1½.
Puerco, Pwę́*r*-kɷ, *r* N-Mex., 200 m.
Puerto Bello, Pwę́*r*-tɷ, Bél-yɷ, *s-pt t* N-Gran.
Puerto Cabello, Pwę́*r*-tɷ Ka-bél-yɷ, *s-pt t* Ven.
Puerto de La Cruz de Oratava, Pwę́*r*-tɷ da Lq Krɷs da Ɑ-rq-tq̧-vq, *s-pt t* Canary Is., 3½.

Puerto del Padre, Pwę́*r*-tɷ del Pq̧-dra, *har* Cuba.
Puerto de Santa Maria, Pwę́*r*-tɷ da Sqn-tq-Mq-ré-q, *c* Sp., 18.
Puerto Principe, Prén-si-pa, *c* Cuba, 49.
Puget (Pq̧-get) Sound, *b* Wash. Ter.
Pughman, Pɷg-mq̧n, *m* Afg., 13,000.
Pulaski, Pq-lás-ki, *vs* N-Y., 1; Pa., 1¾; Io., Ill.; *co t* Tenn., 1½.
Pultusk, Pól-tɷsk, *t* Pol., 4½.
Puna, Pɷ-nq̧, *i* Ecuador.
Punderpoor, Pun-der-pɷr, *t* Ind., 25.
Pungudutive, Puŋ-gɷ-dɷ-tév, *i* n. of Ceylon, 2½.
Punjab, Pun-jq̧b, *ter* of N. W. Hind.; area 210,000, pop. 4,740,000, inhabited by Sikhs, Cashmerians, and Afghans.
Punnair, Pu-nq̧r, *r* S. Ind., 220 m.
Puno, Pq̧-nɷ, *c* Peru, 9.
Puntas Arenas, Pón-tqs Ɑ-rá-nqs, *pt* Costa Rica.
Purbeck, (Púr-bek,) Isle of, Eng.
Purdy (Púr-di) Islands, S. Pac.
Purneah, Púr-nε-ɑ, *t* Br. Ind., 40.
Purus, Pó-rɷs, *r* S. Am., 400 m.
Putnamville, Pút-nam-vil, *vs* Ia., Mo.
Putney, Pút-ni, *r* Eng., 5¼.
Putumayo, Pɷ-tɷ-mí-ɷ, *r* S. Am., 700 m.
Putzig (Pút-si*h*) Bay, an arm of the Gulf Dantzic.
Puy, Le, Lę Pwε, *t* Fr., 15¾.
Puy de Dome, Pwε dę Dɷm, *dep* Fr., 596¾; *m* do. 4806 ft.
Puylaurens, Pwε-lɷ-róṅ, *t* Fr., 6¼.
Pwllheli, Pɷ*l*-há-lε, *bor* and *s-pt t* N. Wales, 2¾.
Pyramid (Pír-a-mid) Lake, Utah Ter., 35 by 15.
Pyrenees, Pír-en-εz, *ms* bet. Fr., and Sp., 11,168 ft.

# Q.

Qua, Kwq, *m* Guinea, 5000 ft.
Quaco, Kwq̧-kɷ, *v* and *light-house* Bay of Fundy.
Quakertown, Kwá-ker-tɘn, *v* N-J., ¾.
Quampanissa, Kwqm-pq-nís-q, *t* Dahomey, 12.
Quang-See, Kwqŋ-Sé, *c* and *prov* China, pop. 7,313,895.
Quang-Tong, Kwqŋ-Tóŋ, *prov* China, pop. 19,147,030.
Quarnero, (Kwq*r*-ná-rɷ,) Gulf of, Adriatic Sea.
Quarto, Kwq̧*r*-tɷ, *r* La Plata, 280 m.
Quarto, Kwq̧*r*-tɷ, *t* Sardinia, 5¾.
Quasqueton, Kwás-kε-ton, *v* Io.

Quathlamba, Kwqt-lq̧m-bq, *m* Af.
Quatre Bras, Kq̧t-r Brq, *v* Belg.
Quebec, Kwε-bék, *c*, *cap* of the two Canadas, 42.
Queda, Ká-dq, *st* Malay Pen., 21.
Quedlingburg, Kwéd-lin-bɷr*h*, *t* Prus. Sax., 14¼.
Queen Charlotte (Σq̧r-lot) Island, S. Pac. Oc.; also numerous *is* Br. N. Am.
Queen Charlotte Sound, w. of N. Am.
Queenstown, *v* C. W., ½.
Quelpaert, Qwél-pqrt, *i* Yellow Sea.
Quenu, Ka-nó, *i* Chili.
Quequay, Ka-kwí, *r* Uruguay, 100 m.

Queretaro, Ka-rá-tq-rɷ, *st* Mex.; area 2444 s. m., pop. 132,124; *cap* of the above state, 29¾.

Querimba (Ka-rém-bɑ) Islands, e. of [Af.

Quesaltepeque, Ka-sql-tq-pá-ka, *t* Guat., 4.

Quezaltenango, Ka-sql-ta-nq́n-gɷ, *c* [Guat., 14.

Quibebon, Kɛ-bȩ-rôn, *pen* Fr., in Brittany, 3.

Quibo, Ké-bɷ, *i* N-Gran.

Quicara, Kɛ-kq́-rq, *is* N-Gran.

Quilimane, Kɛ-li-mq́-na, *t* E. Af.

Quillota, Kɛl-yó-tq, *t* Chili, 10.

Quimper, Kañ-pą́r, *t* Fr., 11.

Quimperlè, Kañ-per-lá, *t* Fr., 6¼.

Quincy, Kwin-si, *co ts* Fa., 1; Ill., 11; *vs* Mass., 5; Pa., ½; O., ½.

Quincy Point, *v* Mass.

Quindiu, Kɛn-di-ó, *mt* S. Am. [1½.

Quinebaug, Kwin-ɛ-bég, *r* and *v* Conn.,

Quinto, Kén-tɷ, *r* La Plata, 250 m.

Quitman, Kwit-man, *co ts* Miss., Tex.

Quito, Ké-tɷ, *c*, *cap* Ecuador, 70.

Quitta, Kwit-q, *t* N. Guinea, 5.

# R.

Raab, Rqb, *or* Nagy-Györ, Noj-Dyȩr, *t* Hun., 18.

Rabatt, Rq-bq́t, *ft t* Morocco, 27.

Rabinal, Rq-bi-nq́l, *t* Gautemala, 6½.

Racconigi, Rq-kɷ-né-jɛ, *t* N. It., 10.

Racine, Ra-sén, *c* Wis., 7½; *co* Wis.

Racketville, Rák-et-vil, *v* N-Y.

Raccoon, Ra-kɷ́n, *cr* Ind.; *r* Iowa.

Racs, Rqts, *t* Hun., 11¼.

Radnor, Rád-nor, *t* S. Wales, 2½.

Radokala, Ra-dɷ-kq́-lq, *is* N. Pac.

Radom, Rq́-dom, *t* Poland, 5¾.

Ragusa, Rq-gó-sq, *t* Sicily, 21½; *s-pt c* Dalmatia, 6.

Rahway, Ré-wa, *r* and *v* N-J., ¾.

Raiatea, Rį-q-tá-q, one of Society Is.

Rai-Koke, Rį-kó-ka, one of Koorile Is.

Rainy, Rá-ni, *l* and *r* bet. Brit. N. A., and U. S. Territories.

Raisin (Rá-zin,) River, Mich., 140 m.

Rajamahal, Rq-jq-mq-hq́l, *c* Br. Ind. 30.

Raleigh, Ré-li, *cap c* N. C., 4½; *co ts* Miss,, Tenn., Ill.

Ralls, Relz, *co* Mo.

Ralston, Réls-ton, *v* Pa.

Rambè, Rqm-bá, one of Feejee Is.

Rambla, La, Lq Rq́m-blq, *t* Sp., 9.

Ramboullet, Roñ-bɷ-ɛl-yá, *t* Fr., 4¼.

Ramgunga, Rqm-gúŋ-gq, *r* Br. Ind., 250 m. [ft.

Ramne, Rq́m-nɛ, *m* Himalayas, 22,768

Rampoor, Rqm-pɷ́r, *ts* Ind.

Ramsay, Rám-za, *v* Can. West, 3¼.

Ramsey, Rám-zi, *t* and *par* Eng., 2¾.

Ramsgate, Rámz-gat, *s-pt t* Eng., 12.

Ranai, Rq́-nį, one of Sandwich Is.

Randers, Rq́n-derz, *t* Den., 7¾.

Randolph, Rán-dolf, (East and West,) *vs* Mass.; *v* Vt., 2¾; N-Y.

Rangoun, Rqŋ-gɷ́n, *t* Burma, 20.

Rannock, Loch, Loh Rán-oh, *l* Scot.

Rapallo, Rq-pq́l-ɷ, *s-pt t* Sar., 10.

Raphoe, Rq́-fɷ, *t* Ir., 1⅓.

Rapidan, Rap-i-dán, *r* and *v* Va.

Rapides, Rq-péd, *or* Ra-pįdz, *par* La.

Rappahannock, Rap-a-hán-ok, *r* Va., 125 m. [Oc., 4.

Raratonga, Rq-rq-tóŋ-gɑ, *i* S. Pac.

Raritan, Rár-i-tan, *r*, *b* and *v* N-J., 1.

Rasay, Rq́-sa, *i* Hebrides, ⅓.

Rassegoo, Rqs-ɛ-gɷ́, one of Koorile Is.

Rastadt, Rq́s-tqt, *ft t* Baden, 6⅓.

Rat Island, in Aleutian Arch.

Rathboneville, Ráŧ-bɷn-vil, *v* N-Y., ⅓.

Rathenow, Rá-te-nov, *t* Prus., 5⅓.

Rathfarnham, Raŧ-fq́rn-am, *v* Ir., 5½.

Rathkeale, Raŧ-kál, *t* Ir.. 4¼.

Rathlin, Ráh-lin, *i* Ir., 1.

Ratibor, Rq́-ti-bor, *t* Prus. Silesia, 7¾.

Ratisbon, Rát-is-bon, *t* Bavaria, 23.

Ratz Böszörmeny, Rqts Bȩs-ȩr-mény, *t* s. e. Hun., 17.

Ravanusa, Rq-vq-nɷ́-sq, *t* Sicily, 6½.

Ravee, Rq́-vɛ, *r* Punjab, 370 m.

Ravenna, Rq-vén-q, *c* Cen. Italy, 12; Ra-vén-ɑ, *co t* O., 3½.

Rawak, Rq-wq́k, *i* East. Arch.

Rawdon, Ré-don, *v* Can. West., ½.

Rawitsch, Rq́-viq, *t* Prus. Poland, 10.

Raymond, Rá-mond, *v* Me., 1¼; *co t* Miss., Wis.

Raysville, Ráz-vil, *v* Ind.

Ré, Ra, *i* w. of France.

Readfield, Réd-fɛld, *v* Me., 2.

Reading, Réd-iŋ, *bor* and *t* Eng., 21½; *c* Pa., 17; *vs* Conn., O., Ind.

Real, Ra-q́l, *r* Brazil, 160 m. [3.

Realejo, Ra-q-lá-hɷ, *s-pt t* Nicaragua,

Rechnitz, Réh-nits, *t* Hun., 5.

Recife, Ra-sé-fa, *c* Brazil, 18.

Red Bank, *v* N-J.

Red Cedar River, Minn. and Iowa, 300 m.; also Wis.

Red Creek, *v* N-Y., ½.

Reddington, Réd-iŋ-ton, *v* Ind.
Redditch, Réd-iç, *v* Eng., 5.
Red Lake, Minn. Ter., 37 by 16.
Redon, Ra-dóṅ, *t* Fr., 5¾.
Red River, trib. of Miss., coursing Tex., Ark., La., 1200 m.; *rs* Tenn., Ky., Minn., 700 m.
Red Rock, *v* Minn.
Redruth, Réd-rωŧ, *t* Eng., 7.
Red Sea, an inland sea, Asia.
Red Sulphur Springs, *v* and *watering place* Va.
Reedsville, Rédz-vil, *v* Pa.
Refugio, Rɛ-fų́-ji-ω, *co* and *co t* Tex.
Regello, Ra-jél-ω, *v* Tus., 10.
Reggio, Réd-jω, *c* E. Italy, 18½; *c* N. Italy, 17.
Richenau, Rį-ḣe-nɤ, *i* Baden, 1½.
Reichenbach, Rį-ḣen-bqḣ, *ts* Sax., 6¾; Prus. Silesia, 5⅓.
Reichenberg, Rį-ḣen-bęrḣ, *t* Boh., 13⅓.
Reigate, Rį-gat, *bor* and *t* Eng., 5. [1.
Reikiavik, Rį-ki-a-vik, *cap t* Iceland,
Reims, Rɛmz, *c* Fr., 45¾.
Remiremont, Ra-mɛr-móṅ, *t* Fr., 5⅓.
Remscheid, Rém-∫įt, *t* Rhen. Prus., 12.
Renaix, Ra-ná, *t* Belg., 12¾.
Rendezvous, Rén-de-vωz, *i* Borneo.
Rendsburg, Réndz-bωrḣ, *ft t* Den., 10⅓.
Renfrew, Rén-frω, *burgh* Scot., 3.
Reni, Rá-ni, *t* Rus., 6.
Rennes, Ren, *c* Fr., 39½.
Rennsselaer, Rén-se-ler, *co* and *v* N-Y.
Rensselaerville, *v* N-Y., 3¾.
Renton, Rén-ton, *v* Scot., 2⅓.
Republic, Rɛ-púb-lik, *v* O., 1¼.
Requena, Ra-kán-yq, *t* Sp., 11.
Resaca de la Palma, Ra-sq́-kq da lq Pq́l-mq, battle field, Mex.
Reshd, Re∫t, *t* Persia, 50.
Resina, Ra-sé-nq, *t* Naples, 9.
Resinar, Ra-zɛ-nq́r, *v* Transylvania, 6.
Resolution, Rez-ω-lų́-∫on, *i* Hudson's Strait. [200 m.
Restigouché, Res-ti-gω-∫á, *r* Br. N. A.,
Retford, Rét-ford, (East,) *bor* and *t* Eng., 46.
Rethel, Ra-tél, *t* Fr., 8⅓.
Reus, Rá-ωs, *t* Sp., 25.
Reutlingen, Rɤ́t-liŋ-en, *ft t* Würtemberg, 11¼. [6.
Revel, Rév-el, *ft s-pt t* Rus., 24¾; *t* Fr.,
Revello, Ra-vél-ω, *t* N. It., 5¼.
Reynoldsburg, Rén-olz-burg, *v* O.
Rezé, Ra-zá, *t* Fr., 6¾.
Rezende, Ra-zén-da, *t* Brazil, 5.
Rhea, Ra, *co* Tenn.
Rhett (Ret,) Lake, *l* of Cal., 12 by 8.
Rhine, Rįn, noted *r* of Europe, 900 m.
Rhinebeck, Rįn-bek, *v* N-Y., 1⅓.
Rhinns, Rins, *pen* Scot.
Rhode Island, Rωd Ī'land, one of the original U. S., having an area of only 1,306 s. m.; pop. whites, 143,875; colored, 3,672; total, 147,541. [15.
Rhodes, Rωdz, *i* As. Tur., 30; *c* same,
Rhoe, Rω, Shetland Island, ¼.
Rhön, Ręn, *m* Ger.
Rhone, Rωn, *r* Eu., 285 m.
Rhuddlan, Hriđ-lan, *bor* N. Wales, 1¼.
Riazan, Rɛ-q-zq́n, *t* Rus., 9.
Ribeauvillé, Rɛ-bω-vɛl-yá, *t* Fr., 7⅛.
Riccarton, Rík-ɑr-ton, *v* Scot., 4¾.
Riccia, Rít-çq, *t* Naples, 6.
Rice Lake, Canada West.
Richibucto, Ri∫-ɛ-búk-tω, *r* and *port of entry*, N-Brunswick.
Richland, Ríç-land, *v* N-Y., 4; *vs* O., Iowa, Wis.
Richmond, Ríç-mond, *c* and *cap* Va., 32⅓; *c* Ia., 5; *t* and *par* Eng., co of Surrey, 9; *t* Eng., co. of York, 5; *vs* Me., 2; Vt., Mass.; *co ts* N-Y., Ky., Tex., Mo., La.
Richville, Ríç-vil, *v* N-Y. [5.
Rickmansworth, Rík-manz-wurŧ, *t* Eng.,
Riddings, Rid-iŋz, *v* Eng., 4⅙.
Rideau, Rɛ-dó, *r* Canada East.
Ridgefield, Ríj-fɛld, *v* Conn., 2¼.
Ridgeway, Ríj-wa, *co t* Penn.; *vs* N. C., Mich., Wis. [Ger.
Riesengebirge, Ré-zen-ga-bérḣ-a, *ms*
Rieti, Rɛ-á-tɛ, *t* Cen. Italy, 11.
Riga, Ré-gq, *ft c* Rus., 71¼.
Rigaud, Rɛ-gó, *v* and *College* Can. E.
Righi Culm, Ré-gɛ Kωlm, *m* Switz.
Rigolets de bon Dieu, Ríg-ω-lets dę bωṅ Dę, duplicate channel of Red River, La., 50 m.
Rimini, Ré-mɛ-nɛ, *c* Cen. Italy, 17⅓.
Rimouski, Rɛ-mωs-kɛ, *v* Can. East, 4.
Ringkiöbing, Riŋ-kyę-biŋ, *s-pt t* Jutland, 1¼.
Ringwood, Ríŋ-wωd, *t* Eng., 4; *v* N. J.
Rio, Ré-ω, Spanish for "river."
Rio Branco, Ré-ω Brq́n-kω, *r* Brazil, 700 m.
Rio Colorado Chiquito, Kω-lω-rq́-dω Ͼɛ-ké-tω, *r* N-Mex., 500 m. [500 m.
Rio das Mortes, dqs Mór-tes, *r* Brazil,
Rio de Janeiro, da Zq-ná-ɛ-rω, *prov* Brazil; area, 70,630 s. m.; pop. 850,-000.
Rio de la Pasion, Pq-sɛ-ón, *r* Cen. A.
Rio de la Plata, Plq́-tq, *r* S. A., 2500 m.
Rio de los Martires, Mq́r-tɛ-res, *r* Cal.
Rio de San Juan, Sqn Hω-q́n, *r* New Mexico, 350 m.
Rio Dulce, Dωl-sa, *r* or outlet of the Golfo Dulce Honduras.

Rio Grande, Ré-ọ Grán-da, *rs* Senegambia, Af.; Bra., 600 m., also one 250 m.; Bol.; N-Gran.; Mex., 400 m.; Mosquito Ter., 200 m.; (anglicized, Rị-ọ Grand,) *r* N. Am., rises in Mex., and separates Texas from Mex., 1800 m. [1.

Rio Grande (Rị-ọ Grand) City, *t* Tex.,

Rio Grande do Norte, Ré-ọ Grán-da dọ Nór-ta, *prov* Bra.; area 22,784 s. m., pop. 110,000.

Rio Grande do Sul, Ré-ọ Grán-da dọ Sọl, *t* Bra., 3½.

Rioja, Re-ó-*h*a, *prov* Argentine Republic; pop. 19,000; *t* do., 4.

Rio Janeiro, Ré-ọ Za-ná-e-rọ, *or* Rị-ọ Jan-é-rọ, *cap* Bra., 350.

Riom, Re-óñ, *t* Fr., 12½.

Rio Negro, Ré-ọ Ná-grọ, *r* N-Gran. and Bra., 1000 m.; also *rs* S. Am., 600 m.; Uruguay, 250 m., &c.

Rionero, Re-ọ-ná-rọ, *t* Nap., 9⅔. [4.

Rio Vermelho, Ré-ọ Ver-mél-yọ, *t* Bra.,

Ripatransone, Re-pa-tran-só-na, *t* It., 5.

Ripley, Ríp-li, *vs* N-Y. 1¾, O. 1¾.

Ripon, Ríp-on, *c* Eng., 6; *v* Wis.

Risdon, Ríz-don, *v* O., ½.

Rising Sun, *co t* Ia., 2.

Rivarolo, Re-va-ró-lọ, *ts* N. It. 6, Sard. States, 5⅔.

Rive-de-Gier, Rev-de-Ze-á, *t* Fr., 13.

Riverhead, Rív-er-hed, *co t* N-Y., 2½.

Riverton, Rív-er-ton, *v* N-J.

River Trent, Rív-er Trent, *v* C. W., 1.

Rivière-a-Jacques, Re-vi-ár-a-Zak, *r* Minn., 600. [Mo.

Rivière-au-Bœuf, Re-vi-ár-ọ-Bef, *cr*

Rivière-au-Cuivre, Re-vi-ár-ọ-Kwev-r', *r* Mo. [3½.

Rivière Ouelle, Re-vi-ár Ọ-él, *v* C. E.,

Rivoli, Ré-vọ-le, *t* Pied., 5¼.

Roane, Rọn, *co* Tenn.

Roanne, Rọ-án, *t* Fr., 13⅓.

Roanoke, Rọ-an-ók, *v* Va. and N. C., 250 m.; *vs* N-Y., Mo.

Roapoa, Rọ-a-pó-a, Marquesas Is.

Robideaux, Rọ-be-dó, *cr* and *v* Mo.

Rochdale, Róch-dal, *bor* and *t* Eng., 29.

Rochefort, Roʃ-fér, *t* Fr., 24⅓.

Rochelle, La, La Rọ-ʃél, *s-pt t* Fr., 16½.

Rochester, Róch-es-ter, *cs* Eng. 15, N-Y. 44½; *vs* N-H. 3, Pa. 1¼, O., Mich., Ia., Iowa, Wis., &c.

Rockaway, Rók-a-wa, *t* N-J.; *v* N-Y.

Rockbridge, Rók-brij, *co t* Mo.

Rockford, Rók-ford, *c* Ill., 7; *co ts* N. C., Ala.; *v* Ia. [Vt.

Rockingham, Rók-iŋ-ham, *co t* N. C.; *v*

Rock Island City, *co t* Ill., 4.

Rockland, Rók-land, *c* Me., 10.

Rockport, Rók-pọrt, *co ts* Ia., Ark.; *vs* Mass., O., Ill.

Rock River, Wis., 225 m.

Rockton, Rók-ton, *v* Ill., ⅔.

Rockville, Rók-vil, *co ts* Ia. 1½, Md.; *vs* Mass., Conn., O.

Rockwell, Rók-wel, *v* Ill.

Rocky Mount, Rók-i Mѕnt, *co t* Va., ⅓.

Rocky Mountains, cen. N. Am.; length, 3000 m.; highest peaks, Fremont's, 13,570 ft.; Pike's, 11,497 ft.

Rodez, Rọ-dá, *t* Fr., 10¼.

Rodrigues, Rọ-drég, *i* Ind. Oc.

Roermond, Rọr-mónt, *t* Neth., 7¼.

Roeskilde, Rés-kil-da, *t* Den., 3¾.

Rogersville, Rój-erz-vil, *co t* Tenn.

Rokelle, Rọ-kél, *r* Af., 250 m.

Rolandswerth, Ró-landz-vert, *i* Rhine.

Rollo, Ról-yọ, *m* Sp.

Roma, Ró-ma, *i* Malay Arch.; *v* Tex.

Romano, Rọ-má-nọ, *ft t* Lom., 4.

Romans, Rọ-móñ, *t* Fr., 11.

Rome, Rọm, *c* It., and the most celebrated in the world, 175; *co ts* N-Y., 10⅔, Ia. ⅔; *c* Ga., 3; *vs* O., Wis.

Romeo, Ró-me-ọ, *v* Mich., 1¼.

Romford, Rúm-ford, *t* Eng., 3¾.

Romney, (Róm-ni,) New, *t* Eng., 1; *co t* Va.; *v* Ia.

Romöe, Ró-mọ, *i* Den., 1½.

Romorantin, Rọ-mọ-roñ-táñ, *t* Fr., 8.

Romsey, Rúm-zi, *bor* and *t* Eng., 2.

Rona, Ró-na, *i* Hebrides, ⅙.

Ronaldshay, Rón-aldz-ha, (North,) Orkney *i*, ½; —(South,) do., 3⅙.

Ronda, Rón-da, *c* Sp., 16.

Rondout, Ron-dѕt, *v* N-Y., 2½.

Rönne, Rén-a, *s-pt t* Den., 4⅓.

Ronneburg, Rón-e-bur*h*, *t* Ger., 5.

Roostchook, Rọs-chók, *ft c* Eu. Tur., 30.

Roques, Los, Lọs Ró-kes, *i* Carib. Sea.

Rosa Morada, Ró-sa Mọ-rá-da, *t* Mex., 4.

Rosario, Rọ-sá-ri-ọ, *v* is. Teneriffe, 1⅔.

Rosario de Cucuta, Rọ-sá-ri-ọ da Kọ-kó-ta, *t* N-Gran., 5.

Roscoe, Rós-kọ, *vs* O., Ill.

Roscommon, Ros-kóm-on, *t* Ir., 3½.

Roscrea, Ros-krá, *t* Ir., 5⅓.

Rose, Rọz, *v* N-Y.

Roseau, Rọ-zó, *t* is. Dominica, 5.

Rosenau, Ró-ze-nѕ, *ts* N. Hun., 7; Transylvania, 4.

Rosendale, Ró-zen-dal, *vs* N-Y., Wis.

Rosetta, Rọ-zét-a, *s-pt t* Low. Eg., 4.

Ross, Ros, *ts* and *pars* Eng. 2⅔, Ir. 1; — New, *bor* and *t* Ir., 9.

Rossano, Ros-á-nọ, *c* Nap., 15.

Rossie, Rós-e, *v* N-Y., 1½.

Rossiena, Ros-e-á-na, *t* Rus., 5¾.

Rossville, Rós-vil, *vs* O. 2½, N-Y., Ia.

Rostock, Rós-tok, *c* Ger., 20¼.
Rostov, Ros-tóv, two *ts* Rus., 8 and 6.
Rota, Ró-tq, *t* Sp., 8; *i* Pac. Oc.
Rothenburg-an-der-Tauber, Ró-ten-bu*rh*-qn-der-Tȣ-ber, *t* Bav., 5¼.
Rotherham, Róđ-er-am, *t* and *par* Eng., 6⅓. [7¼.
Rothesay, Róŧ-sa, *s-pt t* and *par* Scot.,
Rottee, Rót-ε, *i* Malay Arch.
Rottenburg, Rót-en-bu*rh*, *t* Würt., 6.
Rotterdam, Rót-er-dqm, *c* Neth., 89.
Rotuma, Rɷ-tɷ́-mq, *i* Pac. Oc.
Roubaix, Rɷ́-ba, *t* Fr., 34¾.
Rouen, Rɷ́-en, *c* Fr., 100⅓.
Rouge Bayou, Rɷʒ Bị-ɷ, La.
Rouge (Rɷʒ) River, Mich.
Rough-and-Ready, Ruf-and-Réd-i, *vs* Ga., Ala., Ky., Ill.
Roulers, Rɷ-lá, *t* Belg., 10¼.
Roundhead, Rȣnd-hed, *v* O., ¼.
Rousay, Rɷ́-sa, Orkney *i*, 1¼.
Rouse's (Rȣs-ez) Point, *v* N-Y.
Reveredo, Rɷ-va-rá-dɷ, *t* Tyrol, 8.
Rovigno, Rɷ-vén-yɷ́, *s-pt t* Illyria, 10⅔.
Rovigo, Rɷ-vé-gɷ, *t* Aus. It., 9⅔.
Rowandiz, Rȣ-qn-diz, *t* Tur. Koord.
Rowland's (Ró-landz) Springs, watering place, Ga.
Rowlesburg, Rólz-burg, *v* Va.
Rowley, Rȣ-li, *v* Mass.
Rowno, Róv-nɷ, *t* Rus. Poland, 9¼.
Row's, Rȣz, *v* O.
Roxborough, Róks-bur-ɷ, *co t* N. C.
Roxbury, Róks-ber-i, *c* Mass., 25; *vs* Conn. 1¼, Pa.
Roxo, Róks-ɷ, *v* Wis.
Royal Oak, Rǿ-al Ɵk, *v* Mich.
Royalston, Rǿ-alz-ton, *v* Mass., 1½.
Royalton, Rǿ-al-ton, *vs* Vt., Ia.
Royston, Rǿs-ton, *t* Eng., 2; *v* Ia.
Ruatan, Rɷ-q-tq́n, *i* Bay of Hond., 4.
Rubicon, Rɷ́-bi-kon, *r* Cen. It., 20 m.
Rudgeley, Rúj-li, *t* Eng., 3.
Rudolstadt, Rɷ́-dol-stqt, *t* Ger., 5¾.
Ruffec, Rȩf-ék, *t* Fr., 3⅔.

Rugby, Rúg-bi, *t* Eng., 6⅓,
Rügen, Rȩ́-gen, *i* Baltic, 37.
Rum, Rum, *i* Inner Hebrides, ⅛.
Rumbeke, Rúm-ba-ke, *v* Belg., 6¾.
Rumney, Rúm-ni, *v* N-H.
Rumsey, Rúm-zi, *v* Ky.
Runcorn, Rúŋ-korn, *t* Eng., 8.
Rupert (Rɷ́-pert) River, Br. N. Am., 300 m.
Ruppin, Neu, Nǿ Rɷ-pén, *t* Prus., 10.
Rupununy, Rup-ɷ-nɷ́-nε, *r* Br. Guiana, 250 m.
Rush, Ruʃ, *s-pt t* Ir., 1½; *v* N-Y.
Rushford, Rúʃ-ford, *v* N-Y. [N-Y., O.
Rushville, Rúʃ-vil, *co ts* Ia. 1⅔, Ill.; *vs*
Rusk, Rusk, *co t* Tex.
Russell, Rús-el, *vs* N-Y. 1¾, Mass.
Russellville, Rús-el-vil, *co ts* Ky., Ala.; *vs* O., Tenn., La.
Russia, Rɷ́-ʃi-a, *empire* Eu., and the largest that has ever existed, having the following divisions: European Russia; Asiatic Russia, embracing Siberia and Transcaucasian Provinces; and Russian America. Area, 7,430,125 s. m.; pop. 65,220,580.
Russian America, Rɷ́-ʃan A-mér-i-ka, *ter* n. w. N. Am.; area 394,000 s. m., pop. 61,000, mostly Esquimaux.
Russian Poland, Pó-land, former *k* Poland, and contiguous territory.
Rute, Rɷ́-ta, *t* Sp., 8. [N. C., ⅔.
Rutherfordton, Rúđ-er-ford-ton, *co t*
Rutherglen, Rúg-len, *burgh* and *par* Scot., 6½. [3⅓.
Ruthin, Rɷ́-đin, *bor* and *t* N. Wales,
Rutigliano, Rɷ-tεl-yq́-nɷ, *t* Nap., 5.
Rutland, Rút-land, *co t* Vt., 3¾; *v* O.
Rutledge, Rút-lej, *co ts* Tenn., Miss.
Ruvo, Rɷ́-vɷ, *t* Nap., 8.
Rybinsk, Rib-ínsk, *t* Rus., 10.
Ryde, Rịd, *t* Eng., 7¼.
Rye, Rị, *bor* and *t* Eng., 8½; *v* N-Y.
Rylsk, Rịlsk, *t* Rus., 7.
Rzhev, *R*-ʒev, *t* Rus., 9.

# S.

Saale, Sachsische, Sá*h*-siʃ-e Sq́-le, *r* Ger., 212 m.
Saalfeld, Sq́l-felt, *t* Cen. Ger., 4⅓.
Saarbrück, Sq́*r*-brȩk, *t* Rhen. Prus., 8⅔.
Saar-Louis, Sq*r*-Lɷ́-is, *t* Rhen. Prus.,
Saatz, Sqts, *t* Boh., 5. [4⅓.
Saba, Sq́-bq, Dutch W. Ind., 1⅔.
Sabara, Sq-bq́-rq, *c* Bra., 5.
Sabbionetta, Sq́-bi-ɷ-nét-q, *t* Lom., 7.

Sabine (Sa-bén) Lake, La.
Sabine River, Tex., 500 m.
Sibinetown, Sa-bén-tȣn, *v* Tex.
Sabioncello, Sq-bi-on-ɕél-ɷ, *pen* Dalm.
Sablé, Sq-blá, *t* Fr., 5¼.
Sable Island, Sq́-bla Ɨ́land, *i* At. Oc.
Sables, Sq́b-l, *t* Fr., 6.
Sabrina (Sa-brị-na) Land, Ant. Oc.
Sac, Sɛk, *r* Mo.; *co* Iowa.

Sacarappa, Sak-a-ráp-a, *v* Me.
Sacatecoluca, Sq-kq-ta-kω-ló-kq, *t* San Salvador, 5.
Sacatepec, Sq-kq-ta-pék, *t* Guat., 3.
Saccatoo, Sqk-q-tó, *t* Cen. Af.
Sachem's Head, Sá-çemz Hed, watering place, Conn.
Sackett's Harbor, Sák-ets Hq́r-bor, *v* N-Y., 2.
Saco, Sé-kω, *r* N-Eng.; *t* Me., 5¾.
Sacomango, Sak-ω-mang-gω, *r* N-Y.
Sacramento, Sak-ra-mén-tω, *co t* Wis., ¼.
Sacramento City, *t*, *cap* Cal., 20.
Sacs *or* Sauks, Seks, *Ind tr* Iowa.
Sacui, Sq-kω-é, *r* Bra., 250 m.
Sado, Sq́-dω, *i* Sea of Japan.
Saegerstown, Sá-gerz-tsn, *v* Pa., ½.
Saffee, Sq́f-ε, *s-pt t* N. Af., 12.
Saffron-Walden, Sáf-ron-Wél-den, *bor* and *t* Eng., 6.
Sagan, Sq́-gqn, *t* Prus. Silesia, 6¾.
Saghalien, Sq-gq-lé-en, *i* coast Asia.
Sag Harbor, Sag Hq́r-bor, *v* N-Y., 3½.
Saginaw, Ság-i-nε, *r* Mich.; *b* L. Huron.
Saginaw City, *co t* Mich., 1¼.
Sagua la Grande, Sq́-gwq lq Grq́n-da, *r* and *t* Cuba.
Saguenay, Sqg-a-ná, *r* C. E., 100 m.
Sahara, Sq-hq́-rq, *or* Great Desert, vast uninhabited region of N.-E. Af.; area 2,700,000 s. m.
Saida, Sí-dq, *t* Syria, 6.
Sai-Gon, Sį-Gón, *c* Anam, 180.
Saima (Sį-mq) Lake, Finland.
Saint-Affrique, Sańt-Af-rék, *t* Fr., 6⅔.
Saint Alban's, Sant Θl'banz, *bor* and *t* Eng., 7; *v* Vt.
Saint Alban's Bay, *v* Vt.
Saint-Amand, Sańt-A-móń, two *ts* Fr., 8¼ and 9½.
Saint Ambrose, Sant Am'brωz, *i* Pac.
Saint Andrew, An'drω, *s-pt t* Pr. Ed. Is.
Saint Andrew's, An'drωz, *s-pt c* Scot.; *s-pt t* N-Brun., 8; *vs* C. E. 1¼, Fa.
Saint Anthony, An'tω-ni, *t* Minn., 2.
Saint Anthony City, *v* Minn., ½.
Saint Augustine, Θ'gus-tεn, *c* Fa., 2.
Saint Austell, Θs'tel, *t* Eng., 3½.
Saint Bartholomew, Bqr-ŧól-ω-mq, *i* W. Ind., 18.
Saint-Benoit, Sań-Ba-nwq́, *t* is. Bourbon, 11⅓.
Saint Bernard, Sant Ber-nq́rd, singular *m pass* Alps; *par* La.
Saint-Brieuc, Sań-Brε-ę́, *t* Fr., 14.
Saint Catharines, Sant Káŧ-a-rinz, *t* C. W., 5.
Saint Catharine's Island, coast Ga.
Saint-Césaire, Sań-Sa-zą́r, *v* C. E., 2.
Saint-Chamond, Sań-Σq-móń, *t* Fr., 9.
Saint Charles, Sant Єq́rlz, *v* Ill., 3½; *co t* Mo., 3.

Saint Christopher, Krís-tω-fer, *i* Br. W. Ind.; pop. 1612 whites, 21,521 colored.
Saint Clair, Kląr, *v* Pa., 3; *co t* Mich.; *l* bet. C. W. and Mich.; *r* Mich., 40 m.; — City, *v* Pa.
Saint Clairsville, Klą́rz-vil, *co t* O., 1½.
Saint-Claude, Sań-Klωd, *t* Fr., 6.
Saint-Cloud, Sań-Klω, *t* Fr., 4.
Saint Croix, Sant Krǿ, *r* bet. Me. and N-Brun., 75 m.; *r* Wis., 200 m.
Saint Croix (Krǿ) Falls, *co t* Wis.
Saint Cyprian (Síp-ri-an) Bay, w. Af.
Saint Day, *t* Eng., 2.
Saint-Denis, Sań-De-né, *t* Fr., 15¾; *cap* is. Bourbon, 19.
Saint-Dié, Sań-Dε-á, *t* Fr., 9.
Saint-Dizier, Sań-Dε-zε-á, *t* Fr., 7½.
Sainte-Anne-de-la-Pocatière, Sańt-An-dę-lq-Pω-kq-tε-ą́r, *v* C. E.
Sainte-Anne-des-Plaines, Sańt-An-da-Plan, *v* C. E.
Sainte-Anne-du-Machiche, Sańt-An-dę-Mq-ʃéʃ, *v* C. E., 2.
Sainte Croix, Sańt-Krwq, *or* Santa Cruz, Sq́n-tq Krωs, largest of Virgin Islands; area 100 s. m., pop. 25,600.
Saint Elizabeth, Sant Ɛ-líz-a-beŧ, *v* C. E., 3.
Sainte-Marie, Sańt-Mq-ré, *i* of Madagascar, 5.
Sainte-Marie-aux-Mines, Sańt-Mq-ré-ω-Mεn, *t* Fr., 11⅔.
Sainte-Marie-de-la-Beauce, Sań-Mq-ré-dę-lq-Bωs, *v* C. E., 3¼.
Sainte-Marie-de-Monnoir, Sań-Mq-ré-dę-Mon-wq́r, *v* C. E., 5.
Saintes, Sańt, *t* Fr., 11½.
Saintes, Les, La Sańt, *i* Fr. W. Ind., 1.
Saint-Esprit, Sańt-Es-pré, *v* and *par* C. E., 2¼.
Saint-Etienne, Sańt-Ɛ-ti-én, *t* Fr., 56.
Saint Eustatius, Sant Yų-stá-ʃi-us, *i* Br. W. Ind., 2.
Saint-Flour, Sań-Flωr, *t* Fr., 5¾.
Saint Francis (Sant Frán-sis) River, Mo., 450 m.
Saint Francisville, Frán-sis-vil, *co t* La.; *vs* Ill., Mo.
Saint-François, Sań-Frоń-swq́, *t* Fr. W. Ind., 6⅔; *commune* Fr. is. Martinique, 6.
Saint François, Sant Frán-sis, *co* Mo.
Saint-François-du-Lac, Sań-Frоń-swq́-dę-Lqk, *v* C. E., 7; — Rivière-du-Sud, Rε-vε-ą́r-dę-Sęd, *v* C. E., 1⅓.
Saint Gall, Sań Gql, *t* Swit., 11¼.
Saint-Gaudens, Sań-Gω-dóń, *t* Fr., 5.
Saint Genevieve, Sant Jen-ε-vév, *co t* Mo., 1½.

Saint George, Sant Jerj, *bs* Newfoundland, Nova Scotia; Bermuda Island; *t* on same, 2¾; — Gulf of, e. Pat.
Saint George's, Jérj-ez, *v* Del., ⅓.
Saint George's Channel, the part of the Atlantic separating Eng. from Ir.
Saint George's Island, Gulf of Mexico.
Saint-Germain, Sañ-Ƶer-máñ, *t* Fr., 12.
Saint German, Sant Jẹr-man, *bor* and *t* Eng., 3.
Saint-Gilles-les-Boucheries, Sañ-Ƶɛl-la-Bɷ-ʃe-ré, *t* Fr., 6.
Saint-Grégoire-le-Grand, Sañ-Gra-gwɑ́r-lẹ-Gróñ, *v* C. E., 3.
Saint Helena, Sant Hel-é-nɑ, *i* of Br., S. At. Oc., well known as the place of Napoleon's banishment, from 1816 till his death, May 5, 1821; pop. 5; *par* La.
Saint Helen's, Hél-enz, *t* Eng., 5.
Saint Helen's Mountain, Or., 13,000 ft.
Saint Heliers, Hél-yerz, *cap t* is. Jersey, 21.
Saint-Henri-de-Mascouche, Sañt-Hoñ-ré-dẹ-Mɑs-kɷ́ʃ, *v* C. E., 2½; — de-Quebec, dẹ-Ka-bék, *v* C. E., 2⅔.
Saint-Hippolyte, Sañt-Ɛ-pɷ-lét, *t* Fr., 5¾.
Saint Hyacinthe, Sant Hį-a-sint, *t* C. E., 3⅓.
Saint-Iréné, Sañt-Ɛ-ra-ná, *v* and *par* C. E., 1.
Saint Ives, Sent Ivz, *bor* and *s-pt t* Eng., 10.
Saint-Jacques-de-l'Achigan, Sañ-Ƶɑk-de-Lɑ-ʃɛ-góñ, *v* and *par* C. E., 8.
Saint-Jean-Bonnefond, Sañ-Ƶoñ-Bon-fóñ, *v* Fr., 6⅓.
Saint-Jean-d'Angély, Sañ-Ƶoñ-Doñ-ʒa-lé, *t* Fr., 6½.
Saint-Jean-Molenbeek, Sañ-Ƶoñ-Mɷ-loñ-bák, *t* Belg., 7⅓.
Saint-Jean-Port-Joli, Sañ-Ƶoñ-Pɷr-Ƶɷ-lé, *v* and *par* C. E., 3½.
Saint Joachim, Sañ Ƶɷ-q-káñ, *v* and *par* C. E., 1.
Saint John, Sant Jon, *or* Saint John's, *c* N-Brun., 22¾; *r* do., 450 m.; *c*, *cap* Newfoundland, 21; *l* C. E.
Saint John's, Sant Jonz, *t* C. E., 2½.
Saint Johnsbury, Jónz-ber-i, *c* Vt., 3.
Saint John's River, Fa., 200 m.
Saint Joseph, Jó-zef, *c* Mo., 5; *co t* La.; *v* Mich., 1; *l* Br. N. Am.
Saint Joseph's River, Mich. and Ia., 250 m.
Saint-Junien, Sañ-Ƶẹ-ni-áñ, *t* Fr., 6.
Saint Kilda, Sant Kil-dɑ, *i* At. Oc., ⅛.
Saint Lawrence, Ló-rens, large *r* bet. the U. S. and the Canadas, 2200 m.; *i* Behring Sea.
Saint Leonard Middleton, Lén-ɑrd Míd-l-ton, *t* Eng., 5¾.
Saint-Lo, Sañ-Lɷ, *t* Fr., 8⅓.
Saint Louis, Sant Lɷ́is *or* Sant Lɷ́-i, *c* Mo., 95; *l* C. E.; *i* Senegambia, 14½; *t* is. St. Louis, 12; *t* is. Bourbon, 9¼; *r* Minn., 200 m.
Saint Lucia, Lɷ-sé-q, *i* Br. W. Ind., 25.
Saint Lucie, Lɷ-sé, *co* Fa.
Saint-Malo, Sant-Mɑ́-lɷ, *s-pt t* Fr., 9½.
Saint Margherita di Rapallo, Sañ Mɑr-ga-ré-tɑ dɛ Rɑ-pɑ́l-ɷ, *v* Sard. Sts., 6¼.
Saint Marie, Sant Ma-ré, *v* Ill.
Saint Mark's, Mɑrks, *co t* Fa.
Saint Martin, Mɑ́r-tin, *i* W. Ind., 7¾.
Saint Martinsville, Mɑ́r-tinz-vil, *co t* La., 1½.
Saint Mary, Má-ri, *v* Iowa; Azores *i*, 4⅔; *i* Madagascar, 5¾.
Saint Mary's, Má-riz, *vs* C. W. 1, O. 1, Ga. ¾.
Saint Mary's Strait, unites Lake Superior with Lake Huron, 63 m.
Saint Matthew, Máth-ɥ, *i* Mergui Arch.
Saint Maurice, Sañ Mɷ-rés, *r* C. E., 400 m.
Saint Michael, Sant Mį-kel, *i* Azores, 81.
Saint Michael's, Mį-kelz, *v* Md., 1.
Saint-Mihiel, Sañ-Mɛ-i-él, *t* Fr., 5¼.
Saint-Nazaire, Sañ-Nɑ-zɑ́r, *t* Fr., 5⅓.
Saint Neots, Sant Nɛts, *t* Eng., 3.
Saint Nicholas, Nik-ɷ-las, Cade Verd Is.; *t* Belg., 20.
Saint-Omer, Sañt-ɷ-mɑ́r, *ft t* Fr., 22.
Saint Omer, Sant ɷ'mer, *v* Ia., ½.
Saint Ours, Sañt ɷr, *v* C. E., 3.
Saint Paris, Sant Pár-is, *v* O., 1.
Saint Paul, Pɐl, *c*, *cap* Minn. Ter., 10; Sañ Pɷl, *t* is. Bourbon, 16¼.
Saint Paul de Loanda, Sɤñ Pɤ́-lɷ da Lɷ-ɑ́n-dɑ, *cap* Port. st. in Low. Gui.
Saint Peter, Sant Pé-ter, *l* Canada.
Saint-Peter-le-Port, Sañ-Pɛ-ɑ́r-lẹ-Pɷr, *cap t* land of Guernsey, 16¾.
Saint Petersburg, Sant Pé-terz-burg, (Rus. Pá-ter-bɷrg,) *c*, *cap* Russian Empire, 534.
Saint Peter's River, Minn. Ter., 450 m.
Saint Pierre, Sañ Pɛ-ɑ́r, *i* Lake Bienne, Swit.; *i* s. Newfoundland, 1½; *cap t* is. Martinique, 20½; *i* Ind. Oc.; *t* is. Bourbon, 14⅙.
Saint-Pierre-lès-Calais, Sañ-Pɛ-ɑ́r-la-Kɑ-lá, *t* Fr., 11⅓.
Saint-Pol-de-Léon, Sañ-Pol-dẹ-La-óñ, *t* Fr., 7.
Saint Pölten, Sant Pẹl-ten, *ft t* Aus., 6.
Saint-Quentin, Sañ-Koñ-táñ, *t* Fr., 24⅓.
Saint-Remy, Sañ-Ra-mé, *t* Fr., 6.
Saint Scholastique, Sañ Skɷ-lɑs-ték, *v* C. E., 5⅔.
Saint Sebastian, Sant Sɛ-bást-yan, *ft c* Sp., 13.

Saint-Servan, Sañ-Ser-vóñ, *s-pt t* Fr., 10. [N-Brun.
Saint Stephen's, Sant Stḗ-venz, *s-pt t*
Saint-Suzanne, Sañ-Sẹ-zq̈n, *t* is. Bourbon, 6⅙.
Saint Thomas, Sant Tóm-as, one of the Virgin Islands, 12¾; *i* Gulf of Guinea; *t* C. W., 1¼.
Saint-Trond, Sañ-Trɷñ, *t* Belgian Limbourg, 9½.
Saint-Valery-en-Caux, Sañ-Vq-la-rḗ-oñ-Kɷ, *t* Fr., 5⅓.
Saint Vincent, Sant Vín-sent, Br. W. Ind. Is., 30¼; Cape Verd Is.
Saint-Vincent-de-Paul, Sañ-Vín-sent-dẹ-Pɷl, *v* C. E., 3. [s. Aust.
Saint Vincent (Sant Vín-sent) Gulf,
Saint Xavier, Zāv-i-er, *i* w. Pat.
Saint-Yrieix, Sañ-Ɛ-ri-á, *t* Fr., 7¾.
Sakmara, Sqk-mq́-rq, *r* Rus., 350 m.
Sal, Sql, *rs* Rus., 250 m.; Peru; Cape Verd Is., ⅔.
Sala, Sq́-lq, *t* Nap., 6.
Salado, Rio, Rḗ-ɷ Sq-lq́-đɷ, *rs* Buenos Ayres, 400 m.; La Plata, 1000 m.
Salahieh, Sq́-lq-hḗ-e, *t* Lower Eg., 6.
Salama, Sq-lq́-mq, *t* Guatemala, 5.
Salamanca, Sq-lq-mq́ŋ-kq, *c* Sp., 14.
Salamis, Sál-a-mis, *i* of Greece, Gulf of Ægina, 5.
Salawatty, Sq-lq-wq́t-ɛ, *i* Malay Arch.
Salayer, Sq-lị-er, *i* Malay Arch., 60.
Sale, Sq́-la, *t* Sard. States, 5.
Sale, Sq-lá, *s-pt t* Morocco, 10.
Salem, Sá-lem, *t* Br. Ind., 19; *c* Mass., 21; *co ts* N-J. 4, Ia. 2, Ill. 1, Va.; *cap* Or., 1½; *vs* N-Y. 3, N. C. 1¼, Miss.; *t* O., 2½.
Salemi, Sq-lá-mɛ, *t* Sic., 8.
Salerno, Sq-lẹ́r-nɷ, *c* Nap., 19; *g* Med.
Salford, Sól-ford, *t* and *par* Eng., 63½.
Salgado, Sql-gq́-dɷ, *r* and *t* Bra., 4.
Salghir, Sql-gḗr, *r* Crimea, 100 m.
Salibabo, Sq-li-bq́-bɷ, *is* Malay Arch.
Salina, Sq-lḗ-nq, Lipari Is., Med., 4; — Sa-lị-nq, *v* N-Y., 2.
Saline, Sa-lḗn, *vs* Mich., Mo.; *bayou* La.; *r* Ark., 200 m.
Salineville, Sa-lḗn-vil, *v* O., ½.
Salins, Sq-lāñ, *t* Fr., 7¼.
Salisbury, Sólz-ber-i, *c* Eng., 11⅔; *co t* N. C., 2; *vs* Vt. 1, Mass. 3, Conn. 3, Md. 1½.
Salo, Sq́-lɷ, *t* Aus. It., 5⅔.
Salona, Sq-lɷ́-nq, *t* Greece, 4. [70.
Salonica, Sq-lɷ-nḗ-kq, *s-pt c* Eu. Tur.,
Sal Rey, Sql Ra, Cape Verd Is., 3⅓.
Salsette, Sql-sét-a, *i* Br. Ind., 50.
Salso Maggiore, Sq́l-sɷ Mqd-jɷ́-ra, *v* Parma, 5⅓.
Salta, Sq́l-tq, *c* La Plata, 8.
Saltcoats, Sólt-kɷts, *s-pt t* Scot., 4⅓.
Saltillo, Sql-tél-yɷ, *t* Mex., 6; — Sal-til-ɷ, *vs* Ia., Tenn.
Salt Lake City, *cap* Utah Ter., inhabited by Mormons; pop. 10.
Salt (Sɷlt) Range, *ms* Punjab,
Salt River, *cr* Ky., entering the Ohio below Louisville; *r* Mo.
Saltzburg, Sólts-burg, *v* Ia., ¾.
Salubria, Sa-lū́-bri-a, *v* N-Y.
Saluda, Sa-lū́-da, *r* S. C., 200 m.
Saluria, Sa-lū́-ri-a, *v* Tex.
Saluzzo, Sq-lɷ́t-sɷ, *c* N. It., 14½.
Salvisa, Sal-vị-za, *v* Ky.
Salwin, Sql-win, large *r* Far. Ind. a
Salzburg, Sólts-burh, *c* Up. Aus., 14¼.
Salzungen, Sq́lt-sɷŋ-en, *t* Cen. Ger., 3.
Salzwedel, Sq́lts-va-del, *t* Prus. Sax., 8.
Samakov, Sq-mq-kóv, *t* Eu. Tur., 7.
Samana, Sq-mq-nq́, *pen* Hayti, 1¾; *b* San Domingo.
Samar, Sq-mq́r, *i* Malay Arch., 96½.
Samara, Sq-mq-rq́, two *rs* Rus., 150 and 280 m.; *t* Rus., 11. [50.
Samarang, Sq-mq-rq́ŋ, *ft s-pt t* Java,
Samarcand, Sq-mqr-kq́nd, *c* Independent Toorkistan, 10.
Samarrah, Sq-mq́r-q, *t* As. Tur.
Sambas, Sqm-bq́s, *t* is. Borneo, 10.
Sambor, Sq́m-bɵr, *t* Aus. Poland, 6½.
Sambre, Soñ-br, *r* Fr. and Belg., 100 m.
Sambuca, Sqm-bɷ́-kq, *t* Sic., 8.
Samoan, Sa-mɷ́-an, *or* Navigator's Islands, Pac. Oc., 50.
Samoieds, Sam-ɵ-édz, three nomadic tribes occupying the shores of the Arctic Ocean.
Samos, Sá-mos, *i* w. As. Minor, 50.
Samothraki, Sq-mɷ-ŧrq́-kɛ, *i* Ægean Sea, 1½.
Samozero, Sq-mɷ-zá-rɷ, *l* Rus.
Samsoe, Sq́m-sẹ-e, *i* of Den., 5½.
Samson, Ʃqm-ʃon, *v* Hun., 22¼.
Samsoon, Sqm-sɷ́n, *s-pt t* As. Minor.
Sana, Sq-nq́, *c* Arabia, 40.
San Angel, Sqn Ȃŋ'hel, *t* Mex., 2.
San Antonio, Sqn Ȃn-tɷ́-ni-ɷ, *t* Ven.; one of Cape Verd Islands; — San An-tɷ́-ni-a, *r* and *co t* Tex., 7.
San Antonio de Gibraltar, Sqn Ȃn-tɷ́-ni-ɷ da Hɛ-brql-tq́r, *t* Ven., 3. [1.
San Augustine, San Θ-gus-tḗn, *v* Tex.,
San Bartolomé de Tirajana, Sqn Bqr-tɷ-lɷ-má da Tɛ-rq-hq́-nq, *t* Canary Island, 3½.
San Blas, San Blqs, *s-pt t* Mex., 2.
San Buenaventura, Sqn Bwa-nq-ven-tɷ́-rq, *r* and *t* Cal.
San Carlos, Sqn Kq́r-lɷs, *t* Ven., 10.

San Cataldo, Sqn Kq-tql-dœ, *t* Sic., 9.
San Colombano, Sqn Kœ-lom-bq-nœ, *t* Lombardy, 5.
Sanda, Sán-da, *i* of Scot.
Sandalwood (Sán-dal-wud) Island, populous *i* Malay Arch.
San Damiano d'Asti, Sqn Dq-mi-q-nœ Dqs-te, *t* It., 7.
Sandbach, Sánd-baq, *t* Eng., 2¾.
San Diego, Sqn De-á-gœ, *co t* Cal., 2.
Sandisfield, Sán-dis-feld, *v* Mass., 1¾.
San Domingo, San Dœ-míŋ-gœ, *or* the Dominican Republic, *st* is. Hayti, having the following provinces: San Domingo, Azua de Compostela, Seybo, Santiago de los Caballeros, Concepcion de la Vega; area 22,000 s. m., pop. 126,500; *c, cap* same, 10.
Sandusky, San-dús-ki, *c* O., 12.
Sandwich, Sánd-wiq *or* Sánd-wij, *bor* and *t* Eng., 12¾; *vs* N-H. 2½, Mass., C. W.
Sandwich Islands, *or* Hawaii, Hq-wj-e, 13 *is* N. Pac. Oc.; area 6500 s. m., pop. 73,230.
Sandy Hill, Sán-di Hill, *co t* N-Y.
Sandy River, Va. and Ky., 150 m.
San Felipe, Sqn Fa-lé-pa, *t* Ven., 7; — San Fil-ip, *v* Tex.
San Felipe de Aconcagua, Sqn Fa-lé-pa da A-kon-kq-gwq, *t* Chili, 12.
San Felipe de Jativa, Sqn Fa-lé-pa da *H*q-te-vq, *c* Sp., 13¼.
San Fernando de Apure, Sqn Fer-nqn-dœ da A-pœ-ra, *t* Ven., 6.
San Filippo d'Argiro, Sqn Fe-líp-œ Dqr-jé-rœ, *t* Sic., 7¼.
San Francisco, San Fran-sís-kœ *c* Cal., 60; — Bay, the finest harbor in the world, Pac. Oc., Cal.
San Francisco de la Montana, Sqn Frqn-sís-kœ da lq Mon-tq-nq, *t* N-Gran., 5⅓.
Sangamon, Sáŋ-ga-mon, *r* Ill., 200 m.
Sangar, Sqn-gqr, *str* separating islands Niphon and Yesso.
Sangay, Sqn-gj, *vol m* S. Am.
Sangerhausen, Sqŋ-er-hs-zen, *t* Prus. Sax., 5¾.
San German, Sqn *Her*-mqn, *t* is. Porto Rico, 9¼.
San Germano, Sqn Jer-mq-nœ, *t* Nap., 5.
San Gil, Sqn *H*el, *t* N-Gran., 6.
San Giovanni in Fiore, Sqn Jœ-ván-e in Fe-ó-ra, *t* Nap., 5¾.
Sanguir, Sqn-gér, *i* Malay Arch.
Sang-Koi, Sqŋ-Ko, *r* Far. Ind., 600 m.
San Jacinto, Sqn Ja-sín-tœ, *r* and *v* Texas.
San Jaime, Sqn *H*j-ma, *t* Ven., 7.
San Joaquin, Sqn *H*œ-q-kén, *r* Cal., 350 m.; *co* and *t* do.
San José, Sqn *H*œ-sá, one of Pearl Is., Gulf of Panama; *i* Gulf of California; *co t* Cal., 2.
San José de Buenavista, Sqn *H*œ-sá da Bwa-nq-vés-tq, *t* Phil. Is., 7.
San José del Interior, Sqn *H*œ-sá del En-ta-ri-ór, *t* Costa Rica, 18.
San José del Parral, Sqn *H*œ-sá del Pqr-ql, *t* Mex., 5.
San Juan, Sqn *H*œ-qn, *rs* Nicaragua, 100 m.; Bolivia, 300 m.; Mex., 150 m.; *t* Peru, 18; — Jú-an, *t* Cal.
San Juan de la Frontera, Sqn *H*œ-qn da lq Fron-tá-rq, *prov* La Plata, 25.
San Juan de los Remedios, Sqn *H*œ-qn da lœs Ra-má-di-œs, *t* Cuba, 5¼.
San Juan del Rio, Sqn *H*œ-qn del Ré-œ, *t* Mex., 10.
San Juan de Porto Rico, Sqn *H*œ-qn da Pór-tœ Ré-kœ, *c* is. Por. Ri., 11.
San Lorenzo de la Frontera, Sqn Lœ-rén-zœ da lq Fron-tá-rq, *t* Bol., 4.
San Lucar de Barrameda, Sqn Lœ-kqr da Bqr-q-má-dq, *c* Sp., 17.
San Luis, Sqn Lœ-is, *prov* and *c* La Plata.
San Luis Potosi, Sqn Lœ-is Pœ-tœ-sé, *st* Mex.; pop. 394,592; *c* same, 40.
San Marco in Lamis, Sqn Mqr-kœ in Lq-mis, *t* Nap., 9. [Tex.
San Marcos, Sqn Mqr-kos, *r* and *co t*
San Marino, Sqn Mq-ré-nœ, *t* It., 7½.
San Martin, Sqn Mqr-tén, *v* La Plata, 2.
San Miguel, Sqn Me-gél, two *ts* San Salvador, 8 and 10; *t* Cal.; *vol* state of Salvador; *har* N-Gran. [7¾.
San Nicandro, Sqn Ne-kqn-drœ, *t* Nap.,
San Nicolas, Sqn Né-kœ-lqs, Cape Verde Island, 6.
San Nicolo, Sqn Ne-kœ-ló, *cap t* is. Tinos, Gr. Arch., 4.
San Patricio, Sqn Pq-tré-si-œ, *co* and *co t* Tex. [¼; *pt* Cal.
San Pedro, Sqn Pé-drœ, *t* La Plata 1-
Sanquhar, Sáŋk-er, *t* Scot., 1¾.
San Roque, Sqn Ró-ka, *c* Sp., 7¾.
San Salvador, Sqn Sql-vq-dór, *republic* Cen. Am.; area 7500 s. m., pop. 280,000; *c, cap* of the republic; one of Bahama Is.; *t* S. Guinea, 20.
San Salvador De Bayamo, Da Bqn-mœ, *t* Cuba, 10. [10.
Sansanding, Sqn-sqn-díŋ, *t* Cen. Af.,
San Severo, Sqn Sa-vá-rœ, *t* Nap., 17.
Santa Anna, Sqn-tq An'q, *t* San Sal., 10; *ts* Cal., &c.; — Da Chaves, Da Eq-ves, *cap t* is. of St. Thomas, Gulf of Guinea.

Santa Barbara, Sqn-tq Bqr-bq-rq, *co t* Cal., 1; *t* Bra., 4; — Islands, s. of Cal.
Santa Caterina, Sqn-tq Kq-ta-ré-nq, *ft t* Sicily, 5¾. [12.
Santa Catharina, Kq-tq-ré-nq, *i* Bra.,
Santa Clara, Sqn-tq Klq-rq, *co t* Cal.
Santa Cruz, Sqn-tq Krœs, *r* Pat., 200 m.; *co t* Cal.; — *or* Saint Croix, Sant Krœ, largest of the Virgin Is., 25¾; *t* Brazil, 3; *t* is. Luzon, 5½.
Santa Cruz De La Palma, Da Lq Pql-mq, *cap* is. Palma, 5¾.
Santa Cruz De Los Rosales, Da Lœs Rœ-sq-les, *t* N. Mex.
Santa Cruz De Teneriffe, Da Ten-e-rif, *cap c* Canary Is., 8.
Santa Fè, Sqn-tq Fa, *cap t* N-Mex., 4-¾; *t* Sp., 4¼; *i* and *c* La Plata, 4.
Santagny, Sqn-tqg-nε, *t* is. Majorca, 5.
Santa Inez, Sqn-tq E-nés, *r* and *t* Cal.
Santa Juana, Sqn-tq *Hœ* q-nq, *i* Chili.
Santa Margarita, Sqn-tq Mqr-gq-ré-tq, *t* Sicily, 7; *i* Lower Cal.
Santa Maria, Sqn-tq Mq-ré-q, *i* of the Azores. [Majorca, 5¼.
Santa Maria De Rosal, Da Rœ-sql, *t*
Santa Maria Di Capua, Dε Kq-pœ-q, *t* Naples, 8⅓.
Santa Marta, Mqr-tq, *s-pt* N-Gran., 8.
Santa Maura, Mɤ-rq, Ionian Is., 18.
Santander, Sqn-tqn-dqr, *c* Sp., 16¼; *r* Mex., 110 m. [Brazil, 10.
Santarem, Sqn-tq-rén, *t* Port., 8; *t*
Santa Rita, Ré-tq, *v* Tex., 1¼.
Santa Rosa, Ró-sq, *t* Mex., 4; *t* Chili, 6; *t* N-Gran.; *co* Fa.
Santee, San-té, *r* S. C., 150 m.
Santiago, Sqn-ti-q-gœ, largest Cape Verde Is., 10; *dep* Chili; *r* and *t* Ec.; *r* San Salvador; *v* Mex.
Santiago De Chili, Dę Cil-ε, *cap c* Chili, 80.
Santiago De Compostela, Da Kom-pos-tá-lq, *c* Sp., 29. [24¼.
Santiago De Cuba, Da Kœ-bq, *c* Cuba,
Santiago De Las Vegas, Da Lqs Vá-gqs, *t* Cuba, 5¾.
Santiago Del Estero, Del Es-tá-rœ, *prov* and *t* La Plata, 4.
Santiago De Los Caballeros, Da Lœs Kq-bql-yá-rœs, t Hayti, 12.
Santo Antonio, Sqnt An-tó-ni-œ, Cape de Verde Island.
Santo Antonio De Sa, Da Sq, *t* Bra., 7.
Santo Antonio Dos Guarulhos, Dœs Gwq-rœl-yœs, *t* Bra., 6. [13.
Santorini, Sqn-tœ-ré-nε, *i* Gr. Arch.,
Santos, Sqn-tos, *t* Bra., 8; *t* N-Gran.
Santo Stefano Daveto, Sqn-tœ Stá-fq-nœ Dq-vá-tœ, *t* Sardinian States, 6⅓.
San Vicente, Sqn Vε-sén-ta, *t* Sp., 6¾; *t* San Salvador, 8. [6.
Sao Bernardo, Sɤn Ber-nqr-dœ, *c* Bra.,
Sao Francisco, Sɤn Frqn-sés-kœ, *r* Bra., 1250 m.; *i* Bra.
Sao Joao Del Rei, Sɤn Zœ-ɤn Del Rá-ε *c* Bra., 6; — Do Principe, Dœ Prén-si-pa, *t* Bra., 6.
Sao Jorge, Sɤn Zér-ʒa, one of the Azores Is., 4.
Sao Jorge Dos Ilheos, Sɤn Zér-ʒa Dœs El-yá-œs, *t* Bra., 3.
Sao Jose, Zœ-zá, *t* Bra., 5.
Sao Miguel de Piracicaba, Sɤn Mε-gél da Pε-rq-si-kq-bq, *v* Bra., 11.
Saone, Sœn, *r* Fr., 316 m.
Saone-et-Loire, Sœn-a-Lwqr, *dep* Fr., 3270 s. m., pop., 547,720.
Sao Paulo, Sɤn-Pɤ-lœ, *c* Bra., 22.
Sao Ramao, Rœ-mɤn, *t* Bra., 3.
Sao Roque, Ró-ka, *t* Bra., 4.
Sao Salvador, Sql-vq-dór, *c* Bra.
Sao Sebastiao, Sa-bqs-ti-ɤn, *t* Bra., 3.
Sapan Tagh, Sq-pqn Tqg, *m* As. Tur.
Saparooa, Sq-pq-rœ-q, *is* Malay Arch.
Sapucahi, Sq-pœ-kq-é, *r* Bra., 200 m.
Saquarema, Sq-kwq-rq-mq, *t* Bra., 7.
Sara, Bayou, Bį-œ Sá-ra, La.
Saragossa, Sq-rq-gós-q, *c* Sp., 30.
Sarahsville, Sá-raz-vil, *co t* O., ½.
Saramaca, Sq-rq-mq-kq, *r* Dutch Guiana, 200 m.
Saransk, Sq-rqnsk, *t* Rus., 8¾.
Sarapiqui, Sq-rq-pε-ké, *r* Cen. Am.
Sarapool, Sq-rq-pœl, *t* Rus., 6.
Sarare, Sq-rq-rá, *r* Brazil.
Saratoga (Sar-a-tó-ga) Lake, N-Y.
Saratoga Springs, *v* N-Y., 6⅓.
Saratov, Sq-rq-tóv, *ft t* Rus., 45.
Sarawak, Sq-rq-wqk, *t* is. Borneo, 12.
Sardinia, Sqr-din-i-a, large *i* Med. Sea; area 9235 s. m., pop. 552,665; — Kingdom, s. of Eu., composed of the island of Sardinia, and the Sardinian States on the Continent, namely:— Alessandria, Annecy, Coni or Cuneo, Genoa, Ivrea, Nice, Novara, Savona, Savoy or Chambéry, Turin, Vercelli; area 28,229, pop. 5,090,545; *vs* N-Y., O.
Saree *or* Sari, Sq-ré, *t* Persia, 30.
Sarlat, Sqr-lq, *t* Fr., 6.
Sarmatta, Sqr-mqt-q, *i* Malay Arch.
Sarmiento, Sqr-mi-én-tœ, *m* Terra del Fuego.
Sarnia, Sqr-ni-a, *t* C. W., 1⅓.
Sarno, Sqr-nœ, *t* Nap., 7.
Sarpa, Sqr-pq, *r* Rus., 200 m.
Sarre, Sqr, *r* Fr., and N. Ger., 120 m.
Sarreguemines, Sqr-ga-mén, *t* Fr., 5⅔.

Sarthe, Sqrt, *r* Fr., 145 m.
Sarzana, Sqrd-zq-nq, *t* N. It., 8½.
Sarzeau, Sqr-zó, *t* N. It., 7½.
Sasik, Sq-sik, *l* S. Rus.
Saskatchewan, Sas-káq-ɛ-won, *r* Br. N. Am., 1000 m.
Sassari, Sq-sq-rɛ, *c* is. Sardinia, 24.
Satoralja Ujhely, Sq-tω-rol-yo Ɑ-i-hély, *t* Hun., 7¾. [Ind.
Satpoora (Sqt-pó-rq) Mountains, Cen.
Sattarah, Sqt-tq-rq, *dis* and *cap t* Brit. Ind.
Saucelito, Sə-se-lé-tω, *naval station* Cal., 12 m. of San Francisco.
Saugerties, *or* Ulster, Sé-ger-tiz, *or* Ul'ster, *v* N-Y.
Sauk (Sək) Indians, same as Sacs.
Sauk Rapids, *co t* Min., ¼; *r* do.
Saumur, Sω-mer, *t* Fr., 14¼.
Saundersville, Són-derz-vil, *co t* Ga.
Saut (*or* Sault) Sainte Marie, Sω Sañ Mq-ré, usually Sω Sant Má-rɛ, *v* Mich., 1.
Savage Islands, Pac. Oc.
Savaii, Sq-vj-ɛ, Samoan Island, Pac. Oc., 20.
Savanah, Sa-ván-a, *r* S. C., 450 m.; *c* Ga., 16; *co ts* Tenn., Mo.; *v* Ill.
Save, Sqv *or* Sav, *r* Aus. Em., 550 m.
Saverne, Sq-várn, *t* Fr., 6½.
Savigliano, Sq-vɛl-yq-nω, *ft t* It., 15½.
Savona, Sq-vó-nq, *t* It., 16¼.
Savoo, Sq-vó, *i* S. Pac. Oc., 25.
Savoy, (Duchy of,) Sáv-ơ, one of the Sardinian States, pop. 591,135.
Sawarcarna (Sə-war-kqr-na) River, Mo. Ter., 200 m.
Saxe-Altenburg, Saks-Al'ten-burg, *duchy* Cen. Ger., pop. 132,850.
Saxe-Coburg-Gotha, Saks-Kó-burg-Gó-ta, *duchy* Cen. Ger., pop. 150,412.
Saxe-Meiningen-Hildburghausen, Saks Mj-nin-en Hild-burg-hɤ-zen, *duchy* Cen. Ger., 166,364.
Saxe-Weimar-Eisenach, Saks-Wj-mar-ɪ'zen-ak, *grand duchy* Cen. Ger., pop. 262,524.
Saxon (Sáks-on) Land, s. part Transylvania, pop. 446,700.
Saxony, Sáks-ω-ni, *k* Cen. Ger., pop. 1,987,832; — Prussian, *prov* central part Prussia, pop. 1,781,300.
Saypan, Sj-pqn, Ladrone Island.
Scala Nova, Skq-lq Nó-vq, *s-pt t* As. Min., 20.
Scalpa, Skál-pa, *is* Hebrides.
Scalpay, Skál-pa, *i* Hebribes, ¼.
Scarborough, Skqr-bur-ω, *bor* and *s-pt t* Eng., 13.
Scarp, Skqrp, *i* Outer Hebrides, ⅛.

Scarpanto, Skqr-pqn-tω, *i* Med. Sea.
Schaerbeek, Shqr-bak, *v* Belg., 4½.
Schaffhausen, Σqf-hɤ-zen, *can* and *t* of Swit., 7¾.
Schaghticoke, Σág-ti-kωk, *v* N-Y.
Schässburg, Σés-bωrh, *t* Tran., 6¼.
Scheldt, Skelt, *r* Eu., 200 m.
Schelestadt, Σa-les-tqd, *ft t* Fr., 10⅓.
Schemnitz, Σém-nits, *t* Hun., 19.
Schenectady, Sken-ék-ta-di, *c* N-Y., 9.
Schiedam, Shɛ-dqm, *t* Neth., 12¾.
Schiermonnik-oog, Shér-mon-ik-ωg, *i* N. Sea, ¾.
Schintznach, Σints-nqh, *v* Swit., 1½.
Schio, Ské-ω, *i* Aus. It., 6⅔. [½.
Schlangenberg, Σlqŋ-en-berh, *t* Sib., 4-
Schleisingerville, Σlj-siŋ-er-vil, *v* Wis.
Schleitz, Σljts, *t* Cen. Ger., 4¾.
Schleusingen, Σló-siŋ-en, *t* Prus. Sax. 3¼.
Schluckenau, Σlúk-e-nɤ, *t* Boh., 3¼.
Schmalkalden, Σmql-kql-den, *t* Ger., 4½. [3¾.
Schmiedeberg, Σmé-de-berh, *t* Ger.,
Schneeberg, Σná-berh, *t* Sax., 7¼.
Schneekoppe, Σná-kop-e, *m* Prus. Sil.
Schneidemühl, Σjn-de-mel, *t* Prus. Pol., 4¼. [2⅔.
Schohario, Skω-hár-ɛ, *co* and *v* N-Y.,
Schönheide, Σén-hj-de, *v* Sax., 4½.
Schonlinde, Σón-lin-de, *t* Boh., 6.
Schönwalde, Σen-wql-de, *t* Prus., 2¼.
Schoodic (Skó-dik) Lakes, Me.
Schoolcraft, Skól-kraft, *v* Mich., 1¼.
Schoorisse, Shó-ris-e, *v* Belg., 3⅓.
Schorndorf, Σórn-dərf, *t* Wurt., 3¾.
Schouten (Σó-ten) Island, e. coast of Van Die. Land; *i* Malay Arch.
Schouwen, Skɤ-en, *i* prov. of Zeal.
Schreckhorn, Σrék-hərn, *m* Swiss Alps, 13,492 ft. [the Danube.
Schütt, Σet, (Great and Little,) *i* in
Schuyler, Skj-ler, *cos* Ill., N-Y., Mo.
Schuylerville, Skj-ler-vil, *v* N-Y.
Schuylkill, Skól-kil, *r* Pa., 120 m.
Schuylkill Haven, *bor* Pa., 2½.
Schwabach, Σwq-bqh, *t* Bavaria, 10.
Schwarza, Σwqrt-sq, *rs* Ger.
Schwarzburg-Radolstadt, Σwqrts-burg-Ró-dol-stqt, *princip* Ger., 69,000.
Schwarzburg-Sondershausen, Σwqrts-bωrh-Són-derz-hɤ-zen, *principality* Cen. Ger., 60,847.
Schwatz, Σwqts, *t* Tyrol, 8.
Schwedt, Σwet, *t* Prus., 6½. [13.
Schweidnitz, Σwjd-nitz, *ft t* Prus. Sil.,
Schweinfurt, Σwjn-furt, *t* Bav., 7⅓.
Schwerin, Σwa-rén, *t* N. Ger., 17⅓; *t* Prus., 5½; *i* Ger.
Schwiebus, Σwé-bɤs, *t* Prus.

Schwytz, Σwits, *v* Swit., 5¼.
Sciacca, Σq̈k-q, *s-pt t* Sicily, 12¾.
Sciglio, Σél-yo, *prom* Naples.
Scilly (Sil-i) Islands, s. w. of Eng., 2⅜.
Scio, Σé-o *or* Sj-o, *i* w. of As. Min., 62; *t* of same 14½; *vs* N-Y., 2.; Mich., [1¼.
Sciortino, Σər-té-no, *t* Sicily, 6.
Scioto, Sj-ó-to, *r* O., 200 m.
Scipio, Sip-i-o, *vs* Ia., N-Y.
Scituate, Sit-ų-at, *v* Mass., 2¼.
Sclavonia, Skla-vó-ni-a, *prov* Aus.
Scoglio Grande, Skól-yo Grq̈n-da, largest Brioni Island, Adriatic Sea.
Scotland, Skót-land, northern part of the island of Gr. Brit.; area 29,417, pop. 2,888,742.
Scottsville, Skóts-vil, *vs* N-Y., Va., 1¼; *co ts* Va., Ala., Ky.
Scranton, Skrán-ton, *bor* Pa., 3.
Scriba, Skrj-ba, *v* N-Y., 2¾.
Scriven, Skriv-en, *co* Ga.
Scculltown, Skúl-tɤn, *v* N-J.
Scutari, Skó-tq-rε, *t* As. Min., 50; *t* Eu. Tur., 40.
Seabrook, Sé-brük, *v* N-H., 1¼.
Seacombe, Sé-kumb, *v* Eng., 3.
Seaford, Sé-ford, *v* Del., ¾.
Seal Islands, Pac. Oc., off Peru.
Seal River, Br. N. Am., 200 m.
Searcy, Sér-si, *co* Ark.; *co t* do.
Searsmont, Sérz-mont, *v* Me., ⅓.
Searsport, Sérz-port, *v* Me., 2.
Seattle, Sét-l, *co t* Wash. Ter.
Sebastian, Sε-bást-yan, *co* Ark.
Sebastopol *or* Sevastopol, Sε-bás-tó-pol, *t* Rus., 40.
Se-Beero (Sε-Bé-ro) Island, Ind. Oc.
Sebenico, Sa-bá-ni-ko, *t* Dalmatia, 6.
Secunderabad, Sε-kun-der-q-bq̈d, *t* Ind., 34⅓.
Sedan, Se-dóṅ, *ft t* Fr., 37.
Sedbergh, Séd-berg, *t* Eng., 4½. [2¼.
Sedgefield, Séj-fεld, *t* and *par* Eng.,
Sedlitz *or* Seidlitz, Séd-litz, *v* Boh., mineral springs. [3¼.
Seehausen, Sá-hɤ-zen, *t* Prus. Sax.,
Seekonk, Sé-koŋk, *v* Mass., 2¼.
Seeland *or* Zealand, Zé-lqnd, the largest *i* belonging to Denmark, bet. the Cattegat and the Baltic Sea; area 2840 s. m., pop. 499,400.
Seelyville, Sé-li-vil, *v* Pa., ⅓.
Seevas, Sé-vqs, *t* As. Tur., 24.
Seez, Sa, *t* Fr., 5.
Sego, Sá-go, *l* Rus.; *t* Cen. Af., 30.
Segorbe, Sa-gór-ba, *c* Sp., 6.
Segovia, Sa-gó-vi-q, *c* Sp., 6⅔.
Segre, Sá-gra, *r* Sp., 150 m.
Seguin, Sé-gwin, *co t* Tex. [m.
Segundo, Sa-gón-do, *r* La Plata, 130
Segura, Sa-gó-rq, *r* Sp., 180 m.
Seil, Sεl, *i* Inner Hebrides.
Seiland, Sj-lqnd, *i* n. w. Norway.
Seine, San, *r* Fr., 497 m.; *dep* Fr.; area 185 s. m., pop. 1,420,580.
Seine-et-Marne, San-a-Mqrn, *dep* Fr., area 2154 s. m., 345,076.
Seine-et-Oise, San-a-Wqz, *dep* Fr.; area 2141 s. m., pop. 421,882.
Seine-Inferieure, San-Aṅ-fa-ri-ér, *dep* Fr.; area 2298 s. m., pop. 762,039.
Selangan, Sa-lqn-gq̈n, *t* is. Murdinao, 10.
Selby, Sél-bi, *t* and *par* Eng., 5¼.
Seligher, Sa-li-gq̈r, *l* Rus.
Selime, Sa-lé-ma, *oasis* desert Nubia.
Selimno, Sa-lím-no, *t* Eu. Tur., 20.
Selkirk, Sél-kerk, *t* and *par* Scot., 3⅓.
Selma, Sél-ma, *vs* Ala., 1½; Mo.
Semao, Sa-mq̈-o, *i* Malay Arch.
Semendria, Sε-mén-dri-q, *ft t* Servia, 9.
Semerone, Sε-me-rón, *r* Ind. Ter., 600 m.
Seminole (Sém-i-nol *or* Sem-ín-o-lε) Indians, *tr* Fa.
Semlin, Sem-lén, *t* Aus. Em., 10¼.
Seneca, Sén-ε-ka, *v* C. W., 3¾.
Seneca Falls, *v* N-Y.
Seneca Indians, *tr* w. N-Y.
Seneca Lake, N-Y.; *vs* N-Y., N. C.
Seneffe, Se-néf, *v* Belg., 3½.
Senegal, Sen-ε-gól, *r* W. Af., 1000 m.; Fr. *col* W. Af.
Senegambia, Sen-ε-gám-bi-a, a region W. Af.; the history of the country is too imperfect to obtain its area, and the number of its inhabitants.
Seniavine (Sa-ni-q-vén) Islands, Pac. Oc.
Senjen, Sén-yen, *is* n. w. coast Nor.
Senlis, Soṅ-lés, *t* Fr., 5¾.
Sennaar, Sen-q̈r, *st* and *c* Af., 4.
Sens, Soṅ, *c* Fr., 10¾.
Sentis, Sén-tis, *m* Swit., 8¼ ft.
Sept-Isles, Set-Ɛl, *is* n. Brittany.
Sepulga, Sε-púl-ga, *r* Ala. d
Sequatchie, Sε-kwáq-ε, *r* Tenn., 100 m.
Seraing, Se-ráṅ, *v* Belg., 3½. [⅔.
Serampore, Ser-am-pór, *t* Br. Ind., 12-
Sercq, Sqrk, *i* Eng. Chan.
Seres, Sér-es, *t* Eu. Tur., 30.
Sereth, Ser-ét, *r* Moldavia, 270 m.
Sergipe, Ser-ʒé-pa, *v* and *prov* Brazil, 31,958 s. m.; pop. 175,000.
Serido, Sa-ré-do, *r* Bra., 120 m.
Serinagur, Ser-i-nq-gúr, *cap c* Cashmere, 40. [S. Ind.
Seringapatam, Ser-iŋ-ga-pa-tám, *ft*
Serino, Sq-ré-no, *t* Naples, 6.

Serle (Sẹrl) Island, Pac. Oc., ⅛.
Sermatta, Ser-mą-tą, *i* Malay Arch.
Sermide, Ser-mé-da, *v* Aust. It., 5.
Serpho, Sẹ́r-fo, *i* Gr. Arch., ⅜.
Serpookhov, Ser-po-*h*óv, *t* Rus., 13.
Serravalle, Ser-q-vą-la, *t* It., 5⅓.
Servia, Sẹ́r-vi-a, *cy* Eu., area 20,000 [s. m.
Seskar, Ses-kąr, *i* Gulf of Fin.
Sestri a Levante, Sés-trε A-la-vąn-ta, *t* N. It., 7¼.
Setang, Sε-táŋ, *r* Burmah, 260 m.
Setauket, Sε-té-ket, *v* N-Y.
Setta, Sét-q, *t* Dahomey, 9.
Settle, Sét-l, *t* Eng., 2.
Setubal, Sa-tó-bql, *s-pt c* Port., 15.
Sevastopol *or* Sebastopol, Sev-as-tó-pol, *t* and *naval station* Eu. Rus., 40.
Sevellan, Sa-vel-ąn, *m* N. Per., 13,000 ft.
Sevenoaks, Sev-n-óks, *t* Eng., 1¾.
Severn, Sév-ern, *r* Eng., 210 m.; *r* Md., &c.
Sevier, Sev-ér, *cos* Ark., Tenn.
Seville, Sév-il, *c* Sp., 100½; *v* O.
Sevre-Nantaise, Sevr (*or* Savr) Non-táz, *r* Fr., 70 m.
Sevre-Niortaise, Nε-or-táz, *r* Fr.
Sevres, Sevr *or* Savr, *t* Fr., 4¾.
Sevres, Deux, Dẹ Savr, *dep* Fr.; area 2315 s. m., pop. 323,615.
Sewickleyville, Sų-ik-li-vil, *v* O., ¾.
Seybo, Sį-bo, *t* Hayti, 5.
Seychelles, Sa-ʃél, *is* Ind. Oc., 7.
Seymour, Sé-mer, *vs* Conn., Ia., C. W.
Sezza, Sét-sq, *t* It., 8¾.
Shaduan, Σq-do-ąn, *i* Red Sea.
Shaftsbury, Σáfts-ber-i, *bor* and *t* Eng., 2½; *v* Vt., 2.
Shahpoor, Σq-pór, *r* Persia.
Shalersville, Σá-lerz-vil, *vs* Pa., O.
Shamaka, Old, Old Σą-mą-kq, *v* Rus., 18½.
Shammar (Σam-ąr) Mountains, Arabia.
Shamokin, Σám-ó-kin, *v* Pa., 2.
Shamrock, Σám-rok, *v* O.
Shanesville, Σánz-vil, *v* O., ⅜.
Shang-Hai, Σaŋ-Hį, *s-pt c* China, 190.
Shang-I-Yuen, Σqŋ-E-Yo-én, *t* China, [100.
Shannon, Σán-on, *r* Ir., 224 m.
Shannondale (Σán-on-dal) Springs, *watering-place* Va.
Shannonville, Σán-on-vil, *vs* Pa., C. W., ½.
Shao-Choo, Σq-o-Chó, *c* China, 40.
Shao-Hing, Σq-o-Hiŋ, *c* China.
Shao-King, Σq-o-Kiŋ, *ft c* China.
Shao-Woo, Σq-o-Wó, *ft c* China.
Shapinshay, Σáp-in-ʃa, Orkney Is., ¾.
Sharon, Σá-ron, *vs* Vt., Mass., Conn., Pa., Va., Miss., O., Mich., Ill., Io., Wis.
Sharon Centre, *v* O. [N-Y.
Sharon Springs, *v* and *watering-place*
Sharonville, Σá-ron-vil, *v* O.
Sharpsburg, Σąrps-burg, *vs* Ia., 2; Ky.
Sharpsville, Σąrps-vil, *v* Ia.
Sharptown, Σąrp-tʊn, *v* N-J.
Shasta, Σąs-ta, *co t* Cal.
Shaste, Σąs-tε, *m* Cal., 14,000 ft.
Shatsk, Σqtsk, *t* Rus., 6.
Shawnee (Σó-nε) Indians, *tr* now in Kansas Ter.
Shawneetown, Σó-nε-tʊn, *t* Ill., 2.
Shayuen, Σa-yų-én, *r* Min., 300 m.
Sheboygan, Σε-bó-gan, *r* and *t* Wis.; — Falls, *v* Wis., ¾.
Shediac, Σed-i-ąk, *t* N-Brun., 2.
Sheeraz, Σε-rąz, *c* Per., 30.
Sheerness, Σεr-nés, *s-pt t* Eng., 8½.
Sheffield, Σéf-εld, *par* and *c* Eng.; 135⅓; *vs* Mass., 2¾; Pa., &c.
Shehr, Σe*h*r, *t* Arabia, 6.
Sheilville, Σél-vil, *p o* Ia.
Shelburn, Σél-burn, *vs* Vt., 1¼; N-H.
Shelburne, Σél-burn, *s-pt t* N. Scotia.
Shelburne Falls, *v* Mass., 1.
Shelby, Σél-bi, *vs* N-Y., O.; *co t* N. C.
Shelbyville, Σél-bi-vil, *co ts* Tex. Tenn., 1; Ky., 2; Ia., 1½; Ill., Mo.
Sheldon, Σél-don, *vs* Vt., N-Y.
Sheligov, Σel-i-góv, *l* Rus. Am.
Shelliff, Σél-if, *r* Algeria, 250 m. [m.
Shenandoah, Σen-an-dó-a, *r* Va., 170
Shenango, Σε-nán-go, *cr* Pa. [⅔.
Shepherdstown, Σép-erdz-tʊn, *t* Va., 1-
Sheperdsville, Σép-erdz-vil, *co t* Ky.
Sheppy, Σép-i, *i* Eng., in mouth of Thames.
Shepton-Mallet, Σép-ton-Mál-et, *t* and *par* Eng., 3¾.
Sherborn, Σẹ́r-born, *v* Mass.
Sherborne, Σẹ́r-born, *t* Eng., 3¾.
Sherboro, Σẹ́r-bur-o, *i* off Guinea; *r* Guinea, 230 m.
Sherbrooke, Σẹ́r-bruk, *t* C. E., 1½.
Sherburne, Σẹ́r-burn, *v* N-Y., 2⅔.
Sheridan, Σér-i-dan, *v* N-Y.
Shermon, Σẹ́r-man, *co t* Tex.
Shermansville, Σẹ́r-manz-vil, *v* R. I.
Sherington, Σér-iŋ-ton, *v* C. E., 1¼.
Shetland (Σét-land) Islands, *arch* N. At. Oc., 31.
Shiashkotan, Σε-qʃ-ko-tąn, Koorile *i*.
Shiawassee, Σį-a-wós-ε, *r*, *co* and *v* Mich. [Eng., 29.
Shields, South, Sʊθ Σέldz, *bor* and *t*
Shieldsborough, Σέldz-bur-o, *co t* Miss., 1¼.
Shiel, Loch, Lo*h* Σεl, *l* Scot.
Shienne, Σε-én, *r* Mo., 200 m.
Shiffnal, Σif-nal, *t* Eng., 5⅔.

Shikarpoor, Σik-ar-pǿr, *t* Sinde, 30.
Shiloh, Σį-lɷ, *vs* N-J., N. C.
Shinandoah Σin-an-dǿ-a, *v* N-Y.
Shinnston, Σinz-ton, *v* Va.
Shippensburg, Σip-enz-burg, *bor* Pa.
Shippensville, Σip-enz-vil, *v* Penn.
Shippingport, Σip-iŋ-pɷrt, *v* Ky.
Shirley, Σẹr-li, *v* Mass., 1¼.
Shoa *or* Schoa, Σǿ-q, *state* Abys.
Shoalhaven, Σɷl-há-ven, *r* N. S. Wales.
Shokapee, Σɷ-ká-pɛ, *co t* Minn.
Shokokon, Σɷ-kǿ-kon, *p o* Ill.
Shoneaw, Σǿ-nɛ-ė, *v* Wis.
Shongalo, Σoŋ-gá-lɷ, *v* Miss.
Shoojuabad, Σɷ-jɷ-a-bq̇d, *t* Punjab, 10.
Shoomla, Σǿm-lq, *c* Bulgaria, 21.
Shooster, Σǿs-ter, *c* Persia, 8.
Shoreham, Σǿr-ham, *s-pt t* Eng., 2½; *v* Vt., 1⅔.
Shoshonees, Σɷ-ʃǿ-nɛz, *or* Snake Indians, *tr* Oregon.
Showstown, Σǿz-tɤn, *v* Penn., 1.
Shreveport, Σrév-pɷrt, *co t* La., 3.
Shrewsbury, Σrǿz-ber-i *or* Σrǿz-ber-i, *bor* and *t* Eng., 19¾; *vs* Vt., N-J., Penn. [Scotia.
Shubenacadie, Σǿ-ben-a-ka-dɛ, *r* N.
Shullsburg, Σúlz-burg, *v* Wis., 2⅓.
Shumalari, Σum-a-lár-ɛ, peak of the Himmalaya Mountains, 27,200 ft.
Shuna, Σq̇-na, *i* Inner Hebrides.
Shusan, Σq̇-san, *v* N-Y.
Siah-Koh, Sɛ-a-kǿ, *m* Afghanistan.
Siak *or* Siakh, Sɛ-q̇k, *r* and *st* Sumatra.
Siam, Sį-ám, *king* Asia; area, about 250,000 s. m.; pop., about 5,000,000; *g* Siam, 500 by 300 m.
Siamo, Sɛ-q̇-mɷ, *i* Malay Arch.
Siang-Yang; Sɛ-q̇ŋ-Yqŋ, *c* China.
Siasconset, Sį-as-kón-set, *v* Mass.
Siberia, Sį-bé-ri-a, large territory of North Asia belonging to Russia. Divisions: West Siberia — Tobolsk, Tomsk, Omsk. East Siberia—Yeniseisk, Irkootsk, Yakootsk, Okhotsk, Kamtchatka, Tchooktchee. Area, 4,812,389; pop. 2,887,184.
Sibkah, Al, Al Síb-kq, *salt l* North Africa, 80 by 20 m.
Sibley, Síb-li, *v* Mo.
Sibuyan, Sɛ-bɷ-yq̇n, *i* Malay Arch.
Sicily, Sís-i-li, *i* Mediterranean; area, 10,556 s. m.; pop. 2,041,583.
Siculiana, Sɛ-kɷl-yq̇-nq̇, *t* Sicily, 5⅓.
Sidmouth, Síd-muꝥ, *s-pt t* and *par* Eng., 3⅓.
Sidney, Síd-ni, *vs* Me., N-Y., Ind., Ill., Iowa; *co t* O. [5¼.
Siegen, Ség-en, *t* Prus. Westphalia,
Sienna, Sɛ-én-q, *c* Tuscany, 22.

Sierra, Sɛ-ér-q, Sp. word for "saw," applied to the notched appearance of mountain ridges.
Sierra Acarai, A-kq-rį, *ms* S. Am.
Sierra Blanca, Blq̇ŋ-kq, *m* New Mex.
Sierra de Caballo, da Kq-bq̇l-yɷ, *ms* New Mexico.
Sierra de la Lanterna, da lq Lqn-térnq̇, *m* New Mex. [Ter.
Sierra de la Platte, da lq Plat, *m* Utah
Sierra de la Vinda, da lq Vén-dq̇, *m* cordillera in Peru.
Sierra de los Jumanes, da lɷs Hɷ-mq̇-nes, *ms* New Mex. [New Mex.
Sierra de San Juan, da Sq̇n Hɷ-q̇n, *ms*
Sierra Leone, Lɛ-ǿ-nɛ, British colonial settlement, West Africa, 44½.
Sierra Madre, Mq̇-dra, *ms* Mexico.
Sierra Morena, Mɷ-rá-nq, *ms* Spain.
Sierra Morina, Mɷ-ré-nq, *ms* Cal.
Sierra Nevada, Na-vq̇-dq, *ms* Sp. Pen.; — Na-vq̇-dq, *ms* Cal. [Am.
Sierra Pacaraima, Pq-kq̇-rį-mq, *ms* S.
Sigourney, Síg-ur-ni, *v* Iowa, ¾.
Siguenza, Sɛ-gwén-ꝥq, *t* Sp., 5.
Sikhs *or* Seiks, Sɛks, warlike nation, Br. India. [⅓.
Sikino, Sɛ-ké-nɷ, *i* Grecian Arch.;
Sikokf, Sɛ-kókf, *i* Japan.
Silesia, Sį-lé-ʃi-a, *prov* Prus.; area, 15,820 s. m.; pop. 3,060,593.
Silesia, Austrian, part of Silesia subject to Austria.
Silistria, Si-lis-tri-a, *c* Eu. Tur., 20.
Siljan, Síl-yqn, *l* Sweden.
Silvan, Sil-van, *v* Mich., 1.
Silver Creek, *v* N-Y.
Silver Spring, *v* Penn., 2.
Simabara, Sɛ-mq-bq̇-rq, *g* Japan.
Simbeersk *or* Simbirsk, Sim-bérsk, *gov* Russia; area, 27,944 s. m.; pop. 1,-024,236; *cap c* of above, 35⅓.
Simcoe, Sím-kɷ, *l* and *t* Can. W., 1¾.
Simferopol *or* Simpheropol, Sim-ferǿ-pol, *t* S. Russia, 8.
Simooseer, Sɛ-mɷ-sér, Koorile island.
Simplon, Sañ-plɷñ, *m* Switz.
Simpsonville, Símp-son-vil, *v* Ky.
Simsbury, Símz-ber-i, *v* Conn., 2.
Sinai, Sį-na *or* Sį-na-į, Mount, Scripture *m*, Arabia; *pen* bet. Gulfs of Suez and Akabah.
Sind, Sind, *r* Hind., 220 m.
Sinde, Sind, *ter* British India; area, 52,120 s. m.; pop. 1,275,000.
Singapore, Siŋ-ga-pǿr, British settlement in S. E. Asia; pop. 52,891; *c*, *cap* of above, 26.
Sing Sing, Siŋ Siŋ, *v* N-Y., seat of one of the state prisons, 3.

Sinigaglia, Sɛ-nɛ-gą́l-yq, *s-pt t* Pontif. States, 22.
Sinna, Sín-q, *t* Persia, 20.
Sinnimari, Sɛn-q-mq-ré, *r* Fr. Guiana, 200 m.
Sinope, Sín-ɷ-pɛ, *s-pt t* As. Minor, 8.
Sinu, Sɛ-nɷ́, *r* New Granada, 200 m.
Sioot, Sɛ-ɷ́t, *t* Upper Egypt, 20.
Sioux Indians, Sɷ In'di-anz, *tr* Nebraska territory; *r* Minn. ter., 300 m.
Sipan Dagh, Sɛ-pą́n Dqg, *m* Tur. Ar.
Siphanto, Síf-an-tɷ, *i* Grec. Arch., 5.
Sipotuba, Sɛ-pɷ-tɷ́-bq, *r* Brazil.
Sippican, Síp-i-kan, *v* Mass.
Siskiyou, Sís-ki-yɷ *or* Sís-i-kɷ, *co* Cal.
Sisteron, Sis-te-rɷ́ń, *ft t* Fr., 4½.
Sisterville, Sís-ter-vil, *v* Va., 1.
Sistova, Sis-tɷ́-vq, *t* Eu. Tur., 20.
Sitka, Sít-kɑ, *i* w. N. Am.
Sitkhin, Sít-*k*in, Aleutian island.
Sittingbourne, Sít-iŋ-burn, *t* and *par* Eng., 3.
Siue-Foong-Shan, Sé-ɷ-a-Fɷŋ-Σqn, *m* [China.
Siue-Shan, Sé-ɷ-a-Σqn, *m* China.
Sivana, Sɛ-vą́-nq, *i* Br. Ind.
Skagen, Ską́-gen, *cape* Jutland 1⅓.
Skager Rack *or* Skagerrak, Skág-er Rak, arm of North Sea.
Skagtöls-Tind, Ską́g-tęlz-tínd, *m* Nor.
Skalits, Ską́-lits, *t* Hun., 8¾.
Skamania, Ska-má-ni-ɑ, *co* Wash. ter.
Skaneateles, Skan-ɛ-át-les, *v* N-Y., 1⅔; *l* N-Y., 16 by 2 m.
Skegness, Skeg-nés, *v* and *par* Eng.
Skerries, Skér-iz, *t* Ir., 2⅓.
Skiatho, Ské-q-ŧɷ, *i* Grec. Arch.
Skiberbeen, Skíb-er-bén, *t* Ir., 4.
Skipton, Skíp-ton, *t* Eng., 5.
Skopelo, Skɷ-pá-lɷ, one of the North Sporades Islands, Ægean Sea, 2½.
Skopin, Skɷ-pín, *t* Rus., 6.
Skowhegan, Skɤ-hé-gan, *v* Me., 1¾.
Skunk (Skuŋk) River, Iowa, 250 m.
Skye, Skį, *i* Inner Hebrides, 21½.
Skyros, Ské-ros, *i* Grec. Arch., 2⅔.
Slatersville, Slá-terz-vil, *v* R. I., 1½.
Slavonia, Slq-vɷ́-ni-q, *or* Sclavonia, Sklq-vɷ́-ni-q, *ter* Aus.; area, 3,656 s. m.; pop. 336,000.
Sleaford, Slé-ford, New, *t* Eng., 3⅔.
Sleswick, Slés-wik, *duchy* Den., pop. 363,000; *t* Den., cap. of above, 11⅔.
Sleydinge, Slį-diŋ-e, *v* Belgium, 5¾.
Sligo, Slį-gɷ, *bor* and *s-pt t* Ir., 11¼; *vs* Tenn., O.
Slobdosk, Slob-dósk, *t* Rus., 6.
Slonim, Slɷ́-nim, *t* Rus. Poland, 7½.
Slootsk, Slɷtsk, *t* Rus. Poland, 8.
Smethport, Sméŧ-port, *co t* Penn.
Smithborough, Smíŧ-bur-ɷ, *v* N-Y.
Smithfield, Smíŧ-fɛld, *co ts* Va., 1; N. C.; *v* Ind.
Smithland, Smíŧ-land, *co t* Ky.
Smith's Falls, *t* Can. West, 1.
Smith's Sound, n. Baffin's bay.
Smithville, Smíŧ-vil, *co ts* N. C., Ark., Tenn.; *vs* N-Y., Miss., Can. West.
Smolensk, Smɷ-lénsk, *t* Rus., 13.
Smyrna, Smęr-nɑ, *c* Asia Minor, 150; *vs* N-Y., 2; Del., 2; Tenn., O.; *g* Ægean Sea.
Sneedsville, Snédz-vil, *co t* Tenn.
Sneek, Snak, *t* Netherlands, 7¾.
Sniatyn, Snɛ-ą́-tin, *t* Aus. Pol., 6⅓.
Snowdon, Snɷ́-don, *m* Wales.
Snow Hill, *co ts* Maryland, 1¼; N. C.
Society (Sɷ-sį-ɛ-ti) Islands, S. Pac., the principal of which are, Tahiti, Eimeo, Osnaburg; pop. 10,000.
Socorro, Sɷ-kór-ɷ, *t* New Granada, 12.
Socotra, Sók-ɷ-trq, *i* Ind. Oc., 4.
Soda (Sɷ́-dɑ) Lake, La.
Sodus, Sɷ́-dus, *v* N-Y., 4½; *b* 35 m. e. of Rochester, N-Y.
Sodus Point, *v* N-Y.
Soerabaya, Sɷ-rq-bį-q, *s-pt t* Java, 60.
Soerakarta, Sɷ-rq-ką́r-tq, *t* Java, 10.
Soest, Sęst, *t* Prus. Westphalia, 8¾.
Sofala, Sɷ-fą́-lq, *r* E. Africa, 200 m.
Soham, Sɷ́-ham, *t* Eng., 2¾.
Soignies, Swqn-yé, *t* Belgium, 6⅓.
Soissons, Swq-sɷ́ń, *ft t* Fr., 9½.
Solano, Sɷ-lą́-nɷ, *co* Cal.
Solesmes, Sɷ-lám, *t* Fr., 5¾.
Soleure, Sɷ́-lęr, *t* Switz., 5⅓. [6⅓.
Solingen, Sɷ́-liŋ-en, *t* Rhen. Prus.,
So-ling-shan, Sɷ-liŋ-ʃą́n, *m* China.
Soller, Sɷl-yą́r, *t* is. Majorca, 7.
Solo, Sɷ́-lɷ, *r* Java, 356 m.
Solofra, Sɷ-lɷ́-frq, *t* Naples, 5½.
Solomon (Sól-ɷ-mon,) Islands, Pacific Oc.; *is* Indian Oc.
Solon, Sɷ́-lon, *v* Me., 1; Iowa.
Solor, Sɷ-lér, *i* Malay Arch.
Solt, Solt, *t* Hun., 7.
Solta, Sól-tq, *i* Dalmatia, 1⅓. [Sea.
Solway Prith, Sól-wa Friŧ, *inlet* Irish
Somerford, Súm-er-ford, *v* O.
Somers, Súm-erz, *vs* Conn., N-Y.
Somerset, Súm-er-set, *v* Mass.; *bor* Penn., 1; *co ts* Ky., O., 1¼.
Somers Point, *v* N-J.
Somerton, Súm-er-ton, *t* and *par* Eng., 2¼; *vs* Va., O.
Somerville, Súm-er-vil, *v* Mass., 5; *co ts* N-J., 1; Ala., Tenn.; *vs* N-Y., O.
Sommariva del Bosco, Som-q-ré-vq del Bós-kɷ, *t* Pied., 5⅓.
Somme, Som, *dep* and *r* Fr., 117 m.
Sommen, Sóm-en, *l* Sweden.

Sommerfeld, Súm-er-felt, *t* Prus., 3¾.
Somonauk, Som-ꝏ-nék, *v* Ill.
Sondershausen, Són-derz-hʊ-zen, *t* Cen. Ger., 3½.
Sone, *or* Soane, Sꝏn, *r* Ind., 440 m.
Song-Kiang, Soŋ-Ke-ꞓŋ, *c* China.
Sonneberg, Són-a-bęrh, *t* Ger., 3¾.
Sonnenburg, Són-en-burh, *t* Prus., 3.
Sonoma, Sꝏ-nó-ma, *co* and *t* Cal., 1.
Sonora, Sꝏ-nó-ra, *co t* Cal., 2½; *r* Mex., 300 m.; *state* Mexico; area, 123,466 s. m.; pop. 147,133; *t* state of Sonora, 8.
Sonsonate, Son-sꝏ-nꞓ-tá, *t* San Salvador, 10.
Soo-Chow-Foo, Sꝏ-Ꞓʊ-Fó, *t* China, pop. 2,000,000.
Soodan *or* Soudan, Sꝏ-dꞓn, undefined region of Central Africa.
Sooja, Só-jq, *t* Russia, 7.
Sook-el-Shooyookh, Sꝏk-el-Σꝏ-yꝏh, *t* As. Tur.
Sookhona, Sꝏ-hó-nq, *r* Rus., 250 m.
Soolina, Sꝏ-lé-nq, branch of the Danube in Bessarabia.
Sooloo (Sꝏ-ló,) Islands, *arch* Ind. Oc., pop. 200,000; *t* Sooloo Arch., 6.
Soomshoo, Sꝏm-ʃꝏ, Koorile Island.
Soomy, Só-me, *t* Rus., 12; *l* Siberia.
Soongaree, Sꝏn-gq-ré, *r* Mant., 800 m.
Soongaria, Sꝏŋ-gꞓ-ri-q, part of the Chinese Empire in Central Asia.
Soosa, Só-sq, *s-pt* Tunis, 10.
Sophia, Sꝏ-fé-q, *c* Eu. Tur., 50.
Sora, Só-rq, *c* Naples, 8.
Soragno, Sꝏ-rꞓn-yq, *t* Italy, 5⅓.
Sorau, Só-rʊ, *t* Prus., 6¾.
Sorel, Sꝏ-rél, *v* Can. East, 3½.
Soresina, Sꝏ-ra-sé-nq, *t* Lom., 5.
Sorocaba, Sꝏ-rꝏ-kꞓ-bq, *t* Brazil, 12.
Soröe, Só-rę-e, *i* Norway.
Sorrento, Sor-én-tꝏ, *t* Naples, 10.
Sosnitsa, Sos-nít-sq, *t* Rus., 5.
Sosva, Sós-vq, *r* Siberia, 350 m.
Sotoanne, Sꝏ-tꝏ-ꞓn, Caroline Is.
Soucook, Só-kuk, *r* N-H.
Souhegan, Sꝏ-hé-gan, *r* Mass.
Sound, Sʊnd, *or* Oeresund, Er-a-sónd, *str* between Denmark and Sweden.
South Abingdon, Sʊŧ Ab'iŋ-don, *v* Mass.
South Acton, Ak'ton, *v* Mass.
South Adams, Ad'amz, *v* Mass.
South Albion, Al'bi-on, *v* Me.
South Amboy, Am-bó, *v* N-J., 2¼.
Southampton, Suŧ-hámp-ton, *bor* and *s-pt t* Eng., 35⅓; *v* Mass., 1; *i* Br. N. Am.
South Australia, Ꝋs-trál-yq, British colony of Australia; area, 300,000 s. m.; pop. 68,663.
South Bend, *co t* Ind., 2.
South Berwick, Bęr-wik, *v* Me., 2¾.
South Bloomfield, Blóm-feld, *v* O.
Southborough, Sʊŧ-bur-ꝏ, *v* Mass., 1⅓.
South Braintree, Brán-tre, *v* Mass.
Southbridge, Sʊŧ-brij, *v* Mass., 3.
South Bridgewater, Brij-we-ter, *v* Mass.
South Bristol, Brís-tol, *v* N-Y., 1¼.
South Britain, Brít-en, *v* Conn.
Southbury, Sʊŧ-ber-i, *v* Conn.
South Butler, Bút-ler, *v* N-Y.
South Canaan, Ká-nan, Conn.
South Candor, Kán-dor, *v* N-Y.
South Carolina; Kar-ꝏ-lį-nq, one of the original U. S.; area, 30,213 s. m.; pop., whites, 274,563; free colored, 8,960; slaves, 384,984; total, 668,507.
South Carrollton, Kár-ol-ton, *v* Ky.
South Charleston, Ꞓꞓrlz-ton, *v* O.
South Charlestown, Ꞓꞓrlz-tʊn, *v* N-H.
South Corinth, Kór-inŧ, *v* N-Y.
South Cortland, Kórt-land, *v* N-Y.
South Coventry, Kúv-en-tri, *v* Conn.
South Danvers, Dán-verz, *v* Mass.
South Dartmouth, Dꞓrt-muŧ, *v* Mass.
South Dedham, Déd-ham, *v* Mass.
South Deerfield, Dér-feld, *vs* N-H., Mass.
South Dennis, Dén-is, *v* Mass.
South Dorset, Dór-set, *v* Vt.
South Dover, Dó-ver, *v* N-Y.
South Easton, Ɛs'ton, *t* Penn.
South English, Iŋ'gliʃ, *v* Iowa.
South Fairfax, Fꞓr-faks, *v* Vt.
South Fitchburg, Fiꞓ-burg, *v* Mass.
South Framingham, Frám-iŋ-ham, Mass.
South Gardiner, Gꞓr-di-ner, *v* Mass.
South Genesee, Jén-e-sé, *v* Wis.
South Glastenbury, Glás-ten-ber-i, *v* Conn.
South Hadley, Hád-li, *v* Mass., 2½.
South Hampton, Hámp-ton, *v* N-Y., 5.
South Hartford, Hꞓrt-ford, *v* N-Y.
South Harwich, Hꞓr-wiꞓ, *v* Mass.
South Hawley, Hó-li, *v* Mass.
South Hingham, Híŋ-ham, *v* Mass.
Southington, Sʊŧ-iŋ-ton, *v* Conn., 2¼.
South Keene, Ken, *v* N-H.
South Lee, Le, *v* Mass.
South Lincoln, Líŋk-on, *v* Me.
South Livonia, Li-vó-ni-q, *v* N-Y.
South Malden, Mál-den, *v* Mass., 1.
South Merrimack, Mér-i-mak, *v* N-H.
South Middleborough, Míd-l-bur-ꝏ, *v* Mass.
South Milford, Míl-ford, *v* Del.
South Nashville, Náʃ-vil, *t* Tenn., 3.
South Newmarket, Nų-mꞓr-ket, *v* N-H.
South Norwalk, Nór-wek, *v* Conn.
Southold, Sʊŧ-ꝏld; *v* N-Y.

South Orange, Or'anj, *v* N-J.
South Orrington, Or'iŋ-ton, *v* Me.
South Paris, Pár-is, *v* Me.
South Perry, Pér-i, *v* O. [2½.
South Pittsburg, Pits-burg, *bor* Penn.,
South Point, Pɵnt, *v* Mo.
Southport, S𝔲ð-pɵrt, *vs* Conn., 1¼; N-Y., 2¼; Ind.
South Reading, Réd-iŋ, *v* Mass., 2¼.
South Royalston, Rɵ́-alz-ton, *v* Mass.
South Royalton, Rɵ́-al-ton, *v* Vt.
South Salem, Sá-lem, *vs* N-Y., O.
South Sandwich, Sánd-wiç, *v* Mass.
South Schodac, Skɵ-dák, *v* N-Y.
South Scituate, Sít-yɥ-at, *vs* Mass., R. I.
South Seekonk, Sẹ́-koŋk, *v* Mass.
South Shaftsbury, Σáfts-ber-i, *v* Vt.
South Shetland, Σét-land, *arch* South Atlantic. [1½.
South Thomaston, Tóm-as-ton, *v* Me.,
South Vernon, Vẹ́r-non, *v* Vt.
Southville, S𝔲ð-vil, *vs* Conn., N-Y.
Southwark, Sút-ark, *bor* Eng., 173.
Southwell, S𝔲ð-wel, *t* and *par* Eng., 3½.
South Wellfleet, Wél-flɛt, *v* Mass.
South Weymouth, Wa-muð, *v* Mass.
South Wilbraham, Wíl-bra-ham, *v* Mass. [Mass.
South Williamstown, Wil-yamz-t𝔲n, *v*
South Windham, Wind-ham, *v* Conn.
South Woburn, Wó-burn, *v* Mass.
Southwold, S𝔲ð-wold, *bor* and *s-pt* *t* Eng., 2¼.
South Yarmouth, Yɑ́r-muð, *v* Mass.,
Sovicille, Sɵ-vɛ-çɛ́l-a, *v* Tus., 6½.
Soxville, Sóks-vil, *v* Penn.
Spa, Spe, *t* Belg., 3¾.
Spain, Span, *king* S. W. Europe, composed of the following divisions:—New Castile, Old Castile, Leon, Asturias, Galicia, Estramadura, Andalusia, Aragon, Murcia, Valencia, Catalonia, Navarre, Basque Provinces, Balearic Islands, Canary Islands. In America—Cuba, Porto-Rico, Virgin Islands. In Asia—Philippine Islands. In Africa—The Presidios, Guinea Islands. In Oceanica—Part of the Ladrone Islands. Total area, 286,279 s. m.; pop. 18,144,-509. [10⅓.
Spalato, Spɑ-lɑ́-tɵ, *s-pt* *c* Dalmatia,
Spalding, Spéld-iŋ, *t* and *par* Eng., 9.
Spalmadore, Spɑl-mɑ-dó-ra, *is* As. Tur.
Spandau, Spɑ́n-d𝔲, *ft* *t* Prus., 6¼.
Spanish Town, *or* Santiago de la Vega, Sɑn-tɛ-ɑ́-gɵ da lɑ Vá-gɑ, *cap* *t* Jamaica, 6.
Sparta, Spɑ́r-tɑ, *co ts* Ga., Ala., La., Tenn.; *vs* N-J., Ky., O., Ill., Mo.
Spartanburg, Spɑ́r-tan-burg, *co t* S. C.
Spask, Spɑsk, *t* Rus., 6.
Speedsville, Spẹ́dz-vil, *v* N-Y.
Spencer, Spén-ser, *co ts* Tenn., Ind.; *vs* Mass., 1¼; N-Y., O.
Spencer Gulf, *b* South Australia.
Spenserport, Spén-ser-pɵrt, *v* N-Y.
Spencerville, Spén-ser-vil, *v* Ind.
Sperryville, Spér-i-vil, *v* Va.
Spesshardt, Spés-hɑrt, *ms* Ger.
Spey, Spa, *r* Scot., 110 m.
Speyer, Spį-er, *c*, *cap* Rhen. Bav., 9¼.
Spezia, La, Lɑ Spéd-zi-ɑ, *t* It., 9¾.
Spezzia, Spét-si-ɑ, *i* Greece, 8.
Spirit Lake, Iowa.
Spitalfields, Spit-al-fɛldz, section of London, Eng. [Eng.
Spithead, Spit-hed, *roadstead* coast of
Spitzbergen, Spits-bẹ́r-gen, *i* Arc. Oc.
Spoleto, Spɵ-lá-tɵ, *c* Cen. It., 6¼.
Spoon River, Ill., 100 m.
Spottsville, Spóts-vil, *v* Ky.
Spottswood, Spóts-wɯd, *v* N-J.
Spree, Spra, *r* Ger., 220 m.
Spremberg, Sprém-bẹrh, *t* Prus., 4½.
Spring Bay, *v* Ill.
Springborough, Spríŋ-bur-ɵ, *v* O., ¾.
Springdale, Spríŋ-dal, *v* Miss.
Springfield, Spríŋ-fɛld, *c* Mass., 13¾; *c* O., 8; *cap* *c* Ill., 7; *vs* Vt., 2¾, N-J., 1⅓; Mo., 1, &c.
Spring Hill, *vs* Ala., Tenn., Ind., Ill.
Spring Hills, *v* O., ½.
Spring Mill, *v* Penn.
Spring Place, *co t* Ga.
Spring Prairie, Prá-ri, *v* Wis.
Spring River, *r* Mo., and Ark.; *v* Mo.
Spring Valley, *v* O., ½.
Springville, Spríŋ-vil, *vs* N-Y., 1½; Penn., Ky., Ind., Ill., Mo., Wis.
Springwater, Spríŋ-wɵ-ter, *v* N-Y.
Spring Wells, *v* Mich., 2.
Sprottau, Sprót-𝔲, *t* Prus. Silesia, 4¼.
Squam (Skwom) Lake, N-H. [H.
Squammagonic, Skwom-a-gón-ik, *v* N-
Stade, Stɑ́-da, *ft t* Hanover, 6.
Staeden, Stɑ́-den, *v* Belg., 4⅔.
Staffa, Stáf-ɑ, *i* Inner Hebrides.
Stafford, Stáf-ord, *bor* and *t* Eng., 12; *v* N-Y., 1. [Dalmatia, 5½.
Stagno Grande, Stɑ́n-yɵ Grɑ́n-da, *t*
Stalimni, Stɑ-lím-nɛ, *i* Grec. Arch., 8.
Stamford, Stám-ford, *bor* and *t* Eng., 9; *bor* Conn., 5; *vs* N-Y., Can. W., 2¼.
Stampalia, Stɑm-pɑ-lɛ́-ɑ, *i* Grec. Arch., 1½.
Stanardsville, Stán-ardz-vil, *co t* Va.
Stanford, Stán-ford, *co t* Ky., 1.

Stanhope, Stán-hop, v N-J.
Stanislawow, Stán-is-la-vov, ft t Aus. Galicia, 9¼.
Stanley, Stán-li, v Eng., 7¼.
Stanovoi, Sta-no-vó, ms East Asia.
Stanstead, Stán-sted, t Can. East, 1.
Stapleton, Stá-pl-ton, v N-Y. [8¾.
Staraia-Roossa, Sta-ri-a-Róós-a, t Rus.,
Stargard, Stár-gart, t Prus., 13¼.
Starkey, Stár-ki, v N-Y., 3.
Starkville, Stárk-vil, co ts Ga., Miss.
Starling Medical College, Columbus, O.
Starodoob, Sta-ro-dóób, t Rus., 9.
Staten (Stát-en) Island, N-Y. Bay; i Terra del Fuego.
Statesborough, Státs-bur-o, co t Ga.
Statesville, Státs-vil, co t N. C.
Staunton, Stán-ton, r Va., 200 m.; co t Va., 2½; vs O., Ill.
Stavropol, Stav-ró-pol, t Rus., 7.
Steelsville, Stélz-vil, vs Mich., Mo.
Steilacoom, Stí-la-koom, co t Wash. ter.
Steinhude, Stín-hoo-da, l N. Ger.
Stendal, Stén-dal, t Prus. Sax., 6¾.
Stephens' (Sté-venz) Point, v Wis., ½.
Sterling, Stér-ling, vs Mass., 1; Conn., 1; N-Y., 2; co t Ill.
Sternberg, Stérn-berh, t Ger., 8.
Stettin, Stet-én, ft t Prus., 47¼.
Steubenville, Stú-ben-vil, t O., 6¼.
Stewarton, Stú-art-on, t Scot. 3¼.
Stewartstown, Stú-arts-tŏn, v Pa., 1½.
Stewartsville, Stú-arts-vil, v N-J., ½; Penn., N. C.
Steyer, Stí-er, t Upper Aus., 10.
Stilesville, Stílz-vil, v Ind.
Still Valley, v N-J.
Stillwater, Stíl-we-ter, vs N-Y., N-J., co t Minn., 1½.
Stirling, Stér-ling, t Scot., 9⅓.
Stockbridge, Stók-brij, v Mass., 2. [93.
Stockholm, Stok-hom, c, cap Swed.,
Stockorn, Stók-hern, m Switz.
Stockport, Stók-port, bor and t Eng., 54; vs N-Y., Penn.
Stockton, Stók-ton, co t Cal., 9.
Stockton-on-Tees, Stók-ton-on-Tez, s-pt t and par Eng., 10½.
Stokesley, Stóks-li, t and par Eng., 2½.
Stoke-upon-Trent, t and par Eng., 84.
Stolpe, Stól-pa, t Prus., 8⅔.
Stone, Ston, t Eng., 3½.
Stoneham, Stón-ham, v Mass., 1¼.
Stonehaven, Ston-há-ven, s-pt t Scot., 3¼.
Stoneleigh, Stón-le, v Eng., 1⅓.
Stone Mountain, v Ga., ⅓.
Stonington, Stó-ning-ton, t Conn., 3.
Stornoway Stór-no-wa, s-pt and par Hebrides, 2⅓.
Storsiön, Stór-si-en, l Swed.
Stoughton, Stó-ton, vs Mass., Wis.
Stour, Stoor, four rs Eng.
Stourbridge, Stúr-brij, t Eng., 8.
Stourport, Stúr-port, t Eng., 3.
Stoutsville, Stŏts-vil, v N-J.
Stow, Sto, v Mass., 1½. [Eng., 3¼.
Stowmarket, Stó-mar-ket, t and par
Strabane, Stra-bán, bor and t Ir., 5.
Stradbally, Strad-bál-i, t Ir., 1⅓.
Stralsund, Strál-sunt, ft t Prus., 19¼.
Stranraer, Stran-rér, s-pt t and par Scot., 5¾.
Strasbourg, Stras-bóór, c Fr., 65.
Strasburg, Strás-burh, t Prus., 4½; — Strás-burg, t Pa., 1; vs Va., O.
Stratford, Strát-ford, co t C. W.; vs Conn., O. [Eng., 3½.
Stratford-upon-Avon, A'von, bor and t
Stratford le Bow, le Bo, t Eng., 7.
Strattonville, Strát-on-vil, v Pa.
Straubing, Strŏ-bing, t Lower Bav., 9.
Strausberg, Strŏs-berh, t Prus., 3½.
Strawberry Plains, Stré-ber-i Planz, v Tenn.
Strawtown, Stré-tŏn, two vs Ia.
Streefkerk, Stráf-kerk, v Neth., 1⅓.
Strehlen, Strá-len, t Prus. Sil., 4¾.
Strelitz, Alt, Alt Strá-lits, t Mecklenburg-Strelitz, 3.
Striegau, Stré-gŏ, t Prus. Sil., 5¼.
Stromboli, Stróm-bo-li, Lipari Is., 1¼.
Stromness, Strom-nés, s-pt t Scot., 2.
Strongville, Stróng-vil, v O., 1¼.
Stronsa, Strón-sa, Orkney Is., 1.
Stroud, Strŏd, t and par Eng., 36½.
Stroudsburg, Strŏdz-burg, co t Pa., 1.
Stuhlweissenburg, Stool-ví-sen-burh, t Hun., 21.
Sturbridge, Stúr-brij, v Mass., 2¼.
Sturge, Sturj, i Ant. Oc.
Sturgeon, Stúr-jon, l Br. N. Am.
Sturgis, Stúr-jis, v Mich., ¾.
Stuttgart, Stút-gart, c, cap Würt., 30.
Stuyvesant, Stí-ves-ant, v N-Y., 1½.
Styria, Stír-i-a, prov Aus., 950,612.
Suakin, Swá-kin, s-pt t is. Red Sea, 8.
Subiaco, Soo-bi-á-ko, t Cen. It., 6.
Subtiava, Soob-ti-á-va, t Nicaragua, 5.
Subzulcote, Sub-zul-kót, t Sinde.
Suchiltepec, Soo-chel-ta-pék, t Guat.
Suczawa, Soo-chá-va, ft t Aus., 5.
Sudbury, Súd-ber-i, t and par Eng., 6; v Mass., 1¼. [ga, m Ger.
Sudeten-Gebirge, Só-da-ten-Ga-bér-
Sueca, Swá-ka, t Sp., 9.
Suez, Só-ez, s-pt t Egypt, 2; g w. arm Red Sea; ist uniting As. and Af.
Suffeed Koh, Suf-éd Ko, m Afg.
Suffern's, Súf-ernz, v N-Y.

Suffield, Súf-ɛld, *v* Conn., 2.
Suffolk, Súf-ok, *co t* Va., 1½.
Sugar (Σúg-ɑr) Creek, *streams* N. C., Ia., Ill., &c.
Sugar Grove, *vs* Pa., O., Iowa.
Sugar River, *rs* N-H., Wis.
Suhl, Sœl, *t* Prus. Sax., 8.
Suir *or* Sure, Σųr, *r* Ir.
Suisoon, Sœ-ɛ-sœ́n, *b* Cal.
Suleiman, Sœ-la-mɑ́n, *ms* E. Afg.
Sulen (Sœ́-len) Islands, w. Norway.
Sullivan, Súl-i-van, *co t* Ia.; *vs* N-Y., Pa. 1½, O., Ill., Iowa.
Sulmona, Sœl-mṓ-nɑ, *ft t* Nap., 6.
Sultaneeyah, Sœl-tɑ-nḗ-ɑ, anc. *c* Per.
Sulze, Súlt-sa, *t* Meck.-Schwerin, 3⅔.
Sumatra, Sœ-mɑ́-trɑ, *i* Indian Sea; area 140,000 s. m., pop. 5,000,000.
Summer Hill, Súm-er Hil, *v* Pa., 1½.
Summer Islands, 30 *is* w. Scot.
Summerville, Súm-er-vil, *co ts* Va., Ga.; *vs* S. C., O., Ill., Mich., Wis.
Summit, Súm-it, *v* Pa.
Sumner, Súm-ner, *v* Me., 1¼.
Sumterville, Súm-ter-vil, *co t* S. C.; *vs* Ga., Ala.
Sunapee (Sún-a-pɛ) Lake, N-H.
Sunbury, Sún-ber-i, *co t* Pa., 1¼; *vs* O., Ill.
Sunda (Sún-dɑ) Isles, Malay Arch.
Sunday (Sún-da) River, Cape Colony, Af., 200 m.
Sundeep, Sun-dḗp, *i* of Hindostan.
Sunderland, Sún-der-land, *t* and *par* Eng., 67½.
Supaiwasi, Sœ-pį-wɑ́-sɛ, *m* Bol.
Superior, Sų-pḗ-ri-or, *l* n. w. U. S., the largest fresh water lake on the globe; area 32,000 s. m.; — City of, *v* Minn. and Wis.
Surat, Sœ-rɑ́t, *c* Br. Ind., 157.
Surinam, Sœ-rin-ám, *r* Dutch Guiana, 300 m.
Surry (Súr-i) Court-House, *co t* Va.
Susa, Sœ́-sɑ, *t* It., 3½.
Susannah (Sų-zán-ɑ) Island, Mergui Arch.
Suspension Bridge, *v* N-Y., 1.
Susquehanna, Sus-kwɛ-hán-ɑ, *r* Pa., 150 m.; *v* Pa., 1½.
Sussex, Sús-eks, *v* Wis.
Sussex Court-House, *co t* Va.
Sutlej, Sút-lej, *r* Punjab, 1000 m.
Suttersville, Sút-erz-vil, *v* Cal.
Sutton, Sút-on, *v* Mass., 2; *co t* Va.
Sutton-Coldfield, — Kṓld-fɛld, *t* Eng.
Sutton, Long, *par* and *t* Eng., 6½.
Suwalki, Sœ-wɑ́l-kɛ, *t* Poland, 5.
Suwanee, Sų-wḗ-nɛ, *r* and *v* Ga.

Sveaborg, Svá-ɑ-borg, *ft t* Rus. Finland, 4.
Sveer *or* Svir, Svɛr, *r* Rus., 130 m.
Sviaga, Svɛ-ɑ́-gɑ, *r* Rus., 200 m.
Sviazhsk, Svɛ-ɑ́ʒk, *t* Rus., 4.
Swabian (Swá-bi-an) Alps, *ms* Würt.
Swaffham, Swáf-am, *t* and *par* Eng., 4.
Swale, Swal, *r* Eng., 70 m.
Swanage, Swón-aj, *or* Swanwick, Swón-wik, *t* and *par* Eng., 2.
Swan Quarter, — Kwór-ter, *co t* N. C.
Swan River, Swon River, *r* W. Aust.
Swansea, Swón-sɛ, *s-pt t* and *par* S. Wales, 25.
Swanton, Swón-ton, *vs* Vt., O.
Swanzey, Swón-zi, *v* N-H., 2.
Swartwout, Swórt-wɤt, *v* Tex.
Swatara, Swa-tɑ́-rɑ, *cr* Pa.
Swavesey, Swáv-zɛ, *par* Eng.
Sweden, Swḗ-den, *k* N. Eu.; area 128,076 s. m., pop. 3,482,541.
Swedesborough, Swḗdz-bur-œ, *v* N-J.
Sweet Springs, *v* Va.
Swindon, Swín-don, *t* and *par* Eng., 5.
Swinemünde, Swḗ-na-mẹn-da, *t* Prus., [4⅔.
Swineshead, Swįnz-hed, *t* Eng., 2.
Switzerland, Swít-zer-land, *rep* Cen. Eu.; area 15,261, pop. 2,390,116.
Swords, Sœrdz, *t* and *par* Ir., 3.
Sycamore, Sík-a-mœr, *co t* Ill.
Sydney, Síd-ni, *s-pt c* Aust., and *cap* N-S. Wales, 100; *s-pt t* Nova Scotia; *v* Me., 2.
Syltöe, Síl-tœ, *i* of Den., 2⅔.
Sylva, Síl-vɑ, *r* Rus., 300 m.
Sylvania, Sil-vá-ni-ɑ, *co t* Ga.
Sylvester, Sil-vés-ter, *v* Wis., ⅓.
Symi, Sḗ-mɛ, *i* w. As. Minor, 7; *g* do.
Symsonia, Sim-sṓ-ni-ɑ, *v* Ky.
Syra, Sḗ-rɑ, *i* Grecian Arch., 30; *c*, *cap* same, 20. [Y., 25¼.
Syracuse, Sír-a-kųs, *ft c* Sic., 11; *c* N-
Syria, Sír-i-ɑ, *cy* As. Tur.; area 50,000 s. m., pop. 2,000,000.
Sysola, Si-sṓ-lɑ, *r* Rus., 200 m.
Syzran, Siz-rɑ́n, *t* Rus., 8.
Szamos, So-mṓʃ, *r* Transylvania, 200 m.
Szarogrod, Σɑ-rœ-gród, *t* Rus., 6¾.
Szasz-Regen, Sɑs-Ra-gén, *t* Trans., 5.
Szathmar, Nemeth, Na-mét Sot-mɑ́r, *t* E. Hun., 15.
Szegedin, Ség-ed-in, *t* Hun., 34.
Szent Miklos, Nagy, Noj Sent Mé-kloʃ, *t* Hun., 14¼.
Szexard, Seks-órd, *t* Hun., 8¼.
Szigeth, Sé-get, *t* Hun., 7.
Szoboszlo, Sœ-bós-lœ, *t* Hun., 14.
Szolnok, Sol-nók, *t* Hun., 11⅔.
Szurul, Sœ-rœ́l, *m* Transylvania.

# T.

Taasinge, Tó-siŋ-ga, *i* Den., 4⅓.
Tabarca, Tq-bq́r-kq, *i* Med. Sea, ½.
Tabareeyeh, Tqb-a-ré-ye, *l* Pal.
Tabasco, Tq-bás-kω, *st* Mex.; area 15,-609 s. m., pop. 63,580; *r* do., 250 m.
Taberg, Tá-berg, *v* N-Y.
Tabernacle, Táb-er-nak-l, *v* N-J.
Tabernas-de-Valldigna, Tq-bér-nqs-da-Valy-dég-nq, *t* Sp., 5.
Tablas, Tq́-blqs, Philippine Is.
Table Bay, Tá-bl Ba, s. w. Af.
Tabor, Tq́-bor, *t* Boh., 4.
Tabreez, Tq-bréz, *c* Persia, 60.
Tacloban, Tq-klω-bq́n, *t* Phil. Islands.
Tacna, Tq́k-nq, *t* Peru, 10.
Tacora, Tq-kó-rq, *m* Bol.
Tacunga, Tq-kóŋ-gq, *t* Ec., 10.
Tadcaster, Tád-kas-ter, *t* Eng., 2½.
Taganrog, Tq-gqn-róg, *t* Rus., 16.
Tagodast, Tq-gω-dq́st, *t* Morocco, 7.
Tagus, Tá-gus, *r* Iberian Pen., 540 m.
Tahiti, Tq-hé-tε, Society Is., 9.
Tahoora, Tq-hώ-rq, Sandwich Is.
Tahoorowa, Tq-hω-ró-wa, Sandwich Is.
Tain, Tan, *t* Scot., 2⅔.
Tai-Ping, Tį-Piŋ, *cs* China.
Tai-Wan, Tį-Wén, *cap* is. Formosa.
Takinos (Tq-kε-nós) Lake, Eu. Tur.
Talanda (Tq-lq́n-dq) Channel, *arm sea* in Greece.
Talavera de la Reyna, Tq-lq-vá-rq da lq Ra-é-nq, *c* Sp., 6⅓.
Talbotton, Tál-bot-on, *co t* Ga.
Talca, Tq́l-kq, *t* Chili, 14½.
Taliabo, Tq-li-q́-bω, *i* Malay Arch.
Taliaferro, Tól-i-ver, *co* Ga.
Talladega, Tal-a-dé-ga, *co t* Ala.
Tallahassee, Tal-a-hás-ε, *c*, *cap* Fa., 2.
Tallahatchie, Tal-a-háç-ε, *r* Miss, 250 m.
Tallahoma, Tal-a-hó-ma, *r* Miss.
Tallaloosa, Tal-a-ló-sa, *v* Miss.
Tallapoosa, Tal-a-pó-sa, *r* Ga. and Ala., 250 m.; *v* Ga.
Tallassee, Tal-a-sé, *v* Ala.
Tallow, Tál-ω, *i* Ir., 4.
Tallulah, Ta-lq́-la, *co t* Miss.
Tama, Tq́-ma, *co* Iowa.
Tamandua, Tq-mq́n-dω-q, *t* Bra., 8.
Tamaqua, Ta-mé-kwa, *t* Pa., 6.
Tamar, Tá-mar, *r* Eng., 60 m.
Tamara, Tq-mq́-rq, *i* w. Af.
Tamaulipas, Tq-mɤ-lé-pq́s, *st* Mexico; area 30,334 s. m., pop. 100,064.
Tambov *or* Tambow, Tqm-bóv, *gov* Rus.; area 25,542 s. m., pop. 1,666,505; *c*, *cap* same, 20¼.
Tamiagua, Tq-mε-q́-gwq, *l* Mex.
Tamise, Tq-méz, *t* Belg., 7⅔.
Tampa Bay, Tám-pa Ba, *b* Fa.
Tampico, Tqm-pé-kω, *s-pt t* Mex., 7; *r* do., 200 m.; *l* do.
Tamworth, Tám-wurŧ, *t* Eng., 8⅔.
Tanaga, Tq-nq́-gq, Aleutian Is.
Tanah-Pileh, Tq́-nq-Pé-le, *t* is. Sumatra, 4.
Tanakeke, Tq-nq-ká-ka, *is* Malay Arch.
Tangermunde, Tq́ŋ-er-męn-da, *t* Prus. Sax., 4¼.
Tangier, Tqn-jér, *s-pt t* Morocco, 10.
Tangipaha, Tan-ji-pa-hé, *r* La.
Tanjore, Tan-jór, *c* Br. Ind., 40.
Tanna, Tán-a, *i* N-Heb., Pac. Oc.
Tantalem, Tqn-tq-lém, *i* Gulf of Siam.
Taos, Tq́-ωs, *co* and *t* N-Mex.; *v* Tex.
Tapajos, Tq-pq́-ʒωs, *r* Bra., 500 m.
Tapisi, Tq-pi-sé, *r* S. Am., 200 m.
Tappahannock, Tap-a-hán-ok, *co t* Va., ⅓. [and 140 m.
Taquari, Tq-kwq-ré, two *rs* Bra., 400
Taranto, Tq́-rqn-tω, *c* Nap., 15; *g* Med.
Tarare, Tq-rq́r, *t* Fr., 10⅓.
Tarascon, Tq-rqs-kóñ, *t* Fr., 12½.
Tarazona, Tq-rq-ŧó-nq, *t* Sp., 6.
Tarazona de la Mancha, Tq-rq-ŧó-nq da lq Mq́n-çq, *t* Sp., 6.
Tarbagatai, Tqr-bq-gq-tį, *t* Chi. Toork.
Tarbes, Tqrb', *t* Fr., 14.
Tarborough, Tq́r-bur-ω, *co t* N. C., 1.
Tarentum, Ta-rén-tum, *v* Pa., 1¼.
Tarifa, Tq-ré-fq, *s-pt t* Sp., 8¼.
Tariffville, Tár-if-vil, *v* Conn., 2.
Tarki, Tq́r-kε, *t* Rus., 8.
Tarma, Tq́r-mq, *t* Peru, 8.
Tarn, Tqrn, *dep* and *r* Fr., 220 m.
Tarn-et-Garonne, Tqrn-a-Gq-rón, *dep* Fr., pop. 237,553. [3⅔.
Tarnowitz, Tq́r-nω-vits, *t* Prus. Silesia,
Tarporley, Tq́r-por-li, *t* Eng., 2¾.
Tarragona, Tqr-q-gó-nq, *s-pt c* Sp., 13.
Tarrakai, Tqr-a-kį, *b* Sea of Japan.
Tarrant, Tár-ant, *co t* Tex.
Tarrasa, Tqr-q́-sq, *t* Sp., 5.
Tarrinsay, Tár-in-sa, *i* Outer Hebrides.
Tarrytown, Tár-i-tɤn, *v* N-Y., 5.
Tarsus, Tq́r-sus, *c* As. Minor, 7.
Tartary, Tq́r-ta-ri, ext. *reg* As. and Eu.
Tashkend, Tqʃ-kénd, *t* Indep. Toork., 40.
Tasman's (Tás-manz) Peninsula, Van Diemen's Land.
Tatay, Tq-tį, *s-pt t* Phil. Is., 3.
Tat-Seen-Loo, Tqt-Sén-Lω, *ft t* China,
Tatta, Tq́t-q, *t* Sinde, 10. [500.

Taunton, Tén-ton, *t* Eng., 14¼; *co t* Mass., 12; *r* do.
Taunus, Tɤ́-nus, *m* Hesse-Darmstadt.
Taurus, Tó-rus, *ms* As. Tur.
Tauss, Tɤs, *t* Boh., 6½.
Tavira, Tq-vé-rq, *t* Port., 8¾.
Tavistock, Táv-is-tok, *t* Eng., 8¼.
Taw, Tɵ, *r* Eng.
Tawee, Tq́-wɛ, *i* Malay Arch.
Tay, Ta, *r* and *est* Scot., 160 m.
Tayabas, Tį-q́-bqs, *t* Phil. Is., 21½.
Taycheeda, Ta-çé-da, *v* Wis.
Taylor's Falls, Tá-lorz Fɵlz, *v* Minn.
Taylorsport, Tá-lorz-pɷrt, *v* Ky.
Taylorsville, Tá-lorz-vil, *co ts* N. C., Tenn., Ky., Ill. 1; *vs* Pa., Md., Va., O. 1., Ia.
Taz, Tqz, *r* Siberia, 300 m.
Tazewell, Táz-wel, *co t* Tenn.; *co* Ill.
Tchad, Ȼqd, *l* Cen. Af.
Tchadobets, Ȼq-dɷ-béts, *r* Sib., 200 m.
Tchao-Naiman-Soome, Ȼq́-ɷ-Nį-mq́n-Sɷ́-ma, *c* Mongolia.
Tcharytch, Ȼq-ríç, *r* Sib., 220 m.
Tcheboksari, Ȼa-bok-sq́-rɛ, *t* Rus., 5.
Tcherkask, Staroi, Stq-rɵ́ Ȼer-kq́sk, *t* Rus., 15.
Tchernigov, Ȼęr-nɛ-góv, *t* Rus., 7½.
Tchesme, Ȼés-ma, *v* As. Minor, 6.
Tchoogooev, Ȼɷ-gɷ-év, *ft t* Rus., 9.
Tchooi, Ȼɷ́-ɛ, *r* Asia, 700 m.
Tchooktchees, Ȼɷ́k-çɛz, *tribe* E. Sib.
Tchooroom, Ȼɷ-rɷ́m, *t* As. Minor, 7⅜.
Tchoruk, Ȼɷ-rúk, *r* Turkish Armenia, [200 m.
Teano, Ta-q́-nɷ, *t* Nap., 8.
Tebesse, Ta-bés-q, *t* Algeria, 15.
Teche, Teʃ, *bayou* La.
Tecumseh, Tɛ-kúm-se, *v* Mich., 1.
Tedsi, Téd-sɛ, *t* Morocco, 14.
Tedzen, Ted-zén, *r* Persia, 250 m.
Tees, Tɛz, *r* Eng., 90 m.
Teglio, Tál-yɷ, *v* Aus. It., 5½.
Tegucigalpa, Ta-gɷ-sɛ-gq́l-pq, *t* Honduras, 10.
Teheran, Te-her-q́n, *c*, *cap* Persia, 10.
Tehuacan, Ta-wq-kq́n, *t* Mex., 12.
Tehuantepec, Ta-wqn-tq-pék, *st* Mex., pop. 82,395; *ist* and *g* do.; *t* do., 8.
Teign, Tan, *r* Eng., 45 m.
Teignmouth, Tán-muþ, *t* Eng., 5.
Telde, Tél-da, *c* Canaries, 12. [Mex., 5.
Temascaltepec, Ta-mqs-kql-ta-pék, *t*
Temesvar, Tem-eʃ-vq́r, *c* Hun., 19¼.
Temiscaming, Tɛ-mís-ka-miŋ, *l* C. E.
Temiscouata, Tem-is-kɷ-q́-tq, *l* C. E.
Temperanceville, Tém-per-ans-vil, *t* Pa., 2½.
Tempio, Tém-pi-ɷ, *t* is. Sardinia, 9½.
Templemore, Tem-pl-mɵ́r, *t* Ir., 9½.
Templeton, Tém-pl-ton, *v* Mass., 1¼.
Tenasserim, Ten-ás-e-rim, *r* Far. Ind., 220 m.
Tenasserim Provinces, Br. India.
Tenbury, Tén-ber-i, *t* and *par* Eng., 2.
Tenby, Tén-bi, *s-pt t* S. Wales, 3.
Tendra, Tén-drq, *i* Black Sea.
Tenedos, Tén-ɛ-dos, *i* w. As. Minor.
Teneriffe, Ten-er-íf, largest of the Canary Islands, 85; *m peak* 12,182 ft.
Te-Ngan, Ta-ńgq́n, *c* China.
Teng-Tchoo, Teŋ-Ȼɷ́, *c* China.
Tenian, Ta-ni-q́n, Ladrone Is.
Tenimber, Tɛ-ním-ber, *is* Malay Arch.
Tennessee, Ten-e-sé, one of the U. S.; area 45,600 s. m.; pop. 756,826 whites, 6422 free colored, 239,459 slaves—total, 1,002,717; *r* Tenn., 800 m.
Tenterden, Tén-ter-den, *t* and *par* Eng., 4. [Mex.
Teotihuacan, Ta-ɷ-ti-wq-kq́n, *plateau*
Tepic, Ta-pék, *t* Mex., 10.
Teramo, Tér-q-mɷ, *c* Nap., 10.
Terceira, Ter-sá-ɛ-rq, Azores Is., 40.
Tercero, Ter-sá-rɷ, *r* La Plata, 100 m.
Terek, Ta-rék, *r* Rus., 350 m.
Tergovist, Tér-gɷ-vist, *t* Wallachia, 5.
Terlizzi, Ter-lít-sɛ, *t* Nap., 12.
Termini, Tér-mi-nɛ, *s-pt t* Sic., 13.
Terminos, Tér-mi-nɷs, *inlet* Carib. Sea.
Terminos, Laguna de, Lq-gɷ́-nq da Tér-mi-nɷs, *s-pt t* Yucatan, 2.
Ternate, Ter-nq́-ta, *i* Malay Arch.
Terni, Tér-nɛ, *t* Pontifical Sts., 9¼.
Terodant, Ta-rɷ-dq́nt, *t* Morocco, 21.
Teror, Ta-rér, *t* Canaries, 6.
Terra del Fuego, Tér-q del Fwá-gɷ, *is* s. S. Am.
Terranova, Ter-q-nɵ́-vq, *s-pt t* Sic., 10.
Terre aux Bœufs, Ter ɷ Bęf, *v* La.
Terre Bonne, Tęr Bón *or* Tqr Bɷn, *bayou* and *par* La.; *co t* C. E.
Terre Coupee, Tér-e Kɷ-pé, *v* Ia.
Terre Haute, Tér-e Hɷt, *co t* Ia., 7.
Terschelling, Ter-*sh*él-iŋ, *i* N. Sea, 2½.
Teruel, Ta-rɷ-él, *t* Sp., 6¾.
Teschen, Téʃ-en, *t* Aus. Silesia, 6½.
Teshoo-Loomboo, Teʃ-ɷ́-Lɷm-bɷ́, *t* Thibet, 4.
Tesouras, Ta-sɵ́-rqs, *r* Bra., 200 m.
Tetbury, Tét-ber-i, *t* and *par* Eng., 3⅓.
Tetooan, Tet-ɷ-q́n, *t* Morocco, 16.
Teutopolis, Tų-tóp-ɷ-lis, *v* Ill. [Eng., 6.
Tewkesbury, Tų́ks-ber-i, *t* and *par*
Tewksbury, Tų́ks-ber-i, *v* Mass., ¼.
Texana, Teks-q́-na, *co t* Tex.
Texas, Téks-as, one of the s. w. U. S.; area 237,504 s. m.; pop. 154,024 whites, 397 free colored, 58,161 slaves—total, 212,592; *vs* N-Y., O., Ia., Ill.

Texel, Téks-el, *i* North Sea, 5.
Teza, Tá-zq, *t* Morocco, 11.
Tezcoco, Tes-*h*ó-kꝏ, *t* Mex., 5.
Thame, Tem, *t* and *par* Eng., 3¼.
Thames, Temz, *rs* Eng., 215 m.; C. W.
Thanet, Hán-et, Isle of, *i* Eng., 32.
Thann, Tqn, *t* Fr., 6.
Thaso, Hq́-sꝏ, *i* Ægean Sea, 6. [*co t* Ill.
Thebes, Hɛbz, anc. *c* and *cap* Egypt;
Thebes, Hé-va, *t* Greece, 9.
Theiss, Tįs, *r* Hun., 500 m.
Themsche, Tém-*sh*e, *t* Belg., 6¼.
Theresa, Tɛ-ré-sa, *v* N-Y. [40.
Theresienstadt, Ter-a-zi-en-stq́t, *t* Aus.,
Thermia, Her-mé-q, *i* Grecian Arch., 6.
Thermopylæ, Her-móp-i-lɛ, celebrated *pass* Greece.
Thessaly, Hés-a-li, *prov* Eu. Tur.
Thetford, Hét-ford, *t* Eng., 4; *v* Vt., 2.
Thian-Shan, Tɛ-q́n-Σqn, *ms* China.
Thibet *or* Tibet, Tíb-et, large *region* As.
Thibodeaux, Tib-ꝏ-dó, *co t* La.
Thielt, Tɛlt, *t* Belg., 12⅔.
Thiers, Tɛ-ą́r, *t* Fr., 14.
Thionville, Tɛ-ꝏń-vél, *t* Fr., 8½.
Thirlamere, Hę́r-la-mɛr, *l* Eng.
Thirsk, Hęrsk, *t* and *par* Eng., 5⅓.
Thogji-Chumo, Hóg-jɛ-Cʰó-mꝏ, salt *l* West Himalayas, 15,500 feet above the sea.
Thomaston, Tóm-as-ton, *co t* Ga.
Thomastown, Tóm-as-tɤn, *t* and *par* Ireland, 2¼.
Thomasville, Tóm-as-vil, *co t* Ga.
Thompson, Tómp-son, *vs* Conn., Ga.
Thompsonville, *vs* Conn. 2, Pa., Va.
Thonon, Tꝏ-nóń, *t* Savoy, 4½.
Thorda, Tór-dq, *t* Transylvania, 8¼.
Thorn, Tɵrn, *t* W. Prus., 12¾.
Thornapple, Hórn-ap-l, *r* Mich., 80 m.
Thornbury, Hórn-ber-i, *t* Eng., 4¾.
Thorne, Hɵrn, *t* and *par* Eng., 3½.
Thorn Hill, Hɵrn Hil, *v* C. W., ½.
Thornton, Hórn-ton, *vs* Pa., Ill.
Thorntown, Hórn-tɤn, *v* Ia., ¾.
Thorold, Hór-ꝏld, *t* C. W., 1¼.
Thourout, Tꝏ-ró, *t* Belg., 8½.
Thousand Isles, Hɤ́-zand Ilz, 1500 rocky *islets* river St. Lawrence.
Thrace, Hras, *or* Thracia, Hrá-ʃi-a, a name applied to Turkey in Eu., or that part of Turkey bet. Bulgaria and the Archipelago. [1¼.
Thrapston, Hráps-ton, *t* and *par* Eng.,
Three Kings, *or* Manawa-Tawi, Mán-a-wq-Tq-wé, *i* S. Pac. Oc.
Three Rivers, Hrɛ Rív-erz, *vs* Mass., Mich.; *t* C. E., 6½.
Thsieoo-Shan, Hsɛ-ꝏ-Σq́n, *m* China.
Thun, Tꝏn, *l* and *t* Swit., 5.

Thunder Bay, Hún-der Ba, Lake Huron, n. e. Mich.
Thuringian Forest, Hq-rín-ji-an Fórest, *ms* Cen. Ger.
Thurles, Hurlz, *t* and *par* Ir., 6.
Thurso, Húr-sꝏ, *par* and *s-pt t* Scot., 5.
Tibagi, Tɛ-bq-ʒé, *r* Bra., 200 m.
Tiber, Tį́-ber, *r* Cen. It., 185 m.
Ticao, Tɛ-kq́-ꝏ, Philippine Is.
Tichfield-with-Crofton, Tíq-fɛld-wiđ-Króf-ton, *t* and *par* Eng., 4. [2⅔.
Ticonderoga, Tį-kon-der-ó-ga, *v* N-Y.,
Tideswell, Tį́dz-wel, *t* Eng., 3½.
Tidor, Tɛ-dór, *i* Malay Arch.
Tien-Tsin, Tɛ-en-Tsén, *c* China.
Tiete, Tɛ-á-ta, *r* Bra., 500 m.
Tiffin, Tif-in, *co t* O., 4.
Tiflis, Tif-lis, *c*, *cap* Ga. in Asia, 50.
Tigris, Tį́-gris, *r* As. Tur., 1150 m.
Tilburg, Tíl-bu*rh*, *t* Neth., 13⅓.
Tillanchong, Til-qn-ϙóŋ, Nicobar Isle.
Tilsit, Tíl-sit, *t* Prus., 13¾.
Tim, Tɛm, *r* Siberia, 250 m.
Timbuctoo, Tim-búk-tꝏ, *t* Cen. Af., 12.
Timor, Tɛ-mór, *i* Malay Arch.
Timor Laut, Tɛ-mór Lɤt, *i* Mal. Arch.
Tinajo, Tɛ-nq́-*h*ꝏ, *t* Canaries, 1¼.
Ting-Hai, Tiŋ-Hį́, *c* is. Chusan.
Tino, Té-nꝏ, *i* Grecian Arch., 22.
Tiœrn, Tɛ-ę́rn, *i* of Swed.
Tioga, Tį-ó-ga, *vs* N-Y. 1, Pa.
Tioomen, Tɛ-ꝏ-mén, *t* Sib., 12.
Tippecanoe, Tip-ɛ-ka-nꝏ́, *v* O.; *r* Ia.
Tipperary, Tip-er-á-ri, *co* Ir.; *t* do., 8¼.
Tipton, Típ-ton, *co ts* Ia. ¼, Iowa.
Tirajana, Tɛ-rq-*h*q́-nq, *t* Canaries, 3⅜.
Tirana, Tɛ-rq́-nq, *t* Eu. Tur., 10.
Tiraspol, Tɛ-rq́s-pol, *ft t* Rus., 5.
Tiree, Tir-é, *i* Inner Hebrides, 3¾.
Tirlemont, Tɛrl-móń, *t* Belg., 8⅓.
Tirnova, Tír-nꝏ-vq, *t* Eu. Tur., 8.
Tishemingo, Tiʃ-ɛ-míŋ-gꝏ, *co* Miss.
Tiskilwa, Tis-kil-we, *v* Ill.
Titicaca (Tɛ-ti-kq́-kq) Lake, S. Am.
Tittibawassee, Tit-i-ba-wós-ɛ, *r* Mich., nav. 80 m.
Titusville, Tį́-tus-vil, *vs* N-J., Pa.
Tiverton, Tív-er-ton, *t* and *par* Eng., 11; *v* R. I., 2½.
Tivoli, Tív-ꝏ-lɛ, *t* Cen. It., 6½.
Tivoli, Ti-vó-li, *vs* N-Y., Iowa.
Tizzana, Tit-sq́-nq, *t* Tus., 7¾.
Tlapa, Tlq́-pq, *t* Mex.
Tlascala, Tlqs-kq́-lq, *t* Mex., 4.
Tlemcen, Tlem-sén, *t* Algeria, 9½.
Tnilaia, Tnɛ-lį́-q, *r* Rus., 120 m.
Tobago, Tꝏ-bá-gꝏ, *i* Br. W. Ind., 14¾.
Tobarra, Tꝏ-bq́r-q, *t* Sp., 6½.
Tobermory, Tꝏ-ber-mó-ri, *s-pt t* Scot.,
Tobol, Tꝏ-ból, *r* Sib., 500 m. [1½.

Tobolsk, Tɷ-bólsk, *gov* Sib.; area 1,000,000 s. m., pop. 685,000; *c, cap* W. Sib., 20. [*t* do.
Tocantins, Tɷ-kqn-ténz, *r* Bra., 1000 m.;
Tocoa, Tɷ-kɷ́-ɑ, *r* Ga. and Tenn.
Tocuyo, Tɷ-kꝏ́-yɷ, *r* Ven., 200 m.; *t* do.
Toddington, Tód-iŋ-ton, *t* and *par* Eng., 2½.
Todmorden-with-Wafsden, Tód-mer-den-wiđ-Wáfs-den, *t* Eng., 4½.
Tokat, Tɷ-kqt, *c* As. Minor, 26¾.
Tokay, Tɷ-ká, *t* N.-E. Hun., 5¾.
Toledo, Tɷ-lá-đɷ, *c* Sp., 14; — Tɷ-lé-dɷ, *c* O., 11⅓; *v* Ill.
Tolentino, Tɷ-len-té-nɷ, *t* It., 9½.
Tolland, Tól-and, *co t* Conn.
Tolna, Tól-no, *t* Hun., 5¾.
Toloar, Tɷ-lɷ-qr, *i* Malay Arch.
Toluca, Tɷ-lꝏ́-kq, *t* Mex., 12.
Tolu, Santiago de, Sqn-ti-q-gɷ da Tɷ-lꝏ́, *s-pt t* N-Gran.
Tomaszow, Tɷ-mq-ʃov, *t* Poland, 5.
Tombigbee, Tom-big-bɛ, *r* Miss. and Ala., 450 m. [*v* N-Y.
Tompkinsville, Tómp-kinz-vil, *co t* Ky.;
Tomsk, Tomsk, *gov* Sib.; *c, cap* same, 24.
Tom's (Tomz) River, *co t* N-J., 1; *r* do.
Tonawanda, Ton-a-wón-dɑ, *v* NY., 1½.
Tondern, Tón-dern, *t* Den., 6½.
Tondja, Tón-jɑ, *r* Eu. Tur., 150 m.
Tondo, Tón-dɷ, *t* is. Luzon, 17½.
Tone, Tɷn, *r* Eng.
Tonga (Tóŋ-gɑ) Islands, Pac. Oc., 18¼.
Tongataboo, Toŋ-a-tq-bꝏ, *i* Pac. Oc., 8.
Tongres, Tɷń-gr, *t* Belg., 6¼.
Tongue (Tuŋ) River, Mo. Ter., 300 m.
Tonneins, Ton-áń, *t* Fr., 7½.
Tonnerre, Ton-qr, *t* Fr., 4⅔.
Tonquin, Ton-kén, *g* China Sea, 300 m.
Toobonai, Tꝏ-bɷ-nį, *i* Pac. Oc.
Toola, Tꝏ́-lq, *gov* Eu. Rus.; area 11,875 s. m., pop. 1,092,473; *cap* same, 55.
Toolcha, Tꝏ́l-ʒq, *ft t* Eu. Tur.
Toolsborough, Tꝏ́lz-bur-ɷ, *v* Iowa.
Toombuddra, Tꝏm-búd-rɑ, *r* Ind., 400 m
Toong, Tꝏŋ, *r* China, 250 m.
Toora, Tꝏ́-rq, *r* Sib., 300 m.
Toorkistan, Tꝏr-kis-tqn, *reg* Cen. Asia; — Chinese, area 500,000 s. m.; — Independent, *or* Independent Tartary, area 720,800 s. m., pop. 4,000,000.
Tooz-Golee, Tꝏz-Gɷ́-lɛ, *salt l* As. Min.
Topeka, Tɷ-pé-kɑ, *cap* Kanzas Ter.
Topsfield, Tóps-fɛld, *v* Mass., 1¼.
Topsham, Tóps-am, *s-pt t* Eng., 2¾; *v* Me., 1½.
Torbay, Tér-ba, *b* Eng.
Torda, Tér-dq, *t* Transylvania, 7.
Torgau, Tér-gɤ, *ft t* Prus. Sax., 6½.
Torget, Tér-get, *i* of Norway.

Tornea, Tér-nɛ-ɷ, *r* Scan., 230 m.
Toro, Tɷ́-rɷ, *t* Sp., 7.
Toronto, Tɷ-rón-tɷ, *c, cap* C. W., 50.
Toropetz, Tɷ́-rɷ-pets, *t* Rus., 8.
Torquay, Tér-kɛ, *t* Eng., 8.
Torre del Greco, Tér-a del Grá-kɷ, *t* Nap., 13.
Torre dell' Annunziata, Tér-a del Lq-nꝏn-zɛ-q-tq, *t* Nap., 10.
Torre Don Jimeno, Tér-a Don *H*ɛ-má-nɷ, *t* Sp., 5¾. [6½.
Torrejoncillo, Ter-a-*h*on-tél-yɷ, *t* Sp.,
Torren's (Tór-enz) Lake, S. Aust.
Torrente, Tor-én-ta, *t* Sp., 5.
Torrington, Great, Grat Tór-iŋ-ton, *t* Eng., 3⅓.
Tortola, Tor-tɷ́-lɑ, Virgin Island, 8½.
Tortona, Tor-tɷ́-nq, *t* Sard. St., 10¾.
Tortosa, Tor-tɷ́-sq, *t* Sp., 20½.
Törtsvar, Terts-vqr, *v* Tran., 6⅔.
Tortuga, Tor-tꝏ́-gɑ, *i* W. Ind.
Tortugas, Tor-tꝏ́-gqs, *i* W. Ind.
Torzhok, Tor-ʒók, *t* Rus., 15½.
Totana, Tɷ-tq-nq, *t* Sp., 8½.
Totness, Tót-nes, *t* Eng., 4½. [12.
Totonicapan, Tɷ-tɷ-nɛ-kq-pán, *t* Guat.,
Toubouai, Tꝏ-bꝏ-į, *i* S. Pac. Oc.
Toul, Tꝏl, *ft t* Fr., 8½.
Toulon, Tꝏ-lɷ́ń, *s-pt c* Fr., 69½.
Toulouse, Tꝏ-lꝏ́z, *c* Fr., 93⅓.
Tourcoing, Tꝏr-kwáń, *t* Fr., 27⅔.
Tournay, Tꝏr-ná, *ft t* Belg., 33.
Tournus, Tꝏr-nés, *t* Fr., 5½.
Tours, Tꝏr, *c* Fr., 33½.
Towanda, Tɤ-án-dɑ, *bor* Pa., 1¼.
Towcester, Tɤ́s-ter, *t* Eng., 2⅔.
Towyn, Tɷ́-win, *v* N. Wales, 2¾.
Traina, Trį-nq, *t* Sicily, 7½.
Traitor's (Trát-orz) Island, one of Navigators' Is.
Tralee, Trq-lé, *bor* and *s-pt t* Ir., 13¾.
Trani, Trq-nɛ, *s-pt t* Naples, 14.
Transcaucasia, Trans-ke-ká-ʃi-ɑ, *cy* As. Rus.; area 66,300 s. m., pop. 1,625,000.
Transylvania, Tran-sil-vá-ni-ɑ, *principality* Aus. Empire; area 23,078 s. m., pop. 2,074,202.
Trapani, Trq-pq-nɛ, *s-pt t* Sicily, 25.
Travancore, Trav-an-kɷ́r, *st* Ind.; area 6710 s. m., pop. 1,300,000.
Travi, Trq-vɛ, *v* Parma, 5⅓.
Travnik, Trqv-ník, *t* Eu. Tur., 8½.
Trebigne, Tra-bén-ya, 10.
Trebitsch, Trá-biç, *t* Moravia, 5. [40.
Trebizond, Tréb-i-zond, *s-pt c* As. Tur.,
Tredegar, Tréd-ɛ-gɑr, *t* Eng., 17⅔.
Tremiti (Trém-i-tɛ) Isles, Adriatic Sea.
Tremont, Tré-mont, *v* Pa., 1.
Trent, Trent, *r* Eng., 140 m.; *c* Aus., 13¼.

Trenton, Trén-ton, *c, cap* N-J., 6½.
Trenton, *t* C. W., 1½.
Tresco, Trés-kœ, Scilly Island, ½.
Trevanion, Trɛ-vá-ni-on, *i* S. Pac.
Treves, Trɛvz, *c* Rhenish Prus., 19⅔.
Treviglio, Tra-vél-yœ, *t* Aus. It., 6½.
Treviso, Tra-vé-sœ, *c* Aus. It., 19½.
Tricarico, Trɛ-ká-rɛ-kœ, *t* Nap., 5.
Trichinopoly, Triç-in-óp-œ-li, *t* Brit. Ind., 100.
Triest, Trɛ-ést, *s-pt c* Aus., 64.
Trikeri, Tré-ka-rɛ, *t* Tur., 5.
Trikhala, Tré-kq-lq, *t* Eu. Tur., 10.
Trim, Trim, *bor* and *t* Ir., 6¼.
Tring, Triŋ, *t* Eng., 4¾.
Tringany, Trin-gá-nɛ, *t* Malay pen., 15.
Trinidad, Trin-i-dád, (Sp. Trɛ-nɛ-) đáđ, one of the W. Ind. Is.; area 1,-536,000 acres, pop. 68,645. [*v* La.
Trinity, Trín-i-ti, *rs* Tex., 550 m., Cal.,
Trino, Tré-nœ, *t* Sardinian States, 8¼.
Triora, Trɛ-ó-rq, *v* Sardinian States, 4¾.
Tripoli, Tríp-œ-lɛ, *cy* n. Af., area, 105,-000 s. m., pop. 1,500,000. [15.
Tripoli, Tríp-œ-lɛ, *s-pt ts* Af., 20; Syria,
Tripolitza, Trɛ-pœ-lít-sq, *t* Gr.
Tristan D'Acunha, Tris-tán Dq-kóón-yq, *i* S. At.
Trobriand, Trœ-bri-ánd, *is* Louisiade Arch.
Troia, Tró-yq, *t* Naples, 5.
Trois Rivières, Trwq Rɛ-vi-ár, *t* is. Guadeloupe, 3¼.
Troitzkoi, Trót-skɵ, *t* Rus., 7.
Trondhjem, Trónd-yem, *s-pt t* Norway, 13¾.
Tropea, Trœ-pá-q, *t* Naples, 4½.
Troppau, Tróp-ɤ, *ft t* Aus. Silesia, 11.
Troupville, Tróóp-vil, *co t* Ga.
Trowbridge, Tró-brij, *t* and *par* Eng., 11¼.
Troy, Trɵ, ruined *c* As. Min.; *c* N-Y., 45; *t* O., 2; *co ts* N. C., Ala., Tenn., O., 2; Mo.; *vs* Ia., Ill., Pa., Ga., Wis.
Troyes, Trwq, *c* Fr., 27⅓.
Trujillo *or* Truxillo, Trœ-*hél*-yœ, *c* Sp., 6; *t* Peru, 8; *c* Ven., 4; *s-pt t* Hond., 4.
Trumansburg, Tróó-manz-burg, *v* N-Y., 1.
Truro, Tróó-rœ, *bor* and *s-pt t* Eng., 10-¾; *v* Mass., 1; *s-pt t* N. Scotia.
Tsaritsin, Tsq-rit-sín, *ft t* Rus., 4⅔.
Tsarskoe-Selo, Tsárs-kœ-a-Sá-lœ, *t* Rus., 10¼.
Tsong-Gan-Hien, Tsoŋ-Gqn-Hɛ-én, *t* China, 10.
Tsoosima, Tsœ-sé-mq, *i* Japan.
Tsung-Ming, Tsuŋ-Míŋ, *i* China.
Tuam, Tú-am, *t* and *par* Ir., 7¾.
Tübingen, Tę-biŋ-en, *t* Würt., 7½.
Tuckahoe, Tuk-a-hó, *r* Md.; *v* N-J., ⅜.
Tuckerton, Túk-er-ton, *v* N-J.
Tucopiu, Tœ-kó-pi-q, *i* S. Pac. Oc., ½.
Tucuman, Tœ-kœ-mán, *prov* La Plata, 44,000; *t* do. 12.
Tudela, Tœ-đá-lq, *c* Sp., 6¾.
Tulare, Tœ-lá-rɛ, *co* Cal.
Tule, Tóó-lɛ, *l* Cal.
Tullahoma, Tul-a-hó-mq, *v* Tenn.
Tullamore, Tul-a-mór, *t* Ir., 4⅔.
Tülle, Tęl, *t* Fr., 11¾.
Tulln, Tœln, *t* Aus., 1¾.
Tullow, Túl-ó, *t* and *par* Ir., 3.
Tully, Túl-i, *vs* N-Y., Mo., ⅔.
Tulmaro, Tœl-má-rœ, *t* Ven., 8.
Tulpehocken, Tul-pɛ-hók-en, *cr* Pa.
Tunamaguont, Tœ-nam-a-gwónt, *v* Pa.
Tunbridge, Tún-brij, *t* and *par* Eng., 4½.
Tunbridge Wells, *t* and *watering-place* Eng., 10½.
Tuncha, Tun-çá, *t* China, 150.
Tung-Chang, Tœŋ-Çáŋ, *c* China.
Tunis, Tú-nis, *st* N. Af., area 70,000, pop. 2,500,000; *s-pt t, cap* Tunis, 150; — Gulf, Med.
Tunja, Tóóŋ-*h*q, *t* N-Gran., 7. [½.
Tunkhannock, Tuŋk-hán-ok, *co t* Pa.;
Tunstall-Court, Túns-tɵl-Kœrt, *t* Eng., 9½.
Tunuyan, Tœ-nœ-yán, *r* S. Am., 200 m.
Tuolumne, Twól-um-nɛ, *r* Cal.
Tuparro, Tœ pár-œ, *r* N-Gran., 200 m.
Tupisa, Tœ-pé-sq, *t* Bol., 5.
Tura, Tóó-ro, *t* W. Hun., 6½.
Turaboo, Tur-a-bóó, Society Is., 2.
Turin, Tú-rin, (Fr. Tę-ráṅ,) *c, cap* Sardinian States, 143¼; *v* N-Y.
Tur-Kevi, Tœr-Ka-vé, *v* Hun., 9½.
Turkey, *or* The Ottoman Empire, Túr-ki *or* Ot'œ-man Em'pįr, extensive countries in Eu., As., and Af.; the following are the prominent divisions;— Room-Elee, Bosnia, Silistria, Jezayr, Is. of Gallipoli, Candia, Gozzo, Standie, Thasos, Samothraki, Imbro, Stalimni or Lemnos, Strati, &c.; Wallachia, Servia, Moldavia, Asia Minor, Armenia and Koordistan, Syria or Sham, Irak and Mesopotamia, Jidda in Arabia, Egypt, Tripoli, Tunis; area 2,095,194, pop. 35,360,000.
Turner, Túr-ner, *v* Me., 2.
Turnhout, Turn-hɤt, *t* Belg., 13¼.
Turquino, Tœr-ké-nœ, *m* Cuba.
Turriff, Túr-if, *t* and *par* Scot., 1¾.
Turyassu, Tœ-rɛ-q-sóó, *r* Bra., 350 m.
Tuscahoma, Tus-ka-hó-mq, *v* Ala.,
Tuscaloosa, Tus-ka-lóó-sq, *co t* Ala., 3½.

Tuscany, Tús-kan-i, *grand duchy* N. It.; having as divisions:— Florence, Lucca, Pisa, Sienna, Arezzo, Grossetto, Leghorn, with is. of Gorgona, Elba and adjacent islands; area 8,586, pop. 1,778,021. [*v* O.
Tuscarawas, Tus-ka-ré-was, *r*, *co* and
Tuscarora, Tus-ka-ró-ra, *crs* Pa., Va.; *v* N-Y., Pa., ⅔.
Tuscola, Tus-kó-la, *co* and *v* Mich.
Tuscumbia, Tus-kúm-bi-a, *v* Ala.; *co t*
Tuskegee, Tus-ké-gɛ, *co t* Ala. [Mo.
Tutbury, Tút-ber-i, *v* Eng., 1¾.
Tuxford, Túks-ford, *t* and *par* Eng., 1¼.
Tuxtla, Tókst-lq, *t* Mex., 5.
Tuy, Twɛ, *t* Sp., 4¼; *r* S. Am.
Tyer, Tyér, *c* Rus., 24.
Tvertsa, Twért-sq, *r* Rus., 110 m.
Tweed, Twɛd, *r* Scot. and Eng., 95 m.
Tweedmouth, Twéd-muth, *v* Eng., 5¾.
Twickenham, Twik-en-ham, *v* and *par* Eng., 6¼.
Twofold Bay, e. coast of Aust.
Two Rivers, *v* Wis., 1.
Tygart's Valley (Tį-garts Vál-i) River, Va., 150 m.
Tyler, Tį-ler, *co t* Tex.; *v* Ill.
Tymochte, Tį-mók-tɛ, *v* O.
Tyne, Tįn, *r* Eng., 80 m.
Tynemouth-with-North Shields, (Tįn-muth,) two *ts* Eng., 30½.
Tyngsborough, Tiŋz-bur-ω, *v* Mass.
Typinsan, Tį-pin-sqn, Madjicosima Is.
Tyri-Fiord, Tę-ri-Fɛ-órd, *l* Nor.
Tyrnau, Tír-nɤ, *t* Hun., 5¾.
Tyrol, Tír-ol, *prov* Aus.; area 11,084 s. m., pop. 859,706.
Tyrone, Tį-rón, *vs* N-Y., Pa.

# U.

Uanapu, Ꝏ-q-nq-pó, *r* Bra., 400 m.
Uatuma, Ꝏ-q-tó-mq, *r* Bra., 350 m.
Uaupes, Wɤ-pes, *r* Bra.
Ubatuba, Ꝏ-bq-tó-bq, *t* Bra., 6.
Ubeda, Ꝏ-bá-dq, *t* Sp., 13¾.
Ubrique, Ꝏ-bré-ka, *t* Sp., 5½.
Ucayale, Ꝏ-kį-q-la, *r* Peru, 500 m.
Udine, Ꝏ'dɛ-na, *t* Aus. It., 26¾.
Uelzen, Elt'sen, *t* Han., 3.
Uerdingen, Er'diŋ-en, *t* Rhen. Prus., 3.
Ugliano, Ꝏl-yq-nω, *i* in Adriatic Sea.
Uhricksville, Yq-riks-vil, *v* O., 1.
Uist, (Wist *or* Est,) North, *i* Outer Hebrides, 3½.
Uist, South, *i* Outer Hebrides, 4.
Uithuizen, Ꝏt-hé-zen, *v* Neth., 3¼.
Ujhely-Satoralja, Ꝏ'ɛ-hely-Sq-tω-ról-yo, *t* Hun., 6⅓.
Uleaborg, Ꝏ'lɛ-ω-berg, *s-pt t* Fin., 5.
Ulea-Trask, Ꝏ'lɛ-ω-Trqsk, *l* Fin.
Ulloa, Ꝏl-yó-q, *r* Hond., 100 m.
Ullswater, Ulz'wo-ter, *l* Eng.
Ulm, Ulm, *t* Würtemberg, 13½.
Ulster, Ul'ster, *r* Ger.; Ul'ster, *co* and *p o* N-Y.
Ulva, Ul'va, *is* Inner Hebrides, ¾.
Ulverstone, Ul'ver-stωn, *t* and *par* Eng., 6½.
Umbagog (Um'ba-gog) Lake, N-Eng.
Umea, Ꝏ'mɛ-ω, *r* Swed., 250 m.
Umpqua (Ump'kwe) City, *v* Or. Ter.
Una, Ꝏ'nq, four *rs* Bra., 60 m.
Unadilla, Un-a-díl-a, *r* N-Y.; *vs* N-Y., Mich.
Unare, Ꝏ-nq-ra, *r* Ven., 120 m.
Uncasville, Un'kas-vil, *v* Conn.
Unghvar, Ꝏŋ-vqr, *t* Hun., 5.
Unie, Ꝏn'ya, *i* Adriatic Sea, ⅓.
Union, Yqn-yon, *co ts* Va., Mo.; *vs* N-Y., Ia., Mich., N-C.
Union City, *v* Mich.
Union Mills, *vs* Pa., Va., Ia., Io.
Union Springs, *vs* N-Y., 1; Ala. [Ill.
Uniontown, *co t* Pa., 2¾; *vs* Ala., Ia.,
Union Village, *v* N-Y.
Unionville, *co t* S. C.; *vs* Conn., Pa., O.
United States, Yq-nįt-ed Stats, Rep. N. Am., occupying more than half of the territory of the North Temperate Zone, and presenting in the unity of its States, the most perfect government the world ever witnessed. The face of the country is of every variety—valley, mountain, and plain. Topographically considered, the United States are divided as follows: 1. The Atlantic, or Alleghany Slope; 2. The Mississippi Valley; 3. The Pacific, or Rocky Mountain Slope. The first, the oldest, and comprising the original states of the confederacy, possessing the greatest number of inhabitants, farthest advanced in the arts and sciences, commercial and educational improvements, steadily furnishes the states and territories of the other two divisions with "bone, sinew" and mind, for their settlements. The second comprises the richest and most extensive agricultural country in the world; while the other,

yet in embryo, contains beneath its hills great mineral wealth, and in its mountain streams undreamed of manufacturing power.

| States and Territories. | Area in s. ms. | Total populat'n. |
|---|---|---|
| Maine, | 31,766 | 583,169 |
| New Hampshire, | 9,280 | 317,976 |
| Vermont, | 10,212 | 314,120 |
| Massachusetts, | 7,800 | 994,514 |
| Rhode Island, | 1,306 | 147,545 |
| Connecticut, | 4,674 | 370,792 |
| New York, | 47,000 | 3,097,394 |
| New Jersey, | 8,320 | 489,555 |
| Pennsylvania, | 46,000 | 2,311,786 |
| Delaware, | 2,122 | 91,532 |
| Maryland, | 11,124 | 583,034 |
| Dis. of Columbia, | 60 | 51,687 |
| Virginia, | 61,352 | 1,421,661 |
| North Carolina, | 50,704 | 869,039 |
| South Carolina, | 29,385 | 668,507 |
| Georgia, | 58,000 | 906,185 |
| Florida, | 59,268 | 87,445 |
| Alabama, | 50,722 | 771,623 |
| Mississippi, | 47,156 | 606,526 |
| Louisiana, | 41,255 | 517,762 |
| Texas, | 257,504 | 212,592 |
| Arkansas, | 52,198 | 209,897 |
| Tennessee, | 45,600 | 1,002,717 |
| Kentucky, | 37,680 | 982,405 |
| Ohio, | 39,964 | 1,980,329 |
| Michigan, | 56,243 | 397,654 |
| Indiana, | 33,809 | 988,416 |
| Illinois, | 55,405 | 851,470 |
| Missouri, | 67,380 | 682,044 |
| Iowa, | 50,914 | 192,214 |
| Wisconsin, | 53,924 | 305,391 |
| California, | 155,980 | 92,597 |
| Kanzas Territory, | 114,798 | ...... |
| Nebraska Ter., | 335,882 | ...... |
| Minnesota Ter., | 166,025 | 6,077 |
| New Mexico Ter., | 207,007 | 61,547 |
| Utah Ter., | 299,170 | 11,380 |
| Oregon Ter., | 185,030 | 13,294 |
| Washington Ter. | 123,022 | ...... |
| Total, | 2,936,166 | 23,191,876 |

The rapidity with which population increases in the United States is remarkable: at the rate of increase for the preceding ten years, up to 1850, the present population would be (1856) 28,753,062. The number of persons to the square mile in the non-slaveholding states were 21.91; slaveholding, 11.35.

The educational system is unequalled by that of any country (excepting Prussia) in the world. The number of public and private schools, colleges and academies, is 87,162; of students in attendance 4,089,597, and the proportion at school is 1 to 4.9, not including slaves, and greater than that of any other country. The ratio of those over twenty years of age unable to read or write is 1 in 40 in the non-slaveholding states, and 1 in 12 in the slaveholding states. In the New England states, 1 in 400. The number of papers published, 2,526; while other publications, such as books, pamphlets, etc., exceed, probably, all other countries together.

American ships are found on every sea, and in its ports the productions of every clime are received. There entered from foreign ports, in 1854, 19,103 vessels, with a tonnage of 5,884,339 tons; cleared, in the same period, 19,073, with a tonnage of 6,019,194; value of imports, $304,562,384; exports, $278,241,064.

Unity, Yú-ni-ti, *vs* O., Ill.

Unna, Un'a, *t* Prus. Westphalia, 5⅓; *r* Turkish Croatia, 110 m.

Unst, Unst, Shetland Island, 3.

Upland, Up'land, *v* Pa., ½.

Upolou, Œ-pœ-ló, Samoan Is., Pac. Oc., area 60 s. m., pop. 25,000.

Upper *or* New California, (Kal-i-fér-ni-a,) former ter. of the state of Cal.

Upper Iowa, *r* Min. and Io.

Upper Marlborough, Márl-bur-œ, *co t* [Md.

Upper Sandusky, *or* Fremont, *co t* O., 1.

Upper Swatara, Swa-tá-ra, *tp* Pa.

Upperville, Up'er-vil, *v* Va., ¾.

Upsal, Up'sal, *t* Swed., 5.

Upshur, Up'ʃur, *v* O.

Upton-upon-Severn, Up'ton-up-on-Sév-ern, *t* and *par* 2⅜.

Ural, Yú-ral, *r* Rus., 1800 m.; *ms* do.

Urbanna, Ur-bán-a, *co ts* Va., O., Ill., Mo. [7.

Urbino, Œr-bé-nœ, *c* Pontifical States,

Urghundaub, Ur-gun-dób, *r* Afg., 230 m.

Urquhart, Urk'hart, *par* Scot.

Ursa, Ur'sa, *v* Ill.

Urubamba, Œ-rœ-bám-ba, *t* Peru, 4.

Urucaia, Œ-rœ-kí-a, *r* Brazil., 200 m.

Uruguay, Œ-rœ-gwí, *r* S. Am., 800 m.

Uruguay, a republic S. Am.; area 75,000 s. m., pop. 1,120,000.

Usedom, Œ'ze-dom, *i* Prus. Pomerania.

Ushant, Uʃ'ant, *i* off Brittany, 2¼.

Uskup, Œs'kup, *t* Eu. Tur., 10.

Ustica, Œs'ti-ka, *i* Med. [400 m.

Usumasinta, Œ-sœ-ma-sin-ta, *r* C. Am.,

Utah, Yú-tə, *or* Yú-tq, *ter* U. S.; area 269,170, s. m., pop., whites, 11,330; free colored, 24; slaves, 26; total, 11,-380, mostly Mormons.
Utah Lake, central part ter. 30 by 10 m.
Utica, Yú-ti-kq, *c* N-Y., 22¼; *vs* Pa., Miss., O., 1; Mich., 1; Ia., Ill., Mo.
Utiel, Ꝏ-tɛ-él, *t* Sp., 5¾.
Utilla, Ꝏ-tél-yq, *i* Caribbean Sea.
Utrecht, Yú-trekt, *t* Hol., 49¼; *prov* Neth., pop. 155,224.
Utrera, Ꝏ-trá-rq, *t* Sp., 12¾.
Uttoxeter, Uks'ɛ-ter, *t* and *par* Eng., 5.
Uvalde, Ꝏ-vql-da, *co* Tex.
Uxbridge, Uks'brij, *t* Eng., 3¼; *v* Mass., 2.
Uyea, Ꝏ-yá, one of Shet. Is.
Uzes, E-zás, *t* Fr., 7.
Uzzano, Ꝏt-sq-nꝏ, *t* Tuscany, 4.

# V.

Vaagen, Vq-gen, (East and West,) two of the Loffoden Is., Nor., 4.
Vache, (Vqʃ) Island, W. Ind.
Vadavate, Vq-dq-vq-ta, *r* S. Hind., 200 m.
Vaga, Vq-gq, *r* Rus., 250 m.
Vaigats, Vį-gqts, *i* Artic Oc., large and inhabited.
Vaila, Vá-lq, Shetland Island.
Vahk, Vqk, *r* Siberia, 350 m.
Valatie, Vál-a-tɛ, *v* N-Y.
Valbenoite, Vql-be-nwqt, *v* Fr., 6.
Valdepenas, Vql-da-pán-yqs, *t* Sp., 9¾.
Valdes, Vql-des, *i* Gulf of Georgia.
Valdivia, Vql-dé-vi-q, *r* Chili, 120 m.
Valença, Vq-lén-sq, *t* Brazil, 3.
Valence, Vq-lóns, *t* Fr., 16¼.
Valencia, Vq-lén-ʃi-q, *prov* Sp.; *c*, *cap* of same, 70; *c* Ven., 17; — Lake, do.
Valenciennes, Vq-lon-sɛ-én, *t* Fr., 23¼.
Valentia, Vq-lén-ʃi-q, *i* w. of Ir.; *t* do. 2½.
Valenza, Vq-lén-zq, *t* Sard. States, 7½.
Valetta, Vq-lét-q, *s-pt c* is. Malta, 30.
Valki, Vql-kɛ, *t* Rus., 9.
Valladolid, Vql-yq-đꝏ-léđ, *c* Sp., 30; *c* Mex., 18; *c* Yucatan, 15.
Vallay, Vál-a, *i* Outer Hebrides.
Valle-Hermoso, Vql-ya-Er-mó-sꝏ, *t* Canaries, 3.
Valognes, Vq-lóny, *t* Fr., 6.
Valpariso, Vql-pq-rį-sꝏ, *c cap* Chili, 50; Val-pa-rá-zꝏ, *co t* Ia.
Van, Vqn, *c* Turkish Armenia, 40.
Van, Lake, salt lake, As. Tur.
Van Buren, Van Bú-ren, *co ts* Ark., 1⅓; Mis.
Vanceburg, Váns-burg, *vs* Ky., ¼; Ill.
Vancouver's, Van-kó-verz, *i* w. Br. N. Am., 11.
Vancouver, Fort, *settlement* Hudson's Bay Company, Wash. Ter.
Vandalia, Van-dá-li-q, *co t* Ill., 1.
Van Deusenville, Van Dú-zen-vil, *v* Mass.
Van Diemen's (Van Dé-menz) Gulf, n. w. Aust.
Van Diemen's Land, *i* s. e. Aust.; area 24,000 s. m., pop. 80,000.
Vandola, La, Lq-Vqn-dó-lq, Admiralty Island.
Vanikoro, Vq-ni-kó-rꝏ, *i* S. Pac., 1½.
Vannes, Vqn, *s-pt t* Fr., 13½.
Vanua-Valavo, Vq-nó-q-Vq-lq-vꝏ, *i* S. Pac., 1.
Van Wert, Van Wert, *co t* O., 1.
Var, Vqr, *dep* Fr., pop. 357,967.
Varazze, Vq-rqt-sa, *t* Sard., 7¾.
Varel, Fq-rel, *t* Ger., 3¼.
Varinas, Vq-ré-nqs, *t* Ven., 12.
Varna, Vqr-nq, *ft s-pt t* Eu. Tur., 14.
Varoqua, Var-ó-kwa, *co t* Wis.
Vasa, Vq-sq, *s-pt t* Fin., 3⅓.
Vasarhely, Hold-Mezo, Hꝏld-Má-zꝏ, Vq-ʃqr-hely, *t* Hun., 26¼.
Vasarhely, Somlyo, Σóm-lyꝏ Vq-ʃqr-hely, *t* Hun., 25.
Vashka, Vqʃ-kq, *r* Rus., 200 m.
Vasilkov, Vq-sil-kóv, *t* Rus., 8.
Vasioogan, Vq-sɛ-ꝏ-gqn, *r* As. Rus., 170 m.
Vassalborough, Vás-al-bur-ꝏ, *v* Me., 3.
Vasto, Vqs-tꝏ, *t* Naples, 9.
Vatersa, Vqt-er-sq, *i* Outer Hebrides.
Vaucluse, Vꝏ-kléz, *dep* Fr., 264,618.
Vaud, Vꝏ, *or* Pays-de-Vaud, Pá-e-de-Vꝏ, *canton* Switz.
Vaudreuil, Vꝏ-drély, *co* C. E.
Vauxhall, Vꝏ-hél, *suburb* London.
Vavao, Vq-vq-ꝏ, Friendly Island, 6.
Veglia, Vál-yq, *i* Adriatic Sea, 15.
Vejer, Va-ħqr, *t* Sp., 8⅓.
Velez, Vá-les, *t* N-Gran., 7½.
Velez Blanco, Vá-leŧ Blqn-kꝏ, *t* Sp., 7½.
Velez Malaga, Mq-lq-gq, *t* Sp., 16.
Velez Rubio, Ró-bɛ-ꝏ, *t* Sp., 12⅓.
Velikaia, Va-lɛ-kį-q, *r* Rus., 160 m.
Velino, Va-lé-nꝏ, *r* It.
Velizh, Va-lįʒ, *t* Rus. Pol., 6¾.
Velletri, Ve-lá-trɛ, *t* Pontificial St., 10.
Venado, Va-nq-đꝏ, *t* Mex., 8.
Venango, Vɛ-náŋ-gꝏ, *v* Pa.

Vendome, Voṅ-dóm, *t* Fr., 9⅓.
Vendotena, Ven-dɷ-tá-nq, *i* Med., ½.
Venezuela, Ven-ez-wé-la, (Sp. Va-neð-wá-lq, *rep* S. Am., area 400,000 s. m., pop. 1,419,289.
Venice, Vén-is, *c* Aus. It., 110; *v* O.
Venloo, Ven-ló, *ft t* Neth., 7¼.
Venosa, Va-nó-sq, *t* Naples, 6.
Ventnor, Vént-nor, *t* Isle of Wight.
Vera, Vá-rq, *t* Sp., 8½.
Vera Cruz, Vá-rq-Krɷs, *st* Mex., area 27,595 s. m., pop. 274,686; *s-pt t* Mex., 8¼.
Veragua, Va-rq́-gwa, *t* N-Gran., 5.
Vercelli, Ver-çél-ε, *c* Sard. Sts., 18¼.
Verden, Fér-den, *t* Ger., 4¾.
Verdun, Ver-dúṅ, *t* Fr., 14.
Vereya, Va-rá-yq, *t* Rus., 6.
Vergennes, Ver-jénz, *c* Vt., 1⅓.
Veria, Ve-ré-q, *t* Eu. Tur., 8.
Vermejo, Ver-má-*h*ɷ, *r* S. Am., 750 m.
Vermilion, Ver-míl-yon, *v* O., 1, *rs* La., Ill. and Ia.
Vermilionville, Ver-míl-yon-vil, *co t* Louisiana.
Vermont, Ver-mónt, one of the U. S., the first admitted after the union; area 10,212 s.m., pop. whites, 313,402, colored 982, total 314,120; *v* Ill., 1½.
Vernon, Ver-nóṅ, *t* Fr., 6½; Vér-non, *co t* Ia., 1; *vs* Conn., N-Y., Wis., Cal.
Verona, Va-ró-nq, *ft c* Aus. It., 48; Vε-ró-na, *v* N-Y., 5½.
Verret (Vér-et) Lake, La.
Versailles, Ver-sálz, *c* Fr., 35⅓; *co ts* Ky., Ia., Mo.
Versecz, Vér-ʃets, *t* Hun., 15¾.
Vertou, Ver-tó, *v* Fr., 6.
Vervick, Vér-vik, *t* Belg., 5¾.
Verviers, Ver-vε-á, *t* Belg., 20.
Vesoul, Va-zól, *t* Fr., 6⅔.
Vesuvius, (Vε-sū́-vi-us,) Mount, active *vol* It.
Veszprim, Vés-prim, *t* Hun., 9.
Vetlooga, Vet-ló-gq, *r* Rus., 300 m.
Vevay, Vε-vá *or* Vé-va, *co t* Ia., 2.
Viana, Vε-q́-nq, *s-pt t* Port., 8.
Viatka, Vε-q́t-kq, *gov* Rus.; area 53,-493 s. m., pop. 1,818,752; *c, cap* same, 7; *r* do., 500 m.
Viazma, Vε-q́z-mq, *t* Rus., 12.
Viborg, Vé-borg, *s-pt t* Finland, 3½.
Viborg, Vé-bor*h*, *t* Den., 5½.
Vicenza, Vε-sén-zq *or* Vε-çén-zq, *c* Aus. It., 33.
Vich, Vik, *c* Sp., 10⅔.
Vichada, Vε-çq́-đq, *r* N-Gran., 260 m.
Vicksburg, Víks-burg, *c* Miss., 3⅜.
Vico Equense, Vé-kɷ Ɑ-kwén-sa, *t* It., 9¾.

Victoria, Vik-tó-ri-a, Br. *col* Australia; area 160,000 s. m., pop. 320,000; *co t* Tex.; *v* Ill.; *t* Mex., 5½; — Vεk-tó-ri-q, *t* Bra., 5.
Victoria Lake, S. Aust.
Victoria Land, Antarctic *ter*, supposed to be discovered by Sir James Ross.
Victoria River, N. Aust.
Victoria Strait, Arc. Oc.
Victory, Vík-tɷ-ri, *v* N-Y.
Vidalia, Vi-dá-li-a, *co t* La.
Vieille-Vizne, Vε-ály-Vεny, *v* Fr., 5½.
Vienna, Vi-én-a, *c, cap* Aus., 408; *co ts* Ga., Ill.; *vs* N-Y. 2⅛, Ala., O., Ia., Wis., C. W.
Vienne, Vε-én, *dep* Fr., pop. 317,305; *c* do., 20¾; *r* do., 220 m.
Vieque, Vε-á-ka, *i* Br. W. Ind.
Vierzon, Vε-er-zóṅ, *t* Fr., 6¾.
Viesti, Vε-és-tε, *t* Nap., 6.
Vigan, Vε-gq́n, *s-pt t* Phil. Is., 17¼.
Vigevano, Vε-já-vq-nɷ, *t* Sard., 15¼.
Viggiano, Vid-jq́-nɷ, *t* Nap., 5¾.
Vigo, Vé-gɷ, *s-pt t* Sp., 4¼; *l* Rus.; — Vị-gɷ, *co* Ia.
Vilaine, Vε-lán, *r* Fr., 130 m.
Vilcanota, Vεl-kq́n-yó-tq, *m* Andes.
Vilkomeer, Vil-kɷ-mér, *t* Rus. Pol., 5.
Villa-Bella-da-Princeza, Vél-q-Bél-q-dq-Prεn-sá-zq, *t* Bra., 3.
Villa del Fuerte, Vél-yq del Fwér-ta, *t* Mex., 5.
Villa del Principe, Vél-yq del Prén-si-pa, *t* Cuba, 30.
Villa do Rio Pardo, Vél-q dɷ Ré-ɷ Pq́r-dɷ, *t* Bra., 5.
Villa Franca, Vél-q Frq́ŋ-kq, *t* Bra., 4.
Villafranca de los Barros, Vél-yq-frq́ŋ-kq da lɷs Bq́r-ɷs, *t* Sp., 6.
Villafranca de Panades, Vεl-yq-frq́ŋ-kq da Pq-nq́-đes, *t* Sp., 5½.
Villafranca de Xira, Vεl-q-frq́ŋ-kq da Σé-rq, *t* Port., 5.
Villafranca di Piemonte, Vil-q-frq́ŋ-kq dε Pε-a-món-ta, *t* Sard., 8½.
Villajoyosa, Vεl-yq-*h*ɷ-yó-sq, *t* Sp., 8.
Villanova de San Antonio, Vεl-q-nó-vq da Sqn Ɑn-tó-ni-ɷ, *t* Bra., 4.
Villanueva de Cordova, Vεl-yq-nwá-vq da Kór-dɷ-vq, *t* Sp., 6½.
Villanueva de la Serena, Vεl-yq-nwá-vq da lq Sa-rá-nq, *t* Sp., 9.
Villanueva y la Geltru, Vεl-yq-nwá-vq ε lq *H*el-tró, *t* Sp., 10⅓.
Villa Real, Vél-yq Ra-q́l, *t* Sp., 8¼.
Villa Real de Concepcion, Vél-yq Ra-q́l da Kon-ðep-ðε-ón, *t* Paraguay, 4.
Villa Viçosa, Vél-q Vε-só-sq, *t* Bra., 5.
Villefranche-de-Rouergue, Vεl-fróṅʃ-dẹ-Rɷ-q́rg, *t* Fr., 9½.

Villefranche-sur-Saöne, Vεl-fróṅʃ-sęr-Sωn, *t* Fr., 8.
Villena, Vεl-yá-nq, *t* Sp., 8¼.
Villeneuve-le-Roi, Vεl-nęv-lę-Rwq́, *t* Fr., 5¼. [Fr., 13¼.
Villeneuve-sur-Lot, Vεl-nęv-sęr-Lω, *t*
Villette, La, Lq Vεl-ét, *v* Fr., 18⅔.
Vilna, Víl-nq, *c* Rus. Poland, 52¼.
Vilvoorden, Vil-vωr-den, *t* Belg., 5¼.
Vinaroz, Vε-nq-rót, *t* Sp., 10⅔. [2.
Vincennes, Vin-sénz, *t* Fr., 8½; *co t* Ia.,
Vindhya (Vínd-yq) Mountains, Hin.
Vinnitsa, Vin-ít-sq, *t* Rus., 7½.
Vintimiglia, Vin-ti-mél-yq, *ft t* Sard., 5.
Vire, Vεr, *t* Fr., 7¼. [Ind.
Virgin Gorda, Vęr-jin Gér-dα, *i* Br. W.
Virginia, Ver-jín-i-α, one of the original U. S.; area 61,352 s. m.; pop. 894,800 whites, 54,333 free colored, 472,528 slaves—total, 1,421,661.
Virgin (Vęr-jin) Islands, W. Ind.
Virtzerv (Virt-zęrv) Lake, Rus.
Viseu, Vé-sa-ω, *c* Port., 9¼.
Vishera, Viʃ-a-rq́, *r* Rus., 260 m.
Vishnee, Víʃ-nε, *t* Rus., 9.
Viso, Monte, Món-ta Vé-sω, *peak* Alps.
Vistula, Vís-tŋ-lα, *r* Eu., 530 m.
Vitchegda, Vε-çég-dq, *r* Rus., 380 m.
Vitebsk, Vε-tébsk, *t* Rus. Pol., 30.
Viterbo, Vε-tęr-bω, *c* Cen. It., 14.
Vitoria, Vε-tώ-ri-q, *t* Sp., 10¼.
Vitré, Vε-trá, *t* Fr., 8¾.
Vitry-le-François, Vε-tré-lę-Froṅ-swq́, *ft t* Fr., 8¼. [11.
Vittoria, Vi-tώ-ri-α, *ts* C. W. ⅔, Sic.
Vivero, Vε-vá-rω, *t* Sp., 4⅔.
Vlaardingen, Vlq́r-diŋ-en, *t* Neth., 7¼.
Vladimeer, Vlq-di-mér, *gov* Rus.; area 18,445 s. m., pop. 1,168,303; *t* do., 7½.
Vlieland, Vlé-lqnt, *i* Zuyder-Zee, ¾.
Vodla, Vód-lq, *l* and *r* Rus., 120 m.
Voghera, Vω-gá-rq, *t* Pied., 10¾.
Voiron, Vwq-róṅ, *t* Fr., 8½.
Volcan de Agua, Vol-kq́n da A'gwq, *vol* Guat.
Volcano, Vol-ká-nω, *i* S. Pac. Oc.
Volga, Vól-gq, *r* Rus., 2500 m.
Volhynia, Vol-hín-i-α, *gov* Rus. Pol.; area 27,742 s. m., pop. 1,469,442.
Volo, Vó-lω, Gulf, inlet of Ægean Sea.
Vologda, Vω-lóg-dq, *gov* Eu. Rus.; area 148,674 s. m., pop., 864 268; *c* same, 14.
Volta, Vól-tq, *r* Guinea, 360 m.
Voltchansk, Vol-çq́nsk, *t* Rus., 7.
Volterra, Vol-tér-q, *t* Tus., 4½.
Volturno, Vol-tώr-nω, *r* Nap., 90 m.
Voorn, Vωrn, *i* of S. Holland.
Vorms, Vorms, *i* Baltic.
Vorona, Vω-rώ-nq, *r* Rus., 220 m.
Voronezh, Vω-rω-néʒ, *gov* Rus.; area 25,878 s. m., pop. 1,629,741; *c* do., 44.
Vosges, Vωʒ, *dep* Fr.; area 2230 s. m., pop. 427,409; *ms* Fr. and Ger.
Votka, Vót-kq, *t* Rus., 9.
Vozh, Voʒ, *l* Rus.
Vracene, Vrq́-sa-na, *v* Belg., 5½.
Vukovar, Vω-kω-vq́r, *t* Aus., 5⅔.
Vulcano, Vωl-kq́-nω, Lipari Is., Med.
Vuna, Vώ-nq, Feejee Is., 7.
Vuoxen, Vω-óks-en, *r* Finland, 350 m.

# W.

Waag, Wqg, *r* Hun., 200 m. [2.
Wabash, Wé-baʃ, *r* Ia., 550 m; *co t* Ia.,
Wabashaw, Wé-ba-ʃə, *co t* Minn.
Wachusett (Wə-çq́-set) Mt., Mass.
Wacoochee, Wə-kώ-çε, *v* Ala.
Wacousta, Wa-kώs-tα, *v* Mich.
Waday, Wé-dį, *cy* interior Af.; pop. unknown.
Waddington, Wód-iŋ-ton, *v* N-Y., ⅔.
Wadebridge, Wád-brij, *t* Eng., 1.
Wädensweil, Vá-denz-vįl, *v* Swit., 5.
Wadesborough, Wádz-bur-ω, *co t* N. C., 1½; *v* Ky.
Wadesville, Wádz-vil, *v* Va.
Wadjier, Wqd-jér, Arroo *i*.
Waereghem, Wq́-re-gem, *v* Belg., 5.
Wagram, Wq́-gram, *v* Lower Aus.
Wahkiacum, Wq-ki-ák-um, *co* Wash. Ter.
Wahlahgas, Wq-lq́-gas, *r* Me.
Wahsatch (Wq-sáç) Mountains, Utah
Waia, Wį-q́, Feejee Is., 3. [Ter.
Waiblingen, Vį-bliŋ-en, *t* Würt., 3.
Waikato, Wį-kq́-tω, *r* N-Zeal., 250 m.
Waiping, Wį-piŋ, *t* China, 150.
Waitzen, Wįt-sen, *t* Hun., 11¼.
Wakefield, Wák-fεld, *t* and *par* Eng., 33; *vs* R. I., Md.
Wakulla, Wa-kúl-α, *r* and *co* Fa.
Walbridgeville, Wél-brij-vil, *v* Vt.
Walcheren, Vq́l-ker-en, *i* of Neth., 45.
Waldeck-Pyrmont, Wól-dek-Pír-mont, *prin* Ger., pop. 59,697.
Waldenses, Wol-dén-sεz, a Protestant people in Piedmont.
Waldo, Wól-dω, *vs* O. [4½.
Waldoborough, Wól-dω-bur-ω, *t* Me.,
Waldürn, Vq́l-dęrn, *t* Baden, 3¼.

Wales, Walz, *div* Gr. Br.; area 7,398 s. m., pop. 1,005,721.
Walker's (Wék-erz) Lake, Utah Ter.
Walkersville, Wé-kerz-vil, *v* Pa.
Wallachia, Wol-á-ki-a, *prin* Eu. Tur.; area 27,000 s. m., pop. 2,000,000.
Walla Walla, Wol-a Wól-a, *r*, *co* and *co t* Wash. Ter.
Wallenstadt, Vql-en-stqt, *l* Swit.
Wallingford, Wól-iŋ-ford, *t* and *par* Eng., 2¾; *vs* Vt., Conn., Ill.
Wallis (Wól-is) Lake, N-S. Wales.
Walloostook (Wol-ꝏ-stꝏk) River, Me.
Wallsend, Wél-send, *v* Eng., 5¾.
Walpole, Wól-pꝏl, *vs* N-H. 1, Mass. 1.
Walsall, Wól-sel, *t* and *par* Eng., 8¾.
Walsham, Wóls-ham, North, *t* and *par* Eng., 3.
Waltenberg, Vql-ten-berh, *t* Tran., 8½.
Waltersborough, Wél-terz-bur-ꝏ, *co t* S. C.
Waltershausen, Vql-terz-hʊ-zen, *t* Saxe-Coburg-Gotha, 3¼.
Waltham, Wól-tam, *v* Mass., 2½.
Waltham-Abbey, Wélt-am-Ab'i, *t* Eng., 2⅓; —, Bishop's, *t* and *par* Eng., 2¼.
Walthourville, Wol-tꝏr-vil, *v* Ga.
Walton, Wél-ton, *vs* N-Y. 1, Ky. ¼.
Walvisch, Wql-viʃ, *b* S. Af.
Walworth, Wól-wurt, *vs* N-Y., Wis.
Wanchow, Wqn-qʊ, *s-pt t* China, 200.
Wandsworth, Wónz-wurt, *par* and *v* Eng., 9½.
Wangeroog, Vqŋ-er-ꝏg, *i* of N. Ger., ¼.
Wanlock-Head, Wón-lok-Hed, *v* Scot, 1.
Wantage, Wón-taj, *par* and *t* Eng., 3.
Wanzleben, Vqnts-la-ben, *t* Prus. Saxony, 3.
Wapahkonetta, Wop-a-kꝏ-nét-a, *co t* O.
Wapello, Wa-pél-ꝏ, *co* and *co t* Io., ¾.
Wapsipinicon, Wap-si-pin-i-kon, *r* Io., 200 m.
Warasdin, Vq-rqs-din, *t* Aus. Croatia, 9.
Wardsville, Wérdz-vil, *t* C. W., ¾.
Ware, Wqr, *t* and *par* Eng., 5; *v* Mass., 2.
Wareham, Wqr-ham, *bor* and *t* Eng., 3.
Waren, Vq-ren, *t* Meck.-Schwerin, 5.
Waresborough, Wqrz-bur-ꝏ, *co t* Ga.
Warminster, Wér-min-ster, *t* and *par* Eng., 4¼.
Warm Springs, Werm Springs, *co t* Va.; *vs* N. C., Ga.
Warner, Wér-ner, *v* N-H.
Warneton, Vqrn-tóñ, *t* Belg., 6.
Warren, Wór-en, *co ts* Me. 2½, Ark ⅔, O. 3; *vs* Mass., R. I. 2, Conn., Pa. 1, Ia. ⅓, Ill.
Warrensburg, Wór-enz-burg, *co t* Mo.; *v* N-Y.
Warrenspoint, Wor-enz-pꝏnt, *t* and *par* Ir., 1¾.
Warrenton, Wór-en-ton, *co ts* Va. 1½, N. C. 1¼, Ga., Ala., Mo.; *vs* Miss., Ky., O., Ia.
Warrentown, Wór-en-tʊn, *v* Pa.
Warrington, Wór-iŋ-ton, *t* and *par* Eng., 23⅓. [½.
Warrior's Mark, Wér-i-orz Mqrk, *v* Pa.,
Warsaw, Wér-se, *c* Rus. Pol., 164½; *co ts* N-Y., Va., Ky. 1, Ia., Mo.; *t* Ill., 3.
Warta, Vqr-tq, *r* Ger., 450 m.
Wartenburg, Vqr-ten-bꝏrh, *t* Prus., 3.
Warwick, Wér-wik, *bor* and *t* Eng., 11; *co t* Va.; *vs* N-Y., Pa.
Washa, Wóʃ-a, *l* La.
Washington, Wóʃ-iŋ-ton, n. w. *ter* U. S.; area 123,022 s. m.; pop. chiefly Indians; some few whites, mostly traders, occupying a part of the Territory.
Washington, *c*, and seat of government of the United States, situated in the District of Columbia; pop. 55; *co ts* Pa. 2¾, O., Ia. 1¼, Io., Ky., Tenn., Ark.; *vs* Mass., Conn., N-J., Pa., O., Ia., Ill., Mo.
Washington, *land* Arc. Oc., discovered by Dr. Kane, in 1854; — *or* Uahuga, ꝏ-q-hꝏ-gq, Marquesas Is. [500 m.
Washita *or* Ouachita, Wóʃ-i-te, *r* Ark.,
Watab, Wé-tab, *v* Minn.
Watauga, We-té-ga, *r* and *co* N. C.
Wateeo, Wa-té-ꝏ, one of Harvey Is.
Waterbury, Wé-ter-ber-i, *c* Conn., 7; *v* Vt., 2. [than 200 m.
Wateree, We-ter-é, *r* S. C., nav. more
Waterford, Wé-ter-ford, *c* Ir., 25½; *vs* Conn. 2½, N-Y. 1, Pa. ½, Va., O., Ia., Ill., Wis., Miss.
Waterloo, We-ter-lꝏ, *v* Belg., 2¾; *co ts* N-Y. 3½, Ill.; *vs* Va., Ala., Ia., Wis., C. W.
Watertown, Wé-ter-tʊn, *c* Wis., 4; *co t* N-Y., 7¾; *vs* Mass., Conn.
Waterville, Wé-ter-vil, *vs* Me. 4, Conn., N-Y., O.
Watford, Wót-ford, *t* and *par* Eng., 4.
Watkinsville, Wót-kinz-vil, *co t* Ga.
Watling's (Wót-liŋz) Island, Bahamas.
Watlington, Wót-liŋ-ton, *t* and *par* Eng., 2. [Ter., 80 m.
Watonwan (Wót-on-wan) River, Minn.
Watsontown, Wót-son-tʊn, *v* Pa.
Watton, Wót-on, *t* and *par* Eng., 1⅓.
Wattsburg, Wóts-burg, *v* Pa., ¼.
Waukau, We-ké, *v* Wis., ½.
Waukegan, We-ké-gan, *co t* Ill., 4½.
Waukesha, Wé-kε-ʃe, *co t* Wis., 4.
Waupacca, We-pák-a, *co* and *r* Wis.

Waupun, Wé-pun, *v* Wis., ½.
Wausau, Wé-sə, *co t* Wis., 1.
Waushara, Wə-ʃár-ɑ, *v* Wis., ⅓.
Wauwatosa, Wə-wa-tó-sɑ, *v* Wis., 1.
Waveland, Wáv-land, *v* Ia., ⅓.
Waveney, Wá-ven-i, *r* Eng., 50 m.
Waverley, Wá-ver-li, *v* N-Y.
Wavre, Wɑv-r, *t* Belg., 5¼.
Waxahachie, Waks-a-háç-ɛ, *co t* Tex.
Wayne, Wan, *v* N-Y., 1.
Waynesborough, Wánz-bur-ɷ, *co ts* Ga., Tenn.; *vs* Pa. 1, Va., N. C.
Waynesburg, Wánz-burg, *co t* Pa., 1¼; *v* O., 1.
Waynesville, Wánz-vil, *co ts* N. C., Ga., Mo.; *vs* O. 1, Ill.
Wazemmes, Vɑ-zém, *t* Fr., 13.
Wea, Wé-ə, *v* Ia.
Wear, Wɛr, *r* Eng., 67 m.
Weaverville, Wé-ver-vil, *t* Cal., 2⅓.
Webster, Wéb-ster, *vs* Ia., Mo., Cal.
Wednesbury, Wénz-ber-i, *t* and *par* Eng., 12.
Weedowwee, Wɛ-dɤ́-wɛ, *co t* Ala.
Weedsport, Wédz-pɷrt, *v* N-Y.
Weerdt *or* Weert, Vɑrt, *t* Dutch Limburg, 6¼.
Weerselo, Vɑr-se-ló, *t* Neth., 5.
Wehlau, Vá-lɤ, *t* Prus., 3½. [4.
Weichselburg, Vík-sel-bu*rh*, *t* Illyria,
Weida, Vị-dɑ, *t* Saxe-Weimar, 3⅗.
Weighton (Wá-ton) Market, *t* and *par* Eng., 2½.
Weilheim-an-der-Teck, Vịl-hịm-ɑn-der-Tek, *t* Würt., 3⅓. [11.
Weimar, Vị-mɑr, *c*, *cap* Saxe-Weimar,
Weingarten, Vịn-gɑr-ten, *v* Baden, 3.
Weinheim, Vịn-hịm, *t* Bad., 5⅓.
Weissenburg, Vị-sen-bu*rh*, *ft t* Bav., 4.
Weissenfels, Vị-sen-fels, *t* Prus. Sax., 8⅓.
Weisskirchen, Vịs-kẹ*rh*-en, *t* Aus., 5½; *t* Moravia, 5⅓.
Weissport, Wịs-pɷrt, *v* Pa.
Weldon, Wél-don, *v* N. C.
Welland, Wél-and, *r* Eng., 70 m.
Welland Canal, connecting Lake Erie with Lake Ontario.
Wellborn, Wél-born, *co t* Ala.
Wellersburg, Wél-erz-burg, *v* Pa.
Wellesley (Wélz-lɛ) Islands, Gulf of Carpentaria, n. Australia.
Wellfleet, Wél-flɛt, *v* Mass., 2.
Wellingborough, Wél-iŋ-bur-ɷ, *t* and *par* Eng., 5.
Wellington, Wél-iŋ-ton, *ts* and *pars* Eng., 4⅔ and 4; *vs* Mo., C. W.; *set* N-Zeal.; *i* w. S. Am. [do., 3⅗.
Wells, Welz, *c* Eng., 4¾; *s-pt t* and *par*
Wellsborough, Wélz-bur-ɷ, *co t* Pa.
Wellsburg, Wélz-burg, *co t* Va., 3; *v* N-
Wells' River, *v* Vt. [Y.
Wellsville, Wélz-vil, *vs* N-Y. ⅔, O. 1¾.
Wels, Vels, *t* Upper Aus., 4⅓.
Welshpool, Wélʃ-pɷl, *t* and *par* North Wales. [2.
Wendover, Wén-dɷ-ver, *t* and *par* Eng.,
Wener, Vá-ner, *or* Wenner, Vén-er, *l* Sweden.
Wenham, Wén-ham, *v* Mass., ½.
Wenlock, Wén-lok, *t* and two *pars* Eng., 20½.
Wentworth, Wént-wurt̵h, *co t* N. C.
Werdau, Wẹ́r-dɤ, *t* Sax., 6¼.
Werden, Vẹ́r-den, *t* Rhen. Prus., 5⅗.
Werl, Vẹrl, *t* Prus. Westphalia, 4.
Wernigerode, Vẹr-ni-ga-ró-da, *t* Prus. Sax., 5½.
Werra, Wér-ɑ, *r* Cen. Ger., 150 m.
Wertheim, Vẹ́rt-hịm, *t* Baden, 3½.
Wesel, Nieder, Né-der Vá-zel, *ft t* Rhen. Prus., 12¼.
Weser, Vá-zer, *r* Ger., 250 m.
Wesley City, Wés-li Sít-i, *v* Ill.
Wesleyville, Wés-li-vil, *v* Pa., ¼.
Wessel (Wés-el) Islands, off N. Aust.
West Alburg, West Əl'burg, *v* Vt.
West Alexandria, Al-eks-án-dri-ɑ, *vs* Pa., O.
West Alton, Əl'ton, *v* N-H.
West Amesbury, Ɛmz'ber-i, *v* Mass.
West Andover, An'dɷ-ver, *v* N-H.
West Barnstable, Bɑrn-sta-bl, *v* Mass.
West Baton Rouge, Bát-on Rɷʒ, *par* La.
West Bend, *v* Wis., 1.
West Bloomfield, Blóm-fɛld, *v* N-Y.
Westborough, Wést-bur-ɷ, *vs* Mass., O.
Westbrook, Wést-brɷk, *v* Conn., 1.
West Brownsville, Brɤnz-vil, *v* Pa., ½.
Westbury, Wést-ber-i, *t* and *par* Eng., 7. [2.
West Cambridge, Kám-brij, *v* Mass.,
West Camden, Kám-den, *v* N-Y.
West Carlisle, Kɑr-lịl, *v* O. [O.
West Charleston, Çɑrlz-ton, *vs* Me., Vt.,
Westchester, Wést-çes-ter, *v* N-Y.
West Chester, Çés-ter, *co t* Pa., 4½.
West Columbia, Kɷ-lúm-bi-ɑ, *v* Va.
West Concord, Kóŋ-kord, *vs* N-H., Vt.
West Cornwall, Kérn-wəl, *v* Conn.
Westecunk, Wés-tɛ-kuŋk, *v* N. J.
West Elizabeth, Ɛ-líz-a-bet̵h, *v* Pa., ½.
Westeras, Wés-ter-os, *t* Swed., 3⅓.
Westerham, Wést-er-ham, *t* and *par* Eng., 1¼.
Westerly, Wést-er-li, *v* R. I., 1¾.
Western Australia, Wést-ern Əs-trál-yɑ, Br. *col* Australia, 10½.
Western Port, *inlet* s. Australia.
Western Saratoga, Sar-a-tó-gɑ, *v* Ill.

Westervik, Vés-ter-vik, *t* Swed., 3.
West Farms, *v* N-Y., 2¾.
West Feliciana, Fɛ-liʃ-i-ân-ɑ, *par* La.
Westfield, Wést-fɛld, *vs* Mass. 4, N-Y. 2, N-J.
West Fitchburg, Fiç-burg, *v* Mass.
Westford, Wést-ford, *v* Mass.
West Gilead, Gil-ɛ-ad, *v* O.
West Gloucester, Glós-ter, *v* R. I.
West Glover, Glúv-er, *v* Vt.
West Greenville, Grén-vil, *v* Pa., 1.
West Hartford, Hɑ́rt-ford, *v* Conn., 4½.
West Haven, Há-ven, *v* Conn.
West Indies, West In'dɛz, *or* Antilles, An-tél, *is* At. Oc., s. U. S., embracing the following groups: Greater Antilles; Lesser Antilles; Caribbee; Virgin; Bahama, &c.; of which Cuba, Hayti, Porto Rico, and Jamaica, of the first group, are the principal. Area 95,000 s. m., pop. 3,500,000.
West Isles, *is* At. Oc., near Me.
West Jefferson, Jéf-er-son, *v* O., ½.
West Killingly, Kil-iŋ-li, *v* Conn., 2½.
West Lebanon. Léb-a-non, *v* N-H.
West Liberty, Lib-er-ti, *co t* Ky.; *t* O., 1.
West Meriden, Mér-i-den, *v* Conn., 1½.
Westminster, Wést-min-ster, *div* London, Eng.; *co t* Md., 1; *vs* Mass., O. ⅓.
West Needham, Néd-ham, *v* Mass.
West Newton, Nú-ton, *v* Mass., 1⅓.
Weston, Wés-ton, *c* Mo., 3; *co t* Va.; *vs* Vt., Mass., Conn.
Weston-Super-Mare, Wés-ton-Sú-per-Má-rɛ, *t* and *par* Eng., 4.
Westphalia, West-fá-li-ɑ, *prov* Prus.; area 7848 s. m., pop. 1,464,921; *v* Mo.
West Point, 52 miles n. of N-Y. City, on the Hudson River, site of the U. S. Military Academy; *vs* Ga., Tenn., Ky., Ia., Mo., Iowa, 1.
Westport, Wést-port, *s-pt t* Ir., 4; *vs* N-H., Mass., Conn., N-Y., Ky., Ia.; *t* Mo., 1½.
West Poultney, Pólt-ni, *v* Vt.
Westray, Wés-tra, Orkney Is., 2.
West Rumney, Rúm-ni, *v* N-H.
West Rutland, Rút-land, *v* Vt.
West Springfield, Spriŋ-fɛld, *v* Mass.
West Stockbridge, Stók-brij, *v* Mass.
West Union, Yún-yon, *co ts* Va., O., Iowa; *v* Ia. [Ia.; *co t* Miss.
Westville, Wést-vil, *vs* Conn., 1¼, O.,
West Wheeling, Hwél-iŋ, *v* O., ⅓.
Wetherby, Wéđ-er-bi, *t* Eng., 1½.
Wetta, Wét-ɑ, *i* Malay Arch.
Wetter, Vét-er, *l* Sweden.
Wetteren, Wét-er-en, *t* Belg., 8⅓.
Wetterhorn, Vét-er-horn, one of the Alpine Mountains.
Wettin, Vet-én, *t* Prus. Sax., 3⅓.
Wetumpka, Wɛ-túmp-kɑ, *c* Ala., 3½.
Wetzlar, Véts-lɑr, *t* Rhen. Prus., 5.
Weverton, Wé-ver-ton, *v* Md., 2½.
Wexford, Wéks-ford, *s-pt t* Ir., 13.
Wexio, Wék-ʃɛ-ę, *t* Swed., 2¼.
Wey, Wa, *r* Eng.
Weymouth, Wá-muŧ, *s-pt* Eng., 3; *s-pt t* Nova Scotia; *v* N-J.
Whaleysville, Hwá-liz-vil, *v* Md.
Whalsay, Hwál-sa, Shetland Is., ⅔.
Wharton, Hwór-ton, *co t* Tex.
Whartonsburg, Hwór-tonz-burg, *v* O.
Wheatland, Hwét-land, *v* Wis.
Wheaton, Hwé-ton, *v* Ill.
Wheelersburg, Hwél-erz-burg, *v* O., ¾.
Wheeling, Hwél-iŋ, *c* Va., 11½.
Whidby's (Hwíd-biz) Island, *i* n. w. Wash. Ter.
Whiddy (Hwíd-i) Island, s. Ir., ½.
Whippany, Hwip-a-ni, *v* N-J., ¾.
Whitby, Hwit-bi, *bor*, *t* and *par* Eng., 11.
Whitchurch, Hwit-çurç, *ts* and *pars* Eng., 2 and 3⅔.
White Creek, Hwit Krɛk, *v* N-Y., 1.
Whitehall, Hwit-hɑl, *vs* N-Y. 4, N. C., Ill. [*pt t* Eng., 19.
Whitehaven, Hwit-há-ven, *bor* and *s-*
White Haven, Há-ven, *v* Pa.
White House, Hʊs, *v* N-J.
White Mountains, N-H., 6226 ft.
White Oak Springs, Ok Spriŋz, *v* Wis.,
White Pigeon, Pij-on, *v* Mich., 1. [⅓.
White Plains, Planz, *co t* N-Y.
White River, Ark. and Mo., 800 m.; Ia.
Whitesborough, Hwits-bur-o, *co t* N-Y., 2¼.
Whitesburg, Hwits-burg, *co t* Ky.
White Sea, *or* Gulf of Archangel, *g* Arc. Oc.
White Sulphur Springs, *vs* Va., La.
Whitesville, Hwits-vil, *co t* N. C.; *v* Tenn.
Whitewater, Hwit-wo-ter, *v* Wis., 1¼.
Whitewater River, Mo., 250 m. [1⅔.
Whithorn, Hwit-horn, *t* and *par* Scot.,
Whitneyville, Hwit-ni-vil, *v* Conn.
Whitstable, Hwit-stá-bl, *t* and *par* Eng., 3.
Whittlesey, Hwit-l-si, *t* Eng., 5½; *v* O.
Wick, Wik, *s-pt t* and *par* Scot., 12.
Wickford, Wik-ford, *v* R. I.
Wicklow, Wik-lo, *s-pt t* Ir., 3.
Wiconisco, Wik-o-nis-ko, *v* Pa., 1.
Widin, Vid-in, *ft t* Eu. Tur., 25.
Wieliczka, Vɛ-líç-kɑ, *t* Aus. Pol., 4½.
Wiesbaden, Vés-bɑ-den, *t* Ger., 12¼.
Wigan, Wig-an, *t* and *par* Eng., 32.
Wigton, Wig-ton, *t* and *par* Eng., 4¼.
Wigtown, Wig-tʊn, *t* and *par* Scot.

Wilbraham, Wil-bra-ham, *v* Mass.
Wildervank, Wil-der-vqŋk, *v* Neth., 4.
Wilkesbarre, Wilks-bar-ɛ, *bor* Penn., 3.
Wilkesborough, Wilks-bur-ꝏ, *co t* N. C.
Wilkesville, Wilks-vil, *v* O., 1. [m.
Willamette, Wi-lq-met, *r* Or. ter., 200
Williamsburg, Wil-yamz-burg, *c* Long Island, 50; *co ts* Va., 1½; Miss., Ky., *vs* O., 1¾; Pa.
Williamson, Wil-yam-son, *v* N-Y., 1⅓.
Williamsport, Wil-yamz-pꝏrt, *co ts* Pa., 2½, Va., Ia.
Williamstown, Wil-yamz-tʊn, *co ts* N. C., Ky.; *vs* Mass., 1, Mich., ½.
Williamsville, Wil-yamz-vil, *vs* N-Y., 1; Vt. [3½.
Willimantic, Wil-i-mán-tic, *t* Conn.,
Willington, Wil-iŋ-ton, *vs* Conn., ⅓; S. C.
Willingston, Wil-iŋ-ston, *v* Vt.
Willoughby, Wil-ꝏ-bi, *v* O., 1.
Willow Grove, Wil-ꝏ Grꝏv, *v* Pa.
Willsborough, Wilz-bur-ꝏ, *v* N-Y., 1.
Willshire, Wil-ʃɛr, *v* O.
Wilmington, Wil-miŋ-ton, *c* Del., 16¼; *c* N. C., 10; *vs* O., 1¼, Ia., Ill.
Wilson, Wil-son, *v* N-Y., ¾; *co t* N. C.
Wilton, Wil-ton, *t* and *par* Eng., 1¾; *vs* N-H., 1¼, Conn.
Wimborne-Minster, Wim-born-Min-ster, *t* and *par* Eng., 2¼.
Wincanton, Win-kán-ton, *t* and *par* Eng., 2½. [Eng., 2.
Winchcombe, Winq-kum, *t* and *par*
Winchester, Win-ɕes-ter, *c* Eng., 13¾; *vs* N-H., 2⅓; Mass., 1; *co ts* Va., 4½, Ia., 1, Ill., 1, Tenn.
Windermere (Win-der-mɛr) Lake, Eng.
Windham, Wind-ham, *v* Conn.
Windsor, New, Nŭ Win-zor, *t* and *par* Eng., 9½.
Windsor, *co ts* N-C.; *vs* N-Y., Vt., 1, O., Ia., Ill., Wis.; *s-pt t* N. Scotia; *t* C. W. [sovereigns.
Windsor Castle, residence of British
Windsor Locks, *v* Conn., 1¼. [1½.
Winfield, Win-fɛld, *co t* Va.; *v* N-Y.,
Winnebago Win-ɛ-bá-gꝏ (Lake,) Wis., 28 by 10 m.
Winneconna, Win-ɛ-kón-ɑ, *v* Wis.
Winneshiek, Win-ɛ-ʃɛk, *co* and *p o* Io.
Winnipeg, Win-i-peg, *l* Br. N. Am., 240 by 55 m.
Winnipegoos, Win-i-pɛ-gꝏs, *l* Br. N. Am., 125 by 25 m.
Winnipiseogee, Win-i-pɛ-sóg-ɛ, *l* N-H., 23 by 10 m; — River, do. [La.
Winnsborough, Wins-bur-ꝏ, *co ts* S. C.,
Winooski, Win-ꝏ́s-ki, *v* Vt.
Winslow, Winz-lꝏ, *vs* Me., N-J., Ia.

Winstead, Win-sted, *v* Conn.
Winston, Win-ston, *co t* N. C.
Winterset, Win-ter-set, *co t* Io. 5⅔.
Winterswyk, Win-terz-wįk, *v* Neth.,
Winton, Win-ton, *co t* N. C.
Winyaw (Win-yə) Ba, S. C.
Wiota, Wį-ó-tɑ, *v* Wis.
Wirksworth, Wẹrks-wurŧ, *t* and *par* Eng., 2⅔. [½.
Wisbeach, Wis-bɛɕ, *bor* and *t* Eng., 10-
Wiscasset, Wis-kás-et, *t* Me.
Wisconsin, Wis-kón-sin, *r* Wis., 200 m.
Wisconsin, one of the n. w. U. S., recently admitted into the Confederacy; area, 53,924 s. m.; the increase of the pop. in this state is unexampled; in 1850, its inhabitants, numbered 305,391; whites, 304,756, colored, 630.
Wismar, Wis-mɑr, *s-pt t* Mecklenburg-Schwerin, 11⅓.
Wissembourg, Vɛs-em-bꝏ́r, *t* Fr., 6.
Wiston, Wis-ton, *v* and *par* Wales, ¾.
Witham, Wiŧ-am, *r* Eng., 80 m; *t* and *par* do. 3⅓.
Withamsville, Wiŧ-amz-vil, *v* O.
Withlacoochee, Wiŧ-la-kꝏ́-ɕɛ, *rs* Ga., Florida.
Witney, Wit-ni, *t* and *par* Eng., 3.
Wittenberg, Wit-en-bẹ*rh*, *ft t* Prus. Sax., 8¾. [⅔.
Wittenberge, Wit-en-bẹ*rh*-ẹ, *t* Prus., 4-
Wittstock, Vit-stok, *t* Prus., 6½.
Wittzenhausen, Vit-sen-hʊ-zen, *t* Hesse-Cassel, 3¼. [Eng., 3.
Wiveliscombe, Wils-kum, *t* and *par*
Wivenhoe, Wiv-en-hꝏ, *t* and *par* Eng., 1⅔. [*v* Mass.
Woburn, Wó-burn, *t* and *par* Eng., 2;
Wohlau, Vó-lʊ, *t* Prus. Silesia, 3.
Wokingham, Wó-kiŋ-ham, *t* Eng., 2¼.
Wolcott, Wól-kot, *vs* Vt., N-Y.
Wolcottville, Wól-kot-vil, *vs* Conn., 1-¼; Ia.
Woldenberg, Vól-den-bẹ*rh*, *t* Prus., 3.
Wolfborough, Wúlf-bur-ꝏ, *v* N-H.
Wolfenbuttel, Vól-fen-bẹt-el, *t* Ger., 9.
Wolf River, Wis., 150 m.
Wolgast, Vól-gqst, *s-pt t* Prus., 5¼.
Wollin, Vol-én, *s-pt t* Prus., 4½; *i* do.
Wollmirstadt, Vól-mer-stet, *t* Prus. Sax., 3¾. [Eng., 4½.
Wolsingham, Wól-siŋ-ham, *t* and *par*
Wolverhampton, Wol-ver-hámp-ton, *t* and *bor* Eng., 50. [2½.
Wolverley, Wúl-ver-li, *v* and *par* Eng.,
Woodbridge, Wúd-brij, *t* and *par* Eng.,
Woodburn, Wúd-burn, *v* Ill. [5¼.
Woodbury, Wúd-ber-i, *co ts* N-J., 1; Tenn., Ill.; *v* Conn.
Woodsfield, Wúdz-fɛld, *co t* O., ¾.

Woodstock, Wúd-stok, *t* Eng., 1¼; *co ts* N-H., Vt., 1½; Va., 1¼; Ill., N-Brun., C. W., 2; *vs* N-Y., Ga., O.
Woodstown, Wúdz-tɵn, *v* N-J.
Woodville, Wúd-vil, *co ts* Miss., Tex.; *vs* O., Ia., Ill., Mo., Va., Ga., Ala.
Woodwardsville, Wúd-wardz-vil, *v* N-J.
Wooler, Wúl-er, *t* and *par* Eng., 2.
Woolwich, Wúl-iç *or* Wúl-ij, *t* and *par* Eng., 32¾.
Woonsocket, Wun-sók-et, *v* R. I., 6½.
Wooster, Wús-ter, *co t* O., 4.
Wootton-Basset, Wút-on-Bás-et, *t* and *par* Eng., 2¼.
Worcester, Wús-ter, *c* Eng., 27½; *c* Mass., 20¾; *v* N-Y., Ill.
Workington, Wúrk-iŋ-ton, *s-pt* and *par* Eng., 7¼. [¼.
Worksop, Wúrk-sop, *t* and *par* Eng., 7-
Workum, Vór-kum, *t* Neth., 3¼.
Wormditt, Vórn-dit, *t* Prus., 3½.
Worms, Wurmz, *anc c* Hesse-Darmstadt, 9½.
Worthing, Wúrđ-iŋ, *t* Eng., 5⅓.
Worthington, Wúrđ-iŋ-ton, *vs* Pa., Ky., O., ½.
Worthsville, Wúrđs-vil, *v* Ia.
Wragby, Rág-bi, *t* and *par* Eng., ⅔.
Wrangel, Ráŋ-el, *i* Rus., 1⅛.
Wrexham, Réks-ham, *t* and *par* N. Wales, 15½.
Wrietzen, Vrét-sen, *t* Prus., 6.
Wrightsville, Rįts-vil, *bor* Pa., 1⅓.
Wrington, Ríŋ-ton, *t* and *par* Eng., 1⅔.
Wrockwardine, Rók-war-dįn, *v* and *par* Eng., 3¼. [¼.
Wrotham, Rót-ham, *v* and *par* Eng., 3-
Wulur, Wúl-er, *l* Cashmere.
Wunsiedel, Vún-sɛ-del, *t* Bavaria, 4.
Wunzen, Wǿn-zen, *vol* Japan.
Wurdah, Wúr-da, *r* Ind., 300 m.
Wurno, Wúr-nɷ, *t* Cen. Af., 13.
Würtemberg, Vęr-tem-berh, *k* Ger.; area 7554 s. m., pop. 1,733,263.
Wurzburg *or* Wurtzburg, Vęrts-burh, *ft t* Bavaria, 26¾.
Wurzen, Vúrt-sen, *t* Saxony, 4¼.
Wyalusing, Wį-a-lú-siŋ, *v* Wis.
Wyandot, Wį-an-dót, *v* O. [Eng., 7¼.
Wycombe, Wik-um, Chipping, *t* and *par*
Wye, Wį, *r* Eng. and Wales, 130 m.; *par* and *v* Eng., 1¾.
Wyhe, Vį-e, *v* Neth., 11¾.
Wymondham, Wį-mond-ham, *t* and *par* Eng., 5¼.
Wynantskill, Wį-nants-kil, *v* N-Y.
Wyne-Gunga, Wįn-Gún-ga, *r* Ind., 230 [m.
Wyngene, Wíŋ-ha-ne, *v* Belg., 7.
Wyoming, Wį-ó-miŋ, *vs* Pa., N-Y., Ky., Ia., Ill., Io.
Wythe, Wiŧ, *co* Va.; *p o* Ill.
Wytheville, Wiŧ-vil, *co t* Va., 1.
Wytoonee, Wé-tɷ-nɛ, one of the Disappointment Is.

# X.

☞ Many names beginning with X, will be found under J, as the more recent orthography. [pék, *t* Mex., 4.
Xamiltepec *or* Jamiltepec, Hq-mɛl-ta-
Xanten, Ksán-ten, *t* Rhenish Prus., 3.
Xanthus, Zán-ŧus, *r* As. Min.; anc. *c* As. Min.
Xenia, Zé-ni-a, *co t* O., 3½; *v* Ill.
Xingu *or* Chingu, Σiŋ-gǿ, *r* Brazil, 1300 m.
Xochimilco, Hɷ-çɛ-mél-kɷ, *v* Mex.
Xochitepec, Hɷ-çɛ-ta-pék, *v* Mex.
Xorullo, Hɷ-rǿl-ɷ, *vol* Mex.
Xulla, Zǿl-q, *is* Malay Arch.

# Y.

Yablonoi, Yq-blɷ-nǿ, *ms* E. As.
Yadkin, Yád-kin, *r* N-C., 200 m.
Yakoono Seema, Yq-kǿ-nɷ Sé-mq, *i* [Jap.
Yakootsk, Yq-kǿtsk, *t* Sib., 7.
Yakova, Yq-kó-vq, *t* Eu. Tur., 18.
Yallobusha, Yal-ɷ-bǿ-ʃa, *co* and *r* Miss., nav. 90 m.
Ya-Long-Kiang, Yq-Loŋ-Kɛ-áŋ, *r* China, 600 m.
Yalpookh, Yql-pǿh, *l* Rus.
Yamaska, Yq-mqs-ka, *v* C. E., ⅔.
Yana, Yá-nq, *r* Sib., 600 m.
Yanaon, Yq-nq-óú, *v* Fr. Ind., 6¾.
Yanceyville, Yán-si-vil, *co t* N. C., ⅔.
Yang-Tse-Kiang, Yqŋ-Tsɛ-Kɛ-áŋ, *r* China, 1000 m.
Yanina, Yá-nɛ-nq, *c* Eu. Tur., 36,000.
Yan-Phing, Yqn-Fiŋ, *c* China.

Yaqui, Yq-ké, *r* Mex., 400 m.
Yardley-Hastings, Yq̍rd-li-Hás-tiŋz, *v* and *par* Eng., 1¼.
Yardleysville, Yq̍rd-liz-vil, *v* Pa.
Yarkand, Yqr-kq̍nd, *cap c* Chinese Toorkistan, 100.
Yarkand River, China, 500 m.
Yarmouth, Great, Grāt Yq̍r-muŧ, *s-pt t* and *par* Eng., 30¾.
Yarmouth, Yq̍r-muŧ, *t* and *par* Isle of Wight, ⅓; *s-pt t* N. Scotia.
Yarmouth Port, *v* Mass.
Yaroslav, Yq-rø-slq̍v, *c* Rus., 35.
Yarra-Yarra, Yár-a-Yár-a, *r* Aust.
Yassy, *or* Jassy, Yq̍s-ɛ, *cap t* Moldavia,
Yaxley, Yáks-li, *v* Eng., 1⅓. [20.
Yazoo, Yq-zǿ, *r* Miss., nav. 290 m.; — City, *co t* Miss., 2.
Ybicuy, Ɛ-bi-kwé, *r* Uruguay, 200 m.
Yealmpton, Yélmp-ton, *v* and *par* Eng., 1¼.
Yecla, Yá-klq, *t* Sp., 9⅓.
Yeddo *or* Jeddo, Yéd-ø, *cap c* Japan, 1,500,000; — Gulf, s. e. of the is. of Niphon.
Yefremov, Yef-ra-móv, *t* Rus., 7⅓.
Yeia, Yá-yq, *r* Rus., 140 m.
Yekaterinboorg, Ya-kq-ta-rin-bǿrg, *t* As. Rus., 15. [Rus., 5.
Yekaterinodar, Ya-kq-ta-rɛ-nø-dq̍r, *t*
Yekaterinoslav, Ya-kq-ta-rɛ-nø-sláv, *gov* and *t* Rus., 13½.
Yelagooi, Ya-lq-gǿ-ɛ, *r* Siberia, 200 m.
Yelatom, Ya-lq-tóm, *t* Rus., 5.
Yelets, Ya-léts, *t* Rus., 16½.
Yelisavetgrad, Ya-lɛ-sq-vet-grq̍d, *ft t* Rus., 10.
Yell, Yel, one of the Shetland Is., 2⅔.
Yellow Sea, *inlet* Pac. Oc., n. e. of Ch.
Yellow Springs, *v* O., 1⅓.
Yellowstone River, a tributary of the Missouri, 1000 m.
Yellville, Yél-vil, *co t* Ark.
Yemen, Yém-en, s. w. *div* Arabia.
Yen-Chow-Foo, Yen-Ϭɤ-Fǿ, *c* China, pop. 200.
Yenikale, Yen-i-kq̍-la, *strait* uniting the Sea of Azof with the Black Sea.
Yenisei, Yen-i-sá-ɛ, *r* Siberia, 2500 m.
Yeniseisk, Yen-ɛ-sásk, *gov* and *c* Rus., 6.
Yeoo, Ya-ǿ, *r* Af., 300 m.
Yeovil, Yǿ-vil, *t* and *par* Eng., 6.
Yeshil-Kool, Yéʃ-il-Kǿl, *l* Chinese Toorkistan.
Yesso *or* Jesso, Yés-ø, Japanese Is.
Yeste, Yés-ta, *t* Sp., 6.
Yetholm, Yéŧ-øm, *par* Scot., 1⅓.
Yezd, Yezd, *c* Persia.
Ylopango, Ɛ-lø-pq̍ŋ-gø, *l* Cen. Am.
Yonkers, Yóŋk-erz, *v* N-Y., 4.
Yonne, Yon, *dep* Fr., pop. 380,856.
Yoodoma, Yø-dǿ-mq, *r* Siberia, 170 m.
Yoog, Yøg, *r* Rus., 220 m.
Yoogan, Yø-gq̍n, *r* As. Rus., 228 m.
Yoomadung, Yøm-a-dúŋ, *m* Fur. Ind.
York, Yɘrk, *c* Eng., 36⅓; *co t* Pa., 6¾; *vs* Me., 3, Ill.; *ft* Br. N. Am., w. of Hudson's Bay.
York River, Va., 40 m.
Yorkshire, Yórk-ʃɛr, *v* N-Y.
York Sulphur Springs, *v* Pa.
Yorktown, Yórk-tɤn, *co t* Va.; *v* Ia.
Yorkville, Yórk-vil, *co t* S. C.; *vs* Tenn., Ia., Ill., Wis., C. W., Ia.
Youghal, Yó-hil *or* Yɘl, *s-pt t* and *par* Ir., 7⅓. [Md., Pa.
Youghiogheny, Yo-hø-gá-nɛ, *r* Va.,
Youngstown, Yúŋz-tɤn, *v* N-Y., 1, Pa., ½, O., 1½.
Youngsville, Yúŋz-vil, *v* Pa. [tɤn, *v* Pa.
Youngwomanstown, Yuŋ-wúm-anz-
Yountsville, Yɤnts-vil, *v* Ia.
Ypres, Ɛ'pr, *ft t* Belg., 15¾.
Ypsilanti, Ip-si-lán-ti, *v* Mich., 2½.
Yreka, Ɨ-ré-ka, *t* Cal., 2½.
Ysselmonde, Ɨ'sel-món-da, *i* S. Hol.
Yssingeaux, Ɛ-saṅ-ʒǿ, *t* Fr., 7⅔.
Ystad, Is'tq̍d, *s-pt t* Swed., 4¼.
Ystwith, Ist'wiŧ, *r* Wales.
Yuba, Yǘ-ba, *r* Cal.
Yuba City, *t* Cal.
Yucatan, Yø-kq-tq̍n, *st* Mex., area 52,947 s. m., pop. 668,623; — Bay, n. of Honduras. [400 m.
Yuen-Kiang, Yø-én-Kɛ-áŋ, *r* China,
Yuma, Yǿ-mq, *r* Hayti, 70 m.
Yurung-Kash, Yø-rúŋ-Kqʃ, *r* Chinese Toorkistan, 250 m.
Yverdun, Ɛ-vɘr-dúṅ, *t* Swit., 3⅔.
Yvetot, Ɛv-tǿ, *t* Fr., 10.

# Z.

Zaandam, Zq̍n-dq̍m, *t* Neth., 11¼.
Zab, Zqb, *r* Turk. Koordistan, 200 m.
Zabakano, Zq-bq-kq̍-nø, *t* W. Af., 9.
Zacapa, Sq-kq̍-pq, *t* Cen. Am., Guat., 5.
Zacatecas, Zqk-a-tá-kas, *st* Mex., area 30,507 s. m., pop. 305,551; *c*, *cap* of the same, 25.
Zacatula, Sq-ka-tǿ-lq, *t* Mex.

Zacualpan, Sq-kwql-pǽn, *v* Mex.
Zacualtipan, Sq-kwql-tε-pǽn, *t* Mex.
Zafaran-Boli, Zq-fq-rǽn-Bó-lε, *t* As. Min., 15.
Zaffarin, Zǽ-fq-rén, *is* Med.
Zafra, Hǽ-frq, *t* Sp., 4¾.
Zagros (Zǽ-gros) Mount, As.
Zaisan, Zį-zǽn, *l* Chinese Toorkistan.
Zalesczyky, Zq-leʃ-çik-ε, *t* Aus. Galicia, 5.
Zamora, Hq-mó-rq, *c* Sp., 8¾.
Zamora, Sq-mó-rq, *t* Mex.
Zamosz, Zǽ-moʃ, *t* Pol., 5.
Zanesville, Zánz-vil, *c* O., 10⅓; *v* Ill.
Zanguebar, Zqŋ-ga-bǽr, *ter* of E. Af.
Zante, Zǽn-ta, Ionian Island, 39¼; *t* of same, 20.
Zanzibar, Zqn-zε-bǽr, *or* Zanguebar, Zqŋ-ga-bǽr, *i* e. of Af., 150.
Zapatera, Sq-pq-tá-rq, *is* Lake Nicaragua.
Zapatosa, Sq-pq-tó-sq, *l* N-Gran.
Zara, Zǽ-rq, *cap c* Dalmatia, 6¾.
Zarevokokshaisk, Zq-rá-vɷ-kɷ-ʃįsk, *t* Rus., 5.
Zaria, Zǽ-rε-yq, *cap* Zeg-Zeg, Cen. Af., 40.
Zaslav, Zqs-lǽv, *t* Rus. Pol., 8¼.
Zbarasz, Zbǽ-raʃ, *t* Aus. Galicia, 5⅔.
Zea, Zé-q, *i* Gr. Arch., 9.
Zealand, Zé-land, *prov* Neth., 165.
Zebayer, Zε-bį-er, *is* Red Sea.
Zebeed, Zeb-éd, *ft t* Arabia, 7.
Zebu, Zε-bɷ́, *i* Malay Arch., 8¾.
Zebulon, Zéb-yq-lon, *co t* Ga.
Zeiden, Tsį-den, *t* Transylvania, 3⅓.
Zeitz, Tsįts, *t* Prus. Sax., 12¼.
Zelaya, Sa-lǽ-yq, *t* Mex., 10.
Zele, Zá-le, *t* Belg., 10⅓.
Zell (Zel) Lake, s. part of Baden.
Zengg, Zeŋ, *s-pt t* Croatia, 5.
Zenjan, Zen-gǽn, *t* Persia, 15.
Zenta, Sén-to, *t* Hun., 13⅔.
Zer-Afshan, Zer-Af-ʃǽn, *r* Independent Toorkistan, 400 m.
Zerbst, Tsęrpst, *t* Ger., 8⅓.
Zeulenroda, Tsɵ-len-ró-dq, *t* Ger. 4¾.
Zhitomeer, Ʒit-ɷ-mér, *t* Rus. Pol., 28.
Zhizdra, Ʒís-drq, *t* Rus., 8.
Zielenzig, Tsé-len-tsi*h*, *t* Prus., 4½.
Zierikzee, Zé-rik-za, *t* Neth., 6¾.
Zillerthal, Tsíl-er-tql, *val* Tyrol, 14.
Zilwaukie, Zil-wó-kε, *v* Mich.
Zinder, Zín-der, *t* Bornoo, 10.
Zionsville, Zį-onz-vil, *vs* Ia., Pa.
Zittau, Tsí-tɤ, *t* Saxony, 10.
Znaim, Tsnįm, *t* Moravia, 5.
Zoar, Zɔr, *v* O., settled by Germans, having a community of property.
Zolotchev, Zɷ-lɷ-çév, *t* Rus., 5.
Zombor, Zóm-bor, *t* Hun., 22.
Zschoppau, Tʃóp-ɷ, *t* Sax., 6¼.
Zug, Tsɷ*h*, *canton* Swit.; *c* of same 3⅓.
Zulia, Sɷ́-li-q, *r* S. Am., 180 m.
Zullichau, Tsęl-ε-kɤ, *t* Prus., 4¾.
Zuni, Zɷn-yé, *t* N-Mex.
Zurgena, Hɷr-*h*á-nq, *t* Sp., 12¾.
Zurich, Zų-rik, *canton* Swit.; *cap c* of same, 17; — Lake, Swit.
Zurrah, Zúr-a, brackish *l* Afg.
Zuruma, Sɷ-rɷ́-mq, *t* Ec., 6.
Zutphen, Zút-fen, *t* Neth., 12¼.
Zuyder-Zee, Zį-der-Zε, *g* German Oc.
Zvornik, Zvór-nik, *ft t* Eu. Tur., 15.
Zwickau, Tsvík-ɤ, *ts* Bohemia, 3½; Sax., 12¾; Bohemia, 3¾.
Zwittau, Tsvít-ɤ, *t* Moravia, 3¾.
Zwolle, Zwól-e, *ft t* Neth., 17.

# PERSONAL NAMES.

## INTRODUCTION.

SURNAMES, like Steam Engines, Railroads, and Telegraphs, seem to be of modern origin, the expanse of mind and a rapidly advancing civilization having created the necessity for a definite distinction between the actors in the drama of life. However this may be, the invention seems, to the mass of mankind, to be more perplexing than those mentioned in this connection; but this difficulty is not, let it be borne in mind, in the names *vocally* expressed, but in their *symbolical* representation. Following out the tendencies of a wretchedly imperfect orthography, the good fathers dressed themselves [*i. e.*, their names,] in ill-arranged costumes, which, after the established manner of things temporal, fell to their children, who have since continued to hand them down from generation to generation, with but slight modifications.

If it be true that, "*Sine nomine homo non est*,"* then should the clothing of the name be appropriate—an indication to the eye of what the *thing* is itself. But alas! such is not the case, and in view of the fact, which we cannot look to be changed at present, in any way whatever, we have endeavored, in the pages that follow, to overcome this difficulty to some extent—to place it in the power of the reader to call people by their *right names*. We do not claim for it correctness in *every particular*, for the many difficulties in the way rendered this impossible at first, but we feel confident that the reader of general history, and the student in all the departments of science and literature, will find this list of PERSONAL NAMES an invaluable companion. And, furthermore, to those engaged in commercial, mechanical, or agricultural pursuits, who generally give their spare time each day to the reading of their "paper," this will be found of great use in rendering familiar what they read. The constant intercommunication between the civilized nations of the earth, the numerous travelers following the various directions of the compass, at the present time, render such a work highly important. There are biographical dictionaries, it is true, but while the names given are barely readable to the *savant*, they are unapproachable barriers in the way of the general reader.—Surely this class, as well as

---

* Without a name man is nothing.

all others who are in the habit of reading, will feel grateful for the appearance of this little work, and all other attempts to make intelligible words clothed in a strange orthography. If every Dutchman one meets has not a name so long as *Hans Inkvervankodsdorspanckinkadrachdern*,—or every father of the Church so modest a title as that of "*St. Collen-ap-Gyunawg-ap-Clyndawg-ap-Cowrda-ap-Caradoc-Freichfras-ap-Llynn-Merim-ap-Enion-Yrth-ap-Cunedda-Wledig*,"* still there are many less imposing, of Anglo-Saxon as well as of foreign races, quite unpronouncable without assistance,—to dress these in phonotypy renders them intelligible.

This, as we believe, is the first attempt to give the pronunciation of modern names, and in the absence of such a work of reference the task has been laborious. But no pains have been spared in procuring the correct pronunciation of every name as far as possible, not only as instanced, but by reference to geographical names, poetry, and to works in every department of science and Belles-lettres. For instance, the name of a distinguished Senator from Texas, (Houston,) is pronounced by some public speakers, Hʊ́s-ton, by others, Hώs-ton; now the object to be obtained was to find out how the gentleman pronounced it himself, which was done, and was found to be as last given. It would have been gratifying to the publishers to have been able to have given a more extended notice of the works of the great minds that have passed away, together with those actively engaged at the present time,—to have chatted column after column away about the SHAKESPEARES, NEWTONS and GODWINS, the GŒTHES, KANTS and SCHILLERS, the LA PLACES and FRANKLINS of the past, the HUMBOLDTS, ARAGOS and AGASSIZ, of the present, but this would have alone required a massive volume, and would have defeated the object of the publishers, which was to make a convenient book of reference for every class of persons.

In conclusion, we invoke an honest criticism of our labors, hoping that such errors as are noted will be forwarded in time to make the requisite corrections in the second edition.

W. H. S.

---

* The dedication of the Church of Llangollen in Wales. [Vide Recreative Review, vol. ii. p. 189, Eng.] It appears from the following laughable description of cheese, designed to ridicule this system of nomenclature, that the surnominal adjunct, *ap*, [meaning *of*, or *from*, by descent,] was used in Wales until recently:—

"Adam's own cousin-german by its birth,
Ap-Curds-ap-Milk-ap-Cow-ap-Grass-ap-Earth!"

*English Surnames, vol. i. p.* 18.

# EXPLANATION OF ABBREVIATIONS.

The usual Geographical abbreviations are employed, as explained in the Introduction to the Geographical Names; also, the ordinary abbreviations of Christian names. In order to economize space, an abridged style of expression has been adopted, which when once understood is sufficiently expressive for a book of reference. Thus: "Aaron, *eld br* Moses,"—*elder brother of Moses;* "b. A. M.,"—*born year of the world;* "B. C.,"—*before Christ.* The figures at the close of each paragraph, thus: "1512—1571," are to be read, "born 1512—died 1571;" or if "k." precede the last figures, read "killed 1571;" "g." "guillotined," &c. See "Ainmuller," "1807—," means, born 1807, but not dead, or if so it is not known; "Allen," "—1789," means, the birth is not known, but died in 1789. [Those who own the book, when they hear of the death of any individual mentioned in it, should enter the time of his decease opposite the name.]

*act* ·· for ·· actor.
*adm* ····· admiral.
*adv* ······ advocate.
*ag* ······· agriculturist.
*alch* ····· alchemist.
*anat* ····· anatomist.
*antiq* ····· antiquarian.
*ar* ······· army.
*arc, arch* ·· architect.
*archæ* ···· archæologist.
*art* ······· artist.
*ast, astr* ·· astronomer.
*astrol* ···· astrologer.
*au* ······· author.
*b* ········ born.
*bar* ······ barister.
*ben* ······ benefactor.
*biog* ····· biographer.
*bp* ········ bishop.
*br* ········ brother.
*c* ········· crowned.
*capt* ······ captain.
*cari* ······ caricaturist.
*cel* ······· celebrated.
*cen* ······ century.
*chem* ····· chemist.
*cler* ······ clergyman.
*com* ······ commodore.
*comman* ·· commander.
*commen* ·· commentator.
*conch* ····· conchologist.
*conq* ····· conqueror.
*contr* ····· contributer.
*crit* ······ critic.
*dip* ······ diplomatist.
*dist* ······ distinguished.
*div* ······ divine.
*dram* ···· dramatist.
*ecc* ······ ecclesiastic.
*econ* ····· economist.
*ed* ······· editor.
*em* ······· eminent.
*emb* ······ embassador.
*emp* ······ emperor, empire
*eng* ······ engineer.
*engr* ····· engraver.
*ento* ······ entomologist.
*essa* ······ essayist.
*ethno* ····· ethnologist.
*ex* ······· executed.
*exp* ······ explorer, and experimental.
*fab* ······ fabulous.
*found* ···· founder.
*gen* ······ general.
*geneal* ···· genealogist.
*genre* ····· various.
*geo* ······· geographer.
*geol* ······ geologist.
*gov* ······· governor.
*hist* ······ historian.
*hum* ····· humorist.
*illus* ····· illustrious.
*imp* ······ imposter.
*inq* ······ inquirer.
*j* ········ judge.
*jour* ····· journalist.
*jur* ······ juror.
*k* ········ king, killed.
*law* ······ lawyer.
*lec* ······· lecturer.
*leg* ······· legislator.
*lieu* ······ lieutenant.
*lin* ······· linguist.
*lit* ······· literary.
*l-pt* ······ landscape painter.
*math* ····· mathematical.
*mat med* ·· materia medica.
*meta* ····· metaphysical.
*meteor* ···· meteorologist.
*mil* ······ military.
*min* ······ minister.
*miner* ···· mineralogist.
*misc* ····· miscellaneous.
*mor* ······ moralist.
*mus comp* · music composer.
*na* ······· national.
*nat* ······ naturalist.
*nob* ······ nobleman.
*noncon* ··· nonconformist.
*nov* ······ novelist.
*off* ······· officer.
*or* ······· orator.
*ori* ······· orientalist.
*pa* ······· patron.
*pat* ······ patriot.
*ph* ······· physician.
*phil* ······ philosopher.
*philol* ···· philologist.
*phren* ···· phrenologist.
*phys* ····· physiologist.
*pol* ······· politician.
*pop* ······ popular.
*pr* ······· prince.
*pres* ······ president.
*prof* ······ professor.
*prot* ······ protestant.
*psychol* ··· psychologist.
*pt* ········ painter.
*pub* ······ publisher.
*polit* ····· political.
*ref* ······· reformer.
*rel* ······· religious.
*rep* ······ representative.
*repub* ···· republican.
*schol* ····· scholar.
*sculp* ····· sculptor.
*sh* ········ shot.
*sol* ······· soldier.
*st* ········ statesman.
*sur* ······ surgeon.
*surg* ····· surgical.
*theo* ······ theologian.
*trage* ····· tragedian.
*trans* ····· translator.
*trav* ······ traveler.
*vic* ······· viceroy.
*v-pres* ···· vice-president.
*wr* ······· writer.

# PERSONAL NAMES

OF

# DISTINGUISHED INDIVIDUALS.

---

Aaron, A'ron, *eld br* Moses, first high priest of the Jews, b. A. M., 2434, or 1575 B. C.

Aartsbergen, Alex. Van, Fon Arts'ber-gen, *nob* and *st* of Holl., 17th cen.

Abati, Nicolo, Nik-ó-lω A-bá-tε, *pt* Italy, 1512—1571.

Abbas Pacha, Ab'as Pá-ʃa, *vic* Egypt.

Abbot, Ab'ot, Samuel, *merch* Boston, Mass., 1732—1812. [*aus* Mass.

Abbott, Ab'ot, John S. C. and Jacob,

Abd-El-Kader, Obd-el-Ká-der, *gen* Algeria. [*au* Eng.

A'Beckett, E-Bék-et, Gilbert Abbott,

Abercrombie, Ab-er-króm-bi, John, M. D., *au* and *ph* Scot., 1781—1844.

Abercromby, Ab-er-króm-bi, Sir Ralph, *off* Scot., 1734—1801.

Aberdeen, Ab-er-dén, Geo. Gordon, Earl of, *st* Eng.

Abernethy, Ab'er-nε-ti, John, *sur* and *au* Ir., 1763—1831.

Abinger, Ab'in-jer, James Scarlett, Lord, *j* Eng., 1769—1844. [Chaldea.

Abraham, E'bra-ham, patriarch, b. in

Achilles, A-kil-εz, *fab*, being dipped by his mother in the river Styx, was invulnerable in every part except his right heel, by which she held him; killed at the seige of Troy.

Achilli, Giovanni Giacinto, Jω-vá-nε Ja-gén-tω A-ké-lε, Italian Church reformer.

Actæon, Ak'tε-on, *fab*, a hunter who, discovering Diana bathing, was by her turned into a stag.

Adam, Ad'am, father of the human race, lived 930 years after his expulsion from Paradise.

Adams, Ad'amz, C. B., *geo* and *au* Mass., 1814—1853.

Adams, John, *st*, V-Pres. to Washington, from 1789—to 1798, and Pres. U. S., till 1801; Mass., 1735—1826. V-Pres., Thomas Jefferson.

Adams, John Quincy, son of Pres. John Adams, *st* and sixth Pres. of U. S., from 1825 to 1829, elected by House of Representatives, 1767—1848. V-Pres., J. C. Calhoun. [1722—1803.

Adams, Samuel, Am. *pat* and *st* Mass.,

Adams, J. C., *astr* Eng.

Adanson, A-dán-son, Michel, *bot* and *au* Fr., 1727—1806.

Addison, Ad'i-son, Joseph, *poet* and *au* Eng., *ed* "Spectator," 1672—1719.

Adelung, A'de-lωŋ, John Ch., *philol* Ger., 1734—1806.

Adolphus, A-dól-fus, Frederick II, *k* Sweden, 1710—1771.

Adonis, A-dó-nis, a youth remarkably beautiful, beloved by Venus and Proserpine.

Æneas, E-né-as, Trojan prince, son of Anchises and Venus, —1197 B. C.

Æolus, E'ω-lus, the god of the winds.

Æschines, Es'ki-nεz, *or* cotem. Demosthenes, 730 B. C. [B. C.

Æschylus, Es'ki-lus, *poet* Athens, 274

Æsculapius, Es-ku-lá-pi-us, the god of physic.

Æsop, E'sop, a Greek slave, *au* of the fables that bear his name, 200 B. C.

Agamemnon, Ag-a-mém-non, brother to Menelaus, captain-general of the Greeks at the seige of Troy.

Agassiz, Louis, Ló-i Ag-á-sε, dist. *nat*, born 1807, in Switzerland, now of Mass. — [1747—1822.

Aikin, E'kin, John, M. D., *wr* Eng.

Ainmuller, En'mul-er, Maximilian Emanuel, *art* Ger., 1807 —

Ainsworth, Ɛnz'wurth, W. Harrison, *nov* Eng., 1805—
Ainsworth, Ɛnz'wurth, *comp* English and Latin Dictionary, 1743—
Airy, Ɑr'i, Geo. Bidell, *ast royal* Eng., 1798—
Ajax, Ɛ'jaks, *fab*, one of the princes and heroes at the seige of Troy.
Akenside, Ɛ'ken-sīd, Mark, *poet* and *ph* Eng., 1721—1770.
Alban, Θl'ban, St., first Christian martyr in Britain, 3d cen.
Albert, Al'bert, Franz-August-Karl-Emanuel, Prince Consort, Duke of Saxe-Coburg-Gotha, but better known as "Prince Albert," Eng., 1819—
Alcibiades, Al-si-bī-a-dɛz, Athenian *gen*, slain 404 B. C.
Alembert, Ɑ-lém-ber, John Le Rond d', *math*, died 1783.
Alexander the Great, son of Philip, *k* Macedon, born 365 B. C. At 20 assumed his father's throne, and at 33 had "conquered the world," and died.
Alexander Paulowitch, Al-eks-án-der Pó-lɷ-viç, *emp* Rus., 1777—1825.
Alexander II., present *emp* Russia.
Alfieri, Ɑl-fi-á-rɛ, Count Vittorio, *dramatic poet* It., 1749—1803.
Ali, Pacha, Pɑ́-ʃɑ Ɑ'lī, *prince* Eu. Tur., 1750—1822.
Alison, Al'i-son, Archibald, *hist, adv* and *au* Scot., 1792— [Scot.
Alison, Wm. Pultney, *pol econ* and *ph*
Allen, Ethan, Ɛ'tan Al'en, *off* Am. army, —1789. [—1626.
Alleyn, Al'īn, Edward, *act* Eng., 1566
Allston, Θl'ston, Washington, *pt* Mass., 1779—1843.
Almquist, Ɑlm-kɷ́-ist, Karl Jonas Ludwig, *au* Sweden, 1793—
Alsop, Θl'sop, Richard, *poet* Conn., 1759—1815.
Alva, Ɑl'vɑ, Ferdinand, duke of Alva, *gen* Sp., 1508—1582.
Alvensleben, Ɑl-fenz-lá-ben, Count Albert, *dip* and *min of state*, Prus., 1794—
Ambrose, Am'brɷz, St., father of the Christian church, 333—397.
Ambrosia, Am-brɷ́-ʒi-ɑ, *fab*, the food of the gods.
Amerigo Vespucci, Ɑ-mer-é-gɷ Ves-pɷ́-çɛ, *nav* It., —1512. [1808.
Ames, Ɛmz, Fisher, Am. *st* Mass., 1756
Amici, Giovanni-Batista, Jɷ-vɑ́-nɛ-Bɑ-tís-tɑ Ɑm-é-çɛ, *ast* and *nat ph* It., 1784— [785 B. C.
Amos, Ɛ'mos, *prophet* and *k* Israel, d.
Ampere, Jean-Jacques, Ʒan-Ʒak Ɑṅ-pɑr, *philol* and *au* Fr., 1800—
Amphion, Am-fī-on, a famous musician.
Anacharsis, An-a-kɑ́r-sis, *ph* Scythia, was assassinated for attempting to introduce Grecian customs into his own country, 550 B. C. [B. C.
Anacreon, An-ák-rɛ-on, Greek *poet* 270
Anastasius I., pope of Rome, died 402.
Anaxagoras, An-aks-ág-ɷ-ras, Grecian *ph* 450 B. C.
Anderson, Ɑn'der-son, Hans Christian, Dan. *nov* 1805—
Andral, Ɑṅ'dral, Gabriel, *ph* and *au* Fr., 1797— [1749—1780.
Andre, Ɑn'dr, John, *off* Brit. army,
Andrew, St., An'drɷ, *dis* of John the Baptist, put to death on the cross in Scythia, for preaching the Gospel.
Andromache, An-dróm-a-kɛ, *fab*, the wife of Hector.
Anglesey, Aŋ'gl-sɑ, Henry Wm. Paget, Marquis of, *off* Brit. army, 1768—1854.
Anthon, An'thon, Charles. LL. D., classic *au* N-Y., 1797—
Antonius, Marcus, Mɑ́rk-us An-tɷ́-ni-us, *or* Mark Antony, the Roman triumvir, 40 B. C.
Apis, Ɛ'pis, son of Jupiter and Niobe, taught the Egyptians to sow corn and plant vines; after his death worshipped in the form of an ox, a symbol of husbandry.
Apollonius, Ap-ol-ɷ́-ni-us, Greek *poet* and *rhet*. Also, a Pythag. *ph* 1st cen.
Apollos, A-pól-os, a Jew of Alexandria, convert to Christianity, in the time of Paul.
Appert, Ap'er, Benj. Nicholas Marie, *philan* and *au* France, 1797—
Aquinas, Ak'wi-nas, St. Thomas, Italy, 1224—1274.
Arago, Francois Dominique, Frɑ́ṅ-swe Dom-i-nék Ɑ-rɑ́-gɷ, *ast* Fr., 1786—1853. [Fr.
Arago, Etienne, Ɛ-tén Ɑ-rɑ́-gɷ, *jour*
Arbuthnot, Ɑr'buth-not, Dr. John, *ph* and *au* died 1735. [690 B. C.
Archilochus, Ɑr-kil-ɷ-kus, Greek *poet*
Archimides, Ɑr-kim-i-dɛz, anc. *geom* Sicily, k. 208 B. C.
Argelander, Ɑr-ge-lɑn-der, Fred. Wm. Agustus, *ast* Prus., 1799—
Argus, Ɑr'gus, *fab*, said to have had a hundred eyes.
Ariosto, Lodovico, Lɷ-dɷ-vé-kɷ Ɑ-ri-ós-tɷ, *poet* It., 1474—1533.
Arista, Ɑ-rés-tɑ, Don Mariano, Pres. Mex., 1803—

Aristarchus, Ar-is-tqr-kus, *phil* Greece, the first to maintain that the earth turns upon its centre, and describes a circle round the sun, lived about 200 B. C.

Aristides, A-rís-ti-dεz, Ælius, Roman *sophist* and *trav*, died A. D., 180.

Aristides the Just, Athenian *gen*, 480 B. C.

Aristippus, Ar-is-típ-us, *phil*, 392 B.C., who asserted pleasure to be the object of life.

Aristophanes, Ar-is-tóf-a-nεz, comic *poet* of Athens, 340 B. C.

Aristottle, Ar-is-tót-l, peripatetic *phil*, Athens, 384 B. C.

Arius, Ꞓ'rius, *div* 4th cen., *found* of a sect which denied the Godship of Christ.

Arkwright, Ark'rit, Sir Richard, inventor of the spinning machine, Eng., 1732—

Arlincourt, Ar'lin-kωr, Victor, Vicomte d', *poet* and *au* Fr., 1789—

Arminius, Ar-mín-i-us, James, *found* of the doctrine that God creates men free moral agents, Holl., 1560—1619.

Armstrong, Arm'strong, John, M. D., *ph* and *au* Scot., 1709—1779.

Arne, Arn, Thos. Augustine, *mus comp* Eng., 1710—

Arnold, Benedict, Bén-ε-dikt Ar'nold, *off* and traitor, U. S. army, —1801.

Arnold, Samuel, *mus comp* Eng., 1740 —1802.

Arnold, Thomas, D. D., *au* Eng., 1795 —1842.

Aschbach, Aʃ'bqh, Joseph, *hist* Ger., [1801——

Athanasius, Ꞓ-ŧan-á-ʃi-us, St., born of heathen parents, became *bp* of Alexandria, 326.

Atlas, At'las, *k* Mauritania, *ast*, cotem. with Moses, now represented as an old man bearing the world upon his shoulders.

Atterbom, A'ter-bom, Pe. Dan. Amadens, *poet* Sweden, 1790—

Attwood, At'wud, Thomas, *comp* Eng., 1765—1837.

Auber, Θ'ber, Dan. Francois Esprit, (Es'prε,) *comp* Fr., 1784—

Aubigne, Θ-bén, Theod. Agrippa D', *hist*, *sat* and *poet*, 16th cent.

Audubon, Θ'de-boń, John James, Am. *orni* La., 1782—1851.

Auerbach, Berthold, Bér-tωld Ȣ'erbqh, *wr* and *poet*, Ger.

Auffenberg, Ȣf'en-berh, Joseph, Baron Von, *dram* Ger.

Augereau, Θ-ger-ó, Pierre Francois Charles, *gen* Fr., 1757—1816.

Augustenburg, Ȣ-gús-ten-burh, Christian August, Duke of Schleswig-Holstein, etc., 1798—

Augustine, Θ'gus-tεn, St., *bp* and father of the church, —430.

Augustus, Θ-gús-tus, Caius Julius Cæsar Octavianus, the first Roman Emperor, A. D., 14.

Aurora, Θ-ró-ra, *fab*, the goddess of the morning.

Austria, Emperor of, Francis Joseph Charles, 1830— [Scot.

Aytoun, Ɨ'tωn, William, *ed* and *au*

Azeglio, Adz-ég-li-ω, Massimo D', *au* Italy, 1798—

# B.

Babbage, Báb-aj, Charles, *math* and *phil mech* Eng., 1790—

Bach, Johann Sebastian, Yó-hqn Sabás-tε-qn Bqh, *mas* and *comp* music, Upper Saxony, 1685—1750.

Bachmann, Bqh-mqn, Charles Fred., *coun* and *prof phil*, Ger., 1785—

Bachmann, Gottlob Louis Ernest, *prof* and *au*, Ger., 1792—

Bacon, Bá-kon, Francis, Lord Verulam, Lord Chancellor, &c., *au* Eng., 1560 —1626.

Bahr, Bqr, John Christian Felix, *coun*, *prof* and *au*, Ger., 1798—

Bailey, Bá-li, E. H., *sculp* Eng., 1788—

Bailey, Philip James, *poet* Eng.

Baillie, Bá-lε, Joanna, *poetess* Eng., 1762—1841.

Baily, Bá-li, Jean Sylvain, *wr* and *hist*, Fr., 1736—1793.

Baird, Bqrd, Rev. Robert, D. D., *au* and *cler* Pa., 1798—

Bakewell, Bák-wel, Robert, experimental farmer and cattle-breeder Eng., 1726—1795.

Balboa, Bql-bó-q, Vasco Nunez (Nóneŧ) De, Spanish *nav* 16th cen.

Balbo, Bql-bω, Count Cesare, *st* and *au* Italy, 1789. [Ger., 1804——

Bajza, Bo-é-zo, Anthony, *poet* and *au*

Balzac, Honore De, Hon-ór De Bqlzák, *nov* Fr., 1799—1850.

Bancroft, Bán-kroft, George, Am. *au* and *hist* Mass., 1800—
Bangs, Nathan, D. D., *cler* and *essa* Conn., 1778—
Banks, Sir Joseph, Bart., *bot* and *trav* Eng., 1743—1820.
Banks, N. P., *st* and *Speaker of House of Rep.*, U. S. Cong., 1856, elected after 7 weeks of voting, Mass., 1810—
Barante, Guillaume Prosper Brugière, Gwil-ōm Prós-per Brę-ʒąr Bąr-ąṅt, Baron, *au* and *st*, Fr., 1782.
Barbauld, Bą́r-bəld, Anne L., *poetess* Eng., 1743—1825.
Barbes, Armand, Ar'mąnd Bą́r-ba, a French revolutionist, 1810—
Barclay, Bą́r-kla, Robert, Apologist or Quaker, Eng., 1648—1680.
Barebone, Bą́r-bon, Praise-God, zealot of Cromwell's parliament, Eng., 1653.
Barentz, Bąr-énts, Wm., a Dutch *nav* 16th cen. [1757—1812.
Barlow, Bą́r-lo, Joel, *poet au* Conn.,
Barnes, Bą́rnz, Joshua, *cler, prof* and *poet*, Eng., 1654—1712.
Barnes, Daniel H., Am. *conch* and *au*, —killed, 1818. [—1818.
Barney, Joshua, *com* U. S. Navy, 1759
Baroche, Bąr-óʃ, Jules, *min* and *adv* Fr., 1803. [*st* Fr., —1829.
Barras, Bąr-ą, Faul Francis, Count De,
Barrere De Vieuzac, Bąr-ą́r Dę Vę-zą́k, Bertrand, *pol* Fr., 1755—1841.
Barrot, Odillon, O-dél-yoṅ Bąr-ót, *adm* and *ex-min* Fr., 1790—
Barrow, Bą́r-o, Dr. Isaac, *math* and *div* Eng., 1630—1677.
Barry, Bár-i, John, *com* U. S. Navy, 1745—1803. [1795———
Barry, Sir Charles, R. A., *arch* Eng.,
Barthelemy, St. Hilaire, Saṅ Hil-ąr Bąr-tá-lę-me, *pol jour* Fr., 1792—
Bartlett, Bą́rt-let, Josiah, M. D., *gov* and *st* N. H., 1729—1795.
Bartlett, Josiah, M. D., *ph* and *essa*, Mass., 1759—1820.
Barton, Bą́r-ton, Benj. Smith, M. D., *prof nat hist* and *bot, ed*, &c., Pa., 1766—1815. [1784—1849.
Barton, Bernard, "Quaker poet," Eng.,
Bartram, Wm., *bot* and *orni* Pa., 1739 —1823.
Batthyanyi, Bot-yóny-i, Louis, *nob* and *pat* Hun., 1809—shot, 1848.
Bauer, Bŏ́-er, Bruno, *bib crit* Ger., 1809— [Eng., 1615———
Baxter, Báks-ter, Richard, *div* and *au*
Bayard, Bá-ąrd, Jas. A., Am. *st* Pa., 1767—1815. [1706.
Bayle, Bal, Peter, *crit au*, Fr., 1647—
Bayley, Bá-li, Richard, *ph, med au* and *prof*, Conn., 1745—1801.
Bavaria, Ba-vá-ri-a, Maximilian Joseph, King of, 1811—
Beattie, Bé-ti, James, *poet* and *mor* Scot., 1735—1803.
Beaumont, Bo-mónt, Francis *dram poet* Eng., 1584—1616. [1853.
Beaumont, Bo-móṅ, Gustave De, *pol* and *au* Fr., 1802—
Beaumont, Jean Baptiste Armand Louis Lèonce Elie De, *eng, prof geol*, etc., Fr., 1798—
Beccaria, Bek-á-ri-a, marquis, *wr* "On Crimes and Punishments," Milan, 1735—1794.
Beck, Lewis C., Am. *chem* and *bot* N-Y., 1790—1853.
Beecher, Lyman, D. D., *cler, ref*, etc., Conn., 1775—
Beecher, Henry Ward, LL. D., son of above, *div* and *ref*, Brooklyn, N-Y., 1820—
Beechey, Bé́ç-i, Fred. Wm. *nav capt* and *trav* Eng., 1796—
Beddoes, Béd-oz, Thos. Lovell, *poet* Eng., 1803—1849.
Beethoven, Ba-tó-fen *or* Be-tó-ven, Ludwig. Van, *mus* and *comp* Prus., 1779—1827. [1744.
Behring, Bé-riŋ, Vitus, *nav* Den., —
Bekker, Bék-er, Immanuel, *philol* Ger., 1785— [king, 1831.
Belgians, Leopold, King of the, elected
Belknap, Bél-nap, Jeremy, D. D., *cler* and *wr*, Mass., 1744—1798. [—1842.
Bell, Sir Charles, *physiol*, Scot., 1774
Bell, John, *st* N-H., 1730—1825.
Bellini, Vincenzio, *mus comp* Italy, 1806—1835. [*trav*, —1823.
Belzoni, Bel-dzó-ne, Giovanni, Paduan
Benedektow, Ben-e-dék-tŏ, Wladimir, a Russian lyric poet.
Bentham, Bén-tam, Jeremy, a great thinker and writer, Eng., 1748—1832.
Bentinck, Bén-tiŋk, Lord Geo., *parl leader* Eng., 1802—1848.
Benton, Thos. Hart, Am. *st* Mo., 1783.
Beranger, Bę́r-ąṅ-ʒer, Pierre-Jean De, *song wr* and *poet*, Fr., 1780—
Berenger, Bę́r-en-ʒęr, L. P., *poet, rhet* and *au*, Fr., 1748—1822. [1798—
Beresford, Bér-es-ford, Wm., *st* Eng.,
Berghaus, Bę́rh-hŏs, Henry, *geog* Ger., 1797— [—1753.
Berkeley, Bę́rk-li, George, *bp* Ir.. 1684
Berkeley, Wm., *gov* Va., —1677.
Bermudez De Castro, Bąr-mṓd-at Da Ką́s-tro, Don Salvador, *poet* Spain, 1817—

Bernadotte, Ber-nq-dôt, *k* Sweden and Norway, 1764—1844.
Bernard, Ber-nqrd, Sir Francis, *gov* Mass., and *pa lit* —1779.
Bernhard, Bérn-hqrt, Karl, Danish *nov.*
Bernouilli, Bér-nœ-ε, family name of a cluster of celebrated mathematicians of the 17th and 18th centuries.
Berthollet, Ber-tœ-la, Claude Louis, *chem* Fr., 1748—1822.
Berryer, Bér-i-a, M., *pol* and *adv* Fr.
Berzelius, Berts-á-lε-œs, Jno. Jacob, *chem*, Sweden, 1779—1848.
Bethune, Bét-yqn, Geo. W., Am. *au* and *div* 1805—
Beza, Bé-za, *or* Theodore De Beze, (Baz, Eng. Bεz,) *ed*, *trans* and *commen*, Fr., 1518—1605. [1800—
Biard, Bi-ár, François Aug., *pt* Fr.,
Biermann, Bér-mqn, Chas. Ed., *l-pt* Ger., 1803—
Bickersteth, Bík-er-stet, Ed., *wr rel works*, Eng., 1786—1850.
Biddle, James, Am. *com* 1783—1848.
Biddle, Nicholas, *capt* Am. Navy, 1750 —1778, killed.
Biddle, Nicholas, Am. *fin* and *pres* U. S. Bank, 1786—1844. [—1821.
Bigelow, Bíg-lœ, Timothy, *st* Mass.,
Binder, Bín-der, Wilhelm Chris., *hist* Ger., 1810. [Eng.
Binney, Bín-i, Thos., *noncon preacher*
Bird, William, *mus* Eng., 1540—1623.
Bird, Dr. Robt. Mont., *nov* Pa., 1803—
Bishop, Sir Henry Kent, *mus comp* Eng., 1786—1855.
Bixio, Bíks-ε-œ, M., *ph* and *nat*, Fr.
Black, Joseph, *chem* Scot., 1728—1790.
Blackstone, Sir Wm., *j* and *commen*, Eng., 1722–1780.
Blair, Blqr, Francis P., *pol ed* and *st*, Md., 1791—
Blair, Blqr, Dr. Hugh, Scottish *div* and *au* of "Lectures on Rhetoric," 1718—1800. [—1659.
Blake, Admiral, *adm navy*, Eng., 1599
Blakeley, Johnston, *capt* Am. Navy, perished at sea. [1801—
Blanc, Louis, Lœ́-i Blqń, *pol theo* Fr.,
Blessington, Marg. P., Countess of, *wr* Eng., 1789—1849.
Blomfield, Blóm-fεld, Chas. James *bp* London, 1786— [*wr*, 1809—
Blommaert, Bló-mert, Philip, Flemish
Bloomfield, Blœ́m-fεld, Robert, *poet* Eng., 1766—1823.
Blucher, Blœ́-*h*er, Gebhart Lebrecht Von, *off* Prus. Army, 1742—1819.
Blumenbach, Blœ́m-en-bq*h*, Jean Fred., *anat*, *ph* and *nat* Ger., 1752—1840.

Boas, Bó-qs, Ed., *poet* and *au*, Ger., 1815—
Boccaccio, Bœ-kq́-çœ, Giovanni, It. *poet* and *au*, 1313—1375.
Bodenstedt, Bó-den-stet, Fred. Martin, *wr* Ger., 1819—
Boehmen, Bó-men, Jacob, *rel wr* and *teach*, Ger., 1575—1624.
Boehtlingk, Bót-liŋk, Otto, *philol* Rus., 1815— [1785—
Boekh , Bœ*h*, Augustus, *antiq* Ger.,
Boettcher, Bet-*h*er, Adolf, *poet* and *trans* Ger., 1815—
Boettiger, Bó-ti-ger, Karl Wilhelm, *prof lit* and *hist*, and *au*, Ger., 1790—
Boileau-Despreaux, Bwo-lœ́-De-sprœ́, Nicolas, *sat* Fr., 1636—1711.
Boissonade, Bós-on-q́d, Jean François, Gr. *schol* and *clas ed*, Fr., 1774—
Boker, Geo. H., Am. *poet* and *dram* Pa., 1824—
Bolingbroke, Bó-liŋ-brœk, Henry St. John, Lord, *or*, *st* and *phil essa* Eng., 1678—1751.
Bolivar, Bœ-lε-vq́r, Simon, *liberator* of S. Am., 1783—1830.
Bonaparte, Bó-na-pqrt, Napoleon, *emp* Fr., 1769—1821.
Bonaparte, Joseph, *eld br* Napoleon, *k* Sic. and Sp., 1768—1844. [1846.
Bonaparte, Louis, *br* do., *k* Hol., 1778—
Bonaparte, Lucien, *br* do., *pr* Canino, 1775—1840.
Bonaparte, Louis Napoleon, *son* of Louis Bonaparte, *emp*, Fr., 1808—
Bonaparte, Chas. Lucian, *pr* Canino, and *dist nat*, 1803—
Bond, William C., *ast*, Mass., 1790—
Boniface I., to IX., Popes fr. 422 to 1404.
Bonpland, Aimé, Ɑ-má Bœń-plqń, Fr., *nat*, 1799— [1820.
Boone, Daniel, Am. *pio hunter*, 1730—
Bopp, Bop, Francis, *philol* and *ori schol* Ger., 1791— [1728—1804.
Bordley, Bórd-li, Jno. Beale, *ag au* Md.,
Bornhauser, Bórn-hʊ-zer, Thomas, Swiss *poet*, *pol wr*, etc., 1799—
Borrow, Geo., *au* Eng., 1805—
Boscovich, Bós-kœ viq, Roger Jos., *learned Jesuitical wr*, It., 1711—1787.
Bossuet, Bo-sé *or* Bo-sq-á, Jas. Benigne, Fr. *div* and *au* 1627—1704.
Boswell, Bóz-wel, Jas. *biog* Dr. Johnson, 1740—1795.
Botta, Bœt, Paul 'Emile, Ɑ'mεl, Fr. *archæ* and *trav*.
Boudinot, Bœ́-din-ot, Elias, LL.D., *law* and *edu ben* N-J., 1740—d.
Bougainville, Bœ-gan-vél, L. A. De, *com* Fr. Navy, 1729—1811.

Bourdon, Bꝏr-dóṅ, Leonard J. J., *patron na edu*, Fr., d. about 1810.
Boussingault, Bꝏ-sqṅ-gól, M., *chem* and *au*, Fr.
Bowditch, Bó-diç, Nathaniel, LL.D., *math* and *ast*, Mass., 1773—1838.
Bowdoin, Bó-den, [Fr. Bꝏ-dwóṅ,] Jas. LL.D., *gov* Mass., *ben* Harvard University, etc., 1745—1790.
Bowen, Bó-en, Wm. C., D.D., *chem*, R. I., 1776—1815. [*au*, Mass.
Bowen, Francis, *ed N. Am. Rev.* and
Bowring, Bŏ-riŋ, John, LL.D., *philol*, *poet*, *pol wr*, etc., Eng., 1792—
Boylston, Bŏl-ston, Zabdiel, M.D., F.-R.S., Am. *ph* Boston, 1780—1760.
Braddock, Ed., *maj gen* Br. Army, k. 1775. [1795.
Bradford, Wm., *att-gen* U. S., 1775—
Bradstreet, Anne, *au* first Am. *vol poems*, 1612—
Brahe, Tycho, Tę-kꝏ, Brą-e, *ast* Den., 1546—1601.
Brainard, Brá-nard, John G. C., Am. *poet*, Conn., 1797—d.
Bramante, Bra-mąn-ta, Donato, It. *arch*, 1444—1514.
Brande, Brand, Wm. Thos., *chem* and *wr* Eng., 1780.
Brandis, Brąn-dis, Chris. Augustus, *prof phil* Prus., 1790—
Brant, Joseph, *cel* Indian chief.
Brazil, Pedro, Emp. of, 1825, c. 1840.
Braun, Brŏn, August Emil, *wr* and *archæ*, Ger., 1809—
Breckinridge, J. C., *st* and V-Pres. U. S. to James Buchanan, Ky., 18——
Breithaupt, Brįt-hŏpt, Joh. Aug. Fried., *mineralogist*, Ger., 1791—
Breton De Los Herreros, Bra-tón Da Lꝏs Ar-ąr-ós, Don Manuel, *dram* and *poet*, Sp., 1796.
Brewster, Brꝏ́s-ter, Sir David, *exp*, *phil* and *au*, Scot., 1781—
Brindley, James, *civ eng*, Eng., 1716—1772.
Brissot, Bri-só, Jean Pierre, *or* and *pol wr*, Fr., 1793.
Brodie, Bró-di, Sir Benj. Collins, *sur* and *surg wr* Eng., 1783—
Brongniart, Bróṅ-yqr, Adolphe Theo., Fr. *nat*, 1801—
Bronn, Brꝏn *or* Brun, Heinrich Geo., Ger. *nat*, 1803—
Brooke, Sir James, *rajah* of Sarawak, and *philan*, 1803—
Brooks, John, LL.D,, *gov* Mass., and *lieut-col* U. S. Army, 1752—1825.
Brooks, Maria, Am. *poet* Mass., 1795—1845.
Brooks, Hon. Preston S., who brutally caned Charles Sumner, in the U. S. Senate Chamber, in 1856; South Carolina, 1810—
Brooks, Shirley, *dram wr* and *jour* Eng., 1816—
Brougham, Bró-am, Henry, Lord, *phil*, *st*, *law-ref* and *critic*, Eng.
Brown, Chas. Brockden, Am. *nov*, Pa., 1771—1810. [1775—1828.
Brown, Jacob, *maj-gen* U. S. Army,
Brown, Thomas, *met* and *au*, Scot. 1778—1820. [1814——
Brown, Henry Kirke, Am. *sculp* Mass.,
Browne, Sir Thomas, *au* and *ph* Eng., 1605—1682.
Browing, Robt., *poet* Eng., 1812—
Bruce, James, F.R.S., *exp* of Africa, Scot., 1730—1794. [1767.
Bruce, Michael, Scotch *poet*, 1746—
Bruce, Brꝏs, Robert, Scotch *gen*, elected king in 1306, died, 1329.
Brullow, Brꝏ́-lꝏ, Karl, *hist pt* Rus., 1800—
Brunel, Brę-ná *or* Brꝏ́-nel, Marc I., *civ eng*, Normandy.
Brunelleschi, Brꝏ-nél-es-kɛ, Filippo, It. *arch*, 1377—1446.
Bruno, Giordano, Jꝏr-dą-nꝏ Brꝏ́-nꝏ, It. *rel wr*, an atheist, burnt at the stake, 1600.
Brunswick-Wolfenbuttel, Brúnz-wik-Wólf-en-bꝏ-tl, A. W. M. Frederick, Duke of, 1806—
Brutus, Brꝏ́-tus, Marcus, Rom. *gen* and *pol*, who assassinated Julius Cæsar. He slew himself, 42 B. C.
Bruyare, Brę-yąr, Jean, De La, Fr. *au* Normandy, 1644—1696.
Bryant, Brį-ant, Wm. Cullen, Am. *poet* and *jour*, N-Y., 1794—
Buba, Bꝏ́-bq, Adolf, Ger. *poet*, 1802—
Buch, Bꝏh, Leopold Von, *geol* Prus., 1777—
Buchanan, Bq-kán-an, Geo., Latin *poet* and *hist*, Scot., 1506—1581.
Buchanan, James, Am. *st* and fifteenth Pres. U. S., from 1857 to 1861, Pa., 1791— J. C. Breckenridge, V-Pres.
Buchanan, Dr. J. R., *prof* Physiology, Phrenology, etc., *au*, and *ed* "Journal of Man," Ohio, 181 —
Buchez, Bę-ʃá, Philip Benj. Jos., Fr. *ph* and *jour*, 1796—
Buckingham, Jas. S., *trav*, *wr*, *pol*, Eng., 1786—1855.
Buckingham, Jos. T., *jour*, Mass., 1779—
Buckland, Dr. Wm., *geol* Eng.
Buel, Bų-el, Jesse, Am. *ag*, Conn., 1778—1839.

Buffon, Bẹ-foṅ, Geo. L. Le Clerc, Comte De, *nat* Fr., 1707—1788.
Bulgarin, Bœl-gɋr-én, Thaddeus, *wr* Rus., 1789—
Bull, Bœl *or* Bul, Ole B., *viol*, Norway, 1810—
Bülow, Bḗ-lœv, Karl Edward Von, Ger. *nov*, 1803—
Bulwer, Búl-wer, Sir Edward Lytton, *nov* and *poet* Eng.
Bulwer, Sir Henry Earle Lytton, K.-C. B., *dip* and *au* Eng., 1804—
Bunsen, Bœ́n-sen, Christ. Chas. Josias, Chevalier de, Prus. *emb* and *au*, 1791—
Bunyan, John, *au* "Pilgrim's Progress," Eng., 1628—1688.
Burckhardt, Búrk-hɋrt, J. Ludwig, *trav* Swit., 1783—1817.
Burgkmair, Burgh-mạ́r, Hans, *pt* and *wood-eng* Ger., 1472—1559.
Burgos, Bœr-gṓs, Don Javier De, *st* and *au* Sp., 1778—
Burgoyne, Bur-gœ́n, *lieu-gen* Br. Army,
Burke, Burk, Edmund, *or*, *st* and *phil* Ireland, 1730—1797.
Burleigh, Búr-le, Wm. Cecil, Lord, *st* Eng., 1520—1598.
Burleigh, Chas. C., *wr* and *ref* Pa.
Burmeister, Bur-mį́s-ter, Hermann, Ger. *nat* 1807—
Burnap, Bur-náp, Rev. Geo. W., D.D., *theo* and *gen au* N-H., 1802—
Burnet, Jacob, *j*, *leg* and *au* Ohio, 1771—1853.
Burney, Charles, *mus comp* and *au* Eng., 1726—1815.
Burns, Robert, *poet* Scot., 1759—1796.
Burr, Aaron, *st* and V-Pres. U. S. to Thomas Jefferson, 1756—1836.
Burritt, Búr-it, Elihu, *lec*, *jour* and *lin* Conn., 1811—
Bury, Bẹ-ré, Henri B., Baron de, *au* and *crit* Fr., 1818—
Bush, Rev. Geo., *theo* and *commen* Vt., 1796—
Buss, Bœs, Franz Joseph, *polit econ* and *au* Ger., 1803—
Butler, Richard, *maj-gen* U. S. Army, k. 1791.
Butler, Samuel, *poet sat* Eng., 1612—1680.
Byron, Geo. Gordon, Lord, *poet* Eng., 1788—1824.
Bystrom, Bẹ-strṓm, Johann Nikolaus, Swed. *sculp*, 1783—

## C.

Cabanis, Ka-bɋ-né, Pierre Jean G., *ph* and *phil* Fr., 1757—1808.
Cabet, Ka-ba, Etienne, Fr. *communist*, formed communes in Texas and Ill., 1788—1856.
Cabot, Kɋ́-bœt, John, Venetian *nav*, [15th cen.
Cabot, Sebastian, son of Jno. C., *nav*, and discoverer of the variations of the magnetic needle, 1477—1557.
Cadmus, Kád-mus, *k* of Thebes, introduced 16 letters into Greece, B. C.
Cadwallader, Kod-wól-a-der, John, *brig-gen* Am. army, —1786.
Cæsalpinus, Ka-zɋ́l-pin-us *or* Sa-sɋ́l-pin-us, Andre, *bot* Tus., 1519—1603.
Cæsar, Caius Julius, Ká-yus Jɋ́-li-us Sé-zɑr, Roman *gen* and *hist*, b. 98 B. C.
Cailliaud, Kal-yṓd, Frederic, Fr. *trav* 1797—
Calame, Ka-lɋ́m, Alex., Swiss *l-pt*.
Calderon De La Barca, Kɋ́l-dạr-œn Da Lɋ Bɋ́r-kɋ, Pedro, *poet dram* Sp., 1600—1681.
Calderon, Don Serafin E., *poet* and *orientalist* Sp., 1800—
Calhoun, Kal-hœ́n, John C., V-Pres. U. S. to Andrew Jackson and Martin Van Buren, *st*, etc., South Carolina, 1782—1850.
Caligula, Kal-íg-yɋ-lɑ, Roman *emp* and *tyrant*, began his reign A. D. 37; assas. A. D. 41, aged 29 years.
Callcott, Kél-kot, John Wall, *mus comp* Eng., 1766—1821.
Callimachus, Kal-i-má-kus, Greek *poet*.
Calmet, Augustin, Θ-gus-tɛn Kɋl-ma, Fr. *au*, 1672—1757.
Calvin, John, *rel ref* Fr., 1509—1564.
Camoens, Kɋ-mœ-anz, Luis De, *poet* Portugal, 1527—1579.
Campanella, Kɋm-pan-él-yɋ, Thomas, *meta* Sp., 16th cen.
Campbell, Kám-bel, Thomas, *poet* Scot., 1777—1844.
Campbell, Lord John, *j* and *au* Scot., 1781—
Camper, Kɋṅ-pẹ, Pierre, *anat* and *nat* Fr., 1722—1789.
Candolle, Kaṅ-dóly, Aug. Pyramus De, *bot* Fr., 1778—1841.
Canina, Kɋ-né-nɋ, Luigi, *antiq* Italy.

Canning, Kán-iŋ, Geo., *st* Eng., 1770 —1827.
Cano, Kq́-nœ, Alonso, *pt*, *sculp* and *arch* Sp., 1601—1667. [1757—1822.
Canova, Kq-nó-vq, Antonio, *sculp* It.,
Cantu, Kq́n-tœ, Cesare, *schol* and *au* Italy, 1805—
Capefigue, Kq-pe-fég, Baptiste H. Raymond, *hist* Fr., 1799—
Caracci, Ka-*r*q́-çε, name of a celebrated family of painters in It., 16th cen.
Caravaggio, Kq-*r*q-vq́-jœ, Michelangelo M., *pt* Italy, 1569—1609.
Cardan, Kq*r*-dañ, Jerome, *ph*, *astrol* and *au* Fr., 1501—1576.
Carey, Ká-ri, William, *div*, *oriental philol* and *trans* Eng., 1761—1834.
Carey, Henry C., Am. *polit econ* and *au* N-Y., 1793— [1798———.
Carleton, Kq́rl-ton, Wm., Irish *nov*.
Carlisle, Kqr-lịl, Geo. Wm. F. H., Earl of, *st* and *lec* Eng., 1802—
Carlyle, Kqr-lịl, Thomas, Brit. *au* and *reviewer*, 1796—
Carmichael, Kq́r-mị-kl, William, *dip* and Chargé d'Affaires, U. S., Md., —1795.
Carnicer, Kq*r*-nε-ŧq́*r*, Don Ramon, *opera comp* Sp., 1789—
Carnot, Kq*r*-nó, Lazare Nic. M., *mil engin* and *min of war* Fr., 1753—1823. [1814———.
Carrera, Kq-*r*á-rq, Rafael, *pres* Guat.,
Carroll, Kár-ol, Ckarles, *signer Dec. of Ind.*, Md., 1737—1832.
Cartier, Kq*r*-tε-a, Jacques, Fr. *nav* and *trav* 16th cen.
Carver, John, first *gov* "Plymouth Colony," —1621.
Carvallo, Kq*r*-vq́l-yœ, *min* of Chili in the U. S., 1808—
Casas, Kqs-q́s, Barthol. Las, a misguided *philan*,—originator of African slavery, —1566.
Casati, Kqs-q́-tε, Gobrio, Count, *st* Lombardy, 1798—
Caspari, Kqs-pq́-rε, Karl Paul, *bib crit* Ger., 1814—
Cass, Lewis, *st* Mich., 1782—
Cassini, Ka-sin-ε, family name of several *astrs* Fr., 17th cen.
Cassius, Caius, Ká-yus Káʃ-i-us, *br-in-law* Brutus, and one of Cæsar's murderers, —42 B. C.
Castelli, Kqs-tél-ε, Ignaz Friedr, *hum poet* Ger., 1781—
Castiglione, Kqs-tél-yœ-na, Carlo Ottavio, Count, It. *philol* 1795—
Castillio, Kqs-tél-yœ, Antonio F., Port. *poet*, 1800—
Castlereagh, Kas-l-rá, Robt. Stew., Brit. *st*, 1769—1822.
Castor, Kás-tor, *fab* son of Jupiter and Leda.
Castren, Kq́s-*tr*en, M. Alex., *lin* and *ethno* Finland, 1813—
Catesby, Mark, F.R.S., *nat* Eng., 1679 —1749.
Catharine De Medici, — Dẹ Me-dε-sé, a French *princess*, 1519—1589.
Catharine Alexievna, *empress* Russia, from 1725 to 1727.
Catharine II., *empress* Russia, from 1762—1796.
Catilina, Kát-i-lị-nq, Lucius Sergius, Roman *war*, 62 B. C.
Cato, Marcus Portius, *censor* Rome, b. 233 B. C.
Catwn, John, *j* U. S. Sup. Ct., Tenn.
Cattermole, Kát-er-mœl, Geo., *pt* Eng., 1800—
Cavaignac, Ka-ván-yak, Eugene, Fr. *gen* and *republican*, 1802—
Cavendish, Hon. Henry, *chem* Eng., 1731—1810.
Caxton, Káks-ton, Wm., *introducer of printing*, Eng., 1410—1491.
Cecil, Sé-sil, William, Lord Burleigh, Eng. *st*, 1521—1598.
Cecrops, Sé-krops, Egyptian *found* Athenian monarchy, 1556 B. C.
Cellini, Ɛel-é-nε, Benvenuto, *sculp* It., 1500—1572.
Centaurs, Sén-torz, *fab* half men, half horse, Thessaly. [culture.
Ceres, Sé-res, *fab* the goddess of agri-
Cervantes Saavedra, Ŧq*r*-vqn-tás Sq-vád-*r*q, Miguel De, *au* 'Don Quixote,' (Kε-hó-ta,) Sp., 1547—1616.
Cesare, Ɛe-sq́-*r*a, Giuseppe, Cavalieri di, *hist* Italy, 1783—
Chalmers, Ɛám-erz, Thomas, D.D., L-L.D., *pulpit or* and *div* Scotland, 1780—d.
Chambers, Ɛám-berz, Wm. and Robt., *pubs* and *essayists*, Scot., 1800— and 1801—
Chambord, Σam-bó*r*d, Henri Chas., Duke of Bordeaux, etc., *rep* of the house of Bourbon, 1820—
Chamier, Σam-εr, Fred., *nov* Eng., 1796— [1756—d.
Champe, Σomp, John, Am. *soldier*,
Changarnier, Σañ-gq*r*-ni-a, Gen., *gen* Fr. Army, 1809—
Channing, Ɛán-iŋ, William Ellery, Unitarian *div* and *moral phil*, R. I., 1780—d.
Chantrey, Sir Francis, *sculp* and *ben of art*, Eng., 1781—1841.

Chapman, John G., *artist*, Va.
Chapin, Rev. E. H., LL.D., *pulpit or* and *au*, N-Y., 1814—
Charlemagne, Σąr-lẹ-mań, *k* Fr. and Ger., 8th cen.
Charles, name given to numerous *ks* of Europe; the most prominent of which in history is Charles the XII., of Sweden, who ascended the throne in 1697, at the age of fifteen, and was killed 1718.
Charon, Єá-ron, *fab* ferryman of hell.
Chase, Єas, Samuel, *j* U. S. Sup. Ct., Md., 1741—1811.
Chase, Salmon P., *st* and *gov* Ohio.
Chasles, Σas-la, Victor E. P., *wr* Fr., 1800—
Chateaubriand, Σa-tó-bri-ańd, François A., Vicomte De, French *au*, 1769—1848.
Chatham, Єát-am, William Pitt, Earl of, *or* and *st* Eng., 1708—1778.
Chatterton, Єát-er-ton, Thomas, *au* Eng., 1752—1770.
Chaucer, Єé-ser, Geoffrey, father of English poetry, 1328—1400.
Cheever, Rev. Geo. B., *div* and *au*, Maine, 1807—
Chelard, Σel-ąrd, Andre H. J. B., *mus comp* Fr., 1789—
Cherubini, Σąr-ẹ-bi-nε, Lugi C. Z. S., *mus comp* Fr., 1760—1842.
Chesterfield, Philip D. Stanhope, Earl of, *st* Eng., 1694—1773.
Chevalier, Σẹv-a-li-á, Michel, Fr. *wr*, 1806— [Fr., 1786———.
Chevreul, Σẹ-vr-ẹl, M. Eugene, *chem*,
Choate, Єοt, Rufus, *law* Mass., 1799—
Chodzko, *H*ądʒ-kο, Jacques L., *hist*, Poland, 1800—
Chomiakof, Σom-a-kof, Alexei S., *poet* and *prose wr* Rus.
Chotek, *H*ó-tek, *mus comp* Ger., 1800—
Christina, Kris-té-ną, *queen* Sweden, from 1633 to 1654, when she resigned.
Chrysostom, Kris-ós-tom, John, *bp* of Constantinople in 398, —407.
Cibber, Colley, *comedian*, Eng., 1671—1757.
Cibrario, Єε-brą-rε-ο, Luigi, *hist wr* Fr., 1802—
Cicero, Sis-er-ο, Marcus Tullius, Roman *phil*, *or* and *st*, 107—44 B. C.
Cincinnatus, Sin-sin-á-tus, Lucius Quintus, Roman *dictator*, 456—376 B. C.
Circe, Sẹr-sε, *fab* an enchantress.
Civiale, Siv-i-ál, Jean, *sur* Fr., 1792—
Clair, Arthur St., *gen* Am. army 1734—1818.
Clairaut, Kląr-ó, Alexis C., *math* Fr., 1713—1765.
Clarendon, Klár-en-don, Ed. Hyde, Earl of, *st* and *hist* Eng., 1608—1674.
Clark, Wm., Am. *st* and *explo* Va., 1770—1838.
Clark, Dr. Adam, *bib commen* Ireland, 1760—1832.
Clarke, Dr. Samuel, *met div* Eng, 1675—1729.
Clarkson, Thomas, *philan* and *au* Eng., 1760—1846.
Claudius, Klé-di-us, I. and II., Roman *emps*, d. A. D. 54 and 271.
Clay, Henry, *st* and *or* Ky., 1777—1852.
Clay, Cassius M., *anti-slavery speaker*, Ky., 1810— [1773.
Clayton, John, Am. *bot* and *au*, 1686—
Cleanthes, Klε-án-ϑεz, *stoic phil* Athens, fl. 240 B. C.
Clement, name of 14 Papal rulers.
Cleopatra, Klε-ο-pá-trα, *queen* Egypt, fl. 40 B. C.
Clinton, De Witt, *gov* N-Y., and distinguished for his enterprise in public improvements, 1769—1828.
Clinton, Geo., *gov* N-Y., V-Pres. U. S. to Thos. Jefferson and Jas. Madison, 1739—1812.
Clinton, Henry, *maj-gen* Brit. army, —1795.
Cloquet, Klο-ka, Jules G., Fr. *ph*, 1790
Cobbet, William, *wr* Eng., 1762—1835.
Cobden, Richard, M. P., *free trade adv* Eng., 1800—
Coke, Sir Edward, *commen on law*, and *chief justice*, Eng., 1552—1634.
Colbert, Jean B., *st* Fr., 1619—1683.
Coleridge, Kól-rij, Samuel Taylor, *poet* and *meta* Eng., 1772—1834.
Collier, Kól-yer, John Payne, *crit* and *compiler*, Eng., 1789—
Colton, Calvin, *cler* and *au* Mass.
Collins, Wm., *poet*, Eng., 1720—1756.
Columbus, Christopher, *disc* of the Western continent, an Italian, 1435—1506.
Combe, Kοm, Andrew, M. D., *med wr* and *phren* Scot., 1797—1847.
Combe, Geo., *champion of phil* and *phren* Scot., 1788—
Comte, Komt, Auguste, founder of what is termed *positive philosophy*, Fr., 1797—
Condillac, Kon-dεl-yák, Etienne Bonnet De, *meta* Fr., 1715—1780.
Condorcet, Koń-der-sa, Marie Jean A., *math* and *pol wr* Fr., 1743—1794.
Confucius, Kon-fų-ʃi-us, Chinese *phil*, 551 B. C.

Congreve, Kóŋ-grɛv, Wm., *poet* and *humorist*, Eng., 1669—1729.
Constant De Rebecque, Koṅ-staṅt Dẹ Rẹ-bak, Benj., Fr. *pol, au* and *poet*, 1767—1831.
Constantin, Abraham, Swiss *porcelain pt*, 1785—
Constantine, Kón-stan-tịn, the Great, first Christian *emp* Romans, 272—337; succeeded by twelve others.
Cook, Capt. James, Brit. *nav*, 1728—1779, killed. [1812.
Cooke, Geo. Fred., *tragic actor*, 1756—
Cooper, Jas. Fenimore, Am. *nov* N-J., 1789—1851.
Cooper, Thos. Sidney, *art* Eng., 1803—
Copernicus, Kɷ-pẹ́r-ni-kus, Nicolas, (*or* Zepernich,) *ast* Prus., 1473—1543.
Corbiere, Kər-bi-ąr, Edward, *poet* and *nov* Fr., 1795—
Corday, Kər-da, Charlotte, French *repub martyr*, 1768—1793, guillotined.
Corelli, Kor-él-ɛ, Arcangelo, *found* Roman school of music, 1653—1713.
Coriolanus, Kɷ-ri-ɷ-lá-nus, C. Marcius, Roman *capt*, banished and killed as traitor.
Cormenin, Kə́r-mẹ-náṅ, M., *pol wr* Fr., 1789—
Corneille, Kər-na-ɛ, Pierre, *wr* Fr., 1606—1684.
Cornelius, Kər-ná-lɛ-us, Peter Von, *art* Ger., 1787—
Cornwallis, Chas., Lord, Brit. *gen* in American Revolution, 1738—1805.
Correggio, Kor-á-jɷ, *pt* It., 1493—1534.
Cortez, Kər-táŧ, Hernando, Spanish *conq* of Mexico, 1485—1547.
Corwin, Thomas, Am. *st* Ohio.
Corvin-Wiersbitzky, Kər-fɛn-Vɛrz-bits-ki, Otto J. B. Von, *hist wr* Ger., 1810—
Cotta, Kót-ą, Bernhard, *geol* Ger., 1808
Cousin, Kɷ-sáṅ, Victor, *meta phil* Fr., 1791—
Couthon, Kɷ-toṅ, Georges, French *jacobin*, 1756—guillotined. [—1800.
Cowper, Kɤ-per, Wm., *poet* Eng., 1731
Cox, David, *pt* Eng., 1783—
Crabbe, Krab, Geo., *poet* Eng., 1754—1832.
Cranmer, Thomas, Eng. *archbp*, martyr to protestantism, 1489—1555.
Crawford, Wm. Harris, Am. *st* and *j* Va., 1772—1834.
Crawford, Thomas, Am. *sculp* N-Y., 1814—
Cremieux, Kra-mɛ-ẹ, M., French *leg* and *min of justice*.
Crittenden, Krít-en-den, John J., Am. *st* Ky., b. about 1792—
Crœsus, Kré-sus, *ruler* Lydia, 548 B. C.
Croker, John Wilson, *pol* and *au* Eng., 1780— [Ireland.
Croly, Rev. Dr. Geo., *poet, au* and *cler*
Cromwell, Oliver, *Lord Protector*, Great Britain, 1599—1659.
Cruden, Krɷ́-den, Alexander, *au* Concordance Scripture, 1701—1770.
Cruikshank, Krúk-ʃaŋk, Geo., *art* and *cari* Eng., 1794—
Cruveilhier, Krẹ-val-i-a, Jean, *med prof* and *au* Fr., 1791—
Csaplovics, Ȼop-lɷ-viç, Johanŋ, *au* Hungary, 1780—
Csaszar, Ȼo-sąr, Franz, *prose wr* and *poet* Hungary, 1807—
Cubitt, Sir Wm., *engin* Eng., 1785—
Cudworth, Kúd-wurŧ, Ralph, *phil* Eng., 1617—1688. [1790.
Cullen, Wm., M. D., *ph* Scot., 1712—
Culpeper, Kúl-pep-er, Thomas, Lord, *gov* Va., —1719.
Cupid, Kų́-pid, *fab* son of Mars and Venus; the god of love, smiles, &c.
Curran, Kur-án, John Philpot, *bar, or* and *patriot*, Ireland, 1750—1817.
Curtis, George W., Am. *au* and *lect* N-Y.
Curtius, Kɷr-ti-ɯs, Ernst, *archæ* Ger., 1814—
Curtius, George, *philol* Ger., 1820—
Cusa, Kẹ-są, Nicholas De, *astr*, 1401—1464.
Custine, Kẹs-tɛn, Aristolphe, Marquis de, French *nov, poet* and *trav*, 1793—
Cuvier, Kẹ-vi-a, Georges Leopold Ch. Fred., *nat* Fr., 1769—1832. (The most distinguished naturalist the world ever produced.)
Cybulski, Tsib-úl-ski, Adelbert, Sclavic *au*, 1812—
Cyclops, Sị́-klops, *fab* Vulcan's workmen, with only one eye, in the middle of their forehead.
Cynthia, Sín-ŧi-a, poetically applied to the moon.
Cypria, Síp-ri-a, Cytherea, Siŧ-ɛ-ré-a, *fab* titles of Venus.
Cyrus, Sị́-rus, *found* ancient Persian empire, —530 B. C.
Czartoryiski, Ȼąr-tɷr-i-és-kɛ, Adam, Prince, Polish *nob* and *patriot*, 1770—
Czerny, Tsẹ́r-ni, Karl, *comp* Ger., 1791—
Czetz, Tsets, Johann, Hungarian *au*, 1822—
Czuczor, Tsɷ-tsɷr, Geo., Hungarian *prose wr, poet* and *lin*, 1800—

# D

Daguerre, Da-gâr, L. J. M., *pt* and inventer of Daguerreotyping, Fr., 1789—1851. [1788——.
Dahl, Dâl, Johann C. C., *l-pt* Nor.,
Dahl, Dâl, Waladimir I., *au* Rus.
Dahlborn, Dâl-born, Anders G., *ento* Swed., 1806—
Dahlmann, Dâl-mân, Fred. Christoph, *prof hist* and *pol science*, at Bonn, Ger., 1785—
D'Alembert, Dal-ám-ber, Jean Le Rond, *math* and *ast* Fr. 1717—1783.
Dallas, Dál-as, George M., Am. *st* and *min* Pa., 1792—
Dalton, Dól-ton, John D. C. L., *chem* and *math* Eng., 1767—1844.
Damon, Dá-mon, Pythagorean *phil* and friend of Pythias.
Dampier, Dám-per, Wm. *nav* and *nat* Eng., 1652—d.
Dana, Dá-na, Francis LL. D., Am. *st* Mass., 1742—1811.
Dana, Richard H., son of F. D., *poet* and *nov* Mass., 1787—
Dana, Richard H. jr., son of R. H. D., *law* and *au* Mass. [Fr., 1800——.
Dantan, Dáñ-tañ, Jean-Pierce, *sculp*
Dante, Dán-ta, Alighieri, It. *poet*, 1265—1321.
Danton, Dán-ton, Georges Jacques, *st* and *demagogue*, Fr., 1759—1794.
D'Antonelle, Dán-ton-el, Pierre A., Marquis, Fr. *pat*, 1747—*ex.* 1819.
Darius, Dá-ri-us, three *ks* of Persia, 404 B. C.
Darley, Dâr-li, Felix O. C., *art* of N-Y. City, born in Phila. 1822—
Darwin, Dâr-win, Erasmus, *poet* and *bot* Eng., 1731—1802.
Daubenton, Do-bañ-toñ, Louis J. M. *anat* and *nat* Fr., 1716—1799.
D'Aubigne, Do-bén, J. H. Merle, *pres.*, the school, Geneva, and *au* History of the Reformation.
Daumer, Dé-mer, Geo. Fred. *phil wr* Ger., 1800—
Daumier, Dó-mi-á, Henri, Fr. *caracaturist*, 1810. [1748—1825.
David, Dá-ved, Jacques Louis, *pt* Fr.,
David, Pierre Jean, *sculp* Fr., 1793—
David, Felicien, *mus comp* Fr., 1810—
David, Ferdinand, *viol* Ger., 1810—
Davis, Dá-vis, Andrew Jackson, *seer* and *clair* N-Y., 1826—
Davy, Dá-vi, Sir Humphry, Bart., *chem phil* Eng., 1778—1829.
Dawson, Dé-son, Geo., *lec* Eng., 1821—
Deane, Den, Silas, U. S. *min* to Fr., —1789.
Dearborn, Dér-born, Henry, *major gen* U. S. army, N-H., 1751—1829.
Decamps, Da-kámp, Alex. G., a Fr. *genre* and *l-pt* 1803—
Decatur, De-ká-tur, Stephen, *com* U. S. Navy, Md., 1759—1820.
De Foe, De Fo, Daniel, *au* "Robinson Crusoe," etc., Eng., 1661—1731.
Deger, Dá-*her*, Ernst, *pt* Ger., 1809.
Dehn, Dan, Siegfried W., Ger. *wr* on the theory of *mus*, 1799.
Delaine, De-lán, John, *jour* and *ed* "London Times."
Delambre, De-lám-br, M., *astr* Fr., 1749—1822. [1797——.
Delaroche, De-lar-oʃ, Paul, *pt* Fr.,
Demetrius, De-mé-tri-us, *phil* Athens, 284 B. C. [Thrace, 460 B. C.
Democritus, De-mók-ri-tus, *phil* of
Demoivre, De-mwó-vr, Eng. *math* and *au* 1667—1754. [ens, 370 B. C.
Demosthenes, De-mós-then-ez, *or* Ath-
Denman, Dén-man, Lord Thomas, Eng. *j* and *legis*, 1779—1854.
Denmark, Dén-mârk, Charles Christian Frederick, King of, 1808—
Derby, Dér-bi, Edward Geof. S. Stanley, *st* Eng., 1799—
Descartes, Da-kâr-ta, Rene, *met phil* Fr., 1596—1650.
Desmoulins, Da-moo-láñ, Benedict Camille, Fr. *repub or* and *martyr*, 1762—1794. [City, 1794——.
Dewey, Dû-i, Orville, D. D., *div* Wash.
De Quincey, De Kwín-si, Thomas, *phil wr* of Eng.
De La Beche, De La Bes, Sir Henry Thomas, *geol* Eng., 1796—
Diagoras, Dí-ág-o-ras, surnamed the Atheist, *fl* 412 B. C.
Dick, Dik, Thomas, LL. D., *wr* on *pop science*, Scot., 1772—
Dickens, Dík-enz, Chas., Eng. *au*, 1812—
Dickinson, Dík-in-son, Daniel S., *pol* of N-Y., 1800—
Diderot, Díd-er-o, Dionysius, Fr. *poet* and *wr* on physics, 1713—1784.
Didot, Dé-do, Firman, *inv* of Stereotyping, Fr., 1764—1836.
Didymus, Díd-i-mus, of Alexandria, *wr* 4th century.
Diez, Dets, Friedr. Christian, *foun* of romance, *philol* Ger., 1794.

Dilke, Dilk, Charles Went., once *ed* and now *propri* of the London "Athenæum," 1789—
Dilworth, Díl-wurt, Thomas, *teacher* and *compiler* of school-books, Eng., —1781.
Dingelstedt, Díŋ-el-stedt, Franz, *poet* of Ger., 1814—
Dioclesian, Dį-ɷ-klé-ʃi-an, Caius Valerius, Roman *emp* who persecuted Christians, 233—314.
Diodorus Siculus, Dį-ɷ-dó-rus Sík-yų-lus, *hist* Sicily, *fl* in the times of Cæsar and Augustus.
Diogenes, Dį-ój-en-ez, *phil* Babylon, 200 B. C.
Diogenes, the Cynic, an austere *phil*, who for a time lodged in a tub, b. 413 B. C.
Dionysius, Dį-ɷ-níʃ-i-us, I., *tyrant* of Sicily, died 366 B. C.
Dionysius, Halicarnassensis, *hist* and *critic* of antiquity. [1766—1848.
D'Israeli, Diz-ra-él-į, Isaac, *au* Eng.,
D'Israeli, (sometimes written Disraeli,) Benj., *au* and chancellor of exchequer, Eng., 1805—
Doddridge, Dód-rij, Philip, D. D., *div* Eng., 1702—1751.
Donizetti, Don-idz-ét-e, Gaetano, *mus comp* It., 1798—1848.
Dorn, Dɷrn, Heinrich Lud. E., *mus comp* Ger., 1804—
Doughty, Dót-i, Thomas, Am. *l-pt* Pa., 1793—
Douglas, Dúg-las, Frederick, *ed* and *or*, who was a slave until 21 years old, N-Y. [1813—
Douglas, Stephen Arnold, *pol* Ill.,
Dow, Dɤ, Gerard, Dutch *geure pt*, 1613 —1680. [er, —1834.
Dow, Lorenzo, an eccentric Am. preach-
Dozy, Dóts-i, Reinhart, *orientalist* Ger., 1820———. [1546—1596.
Drake, Drak, Sir Francis, Eng. *nav*,
Drake, Freidrich, *sculp* Ger., 1805—
Draper, Dráp-er, John Wm., *ph* and *chem* N-Y., 1811—
Draysen, Drá-sen, Joh. Gustav, Ger. *hist*, 1808— [—1700.
Dryden, Drį-den, John, *poet* Eng., 1631
Dubner, Dɷ́b-ner, Frederick, *phil* and *critic* Ger., 1802— [1805———.
Duchatel, Deʃ-a-tél, M., *min* Fr.,
Ducpetiaux, Dék-pa-tɷ, Edouard, Belgian *philan* and *wr* 1804—
Duller, Dúl-er, Edouard, *poet*, *nov* and *hist* Ger., 1809—
Dumas, De-mą, Jean Baptiste, *chem* Fr., 1800— [1803———.
Dumas, Alexander, *dram* and *nov* Fr.,
Dumont D'Urville, De-móṅ Der-vél, Jules S. C., Fr. *nav* 1791—1842.
Duncker, Dɷ́ŋ-ker, Max. Wolfgang, Ger. *hist* 1812—
Dunglison, Dúŋ-gli-son, R., M. D., LL. D., *prof mat med*, *au*, etc., Pa., born Eng., 1798—
Dunlap, Dún-lap, Wm., Am. *art* and *wr* N-J., 1760—1839.
Duntzer, Dɷ́nts-er, Joh. Heinr. Joseph, Ger. *philol* and *hist* 1813—
Dupin, De-paṅ, Andre M. J. J., *st* Fr., a champion of the middle classes.
Dupont De L'Eure, De-poṅ De Ler, *st* Fr., 1770—
Dupont, Pierre, *poet* Fr., 1826—
Dupuytren, De-pe-i-tran, Wm., Baron, *sur* Fr., 1777—1835.
Duran, Dɷ-rąn, Augustin, Sp. *critic*, 1800—
Durand, Dɷ-rąnd, Asher Brown, *art* and *pres* of the National Academy of design, N-J., 1796—
Durer, Dɷ-rąr, Albrecht, Ger. *pt* 1471 —1529.
Dwight, Dwįt, Timothy, S. T. D., LL. D., *poet*, *au* and *pres* Yale College, 1752—1818. [1797———.
Dyce, Dįs, Alex., Eng. *au* and *ed*

# E.

Eastlake, Est'lak, Sir Charles Lock, *pt* Eng., 1800—
Eckersberg, Ek'erz-berg, Christoph Wilhelm, *hist pt* Den., 1783—
Edgeworth, Ej'wurt, Richard Lovell, *phil* and inventor of the old telegraph, 1744—1817.
Edgeworth, Maria, daughter of above, *au* Eng., 1767—1849.
Edmonds, Ed'mondz, Francis W., *banker* and *art* N-Y., 1806—
Edmondson, Ed'mond-son, Joseph, *heraldic wr* Eng., —1786.
Edward, Ed'ward, name of numerous Saxon kings. [*div au* —1758.
Edwards, Ed'wardz, Jonathan, Am.
Edwards, Jonathan, D. D., son of the above, *scholar*, *theo* and *wr* —1801.

Egerton, Ej'er-ton, Francis, earl of Ellesmere, *au* and *patron* of the arts, Eng., 1800— [1781——.
Eichhorn, Ik'hern, Karl Fried., *st* Ger.,
Elizabeth, E-liz-a-beth, queen of Eng., 1533—1603. Also the name of other European queens.
Ellenborough, El'en-bur-o, Ewd. Law, Lord, Eng. *law* and *j*, 1748—1818.
Ellery, El'er-i, Wm., *signer Dec. of Ind.*, *mem* of Cong. R. I., 1727—1820.
Elliot, El'i-ot, Charles L., Am. *por-pt* N-Y., 1822—
Ellis, El'is, John, *nat* Eng., 1710—1776.
Ellis, Alex. John, one of the inventors of the phonetic alphabet, and a *philol*, Eng., 18—
Ellsworth, Elz'wurth, Oliver, LL. D., *chief justice* Sup. Ct. U. S., Conn., 1745—1807.
Emerson, Em'er-son, Ralph Waldo, Am. *meta* and *au* Mass., 1803—
Emmet, Em'et, Robert, *repub* and *martyr*, Ir., 1780—*ex.* 1803.
Emmet, Thomas Addis, *law* and *or* Ir., latterly of N-Y., 1764—1827.
Encke, Eŋk'a, Johann Franz, *astr* director of the Royal Observatory, and Secretary of the Academy of Sciences, Berlin, Prus., 1791—
Engelbrecht, Eŋ'el-brekt, John, Ger. *visionary* 1549—1642.
Epictetus, Ep-ik-té-tus, *phil* and *au* of great humility, born 68 A. D.
Epicurus, Ep-i-kú-rus, *phil* who taught that the happiness of man consists in pleasure, born 340 B. C.
Epimenides, Ep-i-mén-i-dez, *anc poet* and *phil*, Greece, B. C.
Erasmus, E-ráz-mus, Desiderius, *schol* and *au* Hol., 1467—1536.
Erebus, Er'e-bus, *fab* an infernal deity, son of Chaos and Nox; river of hell.
Ericsson, Er'ik-son, John, Swed. *mechanician*, inventor (in U. S.) of a "coloric engine," 1803—
Erostratus, E-rós-tra-tus, *fab*, he who, to perpetuate his name, set fire to the celebrated temple of Diana at Ephesus.
Erskine, Ers'kin, Thomas, Baron, *law* and *or* Scot., 1748—1823.
Eschenmayer, Eʃ'en-mir, C. A., *prof*, *phil*, and *au*, Ger., —1822.
Espartero, Es-par-tá-ro, General, ex-regent of Sp.
Etty, Et'i, Wm. R. A., *pt* of Eng., 1787—1849.
Euler, Yú-ler, Leonard, *analist*, posthumous *wr* on math. and physical sciences, Fr., 1707—1783.
Euclid, Yú-klid, *math* and *ast*, when born, and in what country, we have no account; but he *fl* about 277 B. C.
Eunomius, Yu-nó-mi-us, *foun* of a Christian sect, died 394.
Euripides, Yu-ríp-i-dez, Gr. *poet* 240 B. C. [Orpheus.
Eurydice, Yu-ríd-i-se, *fab*, the wife of
Eusebius, Yu-sé-bi-us, Pamphilus, *ecc hist*, Palestine, bishop of Cæsarea, died in 338.
Eustachius, E-o-sta-ké-us, *or* Yu-sta-ké-us, Bartholomew, It. *anat*, —1570.
Eutropius, Yu-tró-pi-us, Flavius, It. *sophist* and *hist*, *fl* 364.
Evadne, E-vád-ne, daughter of Mars and Thebe, who threw herself on the funeral pile of her husband Cataneus, from affection.
Evelyn, Ev'e-lin, John, *nat* and *wr* on archi. and numismatics, Eng., 1620—1706.
Everett, Ev'er-et, Edward, Am. *or*, *schol* and *dip*, Mass., 1794—
Ewbank, Yú-bank, Thomas, *wr* on prac. mechanics, and U. S. com. of patents, N-Y., 1792—
Exmouth, Eks'muth, Edward, Pellew, Lord, *com* Br. navy, 1757—1832.
Eyck, Ik, Huber and John Van, *pts* of Bruges, 14th cen.

# F.

Fabricius, Fa-bré-ki-us, Jean Chre., Ger. *ento*, 1742—1807.
Fahrenheit, Fá-ren-hit, Gabriel D., *phil* and inventor of the Thermometer and Barometer, Prus., 1686—1736.
Fairfax, Fár-faks, Ewd., *poet* and *classic trans*, Eng., —1632.
Fairfax, Thomas, Lord, officer in the times of the parlimentary revolution, 1608—1671.
Falconer, Fál-kon-er, W., Eng. *chem* and *disc* of the property of carbonic acid gas, 1743—1824.
Fallopius, Fal-ó-pi-us, Gabriel, *ph*, *bot*, *anat* and *dis* of what are called "Fallopian tubes," Modena, 1490—1563.

Faraday, Fą̈r-a-da, Michael, Eng. *chem* 1794— [1779—1853.
Farrar, Fár-qr, John, Am. *math* Mass.,
Fatio Duiller, Fą̈-si-o Dęl-yę, N., *math* and *art* Fr., 1664—1753.
Faucher. Fó-ʃąr, Leon, *ex-min* of Fr.
Faust, Fqst, John, *theo* and *chem* of Ger., 15th. Cen.
Faustus *or* Fust, Fés-tus *or* Fust, John, one of the inventors of printing, in 1460, in Ger., —1466.
Fellenberg, Fél-en-bęrg, Philippe Emanuel De, *agri, bene* of Edu., and *au* Switz., 1771—d.
Fenelon, Fañ-a-lóñ, (*or* Fén-ε-lon,) Francis De S. De La Motte, *priest* and *au* Fr., 1651—1684.
Ferdinand, Fęr-di-nand, tittle of several *emps* of Ger., and *ks* of Sp.
Ferguson, Fęr-gų-son, Adam, *phil* and *au* Scot., 1724—1816. [1774.
Ferguson, Robert, *poet* of Scot., 1750—
Fermat, Fer-mą̈, Pierre, Fr. *math* 1595—1667.
Fessenden, Fes-én-den, Thomas G., *au* N-H., 1771—1837. [Congress, Me.
Fessender, Wm. Pitt, *st* and *mem* of
Feuillee, Fóly-a, Louis, *nat* Fr., —1732.
Fichte, Fík-ta, Johann Got., *meta phil* Ger., 1762—1814.
Fielding, Féld-iŋ, Henry, *nov* and *dram poet* Eng., 1706—1754.
Filicaija, Fil-ε-kq-é-yq, Vincenzo, Da, *poet* Florence, 1642—1707.
Fillmore, Fíl-mor, Millard, *V-Pres* U. S., with Gen. Taylor, after whose death he served as Pres., bet. 1850 and 1854, b. 1800—
Finiquerra, Fin-εk-o-á-rq, Tommaso, *inv* of metal plate printing, Florence, 1426—1464.
Fitch, Fiç, John, *inv* of the steamboat, Conn., 1743—1798. [1646—1719.
Flamsteed, Flám-stεd, John, *astr* Eng.,
Flaxman, Fláks-man, John, *sculp* Eng., 1755—1826.
Fleischer, Flį-ʃer, Heinr. Leber., *prof* oriental lang., Leipzig, Ger., 1801—
Fletcher, Fléç-er, John and F. Beaumont, *dram wrs* Eng., 1579—1616, 1585—1625. [1760—1814.
Flinders, Flín-derz, Mathew, Eng. *nav*
Flora, Fló-rq, *fab*, goddess of flowers.
Flores, Fló-rεz, General Don Juan Jose, founder and preserver of the republic of Ecuador, 1800—
Fludd, Flud, Robert, Eng. *ph* and Rosicrucian *phil*, 1574—1637.
Fonblanque, Foñ-blañk, Albany, *jour* Eng., 1800—

Fontaine, Foñ-tan, Jean De La, *poet* and *wr* Fr., 1621—1695.
Fontenelle, Foñ-ta-nel, Bernard Le B. De, *lil savant* and *math* Fr., 1657—1757. [1640.
Ford, Ford, John, *dram* Eng., 1586—
Forrest, Fór-est, Edwin, Am. *actor*, Pa., 1806—
Forster. Fórs-ter, John Reinhold, *nat, philol* and *geog* Prussia, 1729—1798.
Forster, John, *au* and *jour*, *ed* of the Examiner, Eng., 1812—
Förster, Fęr-ster, Ernst J., *art* and *wr* Ger., 1800—
Fortuna, Fer-tų̈-nq, *fab* goddess of happiness, &c., said to be blind.
Fosbrooke, Fós-bruk, Rev. Th. Dudley, *antiq wr* and Saxon scholar, Eng., 1770—1842.
Foscolo, Fos-kó-lo, Ugo, It. *poet, dram wr* and *lit savant*, 1776—1827.
Fourier, Fó-ri-a, Charles, *socialist* and *au* Fr., 1772—1837.
Fox, Foks, W. J., an Eng. *pol* and *lect* 1786—
Fox, Chas. James, *st* Eng., 1749—1806.
Fox, George, *found* of the Society of Friends, Eng., 1624—1690.
Francia, Frqn-çé-q, Ruibolini, *pt* of It., 1450—1518.
Francia, Frqn-sé-q, Don Gasper R. De, *dictator* of Paragua, 1757—1840.
Francis, Frán-sis, I., II., etc., *emps* Ger., and *ks* of Fr., from 15th to the 19th century.
Francis, Philip, *clas trans, trage,* and *pol wr* Eng., —1773.
Francis, Frán-sis, John W., M. D., LL. D., *ph* and *med wr* N-Y., 1789—
Franklin, Fráŋk-lin, Benj. Am. *moralist, phil,* and *st*, *signer Dec. of Ind.*, Pa., born in Boston, 1706—1790.
Franklin, Fráŋk-lin, Sir John, Eng. Artic *nav*, 1786—per. Arc. reg., 1852-4.
Frauenhofer, Frŏ-en-hóf-er, Jos. Von, *optician* and *phil* Ger., 1787—1826.
Frederick, Fréd-er-ik, II., *k* of Prussia, called Frederick the Great, b. 1712, began to reign 1740, died 1786; this is also the title of numerous German emperors from the 12th to the 14th cen., also of other Eu. monarchies.
Freiligrath, Frį-li-grqt, Ferd, *poet* of Ger., 1810—
Fremont, Frε-mónt, John C., *explorer* and *contr* to the Physical Sciences, Cal., 1813— [1675—1728.
Friend, John, *ph* and *med wr* Eng.,
Frisi, Fré-sε, Paolo, *math phil* and *astr au* Milan, 1727—1784.

Frobisher, Fró-biʃ-er, Sir Martin, Eng. *nav* —1594.
Frost, Frost, John, *off* Am. army, Me., 1738—1810.
Frost, Frost, Wm. Ed., *pt* Eng., 1810—
Fry, Frį, Mrs. Elizabeth, *philan* Eng., 1780—1844.
Führich, Fę-rik, *or* Fé-rik, Jos., *hist pt* Ger., 1800—
Fulton, Fúl-ton, Robert, Am. *engin*, and first to practically apply steam to vessels, Pa., 1765—1815.
Furies, Fų-riz, *fab*, the three daughters of Nox and Acheron, with hair composed of snakes, and armed with whips, chains, &c.
Furness, Fúr-nes, Rev. Dr. Wm. Henry, *div* and *wr* Pa.

# G.

Gaertner, Gą̇rt-ner, Joseph, *bot* Ger., 1732—1791.
Gagern, Gą̇-hern, Baron Hein. Von, premier *min* Ger., 1799—
Gainsborough, Gánz-bur-ω, Thomas R. A., *pt* Eng., 1727—1788.
Galen, Gá-len, Claudian, Greek *ph*, *sur*, and *au* of 500 books on physic, 131—201.
Galiano, Gą-lε-ą̇-nω, Don A. A., *review*, *pam*, *poet* and *or* Sp., 1789—
Galileo, Gal-i-lé-ω, Galilei, *astr* and inventer of the telescope, Italy, 1564—1642.
Gall, Gąl, Francis Joseph, *found* Phrenology, Ger., 1758—1828.
Gallatin, Albert, *st* Pa., 1761—1849.
Galvani, Gal-vą̇-nε, Luigi, *ph* and *physiol*, and *disc* galvanism, Italy, 1737—1798.
Gama, Gą̇-mą, Vasco De, *nav* Portugal, —1525.
Gambart, Gam-bą̇r, Jean F. A., *astr* France, 1800—1836.
Gans, Gąns, Edward, *jurist* and *legal au* Prussia, 1798—1839.
Garcia Gutierrez, Gąr-θé-ą Gω-tε-á-reθ, Don Antonio, *dram* Sp., 1813—
Garden, Alex., *bot* and *zool* Scot., 1730—1791.
Garnett, Dr. Thos., Eng. *ph* and *nat phil*, 1766—1802.
Garrick, David, *actor* Eng., 1716—1779.
Garrison, Wm. Lloyd, leader of the Abolition party, and *ed* "Liberator," Mass.
Gartner, Friedr. Von, *arch* and *wr* Ger., 1792—
Gassendi, Ga-sáṅd, Pierre, *meta phil* Fr., 1592—1655.
Gates, Horatio, *maj-gen* Am. army, Va., 1728—1806.
Gatterer, Gą-tą̇r-er, John Chris., Ger. *hist*, —1799.
Gauss, Gʊs, *ast* Ger., 1777—1855.
Gavard, Ga-vą̇rd, Hyacinthe, *anat* France, 1753—1802.
Gavarni, Ga-vą̇r-nε, the *nom de crayon* of a French *artist*, 1801—
Gavazzi, Ga-vą̇t-sε, Padre A., Italian *church ref*, 1809—
Gay, John, *ballad wr* Eng., 1688—1732.
Gay Lussac, Ga Lų-sák, N. F., *chem*, and discoveror of chemical principles and compounds, Fr., —1850.
Ged, Wm., *inv* stereotyping, Eng., —1749.
Genii, Jé-ni-į, *fab* guardian angels.
Geoffroy, Ʒa-of-r-wó, Stephen F., *ph* and *chem* Fr., 1672—1731.
Geoffroy St. Hilaire, — Saṅ Hil-ą̇r, Etienne, *zool* Fr., 1772—1844.
George, name of several *ks* Eng., from 16th to 18th centuries.
Gerando, Ʒa-ráṅd, Marie Joseph De, French *meta*, 1772—1842.
Gerard, Jε-rą̇rd, Alex., *div* and *essa* Scot., 1728—1795.
Gericault, Ʒąr-ε-kωl, Jean L. T. A., *pt* Fr., 1790—1824.
Germany, J-B. Joseph Sebastin, Archduke of Austria, Ex-Regent of, 1782—
Gerry, Jér-i, Elbridge, V-Pres. U. S. to Jas. Madison; Mass., 1744—1814.
Gesenius, Ges-á-nε-us, Fred. Henry Wm., *philol* and *ori scholar* Ger., 1786—1812.
Gesner, Jés-ner, Abraham, M. D., *geol* [Nova Scotia.
Ghiberti, Gε-bér-tε, Lorenzo, Florentine *sculp*, 1381—1455.
Giardini, Jąr-dé-nε, Felice, *viol* Eng., 1716—1796.
Girardin, Ʒir-ąr-daṅ, Emile De, *jour*, and *ed* "La Presse," Paris, 1802—
Girardin, Saint-Marc, *jour* and *au* Fr., 1800—
Gibbon, Edward, *hist* Eng., 1737—1794.
Gibbons, Grinling, *carver in wood*, Holland, 1648—1721.

Gibbons, Orlando, *mus comp* Eng., 1583—d.
Gibson, John, *sculp* Eng., 1790—
Gifford, Wm., *poet* and *ed* Eng., 1756—1826.
Gilbert, Wm., Eng. *ph* and *exper phil*, 1540—1603.
Gilfillan, Rev. George, *critic* and *au* Scot., 1813—
Gil y Zarate, *Hel* ɛ Hqr-ʠ-ta, Don Antonio, Sp. *poet* and *dram*, 1793—
Gioberti, Jɷ-bę́r-tɛ, Vincento, Italian *ref* and *au*, 1803—
Girard, Jir-ʠrd, Stephen, *found* "Girard College," Phila., Pa., 1746—1831.
Gladstone, Rt. Hon. Wm. E., Eng. *st*, 1809—
Glauber, Glɤ-ber, John Randolph, Ger. *exp chem*, 16th cen.
Gleig, Glɛg, Rev. Geo. Robt., Eng. *au*, 1796—
Gleim, Glim, Fred. Wm. Louis, *poet* Ger., 1719—1813.
Glendower, Owen, last *prince* Wales, 1349—1415.
Gluck, Christoph, *comp mus* Ger., 1714—1787.
Godwin, Gód-win, William, *ref*, *essa*, *au*, etc., Eng., 1756—1836.
Godwin, Mary Wollstonecraft, *wr* on "rights of women," and on morals, educa. and pol., 1768—1797.
Godwin, Parke, Am. *essa* N-Y.
Goethe, Gę́-te, Johann Wolfgang Von, Ger. *poet* and *au*, 1749—1833.
Goldsmith, Oliver, Brit. *poet* and *prose wr*, 1728—1774.
Goodall, Fred., Eng. *pt*, 1822—
Goodrich, Samuel G., *au* and *pub* Conn., 1800—
Gordon, Lord George, a factious *st* Eng., 1750—1793, died in Newgate prison.
Gore, Christopher, Am. *st* Mass., 1758—1827.
Görgey, Gɷr-gę-y, Arthur, Hungarian *gen*, 1818—
Gorgons,—Medusa, Euryale, and Stheno, *fab*, who could change into stone those upon whom they looked.
Goszezynski, Gɷʃ-ҫins-ki, Seweryn, Polish *poet*, 1803—
Gough, Gof, Am. temperance *lec*.
Gould, Gɷld, John, Eng. *ornith*, 1804—
Gower, John, Eng. *law* and *poet*, 1320—1402.
Gräberg, Von Hemso, Grá-bęrg Fɷn Hém-sɷ, Jacob, Swedish *au*, 1776—
Gracchi, Grák-į, The, Tiberius and Caius, brothers, elected tribunes of the Roman people, secured a law by which all persons possessing more than 500 acres of land, should yield the surplus for the benefit of the poor citizens. Both suffered violent deaths by their enemies, 133 and 121 B. C.
Graham, Sir James Robt. Geo., Bart., Eng. *st*, 1792—
Gramont, Gra-móṅ, name of an illustrious French family.
Granville, G. G. L. Gower, Earl, Eng. *st*, 1815—
Grattan, Grát-an, Henry, Irish *st* and *law*, 1750—1820.
Gray, Thomas, Eng. *poet*, 1716—1771.
Gray, Asa, M. D., *nat* and *prof* at Cambridge, Mass., 1810—
Greece, Otho I., King of, 1815—crowned 1832.
Greeley, Horace, *jour*, and chief *ed* "N-Y. Tribune," 1811—
Greene, Nathaniel, *maj-gen* U. S. army, R. I., 1742—1785.
Greenough, Grḗn-ɷ, Horatio, Am. *sculp* Mass., 1805—1852.
Gregory, an illustrious Scotch family name, as well as names of numerous popes and saints of Rome.
Gregory, O. Gilbert, LL.D., *math* and *au* Eng., 1774—1841.
Grenville, Richard, Earl Temple, Eng. *st*, author of the American Stamp Act, and reputed by some as the original "Junius," 1711—1779.
Grenville, George, Eng. *st*, 1712—1770.
Grew, Nehemiah, Eng. *ph*, *bot* and *au*, 1628—1711.
Grey, Charles Earl, Eng. *st*, 1764—1845.
Grey, Lady Jane, a talented and beautiful English lady, 1537—exec. 1554.
Griffin, Edmund D., *wr* Pa., 1804—1830.
Grimke, Grím-kɛ, Thos. Smith, *law*, *au*, and *spell ref*, S. C., 1778—1834.
Grimm, Fred. M., Baron De, French *au*, 1723—1807.
Grimm, Jakob Lud., elder of the "Brothers Grimm," Ger. *au*, 1785—
Grimm, Wilhelm Karl, younger of the "Brothers Grimm," Ger. *au*, 1786—
Griswold, Roger, LL.D., *law*, *j* Sup. Ct., &c., Conn., —1812.
Griswold, Rufus Wilmot, D. D., Am. *biog* Vt., 1816—
Grote, George, *banker*, *pol ref* and *au*, Eng., 1794—
Grotefrend, Grɷ-ta-frend, Geo. Fried., Ger. *phil* and *antiq*, 1775—1853.
Grotius, Grɷ́-ʃi-us, Hugo, *jur*, *div* and *hist*, Holland, 1583—1645.

Guido, Gį-dœ, Aretinus, *monk*, beginning 11th cen., who introduced the present mode of writing music on the scale, and composing in different parts.
Guise, William, Eng. *div*, and *trans* of oriental languages, 1653—1683.
Guizot, Gę-zó, François-Pierre-G., Fr. *hist* and *ex-min*, 1787—
Gunter, Edmund, Eng. *math*, *ast*, and *inv* "Gunter's Scale," 1581—1626.
Gustavus Adolphus, *k* Sweden, 1594—crowned 1611—killed 1632.
Guttenberg, John, *disc* art of printing, Ger., 1400—1468.
Guy, Thos., *found* Guy's Hospital, London, and most liberal benefactor in England, —1724.
Guyon, Gę-i-óṅ, Madame Jeanne M. R. De La Mothe, Fr. *seer* and *au*, 1642—1717.
Guyon, Gœ-yón, General, *comman* in the patriotic Hungarian army, 1815—
Guyton De Morveau, Gę-i-tóṅ Dę Mer-vœ, Louis B., Fr. *chem* and *au*, 1736—1816.
Gutzkow, Góts-kœv, Karl, Ger. *au*, *jour* and *dram*, 1811—
Gyllenborg, Gęl-en-berg, Chas., Count, Swed. *sen* and *man of letters*, —1746.

# H.

Hagedorn, Hág-a-dern, Fred. Von, Ger. *poet* and *au*, 1708—1754.
Hahnemann, Háṅ-a-mąn, Sam'l, *found* Homœopathy, Ger., 1755—1843.
Haldane, Robert and James Alex., Eng. *navs*, 1764—1842, 1768—1851.
Hale, Sir Mathew, Eng. *j* and constitutional *law*, 1609—1676.
Hale, Nathan, *off* Am. army, and executed by the British, as a spy, 1776.
Halevy, Hál-av, Fromenthal, Fr. *mus comp*, 1800—
Haliburton, Judge, T. C., *hum au* Nova Scotia, *alias* "Sam Slick."
Halifax, Geo. Saville, Marquis of, Eng. *st*, 1630—1695.
Hall, Rev. Robt., *preacher*, Eng., 1764 [—1831.
Hall, Samuel C., Eng. *au*, and *ed* "London Art Journal." 1800—
Hall, James, *geol* N-Y., 1811—
Haller, Albert, M. D., *anat* and *physiol* Swit., 1708—1777.
Halley, Edmund, Eng. *ast*, 1656—1742.
Hallam, Henry, Eng. *hist*, 1778—
Halleck, Hál-ek, Fitz-Green, Am. *poet*, Conn., 1795—
Hamilton, Alexander, Am. *st*, *jur*, *financier*, etc., N-Y., 1757—1804, killed in a duel with Aaron Burr.
Hamilton, Sir Wm., Bart., Scotish *met phil*, and present Professor of Logic in the University of Edinburgh.
Hammerich, Hám-er-ɛh, Fred., Danish *poet* and *prose wr*, 1809—
Hampden, John, Brit. *st*, 1594—1643.
Hancock, John, LL.D., Am. *st*, *pres* of the Continental Congress, and the first to sign the Declaration of Independence; Mass., 1737—1793.
Handel, Háṅ-del, Geo. Fred., *mus comp* Ger., 1684—1759.
Hannibal, Carthaginian *gen*, who after numerous successful victories against the Romans, was defeated, and poisoned himself, 182 B. C.
Hanover, Geo.-Fred.-Alex.-Ch.-E.-Augustus, King of, 1819— commenced his reign 1851.
Harding, J. D., Eng. *art*, 1797—
Hare, Dr. Robt., M. D., M. A., P. S., *chem*, associate of the Smithsonian Institute, spiritualist, etc., Pennsylvania, 1781—
Haring, Hár-iŋ, Wilhelm, Ger. *nov*, 1798—
Harispe, Har-ɛsp, Marshal, Fr. *gen*, [1771———.
Harpies, *fab*, three monsters, with the faces of virgins, bodies of vultures, and hands of claws.
Harrison, Gen. Wm. Henry, ninth Pres. U. S., from Ohio; 1773—1841, a month after assuming his duties. John Tyler, V-Pres.
Hartley, David, Eng *meta* and *au*, 1705—1757.
Hartzenbusch, Art-ṫan-bóʃ, Don Juan Eugenio, Sp. *poet* and *dram*, 1806—
Harvard, John, *found* Harvard College, Mass., —1688.
Harvey, William, M. D., *disc* of the circulation of the blood, Eng., 1578—1657.
Hastings, Warren, Brit. East India *pol*, 1733—1818.
Hauy, Hœ. Rene Just, Fr. *mineralogist*, 1743—1822.
Hawes, Hez, Dr. Wm., *found* Royal Humane Society, Eng., 1736—1808.

Hawks. Heks, Francis L., D. D., LL.D., *pulpit or* and *div* N-Y., 1798—
Hawley, Joseph, *st* Mass., 1724—1788.
Hawthorne, Hé-torn, Nathaniel, Am. *au* Mass., 1809—
Haydn, Hį-dn, Francis Joseph, Aus. *mus comp*, 1732—1809.
Haydon, Há-don, Benj. Robt., English *pt* and *lec*, 1786—1846.
Haynau, Hį-nɤ, Baron, brutal Aus. *comman*, 1786—
Hayne, Han, Robert Y., Am. *law* and *st* S. C., 1791—1839.
Hayti, Faustin-Soulouque, (-Sɷ-lɷ́k,) Emperor of, b. a slave, about the year 1789—
Hazlitt, Ház-lit, William, Eng. *crit, essa* and *au.*, 1778—1830. [and *au.*
Head, Hɛd, Sir Francis B., Eng. *maj*
Headley, J. T., Am. *wr* N-Y., 1814—
Hebe, Hé-bɛ, *fab* goddess of youth.
Hector, most valliant of the Trojans.
Hegel, Há-gel, Geo. Wm. Fred., Ger. *phil*, 1770—1830.
Heiberg, Hį-bę́rg, Johann Ludwig, Danish *poet* and *dram*, 1791—
Heideloff, Hį-del-of, Karl Alex., Ger. *arch* and *wr*, 1788—
Heine, Hį-na *or* Hįn, Heinrich, Ger. *critic, poet*, and *prose wr*, 1799—1853.
Helena, Hél-ɛ-na, *fab*, the most beautiful woman of the world, who running away with Paris occasioned the Trojan war.
Helmont, Jean Baptist Van, *alch* Brussels, 1577—1644.
Helvetius, Hel-vé-ʃi-us, Claude Adrian, *materialistic au*, Fr., 1715—1771.
Heliodorus, Hɛ-li-ɷ-dɷ́-rus, Phœnician romance *wr*, fl. 398. [1835.
Hemans, Mrs. Felicia, Eng. *poet*, 1794—
Henry, name of *ks* England, France and Castile, and of *emps* Germany.
Henry, Mathew, *bib commen* Eng., 1662—1714.
Henry, Patrick, Am. *or* Va., 1736—1799.
Herault-De-Séchelles, Her-ɷl-Dę-Sá-ʃę-la, Marie Jean, Fr. *pat* and *au*, 1760—1794, guillotined.
Herbert, Hę́r-bert, Edward, Lord, Eng. *meta wr*, 1581—1648.
Herbert, Henry William, *wr* N-Y., 1807—
Hercules, Hę́r-kų-lɛz, *fab* son of Jupiter and Alcmena; the man of great strength.
Herder, Hę́r-der, Johann G. Von, Ger. *au*, 1744—1803.
Hermann, Hę́r-mąn, Karl Heinrich, Ger. *hist pt*, 1801—
Hermes, Hę́r-mɛz, Egyptian *leg, priest* and *phil*, year of the world 2076, soon after Moses.
Herodotus, Hɛ-ród-ɷ-tus, Greek *hist*, 484—413 B. C. [1591—1660.
Herrick, Robert, Eng. *clerg* and *poet*,
Herschel, Sir William, *astr* Eng., 1738—1822.
Herschel, Sir John Fred. Wm., son of Wm. H., *astr* Eng., 1790—
Hervey, James, Eng. *div* and *au*, 1714—1758.
Herwegh, Hę́r-veg, George, Ger. *poet*, 1816— [not known.
Hesiod, Hé-ʒi-od, Greek *poet*, his time
Hesperides, Hes-pér-į-dɛz, *fab* daughters of Hesperus: who had a garden bearing golden apples, watched by a dragon, which Hercules slew, and bore away the fruit. [1802———.
Hesse, Fred.-William IV., Elector of,
Heyne, Hį-na, Christ. Gottlob, Ger. *au*, 1729—1812. [5th cen.
Hierocles, Hį-ér-ɷ-klɛz, Platonic *phil*,
Hill, Rowland, *ecc div* Eng., fl. 1800-30.
Hill, Rowland, *Post-Office ref*, Eng., about 1810—
Hipparchus, Hip-ą́r-kus, first to reduce astronomy to science, fl. at Nice, bet. 160 and 125 B. C.
Hippocrates, Hip-ók-ra-tɛz, father of physic, a Grecian, 440 B. C.
Historia, His-tɷ́-ri-a, *fab*, the goddess of history.
Hitchcock, Edward, D. D., LL.D., *geol*, and *pres* Amherst College, Mass., 1793—
Hobbes, Hobz, Thomas, *meta phil* Eng., 1588—1679. [1800.
Hoche, Hoʃ, Lazare, Fr. *gen*, 1768—
Hofer, Andrew, *chief* of the Tyrolese, in war against the French and Bavarians, —1810, shot. [1784—1854.
Hoffman, David, Am. *law* and *au*,
Hoffman, Charles Fenno, Am. *poet* and *prose wr* N-Y., 1806—
Hofland, Mrs., Eng. *au*, 1770—1844.
Hogan, John, Eng. *sculp*, 1800—
Hogarth, Hɷ́-gąrθ, William, Eng. *pt*, 1697—1764. [—1835.
Hogg, James, Scotish *au* and *poet*, 1772
Holbach, Hɷ́l-bąh, Paul T., Baron Von, Ger. *miner* and *nat phil*, Paris, 1723—1789.
Holland, Henry Richard V. F., Lord, Brit. *st*, 1773—1840.
Holland, William III., Alex. Paul Fred. Louis, King of, Prince of Orange—Nassau, Grand Duke of Luxembourg, etc., 1817—c. 1849—

Holmes, Hɷmz, Oliver Wendell, M. D., Am. *ph* and *poet*, 1809—

Holt, Sir John, Eng. *j* 1642—1709.

Homer, Hó-mer, the most ancient and best of the Greek *poets*, whose only remaining works are the "Illiad," and Odyssey;" fl. 920 B. C.

Hood, Thomas, *hum* and *humanitary poet*, Eng., 1798—1845.

Hooke, Robt., *math* and *exp phil*, 1635—1703.

Hooker, Richard, *au* "Ecclesiastical Polity," Eng., 1553—1600.

Hopkins, Stephen, *signer Dec. of Ind.*, R. I., 1742—1785.

Hopkinson, Francis, Am. *j*, and *signer Dec. of Ind.*, Pa., 1738—1791.

Horace, Hór-as, (*or* Horatius, Quintus Flaccus,) Roman *lyric* and *sat poet*, fl. 65 B. C.

Horne, Geo., Eng. *prelate* and *au*, 1730—1792.

Horne, Richard Henry, Eng. *poet* and *critic*.

Horrox, Jeremiah, *astr*, *disc*, and *au* of a theory of lunar motion, 1619—1641.

Hortense Eugenie De Beauharnais, Her-táñs E-ʒe-ne De Bɷ-hɑr-ná, daughter of Empress Josephine, and wife of Louis Bonaparte, 1783—1837.

Houston, Hɷ́s-ton, Gen. Samuel, Am. *st* and U. S. *sen*, Texas, 1793—

Houssaye, Hɷ́-sa, Arsene, Fr. *poet* and *au*, 1815—

Howard, John, *philan* Eng., 1726—1790.

Howe, Admiral Earl, *adm* Eng. navy, 1725—1799.

Howit, Hɤ-it, William, Eng. *poet* and *descri wr*, 1795—

Huber, He-bɑr, François, *nat* Swit., 1750—1831.

Hubner, Hɷ́b-ner, Rud. Jul. Benno, Ger. *hist*, 1806—

Hudson, Henry, Eng. *nav*, —1610, perished at sea.

Hughes, Hɥz, Rev. John, D. D., *arch-bp* N-Y., 1798—

Hugo, Hé-gɷ, Victor, *repub pol*, *poet* and *au*, forbidden, on account of his sentiments, to enter France, 1802—

Hull, Isaac, Am. *com* Conn., 1775—1843.

Humboldt, Húm-bɷlt, William Von, Ger. *phil* and *st*, 1767—1835.

Humboldt, Alexander Von, Baron, brother of the preceding, Ger. *nat* and *trav*, *au* of that great work, "Cosmos," the best product of his towering genius, 1769—

Hume, David, Scottish *phil* and *hist*, 1711—1776

Hume, Joseph, Eng. *st* and *ref*, 1777—1855.

Humphreys, David, LL.D., *sol rev*, *amb* to Lisbon, *min* to Spain, *pat wr*, U. S., —1818.

Hunt, Fred. Knight, Eng. *jour*, *ed* "Daily News," 1814—

Hunt, Leigh, *jour* and *poet* Eng., 1784—

Hunt, Robert, Brit. *au*, 1814—

Hunter, John, Scottish *surg* and *anat*, 1728—1793.

Hunter, William, elder brother of the above, *anat*, *physiol* and *ph*, Scot., 1717—1783.

Huntington, Samuel, *gov* Conn., and *signer Dec. of Ind.*, 1732—1796.

Huntington, Daniel, *art* N-Y., 1816—

Hurd, Richard, Eng. *au*, 1720—1808.

Huskisson, Hús-ki-son, Wm., Brit. *st*, 1770—1830.

Huss, Hɥs, John, Ger. *church ref*, 1370—1415, burnt at the stake.

Hutchinson, John, Eng. *wr* in opposition to the theories of Sir Isaac Newton, 1674—1737.

Hutton, Charles, LL.D., Eng. *math* and *wr*, 1737—1823.

Hutton, Dr. James, Scottish *geol*, and *found* of Psychometry, 1726—1797.

Huyghens, Hɤ́-ħenz, Christian, Dutch *math*, *astr*, etc. In Geometry he gave theorems for the quadrature of the Hyperbola, the Ellipsis, and the Circle; he discovered the Saturn's ring; he laid down the theory of the pendulum, and its application to the clock; he discerned the synchronism of the Cycloid, invented the theory of Involutes and Evolutes of Curves, etc., 1629—1695.

Hydra, Hį-drɑ, *fab*, a serpent, which had seven heads.

Hygeia, Hį-jé-yɑ, *fab*, the goddess of health.

Hymen, Hį-men, *fab*, the god of marriage.

Hypatia, Hį-pá-ʃi-ɑ, female *teacher* in Alexandria, 4th cen.

Hyperides, Hį-pér-i-dez, a disciple of Plato who procured the punishment of Socrates, 320 B. C.

# I.

Ianthe, Ɨ-án-tɛ, *fab*, the beautiful wife of Iphis.

Ibraham Pasha, Ɛb'rq-ham Pa-ʃé, *emp* Egypt, 1789—1848.

Ignatius, Ig-ná-ʃi-us, *bp* Antioch, torn to pieces by lions, at Rome, by order of the emperor Trajan, A. D. 107.

Ingersoll, Iŋ'ger-sol, Jared, LL.D., *j, law*, etc., Pa., —1822.

Ingres, Aṅ-*gra*, Jean Dominique A., Fr. *pt*, 1780—

Innocent, from I. to XIII., *popes* between A. D. 402 and 1724.

Irving, Er'viŋ, Rev. Edward, *pulpit or* and *div*, Scotland, 1792—d.

Irving, Washington, Am. *au*, N-Y., 1783—

Irving, Theodore, LL.D., nephew of Wash. Irving, *au* N-Y.

Isabella of Castile, *queen* of Spain, 1450—1504.

Isturiz, Ɛs-tɷ-réθ, Don Xavier De, Sp. *pol*, 1790—

Iturbide, Ɛ-tɷr-béd, Don Augustus, *emp* Mexico, 1784—sh. 1824.

Ixion, Iks'i-on, *fab*, the son of Phlegyas, who for some vice, was fastened in hell to a wheel perpetually turning round.

Izard, Ralph, Am. *st* S. C., 1738—1804.

# J.

Jackson, Gen. Andrew, seventh Pres. U. S., from 1829 to 1837; Tenn., 1767—1845. V-Pres., J. C. Calhoun and Martin Van Buren.

Jacobi, Yq-kɷ-bɛ, Fred. Henry, Ger. *meta phil* and *wr*, 1743—1819.

Jacobs, Yq-kɷbz, Frederick, Ger. *crit*, 1764—1847.

Jacquard, Ʒa-kqrd, Marie Joseph, *inv* a loom for weaving damasks, France, 1752—1834.

James, name of Scottish and English *ks.*

James, Wm., Eng. *naval hist*, —1827.

James, G. P. R., Eng. *au*, now of N-Y., 1800—

Jameson, Jám-ɛ-son, Robert, *nat* Scot., 1774—1854.

Janin, Ʒa-naṅ, Jules, *au* and *jour*, France, 1804—

Jarvis, Jqr-vis, John Wesley, *por-pt* N-Y., 1780—1834.

Jasmin, Ʒas-maṅ, Jacques, "*barber poet*," France, 1798—

Jay, John, Am. *st*, and first *chief justice* U. S., *signer Dec. of Ind.*, *foreign min*, etc., N-Y., 1745—1829.

Jefferson, Thomas, Am. *st* and *scholar*, draftsman of the Declaration of Independence, author of the ordinance of '87, and third Pres. U. S., from 1801 to 1809; Va., 1743—1826. V-Pres., Aaron Burr and Geo. Clinton.

Jeffrey, Jéf-ri, Francis, Scottish *wr*, *critic*, and *ed Edinburgh Review*, 1773—1850.

Jeffreys, George, Lord, Eng. *law* and *j*, notorious for his infamous cruelty, 1648—1689.

Jellachich, Σe-lq*h*-i*h*, Jos. Baron Von, *ban* of Croatia, Sclav. and Dalmatia, *off* Aus. army, 1801—

Jenner, Edward, M. D., F. R. S., *disc* of vaccination, Eng., 1749—1823.

Jenyns, Jén-inz, Soame, *pol* and *wr* Eng., 1704—1787.

Jerome, of Prague, disciple of Huss, and *prot martyr*, —1416.

Jerrold, Jér-old, Douglas, Eng. *au* and *satirist*, 1805—

Joan d'Arc, Ʒɷ-aṅ Dqrk, (*or* Joan of Arc,) the "virgin-martyr of French liberty," 1410—1431, burnt at stake.

Johnson, Richard M., V-Pres. U. S. to Martin Van Buren; Ky., —1850.

Johnson, Dr. Samuel, *lex*, *au* and *crit*, Eng., 1709—1784.

Joinville, Ʒwoṅ-vɛl, François-Ferd.-Ph.-L.-M. D'Orleans, Prince de, of the house of Orleans; 1818—

Jones, Jacob, *com* Am. navy, Del., 1770—1850.

Jones, Paul, *comman* Am. navy, Scot., [1736—1792.

Jones, Sir William, *ori* and *trans*, Eng., 1746—1794.

Jonson, Benjamin, *dram wr*, contemporary of Shakspeare, Eng., 1573—1637.

Jordan, Dorothea, Eng. *actress*, 1762—1816.

Josephine, first wife of Nap. Bonaparte, and *empress* of France, 1763—1814.

Josephus, Jω-sé-fus, Flavius, *hist* of the Jews, Jerusalem, A. D. 37—93.
Jouffroy D'Albans, Zω-frwo Dɑb-añ, Cl. F. D., Marquis De, Fr. *machanician*, to whom the Academy of Sciences has awarded the honor of having first applied steam to navigation, instead of Fulton; 1751—1832. [1813—1853.
Judd, Rev. Sylvester, Am. *au* Mass.,
Judson, Emily C., ("Fanny Forester,") Am. *au* and *poet* N-Y., —1854.
Julian, Jų-li-an, Roman *emp*, styled the Apostate, for turning anti-Christian after ascending the throne; killed, 363.
Junius, Letters of, famous Eng. *pol writings*, supposed to have been written by Hugh Boyd, who d. 1794.
Juno, Jų-nω, *fab*, the sister and wife of Jupiter.
Jupiter, Jų-pi-ter, *fab*, a son of Saturn and Ops; the supreme deity of the heathens.
Jussieu, Zę-sę, Atoine De, Fr. *bot*, 1686—1758.
Jussieu, Bernard De, brother of the above, *bot*, 1699—1777.
Jussieu, Antoine L. De, nephew of the above, *bot*, 1748—1836.
Justin, Jús-tin, ancient Latin *hist*, fl. A. D. 250.
Justin, the Martyr, *wr* Chris. Church, and for his faith beheaded, 167.
Justinian, Jus-tín-i-an, Roman *emp*, who collected and arranged the laws of the nation, 541. [youths.
Juventa, Jų-vén-ta, *fab*, a goddess of

# K.

Kaempfer, Kámp-fer, Engelbert, Ger. *trav* and *nat*, 1651—1716.
Kaestner, Kást-ner, Abraham Gott., Ger. *math*, *astr* and *au*, 1719—1800.
Kalb, Kɑlb, Baron De, Polish *maj-gen* Am. army, —1780, killed.
Kalm, Kɑlm, Peter, Swedish *nat*, 1715—1779.
Kane, Dr. Elisha Kent, U. S. Navy, *sur*, *nat*, and Arctic explorer, Pa., 1822—
Kant, Kɑnt, Immanuel, Ger. *meta*, *phil* and *critic*, 1724—1804.
Kaulbach, Kȣl-bɑh, William, Ger. *art*, 1804— [1790—1833.
Kean, Kɛn, Edmund, Eng. *tragic act*,
Kean, Chas. John, son of the above, *act*, 1811— [1820.
Keats, Kɛts, John, Eng. *poet*, 1796—
Kemble, Charles, Eng. *act*, 1775—1854.
Kemble, John P., Eng. *act*, 1757—1823.
Kemp, Joseph, *mus comp* Eng., 1778—1824.
Kemp, Kenneth, Scotch *chem*, was the first to solidify carbonic acid gas, and was the introducer of amalgamated zinc plates into the galvanic battery, 1807—1843.
Kennedy, John Pendleton, Am. *nov* Md., 1795—
Kenrick, Wm., *compiler* of an English dictionary, —1779.
Kenrick, John, Eng. *hist* and *philol*.
Kent, James, Am. *jurist* N-Y., 1763—1847.
Kepler, Kép-ler, John, Ger. *astr* and *au*, 1571—o. s. 1631.
Keyser, Kį-ser, Nicaise De, *hist pt* Belgium, 1813—
King, Rufus, Am. *st* Me., 1757—1827.
King, William R., V-Pres. U. S. to Franklin Pierce; N. C., —1853.
Kingsley, Charles, Brit. *poet* and *au*.
Kinkel, Kiŋ-kel, Gottfried, Ger. *wr* and *repub*.
Kirby, Kér-bi, Rev. Wm., *ento* Eng., 1759—1850. [1710.
Kirch, Kirh, Gottf., Ger. *astr*, 1639—
Kirwan, Kér-wan, Richard, *chem* Scot., 1750—1812.
Klaproth, Kláp-rut, Heinrich J. Von, *ori schol* and *crit*, Ger., 1783—1835.
Klaproth, Martin Henry, Ger. *chem*, the discoverer of uranium, zirconia, titanic acid, etc., 1743—1817.
Klopstock, Klóp-stok, Friedrich, Ger. *poet*, 1724—1803.
Knowles, Nωlz, Jas. Sheridan, Irish *dram poet*, 1784—
Knox, Noks, Henry, *maj-gen* Am. army, Mass., 1750—1806.
Knox, John, Scotch *cler*, and *church ref*, 1505—1572.
Kock, Kωk, Chas. Paul De, Fr. *nov*, 1794—
Koekkoek, Kωk-kωk, Bernard C., Dut. *l-pt*, 1803—
Kosciusco, Kusts-ɛ-ős-kω *or* Kos-i-ús-kω, Thaddeus, Polish *patriot* and Am. *gen*, 1756—1817.

Kossuth, Ko-ʃüt, Louis, *ex-gov* Hungary, and *or*, 1806—
Kotzebue, Kóts-e-bǿ-a, August Von, Ger. *dram*, 1761—1819.
Krause, Krȣ-sa, Chas. Christ. Fred., Ger. *meta*, 1781—1832.
Kruseman, Krę-sa-man, Cornelius, Dutch *hist pt*, 1797—
Kugler, Kǿg-ler, Franz. Theod., Ger. *poet* and *au*, 1808—
Kunckell, Kǿŋ-kel, John, Ger. *chem*, 1630—1703.
Kyan, Kį-an, John H., the *inv* of the process of Kyanized wood, Eng., —1859.

# L.

Labitzky, Lą-bits-ki, Joseph, Ger. *mus comp*, 1802—
La-Caille, Lą-Kaly, Nich. Louis De, Fr. *astr observer*, 1713—1762.
Lacepede, Lą-są-pád, Bernard G. Etie. De La, Fr. *nat*, 1756—1825.
Lafayette, Lą-fa-ét, Marie Paul J. R. Y. G. M., Marquis De, Fr. *off*, *st* and *patriot*, who assisted in the American Revolutionary War, 1757—1834.
Lagrange, Lą-gráṅʒ, Joseph Louis, *math*, and *geom* and *astr au*, France, 1736—1813.
Laharpe, Lą-hąrp, Jean F. De, Fr. *crit* and *au*, 1739—1803.
Lahire, Lą-hér, Philip De, Fr. *math* and *astr*, 1640—1719.
Lalande, Lą-laṅd, Joseph J. Le F. De, *astr obs* and *wr*, Fr., 1732—1807.
Lamarck, Lą-mąrk, *or* Jean B. P. A. De Monet, Fr. *nat*,—*conch*, *zool* and *bot*, 1744—1829.
Lamartine, Lam-ąr-téṅ, Alphonse De, *poet*, *or*, *hist* and *pol*, Fr., 1790—
Lamb, Charles, Eng. *humor*, *critic* and *essa*, 1775—1834.
Lambert, Ląm-bert. John Henry,Ger. *math* and *phil*, 1728—1777.
Lamennais, Lą-maṅ-a, Félicité Robert, (Fa-lɛ-si-ta,) Fr. *ecc*, *pol* and *au*, 1782—1853.
La-Motte-Fouque, Lą-Mot-Fœk, Fred. Hein. Karl, Baron De, Normo-Ger. *poet* and *nov*, 1777—1843.
Lancisi, Ląn-çé-sɛ, Giammaria, Italian *anat* and *physiol*, 1654—1720.
Lander, Richard and John, Eng. *exps* of Africa, 1804—1832; 1806—
Landon, Lititia Elizabeth, Eng. *poet*, —1838. [*au*, 1775——.
Landor, Lán-dor, Walter Savage, Eng.
Landseer, Sir Edwin, Eng. *pt*, 1801—
Lane, Edward Wm., Arabic and *ori schol*, Eng., about 1800—
La Perouse, Lą Pa-rǿs, Jean F. G. De, Fr. *nav*, 1741—1789.
La Place, Lą Pląs, Pierre S., Marquis De, Fr. *geom*, and *astr au*,1749—1827.
Lares, Lá-rɛz, *fab*, sons of Mercury and Lara, worshipped as household gods.
Las Cases, Ląs Ką-sá, Fr. *naval comman*, 1766—1842.
Latham, Lá-tam, John, Eng. *orni* and *antiq*, 1740—1837.
Latimer, Hugh, Eng. *church ref*, 1472 burnt at the stake, 1555.
Laube, Lȣ-be, Heinrich, Gęr. *nov* and *dram*, 1806—
Lauder, Lǿ-der, Robt. Scott, Scottish *pt*, 1803— [1724—1792.
Laurens, Lǿ-renz, Henry, Am. *st* S. C.,
Lavater, Lą-vą-ter, John Gasper, *wr* on Physiognomy, Ger., 1741—1801.
Lavoisier, La-vwó-si-a, Antoine Lan., Fr. *chem*, contributing to this science, among other things, the chemical nomenclature now in use; 1743—1794, guillotined.
Law, John, Scotch *finan*, projecter of the French money bubble, 1670—1729.
Law, Wm., Eng. *relig wr*, 1686—1761.
Lawrence, James, Am. *nav off* N. J., 1781—1813.
Lawrence, Sir Thomas, P. R. A., Eng. *por-pt*, 1769—1830.
Lawrence, Abbott, Am. *merch* Mass., 1792—1855.
Layard, Lá-ąrd, Henry Austin, Eng. *trav* and *au*, 1817—
Le Conte, Lɛ Kónt, John L., M. D., Am. *nat* N-Y., 1825— [*pt*.
Lécurieux, La-kę-rę, Jacques, Fr. *hist*
Ledyard, John, Am. *trav* Conn., 1751 —1788.
Lee, Anne, *found* of the "Shakers," Eng., 1735—1784.
Lee, Arthur, Am. *st*, and *pol wr*, Va., 1740—1792. [—1782.
Lee, Charles, *maj-gen* Am. army, Pa.,
Lee, Francis Lightfoot, *signer Dec. of Ind.*, Va., 1734—1797.

Lee, Henry, *off* Am. army, Va., 1756—1818.
Lee, Richard Henry, Am. *st* and *signer Dec. of Ind.*, Va., 1732—1794.
Lee, ———, Eng. *l-pt.*
Legendre, La-ʒáṅ-dr, Adrian Marie, Fr. *geom*, and *math au*, 1751—1833.
Lehmann, Lá-mąn, Prof., Rus. *nat*, 1814—1842.
Leibnitz, Lḭb-nits, Godfrey William, Ger. *meta* and *math phil*, 1646—1716.
Lemon, Mark, Eng. *jour*, *ed* "Punch," 1810—
Lennep, Lá-nap, Jacob Van, Dutch *poet* and *nov*, 1802—
Leo X., Pope Giovanni De Medici, 1475—1521.
Leonhard, Lá-on-hąrt, Karl Casar Von, Ger. *miner* and *geol*, 1779—
Leopold I., *emp* Austria, 1640—1705.
Leopold II., *emp* Germany, 1747—1792.
Lepsius, Lép-si-us, Karl Rich., Ger. *ori*, 1811—
Lerminier, Ląr-maṅ-i-a, Jean Louis E., Fr. *phil* and *wr*, 1803—
Leroux, La-rő, Pierre, Fr. *soc phil*, 1805—
Le Sage, Lẹ Sáʒ, Alain, Fr. *nov* and *dram*, 1668—1747.
Leslie, Lés-li, Sir John, Eng. *math* and *wr*, 1766—1832.
Leslie, Chas. Robert, Eng. *pt*, 1794—
Lessing, Gotthold Ephraim, Ger. *crit*, *phil*, *dram wr* and *au*, 1729—1781.
Lessing, Karl Fred., Ger. *pt*, 1808—
Leutze, Lőts-a, Emanuel G., Ger. *art.*
Leuwenhoeck, Lő-ven-hẹk, Atoine, Ger. *nat*, 1632—1723.
Leverrier, La-vá-ri-a, M., Fr. *astr*, and *disc* of the planet Neptune.
Lewis, Samuel, *pioneer* in the cause of education in the west, and anti-slavery *ref*, Ohio, --1853.
Lieber, Lé-ber, Francis, LL. D., Ger. *repub* and *au*, and *pres* Columbia College, Ga., 1800—
Lilbume, John, Eng. *repub*, 1613—1657.
Lilly, William, Eng. *astrol*, 1602—1681.
Lincoln, Líŋ-kon, Benjamin, *gen* Am. army, Mass., 1733—1810.
Lindley, Lind-li, John, English *bot*, 1800—
Linley, Thomas, *vocal comp*, Eng., —1795.
Linnæus, Lin-ɛ-us, Charles, *bot* and *au* Sweden, 1707—1778.
Liszt, Lɛst, Franz, Hungarian *pianist*, 1811—
Livingston, Lív-iŋ-ston, Edward, Am. *jurist* and *st* N-Y., 1764—1836.
Livingston, Robert R., Am. *law* and *st*, and *signer Dec. of Ind.*, N-Y., 1746—1813.
Livius, Liv-i-us, Titus, best Roman *hist*, most of whose books are lost, b. 59 B. C.
Locke, John, Eng. *meta phil*, 1632—1704.
Lockhart, John G., Scottish *au*, and *ed* "Quarterly Review," 1794—1854.
Logan, John, *poet* Scot., 1748—1788.
Lollard, Walter, *found* of a sect who denied the use of the mass, baptism, &c.; was burnt for heresy, 1322.
Lomenie-De-Brienne, Lo-maṅ-ɛ - Dẹ-Brɛ-áṅ, Stephen Chas. De, *finance min* of Louis XVI., Fr., 1727—1794.
Longfellow, Henry Wadsworth, Am. *poet* Mass., 1807—
Longueville, Loṅ-gẹ-vɛl, the name of a celebrated French family of the 15th century.
Lope De Vega, Lɷ-pa Da Vá-gą, Sp. *dram*, 1562—1635.
Lortzing, Lɷr-tsiŋ, Albrecht Gus., Ger. *mus comp*, 1803—
Louis XIV., (Lő-i,) Bourbon *k*, 1638—1715.
Louis XVI., *k* France, 1754—g. 1793.
Louis Philippe, Lő-i Fil-ép, *k* France, 1773—1850.
Lovejoy, Rev. Elijah P., *ed* "Alton Observer," an anti-slavery paper, and became a martyr to that cause and a free press, in defending his paper from a mob; Ill., 1802—1837.
Lover, Samuel, Irish *au* and *art.*
Lowe, Lɤ, Lieut. Gen. Sir Hudson, K. C. B., *guardian* of Napoleon at St. Helena, 1769—1844.
Lowell, Lő-el, James Russell, Am. *poet* and *wr* Mass., 1819—
Loyola, Lo-ɛ-ő-lą, Ignatius, *found* of the Order of Jesuits, Sp., 1491—1556.
Lucian, Lų́-ʃi-an, Greek *crit* and *sat*, 90—180.
Lucifer, Lų́-si-fer, *fab*, son of Jupiter and Aurora, made the morning star.
Lucius, Lų́-ʃi-us, I., II., III., *popes*, 253, 1144, 1181.
Lucretia, Lų-kré-ʃi-ɑ, Roman matron who was the cause of the revolution, 509 B. C.
Lucretius, Lų-kré-ʃi-us, Titus Carus, Roman *phil* and *poet*, 96—54 B. C.
Lully, Lő-li, Jean B., *mus comp* Italy, 1634—1687.
Luna, Lų́-nɑ, *fab*, Diana's name in heaven.
Luther, Martin, Ger. *church ref*, 1483—1546.
Lycurgus, Lḭ-kúr-gus, Spartaŋ *leg*, 870 B. C.;—Athenian *or*, 408 B. C.

Lyell, Lịl, Sir Charles, *geol* Scot., 1797—

Lyndsay, Lind-sa, Sir David, Scottish *poet*, 1490—1555.

Lysander, Lị-sán-der, Spartan *gen*, who defeated the Athenian fleet, and ended the 27 years' war, 396 B. C.

Lyttleton, Lít-l-ton, George Lord, Eng. *au* and *st*, 1709—1773.

# M.

Mabuse, Mq-bó-sa, Jan De, an It. *pt* 1470—1532.

Macaulay, Ma-ké-la, Catherine, *hist* and *pol wr* Eng., 1734—1791.

Macaulay, Thomas Babington, Br. *hist*, *essa*, *poet* and *pol*, 1800—

Macbeth, Mak-béth, *usurper* of the Scot. crown, slain —1054.

Maccabees, Mák-a-bez, seven brothers, Jews, with their mother, put to death, at Antioch, 168 B. C.

Macdonough, Mak-dón-o, Thomas, *commo* Am. navy, 1784—1825.

Macfarlane, Mak-fqr-lan, Henry, *pol* and *misc wr* Scot., 1734—1804.

Machiavelli, Mq-ke-q-vél-e, Nicolo, an It. *pol wr* and *au* 1469—1527.

Mackay, Ma-ká, Charles, Br. *poet* and *jour*, 1812—

Mackenzie, Ma-kén-zi, Sir. Alex., Br. *nav*, ——d. [—1831.

Mackenzie, Henry, Scottish *nav*, 1745

Mackintosh Mák-in-tosh, Sir. James, Scottish *au* and *law*, 1765—1832.

Macklin, Mák-lin, Chas., *act* and *dram* Ir., 1690—1797.

Maclise, Ma-klíz, Daniel, Irish *art* 1811—

M'Clintock, Ma-Klin-tok, John, D.D., *ed*, *trans* and *au* of Greek and Latin text books, Pa., 1814—

M'Lean, Mak-Lán, John, *chief justice* U. S. *Sup Ct* O., 1785—

Maclaurin, Mak-lé-rin, Colin, Scottish *math* 1698—1746.

Macomb, Ma-kómb, Alex., *com in-chief* of the Am. army, 1782—1841.

Macon, Má-kon, Nathaniel, Am. *st* N. C., ——d.

Macpherson, Mak-fér-son, James, *ed* of "Ossian," *wr* Scot., 1738—1796.

M'Cullah, Ma-kúl-a, Wm. Torrens, *pol* and *au* Ir., 1813—

M'Culloch, Ma-kúl-ok, J. R., *wr* on *pol econ* Scot., 1790—

Madison, Mád-i-son, James, Am. *st* and fourth *pres* U. S., from 1809 to 1817; Va., 1758—1836. V-Pres. George Clinton, and Elbridge Gerry.

Madrazo, Mqd-rq-tho, Don Pedro, Sp. *poet*, *jour*, *critic* and *pt* 1816—

Madvig, Mqd-vig, Johann N., Ger. *class wr* and *prof* 1804—

Magellan, Ma-gél-an, (*or* Magalhaens, Mq-gql-yq-énz,) Fernando, Port., *nav* the first to circumnavigate the globe, 1470—1521, killed by natives at Philippine is.

Maginn, Máj-in, William, Irish *wr*, *foun* of "Fraser's Magazine," 1794—1842.

Mahmoud, Mq-mod, the name of Turkish Sultans.

Mahomet, Ma-hóm-et, the *au* of the "Koran" and *foun* of a new religion. A name applied since, to Turkish emperors, who ruled from the 13th to the 17th century.

Mahon, Mq-hón *or* Mq-ón, Philip H., Viscount, an Eng. *hist wr* 1805—

Mahoney, Mq-hó-ni, Francis, Br. *jour* and *au*, 1800—

Mailath, Mq-él-qt, Count Johann, Hun. *au*, 1786—

Mars, Mqrz, *fab*, god of war.

Mechain, Me-shán, Pierre Francis A., Fr. *astr* and *math*, 1774—1805.

Mecklenburg-Schwerin, Mék-len-burg-Shwa-rén, Frederick Francis, Grand Duke of, 1823— assumed government 1842.

Mecklenburg-Strelitz, Strá-litz, Frederick Chas. Joseph, Grand Duke of, b. 1779; he is a distinguished governor, and a great friend of education and human rights.

Medici, Ma-dé-se, an *illus.* Florentine family, from the 14th cen. to the present time.

Mehemet Ali, Me-hém-et A'le, Eg. *pasha*, 1765—1848. [—1730.

Mehemet-Effendi, Ef-én-de, Turk. *st*

Meigs, Megz, Return Jonathan, Am. *off* O., —1828.

Melanchthon, Mel-ánk-thon, (Ger. Mel-qnk-ton,) Philip, *colleague* of Luther in the Reformation, 1497—1568.

Melbourne, Mél-burn, Wm. Lamb, Viscount, Eng. *st*, 1779—1843.

**Melitus**, Mɛ-lį-tus, Greek *or* and *poet*, accuser of Socrates, ex. 400 B. C.
Mellen, Mél-en, Grenville, Am. *poet* and *misc wr*, 1800—1841.
Melville, Mél-vil, Andrew, Eng. *div* and *au* 1545—1622.
Melville, Henry Dundas, Lord Viscount, Eng. *st* 1740—1811.
Melville, Herman, Am. *au* N-Y., 1819—
Mendelssohn, Mén-del-son, Dr. Felix Bartholody, Ger. *mus comp* and *performer*, 1809—1847.
Mendelssohn, Moses, a Jewish *phil* and *mor* Ger., 1729—1786.
Menelaus, Men-ɛ-lá-us, *k* of Mycenæ, *hus* of Helena.
Mengs, Meŋz. Antony Raphael, Bohemian *pt*, 1729—1779.
Mercator, Mer-ká-tor, Gerard, *math* and *geog* Flanders, 1512—1594.
Mercer, Mér-ser, Hugh, a *brig gen* in the Am. army, —1777.
Mercury, Mér-kq-ri, *fab*, messenger of the gods, inventor of letters, god of eloquence, &c. [1800———.
Merimèe, Mer-ɛ-má, Prosper, Fr. *au*
Mesmer, Més-mer, Fred. Anthony, a promoter of animal magnetism, Ger., 1734—1815.
Mesonero y Romanos, Ma-sɷn-á-rɷ ɛ Rɷ-mqn-ɷ́s, Don Ramon De, Sp. *au* 1803—
Metastasio, Ma-tqs-tás-ɛ-ɷ, Pietro, It. *dram*, 1698—1782.
Metternich, Mét-er-ni*h*, Clemens, W. N. L., Prince, Aus. *st* and *dip*, 1773—
Meursius, Mér-si-ęs, John, Dutch *critic philol* and *hist*, 1579—1639.
Meyer, Mį-er, Philippe, Ger. *mus comp* 1737—1819.
Meyerbeer, Mį-er-bar, Giacomo, Ger. *mus comp*, 1794—
Mezerai, Ma-za-rá, Francis E. De, Fr. *hist* 1610—1683.
Michaelis, Mi*h*-q-él-is, John David, Ger. *orien* and *bib critic*, 1717—1791.
Michelangelo Buonarroti, Mɛ-ka-lqn-gá-lɷ Bɷ-ɷ-nqr-ɷ́-tɛ, *or* anglicized, Michael Angelo, Mį-ka-el An'jɛ-lɷ, It. *art*, 1475—1564. [1798———.
Michelet, Miʃ-a-lá, Jules, Fr. *hist*
Mickiewicz, Mɛts-kɛ-á-vɛç, Adam, Polish *poet*, 1798—
Middleton, Mid-l-ton, Conyers, *polem wr* and *critic* Eng., 1683—1750.
Middleton, Arthur, *signer Dec. of Ind.*, S. C., 1743—1787. [—1846.
Middleton, Henry, Am. *st* S. C., 1771
Mignet, Mɛg-ná, Francois Au. Alexis, Fr. *hist*, 1796—

Mill, Mil, James, Scottish *phil* and *st*, 1773—1836.
Millar, Mil-ar, James, Scot. *ph* and *chem*, 1762—1827.
Miller, Edward, *ph* and *med au* N-Y., 1760—1812.
Miller, Wm., *found* of the sect called the "Millerites," —1849.
Miller, Hugh, Scot. *geol* and *au*, 1805—
Miller, Thomas, Eng. *poet* and *nov* 1809—
Millin, Mil-in, Aubin Louis, Fr. *archæ*, *nat* and *au*, 1759—1818.
Milman, Mil-man, Henry Hart, Eng. *au* and *clerg*, 1791—
Milnes, Mil-nes, Richard Monckton, Eng. *poet*, 1806—
Milton, Mil-ton, John, Eng. *poet* whose writings have given a name to the English language, 1608—1675.
Mina, Mé-nq, Don Francisco E. y, Sp. *gen*, 1782—1836. [wisdom.
Minerva, Min-ér-va, *fab*, goddess of
Minot, Min-ot, Laurence, Eng. *poet* 14th cen.
Minto, Min-tɷ, Walter, *math* and *nat phil* Scot., —1796.
Mirabeau, Mir-q-bɷ, Honore G. R. Comte De, *or* and *repub* Fr., 1749—1791.
Mirabeau, Mir-q-bɷ, Victor Riquetti, Marquis De, *au* and *foun* of *pol sect* of Economists, Fr., —1790.
Miranda, Mir-án-dq, Don Francisco, Sp. S. Am. *liberator* —1816.
Miraflores, Mɛr-q-flɷ́-ras, Don Manuel P. F. De P. M. y D., *st*, *min* and *au* Sp. 1792— [1810———.
Mitchel, Miç-el, O. M., Am. *astr* O.,
Mitchell, John, Am. *nat* and *au*, —1772.
Mitchell, Thomas, Eng. *philol*, 1783—1845. [1822———.
Mitchell, Donald G., Am. *wr* Conn.,
Mitchell, John, Irish "patriot," exiled, now in U. S., 1814—
Mitford, Mit-ford, John, *misc wr* Eng., —1831. [1827.
Mitford, Mary Russel, Eng. *au*, 1786—
Mitford, William, *hist* and *philol* Eng., 1784—1827.
Mittermaier, Mit-er-mį-er, Charles J. Anthon, *jurist* and *au*, a friend of popular freedom, Ger., 1787—
Mitzler, Mits-ler, Lan. Chas. de Kolof, Ger. *mus comp*, 1711—1778.
Modena, Mɷ-dá-nq, Francis Ferd. Gemimen, Duke of, b. 1819, commenced to govern, 1846.
Moir, Mwer, David Macbeth, Scottish *wr* and *au*, 1798—1851.

Mole, Mōl, John, an Englishman, eminent for his skill in the science of Algebra, —1827.

Moliere, Mōl-i-ār, Jean B. Poquelin, Fr. *actor* and *comic wr*, 1622—1668.

Moliers, Mol-i-ār-á, Joseph P. De, *phil wr* Fr., 1677—1742. [1777——.

Molina, Mō-lé-nā, Pedro, *st* Guat.,

Moltke, Mólt-ke, Adam Wm., Count, Danish *st*, 1785—

Molyneux, Mól-i-nō, Wm., an ingenious, *math* Ir., 1656—d.

Molza, Mól-dzā, Francis Maria, Italian *poet*, 1489—1544.

Monardes, Mō-nār-das, Nicholas, Sp. *ph* and *bot*, —1578.

Monbeillard, Moṅ-bal-yārd, Philibert Gue., Fr. *nat*, 1720—1785.

Moncey, Moṅ-sa, Adrien, Fr. *off* and *st*, 1754—1842.

Monge, Moṅz, Gaspard, an illustrious scientific man, *geom*, *au* of the method known as "*Descriptive Geometry*," Fr., 1746—1818.

Monk, Muŋk, George, Eng. *gen* and *pol*, 1608—1670.

Monmouth, Món-muth, James, Duke of, a pretender for the throne of Great Britain; the attempt to seize which was the foundation of the revolution, in 1688; b. 1619—1685, beheaded.

Monnet, Moṅ-ét, Anthony Grim, Fr. *chem*, 1734—1817.

Monro, Mon-ró, Alexander, Eng. *ph* and *anat*, 1697—1767.

Monroe, Mon-ró, James, Am. *st* and fifth *pres* U. S., from 1817 to 1825; Va., 1758—1831. V-Pres., D. D. Tompkins.

Montague, Mon-tág, Charles, earl of Halifax, Eng. *st*, 1661—1715.

Montague, John, fourth earl of Sandwich, *dip*, *st* and *au*, Eng.,1718—1792.

Montague, Basil, an English *law* and *wr*, 1770—1851.

Montague, Lady Mary Wortley, an English *wr* and friend of Addison, Pope, etc., 1690—1762. [1800.

Montague, Elizabeth, *wr* Eng., 1720—

Montaigne, Moṅ-táṅ, Michel, Seigneur De, French *essa*, 1533—1592.

Montcalm, Moṅt-kām, Louis Jos. De, Marquis of St. Krau, French *gen*, 1712—1759.

Montecuculli, Mōn-ta-kō-kó-le, Raymond De, Modenese *gen* Ger., 1608—1680.

Montesquieu, Móṅ-tas-kę, Carl De S., Baron De, Fr. *phil* and *au*, 1689—1755.

Montezuma, Mon-ta-zū-ma, *or* Mon-ta-tó-mā,) last Indian *emp* of Mex., stoned to death at the time of the Spanish invasion, —1520.

Montfaucon, Moṅt-fō-kón, Bernard De, Fr., *critic* and *antiq*, 1655—1741.

Montgolfier, Mont-gōl-fi-a, Jacques Etie., the inventor of air-balloons, 1745—1799.

Montgomery, Mont-gúm-er-i, James, *poet* Eng., 1771—1854.

Montgomery, Richard, *major-gen* Am. army, 1737—k. 1775.

Montgomery, Geo. Wash., Am. *nov* and *trans*, —1841. [—1828.

Monti, Món-te, Vincenso, *poet* It., 1753

Monti, Raffaelle, Italian *sculp*, 1819—

Montmorency, Moṅt-mō-rāṅs, Duke of, Henry II., French *adm*, 1595—1632.

Montrose, Mont-róz, James G., Marquis of, dist. *royalist* under Charles I., Eng., —1645.

Montucci, Mon-tó-ke, Antonio, *philol* and *au*, Italy, 1762—1829. [1799.

Montucla, Móṅ-tę-klā, Fr. *math*, 1725—

Moore, Mōr, Edward, an English *poet* and *dram wr*, 1712—1757. [1802.

Moore, John, *ph* and *au* Scot., 1730—

Moore, Sir John, Brit. *gen*, and the subject of the celebrated stanzas of Wolf, 1761—k. 1809.

Moore, Thomas, British *poet* and *wr*, 1780—1852.

Mora, Mó-rā, Joseph J., Sp. *poet* and *au* S. Am., 1783.

Moratin, Mō-rā-ten, N. F. De, and L. F. De, Sp. *dram poets*, 1737—1760, 1780—1828. [1833.

More, Mōr, Hannah, Eng. *wr*, 1744—

More, Henry, Eng. *div*, 1614—1687.

More, Sir Thomas, Eng. *au* and *st*, 1480—1535.

Moreau, Mor-ó, Jean Michel, *designer* and *engraver* Fr., 1741—1814.

Moreau, Jean Victor, Fr. *gen*, 1763—1813.

Morell, Mór-el, Thomas, Eng. *critic* and *lexicog*, 1703—1784.

Moreto y Cabana, Mō-rá-tō e Kā-bā-nā, Don Augustin, Sp. *dram poet* 17th cen. [1755—1799.

Morgan, Mér-gan, Daniel, Am. *gen* Va.,

Morgan, Wm., Eng. *math* and *wr*, —1833.

Morghen, Mór-gan, Raphael, *engraver* Naples, 1758—d.

Morier, Mór-er, James, Eng. *trav* and *nov*, 1780—1648.

Morison, Mór-i-son, Robert, Eng. *ph* and *bot*, 1620—1383.

Moritz, Mór-its, Charles, P., Ger. *wr* 1757—1793. [1764—1804.

Morland, Mór-land, George, Eng. *pt*

Morland, Sir Samuel, Eng. *st* and *mech*, 1625—1596.

Mornay, Mór-na, Philip de, Fr. *st* and *wr*, 1549—1623. [dreams, &c.

Morpheus, Mór-fe-us, *fab*, god of sleep,

Morris, Mór-is, Gouverneur, Am. *st* and *wr* N-Y., 1752—1816.

Morris, Robert, *supt* of the finances of the U. S., during the Revolutionary war, and *signer Dec. of Ind.*, Pa., —1806.

Morris, George P., Am. *wr* N-Y., 1802—

Mors, Mors, *fab*, goddess of death.

Mortier, Mór-ti-a, Edmund, A. C. J., Fr. *marshal*, 1768—1835.

Morton, Mór-ton, Nathaniel, Am. *au* Mass., 1612—1685.

Morton, Mór-ton, Samuel G., Am. *nat* and *ethno*, Pa., —1851. [1838.

Morton, Thomas, Eng. *dram*, 1764—

Moses, Mó-zez, *lawgiver* of the Jews, Eg., 1571 B. C.

Mosheim, Mos-hīm, John L. Von, Ger. *hist* and *phil wr*, 1694—1755.

Motherwell, Múth-er-wel, Wm., Scottish *poet* and *ed*, 1798—1835.

Mott, Mot, Valentine, M. D., LL. D., Am. *surgeon* N-Y., 1785.

Motley, Mót-li, John Lothrop, Am. *hist* who has recently distinguished himself by a very able and beautifully written history of "The Rise of the Dutch Republic." N-Y.

Mottley, Mót-li, John, Eng. *biog wr*, 1692—1750.

Mortimer, Mór-ti-mer, Thomas, commercial *wr* and *au* Eng., 1740—1809.

Moultrie, Mól-tre, Wm., Am. *off* S. C., —1805. [N-Y., 1807———.

Mount, Mownt, William S., Am. *art*

Mountfort, Mównt-fort, William, Eng. *actor* and *dram wr*, 1659—k. 1692.

Mourad-Bey, Mo-rad-Ba, *chief* of the Mamelukes, 1750—1801.

Mozart, Mó-zqrt, (*or* Ger. Móts-qrt,) Johann, C. W. Gott., *master of mus*, and *mus comp*, Ger., 1756—1792.

Mudie, Mó-de, Robert, Scot. *au* in *nat hist*, 1777—1842.

Mudge, Muj, M. D., F. R. S., *mech* and *au*, —1793.

Muller, Múl-er, Carl Ottfried, Ger. *archæ* and *au*, 1797—1840.

Muller, Gerard Fred., Ger. *trav* and *wr* and Rus. *hist*, 1705—1783.

Muller, John, Ger. *ast*, 1436—1476.

Muller, John Von, Swiss. *hist* 1752—1809. [—1784.

Muller, Othon Fred., Danish *nat*, 1730

Muncer *or* Muntzer, Mónt-ser, Saxon *div*, *church ref* and social *leveller*, beheaded 1525.

Munro, Alex., M. D., a skilful *anat* and *ph* Scot., 1733—1817. [—1836.

Munster, Mún-ster, Coun, *st* Hanover,

Muntz, Munts, George Fred., Eng., *merch* and *pol reformer*, 1794—

Murat, Mẹ-rq, Joachim, Fr. *gen* and *k* of Naples, 1767—sh. 1815.

Muratori, Mo-rq-tó-re, Louis Anthony, It. *hist* and *antiq*, 1672—1750.

Murillo, Mo-rél-yo, Bartholome E., Sp. *pt*, 1618—1682.

Murphy, Múr-fi, Arthur, *dram* and *misc wr*, Ir., 1727—1805.

Murray, Múr-a, Alexander, Scotch *linguist* and *au*, 1775—1813.

Murray, Hugh, Scot. *geo wr*, 1779—1846. [—1820.

Murray, John, *ph*, *chem* and *wr* Scot.,

Murray, Rev. John, father of the Universalist denomination, b. Eng., 1741 —1815, U. S.

Murray, John, F. S. A., Eng. *pub*, 1778—1843. [1826.

Murray, Lindley, Eng. *gram*, 1745—

Murray, Wm. Vans, Am. *dip* Md., 1762 —1803.

Murray, Nicholas, D. D., Am. *wr* N-Y., better known by the *nom de plume*, "Kirwan;" b. 1802—

Muses, Mụz-ez, *fab*, nine daughters of Jupiter, mistresses of all the sciences, presidents of musicians, and poets, and governesses of the feasts of the gods.

Musgrave, Mús-grav, Sir Richard, *bart*, an Ir. *hist*, 1753—1818.

Musschenbroek, Mús-hen-brok, Peter Van, Dutch *nat*, *phil* and *math*, 1692—1761.

Musset, Mẹ-sa, Alfred De, Fr. *poet*, 1810—

Mustapha, Mús-tq-fq, I., ascended the Turkish throne, 1617—strangled 1623. — II., asc. 1695—dethroned 1703. — III., asc. 1757—1774.

Mutis, Mo-tés, Joseph Celestino, Sp. *nat*, 1731—1808.

# N.

Nahl, Nql, Johann Aug., Prussian *sculp*, 1710—1781. [ers, &c.

Naiades, Ná-ya-dɛz, *fab*, nymphs of riv-

Napier, Na-pḗr, Lieut. Gen. Sir Chas. James, *off* Br. army, 1782—1853.

Napier, Sir Charles, *adm* Br. navy, 1786—

Napier, John, Baron of Merchiston, *inv* of logarithms, and *math au*, Scot., 1550—1617.

Napier, Macvey, *ed* "Encyclopedia Britannica," and of the "Edinburgh Review," Scot., —1847.

Naples, Ná-plz, Ferdinand II., *k* of the two Sicilies, b. 1810— succeeded to the throne in 1830.

Napoleon Bonaparte, Na-pṓ-lɛ-on Bṓ-na-pqrt, *emp* Fr., 1768, died at St. Helena, 1821.

Narbonne Lara, Nqr-bṓn Lq-rq, Louis Count, *aid-de-camp* to Napoleon, 1755—1813.

Narcissus, Nqr-sís-us, *fab*, a beautiful youth, who, falling in love with his own shadow in the water, pined away into a daffodil. [1555.

Nardi, Nq́r-dɛ, Jacopo, It. *hist*, 1476—

Nares, Nqrz, Robert, Eng. *critic* and *theol*, —1829.

Naruszewicz, Nqr-ɷʃ-á-vɛq, Adam Stamslans, *hist* and *poet* Poland, —1796.

Narvaez, Nqr-vq-áð, Don Ramon, Duke of Valencia, Sp. *pol*, 1795—

Nash, Naʃ, Francis, *brig-gen* Am. army, —1777 killed.

Nash, John, Eng. *arch*, 1752—1835.

Nasmyth, Ná-smið, Alex., Scot. *l-pt*, 1757—1840.

Nassau, Na-sṓ, Adolph, Duke of, 1817 — assumed government 1839.

Naude, Nɤ́-de, Philip, Ger. *math*, 1654 —1745.

Naudet, Nṓ-da, Thomas Chas., Fr. *l-pt* 1774—1810.

Naumann, Nɤ́-mqn, Johann Got., Ger. *mus comp*, 1741—1801.

Navarre, Na-vq́r, Henry of, [Henry IV.] *k* of Fr., 1553— ascended the throne 1610.

Neal, Nɛl, Joseph C. an Am. *wr*, *au* of the "Charcoal Sketches," Pa., 1807 —1847.

Neal, John, Am. *wr* Me., 1794—

Neander, Na-q́n-der, Johann Aug., Church *hist*, Ger., 1789—1850.

Necker, Nék-er, James, Fr. *min* and *pol*, 1732—1804.

Necker, Madame, wife of the above, dist. for her philanthropy and learning, 1739—1796.

Nelson, Nél-son, Horatio, Eng. *adm*, 1758—1805. [*ed*, 1759———.

Nelson, Samuel, an "Irish patriot" and

Nelson, Thomas, Am. *gen*, and *gov* Va., *signer Dec. of Ind.*, 1738—1789.

Nepos, Nɛ́-pos, Cornelius, Latin *hist*, fl. 75 B. C.

Neptune, Nép-tqn, *fab*, god of the sea.

Nero, Claud. Domit. Cæsar, *emp* and *tyrant* Rome, slew himself A. D. 68.

Nestor, *comman* at siege of Troy, said to have lived 300 years. [—1737.

Neumann, Nɤ́-mqn, Caspar, Ger. *chem*,

Neureuther, Nɤ-rɤ-tqr, Eugene, Ger. *art*, 1806—

Newcomen, Nq́-kɷ-men, Thomas, the first to improve the steam-engine, Eng., 17th cen.

Newland, Peter, Dutch *math* and *au*, 1764—1794.

Newton, Sir Isaac, *math* and *nat phil*, *au* "Principia," etc., Eng., 1642 o. s. —1727.

Ney, Na, Michel, Marshal of the French emp., Duke of Elchingen, Prince of the Moskwa, 1769—sh. 1815. [B. C.

Nicander, Greek *poet* and *med wr*, 140

Niceron, Nɛs-a-rṓn, John Peter, Fr. *biog au*, 1685—1738.

Nicholas, Paulovitch, *emp* Russia, 1796 —c. 1824—1855.

Nicholls, Charlotte, ["Currer Bell,"] Eng. *au*, —1855.

Nicholls, Frank, M. D.. F. R. S., Eng. *ph* and *au*, 1699—1779.

Nichols, John, *antiq* and *misc wr*, conductor of the "Gentleman's Magazine," 1744—1828.

Nicholson, James, *off* Am. navy, Md., 1737—1804.

Nicholson, John B., Am. *com*, —1846.

Nicholson, William, *wr* on chem. and nat. philos., Eng., 1758—1815.

Nicolai, Ník-ɷ-la, Chris. Fred., Ger. *au* and *bookseller*, 1733—1811.

Nicolas, Sir Nicholas Harris, *antiq* Scot., 1799—1848.

Nicole, Francis, Fr. *math*, 1683—1748.

Niebuhr, Nɛ́-bur, Carsten, Ger. *trav*, 1733—1815.

Niebuhr, Barthold Geo., son of the preceding, *hist*, *philol* and *dip*, 1776—1831.

Nield, James, Eng. *philan*, 1744—1814.

Niemeyer, Nε-mį-er, Aug. Herman, Ger. educational and miscellaneous *wr*, 1754—1828.

Nieuwlend, Nε-ω-lqnd, Peter, Dutch *wr* on nat. phil. and mathematics, 1764—1794.

Ninus, Nį-nus, *found* Assyrian empire, husband of Semiramus, 2164 B. C.

Niobe, Nį-ω-bε, *fab*, wife of Amphion, who, preferring herself to Latona, had her 14 children killed by Diana and Apollo, and wept herself into a statue. [—2029 B. C.

Noah, Nó-ɑ, saved from the flood,

Noah, Mordecai M., Am. *jour* N-Y., 1785—1851. [1784—1827.

Noble, Mark, Eng. *hist* and *biog wr*,

Noehden, Nę-den, George Henry, Ger. *wr*, 1770—1826. [1823.

Nollekens, Joseph, Eng. *sculp*, 1737—

Nollet, Nól-a, John Antoine, Fr. *nat phil*, 1770—d.

Noodt, Nωdt, Gerard, *civilian* Holland, 1647—1725.

Norris, John, Eng. *meta phil* and *div*, 1657—1711.

North, Frederic, Earl of Guildford, Lord, Eng. *st*, 1732—1792.

Northcote, Nórϑ-kωt, James, Eng. *pt*, 1746—1831.

Norton, Andrews, Am. *poet* and *prose wr* Mass., 1786— [*wr*.

Norton, Mrs. Caroline, Eng. *poet* and

Nott, John, M. D., *poet* and *ori* Eng., 1751—1826.

Nott, Eliphalet, D. D., *wr*, and *pres* Union College, N-Y., 1773—

Nox, Noks, *fab*, the most ancient of deities.

Nuck, Nęk, Anthony, Dutch *anat* and *med wr*, —1692.

Nunez De Balboa, Nó-neϑ Da Bql-bó-q, Sp. *disc* Pacific Ocean, by crossing the Isthmus of Darien, in 1513.

# O.

Oberlin, John Fred., "Pastor of Waldbach," an earnest laborer in the cause of education and the arts of civilization; Ger., 1740—1826.

Oberlin, Jeremiah James, Ger. *philol* and *antiq*, 1735—1806.

O'Brien, Ω-brį-en, Wm. Smith, "Irish *patriot*," 1806—

Ockham, Ωk'am, William of, British *meta phil*, 14th cen.

Ockley, Ωk'li, Simon, *ori* and *au* Eng., 1678—1720.

O'Connell, Ω-kón-el, Daniel, Irish *or* and *patriot*, 1775—1847.

Odescalchi, Ω-dɑs-kql-kε, Marc A., It. *philan*, —1670.

Odin, *war*, *poet*, *priest* and *monarch*, Den., after death worshipped as a god, 70 B. C.

Oeder, E'der, Geo. Christ., *ph*, *bot* and *au*, Ger., 1728—1791.

Oehlenschloeger, Ω-len-sló-ger, Adam, Danish *dram poet*, 1777—1850.

Oetinger, E'tin-ћer, Fred. Christopher, Ger. *philol*, 1702—1782.

Ogé, Ω-ʒá, a creole of St. Domingo, *founder* of the Haytian revolution, —1790, killed.

Oglethorpe, Ω'gl-ϑerp, James, Brit. *gen*, *found* Georgia, died in Eng., 1785.

O'Keefe, Ω-ké-fε, John, *dram* Ireland, 1748—1833.

Oken, Ω'kn, Lorenz, Swiss *nat* and *au*, 1778—1851.

Olafsen, Ω-lqf-sen, Stephen, *trans* the Edda and Voluspa, Iceland, —1688.

Oldenburg, Ol'den-burg, Augustus-Paul-Fred., Grand-Duke of, 1783—

Oldham, John, Eng. *poet*, 1653—1683.

Olivan, Ol-ε-vqn, Don Alesandro De, Spanish *publicist*.

Omar I., *caliph* of the Saracens, assas. 643.

Onosander, Greek *au*, A. D., 50.

Opie, Ω'pε, John, *hist pt*, Eng., 1761—1807.

Opie, Amelia, wife of the above, *au*, 1768—1853.

Orange, William of Nassau, Prince of, *found* Dutch republic, 1533—as. 1584.

Origen, a father of Christian church, Alexandria, 185—254.

Orion, Ω-rį-on, *fab*, a mighty hunter.

Orleans, Θr-le-áṅ *or* Θr'lε-anz, *dukedom*, and titular name borne by the princes of the blood royal in France, of which there are two houses:—1. Commencing with Louis I. of Fr., 1393; 2. Commencing with Philip I., 1660.

Orleans, Louis Philippe Jos., Duc D', father of the late king, and singularly enough, a republican, 1747—ex. 1793.
Orme, Robert, Eng. *hist*, 1728—1801.
Ormond, James B., Duke of, Eng. *st*, 1610—1688.
Orpheus, Θr'fɛ-us, Greek *poet*, *mus* and *ph*, fl. before Homer.
Orville, Θr-věl, James Philip D', *clas wr* Holland, 1696—1751.
Ossian, Oʃ'i-an, Gaelic *poet*, 3d cen.
Ossoli, Os-ó-lɛ, the Countess, better known as Margaret Fuller, Am. *au* Mass., 1810—1850.
Otho I., *k* Greece, 1815—c. 1832—
Otho, Ѡ'tѡ, Marcus Salvius, *emp* of Rome, in 69. — I., II., III., IV., *emps* Ger., 936 to 1218.
Otis, James, Am. *st* Mass., 1725—1783.
Otranto, Ѡ-trɋn-tѡ, Jos. Fouche, Duke of, *min of Police*, Fr., 1763—1820.
Ottley, Ot'li, Wm. Young, F. R. S., Brit. *art* and *au*, 1772—1836.
Otto, O-tó, Louis Wm., Count de Mosloy, Fr. *dip*, 1754—d. [1651—1685.
Otway, Ot'wa, Thomas, Eng. *dram*,
Oudinot, Ѻ-dań-ó, Chas. Nicholas, Duke of Reggio, *marshal* Fr., 1767—1847.
Ouvrard, Ѻv-rɋrd, Réné, Fr. *div*, *poet*, *math* and *mus*, —1694.
Overbeck, Frederick, Ger. *art*, 1789—
Ovid, Ѡ'vid, Publius Naso, Roman *poet*, fl. A. D. 12.
Oviedo, Ѡ-vi-á-đѡ, John G., Spanish *nat*, —1540. [1683.
Owen, John, D. D., Eng. *div*, 1616—
Owen, Robert Dale, Am. *wr*, *pol theorist*, and *pol*, Ia.
Owen, William, Eng. *por-pt*, 1769—1825.
Owen, Robert, *pol theorist* Eng., 1771—
Owen, Richard, F. R. S., Eng , *sur*, *nat* and *au*.
Oxenstierna, Oks-en-stěr-nɋ, Axel, Count, *st* Sweden, 1583—1654.
Ozanam, Oz-a-nɋm, James, Fr. *math*, 1640—1717.
Ozeretzkoffsky, Oz-er-ets-kóf-ski, Nicholas Yak., Rus. *savant* and *wr*, 1751—1827.
Ozeroff, Vladislas Alexandrovitsch, Rus. *tragic poet*, 1707—1816.

# P.

Paaw, Pɋv, Peter, Dutch *ph* and *bot*, 1564—1617.
Pacheco, Pɋ-ɕá-kѡ, Don Joaquin Franz, Sp. *jour*, *au* and *poet*, 1808—
Paciandi, Pɋ-ɕɛ-ɋn-dɛ, Paul Maria, Italian *antiq* and *hist*, 1710—1785.
Paez, Pɋ-áŧ, Jose Antonio, *ex-pres* Venezuela, 1790—
Paganini, Pɋ-gɋ-né-nɛ, Nicolo, Italian *viol*, 1784—1840.
Page, William, Am. *por-pt* N-Y., 1811—
Paine, Robert Treat, Am. *law*, and *signer Dec. of Ind.*, 1731—1811.
Paine, Thomas, *pol wr* and *bib crit*, Pa., 1737—1809.
Paisiello, Pį-zɛ-á-lѡ, Giovanni, Italian *mus comp*, 1741—1818.
Palafox-Y-Meizi, Pɋ-lɋ-fѡ-Ɛ-Ma-é-ŧɛ, Sp. *gen*, the defender of Saragossa, —1847.
Paley, Pá-li, Wm., D. D., Eng. *div* and *wr* on ethics, 1743—1805.
Palissot De Beauvois, Pal-ɛ-sѡ Dȩ Bѡ-vwó, Ambroise M. F. J., Fr. *nat*, 1752—1820.
Palissy, Pɋ-lɛ-sɛ, Bernard De, French *chem*, —1590.
Palladio, Pɋ-lɋ-dé-ѡ, Andrea, It. *arch*, 1518—1580.
Pallas, Pɋ-lɋs, Peter Simon, *trav* and *nat* Ger., 1741—1811. [1781—1850.
Palmella, Pɋm-él-ɑ, Duke of, *st* Port.,
Palmerston, Pám-er-ston, Henry Temple, Viscount, Eng. *st*, 1784—
Pandora, Pan-dó-rɑ, *fab*, the first woman made by Vulcan, and endowed with gifts by all the deities; Jupiter gave her a box containing all manner of evils, war, famine, &c., with hope at the bottom.
Paoli, Pɋ-ó-lɛ, Pascal, Corsican *st*, 1726—1807.
Papin, Pɋ-pań, Denys, Fr. *nat*, *phil* and *ph*, —1710.
Paracelsus, Par-a-sél-sus, Aureolus Philippus Theophrastus, &c., Swiss *ph* and *phil wr*, 1493—1541. [1590.
Pare, Pɋr, Ambrose, Fr. *sur*, 1509—
Pareja, Pɋr-á-hɋ, Juan De, *pt* and *slave*, Sp., 1610—1670. [1729—1799.
Parini, Pɋr-é-nɛ, Joseph, Italian *poet*,
Paris, Pár-is, *fab*, son of Priam, who ran away with Helena, and occasioned the Trojan war.

Park, Mungo, Scottish *trav* and *exp* in Africa, 1771—perished 1806.
Parker, Rev. Theodore, Unitarian *cler*, anti-slavery *ref*, and *wr*, Mass.
Parkes, Samuel, *exper chem* and *au*, Eng., 1759—1825. [1830.
Parkinson, Thomas, *math* Eng., 1745—
Parnassus, Pqr-nás-us, *fab*, a mountain of Phocis, famous for a temple of Apollo, and being the favorite residence of the muses.
Parnell, Pqr-nél, Thomas, Irish *poet* and *au*, 1679—1718.
Parr, Pqr, Samuel, *div* and *scholar*, Eng., 1746—1825.
Parry, Pár-i, Caleb H., M. D., F. R. S., *ph* and *nat*, 1756—1822.
Parry, Sir Wm. Edward, Eng. *nav*, 1790—1855. [1705—1770.
Parsons, James, Eng. *med* and *misc wr*,
Parsons, Theophilus, LL. D., *law* and *chief justice*, Mass., 1750—1813.
Pascal, Pás-kal, Blaise, *math* and *nat phil*, Fr., 1623—1662.
Paskewitch, Pás-ka-viq, Ivan Feod., Prince of Warsaw, 1782—
Pastor Diaz, Pqs-tœr Dε-qθ, Don Nicomedes, Sp. *poet*, 1811—
Patrick, St., *guard saint* of Ireland, native of Wales, carried to Ireland, and converted the people to Christianity, —460. [*geol*, 1742—1815.
Patrin, Pa-trán, Eugene L. M., Fr.
Paulding, Pél-diŋ, James K., Am. *wr* N-Y., 1779— [1801.
Paul, Petrowitz, *tyr emp* Rus., assas.
Paul, Father, *scholar* and *au* "History of the Council of Trent."
Paul, St., originally Saul, put to death by Nero, for preaching Christ, A. D. 66. [1272.
Paulo, Marco, Venetian *trav* in China,
Paxton, Páks-ton, Sir Joseph, *arch* of the Crystal Palace, Scot., 1804—
Payne, Pan, John Howard, Am. *wr* and *dram* N-Y., 1792—1852.
Peabody, Pé-bod-i, Rev. Andrew P., D. D., *div* and *crit wr* Mass., 1811—
Pecquet, Pę-ká, John, Fr. *anat* and *ph*, discoverer of the thoracic duct and the receptacle of the chyle, —1674.
Pedro I., Páđ-rœ *or* Pé-drœ, Antonio Jose D'Al., Don, *ex-emp* Brazil, 1798—1834.
Peel, Sir Robert, Eng. *st*, 1788—1850.
Pegasus, Pég-a-sus, *fab*, winged horse belonging to Apollo and the Muses.
Pelagius, Pε-lá-ji-us, *found* of a sect, Brit., 5th cen. — I. and II., *popes*, 555, 578.

Pellico, Pal-é-kœ, Silvio, It. *wr*, 1789—
Pemberton, Thomas, Am. *hist*, 1728—1807. [household gods.
Penates, Pε-ná-tεz, *fab*, statues or
Pena Y Aguayo, Pá-nq E A-gwq-ε-œ, Don Jose De La, Sp. *law* and *au*, 1801—
Penelope, Pε-nél-œ-pε, *fab*, daughter of Icarus, celebrated for her chastity and fidelity during the long absence of Ulysses.
Penn, William, a "Quaker," *found* Pennsylvania, 1644—1718.
Pennant, Pén-ant, Thomas, Brit. *nat*, 1726—1798.
Pepusch, Pa-pœʃ, John Christ., Ger. *theor mus*, 1667—1752.
Perceval, Pér-sε-val, Spencer, Eng. *law* and *st*, 1762—sh. 1812.
Percival, Pér-si-val, James Gates, Am. *poet* Conn., 1795—
Percy, Pér-si, Thomas, Eng. *ed* and *wr*, 1729—1811. [and *gen*.
Pericles, Pér-i-klεz, Athenian *st*, *or*
Perry, James, Eng. *jour*, *pol wr*, and *ed* "Morning Chronicle," 1756—1821.
Perry, Oliver Haz., *off* Am. navy, R. I., 1785—1820.
Pestalozzi, Pes-tq-lót-sε, Henry, Swiss *educator*, founder of the system of instruction by "objects," and *au*., 1745—d.
Peter, chief of the Apostles, crucified by Nero, head downward, A. D. 66.
Peter, St., *bp* Alexandria, martyred 311.
Peter the First, *czar* Rus., and a promoter of education and the arts of civilization, 1672—1725.
Peter, the Hermit, Fr. *off*, and holy pilgrim, who instigated the war of the Crusaders, —1100.
Pethion De Villeneuve, Pa-tε-ón Dę Vεl-yań-uv, Jerome, Girondist *leader* of the French revolution, —1793.
Petion, Pa-tε-óń, Alex. Salies, a negro, *gen*, and *pres* republic of Hayti, 1770—1818. [—1750.
Petit, Pę-tε, Jean Louis, Fr. *sur*, 1674
Petrarch, Pé-trqrk, Francesco, chief restorer of classical learning, Tuscany, 1304—1374.
Phaeton, Fá-ε-ton, *fab*, son of Sol (Apollo), who asked the guidance of his father's chariot for one day, as a proof of his divine descent; but unable to manage the horses, set the world on fire, and was therefore struck by Jupiter with a thunderbolt into the river Po. [B. C.
Phidias, Fid-i-as, Athenian *sculp*, 432

Philemon, Fi-lé-mon, comic *poet*, Athens, 274 B. C.
Philetus, Fi-lé-tus, Greek *poet*.
Philip II., Fil-ip, *k* Macedon, father of Alex. the Great, assas. 336 B. C.
Philip II., *k* Spain, *bigot* and *tyrant*, 1527—1598.
Philip, St., the first whom Jesus called as a disciple. [—1749.
Philips, Ambrose, Eng. *poet* and *dram*,
Philips, John, Eng. *poet*, 1671—1708.
Philips, Samuel, Eng. *jour* and *misc wr*, 1815—1854. [*ref* Mass.
Philips, Wendell, Am. *savant*, *or* and
Phillpotts, Henry, champion of the Eng. High-Church party, 1777—
Philo, Fi-lo, Indæus, Greek *wr* on mor. philos., fl. A. D. 40.
Philostratus, Fi-los-trá-tus, Greek *sophist* and *crit*, —244.
Phocion, Fó-ʃi-on, Athenian *gen* and *phil*, poisoned 318 B. C.
Piazzi, Pe-át-se, Guiseppe, It. *astr*, discoverer of the planet Ceres, 1746 —1826. [1728—1801.
Piccini, Pe-çé-ne, Nicolai, It. *mus comp*,
Pichler, Pih-ler, Caroline, posthumous Ger. *wr*, 1769—1843.
Pickering, *law*, and *chief j* Sup. Ct. N-H., —1805.
Pictet, Mark Aug., Swiss *nat* and *phil*, 1752—1825. [k. 1815.
Picton, Sir Thomas, K. C. B., Brit. *off*,
Pierce, Pers, Franklin, *pol*, and thirteenth Pres. U. S., from 1853 to 1857; N-H. V-Pres., Wm. R. King, who died before taking his seat.
Pierpont, Pér-pont, Rev. J., Am. *cler*, *poet* and *ref* Mass., about 1776—
Pike, Zebulon Mont., *off* Am. army, N-J., —k. 1813.
Pilate, Pontius, Pón-ʃi-us Pi-lat, Roman *gov* Judea, under whose rule Christ suffered death; he was exiled, and hanged himself A. D. 37.
Pinckney, Piŋk-ni, Chas. Cotesworth, Am. *off* and *dip* S. C., —1825.
Pindar, lyric *poet*, much esteemed, —500 B. C. [1711—1796.
Pingre, Pań-gr, Alex. Guy, Fr. *astr*,
Pinkerton, Píŋ-ker-ton, John, *au* Scot., 1758—1826.
Pinkney, Píŋk-ni, Wm., Am. *st* Md., 1765—1822.
Piranesi, Pe-ra-ń-se, Giambattista, It. *archæ*, 1707—1778.
Pitman, Isaac, *inv* of Phonography, and experimenter in phonetic printing, Eng., 1814— [1771.
Pitot, Pe-to, Henry, Fr. *math*, 1695—
Pitt, Christopher, Eng. *cler* and *poet*, 1699—1748. [1806.
Pitt, William, *st* and *min* Eng., 1759—
Pius the Ninth, Pope, was b. 1792—assumed the gov. 1846—
Pizarro, Pe-zár-o, Francisco, *conq* of Peru, 1517—1541.
Plato, Plá-to, Athenian *phil*, of great repute, 429—348 B. C.
Playfair, Plá-far, John, *math* and *nat phil* Scot., 1749—1819.
Pleiades, Plé-ya-dez, *fab*, the seven daughters of Atlas and Pleione, who were changed into stars.
Pliny, Plín-i, Caius Secundus, most learned of anc. Roman *wrs*, 23—79.
Pliny, Cæcilius Secundus, nephew of the above, *law* and *consul*, 62—113.
Plot, Robert, Eng. *nat*, 1640—1696.
Pluche, Pluʃ, Noel A., Fr. *nat* and *wr*, 1688—1761. [—1854.
Plunket, Wm. C., Lord, Brit. *st*, 1764
Plutarch, Plú-tark, *phil* and *hist* Greece, —140.
Pluto, Plú-to, *fab*, the god of hell.
Pocahontas, Po-ka-hón-tas, Indian *princess* Va., who married Mr. Rolfe, an Englishman; died in Eng., 1616.
Poinsett, Pén-set, Joel R., Am. *st* S. C., —1851. [1646—1719.
Poiret, Pwo-rá, Peter, Fr. mystic *phil*,
Pole, Reginald, Eng. *cardinal*, and friend of Queen Mary, 1500—1558.
Polignac, Pol-eg-nak, Jules, Prince De, *prime min* of Charles X., of France, 1783—1847.
Polk, Pok, James K., eleventh Pres. U. S., from 1845 to 1849; Tenn., —1849. V-Pres., Geo. M. Dallas, Pa.
Pollok, Pól-ok, Robert, Eng. *poet*, 1798 —1827.
Polwhele, Pol-hwé-le, Rev. Richard, *antiq*, *poet*, *hist* and *misc wr* Scot., 1760—1838. [1667—1703.
Pomfret, Póm-fret, John, Eng. *poet*,
Pomona, Po-mó-na, *fab*, the goddess of fruits.
Pompadour, Póm-pa-dor, Jane Antoinette Poisson, a beloved mistress of Louis XV., 1720—1764.
Pompey, Póm-pi, Cneius the Great, rival of Julius Cæsar; being defeated, he fled to Egypt, and was assas., 48 B. C.
Pomponazzi, Pom-po-nát-se, It. *phil*, 1462—1524.
Pond, John, F. R. S., Eng. *astr*, —1836.
Poniatowski, Po-ne-a-túvs-ki, Stanislaus Augustus, last *k* of Poland, 1732 —drowned 1814.

Pope, Alexander, *poet* and *sat* Eng., 1688—1744.
Porson, Pór-son, Richard, Eng. *crit* and *classic au*, 1759—1808.
Porta, Pór-tą, Giovanni B. D., *nat phil* and *math*, inventor of the camera obscura, Italy, 1540—d.
Porter, Anna Maria, *nov* Eng., —1832.
Porter, Jane, Eng. *au*, 1776—1850.
Porter, Sir Robert Ker, Eng. *art* and *wr*, 1780—1842.
Porter, David, *com* Am. navy, Mass., 1780—1843.
Portugal, Maria-Da-Gloria, Queen of, b. 1819—assumed gov. 1834—
Potemkin, Gregory Alexandrovitsch, Rus. *prince* and *off*, 1736—1791.
Potocki, Pœ-tœ-kɛ, Claudia, Countess of, distinguished for her acts of charity in the Polish war, 1802—1836.
Pott, Percival, Eng. *sur*, 1713—1788.
Potter, Jno., *au* "Antiquities of Greece," Eng., 1674—1747.
Potter, Paul, Dutch *pt*, 1625—1654.
Pouschkine, Pɤʃ-kįn-e, Alex., Rus. *poet*, 1799—1837.
Poussin, Pœ-sán, Nicolas, Fr. *pt*, 1594—1665.
Powers, Pɤ-erz, Hiram, Am. *sculp*, O., 1805—
Powhattan, Pɤ-hát-an, Indian *chief*, Va., father of Pocahontas, —1618.
Pozzo Di Borgo, Pót-sœ Dɛ Bér-gœ, Chas. A. Count, *dip* Corsica, 1768—1842.
Prentice, Prén-tis, George D., Am. *poet* and *jour*, *ed* "Louisville Journal," Ky., 1804—
Preissnitz, Prįs-nits, Vincent, *disc* of the Water-Cure, Prus., 1799—1851.
Prescott, Prés-kot, Wm. Hickling, Am. *hist* Mass., 1796—
Prescott, Wm., *off* Am. army, Mass., 1725—1795.
Prevot D'Exiles, Prę-vœ Dąg-zél-a, Anthony Francis, a posthumous Fr. *wr*, 1697—1763.
Priam, Prį-am, *fab*, father of Paris, Hector, &c.; the last king of Troy.
Price, Dr. Richard, Eng. *div*, *essa* and *math*, 1723—1791.
Prichard, Priq-ard, James Cowles, M. D., Eng. *ethno*, 1786—1848.
Priestley, Prést-li, Joseph, *chem*, *theol*, *hist*, *electrician* and *pol*. To him we are indebted for a knowledge of oxygen, carbonic oxide, binoxide of nitrogen, ammonia, muriatic acid, sulphurous acid, fluosilicic acid, etc., Eng., 1733—1804.
Pringle, Prín-gl, Sir John, Eng. *nat phil* and *ph*, 1707—1782.
Prior, Prį-or, Mathew, Eng. *poet*, 1664—1721.
Procter, Prók-ter, Bryan W., better known as "Barry Cornwall," British *poet*.
Prometheus, Prœ-mé-ɫɛ-us, a great *war*, supposed to have been the first discoverer of the art of striking fire by flint and steel, which gave rise to the fable of his stealing fire from heaven; fl. 1687 B. C.
Proserpine, Prós-er-pįn, *fab*, the wife of Pluto.
Proteus, Prœ́-tɛ-us, *fab*, a sea-god, who could transform himself into any shape.
Prudhomme, Pręd-óm, L., *ed* of "Le Journal des Révolutions de Paris," 1752—1830.
Prutz, Prœts, Reinhold E., Ger. *poet* and *lit hist*, 1810—
Prynne, Prįn, William, Puritan *au*, Eng., 1600—1637.
Psyche, Sį-kɛ, *fab*, the goddess of pleasure.
Ptolemy, Tól-ɛ-mi, Claudius, *geog*, *math* and *astr*, b. in Eg., A. D. 138.
Publius Cyrus, Pŭb-li-us Sį-rus, Syrian slave, who distinguishing himself as a poet, was set at liberty, 44 B. C.
Puffendorf, Pœ́f-en-dørf, Samuel, Ger. *nat*, *jurist* and *hist*, 1632—1694.
Pultney, Púlt-ni, Wm., Earl of Bath, *pol* Eng., 1682—1764.
Pulaski, Pœ-lą́s-kɛ, Count, Pole *off* Am. army, —k. 1779.
Purcell, Pur-sél, Henry, Eng. *mus*, 1658—1695.
Putnam, Israel, Am. *maj-gen* Revolutionary war, Mass., 1718—1790.
Pym, Pim, John, Eng. *st*, 1584—1643.
Pyrrhus, Pír-us, *fab*, son of Achilles, remarkable for his cruelty at the siege of Troy.
Pythagoras, Pi-ɫág-œ-ras, Grecian *phil*, 590—497 B. C.
Pytheas, Pít-ɛ-as, Greek *phil*, who discovered the difference in the length of days in different climates, 384 B. C.

# Q.

Querles, Kwq́r-les, Francis, Eng. *poet*, 1592—1614.
Quelinus, Kę-a-lín-ųs, Erasmus, Dutch *pt*, 1607—1678.
Querlon, Kęr-loṅ, Anne Gabriel M. De, Fr. *jour*, 1702—1780.
Quer y Martinez, Kar ε Mqr-tεn-áθ, Joseph, Sp. *bot*, 1695—1764.
Quesnay, Kę́s-na, Francois, Fr. *pol econ*, 1794—1774.
Quesnoy, Kęs-nwó, Francis Du, *sculp* Brussels, 1592—1646.
Quevedo Villegas, Ka-vá-dω Vεl-ya-gq́s, Francisco De, Sp. *poet* and *satirist*, 1570—1647.
Quin, Kwin, James, Br. *act*, 1693—1766.
Quinault, Kę-nól, Philip, Fr. *dram poet*, 1636—1688.
Quincy, Kwín-si, Josiah, Am. *patriot* and *law* Mass., —1775.
Quincy, Josiah, *ex-pres* Harvard University, *st* and *sch* Mass., 1772—
Quincy, Josiah, jr., *law* and *finan* Mass., 1802—
Quinet, Kę-ná, Edgar, Fr. *poet* and *hist* of literature, 1803—
Quintana, Kεn-tq́-nq, Jose Manuel De, Sp. *poet* and *hist*, 1772—
Quita, Ké-tq, Domingos Dos Reis, *poet* Port., 1728—1770.
Quintilian, Kwin-til-i-an, Marcus Fabius, Rom. *law* and *crit*, A. D. 42—131.

# R.

Rabelais, Rq-bel-á, Francois, Fr. *hum*, 1483—1553.
Racan, Rq-káṅ, Honorat De B., Marquis of, Fr. *poet*, 1589—1670.
Racine, Rq-sén, Jean, Fr. *trag dram*, 1639—1699. [1764—1823.
Radcliffe, Rád-klif, Ann, Eng. *nov*,
Radetzky, Rq-déts-ki, Joseph, Count, *comman* Austrian army, 1766—
Radowitz, Rq-dω-véts, Joseph Von, Prus. *min*, 1797—
Raeburn, Rá-burn, Sir Henry, Scot. *art*, 1756—1823.
Rafu, Rq́-fω, Karl Christian, Icelandic *critic* and *antiq*, 1795—
Raglan, Rág-lan, Lord Fitzroy James H. Somerset, Baron, Eng. *gen com*, Crimean forces, 1788—1855.
Ragotsky, Rq-góts-ki, Francis, *prince* of Transylvania, 1676—1735.
Raimondi, Rį-món-dε, Marc Antonis, It. *engraver*, 1478—1540.
Raleigh, Rq́-li, Sir Walter, Eng. *nav*, *exp* and *wr*, 1552— beheaded 1618.
Rameau, Rq-mó, Jean Philippe, Fr. *mus theorist*, 1683—1764.
Ramler, Rq́m-ler, Chas. Wm., Ger. *poet* and *misc wr*, 1725—1798.
Rammohun Roy, Rám-ω-un Rσ, Rajah, *phil* and *reformer*, Br. Ind., 1774—1833.
Ramond De Carbonnieres, Rá-moṅd Da Kq́r-boṅ-ε-ra, Louis F. E., Baron, Fr. *phil* and *geol*, 1775—1827.
Ramsay, Rám-za, Allan, Scottish *poet*, 1685—1758.
Ramsay, David, Am. *ph* and *hist*, S. C., 1749—1815.
Ramsden, Rámz-den, Jesse, *opt* and *math* instrument maker, Eng., 1735—1800.
Ramus, Rq-męs, Peter, Fr. *meta phil*, and *wr*, 1515—1572.
Randolph, Rán-dolf, John, of Roanoke, Am. *st* Va., 1773—1833.
Ranke, Rq́ŋ-ka, Leopold, Ger. *hist*, 1795—
Raphael, Rá-fa-el, Santi, the "prince of painters," It., 1483—1520.
Raphall, Ráf-al, Morris J., M. A., Ph. Dr., a rabbi preacher, N-Y., and em. *wr*, 1798—
Raspail, Rq́s-pal, Francois V., Fr. *wr* on the *nat sciences*, and a *repub ed*, 1794— [1722—1805.
Ratte, Rqt, Etienne Hy. De, Fr. *ast*,
Rauch, Rɤh, Christian, Ger. *sculp*, 1777—
Raumer, Rɤ́-mer, Fred. Lud. Geo. Von, Ger. *hist* and *trav*, 1781—
Ray, Ra, Joseph, *prof* and *au math* works, Ohio, b. Va., 18——1855.
Ray, Rev. John, *bot* and *zool* Eng., 1628—1705.
Raynal, Rá-nql, Wm. Thom. F., Fr. *hist* and *pol wr*, 1711—1796.
Reach, Rεç, Augus B., Scottish *jour* and *au*, 1821—

Reaumur, Ró-me, Rêné An. F. De, *phil nat*, Fr., 1683—d.
Reboul, Ra-bǿl, Jean, "the baker poet," Fr., 1796—
Redesdale, Réd-es-dal, John F. M., Baron, Eng. *law* and *st*, 1748—1830.
Redfield, Réd-fɛld, William C., Am. *meteor* Conn., 1789—
Redgrave, Réd-grav, Richard, Eng. *pt*, 1804— [1626—1698.
Redi, Rá-dɛ, Francis, It., *ph* and *nat*,
Reding, Réd-iŋ, Aloys, Baron Von, Swiss. *gen*, 1755—1818.
Reed, Rɛd, Henry, Am. *wr* Pa., perished at sea, 1854. [1742—1807.
Reed, Isaac, *critic* and *misc wr* Eng.,
Reed, Joseph, Am. *rev* and *mem* of Congress, Pa.,—1781. [1632—1707.
Regis, Rá-ʒɛ, Pierre S., Fr. *meta phil*,
Regius, Ra-*hé*-ɷs, Urban, Ger. *poet* and *controversialist*, —1541.
Regnault, Rán-yɷl, Michel L. S., Fr. *st* 1760—1819. [1736—1814.
Regnault, Noel, *math* and *phil*, Fr.,
Regnier, Rán-yɛr, Maturin, Fr. *poet* and *satirist*, 1573—1613.
Regulus, Rég-yɥ-lus, Marcus Attitius, Rom. *gen*, put to death 251 B. C.
Reicha, Rį-*h*ɥ, Antoine Jos., Ger. *mus comp*, 1770—1836.
Reichardt, Rį*h*-ɥrt, Johann Fried., Ger. *mus comp*, 1752—1814.
Reichenbach, Rį*h*-en-bɥ*h*, George of, an *artist* dist. in *manuf astro* and *philo instruments*, Ger., 1772—1826.
Reichstadt, Rį*h*-stɥt, Napoleon Fran. Chas. Jos. Bonaparte, Duc De, only son of Napoleon, 1811—1832.
Reid, Rɛd, Thomas, Scottish *phil*, 1710—1795.
Reid, Col. Sir William, Royal *eng* and *naut wr*, 1791—
Reinhold, Rįn-hɷlt, Erasmus, Ger. *math* and *ast*, 1511—1553.
Reiske, Rįs-kɛ, John James, *philol* and *orientalist*, Ger., 1716—1774.
Reissiger, Rįs-ig-er, Karl Got., Ger. *mus comp*, 1798— [1733—1790.
Reiz, Rįts, Frederic W., Ger. *philol*,
Rembrandt Van Rhyn, Rem-brɥ́nt Fɥn Rįn, Paul, Dutch *pt* and *engra*, 1606—1674.
Remusat, Ra-mɷ-sɥ́, Jean Pierre A., Fr. *ling*, 1788—1832.
René, Ru-ná, of Anjou, the last of his dynasty who sat on the throne of Naples, 1409—1470. [1761—1821.
Rennie, Rén-ɛ, John, *civil eng* Eng.,
Retz, Ret, Jean F. P. De Gondi, Cardinal De, Fr. *pol* and *wr*, 1614—1679.
Retzsch, Réts-ʃ, Moritz, Ger. *art*, 1779—
Reuchlin, R*ʊh*-lin, John, Ger. *philol*, 1455—1522.
Rey, Rā, John, Fr. *pneumatic chem* and *ph*, —1645.
Reyneau, Rá-nɷ, Chas. René, Fr. *math*, 1656—1728.
Reynolds, Rén-oldz, Sir Joshua, *found* of the Eng. school of painting, 1723—1792.
Rhigas, Ré-gɥs, a modern Greek *patriot*, 1753—1798.
Rhyne, Rį-ne, Wm. Fen., Dutch *ph* and *nat*, 1640—d.
Ricardo, Ri-kɥ́r-dɷ, David, Eng. *pol econ*, 1772—1823.
Rich, Riç, Claudius James, Eng. *trav* and *orientalist*, 1787—1821.
Richard, Riç-ɥrd, I., the "Lion-hearted," b. 1157— *k* of Eng. from 1189 to 1199 the time of his death.
Richard, II., b. 1366— *k* of Eng. from 1366 to 1399.
Richard, III., the most execrable Eng. prince, b. 1452— *k* from 1484 to 1485.
Richard, Claude Louis, Fr. *bot*, 1754—1821. [1761.
Richardson, Samuel, Eng. *nov*, 1689—
Richardson, Wm., *poet* and *misc wr*, Scot., —1814.
Richelieu, Riʃ-el-ę, Armand J. Du Plessis, Cardinal, Fr. *min*, 1585—1642.
Richter, Ri*h*-ter, Jean Paul Friedrich, Ger. *wr* and *au*, 1763—1825.
Riego, Rɛ-á-gɷ, Rafael Del, Sp. *patriot off*, 1785—1823.
Rienzi, Rɛ-énd-zɛ, Nicolas Gabrini de, a man of low estate, who raised himself to sovereign power in Rome, 1310—1354. [—1838.
Ries, Rɛs, Ferdinand, Ger. *mus*, 1784
Rigaud, Ri-gód, Stephen Peter, *ast* Eng., 1775—1839.
Ritchie, Riç-i, Thomas, Am. *pol* and *ed* of "Richmond Enquirer," Va.
Rittenhouse, Rít-en-hɤs, David, *math* Pa., 1732—1796.
Ritter, Rit-er, John Wm., Ger. *phil* and *wr*, 1776—1810.
Rivaroi, Riv-ɥr-wó, Anthony, Count De, Fr. *wr*, 1757—1801.
Rivas, Rɛ-vɥ́s, Angel De S., Duque De, *poet*, *dram* and *pt*, Sp., 1791—
Rivaz, Rɛ-vɥ́, Peter Jos. De, Fr. *mech* and *chronologer*, 1711—1772.
Riviere, Rɛ-vi-ą́r, Mercier De La, Fr. *pol econ*, 1747—1794.
Rivinus, Riv-in-us, Augustus Q., Ger. *bot*, 1652—1723.

Robert, Rob-ąr, Peter Fran. Jos., Fr. *st* and *wr*, 1743—d.
Robert, Hubert, Fr. *pt*, 1732—1808.
Robert-Fleury, — Flęr, Joseph Nicolas, Fr. *pt*, 1797—
Robertson, Rób-ert-son, Dr. Wm., Scottish *hist* and *clerg*, 1729—1793.
Robespierre, Rob-es-pér, Francois Joseph M. J., the chief actor in the French revolution, and celebrated for his cruelty, 1759—guil. 1794.
Robin Hood, Rób-in Hud, *capt* band of robbers, Eng., —1247.
Robins, Rób-inz, Benjamin, Eng. *math wr*, 1707—1751.
Robinson, Rób-in-son, Mary, Eng. *poet* and *misc wr*, 1758—1800.
Robinson, Thomas, Eng. *nat* and *clerg*, —1719.
Robinson, Rób-in-son, Edward, D. D., LL. D., Am. *scholar*, Conn., 1794—
Robison, Rób-i-son, John, Scottish *wr* on *nat phil*, 1739—1805.
Robson, Geo. Fennel, *draughtsman* and *l-pt*, Eng., —1833.
Roby, Ró-bi, John, Eng. *banker, poet,* and *hist*, —1850.
Rochambeau, Ro-ʃam-bó, Jean B. D. De Vimeur, Count De, Fr. *off*, 1725 1807.
Rochejaquelein, Ro-ʃa-ʒa-kę-lán, Henri De La, *chief* of La Vendée, 1773—k. 1794.
Rockingham, Rók-iŋ-ham, Charles W. W., second Marquis of, Eng. *st* and *pol*, 1730—1782
Rodney, Ród-ni, George B., Lord, Eng. *adm*, —1792. [1644.
Roe, Rō, Sir Thomas, Eng. *st*, 1580—
Roebuck, Ró-buk, John, Eng. *ph* and *nat phil*, 1718—1794.
Roebuck, John Arthur, radical Eng. *pol*, 1801—
Roemer, Ré-mer, Olaus, Danish *astr*, discoverer of the velocity of light, 1644—1710. [—1732.
Rogers, Rój-erz, Woods, Eng. *nav*,
Rogers, Samuel, Eng. *poet* and *banker*, 1760—1856.
Rogers, John, Eng. *div* martyred in the persecuting reign of Mary, at Smithfield, —1555.
Rohault, Ro-ól, James, Fr. *math* and *nat phil*, 1620—1675.
Roland De La Platiere, Rol-ąnd Dę Lą Plą-tér, Jean Marie, Girondist *min* of Fr., 1732—1793.
Roland, Manon Jeanne P., the wife of the above and dist. as *pol wr*, 1754—g. 1793.
Rollin, Rol-an, Charles, Fr. *hist*, 1661—1741.
Romanzoff, Ró-man-zof, Peter Alex., Count, Russian *gen*, 1730—1796.
Romanzoff, Michael Paul, Count, Rus. *dip*, —18—.
Rome De L'Isle, Rom Dę Lɛl, John Baptist L., Fr. *miner*, 1736—1790.
Romilly, Róm-i-li, Sir Samuel, Eng. *st*, 1757—1818. [—1302.
Romney, Róm-ni, George, Eng. *pt*, 1734
Romulus, Róm-yų-lus, *found* and first *k* of Rome, —715 B. C.
Rosa, Ró-są, Salvator, Sp. *poet, pt* and *mus*, 1615—1673.
Rosa, Francisco M. De La, *st*, *or*, *poet*, *dram* and *hist* Sp., 1789—
Rosas, Rō-sąs, Don Juan Manuel, the dictator who ruled the Argentine Republic 23 years, b. 1783—
Roscoe, Rós-kō, Wm., Eng. *biog* and *misc wr*, —1831.
Roscoe, Henry, son of the above, Eng. *wr* and *law*, 1800—1836.
Rose, Rōz, George, *st* and *pol wr*, Eng., 1744—1818.
Rosellini, Rō-sel-é-nɛ, Ippolito, It. *archæ*, 1800—1843.
Rosenkranz, Rōz-en-kránts, Johann Karl Fried., Ger. *phil*, 1805—
Ross, Ros, Sir James Clark, Eng. Artic *nav*, 1800—
Rosse, Ros, Wm. Parsons, Earl of, man of science, and projector of the largest telescope constructed up to this time; *pres* of the Royal Society, Eng., 1800—
Rossi, Ró-sɛ, Pellegrino, Count, noble victim of the popular cause in Italy, 1787—1848.
Rossini, Ro-sé-nɛ, Gioachimo, It. *mus comp*, 1792—
Rosslyn, Róz-lin, Alex. W., Earl of, *law* and *st*, Scot., 1733—1805.
Rostopschin, Ros-tóp-skin, Feador, Count, Rus. *st* and *off*, 1760—1826.
Rothermel, Ród-er-mel, Peter F., Am. *art*, b. 1817—
Rothschild, Róts-çild, House of, *found* of this world-controlling financial establishment was Mayer Anselm Rothschild, a native of Frankfort, Ger., and *money-changer*, b. 1740—1812. His sons were five in number, Anselm, Nathan, Solomon, James de, and Charles; all are now living with the exception of Nathan, who died 1836. The heads of the house are stationed at Frankfort, Vienna, Naples, Paris and London.

Rotteck, Ro-ték, Charles Von, Ger. *hist*, 1775—1848.
Roubilliac, Rœ-bel-yi-ák, Louis Francis, Fr. *sculp*, —1762.
Rouelle, Rǿ-el, Wm. Francis, *chem* Fr., 1703—1770.
Rouget De Lisle, Rœ-ʒét Dę Lél, Joseph, *wr* and *comp* of the "Marseillaise," and a Fr. *off*, 1760—1836.
Rousseau, Rœ-sǿ, Jean Baptiste, Fr. *lyric poet*, 1669—17—.
Rousseau, Jean Jacques, *phil* and *poet* Fr., 1712—1778.
Rowe, Rœ, Nicholas, *poet* and *dram wr* Eng., 1673—1718.
Roxburgh, Róks-burg, William, *ph* and *bot* Scot., 1759—1815. [—1847.
Roy, R-wo, Count Antoine, Fr. *st*, 1764
Royer-Collard, R-wo-ąr-Kol-ąrd, Pierre Paul, Fr. *phil*, 1763—1845.
Rozier, Ro-zér, Francis, Fr. *bot* and *agri wr*, 1734—1793.
Rubens, Rǿ-benz, Peter Paul, the great *master-pt*, b. at Cologne, 1577 —1640.
Rubini, Rœ-bé-ne, Giambatista, *tenor opera singer* It., 1795—1854.
Rucellai, Rœ-çél-j, Bernard, It. *st* and *hist*, 1449—1525.
Ruckert, Rǿ-kert, Frederick, Ger. *poet*, 1789—
Rugendas, Rœ-gén-dąs, Geo. Philip, Ger. *battle-pt*, 1666—1742.
Ruhs, Rœz, Frederick, Ger. *hist*, 1780 —1820.
Ruschenberger, Rǿʃ-en-ber-ger, W. S. W., M. D., *surg* and *wr* U. S. navy, Pa., 1807—
Rush, Ruʃ, Dr. Benj., Am. *ph*, *scholar*, *philan*, *patriot*, *au*, and *signer Dec. of Ind.*, Pa., 1741—1813.
Rush, Richard, son of the above, *ex-min* and *pol* Pa., —1780.
Russell, Rús-el, Lord Wm., Eng. *st*, 1639—ex. 1683. [1792———.
Russel, Lord John, Eng. *st* and *min*,
Russia, Rǿ-ʃi-a, Alexander II., *emp* of, succeeded to the government 1855.
Rutherford, Rúđ-er-ford, Daniel, Scot. *nat, phil* and *ph*, 1749—1819.
Rutledge, Rút-lej, Edward, Am. *st*, and *signer Dec of Ind.*, S. C., 1749—1800.
Ruysch, Røs, Frederic, M. D., F. R. S., Dutch *anat*, 1638—1731. [1676.
Ruyter, Rǿ-ter, Dutch *adm*, 1607—
Rysbrach, Rįs-brąh, John M., Dutch *sculp*, 1694—1770.

# S.

Sabatier, Sa-ba-tér, Antoine, Fr. *wr*, 1742—1817.
Sacy, Sąs, Antoine I. S., Baron De, Fr. *scholar* and *au*, 1758—1838.
Sa Da Bandeira, Są Dą Bąn-da-é-rą, Bernardo De, Port. *st*, 1796—
Sadler, Michael Thomas, F. R. S., Eng. *scholar*, *or* and *philan*, 1780—1835.
Sadler, Wm. W., Eng. *æronaut* and *chem*, 1804—k. 1824.
Saint Arnaud, Sań Ar-nód, Jaques Leroy De, *marshal*, and *comman* of the French forces in the Crimea, 1801—1854.
Saint-Clair, Sant-Kląr, *off* Am. army, Pa., —1818.
Saint-Croix, Sań-Krwo, G. E. J., Baron De, Fr. *wr*, 1746—1809.
Sainte-Beuve, Sańt-Bęv, Chas. Augus., Fr. *crit* and *poet*, 1803—
Saintine, Sań-ten, Xavier Bon., Fr. *poet* and *dram*, 1790—
Saint-Just, Antoine, *min* of Robespierre, 1768—1794.
Saint-Mars, Fr. *off*, the Keeper of 'The Man in the Iron Mask,' which to this day remains a historical secret; 17th cen.
Saint-Martin, — Mąr-tań, Louis C. De, Fr. *phil*, 1743—1803.
Saint-Palaye, — Pa-lá, Charles I. C., Abbe De, Fr. *pol wr* and *philan*, 18th cen.
Saint Pierre, — Per, Jacques B. H. De, *phil wr* Fr., 1737—1814.
Saint-Simon, — Si-móń, Claude Henri, Count De, *found* of a school of social science, Fr., 1760—1825.
Saldanha, Sąl-dąn-yą, Oliviera, E. Daun, etc., Duke of, *min* and *off* Portugal, 1780—
Sallust, Caius Crispus, Roman *hist*, 85—35 B. C.
Samson, celebrated in Scripture for his strength, was betrayed and perished with 3000 Philistines in the temple of Dagon, 1117 B. C.
Samuel, *prophet* of Israel, —1057 B. C.

Sancho, Sán-kœ, Ignatius, a negro *wr* and *poet*, born on board a slave-ship, freed in England, 1729—1780.
Sandby, Paul, Eng. *art*, 1732—1809.
Sandford, Sir Daniel K., D. C. L., *classic scholar* and *or*, Scot., —1838.
Sands, Robt. C., *jour* and *poet*, N-Y., 1798—1832.
Sannazarius, Sqn-qd-zqr-ε-ós, Jacopo, Italian *poet*, 1458—1533.
Sansovino, Sqn-sœ-vé-nœ, Giocomo F., Italian *sculp* and *arch*, 1479—1570.
Santa Anna, Sqn-tq Ȧ'nq, Antonio Lopez De, *ex-pres* of the Mexican Confederation, 1790—
Santa Cruz, (Sp. Krœθ, S. Am. Krœs;) *protector* of the Peru-Bolivian Confederacy, b. about 1790—
Sappho, Sáf-œ, Greek *poetess*, whose lover was so cruel to her that she threw herself into the sea.
Sardanapalus, *k* Assyria, who on a revolt of his people, set fire to his palace, and perished in the flames, 820 B. C.
Sardinia, Victor-Emmanuel-A.-E.-F.-Thomas, King of, b. 1820—assumed gov. 1849—
Saumaise, Sœ-más, Claude, *crit*, *archæ* and *ori*, Burgundy, 1588—1658.
Saumarez, Só-ma-rez, Rt. Hon. James, Lord De, *off* Brit. navy, 1757—1836.
Saunders, Són-derz, John C., Eng. *sur*, *oculist* and *med wr*, 1773—1810.
Saunders, Wm., *ph* and *med wr*, 1743—1819.
Saunderson, Són-der-son, Nicholas, a blind *math* Eng., 1682—1739.
Saussure, Sœ-sęr, Horace B. De, *nat* Swit., 1740—1799.
Saussure, Nicholas T. De, son of the above, *nat* and *chem*, 1767—1845.
Sauvages, Sœ-vq-ʒa, Francis B. De, Fr. *bot* and *ph*, —1767.
Sauveur, Sœ-vęr, Joseph, Fr. *math*, 1653—1716.
Savage, Richard, Eng. *poet*, 1698—1743.
Savary, Sa-vq́r, Réné, Fr. *gen*, 1774—1833.
Savonarola, Sqv-on-qr-ó-lq, Franciscan *monk* and *ref*, 1452—k. 1498.
Saxe, Count Maurice of Saxony, Fr. *gen*, —1750.
Saxe, John G., Am. *sat* and *hum poet*, Vt., 18 —
Say, Sa, Jean B., Fr. *wr* on political economy, 1767—1832.
Say, Thomas, Am. *nat*, 1787—1834.
Scanderbeg, Skq́n-der-beg, Albanian *chief*, 1404—1467.
Scarlatti, Skqr-lq́-te, Alessandro, It. *mus comp*, 1658—1728. [—1826.
Scarpa, Skq́r-pq, Antonio, It. *art*, 1746
Schadow, Σq́-dœv, Johann G., Ger. *sculp*, 1764—1852.
Schadow-Godenhaus, — Gó-den-hɤs, Fried. Wilhelm Von, Ger. *hist* and *por-pt*, 1789—
Schaeffer, Σq́f-er, Geof. Heinrich, Ger. *philol*, 1764—1840. [1740—1823.
Schank, Skaŋk, John, Eng. *naval off*,
Scheele, Σę-le, Chas. William, Swed. *chem*. He discovered fluorine, chlorine, malic, molybdic, arsenic, tartaric, oxalic, &c., acids, glycerine and oxygen. 1742—1786.
Scheffer, Σá-fer, Ary, Dutch *art* Fr., 1795—
Schelling, Σél-iŋ, Fred. Wm. Joseph, Ger. *meta phil* and *poet*, 1775—1854.
Schiller, Σil-er, Friedrich, Ger. *poet* and *dram*. It is enough to say that he is the only German poet who can contest the supremacy of Goethe. 1759—1805.
Schirmer, Σi*r*-mer, Johann Wilhelm, Ger. *l-pt*, 1807—
Schloetzer, Σlęt-zer, Aug. Louis, Ger. *hist*, 1737—1809.
Schlosser, Σlós-er, Friedrich Chris., Ger. *hist*, and *prof* at University of Heidelberg, 1776—
Schlegel, Σlá-gel, John Elias, Ger. *poet* and *dram wr*, 1718—1749.
Schlegel, August Wilhelm Von, Ger. *poet*, *crit*, *hist* and *meta phil*, 1767—1845.
Schlegel, Friedrich Von, brother of the above, *crit* and *phil*, 1772—1829.
Schleiermacher, Σlį-er-mq*h*-er, Frederic Daniel E., Ger. *div* and *wr* 1768—1834.
Schoefer, Σę-fer, Peter, one of the inventors of printing, Ger., —1502.
Schoepflin, Σęp-flin, John Daniel, Ger. *hist*, 1694—1771.
Schomberg, Σóm-be*r*g, Isaac, *hist* and *off* Am. navy, —1813.
Schomburgh, Σóm-bu*r*g, Sir Robt. Hermann, Ger. *nat* and *trav*, 1804—
Schoolcraft, Skœl-kraft, Henry Rowe, Am. *trav*, *nat*, *antiq* and *au* N-Y., 1793—
Schopenhauer, Σóp-en-hɤ-er, Johanna, Ger. *authoress*, 1770—1838.
Schrodter, Σród-ter, Adolf, Ger. *pt*, 1805. [1680—1756.
Schroeder, Σrę-der, John Joa., Ger. *ori*,
Schubert, Σœ-bert, Francis, Ger. *mus comp*, 1795—1830.

Schulz, Σɷlts, Wilhelm, Ger. *pol wr*, 1797—
Schumacher, Σó-mqh-er, Heinrich Christian, Ger. *astr*, 1780—1850.
Schumann, Σó-mqn, Robert, Ger. *mus wr*, 1810—
Schuyler, Skị-ler, Philip, *maj-gen* Am. army, N-Y., 1804.
Schwanthaler, Σvqn-tq́-ler, Ludwig Von, Ger. *sculp*, 1802—1848.
Schwartzenberg, Σvq́rts-en-bęrg, Chas. Philip, Prince, Aust. *field-marshal*, 1771—1820.
Scipio, Síp-i-ɷ, Publius Cornelius, Roman *gen*, —180 B. C.
Scott, David, Scottish *art*, 1806—1849.
Scott, Michael, *au* "Tom Cringle's Log," Scot., 1789—1835.
Scott, Sir Walter, Scottish *poet*, *nov* and *misc wr*, 1733—1832.
Scott, Gen. Winfield, *comman-in-chief* Am. army, 1786—
Scribe, Skrɛb, Augustine Eugene, Fr. *lyric poet* and *dram wr*, 1791—
Sebastian, Sɛ-bást-yan, (Port. Sa-bqs-tɛ-q́n,) King of Portugal, 1554—k. in Africa, 1578.
Sedgwick, Séj-wik, Theodore, Am. *wr* Mass., 1730—1839.
Seetzen, Sę́ts-en, Ulric Jaspar, Ger. *trav*, —1811.
Segur, Sa-gę́r, Louis, Count De, Fr. *dip* and *hist wr*, 1753—1830.
Seidl, Sị-dl, John Gabr., Aust. *poet*, 1804—
Selden, Sél-den, John, Eng. *antiq*, *law*, *wr* and *hist*, 1584—1654.
Selkirk, Alex., Scot. *voyager* to the South Seas, 1680—d.
Semiramis, Sɛ-mír-a-mis, *queen* of Assyria, famous for her conquests; put to death by her son Ninyas, 1220 B. C. [1742—1809.
Senebier, Sén-e-bɛr, *nat phil* Swit.,
Seneca, Sén-ɛ-kɑ, Lucius Annæus, *stoic phil*, preceptor of Nero, by whom he was put to death. b. Sp. A. D. 12.
Sergeant, Sę́r-jent, John, Am. *law* and *st* Pa., 1779—1852.
Servetus, Sęr-vɛ́-tus *or* Sęr-vá-tus, Michael, *theol*, burnt at the stake through the instrumentality of Calvin, 1509—1553.
Servius Tullus, sixth *k* Rome, cel. for his laws on rank and property; murdered, 530 B. C. [211.
Severus, Lucius Septimius, Rom. *emp*,
Severus, Sulpitius, *hist*, *au* "Historia Sacra," —420.

Sewall, Sq́-al, Stephen, Am. *scholar* and *au* Mass., 1734—1804.
Seward, Sq́-ard, William H., Am. *st* and *sen*, N-Y., 1801—
Sewell, Sq́-el, George, Eng. *misc wr* and *poet*, —1726. [A. D. 100.
Sextus Empyricus, a Pyrrhonian *phil*,
Seymour, Sɛ́-mɷr, Edward, Duke of Somerset, Eng. *off*, —ex. 1552.
Shadwell, Σád-wel, the Rt. Hon. Sir Lancelot, *vice-chancellor* of England, and *j*, 1779—1850.
Shaftesbury, Σáfts-ber-i, Anthony Ashley Cooper, Eng. *meta phil* and *wr*, 1671—1713.
Shaftesbury, Anthony Ashley C., Earl of, Eng. *philan*, and leader of the Low-Church party, 1801—
Shakspeare, Σáks-pɛr, William, the most illustrious *dram poet* of Anglo-Saxon origin, 1564—1616.
Sharp, Granville, *au*, and projector of the society for the abolition of the slave-trade, Eng., 1734—1813.
Sharp, William, Eng. *engr*, 1749—1824.
Shee, Sir Martin Archer, Irish *art* and *poet* Eng., 1769—1850. [1792—1822.
Shelley, Σél-i, Percy Bysshe, Eng. *poet*,
Shenstone, Σén-stɷn, William, *poet* and *prose wr* Eng., 1714—1763.
Sheridan, Σér-i-dan, Richard Brinsley, Irish *dram*, *st* and *or* Eng., 1751—1816.
Sherman, Σę́r-man, Roger, Am. *st*, and *signer Dec. of Ind.*, Mass., 1721—1793.
Sherwin, John Keyse, *engr* Eng., —1790. [1749—1829.
Shield, Σɛld, William, Eng. *composer*,
Shirley, Σę́r-li, James, Eng. *dram wr* and *poet*, 1594—1666.
Short, James, *nat phil* and *optician* Scot., 1710—1768.
Shrapnel, Σráp-nel, Lieut.-Gen. Henry, *inv* of the spherical case-shot, Eng., —1842.
Sibthorp, Síb-ꝥerp, John, *nat*, and *prof bot* in the University of Oxford, Eng., —1796. [1755—1831.
Siddons, Síd-onz, Sarah, Eng. *actress*,
Siddons, Mrs. H., *actress* of the Theatre Royal, Edinburgh, —18 .
Sidmouth, Síd-muꝥ, Henry, Viscount, Eng. *st*, 1757—1844.
Sidney, Síd-ni, Sir Philip, *gentleman*, *au*, and *comman*, of the reign of Queen Elizabeth, 1554—1586.
Siebold, Sɛ́-bǫld, Philip Franz Von, *wr* on Japan, Ger., 1796—
Sieyes, Sɛ-i-ɑ, Count Emanuel Jos., *vol* of the Fr. revolution, 1748—1836.

Sigaud De Lafond, Sɛ-gɷd Dẹ Lạ-foṅd, Jno. Renatus, Fr. *sur* and *nat phil,* 1740—1810.
Sigismund, Sig-is-mɷnd, *emp* of Ger., 1378—1437; also, names of three Polish kings. [1441—1524.
Signorelli, Sɛg-nɷ-rél-ɛ, Luca, It. *pt,*
Silenus, Sị-lé-nus, *fab,* the foster-father of Bacchus, who lived in Arcadia, rode on an ass, and was drunk every day.
Silliman, Sil-i-man, Benjamin, M. D., LL. D., *prof* of the Natural Sciences in Yale College, and distinguished for his scien. writings, 1779—
Simms, Simz, Wm. Gilmore, Am. *nov, hist* and *poet* S. C., 1806—
Simon Magus, Samaritan *imp,* who pretended to be the Son of God, —A. D. 56.
Simrock, Karl, Ger. *poet,* 1802—
Simson, Robert, *math* Scot., 1687—1768.
Sinclair, Sín-klạr, George, *eng* and *nat phil, au* of works on hydrostatics and the principles of astronomy and navigation, Scot., —1696.
Sinclair, Sir John, Bart., *philan* Scot., 1754—1835.
Sindiah, Sín-di-ạ, Mahadjee, Mahratta *prince,* 1741—1794.
Singh, Síŋ-*h,* Maha Raja Runjeet, *chief* of Lahore and Cachmire, 1779—1839.
Sismondi, Sis-moṅ-dé, Jean Chas. L. S. D', *hist* and *wr* on pol. economy, Swit., 1773—1842.
Sisyphus, Sis-i-fus, *fab,* killed by Theseus, and doomed incessantly to roll a huge stone up a mountain in hell for his perfidy and numerous robberies. [1590.
Sixtus Quintus, *pope* of Rome, 1521—
Skelton, John, *poet-laureate* of Eng., —1529.
Sleidan, Slị-dan, John Philipson, Ger. *hist,* 1506—1556.
Sloane, Slɷn, Sir Hans, Bart., *bot* Ireland, 1660—1752. [1771.
Smart, Christopher, Eng. *poet,* 1722—
Smeaton, Smé-ton, John, *civil eng* Eng., 1724—1792.
Smith, Adam, *meta phil, au* and *pol econ* Scot., 1723—1790.
Smith, Sir James Edward, Eng. *ph* and *nat,* 1759—1828.
Smith, James and Horace, *lit duumvirate* Eng., 1775—1839, 1779—1849.
Smith, Capt. John, *off* and *trav,* connected with the history of Virginia, 1579—1631.

Smith, Rev. Dr. John, *antiq* and Celtic *scholar* and *wr* Scot., 1747—1842.
Smith, Dr. John Pye, *theol wr* Eng., 1775—1851. [1689—1768.
Smith, Robert, *div* and *math* Eng.,
Smith, Sir Wm. Sidney, Brit. *adm,* 1764—1840.
Smith, Rev. Sidney, M. A., *div, essa, crit, wr* and *wit,* the projector of the *Edinburgh Review,* Eng., 1771—1845.
Smith, William, LL. D., F. G. S., Eng. *geol,* 1769—1840.
Smith, Thomas Southwood, *au, ph* and *wr* Eng., 1790—
Smith, Gerritt, Am. *philan, or, scholar,* and anti-slavery *ref,* N-Y.
Smithson, James, *found* of the Smithsonian Institution, Washington, Eng., —1829.
Smollett, Smól-et, Tobias, Eng. *crit* and *nov,* 1721—1771.
Smyth, Smiŧ, William, *hist lec* and *wr* Eng., 1764—1849.
Snell, Rodolph, *math* and *philol wr* Holland, 1547—1613. [—1837.
Soane, Sɷn, Sir John, Eng. *arch,* 1752
Sobiesky, Sɷ-bés-ki, John, *k* of Poland, fam. in the Turkish wars, 1629 —1696.
Socinus, Sɷ-sin-us, Faustus, *champion* of the doctrine of Unitarianism, Italy, 1539—1604.
Socrates, Sók-ra-tɛz, greatest of *anc phil,* put to death by the Athenians on false charge of atheism, 467—400 B. C.
Sol, *fab,* a name of Apollo; the sun.
Solander, Sɷ-lạn-der, Daniel Chas., *nat* Sweden, 1736—1782.
Solomon, Sól-ɷ-mon, son of David, *k* Israel, wrote the books of Proverbs, Eccl., and Canticles, died 975 B. C., aged 58. [80.
Solon, *sage* of Greece, d. 558 B. C., aged
Solvyns, Sol-vinz, Francis B., Dutch *art* and *au,* 1760—1824.
Solyman, Sól-i-man, the Great, Turkish *emp,* 1494—1566.
Somnus, Sóm-nus, *fab,* the god of sleep.
Somoza, Sɷ-mó-ŧa, José, Sp. *pol* and *wr,* 1781—
Sonnini De Manoncourt, Soṅ-aṅ Dẹ Maṅ-on-kɷ́r, Charles N. S., Fr. *trav* and *nat,* 1751—1811.
Sontag, Són-tạg, Henrietta, *opera singer* Ger., 1805—1854.
Sophocles, Sóf-ɷ-klɛz, Greek *poet,* and *chief magistrate* of Athens, 500—410 B. C.
Soulé, Sɷ-lá, Pierre, Am. *ex-sen* La.

Soult, Sɷl, Nicole Jean De D., Duke of Dalmatia, Fr. *marshal* and *off*, 1769—1851.
Southcote, Sŭŧ-kɷt, Joanna, the subject of religious delusion, England, 1750—1814.
Southern, Sŭđ-ern, Thomas, an Irish *dram poet*, 1660—1746.
Southey, Sŭđ-i, Robert, Eng. *poet* and *prose wr;* and in 1813, *poet-laureate*, 1774—1843. [1588—1650.
Spagnoletto, Spɑn-yɷ-lét-ɷ, Italian *pt*,
Spallanzani, Spal-ɑnd-zɑ́n-ɛ, Lazaro, It. *physiol* and *nat*, 1729—1799.
Spanheim, Spɑ́n-hįm, Ezekiel, *wr* and *st* Geneva, 1629—1710.
Sparks, Spɑrks, Jared, Am. *biog* and *misc wr*, and *pres* Harvard College, 1794— [*nat*, 1747—1820.
Sparrmann, Spɑ́r-mɑn, Andrew, Swed.
Spartacus, Spɑ́r-ta-kus, Thracian *shepherd*, and *conq* of some of the Roman armies, 71 B. C. [Y., 1788—1855.
Spencer, John C., Am. *law* and *st* N-
Spencer, John Chas., Earl, promoter of agriculture, Eng., 1782—1845.
Spenser, Edmund, Eng. *poet*, 1553—1599.
Sphinx, Sfiŋks, *fab*, a monster, who destroyed herself because Œdipus solved the enigma she proposed.
Spielmann, Spél-mɑn, James Reinhold, Ger. *chem*, 1722—1782.
Spinoza, Spin-ó-zɑ, Baruch, *meta phil* (atheistical,) Holland, 1632—1677.
Spohr, Spor, Louis, Ger. *mus comp*, 1783—
Spontini, Spon-té-nɛ, Gasparo, It. *mus comp*, 1778—1851.
Sprague, Sprag, Charles, Am. *poet* Mass., 1791—
Spurzheim, Spɷ́rʒ-hįm *or* Spɷ́rts-hįm, *phren*, contemporary of Gall, Ger., 1776—1832.
Squier, Skwįr, Ephram Geo., Am. *wr* and *pol* N-Y., 1821—
Stael-Holstein, Stal-Hól-stįn, Anna Louisa G. Necker, Baroness De, *tragic poet*, *pol* and *romance wr* France, 1766—1817.
Stahl, Stel, Geo. Ernest, Ger. *ph* and *chem*, 1660—1734.
Stallbaum, Stɑl-bŭm, Gottfried, Ger. *classic scholar* and *au*, 1793—
Standish, Stán-diʃ, Frank Hall, Eng. *au* and *poet*, 1798—1840.
Stanfield, Stán-fɛld, Clarkson, Eng. *pt*, 1790—
Stanislaus, Stán-is-lŭs, Augustus, the last *k* of Poland, 1732—1798.
Stanley, Stán-li, Thomas, Eng. *phil hist*, 1625—1678. [—1822.
Stark, John, *gen* Am. army, N-H., 1728
Staudenmaier, Stŭ-den-mį-er, Franz A., Catholic *theol* and *au* Germany, 1800—
Steele, Sir Richard, Brit. *essa*, *pol wr*, *dram poet* and *hum*, 1671—1729.
Steevens, Sté-venz, Geo., *commen* on Shakspeare, Eng., 1736—1800.
Stenbock, Stén-bok, Magnus, Count, Swedish *gen*, 1664—1717.
Stentor, Stén-tor, *fab*, a Grecian, whose voice is reported to have been as strong and as loud as the voices of 50 men together. [*pol wr*, —1832.
Stephen, Sté-ven, James, Eng. *law* and
Stephen, St., first Christian *martyr*, stoned by the Jews, A. D. 33.
Stephens, John Loyd, Am. *trav* and *wr* N-J., 1805—1852.
Stephenson, Sté-ven-son, Geo., Eng. *civil eng*, 1787—1848.
Stephenson, Robert, *eng* Eng., 1803—
Sterling, John, Brit. *essa* and *crit*, 1806—1844.
Sternberg, Stérn-bɛrg, Alexander, Baron Von, Ger. *au*, 1806—
Sterne, Stern, Laurence, Irish *wr* and *hum*, 1713—1768.
Steuben, Stó-ben, (Am. Stú-ben,) Frederic Wm. Aug., Baron, Prussian *off* Am. army, during the Revolutionary war, —1795.
Stevenson, Sté-ven-son, Sir John Andrew, *mus comp* Ireland, 1761—1833.
Stevenson, Robert, *civil eng* Scotland, 1772—1850. [navy, 1778——.
Stewart, Stú-ɑrt, Charles, *com* Am.
Stewart, Dugald, Scottish *meta*, *math* and *au*, 1753—1828.
Stewart, Mathew, D.D., Scottish *math* and *au*, 1717—1785. [1727—1795.
Stiles, Stįlz, Ezra, Am. *div* and *hist*,
Stilling, Heinrich, *pseudonyme* adopted by Heinrich Jung, in a remarkable autobiography. He was a *misc wr* Ger., 1740—1817.
Storch, Storh, Heinrich Fred. Von, *pol econ* Ger., 1766—1835.
Storch, Nicholas, *found* of the sect called Anabaptists, Ger., —1530.
Story, Justice Joseph, Am. *j* and *jur wr* Mass., 1779—1845.
Stothard, Stóđ-ɑrd, Thomas, R. A., Eng. *art*, 1755—1838.
Stowe, Stɷ, Harriet Beecher, Am. *au*, now residing in Maine.
Strakosch, Strák-oʃ, Maurice, *mus comp* and *pianist*, Pol., 1825—

Strafford, Stráf-ord, Thomas Bent., Earl of, *st* Eng., 1593—ex. 1641.
Strange, Stranj, Sir Robt., Brit. *hist engr*, 1721—1792.
Strauss, Strɤs, Dav. Rriedr., Ger. *au*, 1808— [—1849.
Strauss, John, *mus comp* Aust., 1804
Strickland, Strík-land, E., *trav* and *nat* Eng., 1811—1853.
Struensee, Strώ-en-se, John Fred., Count, *ph* and *pol* Denmark, 1737—ex. 1772. [1749—1802.
Strutt, Joseph, *art* and *antiq wr* Eng.,
Struve, Strɷv *or* Strώv-a, Friedr. Geo. Wilh., Russian *astr.*
Stuart, the royal house of Great Britain after the union of Scotland.
Stuart, Daniel, *pol wr*, *ed* " Morning Post," London, 1766—1846. [1786.
Stuart, Gilbert, *hist wr* Scot., 1742—
Stuart, James, Eng. *trav* and *antiq au*, 1713—1788.
Stuart, James, of Duncarn, *pol wr* Scot., 1776—1849.
Stukeley, Stᶙk-li, William, Eng. *antiq* and *au*, 1687—1765.
Sture, Stώ-re, *administrators* of Sweden, from the 14th to the close of the 16th cen.
Sturgeon, Stúr-jon, William, *exp* in the nat. sciences, Eng., 1783—1850.
Stuyvesant, Stέ-ves-ant, Peter, the last Dutch *gov* of New-York, appointed 1664.
Styx, Stiks, *fab*, a river of hell.
Suckling, Sir John, *poet* and *courtier*, Eng., 1609—1641.
Sue, Sę, Eugene, Fr. *nov*, 1808—
Sullivan, Súl-i-van, John, *gen* Am. army, in the Revolutionary war, N-H., 1741—1795.
Sully, Súl-i, Thomas, Eng. *art*, 1783—
Sully, Maximilin De Bethune, Duke of, Fr. *min* and *off*, 1560—1641.
Sumner, Charles, Am. *st*, *or*, *legal wr* and *scholar*, *sen* from Mass., 1811—
Suwarrow, Sɷ-vqr-óv, Peter Alexis V., Count, Russian *gen*, 1730—1800.
Swammerdam, Svᶐm-er-dqm, Jean, Dutch *anat* and *ento*, 1637—1680.
Swartz, Swqrts, Olans, Swedish *bot*, 1760—1817.
Sweden and Norway, Oscar I., King of, 1799—assumed gov. 1844—
Swedenborg, Swέ-den-berg *or* Swá-den-berg, Emanuel, *math* and Christian *phil*, *found* of a sect numerous at the present day; b. at Stockholm, 1688—1772. [1854.
Sweet, John A., Am. *ph* Mass., 1808—
Swift, Jonathan, Brit. *au*, *sat* and *pol wr*, and *hum*, 1667—1745.
Sydenham, Síd-en-ham, Thomas, M. D., Eng. *ph* and *med wr*, 1624—1689.
Sydney, Síd-ni, Algernon, *pol wr* and *repub* Eng., 1621—ex. 1683.
Sylla, Lucius Cornelius, Roman *gen* and *dictator*, scourge of his country, —78 B. C. [woods and forests.
Sylvanus, Sil-vá-nus, *fab*, a god of
Symmes, Simz, John Cleves, *au* of the eccentric Theory of the Earth, that the globe is hollow, with openings at the poles for the admission of light; Ohio, —1829.
Syrens, Sį-renz, *fab*, sea-monsters.

# T.

Tacitus, Tás-i-tus, Marcus Claudius, *emp* Rome, —276.
Talbot, Tél-bot, *or* Tál-bot, John, Earl of Threwsbury, Eng. *off* in the renowned Fr. wars, 1373—1453.
Talfourd, Tál-fɷrd, Sir Thomas Noon, dist. as the *au* of "Ion," and other interesting writings, as a judge, and for his many virtues, Eng., 1795—1854.
Tallard, Tal-ᶐrd, Camille D'H., Duke De, Fr. *marshal*, 1652—1728.
Talleyrand-Perigord, Tál-ɛ-rqnd-Pᶐr-ɛ-gord, Charles Maurice De, the "prince of diplomatists," Fr., 1754—1838.
Tallien, Tal-i-áṅ, Jean Lambert, dist. Jacobine of the Fr. revolution, 1769—1820.
Talma, Tál-mq, Francis Joseph, Fr. *actor*, 1770—1826.
Tamerlane, Tam-er-lán, *emp* of Tartary, 1335—1405.
Taney, Tán-i, Roger B., *chief justice* of the Sup. Ct. U. S., Md., 1777—
Tannahill, Tán-a-hil, Robert, Scottish *lyric poet*, 1774—1810. [*au.*
Tapia, Tᶐ-pé-q, Eugenio, Sp. *jour* and
Tasman, Tas-mᶐn, Abel Janssen, Dutch *nav*, 1600—d. [—1595.
Tasso, Tᶐ-sɷ, Torquato, It. *poet*, 1544.
Tate, Tat, Irish *poet*, 1652—d.

Taylor, Tá-lor, Jane, Eng. *poet* and *prose wr*, 1783—1823.
Taylor, Dr. Jeremy, *bishop* of the Church of Eng., 1613—1667.
Taylor, Thomas, a modern promulgator of the Platonic Philosophy, Eng., 1758—1835.
Taylor, William, *critic* and *trans*, Eng., 1765—1836.
Taylor, Wm. Cooke, LL. D., *misc wr* Ir., 1800—1849.
Taylor, Zachary, Am. *gen*, *pres* of the U. S., from 1849 to 1850; his career being terminated by his sudden death in July of the latter year. He was succeeded in office by his V-Pres., Millard Fillmore; b. La., 1790—1850.
Taylor, Bayard, Am. *trav*, *poet*, and *misc wr*, N-Y., 1825—
Tching Tching Kong, Ꞓiŋ-Ꞓiŋ-Koŋ, Chinese *adm*, 17th cen.
Tefft, Teft, B. F., *au*, Methodist *clerg* and *ed* N-Y., 1813—
Tekeli, Te-kél-ɛ, Emerie, Count De, Hungarian *nob* and *patriot*, 1658—1705.
Telford, Tél-ford, Thomas, *civil eng* Scot., 1757—1834.
Tell, Tel, William, Swiss *hero* of the 14th cen.
Tempelhof, Tém-pel-hof, Geo. Fred., Ger. *off* and *au*, —1807.
Temple, Tém-pl, Sir William, Eng. *st*, 1628—1700.
Teniers, Tén-ɛrz, David, the elder, Flemish *pt*, Belg., 1582—1649.
Teniers, David, the younger, Flem. *pt* Belg., 1610—1694.
Tennant, Tén-ant, William, Scottish *poet* and *philol*, —1843.
Tennant, Tén-ant, Smithson, F. R. S., Eng. *chem*, 1761—1815.
Tennyson, Tén-i-son, Alfred, Eng. *poet*, and now *poet-laureate*, 1810—
Tenterden, Tén-ter-den, Charles Abbot, Lord, Eng. *law*, *j*, and *legal wr*, 1762—1832.
Tertullian, Ter-túl-i-ȧn, Quintus Septimius Florus, *father* and *def* early Christian Church, fl. 211.
Thackery, Hák-er-i, Wm. Makepeace, Eng. *au*, *lect* and *humorist*, 1811—
Thalberg, Tɋl-bɇrg, Sigismund, *mus comp*, Switz., 1812—
Thales, Há-lɛz, *chief* of the seven *sages* of Greece, 640—545 B. C.
Themistocles, Hɛ-mís-tɷ-klɛz, Athenian *gen* and *pat*, being banished to Persia, to avoid taking arms against his county, he slew himself, 465 B. C.
Theodosius, Hɛ-ɷ-dɷ́-ʃi-us, the last Rom. *emp*, a convert to Chris., —395.
Theodotus, Hɛ-ód-ɷ-tus, a *tanner* of Byzantium, who apostatized from Chris. faith to save his life, and formed a sect.
Theon, Hé-on, Greek *sophist*, *au* Treatise on Rhetoric; also, a *math* of Alexandria.
Theophrastus, Hɛ-ɷ-frás-tus, Greek *phil*, 288 B. C.
Thespis, Hés-pis, Greek *tragic poet*, and first actor at Athens, 536 B. C.
Thibaut, Tíb-ɤt, Anton Justus Fried., Ger. *jurist*, 1792—1840.
Thicknesse, Hik-nés, Anne, Eng. *wr*, 1737—1824. [1798———.
Thiers, Tɛr, Adolphe, Fr. *pol* and *hist*,
Thierry, Tɛr, Jacq. Nic. Augustin, Fr. *hist*, 1795—
Thom, Tom, James, *sculp* N-Y., 1799—1850. [1770—1824.
Thom, Walter, *hist* and *misc wr* Scot.,
Thomas, Tóm-as, St., surnamed Didymus, one of Christ's apostles; suffered martyrdom in India.
Thompson, Tóm-son, Alex., *misc wr* and *poet* Scot., 1762—1803.
Thompson, Col. Thomas Peyronnet, *pol reformer* and *au* Eng., 1783—
Thomson, Tóm-son, Anthony Todd, M. D., *med wr*, Scot., 1778—1849.
Thomson, James, Scottish *poet*, *au* of the "Seasons," 1700—1748.
Thomson, Rev. John, Scot. *l-pt*, 1778—1840.
Thomson, Thomas, M. D., Scot. *exp chem*, *lect* and *wr*, 1773—1852.
Thomson, Edward, M. D., D. D., Am. *div*, *wr* and *pres* Ohio Wesleyan University, Ohio, 1810—
Thomson, Samuel, *med ref*, and *au* of "Botanic Family Physician," in 1838, U. S.
Thornton, Hérn-ton, Bonnel, *humorist wr* and *poet* Eng., 1724—1768.
Thornton, John Robt., Eng. *bot*, 1758—1837.
Thorwaldsen, Tor-vɋld-sen, Bertel, Danish *art*, 1770—1844.
Thucydides, Hɥ-síd-i-dɛz, Greek *hist*, —391 B. C.
Thurlow, Húr-lɷ, Edward, Lord, Eng. *pol*, 1732—1806.
Tiarks, Tɛ-ɋrks, John Lewis, F. R. S., Ger. *ast*, Eng., 1789—1837.
Tiberius, Tį-bé-ri-us, Claudius Nero, dissolute *emp* Rome, —37.
Tickell, Tík-el, Thomas, *wr* and *poet*, Eng., 1686—1740.

Ticknor, Tík-nor, George. Am. *schol* and *au*, 1791—

Tieck, Tεk, Ludwig, Ger. *poet* and *nov*, 1773—1853.

Tierney, Tír-ni, *st* and *pol wr*, Eng., [1756—1830.

Tillotson, Tíl-ot-son, Dr. John, *ar-bp* Canterbury, published many valuable sermons; —1694.

Timothy, Tím-ɷ-ŧi, disciple of St. Paul, first *bp* of Ephesus, stoned to death, A. D. 97.

Tindall, Tín-dal, Wm., Eng. *div* and *antiq*, —1804.

Tintoretto, Tin-tɷ-*rét*-ɷ, Jacopo R., *pt* Venice, 1512—1594.

Tippoo Saib, Típ-ɷ Sab, the last *sultan* of Mysore, 1749—k. 1799.

Titian, Tε-tε-án, (*or* Tiziano Vecellio, Tεd-zε-á-nɷ Va-ça-lé-ɷ,) It *pt*, 1477 —1576.

Titus, Tí-tus, Greek disciple of St. Paul, *bp* of Crete.

Tofino De San Miguel, Tɷ-fé-nɷ Da Sqn Mε-*hál*, Sp. *ast*, 1740—1806.

Toland, Tól-and, John, Scot. *meta au*, 1669—1722.

Tompkins, Tóm-kinz, Daniel D., *gov* N-Y. and *V-Pres* U. S., under Mr. Monroe, —1825.

Tone, Tɷn, Theobald W., Irish *revolutionary pol*, 1763—1798.

Tooke, Tuk, John Horne, Eng. *pol*, *gram* and *philol*, 1736—1812.

Toreno, Tor-á-nɷ, Count Jose De, *hist* and *st* Sp., 1786—d.

Torre, Tó-*ra*, Giovanni, M. D., *nat phil* It., —1782.

Torricelli, Tɷ-rε-çá-lε, Evangelista, It. *math*, invented the barometer; 1608—d.

Torrigiano, Tɷ-rε-já-nɷ, Pietro, *sculp* Florence, 1472—1522.

Totten, Tót-en, Joseph G., Am. *military eng*, Conn., 1788—

Totten, George M., Am. *civil eng*, Conn., 1809—

Torrey, Tór-i, John, M. D., LL. D., Am. *bot* and *chem* N-Y.

Tournefort, Tɷ́r-na-fɷr, Joseph Pitton De, Fr. *bot*, 1656—1708.

Toussaint, Tɷ-sáń, L'Ouverture, an illus. and intel. *chief* of the negroes of St. Domingo, after the revolution they affected in that island, was for the greater part of his life a slave, but noted for his kindness and skill. 1743—perished in prison, Fr., 1803.

Trajan, Trá-jan, M. Alpinus Crinitus, Rom. *emp* celebrated for his mild and equitable government, —117.

Trembley, Trém-bli, Abraham, *nat* Swit., 1700—1784.

Trenck, Trenk, Frederick, Baron Von, Prussian *off*, cel. for his adventures and misfortunes, 1726—g. 1794.

Trotter, Trót-er, Thomas, M. D., *med wr* Scot., —1832.

Trumbull, Trúm-bul, Jonathan, *pat* of the Am. Rev., and *gov* Conn., —1785. Son of the same name, Aid to Gen. Washington, *st* and *lieut-gov* Conn., —1809.

Truxton, Trúks-ton, Thomas, *com* Am. navy, N-Y., 1755—1822.

Tschirnhausen, Tʃirn-hɤ-sen, Ehrenfred, W. Von, Ger. *geom* and *exp phil*, 1651—1708.

Tucker, Túk-er, Saint George, Am. *law* and *st*, —1828.

Tuckerman, Henry T., Am. *poet* and *essa*, Mass., 1813—

Tupper, Túp-er, Martin Farquhar, Eng. *au*, 1811—

Turenne, Tu-raň, Henri De La Tour D'Auv. Viscount de, Fr. *gen*, 1611—1675.

Turgot, Tur-gɷ, Anne Robert Jacques, Fr. *st* and *phil*, 1727—1781.

Turner, Túrn-er, Edward, M. D., *chem* and *au* Eng., 1797—1837.

Turner, Joseph M. Wm., Eng. *art*, 1775—1851.

Turner, Sharon, *hist* of the Anglo Saxons, Eng., 1768—1847.

Turner, Túrn-er, William W., *printer* and *philol* Eng., 1810—

Tuscany, Tús-kan-i, Leopold II., Grand Duke of, b. 1797 succeeded to the government 1824. [—1849.

Twiss, Twis, Horace, Eng. *law* and *wr*

Tyler, Tí-ler, John, elected *V-Pres* of the U. S. in 1840, and succeeded to the presidency at the death of Harrison in 1841; Va., 1790—

Tyndale, Tín-dal, Wm., *trans* and *martyr*, Eng., 1484—ex. 1536.

Tytler, Tít-ler, Patric Fraser, *hist*, Scot., 1790—1849.

# U.

Ueoktritz, Eh'trits, (*or* Eh'trits,) Fried. Von, Ger. *dram poet*, 1800—
Uhland, Ѻ'lqnd, Ludwig, Ger. *poet*, 1787—
Uilkens, Ѻl'kenz, James Albert, Dutch *nat*, 1772—1825.
Ulloa, Ѻl-yó-q, Antonio De, Sp. *gen*, *st* and *math*, 1718—1795.
Ulrica, Ѻl-ré-kq, Eleanora, two *queens* of Sweden, from the 17th to the 18th century.
Ulysses, Yu-lís-ez, *fab*, *k* of Ithaca, who, by his subtlety and eloquence, was eminently serviceable to the Greeks, in the Trojan war.
Unzer, Ѻnts'er, John Aug., Ger. *ph*, *psychol* and *phys au*, 1727—1799.
Urban, Ur'ban, I. to VIII., *popes* from 223 to 1644.
Urquhart, Ur'kwqrt, Sir Thomas, Scottish *philol* and *math*, 17th cen.
Urquijo, Ѻr-ké-hѻ, Mariano L. Chevalier De, Sp. *st*, 1768—1817.
Urquiza, Ѻr-ké-ѳq, Gen. Don Justo Jose, *pres* of the Argentine Confederation, 1800—
Ursins, Er-sań, (*or* Ѻr-sénz,) Anna M. De La T., Princes De, a French lady who indirectly governed Spain, in the days of Philip V., —1722.
Usher, Uʃ'er, James, D. D., Irish *div* and *theo wr*, 1580—1656.
Uwins, Yú-inz, David, M. D., Eng. *ph* and *med wr*, 1780—1837.

# V.

Vahl, Vql, Martin, *bot* Norway, 1749 —1804.
Vaillant, Val-yań, Sebastian, Fr. *bot*, [1669—1722.
Valckenaer, Vqlk-en-q̈r, Louis C., Dutch *philol* and *critic*, 1715—1820.
Valerius Maximus, Val-é-ri-us Máks-i-mus, Latin, *hist*, fl. A. D. 30.
Valli, Vq̈l-e, Eusebius, It. *ph*, 1762—1816.
Valperga De Caluso, Vql-párr-gq De Kql-ẹ-sѻ, Piedmontese *math* and *ast*, 1730—1815.
Vanbrugh, Van-bróh, Sir John, Dutch *dram*, 1666—1729.
Van Buren, Van-Bú-ren, Martin, *pol* and eighth *pres* of the U. S., from 1837 to 1841; N-Y., 1782———. V-Pres. R. M. Johnston.
Vancouver, Van-kó-ver, George, Eng. *nav*, —1798.
Vanderlyn, Ván-der-lin, John, Am. *art*, N-Y., 1776—1852.
Vandervelde, Vqn-der-vál-de, William, Dutch *pt*, 1610—1693.
Vandyck, Van-dįk, Antony, Dutch *pt*, 1599—1641.
Vandyk, Van-dík, Harry Stoe, *poet* and *misc wr* Eng., 1798—1828.
Vane, Van, Sir Henry, *rebup*, a champion of the English commonwealth, 1612—ex. 1662.
Van Schouten, Fan Sѻ-u-ten, Dutch *nav*, 17th cen.
Varignon, Var-en-yóń, Pierre, Fr. *math*, 1654—1722.
Vasari, Vq-sq̈-re, Giorgio, It. *au*, 1512 —1574.
Vattel, Va-tél, N., *wr* on *juris* and *meta*, *au* of "Right of Nations;" Swit., —1770. —Emer de, Swiss *wr* on same subjects, —1767.
Vauban, Vѻ-bań, Sebastian L. De Fr. *military-eng*, 1632—1707.
Vaugelas, Vó-gu-lq, Claude F. De, Fr. *wr*, 1585—d. [—1522.
Vaux, Vѻ, Thomas, Eng *off* and *poet*,
Vega, Vá-gq, Lopez De La, Sp. *poet*, 1562—1635.
Veit, Vįt, Philipp, Ger. *pt*, 1793—
Velazquez, Val-qѳ-káѳ, Don Diego R. De Silva Y, Sp. *pt*, 1599—1660.
Venus, Vé-nus, *fab*, the goddess of love and beauty.
Vespasian, Ves-pá-ʃi-an, Titus Flavius, Rom. *gen*, made *emp* A. D. 69—79.
Verboeckhoven, Fer-bѻk-hó-ven, Eugen, Flemish *pt* of animals, 1799—
Vernet, Vẹr-ná, Horace, Fr. *pt*, 1789—
Vernon, Vẹ́r-non, Edward, Eng. *adm*, 1684—1751.
Vernon, Robert, *found* of the Gallery of British Art, 1774—1849.
Verplanck, Vér-plaŋk, Gulian C., Am. *au* N-Y.
Vertot D'Aubœuf, Vq̈r-tѻ Dѻ-bẹf, Rene Aubert De, Fr. *hist*, 1655—d.

Vesalius, Va-sa-le-ŏs, Andreas, *anat*, father of the modern human anatomy, Brussels, 1513—1564.

Vico, Vé-ko, Francis De, It. *ast* and *wr* on *nat phil*, —1848.

Vico, Giovanni Battista, the first to propose a philosophical method of considering human history, Naples, 1668—1744.

Victoria, Vik-tō-ri-a, Queen of Eng., b. 1819—assumed government 1837.

Vigny, Vén-ye, Count Alfred, Fr. *au*, 1799—

Villemain, Vil-a-mán, Abel Francois, Fr. *savant* and *pol*, 1791—

Villoison, Vil-wo-sŏn, Jean Baptiste G. D'Anse De, Fr. *schol*, and discoverer of the manuscripts of Greek authors, 1750—1805.

Vince, Vins, Samuel, Eng. *math* and *ast au*, —1821.

Vincent, Vin-sent, Thomas, Eng. *non-con div*, *au* of "Explanation of Catechism, —1671. [1452—1519.

Vinci, Vén-çe, Leonardo Da, It. *pt*,

Virgil, Vẹr-jil, (*or* Virgilius,) Publius Maro, most excellent of Rom. *poets*, 70—18 B. C.

Virginia, Ver-jín-i-a, daughter of Virginius, was stabbed by her father, to prevent the violence which Appius meditated against her, 450 B. C.

Vivens, Viv-enz, John Louis, one of the revivers of English literature, 1492—1541.

Viviun, Viv-i-un, Richard Hussey, Lord, British *off*, 1775—1842.

Viviani, Ve-ve-á-ne, Vincentio, It. *math*, 1622—1703.

Volkoff, Vól-kof, Theodore, Russian *dram*, 1729—1763.

Volney, Vól-na, Constantine C., Comte De, Fr. *wr*, —1820.

Volta, Vól-ta, Alexander, It. *nat phil*, the inventor of the Voltaic pile, 1745—1829.

Voltaire, Vol-tār, the name assumed by Francois Marie Aronet, Fr. *savant* who was a *phil*, *essa*, *poet*, *hist*, etc., etc., 1694—1778.

Voss, Vos, John Henry, Ger. *poet*, *critic*, *trans*, and *philol*, 1751—1821.

Vossius, Vos-é-us, Gerard John, Dutch *critic*, *phil* and *au*, 1577—1649.

Vulcan, Vŭl-kan, *fab*, the god of subterraneous fire.

# W.

Wackernagel, Vák-ern-á-gel, Karl Heinrich Wilhelm, Ger. *wr* and *poet*, 1806—

Waghorn, Lieut. Thomas, R. N., the projector of steam navigation bet. England and India, 1800—1850.

Wahlenberg, Val-en-bẹrg, George, Ger. *bot*, 1784—1814.

Waldo, Peter, *merch* Lyons, *found* sect Waldenses, 12th cen.

Wales, William, *math* and *astr* Eng., 1734—1798.

Walker, Wé-ker, Adam, *exp phil* and *lect*, 1732—1821.

Walker, John, *lex* Eng., 1732—1807.

Wallace, Wól-as, Horace Binney, Am. *savant*, and *wr* on art, philosophy, &c., Pa., 1817—1852.

Wallace, Sir Wm., Scottish *gen*, who sought to rescue his country from the English yoke, but was betrayed by Sir John Montieth, and ex. 1303.

Wallenstein, Wál-en-stīn, Albert, duke of Friedland, Ger. *comman*, during the first half of the Thirty Years' war; 1583—1634.

Waller, Wól-er, Edmund, Eng. *poet*, 1605—1687.

Walpole, Wól-pol, Sir Robert, Eng. *st* and *pol*, 1676—1745. [—1797.

Walpole, Horace, Eng. *st* and *wr*, 1717

Walsingham, Wól-sing-ham, Sir Francis, Eng. *st*, 1536—1590.

Walter, Wól-ter, John, for many years *proprietor* of the "London Times," to whom its great success is chiefly owing, 1773—1847.

Walton, Wól-ton, Isaac, *wr* on angling, Eng., 1593—1583.

Wappers, Wá-perz, Gustavus, Dutch *pt*, 1803—

Warburton, Wér-bur-ton, Eliot Barth. Geo., Irish *au*, 1810—1852.

Ward, Werd, Robert Plumer, Eng. *au*, 1765—1846.

Ward, Edward Mathew, Eng. *pt*, 1816—

Ware, Wār, Henry, Am. *div* and *poet* Mass., 1794—1843.

Ware, James, Eng. *sur*, *ocultist* and *au*, 1756—1815.

Ware, William, Am. *div* and *misc wr* Mass., 1797—1852.

Waring, Wér-iŋ, Edward, Eng. *math* and *wr*, 1734—1798.
Warren, Wór-en, Dr. Joseph, Am. *off* who fell at the battle of Bunker Hill, 1741--1775.
Warton, Wér-ton, Joseph and Thomas, Eng. *aus* and *poets*, 18th cen.
Warwick, Richard Nevil, Earl of, *gen* and *st* Eng., —1471.
Washington, George, illustrious as the "Father of his Country,"—for his love of liberty, his stern advocacy and defense of human rights, and for his many private virtues; first Pres. U. S., from 1789—1797; Va., 1732—1799. V-Pres., John Adams.
Waterhouse, Benjamin, Am. *ph*, *nat* and *wr*, 1754—1846.
Watt, Wot, James, the author of improvements in the application of steam to motive power, Scot., 1736—1819.
Watts, Isaac, D. D., Brit. *div*, *wr* and *poet*, 1674—1748.
Wayland, Francis, *pres* of Brown University, and *wr*, N-Y., 1796—
Wayne, Wan, Anthony, *maj-gen* Am. army, Pa., 1745—1796.
Webb, James Watson, Am. *jour* and *ed* "N-Y. Courier and Enquirer," 1802—
Weber, Wéb-er, Carl Maria Von, Ger. *mus*, 1786—1826.
Weber, Henry William, *min*, *wr* and *archæ* Scot., 1783—1818. [1852.
Webster, Daniel, Am. *st* Mass., 1782—
Webster, Noah, Am. *lex* Conn., 1758—1843.
Wedel, George Wolfgang, Ger. *ph* and *au*, 1645—1721.
Weed, Thurlow, Am. *jour* and *ed* "Albany Evening Journal," 1797—
Weinbrenner, Vįn-bren-er, Frederic, Ger. *arch*, 1766—1828. [1803———.
Weir, Wɛr, Robert W., Am. *pt* N-Y.,
Weisse, Vįs-e, Christian Felix, Ger. *misc wr* and *dram poet*, 1726—1804.
Wellington, Wél-iŋ-ton, Arthur W., Duke of, Brit. *comman* and *st*, 1769—1852.
Werner, Abraham Gottlieb, *miner* and *geol* Ger., 1750—1817. [1785.
Werner, Paul De, Prus. *gen*, 1707—
Werner, Zacharias, Ger. *dram poet*, 1768—1823.
Wesley, Wés-li, John, *found* of the Arminian branch of Methodists, Eng., 1703—1791.
Wesley, Charles, brother of the above, *preacher*, 1708—1788.
West, Benjamin, Am. *pt*, b. in Pa., 1738—d. in Eng., 1820.
Westall, William, Eng. *art*, 1782—1850.
Westmacott, Wést-ma-kot, Sir Richard, Eng. *sculp*, 1775—
Weyse, Vį-se, Christopher Ernest Fred., Ger. *dramatic* and *lyric comp*, 1774—1842.
Wheaton, Hwé-ton, Henry, Am. *law*, *dip* and *wr*, R. I., 1785—1848.
Whipple, Hwíp-l, Edwin P., Am. *wr* Mass., 1819—
Whiston, Hwís-ton, William, Eng. *div* and *nat phil*, 1667—1752.
White, Rev. Gilbert, Eng. *nat* and *au*, 1720—1793.
White, Henry Kirke, Eng. *poet* of great promise, whose early death was a nation's regret. 1785—1806.
Whitefield, Hwit-fɛld, Rev. George, *found* of the Calvinistic Methodists, Eng., 1714—d.
Whitney, Hwit-ni, Eli, *inv* of the cotton gin, Mass., 1756—1825.
Whittier, Hwít-i-er, John G., Am. *poet* and *prose wr* Mass., 1808—
Wieland, Vé-lqnd *or* Vé-lqnt, Christopher Martin, Ger. *poet*, *dram* and *wr*, 1733—1813.
Wiffen, Jeremiah Holme, Quaker *poet* Eng., 1792—1836.
Wilberforce, Wil-ber-fors, William, Esq., Brit. *st* and *philan*, 1759—1833.
Wilkie, Wíl-kɛ, Sir David, Scottish *pt*, 1785—1841.
Wilkins, Sir Chas., F. R. S., *ori scholar* and *wr* Eng., 1751—1836.
William I., the Conqueror, asc. the Eng. throne 1066—d. 1087.
William III., *k* of Eng., *stadtholder* of Holland, and Prince of Orange, the defender of civil and religious liberty, 1650—1702.
William IV., *k* of Eng., b. 1765—succeeded to gov. 1830—d. 1837.
William I. of Nassau, Prince of Orange, *leader* in the war of Independence that established the Dutch Republic, 1533—k. 1584.
William, two *ks* of Holland, from 1772 to 1848.
Williams, Roger, *pres* of the Colony of Rhode Island, 1599—1683.
Willis, Thomas, Eng. *anat* and *ph*, 1622—1675.
Willis, Nathaniel Parker, Am. *poet* and *jour*, N-Y., 1807—
Wills, Wm. Henry, Eng. *jour*, 1810—
Wilson, Alexander, *ornith* Pa., 1766—1831.

Wilson, James, Am. *law, wr*, and *signer Dec. of Ind.*, Pa., 1742—1798.
Wilson, John, better known by the soubriquet of Christopher North, *poet, wr* and *prof*, Scot., 1788—1854.
Wilson, Sir Robert, Brit. *gen*, 1777—1849.
Wilson, Richard, R. A., Brit. *pt*, —1782.
Wilson, Horace Hayman, *prof* of Sanskrit at the University of Oxford, and *wr*, Eng.
Winclemann, Vĭŋk-le-mɑn, John Joachim, cel. in æsthetical and art literature, Ger., 1718—1768.
Windischgratz, Vĭn-diʃ-grɑts, Prince *generalissimo* of the Austrian troops, 1786—
Winsor, Wĭn-zor, Frederic Albert, the projector of gas-lights, Eng., —1830.
Winthrop, John, first *gov* of Mass., 1587—1676.
Wirt, Wẹrt, Wm., Am. *law* and *misc wr* Va., 1772—1835.
Wirth, Virt, John Geo. Aug., Ger. *pol wr*, 1800—
Withers, George, Eng. *poet*, 1588—1667.
Witherspoon, John, D. D., LL. D., *clerg* Scot., *pres* of Princeton College, U. S., *signer Dec. of Ind.*, &c., —1794.
Withmer, Vĭt-mer, Michael, Ger. *hist pt*, 1803—
Wolcott, Wŏl-kot, John, assumed name *Peter Pindar*,—*sat poet* and *hum* Eng., 1738—1819.
Wolcott, Oliver, *gov* Conn., and *signer Dec. of Ind.*, 1727—1797.
Wolf, Vɷlf, Fred. Augustus, *philol* and *wr* Ger., 1759—1824.
Wolf, John Christian, voluminous *wr* and superficial *phil* Ger., 1679—1754.
Wolfe, Wulf, Charles, Irish *poet, au* of 'Ode on the Death of Sir John Moore,' 1791—1823. [1759.
Wolfe, Gen. James, Brit. *off*, 1726—k.
Wolff, Volf, Emil, Ger. *sculp*, 1802—
Wollaston, Wŏl-as-ton, Wm. Hyde, M. D., Eng. *chem, inv* of the periscopic camera, etc., 1766—1828.
Wolsey, Wúl-zi, Thomas, a powerful *Cardinal* of Eng., 1471—1530.
Woodhouse, Wúd-hɤs, Robert, Eng. *math*, 1773—1827.
Woodhouse, James, Am. *chem* and *ph*, 1770—1809.
Wool, Wul, John E., Am. *gen*, N-Y., 1789— [1785.
Woollett, William, Eng. *engr*, 1735—
Worcester, Wúr-ster, Joseph E., *lex* Mass., 18 —
Wordsworth, Wúrdz-wurθ, William, Brit. *poet*, 1770—1850.
Worth, Wurθ, W. I., *maj-gen* Am. army, N-Y., 1794—1849.
Wouverman, Wɷ́-ver-mɑn, Philip, *pt*, b. at Haarlem, 1620—1668.
Wraxall, Ráks-el, Sir Nathaniel Wm., Eng. *trav* and *hist wr*, 1751—1831.
Wrede, Vréd-e, Field-marshal Prince, Bavarian *soldier* and *st*, 1767—1839.
Wren, Ren, Sir Christopher, dist. as England's greatest *arch*, 1632—1723.
Wright, Rịt, Silas, Am. *st* N-Y., 1795—1847.
Wright, Thomas, Eng. *wr* and *lit ed*,
Wurtemberg, William I., King of, b. 1781—assumed gov. 1816—
Wyatt, Wị-at, R. J., Eng. *sculp*, 1795—1850. [1503—1541.
Wyatt, Sir Thomas, Eng. *st* and *poet*,
Wycherley, Wị-ker-li, Wm., *comic dram* Eng., 1640—1715.
Wycliffe, Wicklyffe, *or* Wiclif, Wiklif, John De, Eng. *div* and *church ref*, 1324—1384.
Wyndham, Wind-ham, Sir William, Eng. *st*, 1687—1763.
Wythe, Wịθ, Am. *st*, and *signer Dec. of Ind.*, 1726—1806.

# X.

Xantippe, Zan-tĭp-ɛ, wife of Socrates, had a morose and violent temper, 460 B. C.
Xantippus, Zan-tĭp-us, Lacedæmonian *gen*, in the service of the Carthagenians.
Xavier, Zá-vi-a, Jerome, *jesuit* and *mis* to East Indies, —1617.
Xenocrates, Zɛ-nók-ra-tɛz, Greek *phil*, 314 B. C.
Xenophon, Zén-ɷ-fon, Athenian *phil*, *sold* and *hist*, 370 B. C.
Xerxes, Zẹ́rks-ɛz, *k* Persia, who entered Greece with an army of 5,283,220; was stopped at Thermopylæ by 300 Spartans under Leonidas; murdered, 454 B. C.

# Y.

Yale, Elihu, native of Conn., went to Eng., became *gov* East India Comp., and gave liberally to establish Yale College, —1721.
Yearsley, Yérz-li, Anne, *dram wr* Eng., 1756—1806.
Yeates, Yats, Thomas, *ori scholar* Eng., 1768—1839.
York, the House of, rival of that of Lancaster, in claim for the crown of England.
York, Frederick, Duke of, *comman* of the British army, 1763—1827.
Yorke, Philip, *geneal* and *hist* Eng., 1743—1804.
Young, Edward, Eng. *poet—au* of "Night Thoughts," 1684—1765.
Young, Mathew, Irish *math* and *au*, 1750—d.
Young, Thomas, Eng. *nat phil.* He is principally distinguished for two things. First, he contests with Fresnel the glory of founding the Undulatory Theory of Light. Second, he was the first to detect the key to phonetic Hieroglyphics; 1773—1829.
Ypsilanti, Ep-sɛ-lɑ́n-tɛ, three Greek *princes*, who have endeavored to achieve the independence of their country; they lived from 1760 to 1832.
Yriarte, Er-ɛ-ɑ́r-ta, Don Juan De, Sp. *archæ* and *philol*, 1702—1771.

# Z.

Zachariah, Zak-a-rī-ɑ, *prophet* of the Messiah, 400 B. C.
Zahn, Tsɑn, Joh. Karl Wilh., *arch, pt*, and prof. of arts, Ger., 1800—
Zaionezek, Zɑ-ɛ-ǿn-ɢek, Joseph, Polish *gen*, 1752—1826. [1802———.
Zaleski, Zɑ-lés-kɛ, Bohdan, Polish *poet*,
Zamoski, Zɑ-mǿs-kɛ, John, a dist. Polander, 16th cen.
Zanotti, Dzɑn-ót-ɛ, J. P., It. *pt* and *poet*, 1674—1765. [15th cen.
Zarco, Zɑ́r-kɷ, John G., Port. *nav*,
Zea, Ħá-ɑ, Don Francisco Aatonio, *bot* and *st*, N-Gran., 1770—1822.
Zendrini, Tsen-drέ-nɛ, Bernardo, *math* and *hydraulic eng*, Aust., 1679—1747.
Zeno, Dzá-nɷ, Nicolo and Antonio, are alleged to have discovered America prior to the voyage of Columbus; 15th cen.
Zeno, Zé-nɷ, *stoic phil*, Cyprus, strangled himself 264 B. C., aged 98.
Zenobia, Zɛ-nó-bi-ɑ, *queen* of Palmyra, and *empress* of the East, —280.
Zimmermann, Tsím-er-mɑn, Eberhard, Augustus W. Von, Ger. *nat* and *au*, 1743—1815.
Zinzendorf, Tsín-tsen-dorf, Nicholas, Louis, Count Von, *found* of the Moravian Brethren, Ger., 1700—1760.
Ziska, Tsís-kɑ, (*or* John Troczнow,) Ger. *leader* in the religious wars, 1380—1425.
Zoroaster, Zɷ-rɷ-ɑ́s-ter, Persian *phil*, *found* Majian religion, said to have predicted the coming of the Messiah.
Zorrilla, Ħɷr-él-yɑ, Jose, Sp. *poet* and *dram*, 1817—
Zschokke, Ts-ʃók-e, Heinrich, Ger. *hist*, *nov* and *dram*, 1771—1848.
Zschukowskii, Ts-ʃɷ-kɤ́-skę, (?) Wassilii Andrejewitsch, Rus. *poet*, 1783—
Zumbo, Dzǿm-bɷ, Gaetano Julio, Silician *art*, 1656—1701.
Zumpt, Tsɷmpt, Karl Gottlob, Ger. *Latinist*, 1792—
Zwingli, Tsvíŋ-glɛ, Ulrick, the great Swiss *reformer* 1484—k. 1531.

# PRONUNCIATION

OF

# SCRIPTURE PROPER NAMES.

---

Aalar, Ɑ'a-lɑr.
Aaron, Ɑ'ron.
Ab, Ab.
Abacuc, Ab'a-kꝗ.
Abadah, Ab'a-dꝗ.
Abaddon, A-bád-on.
Abadias, Ab-a-dị-as.
Abagtha, A-bág-ŧɑ.
Abal, Ɑ'bal.
Abana, Ab'a-nꝗ.
Abarim, Ab'a-rim.
Abaron, Ab'a-ron.
Abba, Ab'ɑ.
Abda, Ab'dɑ.
Abdi, Ab dị.
Abdias, Ab-dị-as.
Abdiel, Ab'di-el.
Abdon, Ab'don.
Abednego, A-béd-nɛ-gω.
Abel, Ɑ'bel.
Abel Bethmaacah, Ɑ'bl Beŧ-má-a-kꝗ.
Abel Maim, Ɑ'bel Má-im.
Abel Meholath, Ɑ'bel Mɛ-hó-laŧ. [ra-im.
Abel Mizraim, Ɑ'bel Míz-
Abel Shittim, Ɑ'bel Σit-im.
Abesan, Ab'ɛ-san.
Abesar, Ab'ɛ-sɑr.
Abez, Ɑ'bɛz.
Abgarus, Ab'ga-rus.
Abi, Ɑ'bị.
Abia, A-bị-ɑ, *or*
Abiah, A-bị-ɑ.
Abialbon, Ɑ-bi-ál-bon.
Abiasaph, A-bị-a-saf.
Abiathar, A-bị-a-ŧꝗr.
Abib, Ɑ'bib.
Abidah, A-bị-dɑ.
Abidan, Ab'i-dan.
Abiel, Ɑ'bi-el.
Abiezer, Ɑ-bi-é-zer.
Abiezrite, Ɑ-bi-éz-rịt.
Abigal, Ab'i-gal.
Abihail, Ab-i-há-il.
Abihu, A-bị-hꝗ.
Abihud, A-bị-hud.
Abijah, A-bị-jɑ.
Abijam, A-bị-jam.
Abilene, Ab-i-lé-nɛ.
Abimael, A-bím-a-el.
Abimelech, A-bím-ɛ-lek.
Abinadab, A-bín-a-dab.
Abinoam, A-bín-ω-am.
Abiram, A-bị-ram.
Abirom, A-bị-rom.
Abisai, A-bís-a-ị.
Abisei, Ab-i-sé-ị.
Abishag, Ab'i-ʃag.
Abishahar, A-bíʃ-a-hꝗr.
Abishai, A-bíʃ-a-ị.
Abishalam, Ab-íʃ-a-lam, *or*
Abishalom, Ab-i-ʃá-lom.
Abishua, A-bíʃ-ꝗ-ɑ, *or* A-bị-ʃꝗ-ɑ.
Abishur, Ab'i-ʃur.
Abisum, Ab'i-sum.
Abital, Ab'i-tal.
Abitub, Ab'i-tub.
Abiud, A-bị-ud.
Abner, Ab'ner.
Abram, Ɑ'bram, *or*
Abraham, Ɑ'bra-ham.
Absalom, Ab'sa-lom
Abubus, A-bꝗ́-bus.
Acaron, Ak'a-ron.
Acatan, Ak'a-tan.
Accad, Ak'ad.
Accaron, Ak'a-ron.
Accho, Ak'ω.
Accos, Ak'os.
Accoz, Ak'oz.
Aceldama, A-sél-da-mꝗ.
Achab, Ɑ'kab.
Achad, Ɑ'kad.
Achaia, A-ká-yɑ.
Achaicus, A-ká-i-kus.
Achan, Ɑ'kan.
Achar, Ɑ'kɑr.
Achaz, Ɑ'kaz.
Achbor, Ak'bǿr.
Achiacharus, Ɑ-ki-ák-a-rus.
Achim, Ɑ'kim.
Achimelech, A-kím-ɛ-lek.
Achior, Ɑ'ki-ør.
Achiram, A-kị-ram.
Achish, Ɑ'kiʃ.
Achitob, Ak'i-tob, *or*
Achitub, Ak'i-tub.
Achitophel, A-kít-ω-fel.
Achmetha, Ak'mɛ-ŧꝗ, *or* Ak-mé-ŧɑ.
Achor, Ɑ'kør.
Achsa, Ak'sɑ.
Achshaph, Ak'ʃaf.
Achzib, Ak'zib.
Acipha, As'i-fꝗ.
Acitho, As'i-ŧω.
Acua, A-kꝗ́-ɑ.
Acub, Ɑ'kub.
Ada, Ɑ'dɑ.
Adad, Ɑ'dad.
Adada, Ad'a-dꝗ,
Adadah, Ad'a-dꝗ.
Adadezer, Ad-ad-é-zer.

Adadrimmon, Ad-ad-rím-on.
Adah, Ɑ'dɑ.
Adaiah, Ad-a-į-ɑ.
Adalia, Ad-a-lį-ɑ.
Adam, Ad'am.
Adama, Ad'a-mą, *or*
Adamah, Ad'a-mą.
Adami, Ad'a-mį.
Adami Nekeb, Ad'a-mį Né-keb.
Adar, Ɑ'dɑr.
Adasa, Ad'a-są.
Adatha, Ad'a-ŧą.
Adbeel, Ad'bɛ-el.
Addan, Ad'an.
Addar, Ad'ɑr.
Addi, Ad'į.
Addin, Ad'in.
Addo, Ad'ɷ.
Addus, Ad'us.
Ader, Ɑ'der.
Adida, Ad'i-dą.
Adiel, Ɑ'di-el.
Adin, Ɑ'din.
Adina, Ad'i-ną.
Adino, Ad'i-nɷ.
Adinus, Ad'i-nus.
Aditha, Ad'i-ŧą.
Adithaim, Ad-i-ŧá-im.
Adlai, Ad'la-į.
Admah, Ad'mɑ.
Admatha, Ad'ma-ŧą.
Adna, Ad'nɑ.
Adnah, Ad'nɑ.
Adonai, Ad'ɷ-na.
Adonias, Ad-ɷ-nį-as.
Adonibezek, A-don-i-bé-zek.
Adonijah, Ad-ɷ-nį-jɑ.
Adonikam, A-dón-i-kam.
Adoniram, Ad-on-į-ram.
Adonizedek, A-don-i-zé-dek.
Adora, A-dɷ́-rɑ.
Adoraim, Ad-ɷ-rá-im.
Adoram, A-dɷ́-ram.
Adramelech, A-drám-ɛ-lek.
Adria, Ɑ'dri-ɑ.
Adriel, Ɑ'dri-el.
Aduel, A-dų́-el.
Adullam, A-dúl-am.
Adummim, A-dúm-im.
Aedias, Ɑ-ɛ-dį-as.
Ægypt, Ɛ'jipt.
Æneas, Ɛ-né-as, (*Virgil.*)
Æneas, Ɛ'nɛ-as, (*Acts* ix.)
Ænon, Ɛ'non.
Ænos, Ɛ'nos.
Agaba, Ag'a-bą.
Agabus, Ag'a-bŭs.
Agag, Ɑ'gag.
Agagite, Ɑ'gag-įt.
Agar, Ɑ'gɑr.
Agarenes, Ag-a-rénz.
Agee, Ag'ɛ-ɛ.
Aggeus, A-gé-us.
Agnothtabor, Ag-noŧ-tá-bor.
Agur, Ɑ'gur.
Ahab, Ɑ'hab.
Aharah, A-hár-ɑ.
Aharal, A-hár-al.
Ahasai, A-hás-a-į.
Ahasuerus, A-has-yų-é-rus.
Ahava, A-há-vɑ.
Ahaz, Ɑ'haz.
Ahazai, A-ház-a-į.
Ahaziah, Ɑ-ha-zį-ɑ.
Ahban, Ɑ'ban.
Aher, Ɑ'her.
Ahi, Ɑ'hį.
Ahia, A-hį-ɑ.
Ahiam, A-hį-am.
Ahiezer, Ɑ-hi-é-zer.
Ahihud, A-hį-hud.
Ahijah, A-hį-jɑ.
Ahikam, A-hį-kam.
Ahilud, A-hį-lud.
Ahimaaz, A-hím-a-az.
Ahiman, A-hį-man.
Ahimelech, A-hím-ɛ-lek.
Ahimoth, A-hį-moŧ.
Ahinadab, A-hín-a-dab.
Ahinoam, A-hín-ɷ-am.
Ahio, A-hį-ɷ.
Ahira, A-hį-rɑ.
Ahiram, A-hį-ram.
Ahiramites, A-hį-ram-įts.
Ahisamach, A-hís-a-mak.
Ahishahur, A-híʃ-a-hur.
Ahisham, A-hį-ʃam.
Ahishar, A-hį-ʃɑr.
Ahitob, A-hį-tob.
Ahitophel, A-hít-ɷ-fel.
Ahitub, A-hį-tub.
Ahiud, A-hį-ud.
Ahlah, Ɑ'lɑ.
Ahlai, Ɑ'la, *or* Ɑ-lá-į.
Ahoe, A-hɷ́-ɛ, *or*
Ahoah, A-hɷ́-ɑ.
Ahoite, A-hɷ́-įt.
Aholah, A-hɷ́-lɑ.
Aholba, A-hól-bɑ.
Aholbah, A-hól-bɑ.
Aholiab, A-hɷ́-li-ab.
Aholibah, A-hól-i-bą.
Aholibamah, Ɑ-hɷ-líb-a-mą.
Ahumai, A-hų́-ma-į.
Ahuzam, A-hų́-zam.
Ahuzzah, A-húz-ɑ.
Ai, Ɑ'į.
Aiah, Ɑ-į-ɑ.
Aiath, Ɑ-į-aŧ.
Aija, Ɑ-į-jɑ.
Aijah, Ɑ-į-jɑ.
Aijalon, Aj'a-lon.
Aijeleth Shahar, Aj'ɛ-leŧ Σá-hɑr.
Ain, Ɑ'in.
Aioth, Ɑ-į-oŧ.
Airus, Ɑ-į-rus.
Ajalon, Aj'a-lon.
Akkub, Ak'ub.
Akrabbim, Ak-ráb-im.
Alamelech, A-lám-ɛ-lek.
Alameth, Al'a-meŧ.
Alamoth, Al'a-moŧ.
Alcimus, Al'si-mus.
Alema, Al'ɛ-mą.
Alemeth, A-lé-meŧ.
Alexandria, Al-eks-án-dri-ą.
Alexandrion, Al-eks-an-drį-on.
Aliah, A-lį-ɑ.
Alian, A-lį-an.
Allelujah, Al-ɛ-lų́-yą.
Allom, Al'om.
Allon Bachuth, Al'on Bák-huŧ.
Almodad, Al'mɷ-dad.
Almon Diblathaim, Al'mon Dib-la-ŧá-im.
Alnathan, Al'na-ŧan.
Aloth, Ɑ'loŧ.
Alpha, Al'fɑ.
Alpheus, Al-fé-us.
Altaneus, Al-ta-né-us.
Altaschith, Al-tás-kiŧ.
Altekon, Al'tɛ-kon.
Alush, Ɑ'luʃ.
Alvah, Al'vɑ, *or*
Alvan, Al'van.
Amad, Ɑ'mad.
Amadatha, A-mád-a-ŧą.
Amadathus, A-mád-a-ŧus.
Amal, Ɑ'mal.
Amalda, A-mál-dɑ.
Amalek, Am'a-lek.
Amalekites, Am'a-lek-įts.
Aman, Ɑ'man.
Amana, Am'a-ną.
Amariah, Am-a-rį-ɑ.
Amasa, A-má-sɑ, *or* Am'a-są.
Amasai, A-más-a-į.
Amashiah, Am-a-ʃį-ɑ.
Amatheis, Am-a-ŧé-is.
Amathis, Am'a-ŧis.
Amaziah, Am-a-zį-ɑ.
Amen, Ɑ-mén.
Ami, Ɑ'mį.
Aminadab, A-mín-a-dab.

Amittai, A-mít-a-ị.
Amizabad, A-míz-a-bad.
Ammadatha, A-mád-a-ȶạ.
Amma, Am'ɑ.
Ammi, Am'ị.
Ammidioi, A-míd-i-ơ.
[el.
Ammiel, Am'i-el, *or* A-mị-
Ammihud, A-mị-hud. [a-ị.
Ammishaddai, Am-i-ſád-
Ammon, Am'on.
Ammonites, Am'on-ịts.
Amnon, Am'non.
Amok, Ā'mok.
Amon, Ā'mon.
Amorites, Am'ω-rịts.
Amos, Ā'mos.
Amplias, Am'pli-as.
Amram, Am'ram.
Amramites, Am'ram-ịts.
Amran, Am'ran.
Amraphel, Am'ra-fel.
Amzi, Am'zị.
Anab, Ā'nab.
Anael, An'a-el.
Anah, Ā'nɑ.
Anaharath, An-á-há-raȶ.
Anaiah, An-a-ị-ɑ.
Anak, Ā'nak.
Anakims, An'a-kimz.
Anamelech, A-nám-ε-lek.
Anamim, An'a-mim.
Anan, Ā'nan.
Anani, An-á-nị.
Ananiah, An-a-nị-ɑ.
Ananias, An-a-nị-as.
Ananiel, A-nán-i-el.
Anath, Ā'naȶ.
Anathema, A-náȶ-ε-mạ.
Anathoth, An'a-ȶoȶ.
Anathothite, An'a-ȶoȶ-ịt.
Andrew, An'drω.
Andronikus, An-drω-nị-kus, *or* An-drón-i-kus.
Anem, Ā'nem, *or*
Anen, Ā'nen.
Aner, Ā'ner.
Anes, Ā'nes.
Aneth, Ā'neȶ.
Aniam, Ā'ni-am.
Anim, Ā'nim.
Anna, An'ɑ.
Annaas, An'a-as.
Annas, An'as.
Annuus, A-nụ-us. [nus.
Antilibanus, An-ti-líb-a-
Antioch, An'ti-ok.
Antiochis, An-tị-ω-kis.
Antiochus, An-tị-ω-kus.
Antipas, An'ti-pas.
Antipatras, An-típ-a-tris.
Antipha, An'ti-fạ.
Antonia, An-tó-ni-ạ.
Antothijah, An-tω-ȶị-jɑ.
Antothite, An'toȶ-ịt.
Anub, Ā'nub.
Anus, Ā'nus.
Apamea, Ap-a-mé-ɑ.
Apharaim, Af-a-rá-im.
Apharsathchites, A-fạr-saȶ-kịts.
Apharsites, A-fạr-sịts.
Aphek, Ā'fek.
Aphekah, A-fé-kɑ.
Apherema, A-fér-ε-mạ.
Apherra, A-fér-ɑ.
Aphiah, A-fị-ɑ.
Aphrah, Af'rɑ.
Aphses, Af'sεz.
Apocalypse, A-pók-a-lips.
Apocrypha. A-pók-ri-fạ.
Apallos, A-pól-os.
Apollyon, A-pól-yon.
Appaim, Ap'a-im.
Apphia, Af'i-ạ.
Apphus, Af'us.
Aquila, Ak'wi-lạ.
Ar, Är.
Ara, Ā'rɑ.
Arab, Ā'rab.
Arabah, Ar'a-bạ.
Arabattine, Ar-a-bát-i-nε.
Arabia, A-rá-bi-ạ.
Arad, Ā'rad.
Aradite, Ā'rad-ịt.
Aradus, Ar'a-dus.
Arah, Ā'rɑ.
Aram, Ā'ram.
Aran, Ā'ran.
Ararat, Ar'a-rat.
Araunah, A-ré-nɑ.
Arba, *or* Arbah, Är'bɑ.
Arbal, Är'bal.
Arbattis, Är-bát-is.
Arbela, Är-bé-lɑ. (*Syria.*)
Arbella, Är-bél-ɑ.
Arbite, Är'bịt.
Arbonai, Är-bó-na-ị.
Archelaus, Är-kε-lá-us.
Archestratus, Är-kés-tra-tus.
Archevites, Är'kε-vịts.
Archi, Är'kị. [roȶ.
Archiataroth, Är-ki-át-a-
Archippus, Är-kíp-us.
Archites, Ärk'ịts.
Ard, Ärd.
Ardath, Är'daȶ.
Ardites, Ärd'ịts.
Ardon, Är'don.
Areli, A-ré-lị.
Arelites, A-ré-lịts.
Areopagite, Ā-rε-óp-a-jịt.
Areopagus, Ā-rε-óp-a-gus, *or* Ar-ε-óp-a-gus.
Ares, Ā'rεz.
Aretas, A-ré-tas.
Areus, A-ré-us.
Argob, Är'gob.
Argol, Är'gol.
Aridai, A-ríd-a-ị.
Aridatha, A-ríd-a-ȶạ.
Arieh, A-rị-e.
Ariel, Ā'ri-el.
Arimathea, Ar-i-ma-ȶé-ɑ.
Arioch, Ā'ri-ok.
Arisai, A-rís-a-ị. [lus.
Aristobulus, Ar-is-tω-bụ-
Arkites, Ärk'ịts. [on.
Armageddon, Är-ma-géd-
Armishadai, Är-mi-ſád-a-ị.
Armon, Är'mon.
Arnan, Är'nan.
Arnepher, Är'nε-fer.
Arnon, Är'non.
Arod, Ā'rod.
Arodi, Ar'ω-dị.
Aroer, Ar'ω-er.
Arom, Ā'rom.
Arpad, Är'pad, *or*
Arphad, Är'fad.
Arphaxad, Är-fáks-ad.
Arsaces, Är'sa-sεz.
Artemas, Är'tε-mas.
Aruboth, Är'yụ-boȶ.
Arumah, A-ró-mɑ.
Arvad, Är'vad.
Arvadites, Är'vad-ịts.
Arza, Är'zɑ.
Asa, Ā'sɑ.
Asadias, As-a-dị-as.
Asael, As'a-el.
Asahel, As'a-hel.
Asaiah, As-a-ị-ɑ.
Asana, As'a-nạ.
Asaph, Ā'saf.
Asaphar, As'a-fạr.
Asara, As'a-rạ.
Asareel, A-sár-ε-el.
Asarelah, As-a-ré-lɑ.
Asbazareth, As-báz-a-reȶ.
Ascalon, As'ka-lon.
Aseas, A-sé-as.
Asebebia, A-seb-ε-bị-ɑ.
Asebia, As-ε-bị-ɑ.
Asenath, As'ε-naȶ.
Aser, Ā'ser.
Aserar, A-sé-rɑr.
Ashabiah, Aſ-a-bị-ɑ.
Ashan, Ā'ſan.

Ashbea, Aʃ'bɛ-ɑ.
Ashbel, Aʃ'bel.
Ashbelites, Aʃ'bel-ịts.
Ashdod, Aʃ'dod.
Ashdothites, Aʃ'doŧ-ịts.
Ashdoth Pisgah, Aʃ'doŧ Piz-gɑ.
Ashean, Ɑ'ʃɛ-an.
Asher, Aʃ'er.
Ashimath, Aʃ'i-maŧ.
Ashkenaz, Aʃ'kɛ-naz
Ashnah, Aʃ'nɑ.
Ashon, Ɑ'ʃon.
Ashpenaz, Aʃ'pɛ-naz.
Ashriel, Aʃ'ri-el.
Ashtaroth, Aʃ'ta-roŧ. [ịts.
Ashtarothites, Aʃ'ta-roŧ-
Ashtemoth, Aʃ'tɛ-moŧ.
Ashuath, A-ʃų-aŧ.
Ashur, Aʃ'ur.
Ashurim, A-ʃų-rim.
Ashurites, Aʃ'ur-ịts.
Asia, Ɑ'ʃi-ɑ.
Asibias, As-i-bị-as.
Asiel, Ɑ'si-el.
Asipha, As'i-fɑ.
Askelon, As'kɛ-lon.
Asmadai, As'ma-dá.
Asmaveth, As'ma-veŧ.
Asmodeus, As-mω-dé-us.
Asmoneans, As-mω-né-anz.
Asnah, As'nɑ.
Asnapper, As-náp-er.
Asochis, A-só-kis.
Asom, Ɑ'som.
Aspatha, As'pa-ŧɑ.
Asphar, As'fɑr.
Aspharasus, As-fár-a-sus.
Asriel, As'ri-el.
Assabias, As-a-bị-as.
Assalimoth, A-sál-i-moŧ.
Assanias, As-a-nị-as.
Assideans, As-i-dé-anz.
Assir, As'er.
Assos, As'os.
Astaroth, As'ta-roŧ.
Astarte, As-tɑ̣r-tɛ.
Astath, As'taŧ.
Asuppim, A-súp-im.
Asyncritus, A-sín-kri-tus.
Atad, Ɑ'tad.
Atarah, At'a-rɑ.
Atargatis, A-tɑ̣r-ga-tis.
Ataroth, At'a-roŧ.
Ater, Ɑ'ter.
Aterezias, At-ɛ-rɛ-zị-as.
Athack, Ɑ'ŧak.
Athaiah, Aŧ-a-ị-ɑ.
Athaliah, Aŧ-a-lị-ɑ.
Atharias, Aŧ-a-rị-as. [us.
Athenobius, Aŧ-ɛ-nó-bi-
Athens, Aŧ'enz.
Athlai, Aŧ'lɑ.
Atroth, At'roŧ.
Attai, At'a.
Attalia, At-a-lị-ɑ,
Attalus, At'a-lus.
Attharates, At-ŧár-a-tɛz.
Augia, Θ'ji-ɑ.
Auranitis, Θ-ra-nị-tis.
Auranus, Θ-rá-nus.
Auteus, Θ-té-us.
Ava, Ɑ'vɑ.
Avaran, Av'a-ran.
Aven, Ɑ'ven.
Avim, Ɑ'vim.
Avims, Ɑ'vimz.
Avites, Ɑ'vịts.
Avith, Ɑ'viŧ.
Azaelus, Az-a-é-lus.
Azah, Ɑ'zɑ.
Azal, Ɑ'zal.
Azaliah, Az-a-lị-ɑ.
Azania, Az-a-nị-ɑ.
Azaphion, A-zá-fi-on.
Azara, Az'a-rɑ.
Azareel, A-zá-rɛ-el.
Azariah, Az-a-rị-ɑ.
Azarias, Az-a-rị-as.
Azaz, Ɑ'zaz.
Azazel, A-zá-zel.
Azaziah, Az-a-zị-ɑ.
Azbazareth, Az-báz-a-reŧ.
Azbuk, Az'buk.
Azekah, A-zé-kɑ.
Azel, Ɑ'zel.
Azem, Ɑ'zem.
Azephurith, Az-ɛ-fų-riŧ.
Azer, Ɑ'zer.
Azetas, A-zé-tas.
Azgad, Az'gad.
Azia, A-zị-ɑ.
Aziei, A-zị-ɛ-ị.
Aziel, Ɑ'zi-el.
Aziza, A-zị-zɑ.
Azmaveth, Az'ma-veŧ.
Azmon, Az'mon. [bor.
Aznoth Tabor, Az'noŧ Tá-
Azor, Ɑ'zor.
Azotus, A-zó-tus.
Azriel, Az'-ri-el.
Azrikam, Az'ri-kam.
Azubah, A-zų-bɑ.
Azur, Ɑ'zur.
Azuran, Az'yų-ran.
Azymites, Az'i-mịts.
Azzah, Az'ɑ.
Azzan, Az'an.
Azzur, Az'ur.

# B.

Baal, Bá-al, *or* Bel, Bel.
Baalah, Bá-a-lɑ.
Baalath, Bá-al-aŧ.
Baalath Beer, — Bé-er.
Baal Berith, Bá-al Bé-riŧ.
Baal Gad, — Gad.
Baal Hamon, — Hám-on.
Baal Hanan, — Hán-an.
Baal Hazor, — Há-zor.
Baal Hernon, — Hẹr-non.
Baali, Bá-al-ị.
Baalim, Bá-al-im.
Baalis, Bá-a-lis.
Baalle, Bá-al-ɛ.
Baal Meon, Bá-al Mé-on.
Baal Peor, — Pé-or.
Baal Perazim, — Pér-a-zim. [ʃɑ.
Baal Shalisha, — Σál-i-
Baal Tamar, — Tá-mɑr.
Baal Zebub, — Zé-bub.
Baal Zephon, — Zé-fon.
Baana, Bá-a-nɑ.
Baanah, Bá-a-nɑ.
Baanan, Bá-a-nan.
Baanath, Bá-a-naŧ.
Baanias, Ba-a-nị-as.
Baara, Bá-a-rɑ.
Baasha, Bá-a-ʃɑ.
Baashah, Bá-a-ʃɑ.
Baasiah, Ba-a-sị-ɑ.
Babel, Bá-bel.
Babi, Bá-bị.
Babylon, Báb-i-lon.
Baca, Bá-kɑ.
Bacchurus, Ba-kų-rus.
Bachrites, Bák-rịts.
Bachuth Allon, Bák-ut Al'on.
Bagoas, Ba-gó-as.
Bagoi, Bág-ω-ị. [ịt.
Baharumite, Ba-há-rum-
Bahurim, Ba-hų-rim.
Bajith, Bá-jiŧ.
Bakbaker, Bak-bák-er.
Bakbuk, Bák-buk.
Bakbukiah, Bak-buk-ị-ɑ.
Balaam, Bá-lam.
Baladan, Bál-a-dan.
Balah, Bá-lɑ.
Balak, Bá-lak.
Balamo, Bál-a-mω.
Balanus, Bál-a-nus.
Balthasar, Bal-ŧá-sɑr.

Bamah, Bá-mɑ.
Bamoth, Bá-moŧ. [al.
Bamoth Baal, Bá-moŧ Bá-
Ban, Ban.
Banaias, Ban-a-ị-as.
Bani, Bá-nị.
Banid, Bá-nid.
Bannus, Bán-us.
Banuas, Bán-yɋ-as.
Barabbas, Ba-ráb-as.
Barachel, Bár-a-kel.
Barachiah, Bar-a-kị-ɑ.
Barachias, Bar-a-kị-as.
Barak, Bá-rak.
Barcenor, Bɋr-sé-nor.
Bargo, Bɋ́r-gɷ.
Barhumites, Bɋr-hɋ́-mịts.
Bariah, Ba-rị-ɑ.
Barjesus, Bɋr-jé-sus.
Barjona, Bɋr-jó-nɑ.
Barkos, Bɋ́r-kos.
Barnabas, Bɋ́r-na-bas.
Barodis, Ba-ró-dis.
Barsabas, Bɋ́r-sa-bas.
Bartacus, Bɋ́r-ta-kus. [mɋ.
Bartholomew, Bɋr-ŧól-ɷ-
Bartimeus, Bɋr-ti-mé-us.
Baruch, Bá-ruk.
Barzillai, Bɋr-zíl-a-ị.
Bascama, Bás-ka-mɋ.
Bashan, Bá-ʃan, *or*
Bassan, Bás-an.
Bashan Havoth Fair, Bá-
ʃan Há-voŧ Fá-er.
Bashemath, Báʃ-ɛ-maŧ.
Baslith, Bás-liŧ.
Basmath, Bás-maŧ.
Bassa, Bás-ɑ.
Bastai, Bás-ta-ị.
Batane, Bát-a-nɛ.
Bath, Baŧ.
Bathaloth, Báŧ-a-loŧ.
Bathrabbim, Baŧ-ráb-im.
Bathsheba, Báŧ-ʃɛ-bɋ.
Bathshua, Baŧ-ʃɋ́-ɑ.
Bavai, Báv-a-ị.
Bealiah, Bɛ-ɑ-lị-ɑ.
Bealoth, Bé-a-loŧ.
Bean, Bé-an.
Bebai, Béb-a-ị.
Becher, Bé-ɕer.
Bechorath, Bɛ-kó-raŧ.
Bechtileth, Bék-ti-leŧ.
Bedad, Bé-dad.
Bedaiah, Bed-a-ị-ɑ.
Beeliada, Bɛ-el-ị-a-dɋ.
Beelsarus, Bɛ-él-sa-rus.
Beeltethmus, Bɛ - el - téŧ-
mus.
Beelzebub, Bɛ-él-zɛ-bub.

Beer, Bé-er.
Beera, Bɛ-é-rɑ.
Beerah, Bɛ-é-rɑ, *or*
Berah, Bé-rɑ.
Beerelim, Bɛ-ér-ɛ-lim.
Beeri, Bɛ-é-rị. [i-rɷ.
Beerlahairoi, Bɛ-er-la-há-
Beeroth, Bɛ-é-roŧ.
Beerothites, Bɛ-é-roŧ-ịts.
Beersheba, Bɛ-ér-ʃɛ-bɋ.
Beeshterah, Bɛ-éʃ-tɛ-rɋ.
Behemoth, Bé-hɛ-moŧ.
Bekah, Bé-kɑ.
Bela, Bé-lɑ.
Belaites, Bé-la-ịts.
Belemus, Bél-ɛ-mus.
Belgai, Bél-ga-ị.
Belial, Bé-li-al.
Belmaim, Bél-ma-im.
Belmen, Bél-men.
Belshazzar, Bel-ʃáz-ɑr. [ɑr.
Belteshazzar, Bel - tɛ - ʃáz-
Ben, Ben.
Benaiah, Bɛ-ná-yɑ.
Benammi, Ben-ám-ị.
Beneberak, Ben-éb-ɛ-rak.
Benejaakam, Ben-ɛ-já-a-
kam. [Ben-há-dad.
Benhadad, Bén-ha-dad, *or*
Benhail, Ben-há-il.
Benhanan, Ben-há-nan.
Beninu, Bén-i-nɋ.
Benjamin, Bén-ja-min.
Benjamite, Bén-ja-mịt.
Benjamites, Bén-ja-mịts.
Beno, Bé-nɷ.
Benoni, Bɛ-nó-nị.
Benui, Bɛ-nɋ́-ị.
Benzoheth, Ben-zó-heŧ.
Beon, Bé-on.
Beor, Bé-or.
Bera, Bé-rɑ.
Berachah, Bér-a-kɋ.
Berachiah, Ber-a-kị-ɑ.
Beraiah, Ber-a-ị-ɑ.
Berea, Bɛ-ré-ɑ.
Bered, Bé-red.
Beri, Bé-rị.
Beriah, Bɛ-rị-ɑ.
Berites, Bé-rịts.
Berith, Bé-riŧ. [nis.
Bernice, Ber-nị-sɛ, *or* Bér-
Berodach Baladan, Bɛ-ró-
dak Bál-a-dan.
Beroth, Bé-roŧ.
Berothai, Bér-ɷ-ŧɑ.
Berothath, Bɛ-ró-ŧaŧ.
Beryl, Bér-il.
Berzelus, Ber-zé-lus.
Besodiah, Bes-ɷ-dị-ɑ.

Besor, Bé-sor.
Betah, Bé-tɑ.
Beten, Bé-ten.
Bethabara, Beŧ-áb-a-rɋ.
Bethebarah, Beŧ-áb-a-rɋ.
Bethanath, Béŧ-a-naŧ.
Bethanoth, Béŧ-a-noŧ.
Bethany, Béŧ-a-ni.
Betharabah, Beŧ-ár-a-bɋ.
Betharam, Béŧ-a-ram.
Betharbel, Beŧ-ɋ́r-bel.
Bethaven, Beŧ-á-ven.
Bethazmaveth, Beŧ-áz-ma-
veŧ. [mé-on.
Bethbaalmeon, Beŧ-ba-al-
Bethbara, Beŧ-bá-rɑ.
Bethbarah, Beŧ-bá-rɑ.
Bethbasi, Béŧ-ba-sị.
Bethbirei, Beŧ-bír-ɛ-ị.
Bethcar, Béŧ-kɑr.
Bethdagon, Beŧ-dá-gon.
Bethdiblathaim, Beŧ-dib-
la-ŧá-im.
Bethel, Béŧ-el.
Bethelite, Béŧ-el-ịt.
Bethemek, Beŧ-é-mek.
Bether, Bé-ŧer.
Bethesda, Bɛ-ŧéz-dɑ.
Bethezel, Beŧ-é-zel.
Bethgader, Beŧ-gá-der.
Bethgamul, Beŧ-gá-mul.
Bethhaccerim, Beŧ - hák-
sɛ-rim.
Bethharan, Beŧ-há-ran.
Bethhoglah, Beŧ-hóg-lɑ.
Bethhoron, Beŧ-hó-ron.
Bethjesimoth, Beŧ - jés - i-
moŧ.
Bethlebaoth, Beŧ-léb-a-oŧ.
Bethlehem, Béŧ-lɛ-hem.
Bethlehem Ephratah, Béŧ-
lɛ-hem Ef'ra-tɋ. [ịt.
Bethlehemite, Béŧ-lɛ-hem-
Bethlehem Judah, Béŧ-lɛ-
hem Jɋ́-dɑ.
Bethlomon, Beŧ-ló-mon.
Bethmaacah, Beŧ - má - a-
kɋ. [ka-boŧ.
Bethmarcaboth, Beŧ-mɋ́r-
Bethmeon, Beŧ-mé-on.
Bethnimrah, Beŧ-ním-rɑ.
Bethoron, Beŧ-ó-ron.
Bethpalet, Beŧ-pá-let.
Bethpazzer, Beŧ-páz-er.
Bethpeor, Beŧ-pé-or.
Bethphage, Béŧ-fa-jɛ.
Bethphelet, Béŧ-fɛ-let.
Bethrabah, Béŧ-ra-bɋ.
Bethrapha, Béŧ-ra-fɋ.
Bethrehob, Béŧ-rɛ-hob.

Bethsaida, Beŧ-sá-i-dq.
Bethsamos, Béŧ-sa-mos.
Bethshan, Béŧ-ʃan.
Bethshean, Beŧ-ʃé-an.
Bethshemesh, Béŧ-ʃɛ-meʃ.
Bethshittah, Beŧ-ʃít-a.
Bethsimos, Béŧ-si-mos.
Bethsura, Beŧ-sų́-ra. [q.
Bethtappua, Beŧ-táp-yų-
Bethuel, Bɛ-ŧų́-el.
Bethul, Bé-ŧul.
Bethulia, Beŧ-yų-lị-q.
Bethzor, Béŧ-zor.
Bethzor, Béŧ-zur.
Betolius, Bɛ-tó-li-us.
Betomestham, Bet-ɷ-més-ŧam.
Betonim, Bét-ɷ-nim.
Beulah, Bɛ-yų́-la.
Bezai, Bé-za.
Bezaleel, Bɛ-zál-ɛ-el.
Bezek, Bé-zek.
Bezer, Bé-zer, *or*
Bozra, Bóz-ra.
Bezeth, Bé-zeŧ.
Biatas, Bị-a-tas.
Bichri, Bík-rị.
Bidkar, Bíd-kar.
Bigthah, Bíg-ŧa.
Bigthan, Bíg-ŧan.
Bigthana, Bíg-ŧa-nq.
Bigvai, Bíg-va-ị.
Bildad, Bíl-dad.
Bileam, Bíl-ɛ-am.
Bilgah, Bíl-ga.
Bilgai, Bíl-ga-ị.
Bilha, *or* Bilhah, Bíl-ha.
Bilhan, Bíl-han.
Bilshan, Bíl-ʃan.
Bimhal, Bím-hal.
Binea, Bín-ɛ-q.
Binnui, Bín-yų-ị.
Birsha, Bẹ́r-ʃa.
Birzavith, Bẹ́r-za-viŧ.
Bishlam, Biʃ-lam.
Bithiah, Bi-ŧị-a.
Bithron, Biŧ-ron.
Bizijothiah, Biz-i-jɷ-ŧị-a.
Bizijothijah, Biz-i-jɷ-ŧị-ja.
Bizjothjah, Biz-jóŧ-ja.
Biztha, Bíz-ŧa.
Blastus, Blás-tus.
Boanerges, Bɷ-a-nẹ́r-jɛz.
Boaz, Bó-az, *or*
Booz, Bó-oz.
Boccas, Bók-as.
Bocheru, Bók-ɛ-rɷ.
Bochim, Bó-kim.
Bohan, Bó-han.
Boscath, Bós-kaŧ.
Bosor, Bó-sor.
Bosora, Bós-ɷ-rq.
Bosrah, Bóz-ra,
Bozez, Bó-zez.
Bozrah, Bóz-ra.
Brigandine, Bríg-an-dịn.
Bukki, Búk-ị.
Bukkiah, Buk-ị-a.
Bul, Bul.
Bunah, Bų́-na.
Bunni, Bún-ị.
Buz, Buz.
Buzi, Bų́-zi.
Buzite, Búz-ịt.

## C.

Cab, Kab.
Cabbon, Káb-on.
Cabhem, Káb-ham.
Cabul, Ká-bul.
Caddis, Kád-is.
Cades, Ká-dɛz.
Cadesh, Ká-deʃ.
Caiaphas, Ká-ya-fas, *or*
Ká-a-fas.
Cain, Kan.
Cainan, Ka-ị-nan.
Cairites, Ká-rịts.
Calah, Ká-la. [a-lus.
Calamolalus, Kal-a-mól-
Calamus, Kál-a-mus.
Calcol, Kál-kol.
Caldees, Kal-déz.
Caleb, Ká-leb.
Caleb Ephratah, Ká-leb Ef'ra-tq.
Calitas, Kál-i-tas.
Calneth, Kál-neŧ.
Calno, Kál-nɷ.
Calphi, Kál-fị.
Calvary, Kál-va-ri.
Camon, Ká-mon.
Cana, Ká-na. [na-an.
Canaan, Ká-nan, *or* Ká-
Canaanites, Ká-nan-ịts, *or*
Ká-na-an-ịts.
Candace, Kán-da-sɛ.
Canneh, Kán-e.
Canveh, Kán-ve. [um.
Capernaum, Ka-pẹ́r-na-
Capharsalamah, Kaf-ar-sál-a-mq.
Caphenatha, Ka-fén-a-ŧq.
Caphira, Ka-fị-ra.
Caphtor, Káf-tor.
Caphtorim, Káf-tɷ-rim.
Caphtorims, Káf-tɷ-rimz.
Cappadocia, Kap-a-dó-ʃi-q. [on.
Carabasion, Kar-a-bá-ʒi-
Carchamis, Kq́r-ka-mis.
Carchemish, Kq́r-kɛ-miʃ.
Careah, Ka-ré-a.
Caria, Ká-ri-a.
Carcas, Kq́r-kas. [anz.
Carmanians, Kar-má-ni-
Carme, Kq́r-mɛ.
Carmel, Kq́r-mel.
Carmelite, Kq́r-mel-ịt. [es.
Carmelitess, Kq́r-mel-ịt-
Carmi, Kq́r-mị.
Carmites, Kq́r-mịts.
Carnaim, Kq́r-na-im.
Carnion, Kq́r-ni-on.
Carpus, Kq́r-pus.
Carshena, Kqr-ʃé-na.
Casiphia, Ka-síf-i-q.
Casleu, Kás-lų.
Caslubim, Kás-lų-bim.
Casphor, Kás-fɛr.
Caspis, Kás-pis, *or*
Casphin, Kás-fin.
Cathuath, Ka-ŧų́-aŧ.
Cedron, Sé-dron.
Ceilan, Sị-lan.
Celemia, Sel-ɛ-mị-a.
Cenchrea, Sén-krɛ-a.
Cendebeus, Sen-dɛ-bé-us.
Centurion, Sen-tų́-ri-on.
Cephas, Sé-fas.
Ceras, Sé-ras.
Ceteb, Sé-teb.
Chabris, Ká-bris.
Chadias, Ká-di-as.
Chæreas, Ké-rɛ-as.
Chalcedony, Kál-sɛ-dɷ-ni.
Chalcol, Kál-kol.
Chaldea, Kal-dé-a.
Chanes, Ká-nɛz. [us.
Channuneus, Kan-yų-né-
Charaathalas, Kar-a-áŧ-a-las.
Characa, Kár-a-kq.
Charasim, Kár-a-sim.
Charcus, Kq́r-kus.
Charea, Ká-rɛ-a.
Charmis, Kq́r-mis.
Charran, Kár-an.
Chaseba, Kás-ɛ-bq.
Chebar, Ké-bqr. [ɷ-mer.
Chederlaomer, Ked-er-lá-
Chelal, Ké-lal.
Chelcias, Kél-ʃi-as.
Chellians, Kél-i-anz.
Chellub, Kél-ub.

Chellus, Kél-us.
Chelod, Ké-lod.
Chelūb, Ké-lub.
Chelubai, Kε-lú-ba.
Chelubar, Kε-lú-bar.
Chemarims, Kém-a-rimz.
Chemosh, Ké-moſ.
Chenaanah, Kε-ná-a-nq.
Chenani, Kén-a-nj.
Chenaniah, Ken-a-nj-a.
Chephar Haamonai, Ké-far Ha-ám-ω-na.
Chephirah, Kε-fj-ra.
Cheran, Ké-ran.
Chereas, Ké-rε-as.
Cherethims, Kér-eŧ-imz.
Cherethites, Kér-eŧ-jts.
Cherith, Ké-riŧ, *or*
Cherish, Ké-riſ.
Cherub, Ké-rub, (*a city.*)
Cherub, Cér-ub.
Cherubim, Cér-yq-bim.
Chesalon, Kés-a-lon.
Chesed, Ké-sed.
Chesil, Ké-sil.
Chesud, Ké-sud.
Chesulloth, Kε-súl-oŧ.
Chetim, Két-im.
Chezib, Ké-zib.
Chidon, Kj-don.
Chilion, Ki-lj-on.
Chiliab, Kíl-ε-ab.
Chilmad, Kíl-mad.
Chimham, Kím-ham.
Chisleu, Kís-lq, Casleu, Kás-lq, *or* Cisleu, Sís-lq.
Chislon, Kís-lon.
Chisloth Tabor, Kís-loŧ Tá-bor.
Chittim, Kít-im.
Chiun, Kj-un.
Chloe, Kló-ε.
Choba, Kó-ba.
Chorasin, Kω-rá-sin, *or*
Chorashan, Kω-rá-ſan, *or*
Chorazin, Kω-rá-zin.
Chosameus, Kos-a-mé-us.
Chozeba, Kω-zé-ba.
Christ, Krjst.
Chub, Kub.
Chun, Kun.
Chusa, Kú-sa, *or*
Chuza, Kú-za.
Chushan Rishathaim, Kúſ-an Riſ-a-ŧá-im.
Chusi, Kú-sj.
Cinnereth, Sin-é-reŧ, *or*
Cinneroth, Sín-ε-roŧ.
Cirama, Sír-a-mq.
Cisai, Sj-sa.
Cisleu, Sís-lq.
Citherus, Siŧ-ε-rus.
Cittims, Sit-imz.
Clauda, Kló-da.
Cleasa, Klε-á-sa.
Clement, Klém-ent.
Cleophas, Klé-ω-fas, *or*
Cleopas, Klé-ω-pas.
Cloe, Kló-ε.
Cnidus, Nj-dus.
Colhozeh, Kol-hó-ze.
Collius, Kól-i-us.
Colosse, Kω-lós-ε.
Colossians, Kω-lóſ-i-anz.
Coniah, Kω-nj-a.
Cononiah, Kon-ω-nj-a.
Cor, Kor.
Corban, Kór-ban.
Corbe, Kór-bε.
Core, Kó-rε.
Corinth, Kór-inŧ.
Corinthians, Kω-rín-ŧi-anz.
Cosam, Kó-sam.
Coūtha, Ká-ŧa.
Coz, Koz.
Cozbi, Kóz-bj.
Cresens, Krés-enz.
Cretans, Kré-tanz.
Crete, Krεt.
Cretes, Krεts.
Cretians, Kré-ſi-anz.
Cubit, Kú-bit.
Cush, Kuſ.
Cushan, Kú-ſan.
Cushan Rishathaim, Kú-ſan Riſ-a-ŧá-im.
Cushi, Kú-ſj.
Cuth, Kuŧ, *or*
Cuthah, Kúŧ-a.
Cutheans, Kú-ŧε-anz.
Cyamon, Sj-a-mon.
Cyrene, Sj-ré-nε.
Cyrenius, Sj-ré-ni-us.

# D.

Dabareh, Dáb-a-re.
Dabbasheth, Dáb-a-ſeŧ.
Daberath, Dáb-ε-raŧ.
Dabria, Dá-bri-a.
Dacobi, Da-kó-bj.
Daddeus, Da-dé-us.
Dagon, Dá-gon.
Daisan, Dá-san.
Dalaiah, Dal-a-j-a.
Dalilah, Dál-i-lq.
Dalmanutha, Dal-ma-nú-ŧa.
Dalphon, Dál-fon.
Damaris, Dám-a-ris.
Damascenes, Dam-a-sénz.
Dan, Dan.
Daniel, Dán-yel.
Danites, Dán-jts.
Danjaan, Dan-já-an.
Dannah, Dán-a.
Danobrath, Dán-ω-braŧ.
Dara, Dá-ra.
Darda, Dár-da.
Darian, Dá-ri-an.
Darkon, Dár-kon.
Dathan, Dá-ŧan.
Dathemah, Dáŧ-ε-mq.
Dathmah, Dáŧ-ma.
David, Dá-vid.
Debir, Dé-ber.
Deborah, Déb-ω-rq.
Decapolis, Dε-káp-ω-lis.
Dedan, Dé-dan.
Dedanim, Déd-a-nim.
Dedanims, Déd-a-nimz.
Dehavites, Dε-há-vjts.
Dekar, Dé-kar.
Delaiah, Del-a-j-a.
Delilah, Dél-i-lq.
Demas, Dé-mas.
Derbe, Dér-bε.
Dessau, Dés-e.
Deuel, Dε-yú-el.
Deuteronomy, Dq-ter-ón-ω-mi.
Diblaim, Díb-la-im.
Diblath, Díb-laŧ.
Dibon, Dj-bon.
Dibon Gad, Dj-bon Gad.
Dibri, Díb-rj.
Dibzahab, Díb-za-hab, *or*
Dizahab, Díz-a-hab.
Didrachm, Dj-dram.
Didymus, Díd-i-mus.
Diklah, Dík-la, *or*
Dildah, Díl-da.
Dilean, Díl-ε-an.
Dimnah, Dím-na.
Dimon, Dj-mon.
Dimonah, Dj-mó-na.
Dinah, Dj-na.
Dinaites, Dj-na-jts.
Dinhabah, Din-ha-bq.
Diotrephes, Dj-ót-rε-fεz.
Dishan, Dj-ſan.
Dishon, Dj-ſon.
Dizahab, Díz-a-hab.
Docus, Dó-kus.
Dodai, Dód-a-j.
Dodanim, Dód-a-nim.
Dodovah, Dód-a-vq.
Dodo, Dó-dω.
Doeg, Dó-eg.

Dophkah, Dóf-kɑ.
Dor, Dɵr.
Dora, Dó-rɑ.
Dorcas, Dér-kas.
Dorymenes, Dω-rím-ɛ-nɛz.
Dositheus, Dω-síŧ-ɛ-us.
Dothaim, Dó-ŧa-im, *or*
Dothan, Dó-ŧan.
Dumah, Dų-mɑ.
Dura, Dų-rɑ.

# E.

Eanas, Ɛ'a-nas.
Ebal, Ɛ'bal.
Ebed, Ɛ'bed.
Ebedmelech, Ɛ-béd-mɛ-lek.
Ebenezer, Eb-en-é-zer.
Eber, Ɛ'ber.
Ebiasaph, Ɛ-bị-a-saf.
Ebronah, Ɛ-bró-nɑ.
Ecanus, Ɛ-ká-nus.
Ecbatana, Ek-bát-a-nq.
Ecclesiastes, Ek-lɛ-zi-ás-tɛz.
Ecclesiasticus, Ek-lɛ-zi-ás-ti-kus.
Ed, Ed.
Edar, Ɛ'dɑr.
Eden, Ɛ'den.
Eder, Ɛ'der.
Edes, Ɛ'des.
Edias, Ɛ'di-as.
Edna, Ed'nɑ.
Edom, Ɛ'dom.
Edomites, Ɛ'dom-ịts.
Edrei, Ed'rɛ-ị.
Eglah, Eg'lɑ.
Eglaim, Eg'la-im.
Eglon, Eg'lon.
Egypt, Ɛ'jipt.
Ehi, Ɛ'hị.
Ehud, Ɛ'hud.
Eker, Ɛ'ker.
Ekrebel, Ek'rɛ-bel.
Ekron, Ek'ron.
Ekronites, Ek'ron-ịts.
Ela, Ɛ'lɑ.
Eladah, El'a-dq.
Elah, Ɛ'lɑ.
Elam, Ɛ'lam.
Elamites, Ɛ'lam-ịts.
Elasah, El'a-sq.
Elath, Ɛ'laŧ.
Elbethel, El-béŧ-el.
Elcia, El'ʃi-q.
Eldaah, El'da-q.
Eldad, El'dad.
Elead, Ɛ'lɛ-ad, *or* Ɛ-lé-ad.
Elealeh, Ɛ-lɛ-á-le.
Eleasah, Ɛ-lé-a-sq.
Eleazer, Ɛ-lɛ-á-zer.
Eleazurus, Ɛ-lɛ-a-zų-rus.
Elelohe Israel, El-ɛ-ló-hɛ Iz'ra-el.
Eleph, Ɛ'lef.
Eleutherus, Ɛ-lų-ŧɛ-rus.
Eleuzai, El-yų-zá-ị.
Elhanan, El-há-nan.
Eli, Ɛ'lị.
Eliab, Ɛ-lị-ab.
Eliada, Ɛ-lị-a-dq.
Eliadah, Ɛ-lị-a-dq.
Eliadun, Ɛ-lị-a-dun.
Eliah, Ɛ-lị-ɑ.
Eliahba, Ɛ-lị-a-bq.
Eliakim, Ɛ-lị-a-kim.
Eliali, Ɛ-lị-a-lị.
Eliam, Ɛ-lị-am.
Elias, Ɛ-lị-as.
Eliasaph, Ɛ-lị-a-saf.
Eliashib, Ɛ-lị-a-ʃib.
Eliasis, Ɛ-lị-a-sis.
Eliatha, Ɛ-lị-a-ŧq, *or*
Eliathah, Ɛ-lị-a-ŧq.
Eliazar, Ɛ-li-á-zɑr.
Elidad, Ɛ-lị-dad.
Eliel, Ɛ'li-el.
Elienai, Ɛ-li-é-na-ị.
Eliezer, Ɛ-li-é-zer.
Elihaba, Ɛ-lị-ha-bq.
Elihæna, El-i-hé-nɑ.
Elihœnai, El-i-hé-na-ị.
Elihoreph, El-i-hó-ref.
Elihu, Ɛ-lị-hų.
Elijah, Ɛ-lị-jɑ.
Elika, El'i-kq.
Elim, Ɛ'lim.
Elimelech, Ɛ-lím-ɛ-lek.
Eliœnai, Ɛ-li-é-na-ị.
Elionas, Ɛ-li-ó-nas.
Eliphal, El'i-fal.
Eliphaleh, Ɛ-líf-a-lq.
Eliphaz, El'i-faz.
Eliphelet, Ɛ-líf-ɛ-let.
Elisabeth, Ɛ-líz-a-beŧ.
Elisæus, El-i-sé-us.
Eliseus, El-i-sé-us.
Elisha, Ɛ-lị-ʃɑ.
Elishah, Ɛ-lị-ʃɑ.
Elishama, Ɛ-líʃ-a-mq.
Elishamah, Ɛ-líʃ-a-mq.
Elishaphat, Ɛ-líʃ-a-fat.
Elisheba, Ɛ-líʃ-ɛ-bq.
Elishua, El-i-ʃų-ɑ.
Elisimus, Ɛ-lís-i-mus.
Eliu, Ɛ-lị-yų.
Eliud, Ɛ-lị-ud.
Elizaphan, Ɛ-líz-a-fan.
Elizur, Ɛ-lị-zur.
Elkanah, El'ka-nq.
Elkoshite, El'kω-ʃịt.
Ellasar, El'a-sqr.
Elmodam, El'mω-dam.
Elnaam, El'na-am.
Elnathan, El'na-ŧan, *or* El-ná-ŧan.
Elon, Ɛ'lon.
Elon Bethhanan, Ɛ'lon Béŧ-ha-nan.
Elonites, Ɛ'lon-ịts.
Eloth, Ɛ'loŧ.
Elpaal, El'pa-al.
Elpalet, El'pa-let.
Elparan, El-pá-ran.
Eltekeh, El'tɛ-ke.
Elteketh, El'tɛ-keŧ.
Eltekon, El'tɛ-kon.
Eltolad, El'tω-lad.
Elul, Ɛ'lul.
Eluzai, Ɛ-lų-za-ị.
Elymais, El-i-má-is.
Elymas, El'i-mas.
Elzabad, El'za-bad.
Elzaphan, El'za-fan.
Emalcuel, Em-al-kų-el.
Emanuel, Ɛ-mán-yų-el.
Emims, Ɛ'mimz.
Emmaus, Em'a-us.
Emmer, Em'er.
Emor, Ɛ'mor.
Enam, Ɛ'nam.
Enan, Ɛ'nan.
Endor, En'dor.
Eneas, Ɛ'nɛ-as.
Eneglaim, En-eg-lá-im.
Enemessar, En-ɛ-més-ɑr.
Enenias, Ɛ-né-ni-as.
Engannim, En-gán-im.
Engedi, En'gɛ-dị.
Enhaddah, En-hád-ɑ.
Enhakkore, En-hák-ω-rɛ.
Enhazor, En-há-zor.
Enmishpat, En-míʃ-pat.
Enoch, Ɛ'nok.
Enon, Ɛ'non.
Enos, Ɛ'nos.
Enosh, Ɛ'noʃ.
Enrimmon, En-rím-on.
Enrogel, En-ró-gel.
Enshemesh, En'ʃɛ-meʃ.
Entappuah, En-táp-yų-q.
Epaphras, Ep'a-fras.
Epophroditus, Ɛ-paf-rω-dị-tus.
Epenetus, Ɛ-pén-ɛ-tus.
Ephah, Ɛ'fɑ.
Ephai, Ɛ'fɑ.

Epher, Ɛ'fer.
Ephes-dammim, Ɛ'fes-dám-im.
Ephesians, Ɛ-fé-ʒi-anz.
Ephlal, Ef'lal.
Ephod, Ɛ'fod.
Ephor, Ɛ'for.
Ephphatha, Ef'a-ŧạ.
Ephraim, Ɛ'fra-im.
Ephraimites, Ɛ'fra-im-ịts.
Ephratah, Ef'ra-tạ.
Ephrath, Ef'raŧ.
Ephrathites, Ef'raŧ-ịts.
Ephron, Ɛ'fron.
Er, Er.
Eran, Ɛ'ran.
Eranites, Ɛ'ran-ịts.
Erastus, Ɛ-rás-tus.
Erech, Ɛ'rek.
Eri, Ɛ'rị.
Esa, Ɛ'sɑ.
Esaias, Ɛ-zá-yas.
Esarhaddon, Ɛ'sɑr-hád-on.
Esau, Ɛ'sɷ.
Esdras, Es'dras.
Esdrelon, Es-dré-lon.
Esebon, Es'ɛ-bon.
Esebrias, Ɛ-sé-bri-as.
Esek, Ɛ'sek.
Eshbaal, Eʃ'ba-al.
Eshban, Eʃ'ban.
Eshcol, Eʃ'kol.
Eshean, Ɛ'ʃɛ-an.
Eshek, Ɛ'ʃek.
Eshkalon, Eʃ'ka-lon.
Eshtaol, Eʃ'ta-ɑl.
Eshtaulites, Eʃ'tɷ-lịts.
Eshtemoa, Eʃ-tém-ɷ-ạ.
Eshtemoth, Eʃ'tɛ-moŧ.
Eshton, Eʃ'ton.
Esli, Es'lị.
Esmachiah, Es-ma-kị-ɑ.
Esora, Ɛ-só-rɑ.
Esril, Es'ril.
Esrom, Es'rom.
Essenes, Es-énz.
Esthaol, Est'ha-ol.
Esther, Es'ter.
Etam, Ɛ'tam.
Etham, Ɛ'ŧam.
Ethan, Ɛ'ŧan.
Ethanim, Eŧ'a-nim.
Ethbaal, Eŧ'ba-al.
Ether, Ɛ'ŧer.
Ethma, Eŧ'mɑ.
Ethnan, Eŧ'nan.
Ethni, Eŧ'nị.
Euasibus, Yụ-ás-i-bus.
Eubulus, Yụ-bụ́-lus.
Eunathan, Yụ́-na-ŧan.
Eunice, Yụ-nị-sɛ.
Euodias, Yụ-ó-di-as.
Eupolemus, Yụ-pól-ɛ-mus.
Euroclydon, Yụ-rók-li-don.
Eutychus, Yụ́-ti-kus.
Eve, Ɛv.
Evi, Ɛ'vị.
Evil Merodach, Ɛ'vil Mɛ-ró-dak, *or* Ɛ'vil Mér-ɷ-dak.
Exodus, Eks'ɷ-dus.
Ezar, Ɛ'zɑr.
Ezbai, Ez'ba-ị.
Ezbon, Ez'bon.
Ezechias, Ez-ɛ-kị-as.
Ezekias, Ez-ɛ-kị-as.
Ezekiel, Ɛ-zé-ki-el.
Ezel, Ɛ'zel.
Ezem, Ɛ'zem.
Ezer, Ɛ'zer.
Ezerias, Ez-ɛ-rị-as.
Ezias, Ɛ-zị-as.
Ezion Gebar, Ɛ'zi-on Gé-bɑr, *or* Ezion-geber, Ɛ'zi-on-jé-ber.
Eznite, Ez'nịt.
Ezra, Ez'rɑ.
Ezrahite, Ez'ra-hịt.
Ezri, Ez'rị.
Ezriel, Ez'ri-el.
Ezril, Ez'ril.
Ezron, Ez'ron.
Ezronites, Ez'ron-ịts.

## F.

Felix, Fé-liks.
Festus, Fés-tus.
Fortunatus, Fɛr-tụ-ná-tus.

## G.

Gaal, Gá-al.
Gaash, Gá-aʃ.
Gaba, Gá-bɑ.
Gabael, Gáb-a-el.
Gabatha, Gáb-a-ŧạ.
Gabbai, Gáb-a-ị.
Gabbatha, Gáb-a-ŧạ.
Gabrias, Gá-bri-as.
Gabriel, Gá-bri-el.
Gad, Gad.
Gadara, Gád-a-rạ.
Gadarenes, Gad-a-rénz.
Gaddes, Gád-ɛz.
Gaddiel, Gád-i-el.
Gadi, Gá-dị.
Gadites, Gád-ịts.
Gaham, Gá-ham.
Gahar, Gá-hɑr.
Gaius, Gá-yus.
Galaad, Gál-a-ad.
Galal, Gá-lal.
Galeed, Gál-ɛ-ed.
Galgala, Gál-ga-lạ.
Galilee, Gál-i-lɛ.
Gallim, Gál-im.
Gallio, Gál-i-ɷ.
Gamael, Gám-a-el.
Gamaliel, Ga-má-li-el.
Gammadims, Gám-a-dimz.
Gamul, Gá-mul.
Gar, Gạr.
Gareb, Gá-reb.
Garizim, Gár-i-zim.
Garmites, Gạ́r-mịts.
Gashmu, Gáʃ-mụ.
Gatam, Gá-tam.
Gath, Gaŧ.
Gath Hepher, Gaŧ Hé-fer.
Gath Rimmon, Gaŧ Rím-on.
Gaulan, Gó-lan.
Gaulon, Gó-lon.
Gaza, Gá-zɑ.
Gazabar, Gáz-a-bạr.
Gazara, Ga-zá-rɑ.
Gazathites, Gá-zaŧ-ịts.
Gazer, Gá-zer.
Gazera, Ga-zé-rɑ.
Gazez, Gá-zez.
Gazites, Gáz-ịts.
Gazzam, Gáz-am.
Geba, Gé-bɑ.
Gebal, Gé-bal.
Gebar, Gé-bɑr.
Geber, Gé-ber.
Gebim, Gé-bim.
Gedaliah, Ged-a-lị-ɑ.
Geddur, Géd-ur.
Geder, Gé-der.
Gederah, Gɛ-dé-rạ.
Gederite, Géd-ɛ-rịt.
Gederoth, Gɛ-dé-roŧ.
Gederothaim, Ged-ɛ-roŧ-á-im.
Gedir, Gé-der.
Gedor, Gé-dor.
Gehazi, Gɛ-há-zị.
Geliloth, Gél-i-loŧ.
Gemalli, Gɛ-mál-ị.
Gemariah, Gem-a-rị-ɑ.
Genesareth, Gɛ-nés-a-reŧ.
Genesis, Jén-ɛ-sis.

Genezar, Gɛ-né-zɑr.
Genneus, Gen-é-us.
Gentiles, Jén-ti̧lz.
Genubath, Gɛ-nų́-baŧ.
Geon, Gé-on.
Gera, Gé-rɑ.
Gerah, Gé-rɑ.
Gerar, Gé-rɑr.
Gerasa, Gér-a-sɋ.
Gergashi, Gęr-ga-ʃi̧.
Gergashites, Gęr-ga-ʃi̧ts.
Gergesenes, Gęr-gɛ-sénz.
Gerizim, Gér-i-zim.
Gerræans, Ger-é-anz.
Gerrinians, Ger-ín-i-anz.
Gershom, Gęr-ʃom.
Gershon, Gęr-ʃon.
Gershonites, Gęr-ʃon-i̧ts.
Gershur, Gęr-ʃur.
Gesem, Gé-sem.
Geshan, Gé-ʃan.
Geshem, Gé-ʃem.
Geshur, Gé-ʃur.
Geshuri, Géʃ-yų-ri̧.
Geshurites, Géʃ-yų-ri̧ts.
Getholias, Geŧ-ɷ-li̧-as.
Gethsemane, Geŧ-sém-a-nɛ.
Gethur, Gé-ŧur.
Geuel, Gɛ-yų́-el.
Gezer, Gé-zer.
Gezerites, Gé-zer-i̧ts.
Giah, Gi̧-ɑ.
Gibbar, Gíb-ɑr.
Gibbethon, Gib-ɛ-ŧon.
Gibea, Gíb-ɛ-ɋ.
Gibeah, Gíb-ɛ-ɋ.
Gibeath, Gíb-ɛ-aŧ.
Gibeon, Gíb-ɛ-on.
Gibeonites, Gíb-ɛ-on-i̧ts.
Giblites, Gíb-li̧ts.
Giddalti, Gid-ál-ti̧.
Giddel, Gíd-el.
Gideon, Gíd-ɛ-on.
Gideoni, Gid-ɛ-ó-ni̧.
Gidom, Gi̧-dom.
Gier Eagle, Ji̧-er E'gl.
Gihon, Gi̧-hon.
Gilalai, Gil-a-la.
Gilboa, Gil-bɷ-ɋ.
Gilead, Gíl-ɛ-ad.
Gileadite, Gíl-ɛ-ad-i̧t.
Gilgal, Gíl-gal.
Giloh, Gi̧-lɷ.
Gilonite, Gi̧-lɷ-ni̧t.
Gimzo, Gím-zɷ.
Ginath, Gi̧-naŧ.
Ginnetho, Gín-ɛ-ŧɷ.
Ginnethon, Gín-ɛ-ŧon.
Girgashi, Gęr-ga-ʃi̧.
Gergashites, Gęr-ga-ʃi̧ts.
Gispa, Gís-pɑ. [fer.
Gittah Hepher, Gít-ɑ Hé-
Gittaim, Gít-a-im.
Gittite, Gít-i̧t.
Gittites, Gít-i̧ts.
Gittith, Gít-iŧ.
Gizonite, Gi̧-zɷ-ni̧t.
Glede, Glɛd.
Gnidus, Ni̧-dus.
Goath, Gó-aŧ.
Gob, Gob.
Gog, Gog.
Golan, Gó-lan.
Golgotha, Gól-gɷ-ŧɋ.
Goliah, Gɷ-li̧-ɑ.
Goliath, Gɷ-li̧-aŧ.
Gomer, Gó-mer.
Gomorrah, Gɷ-mór-ɑ.
Gopherwood, Gó-fer-wɯd.
Gorgias, Gór-ji-as.
Gortyna, Gór-ti-nɋ, *or* Ger-ti̧-nɑ.
Goshen, Gó-ʃen.
Gothoniel, Gɷ-ŧón-i-el.
Gozan, Gó-zan.
Graba, Grá-bɑ.
Grecia, Gré-ʃi-ɋ.
Gudgodah, Gúd-gɷ-dɋ.
Guni, Gų́-ni̧.
Gunites, Gų́-ni̧ts.
Gur, Gur.
Gurbaal, Gur-bá-al.

# H.

Haahashtari, Ha-a-háʃ-ta-
Habaiah, Ha-bá-yɑ. [ri̧.
Habakkuk, Háb-a-kuk.
Habaziniah, Hab-a-zi-ni̧-ɑ.
Habergeon, Ha-bęr-jɛ-on.
Habor, Há-bor.
Hachaliah, Hak-a-li̧-ɑ.
Hachilah, Hák-i-lɋ.
Hachmoni, Hák-mɷ-ni̧.
Hachmonite, Hák-mɷ-ni̧t.
Hada, Há-dɑ.
Hadad, Há-dad.
Hadadezer, Had-ad-é-zer.
Hadad Rimmon, Há-dad Rím-on.
Hadar, Há-dɑr.
Hadashah, Hád-a-ʃɋ.
Hadassa, Ha-dás-ɑ.
Hadassah, Ha-dás-ɑ.
Hadattah, Ha-dát-ɑ.
Hadid Há-did.
Hadlai, Hád-la-i̧.
Hadoram, Ha-dó-ram.
Hadrach, Há-drak.
Hagab, Há-gab.
Hagabah, Hág-a-bɋ.
Hagai, Hág-a-i̧.
Hagar, Há-gɑr.
Hagarenes, Ha-gar-énz.
Hagarites, Há-gar-i̧ts.
Haggai, Hág-a-i̧.
Haggari, Hág-a-ri̧.
Haggeri, Hág-ɛ-ri̧.
Haggi, Hág-i̧.
Haggiah, Ha-gi̧-ɑ.
Haggites, Hág-i̧ts.
Haggith, Hág-iŧ.
Hai, Há-i̧.
Hakkatan, Hák-a-tan.
Hakkoz, Hák-oz.
Hakupha, Ha-kų́-fɑ.
Halac, Há-lak.
Halah, Há-lɑ.
Hali, Há-li̧.
Hallelujah, Hal-ɛ-lų́-yɑ.
Halloesh, Ha-ló-eʃ.
Hallul, Hál-ul.
Ham, Ham.
Haman, Há-man.
Hamath, Há-maŧ, *or* Hemath, Hé-maŧ.
Hamathite, Há-maŧ-i̧t.
Hamath Zobah, Há-maŧ Zó-bɑ.
Hamelech, Hám-ɛ-lek.
Hamital, Hám-i-tal.
Hammath, Hám-aŧ.
Hammedatha, Ha-méd-a-ŧɋ. [keŧ.
Hammoleketh, Ha-mól-ɛ-
Hammon, Hám-on.
Hamonah, Hám-ɷ-nɋ.
Hamon Gog, Há-mon Gog.
Hamor, Há-mor.
Hamoth, Há-moŧ.
Hamoth Dor, Há-moŧ Dor.
Hamuel, Ha-mų́-el.
Hamul, Há-mul.
Hamulites, Há-mul-i̧ts.
Hamutal, Ha-mų́-tal, *or* Hám-yų-tal.
Hanameel, Ha-nám-ɛ-el, *or* Hán-a-mɛl.
Hanan, Há-nan.
Hananeel, Ha-nán-ɛ-el, *or* Hán-a-nɛl. [ná-ni̧.
Hanani, Han-a-ni̧, *or* Ha-
Hananiah, Han-a-ni̧-ɑ.
Hanes, Há-nɛz.
Haniel, Hán-i-el.
Hannah, Hán-ɑ.

Hannathon, Hán-a-ŧon.
Hanniel, Hán-i-el.
Hanoch, Há-nok.
Hanochites, Há-nok-ịts.
Hanun, Há-nun.
Hapharaim, Haf-a-rá-im.
Hara, Há-rɑ.
Haradah, Hár-a-dɑ, *or* Ha-rá-dɑ. [rá-ɑ.
Haraiah, Har-a-ị-ɑ, *or* Ha-
Haran, Há-ran.
Hararite, Há-ra-rịt.
Harbona, Hɑr-bɷ́-nɑ, *or* Hɑ́r-bɷ-nɑ.
Harbonah, Hɑr-bɷ́-nɑ.
Hareph, Há-ref.
Hareth, Há-reŧ.
Harhass, Hɑ́r-has.
Harhata, Hɑ́r-ha-tɑ.
Harhur, Hɑ́r-hur.
Harim, Há-rim.
Hariph, Há-rif.
Harnepher, Hɑ́r-nɛ-fer, *or* Hɑr-né-fer.
Harod, Há-rod.
Harodite, Há-rod-ịt.
Haroeh, Hár-ɷ-e, *or* Ha-rɷ́-e.
Harorite, Há-rɷ-rịt.
Harosheth, Hár-ɷ-ʃeŧ.
Harsha, Hɑ́r-ʃɑ.
Harum, Há-rum.
Harumaph, Ha-rɷ́-maf.
Haruphite, Ha-rɷ́-fịt.
Haruz, Há-ruz.
Hasadiah, Has-a-dị-ɑ.
Hasenuah, Has-ɛ-nų́-ɑ.
Hashabiah, Haʃ-a-bị-ɑ.
Hashabnah, Haʃ-áb-nɑ.
Hashabniah, Haʃ-ab-nị-ɑ.
Hashbadana, Haʃ-bád-a- [nɑ.
Hashem, Há-ʃem.
Hashmonah, Haʃ-mɷ́-nɑ.
Hashum, Há-ʃum.
Hashupha, Ha-ʃų́-fɑ.
Hasrah, Hás-rɑ.
Hassenaah, Has-ɛ-ná-ɑ.
Hasupha, Ha-sų́-fɑ.
Hatach, Há-tak.
Hathath, Há-ŧaŧ.
Hatita, Hát-i-tɑ.
Hattil, Hát-il.
Hattipha, Ha-tị-fɑ.
Hattush, Hát-uʃ.
Hauran, Hɷ́-ran.
Havilah, Háv-i-lɑ.
Havoth Jair, Há-voŧ Já-er.
Hazael, Ház-a-el.
Hazaiah, Ha-zá-yɑ. [ɑr.
Hazar Addar, Há-zɑr Ád'-
Hazar Enan, Há-zɑr É'nan.
Hazar Gaddah, — Gád-ɑ.
Hazer Haticon, — Hát-i-kon.
Hazar Maveth, — Má-veŧ.
Hazaroth, Ha-zá-roŧ. [al.
Hazar Shual, Há-zɑr Σų́-
Hazar Susah, — Sų́-sɑ.
Hazar Susim, — Sų́-sim.
Hazel Elponi, Há-zel El-pɷ́-nị.
Hazerim, Ha-zé-rim.
Hazer Shusim, Há-zer Σų́-sim. [Tá-mɑr.
Hazezon Tamar, Ház-ɛ-zon
Haziel, Há-zi-el.
Hazo, Há-zɷ.
Hazor, Há-zor.
Hazubah, Ház-yɥ-bɑ.
Heber, Hé-ber.
Heberites, Hé-ber-ịts.
Hebrews, Hé-brɷz.
Hebron, Hé-bron.
Hebronites, Hé-bron-ịts.
Hegai, Hég-a-ị.
Hege, Hé-gɛ.
Helah, Hé-lɑ.
Helam, Hé-lam.
Helbah, Hél-bɑ.
Helbon, Hél-bon.
Helchiah, Hel-kị-ɑ.
Heldai, Hél-da-ị.
Heleb, Hé-leb.
Heled, Hé-led.
Helek, Hé-lek.
Helekites, Hé-lek-ịts.
Helem, Hé-lem.
Heleph, Hé-lef.
Helez, Hé-lez.
Heli, Hé-lị.
Helkai, Hél-ka-ị.
Helkath, Hél-kaŧ.
Helkath Hazzurim, Hél-kaŧ Ház-yɥ-rim.
Helkias, Hel-kị-as.
Helon, Hé-lon.
Heman, Hé-man, *or* Hamath, Há-maŧ.
Hemdan, Hém-dan.
Hen, Hen.
Hena, Hé-nɑ.
Henadad, Hén-a-dad.
Henoch, Hé-nok.
Hepher, Hé-fer.
Hepherites, Hé-fer-ịts.
Hephzibah, Héf-zi-bɑ.
Heram, Hé-ram.
Heres, Hé-rɛz.
Heresh, Hé-reʃ.
Hermas, Hẹ́r-mas.
Hermogenes, Her-mɷ́j-ɛ-nɛz.
Hermon, Hẹ́r-mon.
Hermonites, Hẹ́r-mon-ịts.
Herod, Hér-od.
Herodian, Hɛ-rɷ́-di-an.
Herodians, Hɛ-rɷ́-di-anz.
Herodias, Hɛ-rɷ́-di-as.
Heseb, Hé-seb.
Hesed, Hé-sed.
Heshbon, Héʃ-bon.
Heshmon, Héʃ-mon.
Heth, Heŧ.
Hethlon, Héŧ-lon.
Hezeki, Héz-ɛ-kị.
Hezekiah, Hez-ɛ-kị-ɑ.
Hezer, Hé-zer, *or*
Hezir, Hé-zer.
Hezia, Hɛ-zị-ɑ.
Hezion, Hé-zi-on.
Hezrai, Héz-ra-ị.
Hezro, Héz-rɷ.
Hezron, Héz-ron.
Hezronites, Héz-ron-ịts.
Hiddai, Híd-a-ị.
Hiddekel, Híd-ɛ-kel.
Hiel, Hị-el.
Hiereel, Hị-ér-ɛ-el.
Hieremoth, Hị-ér-ɛ-moŧ.
Hierielus, Hị-er-i-é-lus.
Hiermas, Hị-ẹ́r-mas.
Hieronymus, Hị-ɛ-rón-i-mus.
Higgaion, Hi-gá-yon.
Hilen, Hị-len.
Hilkiah, Hil-kị-ɑ.
Hillel, Híl-el.
Hin, Hin.
Hinnom, Hín-om.
Hirah, Hị-rɑ.
Hiram, Hị-ram.
Hircanus, Her-ká-nus.
Hiskijah, His-kị-jɑ.
Hittites, Hít-ịts.
Hivites, Hị-vịts.
Hoba, *or* Hobah, Hɷ́-bɑ.
Hobab, Hɷ́-bab.
Hod, Hod.
Hodaiah, Hod-a-ị-ɑ.
Hodaviah, Hod-a-vị-ɑ.
Hodeva, Hɷ-dé-vɑ.
Hodevah, Hɷ-dé-vɑ.
Hodiah, Hɷ-dị-ɑ.
Hodijah, Hɷ-dị-jɑ.
Hodish, Hɷ́-diʃ.
Hoglah, Hóg-lɑ.
Hoham, Hɷ́-ham.
Holen, Hɷ́-len.
Holofernes, Hol-ɷ-fẹ́r-nɛz.
Holon, Hɷ́-lon.

Homan, Hó-man, *or*
 Heman, Hé-man.
Homer, Hó-mer.
Hophni, Hóf-nį.
Hophra, Hóf-ra.
Hor, Hər.
Horagiddad, Hor-a-gíd-ad.
Horam, Hó-ram.
Horeb, Hó-reb.
Horem, Hó-rem.
Hori, Hó-rį.
Horims, Hó-rimz.
Horites, Hó-rįts.
Hormah, Hór-ma.
Horonaim, Hor-ɷ-ná-im.
Horonites, Hór-ɷ-nįts.
Hosa, Hó-sa, *or*
 Hasah, Hás-a.
Hosanna, Hɷ-zán-a.
Hosea, Hɷ-zé-a.
Hoshaiah, Hoʃ-a-į-a.
Hoshama, Hóʃ-a-mq.
Hoshea, Hɷ-ʃé-a.
Hotham, Hó-ŧam.
Hothan, Hó-ŧan.
Hothir, Hó-ŧer.
Hukkok, Húk-ok.
Hul, Hul.
Huldah, Húl-da.
Humtah, Húm-ta.
Hupham, Hų́-fam.
Huphamites, Hų́-fam-įts.
Huppah, Húp-a.
Huppim, Húp-im.
Hur, Hur.
Hurai, Hų́-ra.
Huram, Hų́-ram.
Huri, Hų́-rį.
Hushah, Hų́-ʃa.
Hushai, Hų́-ʃa, *or* Hų́-ʃa-į.
Husham, Hų́-ʃam.
Hushathite, Hų́-ʃaŧ-įt.
Hushim, Hų́-ʃim.
Hushub, Hų́-ʃub.
Hushubah, Hų-ʃų́-ba.
Huz, Huz.
Huzoth, Hų́-zoŧ.
Huzzab, Húz-ab.
Hydaspes, Hį-dás-pɛz.
Hyene, Hį-é-nɛ.
Hymenous, Hį-men-é-us.

# I.

Ibhar, Ib'har.
Ibleam, Ib'lɛ-am.
Ibneiah, Ib-nį-a.
Ibnijah, Ib-nį-ja.
Ibri, Ib'rį.
Ibzan, Ib'zan.
Ichabod, Ik'a-bod.
Iconium, Ɨ-kó-ni-um.
Idalah, Id'a-lq.
Idbash, Id'baʃ.
Iddo, Id'ɷ.
Iduel, Id'yų-el.
Idumæa, Id-yų-mé-a.
Idumæans, Id-yų-mé-anz.
Igal, Ɨ'gal.
Igdaliah, Ig-da-lį-a.
Igeabarim, Ig-ɛ-áb-a-rim.
Igeal, Ig'ɛ-al.
Ijon, Ɨ'jon.
Ikkesh, Ik'eʃ.
Ilai, Ɨ'la, *or* Il'a-į.
Im, Im.
Imlah, Im'la.
Immah, Im'a.
Immanuel, Im-án-yų-el.
Immer, Im'er.
Imna, Im'na, *or*
Imnah, Im'na.
Imrah, Im'ra.
Imri, Im'rį.
Iota, Ɨ-ó-ta.
Iphedeiah, If-ɛ-dé-ya
Ir, Er.
Ira, Ɨ'ra.
Irad, Ɨ'rad.
Iram, Ɨ'ram.
Iri, Ɨ'rį.
Irijah, Ɨ-rį-ja.
Irnahash, Er'na-haʃ.
Iron, Ɨ'ron.
Irpeel, Er'pɛ-el.
Irshemish, Er'ʃɛ-miʃ.
Iru, Ɨ'rɷ.
Isaac, Ɨ'zak.
Isaiah, Ɨ-zá-ya.
Iscah, Is'kq.
Iscariot, Is-kár-i-ot.
Isdael, Is'da-el.
Ishbah, Iʃ'ba.
Ishbak, Iʃ'bak.
Ishbi Benob, Iʃ'bį Bé-nob.
Ishbosheth, Iʃ'bɷ-ʃeŧ.
Ishi, Ɨ'ʃį.
Ishiah, Ɨ-ʃį-a.
Ishijah, Ɨ-ʃį-ja.
Ishma, Iʃ'ma.
Ishmael, Iʃ'ma-el.
Ishmaelites, Iʃ'má-el-įts.
Ishmaiah, Iʃ-ma-į-a.
Ishmerai, Iʃ'mɛ-ra.
Ishod, Ɨ'ʃod.
Ishpan, Iʃ'pan.
Ishtob, Iʃ'tob.
Ishua, Iʃ'yų-a.
Ishuai, Iʃ'yų-a.
Ismachiah, Is-ma-kį-a.
Ismaiah, Is-ma-į-a.
Ispah, Is'pa.
Israel, Iz'ra-el.
Israelites, Iz'ra-el-įts.
Issachar, Is'a-kqr.
Istalcurus, Is-tal-kų́-rus.
Isui, Iʃ'yų-į.
Isuites, Iʃ'yų-įts.
Italy, It'a-li.
Ithai, Iŧ'a-į.
Ithamar, Iŧ'a-mqr.
Ithiel, Iŧ'i-el.
Ithmah, Iŧ'ma.
Ithnan, Iŧ'nàn.
Ithra, Iŧ'ra.
Ithran, Iŧ'ran.
Ithream, Iŧ'rɛ-am.
Ithrites, Iŧ'rįts.
Ittah Kazin, It'a Ká-zin.
Ittai, It'a-į.
Iturea, It-yų-ré-a.
Ivah, Ɨ'va.
Izehar, Iz'ɛ-hqr.
Izhar, Iz'hqr.
Izharite, Iz'har-įt.
Izrahiah, Iz-ra-hį-a, *or*
Israiah, Iz-ra-į-a.
Izreel, Iz'rɛ-el.
Izri, Iz'rį.
Izrites, Iz'rįts.

# J.

Jaakan, Já-a-kan.
Jaakabah, Ja-ák-ɷ-bq.
Jaala, Ja-á-la.
Jaalah, Ja-á-la.
Jaalam, Ja-á-lam.
Jaanai, Já-a-na.
Jaareoragim, Ja-ar-ɛ-ór-a-
 gim.
Jaasania, Ja-as-a-nį-a.
Jaasau, Já-a-sə.
Jaasiel, Ja-á-si-el.
Jaazah, Ja-á-za.
Jaazaniah, Ja-az-a-nį-a.
Jaazar, Ja-á-zar.
Jaaziah, Ja-a-zį-a.
Jaaziel, Ja-á-zi-el.
Jabal, Já-bal.
Jabbok, Jáb-ok.
Jabesh, Já-beʃ.
Jabez, Já-bez.
Jabin, Já-bin.

Jabneel, Jáb-nɛ-el.
Jabneh, Jáb-ne.
Jachan, Já-kan.
Jachin, Já-kin.
Jachinites, Já-kin-ịts.
Jacob, Já-kob.
Jacobus, Ja-kó-bus.
Jada, Já-dɑ.
Jaddua, Ja-dɥ́-ɑ.
Jadon, Já-don.
Jael, Já-el.
Jagur, Já-gur.
Jah, Jɋ.
Jahaleel, Ja-há-lɛ-el.
Jahalelel, Ja-hál-ɛ-lel.
Jahath, Já-haŧ.
Jahaz, Já-haz.
Jahaza, Ja-há-zɑ.
Jahazah, Ja-há-zɑ.
Jahazia, Ja-há-zi-ɑ.
Jahaziel, Ja-há-zi-el.
Jahdai, Jɋ́-da-ị.
Jahdiel, Jɋ́-di-el.
Jahdo, Jɋ́-dɷ.
Jahleel, Jɋ́-lɛ-el.
Jahleelites, Jɋ́-lɛ-el-ịts.
Jahmai, Jɋ́-ma-ị.
Jahza, Jɋ́-zɑ.
Jahzeel, Jɋ́-zɛ-el.
Jahzeelites, Jɋ́-zɛ-el-ịts.
Jahzerah, Jɋ́-zɛ-rɋ.
Jahziel, Jɋ́-zi-el.
Jair, Já-er.
Jairites, Já-i-rịts.
Jairus, Já-i-rus.
Jakan, Já-kan.
Jakeh, Já-ke.
Jakim, Já-kim.
Jakkim, Ják-im.
Jalon, Já-lon.
Jambres, Jám-brɛz.
Jambri, Jám-brị.
James, Jamz.
Jamin, Já-min.
Jaminites, Já-min-ịts.
Jamlech, Jám-lek.
Jamnaan, Jám-na-an.
Jamnia, Jam-nị-ɑ.
Jamnites, Jám-nịts.
Janna, Ján-ɑ.
Jannes, Ján-ɛz.
Janoah, Ja-nó-ɑ.
Janohah, Ja-nó-hɑ.
Janum, Já-num.
Japhet, Já-fet.
Japheth, Já-feŧ.
Japhiah, Ja-fị-ɑ.
Japhlet, Jáf-let.
Japhleti, Jáf-lɛ-tị.
Japho, Já-fɷ.
Jar, Jɋr.
Jarah, Já-rɑ.
Jareb, Já-reb.
Jared, Já-red.
Jaresiah, Jar-ɛ-sị-ɑ.
Jarha, Jɋ́r-hɑ.
Jarib, Já-rib.
Jarmuth, Jɋ́r-muŧ.
Jaroah, Ja-ró-ɑ.
Jasael, Jás-a-el.
Jashem, Já-ʃem.
Jashen, Já-ʃen.
Jasher, Já-ʃer.
Jashobeam, Ja-ʃó-bɛ-am.
Jashub, Jáʃ-ub.
Jashubi Lehem, Jáʃ-yɥ-bị Lé-hem.
Jashubites, Jáʃ-ub-ịts.
Jasiel, Já-si-el.
Jasubus, Ja-sɥ́-bus.
Jatal, Já-tal.
Jathniel, Jáŧ-ni-el.
Jattir,Ját-er.
Javan, Já-van.
Jazar, Já-zɑr.
Jazer, Já-zer.
Jaziel, Já-zi-el.
Jaziz, Já-ziz.
Jearim, Jé-a-rim.
Jeaterai, Jɛ-át-ɛ-ra. [ɑ.
Jeberechiah, Jɛ-ber-ɛ-kị-
Jebus, Jé-bus.
Jebusi, Jɛ-bɥ́-sị.
Jebusites, Jéb-yɥ-sịts.
Jecamiah, Jek-a-mị-ɑ.
Jecoliah, Jek-ɷ-lị-ɑ.
Jeconiah, Jek-ɷ-nị-ɑ.
Jedaia, Jɛ-dá-yɑ.
Jedaiah, Jɛ-dá-yɑ.
Jeddeus, Jed-é-us.
Jeddu, Jéd-ɥ.
Jedediah, Jed-ɛ-dị-ɑ.
Jedeiah, Jɛ-dị-ɑ.
Jediael, Jɛ-dị-a-el.
Jediah, Jéd-i-ɋ.
Jediel, Jé-di-el.
Jeduthun, Jéd-yɥ-ŧun.
Jeeli, Jɛ-é-lị.
Jeezer, Jɛ-é-zer.
Jeezerites, Jɛ-é-zer-ịts.
Jegar Sahadutha, Jé-gɑr Sa-ha-dɥ́-ŧɑ.
Jehaleel, Jɛ-há-lɛ-el.
Jehalelel, Jɛ-hál-ɛ-lel.
Jehaziel, Jɛ-há-zi-el.
Jehdeiah, Je-dị-ɑ.
Jeheiel, Jɛ-hị-el.
Jehezekel, Jɛ-héz-ɛ-kel.
Jehiah, Jɛ-hị-ɑ.
Jehiel, Jɛ-hị-el.
Jehieli, Jɛ-hị-ɛ-lị.
Jehishai, Jɛ-híʃ-a-ị.
Jehiskiah, Jɛ-his-kị-ɑ́.
Jehoadah, Jɛ-hó-a-dɋ.
Jehoaddan, Jɛ-hɷ-ád-an.
Jehoahaz, Jɛ-hó-a-haz.
Jehoash, Jɛ-hó-aʃ.
Jehohadah, Jɛ-hó-ha-dɋ.
Jehohanan, Jɛ-hó-ha-nan.
Jehoiachin, Jɛ-hǿ-a-kin.
Jehoiada, Jɛ-hǿ-a-dɋ.
Jehoiakim, Jɛ-hǿ-a-kim.
Jehoiarib, Jɛ-hǿ-a-rib.
Jehonadab, Jɛ-hón-a-dab.
Jehonathan, Jɛ-hón-a-ŧan.
Jehoram, Jɛ-hó-ram.
Jehoshabeath, Jɛ-hɷ-ʃáb-ɛ-aŧ.
Jehoshaphat, Jɛ-hóʃ-a-fat.
Jehosheba, Jɛ-hóʃ-ɛ-bɋ.
Jehoshua, Jɛ-hóʃ-yɥ-ɋ.
JEHOVAH, Jɛ-hó-vɑ.
Jehovah, Jireh, — Jị-re.
Jehovah Nissi, — Nís-ị.
Jehovah Shallom, — Σál-om. [Σám-ɑ.
Jehovah Shammah, —
Jehovah Tsidkenu, — Tsíd-kɛ-nɥ.
Jehozabad, Jɛ-hóz-a-bad.
Jehu, Jé-hɥ.
Jehubbah, Jɛ-húb-ɑ.
Jehucal, Jé-hɥ-kal.
Jehud, Jé-hud.
Jehudi, Jɛ-hɥ́-dị.
Jehudijah, Jɛ-hɥ-dị-jɑ.
Jehush, Jé-huʃ.
Jeiel, Jɛ-ị-el.
Jekabzeel, Jɛ-káb-zɛ-el.
Jekameam, Jek-a-mé-am.
Jekamiah, Jek-a-mị-ɑ.
Jekuthiel, Jɛ-kɥ́-ŧi-el.
Jemima, Jém-i-mɋ.
Jemuel, Jɛ-mɥ́-el.
Jephthah, Jéf-ŧɑ.
Jephunneh, Jɛ-fún-e.
Jerah, Jé-rɑ.
Jerahmeel, Jɛ-rɋ́-mɛ-el.
Jerahmeelites, Jɛ-rɋ́-mɛ-el-ịts.
Jerechus, Jér-ɛ-kus.
Jered, Jé-red.
Jeremai, Jér-ɛ-ma.
Jeremiah, Jer-ɛ-mị-ɑ.
Jeremoth, Jér-ɛ-moŧ.
Jeremouth, Jér-ɛ-mȣŧ.
Jeriah, Jɛ-rị-ɑ.
Jeribai, Jér-i-bɑ́.
Jericho, Jér-i-kɷ.
Jeriel, Jé-ri-el.

Jerijah, Je-rj-ja.
Jerimoth, Jér-i-moŧ.
Jerioth, Jé-ri-oŧ.
Jeroboam, Jer-ω-bó-am.
Jerodon, Jér-ω-don.
Jeroham, Jér-ω-ham.
Jerubbaal, Je-rúb-a-al.
Jerubesheth, Je-rúb-e-ſeŧ.
Jeruel, Jér-yų-el.
Jerusalem, Je-ró-sa-lem.
Jerusha, Je-ró-ſa.
Jesaiah, Je-sá-yq.
Jeshaiah, Jeſ-a-j-a.
Jeshanah, Jéſ-a-nq.
Jesharelah, Jeſ-ár-e-lq.
Jeshebeab, Joſ-éb-e-ab.
Jeshebeah, Jeſ-éb-e-q.
Jesher, Jé-ſer.
Jeshimon, Jéſ-i-mon.
Jeshishai, Je-ſiſ-a-j.
Jeshohaiah, Jeſ-ω-há-j-a.
Jeshua, Jéſ-yų-q.
Jeshurun, Jéſ-yų-run.
Jesiah, Je-sj-a.
Jesimiel, Je-sím-i-el.
Jesse, Jés-e.
Jesaa, Jés-yų-q.
Jesui, Jés-yų-j.
JESUS, Jé-zus.
Jether, Jé-ŧer.
Jetheth, Jé-ŧeŧ.
Jethlah, Jéŧ-la.
Jethro, Jé-ŧrω.
Jetur, Jé-tur.
Jeuel, Jé-yų-el.
Jeush, Jé-uſ.
Jeuz, Jé-uz.
Jewry, Jų-ri.
Jezabel, Jéz-a-bel.
Jezaniah, Jez-a-nj-a.
Jezelus, Je-zé-lus.
Jezer, Jé-zer.
Jezerites, Jé-zer-jts.
Jeziah, Je-zj-a.
Jeziel, Jé-zi-el.
Jezliah, Jez-lj-a.
Jezoar, Jéz-ω-qr.
Jezrahiah, Jez-ra-hj-a.
Jezreel, Jéz-re-el.
Jezreelite, Jéz-re-el-jt.
Jezreelitess, Jéz-re-el-jt-es.
Jibsam, Jíb-sam.
Jidlaph, Jíd-laf.
Jim, Jim.
Jimla, Jím-la, *or*
Imla, Ím'la.
Jimna, Jím-na, *or*
Jimnah, Jím-na.
Jimnites, Jím-njts.
Jiphtah, Jíf-ta.
Jiphthahel, Jíf-ŧa-el.
Joab, Jó-ab.
Joachas, Jó-a-kaz.
Joadanus, Jω-a-dá-nus.
Joah, Jó-a.
Joahaz, Jó-a-haz.
Joakim, Jó-a-kim.
Joanna, Jω-án-a.
Joannan, Jω-án-an.
Joash, Jó-aſ.
Joatham, Jó-a-ŧam.
Joazabdus, Jω-a-záb-dus.
Job, Jωb.
Jobab, Jó-bab.
Jochebed, Jók-e-bed.
Joda, Jó-da.
Joed, Jó-ed.
Joel, Jó-el.
Joelah, Jω-é-la.
Joezer, Jω-é-zer.
Jogbeah, Jóg-be-q.
Jogli, Jóg-lj.
Joha, Jó-ha.
Johanan, Jω-há-nan.
John, Jon.
Joiada, Jó-a-dq.
Joiakim, Jó-a-kim.
Joiarib, Jó-a-rib.
Jokdeam, Jók-de-am.
Jokim, Jó-kim.
Jokmeam, Jók-me-am.
Jokneam, Jók-ne-am.
Jokshan, Jók-ſan.
Joktan, Jók-tan.
Joktheel, Jók-ŧe-el.
Jona, Jó-na.
Jonadab, Jón-a-dab.
Jonah, Jó-na.
Jonan, Jó-nan.
Jonas, Jó-nas.
Jonathan, Jón-a-ŧan.
Jonath Elim Rechochim, Jó-naŧ E'lim Re-kó-kim.
Joppa, Jóp-a.
Jora, Jó-ra.
Jorai, Jó-ra-j.
Joram, Jó-ram.
Jordan, Jór-dan.
Joribas, Jór-i-bas.
Jorim, Jó-rim.
Jorkoam, Jór-kω-am.
Josabad, Jós-a-bad.
Josaphat, Jós-a-fat.
Josaphias, Jos-a-fj-as.
Jose, Jó-se.
Josedech, Jós-e-dek.
Joseel, Jó-se-el.
Joseph, Jó-zef.
Josephus, Jω-sé-fus.
Joses, Jó-sez.
Joshabad, Jóſ-a-bad.
Joshah, Jó-ſa.
Joshaphat, Jóſ-a-fat.
Joshaviah, Joſ-a-vj-a.
Joshbekasha, Joſ-bék-a-ſq.
Joshua, Jóſ-yų-q.
Josiah, Jω-sj-a.
Josias, Jω-sj-as.
Josibiah, Jos-i-bj-a.
Josiphiah, Jos-i-fj-a.
Jotbah, Jót-ba.
Jotbath, Jót-baŧ.
Jotbatha, Jót-ba-ŧq.
Jotham, Jó-ŧam.
Jozabad, Józ-a-bad.
Jozachar, Józ-a-kqr, *or*
Jozachar, Jω-zá-kar.
Jozadak, Józ-a-dak.
Jubal, Jų-bal.
Jucal, Jų-kal.
Judæa, Jų-dé-a.
Judah, Jų-da.
Judas, Jų-das.
Jude, Jųd.
Judith, Jų-diŧ.
Juel, Jų-el.
Julia, Jų-li-q.
Junia, Jų-ni-q.
Jushabhesed, Jų-ſáb-he-sed.
Justus, Jús-tus.
Juttah, Jút-a.

# K.

Kab, Kab.
Kabzeel, Káb-ze-el.
Kades, Ká-dez.
Kadesh, Ká-deſ, *or*
Cadesh, Ká-deſ.
Kadesh Barnea, Ká-deſ Bqr-ne-q.
Kadmiel, Kád-mi-el.
Kadmonites, Kád-mon-jts.
Kallai, Kál-a-j.
Kanah, Ká-na.
Kareah, Ka-ré-a.
Karkaa, Kqr-ka-q.
Karkor, Kqr-kor.
Karnaim, Kqr-na-im.
Kartah, Kqr-taŧ.
Kattath, Kát-a.
Kedar, Ké-dar.
Kedemah, Kéd-e-mq.
Kedemoth, Kéd-e-moŧ.
Kedesh, Ké-deſ.
Kehelathah, Ke-hél-a-ŧq.

Keilah, Kị-la.
Kelaiah, Kɛ-lá-ya.
Kelita, Kél-i-tq.
Kelkathhazurim, Kél-kaŧ-ha-zų-rim.
Kemuel, Kɛ-mų́-el.
Kenah, Ké-na.
Kenan, Ké-nan.
Kenath, Ké-naŧ.
Kenaz, Ké-naz.
Kenites, Kén-ịts.
Kennizzites, Kén-iz-ịts.
Kerenhappuch, Ker-en-háp-uk.
Kerioth, Ké-ri-oŧ.
Keros, Ké-ros.
Ketura, Kɛ-tų́-ra.
Keturah, Kɛ-tų́-ra.
Kezia, Kɛ-zị-a.
Keziz, Ké-ziz.
Kibroth Hattaava, Kíb-roŧ Ha-tá-a-vq.
Kibzaim, Kib-za-im.
Kidron, Kíd-ron.
Kinah, Kị-na.
Kir, Kẹr.
Kirharaseth, Ker-hár-a-seŧ.
Kirheresh, Kẹ́r-hɛ-reʃ.
Kiriathaim, Kir-i-a-ŧá-im.
Kirieth, Kír-i-eŧ, *or* Kirjath, Kẹ́r-jaŧ.
Kirioth, Kír-i-oŧ.
Kirjath Aim, Kẹ́r-jaŧ Ȧ'-im.
Kirjath Arba, — Ȧr'ba.
Kirjath Arim, — Ȧ'rim.
Kirjath Arius, — Ȧ'ri-us.
Kirjath Baal, — Bá-al.
Kirjath Huzoth, — Hų́-zoŧ.
Kirjath Jearim, — Jé-a-rim.
Kirjath Sannah, — Sán-a.
Kirjath Sepher, — Sé-fer.
Kish, Kiʃ.
Kishi, Kíʃ-ị.
Kishion, Kíʃ-i-on.
Kishon, Kị-ʃon.
Kithlish, Kíŧ-liʃ.
Kitron, Kit-ron.
Kittim, Kit-im.
Koa, Kó-a.
Kohath, Kó-haŧ.
Kohathites, Kó-haŧ-ịts.
Kolaiah, Kol-a-ị-a.
Korah, Kó-ra.
Korahitas, Kó-ra-ịts.
Korathites, Kó-raŧ-ịts.
Kore, Kó-rɛ.
Korhite, Kór-hịt.
Korhites, Kór-hịts.
Korites, Kór-ịts.
Koz, Koz.
Kushaiah, Kuʃ-á-ya.

# L.

Laadah, Lá-a-dq.
Laadan, Lá-a-dan.
Laban, Lá-ban.
Labana, Láb-a-nq.
Lachish, Lá-kiʃ.
Lacunus, La-kų́-nus.
Ladan, Lá-dan.
Lael, Lá-el.
Lahad, Lá-had.
Lahairoi, La-há-rø.
Lahman, Lq́-man.
Lahmas, Lq́-mas.
Lahmi, Lq́-mị.
Laish, Lá-iʃ.
Lakum, Lá-kum.
Lamech, Lá-mek.
Laodicea, La-od-i-sé-a.
Lapidoth, Láp-i-doŧ.
Lasea, La-sé-a.
Lashah, Lá-ʃa.
Lasharon, La-ʃá-ron.
Lasthenes, Lás-ŧɛ-nɛz.
Lazarus, Láz-a-rus.
Leah, Lé-a.
Lebanah, Léb-a-nq.
Lebanon, Léb-a-non.
Lebaoth, Léb-a-oŧ.
Lebbeus, Leb-é-us.
Lebona, Lɛ-bó-na.
Lechah, Lé-ka.
Lehabim, Lé-ha-bim.
Lehi, Lé-hị.
Lemuel, Lém-yq-el.
Leʃem, Lé-ʃem.
Lettus, Lét-us.
Letushim, Lɛ-tų́-ʃim.
Leummim, Lɛ-ų́m-im.
Levi, Lé-vị.
Leviathan, Lɛ-vị-a-ŧan.
Levis, Lé-vis.
Levites, Lé-vịts.
Leviticus, Lɛ-vít-i-kus.
Libanus, Líb-a-nus.
Libnah, Líb-na.
Libni, Líb-nị.
Libnites, Líb-nịts.
Libia, Líb-i-q.
Lignaloes, Lig-nál-ωz.
Ligure, Lị-gųr.
Likhi, Lík-hị.
Loammi, Lω-ám-ị.
Lod, Lod.
Lodebar, Lód-ɛ-bq̈r.
Log, Log.
Lois, Ló-is.
Lo Ruhamah, Lω Ró-ha-mq́.
Lot, Lot.
Lotan, Ló-tan.
Lothasubus, Loŧ-a-sų́-bus.
Lozon, Ló-zon.
Lubim, Lų́-bim.
Lubims, Lų́-bimz.
Lucas, Lų́-kas.
Lucifer, Lų́-si-fer.
Lucius, Lų́-ʃi-us.
Lud, Lud.
Ludim, Lų́-dim.
Luhith, Lų́-hiŧ.
Luke, Lųk.
Luz, Luz.
Lycaonia, Lik-a-ó-ni-q.
Lycca, Lík-a.
Lydda, Líd-a.
Lydia, Líd-i-a.
Lysanias, Lị-sá-ni-us.
Lysia, Líʃ-ɛ-q.
Lysias, Líʃ-ɛ-as.
Lystra, Lís-tra.

# M.

Maacah, Má-a-kq.
Maachah, Má-a-kq.
Maachathi, Ma-ák-a-ŧị.
Maachahthites, Ma-ák-a-ŧịts.
Maadai, Ma-ád-a.
Maadiah, Ma-a-dị-a.
Maai, Ma-á-ị.
Maaleh Acrabbim, Ma-ál-ɛ A-kráb-im.
Maanai, Má-a-na.
Maarath, Má-a-raŧ.
Maaseiah, Ma-a-sé-a.
Maasiah, Ma-a-sị-a.
Maath, Má-aŧ.
Maaz, Má-az.
Maaziah, Ma-a-zị-a.
Mabdai, Máb-da-ị.
Macalon, Mák-a-lon.
Maccabæus, Mak-a-bé-us.
Maccabees, Mák-a-bɛz.
Machbenah, Mák-bɛ-nq.
Machbenai, Mák-bɛ-na.
Macheloth, Mak-hé-loŧ.
Machi, Má-kị.
Machir, Má-ker.
Machirites, Má-ker-ịts.
Machmas, Mák-mas.
Machnadebai, Mak-na-dé-ba.

Machpelah, Mak-pɛ́-lɑ.
Macron, Má-kron.
Madai, Mád-a-į.
Madiabun, Ma-dį́-a-bun.
Madiah, Ma-dį́-ɑ.
Madian, Má-di-an.
Madmannah, Mad-mán-ɑ.
Madmenah, Mad-mɛ́-nɑ.
Madon, Má-don.
Maelus, Ma-ɛ́-lus.
Magbish, Mág-biʃ.
Magdala, Mág-da-lą.
Magdalen, Mág-da-len.
Magdalene, Mag-da-lɛ́-nɛ, *or* Mág-da-len.
Magdial, Mág-di-el.
Magog, Má-gog.
Magor Missabib, Má-gor Mís-a-bib.
Magpiash, Mág-pi-aʃ.
Mahalah, Má-ha-lą.
Mahalaleel, Ma-hál-a-lɛl.
Mahalath Leannoth, Má-ha-laŧ Lɛ-án-oŧ.
Mahalath Maschil, —Más-kil.
Mahaleel, Ma-há-lɛ-el.
Mahali, Má-ha-lį.
Mahanaim, Ma-ha-ná-im.
Mahaneh Dan, Má-ha-ne Dan.
Mahanem, Má-ha-nem.
Maharai, Ma-hár-a-į.
Mahath, Má-haŧ.
Mahavites, Má-ha-vįts.
Mahaz, Má-haz.
Mahazioth, Ma-há-zi-oŧ.
Mahershalalhashbaz, Má-her-ʃál-al-háʃ-baz.
Mahlah, Mą́-lɑ.
Mahli, Mą́-lį.
Mahlites, Mą́-lįts.
Mahlon, Mą́-lon.
Maianeas, Ma-án-ɛ-as.
Makas, Má-kas.
Maked, Má-ked.
Makeloth, Ma-kɛ́-loŧ.
Makkedah, Ma-kɛ́-dɑ.
Maktesh, Mák-teʃ.
Malachi, Mál-a-kį.
Malcham, Mál-kam.
Malchiah, Mal-kį́-ɑ.
Malchiel, Mál-ki-el.
Malchielites, Mál-ki-el-įts.
Malchijah, Mal-kį́-jɑ.
Malchiram, Mal-kį́-ram.
Malchishuah, Mal-ki-ʃų́-ɑ.
Malchom, Mál-kom.
Malchus, Mál-kus.
Mallas, Mál-as.
Mallothi, Mál-ω-ŧį.
Malluch, Mál-uk.
Mamaias, Ma-má-yas.
Mammon, Mám-on.
Mamnitanaimus, Mam-ni-ta-ná-mus.
Mamre, Mám-rɛ.
Mamucus, Ma-mų́-kus.
Manaen, Mán-a-en.
Manahath, Mán-a-haŧ.
Manahem, Mán-a-hem.
Manahethites, Ma-ná-heŧ-įts.
Manasseas, Man-a-sɛ́-as.
Manasseh, Ma-nás-e.
Manassites, Ma-nás-įts.
Maneh, Má-ne.
Manhanaim, Man-ha-ná-im.
Mani, Má-nį.
Manna, Mán-ɑ.
Manoah, Ma-nó-ɑ.
Maoch, Má-ok.
Maon, Má-on.
Maonites, Má-on-įts.
Mara, Má-rɑ.
Marah, Má-rɑ.
Maralah, Már-a-lą.
Maranatha, Mar-a-náŧ-ɑ.
Mardocheus, Mąr-dω-kɛ́-us.
Mareshah, Ma-rɛ́-ʃɑ.
Mark, Mąrk.
Marisa, Már-i-są.
Marmoth, Mą́r-moŧ.
Maroth, Má-roŧ.
Marrekah, Már-ɛ-ką.
Marsena, Mą́r-sɛ-ną.
Martena, Mą́r-tɛ-ną.
Martha, Mą́r-ŧɑ.
Mary, Má-ri.
Masa, Má-sɑ.
Maschil, Más-kil.
Maseloth, Más-ɛ-loŧ.
Mash, Maʃ.
Mashal, Má-ʃal.
Masman, Más-man.
Masmoth, Más-moŧ.
Masrekah, Más-rɛ-ką.
Massah, Más-ɑ.
Massias, Ma-sį́-as.
Matred, Má-tred.
Matri, Má-trį.
Mattan, Mát-an.
Mattanah, Mát-a-ną.
Mattaniah, Mat-a-nį́-ɑ.
Mattatha, Mát-a-ŧą.
Mattathias, Mat-a-ŧį́-as.
Mattenai, Mat-ɛ-ná-į.
Matthan, Mát-ŧan.
Matthat, Mát-ŧat.
Matthelas, Mat-ŧɛ́-las.
Matthew, Máŧ-yų.
Matthias, Mat-ŧį́-as.
Mattithiah, Mat-i-ŧį́-ɑ.
Mazitias, Maz-i-tį́-as.
Mazzaroth, Máz-a-roŧ.
Meah, Mɛ́-ɑ.
Meani, Mɛ-á-nį.
Mearah, Mɛ-á-rɑ.
Mebunai, Mɛ-bų́-na.
Mecherath, Mék-ɛ-raŧ.
Mecherathite, Mék-ɛ-raŧ-įt.
Medad, Mɛ́-dad.
Medalah, Méd-a-lą.
Medan, Mɛ́-dan.
Medeba, Méd-ɛ-bą.
Medes, Mɛdz.
Media, Mɛ́-di-ą.
Median, Mɛ́-di-an.
Meeda, Mɛ-ɛ́-dɑ.
Megiddo, Mɛ-gíd-ω.
Megiddon, Mɛ-gíd-on.
Mehali, Mɛ-há-lį.
Mehetabel, Mɛ-hét-a-bel.
Mehida, Mɛ-hį́-dɑ.
Mehir, Mɛ́-her.
Meholathite, Mɛ-hól-aŧ-įt.
Mehujael, Mɛ-hų́-ja-el.
Mehuman, Mɛ-hų́-man.
Mehunim, Mɛ-hų́-nim.
Mehunims, Mɛ-hų́-nimz.
Mejarkon, Mɛ-ją́r-kon.
Mekonah, Mék-ω-ną.
Melatiah, Mel-a-tį́-ɑ.
Melchi, Mél-kį.
Melchiah, Mel-kį́-ɑ.
Melchias, Mel-kį́-as.
Melchiel, Mél-ki-el.
Melchisedek, Mel-kíz-ɛ-dek.
Melchishua, Mel-ki-ʃų́-ɑ.
Melea, Mɛ-lɛ́-ɑ.
Melech, Mɛ́-lek.
Melita, Mél-i-tą.
Mellicu, Mél-i-kų.
Melzar, Mél-zar.
Memphis, Mém-fis.
Memucan, Mɛ-mų́-kan.
Menahem, Mén-a-hem.
Menan, Mɛ́-nan.
Mene, Mɛ́-nɛ.
Menith, Mɛ́-niŧ.
Menothai, Mén-ω-ŧa.
Meonenem, Mɛ-ón-ɛ-nem.
Mephaath, Méf-a-aŧ.
Mephibosheth, Mɛ-fíb-ω-ʃeŧ.
Merab, Mɛ́-rab.
Meraiah, Mer-a-į́-ɑ.
Meraioth, Mɛ-rá-yoŧ.
Meran, Mɛ́-ran.
Merari, Mér-a-rį.

Merarites, Mér-a-rjts.
Merathaim, Mer-a-ƀá-im.
Mered, Mé-red.
Meremoth, Mér-ɛ-moƀ.
Merez, Mé-rɛz.
Meriba, Mér-i-bq.
Meribah, Mér-i-bq.
Meribah Kadesh, — Ká-[deʃ.
Meribbaal, Mɛ-ríb-a-al.
Merimoth, Mér-i-moƀ.
Merodach Baladan, Mɛ-ró-dak Bál-a-dan.
Merom, Mé-rom.
Meronothite, Mɛ-rón-ɷ-ƀjt.
Meroz, Mé-roz.
Meruth, Mé-ruƀ.
Mesech, Mé-sek.
Mesha, Mé-ʃa.
Meshach, Mé-ʃak.
Meshech, Mé-ʃok.
Meshelemiah, Meʃ-el-ɛ-mj-a.
Meshezabeel, Mɛ-ʃéz-a-bɛl.
Meshezabel, Mɛ-ʃéz-a-bel.
Meshillamith, Meʃ-i-lá-miƀ.
Meshillemoth, Mɛ-ʃil-ɛ-[moƀ.
Meshoba, Mɛ-ʃó-ba.
Meshullam, Mɛ-ʃúl-am.
Meshullemith, Mɛ-ʃúl-ɛ-miƀ.
Mesobah, Més-ɷ-bq.
Mesobaite, Més-ɷ-ba-jt.
Mesopotamia, Mes-ɷ-pɷ-tá-mi-q.
Messiah, Mes-j-a.
Messias, Mes-j-as.
Meterus, Mɛ-té-rus.
Metheg Ammah, Mé-ƀeg Am'a.
Methredath, Méƀ-rɛ-daƀ.
Methusael, Mɛ-ƀú-sa-el.
Methusela, Mɛ-ƀú-sɛ-lq.
Methuselah, Mɛ-ƀú-sɛ-lq.
Meunim, Mɛ-yú-nim.
Mezahab, Méz-a-hab.
Miamin, Mj-a-min.
Mihbar, Míb-har.
Mibsam, Míb-sam.
Mibzar, Míb-zar.
Micah, Mj-ka.
Micaiah, Mj-ká-yq.
Micha, Mj-ka.
Michael, Mj-ka-el.
Michah, Mj-ka.
Michaiah, Mj-ká-ya.
Michal, Mj-kal.
Michmas, Mík-mas.
Michmash, Mík-maʃ.
Michmethah, Mík-mɛ-ƀq.
Michri, Mík-rj.
Michtam, Mík-tam.
Middin, Míd-in.
Midian, Míd-i-an.
Midianites, Míd-i-an-jts.
Migdalel, Míg-da-lel.
Migdal Gad, Míg-dal Gad.
Migdol, Míg-dol.
Migron, Míg-ron.
Mijamin, Míj-a-min.
Mikloth, Mík-loƀ.
Mikneiah, Mik-nj-a.
Milalai, Mil-a-lá-j.
Milcah, Míl-ka.
Milcha, Míl-ka.
Milchah, Míl-ka.
Milcom, Míl-kom.
Millo, Míl-ɷ.
Mina, Mj-na.
Miniamin, Mi-nj-a-min.
Minni, Mín-j.
Minnith, Mín-iƀ.
Miphkad, Míf-kad.
Miriam, Mír-i-am.
Mirma, Mér-ma.
Misgab, Mís-gab.
Mishael, Míʃ-a-el.
Mishal, Mj-ʃal.
Misham, Mj-ʃam.
Misheal, Mj-ʃɛ-al, *or* Mj-ʃé-al.
Mishma, Míʃ-ma.
Mishmanna, Miʃ-mán-a.
Mishraites, Míʃ-ra-jts.
Mispar, Mís-par.
Mispereth, Míz-pɛ-reƀ.
Mispha, Míz-fa.
Misphah, Míz-fa.
Misraim, Míz-ra-im.
Misrephothmaim, Miz-rɛ-foƀ-má-im.
Mithcah, Míƀ-ka.
Mithnite, Míƀ-njt.
Mithridath, Míƀ-ri-daƀ.
Mizar, Mj-zar.
Mizpah, Míz-pa.
Mizpeh, Míz-pe.
Mizraim, Míz-ra-im.
Mizzah, Míz-a.
Mnason, Ná-son.
Moab, Mó-ab.
Moabites, Mó-ab-jts.
Moadiah, Mɷ-a-dj-a.
Mockmur, Mók-mur.
Mockram, Mók-ram.
Modin, Mó-din.
Moeth, Mó-eƀ.
Moladah, Mól-a-dq.
Molech, Mó-lek.
Moli, Mó-lj.
Molid, Mó-lid.
Moloch, Mó-lok.
Momdis, Móm-dis.
Moosias, Mɷ-ɷ-sj-as.
Morashite, Mó-raʃ-jt.
Morasthite, Mó-ras-ƀjt.
Mordecai, Mór-dɛ-ka.
Moreh, Mó-re.
Moresheth Gath, Mór-eʃ-eƀ Gaƀ.
Moriah, Mɷ-rj-a.
Mosera, Mɷ-sé-ra.
Moserah, Mɷ-sé-ra.
Moses, Mó-zez.
Mosollam, Mɷ-sól-am.
Mosoroth, Mɷ-só-roƀ.
Mosullamon, Mɷ-súl-a-mon.
Moza, Mó-za.
Mozah, Mó-za.
Muppim, Múp-im.
Mushi, Mú-ʃj.
Mushites, Mú-ʃjts.
Muthlabben, Muƀ-láb-en.
Myndus, Mín-dus.
Myra, Mj-ra.
Mytilene, Mit-i-lé-nɛ.

# N.

Naam, Ná-am.
Naamah, Ná-a-mq.
Naaman, Ná-a-man.
Naamathite, Ná-a-ma-ƀjt.
Naamites, Ná-am-jts.
Naarah, Ná-a-rq.
Naarai, Ná-a-ra.
Naaran, Ná-a-ran.
Naarath, Ná-a-raƀ.
Naashon, Na-áʃ-on.
Naathus, Ná-a-ƀus.
Nabal, Ná-bal.
Nabarias, Nab-a-rj-as.
Nabatheans, Na-ba-ƀé-anz.
Nabathites, Ná-baƀ-jts.
Naboth, Ná-boƀ.
Nachon, Ná-kon.
Nachor, Ná-kor.
Nadab, Ná-dab.
Nadabatha, Na-dáb-a-ƀq.
Nagge, Nág-ɛ.
Nahabi, Ná-ha-bj.
Nahaliel, Na-há-li-el.
Nahallal, Na-hál-al.
Nahalol, Ná-ha-lol.
Naham, Ná-ham.
Nahami, Na-hám-a-nj.

Naharai, Na-hár-a-j.
Nahash, Ná-haſ.
Nahath, Ná-haŧ.
Nahbi, Nꝗ-bj.
Nahor, Ná-hor.
Nahshon, Nꝗ-ſon.
Nahum, Ná-hum.
Naidus, Ná-i-dus.
Naim, Ná-im.
Nain, Ná-in.
Naioth, Ná-yoŧ.
Nanea, Na-né-ɑ.
Naomi, Ná-ɷ-mj, *or* Na-ɷ́-mi.
Naphisi, Náf-i-sj.
Naphthali, Náf-ŧa-lj.
Naphthar, Náf-ŧɑr.
Naphtuhim, Náf-tɥ-him.
Napish, Ná-piſ.
Nasbas, Nás-bas.
Nashon, Ná-ſon.
Nasith, Ná-siŧ.
Nasor, Ná-sor.
Nathan, Ná-ŧan.
Nathanael, Na-ŧán-a-el.
Nathanias, Naŧ-a-nj-as.
Nathan Melech, Ná-ŧan Mé-lek.
Naum, Ná-um.
Nave, Ná-vɛ.
Nazarene, Naz-a-rén.
Nazarenes, Naz-a-rénz.
Nazareth, Náz-a-reŧ.
Nazarite, Náz-a-rjt.
Neah, Né-ɑ.
Neariah, Nɛ-a-rj-ɑ.
Nebai, Néb-a-j.
Nebaioth, Nɛ-bá-yoŧ.
Nebajoth, Nɛ-bá-joŧ.
Neballat, Nɛ-bál-at.
Nebat, Né-bat.
Nebo, Né-bɷ.
Nebuchadnezzar, Neb-yɥ-kad-néz-ɑr.
Nebuchadrezzar, Neb-yɥ-kad-réz-ɑr.
Nebuchasban, Neb-yɥ-kás-ban.
Nebuchodonosor, Neb-yɥ-kod-ón-ɷ-sor.
Nebuzaradan, Neb-yɥ-zár-a-dan.
Necho, Né-kɷ.
Necodan, Nɛ-kɷ́-dan.
Nedabiah, Ned-a-bj-ɑ.
Neemias, Nɛ-ɛ-mj-as.
Neginoth, Nég-i-noŧ.
Nehelamite, Nɛ-hél-a-mjt.
Nehemiah, Nɛ-hɛ-mj-ɑ.
Nehemias, Nɛ-hɛ-mj-as.
Nehum, Né-hum.

Nehushta, Nɛ-hɥ́ſ-tɑ.
Nehushtah, Nɛ-hɥ́ſ-tɑ.
Nehushtan, Nɛ-hɥ́ſ-tan.
Neiel, Né-j-el.
Nekeb, Né-keb.
Nekoda, Nɛ-kɷ́-dɑ.
Nemuel, Nɛ-mɥ́-el.
Nemuelites, Nɛ-mɥ́-el-jts.
Nepheg, Né-feg.
Nephi, Né-fj.
Nephis, Né-fis.
Nephish, Né-fiſ.
Nephishesim, Nɛ-fíſ-ɛ-sim.
Nephthali, Néf-ŧa-lj.
Nephthoah, Néf-ŧɷ-ɑ.
Nephtuim, Néf-tɥ-im.
Nephusim, Nɛ-fɥ́-sim.
Ner, Nẹr.
Nereus, Né-rɛ-us.
Nergal, Nẹ́r-gal.
Nergal Sharezer, —Σa-ré-zer.
Neri, Né-rj.
Neriah, Nɛ-rj-ɑ.
Nethaneel, Nɛ-ŧán-ɛ-el.
Nethaniah, Neŧ-a-nj-ɑ.
Nethinims, Néŧ-i-nimz.
Netophah, Nɛ-tɷ́-fɑ.
Netophathi, Nɛ-tóf-a-ŧj.
Netophathites, Nɛ-tóf-a-ŧjts.
Neziah, Nɛ-zj-ɑ.
Nezib, Né-zib.
Nibbas, Níb-as.
Nibshan, Níb-ſan.
Nicodemus, Nik-ɷ-dé-mus.
Nicolaitans, Nik-ɷ-lá-i-tanz.
Nicolas, Ník-ɷ-las.
Nimrah, Ním-rɑ.
Nimrim, Ním-rim.
Nimrod, Ním-rod.
Nimshi, Ním-ſj.
Nineve, Nín-ɛ-vɛ.
Nineveh, Nín-ɛ-ve.
Ninevites, Nín-ɛ-vjts.
Nisan, Nj-san.
Nisroch, Nís-rok.
Noadiah, Nɷ-a-dj-ɑ.
Noah, Nɷ́-ɑ, *or*
Noe, Nɷ́-ɛ.
Nob, Nob.
Nobah, Nɷ́-bɑ.
Nod, Nod.
Nodab, Nɷ́-dab.
Noeba, Nɷ́-ɛ-bɑ.
Noga, Nɷ́-gɑ, *or*
Nogan, Nɷ́-gan.
Nohah, Nɷ́-hɑ.
Nom, Nom.
Nomades, Nóm-a-dɛz.

Nomenius, Nɷ-mé-ni-us.
Non, Non.
Noph, Nof.
Nophah, Nɷ́-fɑ.
Nun, Nun, (*the father of Joshua.*)
Nymphas, Ním-fas.

# O.

Obadiah, Ob-a-dj-ɑ, *or* ɷ-ba-dj-ɑ.
Obal, ɷ'bal.
Obed, ɷ'bed.
Obed Edom, — Ɛ'dom.
Obeth, ɷ'beŧ.
Obil, ɷ'bil.
Oboth, ɷ'boŧ.
Ochiel, ɷ'ki-el.
Ocidelus, Os-i-dé-lus.
Ocina, Os'i-nꝗ.
Ocran, Ok'ran.
Oded, ɷ'ded.
Odollam, ɷ-dól-am.
Odonarkes, ɷd-on-ꝗr-kɛz.
Og, Og.
Ohad, ɷ'had.
Ohel, ɷ'hel.
Olamus, Ol'a-mus.
Olivet, Ol'i-vet.
Olymphas, ɷ-lím-fas.
Omaerus, Om-a-é-rus.
Omar, ɷ'mɑr.
Omega, ɷ-mé-gɑ.
Omer, ɷ'mer.
Omri, Om'rj.
On, On.
Onam, ɷ'nam.
Onan, ɷ'nan.
Onesimus, ɷ-nés-i-mus.
Onesiphorus, On-ɛ-síf-ɷ-rus.
Oniares, ɷ-nj-a-rɛz.
Onias, ɷ-nj-as.
Ono, ɷ'nɷ.
Onus, ɷ'nus.
Onyas, ɷ-nj-as.
Onycha, On'i-kꝗ.
Onyx, ɷ'niks.
Ophel, ɷ'fel.
Opher, ɷ'fer.
Ophir, ɷ'fer.
Ophni, Of'nj.
Ophrah, Of'rɑ.
Oreb, ɷ'reb,
Oren, ɷ'ren, *or* Oran, ɷ'ran.

Orion, Ω'ri-on, *or* Ω-rȷ-on.
Ornan, Θr'nan.
Orphah, Θr'fɑ.
Orthosias, Θr-ŧω-sȷ-as.
Osaias, Ω-zá-yas.
Oseas, Ω-zé-as.
Osee, Ω'zɛ.
Oshea, Ω'ʃɛ-ɋ.
Ospray, Os'prɑ.
Ossifrage, Os'i-fraj.
Othni, Oŧ'nȷ.
Othniel, Oŧ'ni-el.
Othonias, Oŧ-ω-nȷ-as.
Ozem, Ω'zem.
Ozias, Ω-zȷ-as.
Oziel, Ω'zi-el.
Ozni, Oz'nȷ.
Oznites, Oz'nȷts.
Ozora, Ω-zó-rɑ.

# P.

Paarai, Pá-a-rɑ.
Padan, Pá-dan.
Padan Aram, — Ɑ'ram.
Padon, Pá-don.
Pagiel, Pá-gi-el.
Pahath Moab, Pá-haŧ Mó-ab.
Pai, Pá-ȷ.
Palal, Pá-lal.
Palestine, Pál-es-tȷn.
Pallu, Pál-yɋ.
Palluites, Pál-yɋ-ȷts.
Palti, Pál-tȷ.
Paltiel, Pál-ti-el.
Paltite, Pál-tȷt.
Pannag, Pán-ag.
Paradise, Pár-a-dȷs.
Parah, Pá-rɑ.
Paran, Pá-ran.
Parbar, Pɑ́r-bɑr.
Parmashta, Pɑr-máʃ-tɑ.
Parmenas, Pɑ́r-mɛ-nas.
Parnach, Pɑ́r-nak.
Parnath, Pɑ́r-naŧ.
Parosh, Pá-roʃ.
Parshandatha, Pɑr-ʃán-da-ŧɋ.
Paruah, Pár-yɋ-ɋ.
Parvaim, Pɑr-vá-im.
Pasach, Pá-sak.
Pasdammin, Pas-dám-in.
Paseah, Pa-sé-ɑ.
Pashur, Páʃ-ur.
Passover, Pás-ω-ver.
Patara, Pát-a-rɋ.
Pateoli, Pa-té-ω-li.
Patheus, Pa-ŧé-us.
Pathros, Páŧ-ros.
Pathrusim, Paŧ-ró-sim.
Patrobas, Pát-rω-bas.
Pau, Pá-yɋ.
Paul, Pɐl.
Pedahel, Péd-a-hel.
Pedahzur, Péd-a-zur.
Pedaiah, Pɛ-dá-yɑ.
Pekah, Pé-kɑ.
Pekahiah, Pek-a-hȷ-ɑ.
Pekod, Pé-kod.
Pelaiah, Pel-a-ȷ-ɑ.
Pelaliah, Pel-a-lȷ-ɑ.
Pelatiah, Pel-a-tȷ-ɑ.
Peleg, Pé-leg.
Pelet, Pé-let.
Peleth, Pé-leŧ.
Pelethites, Pé-leŧ-ȷts.
Pelias, Pɛ-lȷ-as.
Pelonite, Pél-ω-nȷt.
Peniel, Pɛ-nȷ-el.
Peninnah, Pɛ-nín-ɑ.
Penninah, Pén-i-nɋ.
Pentapolis, Pen-táp-ω-lis.
Pentateuch, Pén-ta-tɋk.
Pentecost, Pén-tɛ-kost.
Pennel, Pɛ-nɋ́-el.
Peor, Pé-or.
Perazim, Pér-a-zim.
Peresh, Pé-reʃ.
Perez, Pé-rez.
Perez Uzza, — Uz'ɑ.
Perga, Pɛ́r-gɑ.
Pergamos, Pɛ́r-ga-mos.
Perida, Pɛ-rȷ-dɑ.
Perizzites, Pér-iz-ȷts.
Permenas, Pɛ́r-mɛ-nas.
Peruda, Pɛ-ró-dɑ.
Pethahiah, Peŧ-a-hȷ-ɑ.
Pethor, Pé-ŧor.
Pethuel, Pɛ-ŧɋ́-el.
Peulthai, Pɛ-úl-ŧɑ.
Phacareth, Fák-a-reŧ.
Phaisur, Fá-sur.
Phaldaius, Fal-dá-yus.
Phaleas, Fa-lé-as.
Phaleg, Fá-leg.
Phallu, Fál-yɋ.
Phalti, Fál-tȷ.
Phaltiel, Fál-ti-el.
Phanuel, Fa-nɋ́-el.
Pharacim, Fár-a-sim.
Pharaoh, Fá-rω.
Pharathoni, Far-a-ŧó-nȷ.
Pharez, Fá-rez.
Pharezites, Fá-rez-ȷts.
Pharisees, Fár-i-sɛz.
Pharosh, Fá-roʃ.
Pharpar, Fɑ́r-pɑr.
Pharites, Fɑ́r-zȷts.
Phaseah, Fá-sɛ-ɋ.
Phaselis, Fa-sé-lis.
Phasiron, Fás-i-ron.
Phebe, Fé-bɛ.
Phenice, Fɛ-nȷ-sɛ.
Phibeseth, Fíb-ɛ-seŧ.
Phicol, Fȷ-kol.
Philarches, Fi-lɑ́r-kɛz.
Philemon, Fi-lé-mon.
Philetus, Fi-lé-tus.
Philistia, Fi-lís-ti-ɋ.
Philistim, Fi-lís-tim.
Philistines, Fi-lís-tinz.
Philologus, Fi-lól-ω-gus.
Philometor, Fil-ω-mé-tor.
Phineas, Fín-ɛ-as.
Phinehas, Fín-ɛ-has.
Phison, Fȷ-son.
Phlegon, Flé-gon.
Phoros, Fó-ros.
Phul, Ful.
Phur, Fur.
Phurah, Fɋ́-rɑ.
Phut, Fut.
Phuvah, Fɋ́-vɑ.
Phygellus, Fi-jél-us.
Phylacteries, Fi-lák-tɛ-riz.
Pihahiroth, Pȷ-ha-hȷ-roŧ.
Pilate, Pȷ-lat.
Pildash, Píl-daʃ.
Piletha, Píl-ɛ-ŧɋ.
Piltai, Píl-ta.
Pinon, Pȷ-non.
Pira, Pȷ-rɑ.
Piram, Pȷ-ram.
Pirathon, Pír-a-ŧon.
Pirathonite, Pír-a-ŧon-ȷt.
Pisgah, Píz-gɑ.
Pison, Pȷ-son.
Pispah, Pís-pɑ.
Pithon, Pȷ-ŧon.
Pochereth, Pók-ɛ-reŧ.
Pontius Pilate, Pón-ti-us Pȷ-lat.
Poratha, Pór-a-ŧɋ.
Potiphar, Pót-i-fɑr.
Potiphera, Pω-tíf-ɛ-rɋ.
Prochoras, Prók-ω-rus.
Pua, Pɋ́-ɑ, *or*
Puah, Pɋ́-ɑ.
Pudens, Pɋ́-denz.
Puhites, Pɋ́-hȷts.
Pul, Pul.
Punites, Pɋ́-nȷts.
Punon, Pɋ́-non.
Pur, Pur, *or*
Purim, Pɋ́-rim.
Put, Put.
Puteoli, Pɋ-té-ω-lȷ.
Putiel, Pɋ́-ti-el.
Pygarg, Pȷ-gɑrg.

# R.

Raamah, Rá-a-mq.
Raamiah, Ra-a-mȷ-ɑ.
Raamses, Ra-ám-sɛz.
Rabbah, Ráb-ɑ.
Rabbat, Ráb-at.
Rabbath, Ráb-aŧ.
Rabbi, Ráb-ȷ.
Rabbith, Ráb-iŧ.
Rabboni, Ra-bɷ́-nȷ.
Rabmag, Ráb-mag.
Rabsaces, Ráb-sa-sɛz.
Rabsaris, Ráb-sa-ris.
Rabshakeh, Ráb-ʃa-ke.
Raca, *or* Racha, Rá-kɑ.
Racab, Rá-kab.
Racal, Rá-kal.
Rachab, Rá-kab.
Rachel, Rá-çel.
Raddai, Rád-a-ȷ.
Ragau, Rá-gɵ.
Rages, Rá-jɛz.
Ragua, Rág-yɥ-q.
Raguel, Ra-gɥ́-el.
Rahab, Rá-hab.
Raham, Rá-ham.
Rakem, Rá-kem.
Rakkath, Rák-aŧ
Rakkon, Rák-on.
Ram, Ram.
Rama, *or* Ramah, Rá-mɑ.
Ramath, Rá-maŧ.
Ramathaim, Ra-maŧ-á-im.
Ramathem, Rám-a-ŧem.
Ramathite, Rá-maŧ-ȷt.
Ramath Lehi, Rá-maŧ Lé-hȷ.
Ramath Mispeh, — Mís-pe.
Rameses, Ra-mé-sɛz.
Ramiah, Ra-mȷ-ɑ.
Ramoth, Rá-moŧ.
Ramoth Gilead, Rá-moŧ Gíl-ɛ-ad.
Rapha, Rá-fɑ.
Raphael, Rá-fa-el.
Raphah, Rá-fɑ.
Raphaim, Ráf-a-im.
Raphon, Rá-fon.
Raphu, Rá-fɥ.
Rassis, Rás-is.
Rathumus, Ráŧ-yɥ-mus.
Razis, Rá-zis.
Reaiah, Rɛ-a-ȷ-ɑ.
Reba, Ré-bɑ.
Rebecca, Rɛ-bék-ɑ.
Rechab, Ré-kab.
Rechabites, Ré-kab-ȷts.
Rechah, Ré-kɑ.
Reelaiah, Rɛ-el-á-yɑ.
Reelias, Rɛ-el-ȷ-as.
Reesaias, Rɛ-sá-yas.
Regem, Ré-gem.
Regemmelech, Rɛ-gém-ɛ-lek.
Regom, Ré-gom.
Rehabiah, Rɛ-ha-bȷ-ɑ.
Rehob, Ré-hob.
Rehoboam, Rɛ-hɷ-bɷ́-am.
Rehoboth, Rɛ-hɷ́-boŧ.
Rehu, Ré-hɥ.
Rehum, Ré-hum.
Rei, Ré-ȷ.
Rekem, Ré-kem.
Remaliah, Rem-a-lȷ-ɑ.
Remeth, Ré-meŧ.
Remmon, Rém-on.
Remmon Methoar, — Méŧ-ɷ-qr.
Remphan, Rém-fan.
Remphis, Rém-fis.
Rephael, Ré-fa-el.
Rephah, Ré-fɑ.
Rephaiah, Ref-a-ȷ-ɑ.
Rephaim, Réf-a-im.
Rephaims, Réf-a-imz.
Rephidim, Réf-i-dim.
Resen, Ré-sen.
Resheph, Ré-ʃef.
Reu, Ré-ɥ.
Reuben, Rɷ́-ben.
Reuel, Rɛ-yɥ́-el.
Reumah, Rɷ́-mɑ.
Rezeph, Ré-zef.
Rezia, Rɛ-zȷ-ɑ.
Rezin, Ré-zin.
Rezon, Ré-zon.
Rhegium, Ré-ji-um.
Rhesa, Ré-sɑ.
Rhoda, Rɷ́-dɑ.
Rhodocus, Ród-ɷ-kus.
Ribai, Rȷ-ba.
Riblah, Ríb-lɑ.
Rimmon, Rím-on.
Rimmon Parez, — Pá-rɛz.
Rinnah, Rín-ɑ.
Riphath, Rȷ-faŧ.
Rispah, Rís-pɑ.
Rissah, Rís-ɑ.
Rithmah, Ríŧ-mɑ.
Rogelim, Rɷ-gé-lim.
Rohgah, Rɷ́-gɑ.
Roimus, Rɷ́-i-mus.
Romantiezer, Rɷ-man-ti-é-zer.
Rosh, Roʃ.
Ruby, Rɷ́-bi.
Rufus, Rɷ́-fus.
Ruhamah, Rɷ́-ha-mq.
Rumah, Rɷ́-mɑ.
Rusticus, Rús-ti-kus.
Ruth, Rɷŧ.

# S.

Sabacthani, Sa-bak-ŧá-nȷ.
Sabaoth, Sáb-a-oŧ.
Sabat, Sá-bat.
Sabatus, Sáb-a-tus.
Sabban, Sáb-an.
Sabbath, Sáb-aŧ.
Sabbatheus, Sab-a-ŧé-us.
Sabbeus, Sa-bé-us.
Sabdeus, Sab-dé-us.
Sabdi, Sáb-dȷ.
Sabeans, Sa-bé-anz.
Sabi, Sá-bȷ.
Sabtah, Sáb-tɑ.
Sabtecha, Sáb-tɛ-kq.
Sacar, Sá-kɑr.
Sadamias, Sad-a-mȷ-as.
Sadas, Sá-das.
Saddeus, Sad-é-us.
Sadduc, Sád-uk.
Sadducees, Sád-yɥ-sɛz.
Sadoc, Sá-dok.
Sahadutha Jegar, Sa-ha-dɥ́-ŧɑ Jé-gɑr.
Sala, Sá-lɑ.
Salah, Sá-lɑ.
Salasadai, Sal-a-sád-a-ȷ.
Salathiel, Sa-lá-ŧi-el.
Salcah, Sál-kɑ.
Salchah, Sál-kɑ.
Salem, Sá-lem.
Salim, Sá-lim.
Sallai, Sál-a-ȷ.
Sallu, Sál-yɥ.
Sallum, Sál-um.
Sallumus, Sa-lɥ́-mus.
Salma, *or* Salmah, Sál-mɑ.
Salmon, Sál-mon.
Salmone, Sal-mɷ́-nɛ.
Salom, Sá-lom.
Salome, Sa-ló-mɛ.
Salu, Sá-lɥ.
Salum, Sá-lum.
Samael, Sám-a-el.
Samaias, Sa-má-yas.
Samaria, Sa-má-ri-q, *or* Sam-a-rȷ-ɑ.
Samaritans, Sa-már-i-tanz.
Samatus, Sám-a-tus.
Sameius, Sa-mé-yus.
Samgar Nebo, Sám-gqr Né-bɷ.

Sami, Sá-mị.
Samis, Sá-mis.
Samlah, Sám-la.
Sammus, Sám-us.
Sampsames, Sámp-sa-mez.
Samson, Sám-son.
Samuel, Sám-yų-el.
Sanabassarus, San-a-bás-a-rus.
Sanasib, Sán-a-sib.
Sanballat, San-bál-at.
Sanhedrim, Sán-he-drim.
Sansannah, San-sán-a.
Saph, Saf.
Saphat, Sá-fat.
Saphatias, Saf-a-tị-as.
Sapheth, Sá-feŧ.
Saphir, Sáf-er.
Sapphira, Sap-fị-ra.
Sapphire, Sáp-fịr.
Sara, Sá-ra, *or*
Sarai, Sá-ra.
Sarabias, Sar-a-bị-as.
Saraiah, Sar-a-ị-a.
Sarah, Sá-ra.
Saraias, Sa-rá-yas.
Saramael, Sa-rám-a-el.
Saramel, Sár-a-mel.
Saraph, Sá-raf. [nus.
Sarchedonus, Sąr-kéd-ɷ-
Sardeus, Sąr-de-us.
Sardis, Sąr-dis.
Sardine, Sąr-dịn.
Sardites, Sąr-dịts.
Sardius, Sąr-di-us.
Sardonyx, Sąr-dɷ-niks.
Sarea, Sá-re-ą.
Sarepta, Sa-rép-ta.
Sargon, Sąr-gon.
Sarid, Sá-rid.
Saron, Sá-ron.
Sarothi, Sa-rɷ́-ŧị.
Sarsechim, Sąr-sé-kim.
Saruch, Sá-ruk.
Satan, Sá-tan. [nez.
Sathrabaznes, Saŧ-ra-báz-
Sathrabouzanes, Saŧ-ra-bɤ-zá-nez.
Saul, Sɘl.
Savaran, Sáv-a-ran.
Savias, Sá-vi-as.
Sceva, Sé-va.
Scribes, Skrịbz.
Scythians, Skiŧ-i-anz.
Scythopolis, Skị-ŧóp-ɷ-lis.
Scythopolitans, Skiŧ-ɷ-pól-i-tanz.
Seba, Sé-ba.
Sebat, Sé-bat.
Secacah Sék-a-ką.

Sechenias, Sek-e-nị-as.
Sechu, Sé-kų.
Sedecias, Sed-e-sị-as.
Segub, Sé-gub.
Seir, Sé-er.
Seirath, Sé-i-raŧ.
Sela, Sé-la.
Selah, Sé-la.
Selah Hammahlekoth, — Ham-a-lé-koŧ.
Seled, Sé-led.
Selemias, Sel-e-mị-as.
Sem, Sem.
Semachiah, Sem-a-kị-a.
Semaiah, Sem-a-ị-a.
Semaias, Sem-a-ị-as.
Semei, Sém-e-ị.
Semelleus, Se-mél-e-us.
Semis, Sé-mis.
Sennaah, Sén-a-ą.
Seneh, Sé-ne.
Senir, Sé-ner.
Sennacherib, Sen-a-ké-rib, *or* Sen-ák-e-rib.
Senuah, Sén-yų-ą.
Seorim, Se-ɷ́-rim.
Sephar, Sé-far.
Sepharad, Séf-a-rad.
Sepharvaim, Sef-ar-vá-im.
Sepharvites, Sé-far-vịts.
Sephela, Se-fé-la.
Serah, Sé-ra.
Seraiah, Se-ra-ị-a.
Seraphim, Sér-a-fim.
Sered, Sé-red.
Seron, Sé-ron.
Serug, Sé-rug.
Sesis, Sé-sis.
Sesthel, Sés-ŧel.
Seth, Seŧ.
Sethar, Sé-ŧar.
Sether, Sé-ŧer.
Shaalabbin, Σa-al-áb-in.
Shaalbim, Σa-ál-bim.
Shaalbonite, Σa-ál-bɷ-nịt.
Shaaph, Σá-af.
Shaaraim, Σa-a-rá-im.
Shaashgas, Σa-áʃ-gas.
Shabbethai, Σa-béŧ-a-ị.
Shachia, Σák-i-ą.
Shaddai, Σád-a-ị.
Shadrach, Σá-drak.
Shage, Σá-ge. [maŧ.
Shahazimath, Σa-ház-i-
Shalem, Σá-lem.
Shalim, Σá-lim.
Shalisha, Σál-i-ʃą.
Shallecheth, Σál-e-keŧ.
Shallum, Σál-um.
Shalmai, Σál-ma-ị.

Shalman, Σál-man. [zer.
Shalmaneser, Σal-ma-né-
Shama, Σá-ma.
Shamariah, Σam-a-rị-a.
Shamed, Σá-med.
Shamer, Σá-mer.
Shamgar, Σám-gar.
Shamhuth, Σám-huŧ.
Shamir, Σá-mer.
Shamma, Σám-a.
Shammah, Σám-a.
Shammai, Σám-a-ị.
Shammoth, Σám-oŧ.
Shammua, Σa-mų́-a.
Shammuah, Σa-mų́-a.
Shamsherai, Σam-ʃe-rá-ị.
Shapham, Σá-fam.
Shaphan, Σá-fan.
Shaphat, Σá-fat.
Shapher, Σá-fer.
Sharai, Σár-a-ị.
Sharaim, Σár-a-im.
Sharar, Σá-rar.
Sharezer, Σa-ré-zer.
Sharmaim, Σąr-ma-im.
Sharon, Σą́-ron.
Sharonites, Σą́-ron-ịts.
Sharuhen, Σa-rɷ́-hen.
Shashai, Σáʃ-a-ị.
Shashak, Σá-ʃak.
Shaul, Σá-ul.
Shaulites, Σá-ul-ịts.
Shausha, Σa-yų́-ʃa.
Shaveh, Σá-ve.
Shaveth, Σá-veŧ.
Sheal, Σé-al.
Shealtiel, Σe-ál-ti-el.
Sheariah, Σe-a-rị-a.
Shearjashub, Σe-ar-já-ʃub.
Sheba, *or* Shebah, Σé-ba.
Shebam, Σé-bam.
Shebaniah, Σeb-a-nị-a.
Shebarim, Σéb-a-rim.
Shebat, Σé-bat.
Sheber, Σé-ber.
Shebna, Σéb-na.
Shebuel, Σéb-yų-el.
Shechaniah, Σek-a-nị-a.
Shechem, Σé-kem.
Shechemites, Σé-kem-ịts.
Shechinah, Σék-i-ną.
Shedeur, Σéd-e-ur.
Sheheriah, Σe-ha-rị-a.
Shekel, Σé-kel.
Shelah, Σé-la.
Shelanites, Σé-lan-ịts.
Shelemiah, Σel-e-mị-a.
Sheleph, Σé-lef.
Shelesh, Σé-leʃ.
Shelomi, Σél-ɷ-mị.

Shelomith, Σél-ɷ-miŧ, *or* Σε-lɷ́-miŧ,
Shelomoth, Σél-ɷ-moŧ.
Shelumiel, Σε-lq̣́-mi-el.
Shem, Σem.
Shema, Σé-mɑ.
Shemaah, Σém-a-q̣.
Shemaiah, Σem-a-ị-ɑ.
Shemariah, Σem-a-rị-ɑ.
Shemeber, Σém-ε-ber.
Shemer, Σé-mer.
Shemida, Σε-mị-dɑ.
Sheminith, Σém-i-niŧ.
Shemiramoth, Σε-mír-a-moŧ.
Shemuel, Σε-mq̣́-el.
Shen, Σen.
Shenazar, Σε-ná-zɑr.
Shenir, Σé-ner.
Shepham, Σé-fam.
Shephatiah, Σef-a-tị-ɑ.
Shephi, Σé-fị.
Shepho, Σé-fɷ.
Shephuphan, Σε-fq̣́-fan.
Sherah, Σé-rɑ.
Sherebiah, Σer-ε-bị-ɑ.
Sheresh, Σé-reſ.
Sherezer, Σε-ré-zer.
Sheshack, Σé-ſak.
Sheshai, Σé-ſa.
Sheshan, Σé-ſan.
Sheshbazzar, Σeſ-báz-ɑr.
Sheth, Σeŧ.
Shethar, Σé-ŧɑr.
Shethar Boznai, — Bóz-na-ị.
Sheva, Σé-vɑ.
Shibboleth, Σib-ɷ-leŧ.
Shibmah, Σib-mɑ.
Shichron, Σị-kron.
Shiggaion, Σi-gá-yon.
Shihon, Σị-hon.
Shihor, Σị-hor.
Shihor Libnath, — Líb-naŧ.
Shiihim, Σị-ị-him.
Shilhi, Σil-hị.
Shilhim, Σil-him.
Shillem, Σil-em.
Shillemites, Σil-em-ịts.
Shiloah, Σi-lɷ́-ɑ.
Shiloh, *or* Shilo, Σị-lɷ.
Shiloni, Σi-lɷ́-nị.
Shilonites, Σi-lɷ́-nịts.
Shilshah, Σil-ſɑ.
Shimea, Σim-ε-q̣.
Shimeah, Σim-ε-q̣.
Shimeam, Σim-ε-am.
Shimeath, Σim-ε-aŧ.
Shimeathites, Σim-ε-aŧ-ịts.
Shimei, Σim-ε-ị.
Shimeon, Σim-ε-on.
Shimhi, Σim-hị.
Shimi, Σị-mị.
Shimites, Σim-ịts.
Shimna, Σim-nɑ.
Shimon, Σị-mon.
Shimrath, Σim-raŧ.
Shimri, Σim-rị.
Shimrith, Σim-riŧ.
Shimron, Σim-ron.
Shimronites, Σim-ron-ịts.
Shimron Meron, Σim-ron Mé-ron.
Shimshai, Σim-ſa.
Shinab, Σị-nab.
Shinar, Σị-nɑr.
Shion, Σị-on.
Shiphi, Σị-fị.
Shiphmite, Σif-mịt.
Shiphra, Σif-rɑ.
Shiphrath, Σif-raŧ.
Shiptan, Σip-tan.
Shisha, Σị-ſɑ.
Shishak, Σị-ſak.
Shitrai, Σit-ra-ị.
Shittah, Σit-ɑ.
Shittim Wood, Σit-im Wɷd.
Shiza, Σị-zɑ.
Shoa, Σɷ́-ɑ.
Shoab, Σɷ́-ab.
Shoah, Σɷ́-ɑ.
Shobach, Σɷ́-bak.
Shobai, Σɷ́-ba-ị.
Shobal, Σɷ́-bal.
Shobek, Σɷ́-bek.
Shobi, Σɷ́-bị.
Shocho, Σɷ́-kɷ.
Shochoh, Σɷ́-kɷ.
Shoham, Σɷ́-ham.
Shomer, Σɷ́-mer.
Shophach, Σɷ́-fak.
Shophan, Σɷ́-fan.
Shoshannim, Σɷ-ſán-im.
Shoshannim Eduth, — Ɛ́-duŧ.
Shua, Σq̣́-ɑ.
Shuah, Σq̣́-ɑ.
Shual, Σq̣́-al.
Shubael, Σq̣́-ba-el.
Shuham, Σq̣́-ham.
Shuhamites, Σq̣́-ham-ịts.
Shuhites, Σq̣́-hịts.
Shulamite, Σq̣́-lam-ịt.
Shumathites, Σq̣́-maŧ-ịts.
Shunamite, Σq̣́-nam-ịt.
Shunem, Σq̣́-nem.
Shuni, Σq̣́-nị.
Shunites, Σq̣́-nịts.
Shupham, Σq̣́-fam.
Shuphamite, Σq̣́-fam-ịt.
Shuppim, Σúp-im.
Shur, Σur.
Shushan, Σq̣́-ſan.
Shushan Eduth, — Ɛ́duŧ.
Shuthalites, Σq̣́-ŧal-ịts.
Shuthelah, Σq̣́-ŧε-lq̣.
Sia, Sị-ɑ.
Siaka, Sị-a-kq̣.
Siba, Sị-bɑ.
Sibbachai, Síb-a-ka.
Sibboleth, Síb-ɷ-leŧ.
Sibmah, Síb-mɑ.
Sibraim, Síb-ra-im.
Sichem, Sị-kem.
Siddim, Síd-im.
Side, Sị-dε.
Sidon, Sị-don.
Sigionoth, Si-gị-ɷ-noŧ.
Siha, Sị-hɑ.
Sihon, Sị-hon.
Sihor, Sị-hor.
Silas, Sị-las.
Silla, Síl-ɑ.
Siloa, Síl-ɷ-q̣, *or*
Siloah, Síl-ɷ-q̣.
Siloam, Síl-ɷ-am, *or* Si-lɷ́-am.
Siloas, Síl-ɷ-as.
Siloe, Síl-ɷ-ε.
Simalcue, Sị-mal-kq̣́-ε.
Simeon, Sím-ε-on.
Simeonites, Sím-ε-on-ịts.
Simon, Sị-mon.
Simri, Sím-rị.
Sin, Sin.
Sinai, Sị-na.
Sinim, Sị-nim.
Sinites, Sín-ịts.
Sion, Sị-on.
Siphmoth, Síf-moŧ.
Sippai, Síp-a.
Sirach, Sị-rak.
Sirah, Sị-rɑ.
Sirion, Sír-i-on.
Sisamai, Sis-ám-a-ị.
Sisera, Sís-ε-rq̣.
Sisinnes, Sị-sín-εz.
Sitnah, Sít-nɑ.
Sivan, Sị-van.
So, Sɷ.
Sochoh, Sɷ́-kɷ.
Socoh, Sɷ́-kɷ.
Sodi, Sɷ́-dị.
Sodom, Sód-om.
Sodoma, Sód-ɷ-mq̣.
Sodomites, Sód-om-ịts.
Solomon, Sól-ɷ-mon.
Sopater, Sóp-a-ter.
Sophereth, Sóf-ε-reŧ.
Sorek, Sɷ́-rek.
Sosipater, Sɷ-sip-a-ter.
Sosthenes, Sós-ŧε-nεz.

Sosthenes, Sós-ŧɛ-nɛz.
Sostratus, Sós-tra-tus.
Sotai, Sɷ́-ta-ị, *or* Sɷ-tá-ị.
Stachys, Stá-kis.
Stacte, Sták-tɛ.
Stephana, Stéf-a-ną.
Stephanas, Stéf-a-nas.
Stephen, Stɛ́-ven.
Suah, Sų́-ɑ.
Suba, Sų́-bɑ.
Subai, Sų́-ba-ị.
Sucaathites, Sų-ká-aŧ-ịts.
Succoth, Súk-oŧ.
Succoth Benoth, —Bɛ́-noŧ.
Sud, Sud.
Sudias, Sų́-di-as.
Sukkiims, Súk-i-imz.
Sur, Sur.
Susa, Sų́-sɑ.
Susanchites, Sų́-san-kịts.
Susannah, Sų-zán-ɑ.
Susi, Sų́-sị.
Sycamine, Sík-a-mịn.
Sycene, Sị-sɛ́-nɛ.
Sychar, Sị́-kɑr.
Syelus, Sị-ɛ́-lus.
Syene, Sị-ɛ́-nɛ.
Synagogue, Sín-a-gog.
Syntyche, Sín-ti-kɛ.
Syria Maacah, Sír-i-ɑ Má-a-ką.
Syrion, Sír-i-on.
Syrophenicia, Sị-rɷ-fɛ-níʃ-i-ą.

# T.

Taanach, Tá-a-nak, *or* Ta-á-nak.
Taanach Shilo, — Σị́-lɷ.
Tabbaoth, Táb-a-oŧ.
Tabbath, Táb-aŧ.
Tabeal, Tá-bɛ-al.
Tabeel, Tá-bɛ-el.
Tabellius, Ta-bél-i-us.
Tabera, Táb-ɛ-rą.
Tabitha, Táb-i-ŧą.
Tabor, Tá-bor.
Tabrimon, Táb-ri-mon.
Tachmonite, Ták-mɷ-nịt.
Tadmor, Tád-mor.
Tahan, Tá-han.
Tahanites, Tá-han-ịts.
Tahapenes, Ta-háp-ɛ-nɛz.
Tahaphanes, Ta-háf-a-nɛz.
Tahath, Tá-haŧ.
Tahpenes, Tą́-pɛ-nɛz.
Tahrea, Tą́-rɛ-ą.
Tahtim Hodshi, Tą́-tim Hód-ʃị. [Kų́-mị.
Talitha Cumi, Tál-ị-ŧą
Talmai, Tál-ma.
Talmon, Tál-mon.
Talsas, Tál-sas.
Tamah, Tá-mɑ.
Tamar, Tá-mɑr.
Tammuz, Tám-uz.
Tanach, Tá-nak.
Tanhumeth, Tán-hų-meŧ.
Tanis, Tá-nis.
Taphath, Tá-faŧ.
Taphenes, Táf-ɛ-nɛz.
Taphnes, Táf-nɛz.
Taphon, Tá-fon.
Tappuah, Táp-yų-ą.
Tarah, Tá-rɑ.
Taralah, Tár-a-lą.
Tarea, Tá-rɛ-ą.
Tarpelites, Tą́r-pel-ịts.
Tarshis, Tą́r-ʃis.
Tarshish, Tą́r-ʃiʃ.
Tarshisi, Tąr-ʃị́-sị.
Tarus, Tą́r-sus.
Tartak, Tą́r-tak.
Tartan, Tą́r-tan.
Tatnai, Tát-na-ị.
Tebah, Tɛ́-bɑ.
Tebaliah, Teb-a-lị́-ɑ.
Tebeth, Tɛ́-beŧ. [hɛz.
Tehaphnehes, Tɛ-háf-nɛ-
Tehinnah, Tɛ-hín-ɑ.
Tekel, Tɛ́-kel.
Tekoa, Tɛ-kɷ́-ɑ, *or*
Tekoah, Tɛ-kɷ́-ɑ.
Tekoites, Tɛ-kɷ́-ịts.
Telabib, Tél-a-bib.
Telah, Tɛ́-lɑ.
Telaim, Tél-a-im.
Telassar, Tɛ-lás-ɑr.
Telem, Tɛ́-lem.
Telharesha, Tel-ha-rɛ́-ʃɑ.
Telharsa, Tel-hą́r-sɑ.
Telmela, Tél-mɛ-lą.
Telmelah, Tél-mɛ-lą.
Tema, Tɛ́-mɑ.
Teman, Tɛ́-man.
Temani, Tém-a-nị.
Temanites, Tɛ́-man-ịts.
Temeni, Tém-ɛ-nị.
Tepho, Tɛ́-fɷ.
Terah, Tɛ́-rɑ.
Teraphim, Tér-a-fim.
Teresh, Tɛ́-reʃ.
Tertius, Tér-ʃi-us.
Tertullus, Ter-túl-us.
Teta, Tɛ́-tɑ.
Tetrarch, Tét-rąrk.
Thaddeus, Ħa-dɛ́-us.
Thahash, Ħá-haʃ.
Thamah, Ħá-mɑ.
Thamnatha, Ħám-na-ŧą.
Thara, Ħá-rɑ.
Tharra, Ħár-ɑ.
Tharshish, Ħą́r-ʃiʃ.
Thassi, Ħás-ị.
Thebez, Ħɛ́-bez.
Thecoe, Ħɛ-kɷ́-ɛ.
Thelasser, Ħɛ-lás-er.
Thelersas, Ħɛ-lér-sas.
Theocanus, Ħɛ-ók-a-nus.
Theodotus, Ħɛ-ód-ɷ-tus.
Theophilus, Ħɛ-óf-i-lus.
Theras, Ħɛ́-ras.
Thermeleth, Ħér-mɛ-leŧ.
Thessalonica, Ħes-a-lɷ-nị́-kɑ.
Theudas, Ħų́-das.
Thimnathath, Ħím-na-ŧaŧ.
Thisbe, Ħís-bɛ.
Thomas, Tóm-as.
Thomoi, Ħóm-ɷ-ị.
Thraseas, Ħra-sɛ́-as.
Thummim, Ħúm-im.
Thyatira, Ħị-a-tị́-rɑ.
Tibbath, Tíb-aŧ.
Tiberias, Tị-bɛ́-ri-as.
Tibni, Tíb-nị.
Tidal, Tị́-dal.
Tiglath Pileser, Tíg-laŧ Pị-lɛ́-ser.
Tikvah, Tík-vɑ.
Tikvath, Tík-vaŧ.
Tilon, Tị́-lon.
Timelus, Tị-mɛ́-lus.
Timna, Tím-nɑ.
Timnath, Tím-naŧ.
Timnathah, Tím-na-ŧą.
Timnath Heres, Tím-naŧ Hɛ́-rɛz.
Timnath Serah, — Sɛ́-rɑ.
Timnite, Tím-nịt.
Timotheus, Tị-mɷ́-ŧɛ-us.
Timothy, Tím-ɷ-ŧi.
Tipsah, Típ-sɑ.
Tiras, Tị́-ras.
Tirathites, Tị́-raŧ-ịts.
Tirhakah, Tér-ha-ką.
Tirhanah, Tér-ha-ną.
Tiria, Tír-i-ą.
Tirshatha, Tér-ʃa-ŧą.
Tirzah, Tér-zɑ.
Tishbite, Tíʃ-bịt.
Tivan, Tị́-van.
Tiza, Tị́-zɑ.
Tizite, Tị́-zịt.
Toah, Tɷ́-ɑ.
Toanah, Tɷ́-a-ną.
Tob, Tob.
Tobiah, Tɷ-bị́-ɑ.

Tobias, Tɷ-bɩ-as.
Tobie, Tɷ́-bi.
Tobiel, Tɷ́-bi-el.
Tobijah, Tɷ-bɩ-jɑ.
Tobit, Tɷ́-bit.
Tochen, Tɷ́-ken.
Togarmah, Tɷ-gą́r-mɑ.
Tohu, Tɷ́-hɥ.
Toi, Tɷ́-ɩ.
Tola, Tɷ́-lɑ.
Tolad, Tɷ́-lad.
Tolaites, Tɷ́-la-ɩts.
Tolbanes, Tól-ba-nεz.
Tolmai, Tól-ma.
Tophel, Tɷ́-fel.
Tophet, Tɷ́-fet.
Tou, Tɷ́-yɥ.
Trachonitis, Trak-ɷ-nɩ-tis.
Tripolis, Tríp-ɷ-lis.
Troas, Trɷ́-as.
Trogyllium, Trɷ-jil-i-um.
Trophimus, Tróf-i-mus.
Tryphena, Trɩ-fé-nɑ.
Tryphosa, Trɩ-fɷ́-sɑ.
Tubal, Tɥ́-bal.
Tubal Cain, — Ká-in.
Tubieni, Tɥ-bɩ-ε-nɩ.
Tyberias, Tɩ-bé-ri-as.
Tychicus, Tik-i-kus.
Tyrannus, Tɩ-rán-us.
Tyre, Tɩr.
Tyrus, Tɩ́-rus.

# U.

Ucal, Yɥ́-kal.
Uel, Yɥ́-el.
Ulai, Yɥ́-la-ɩ.
Ulam, Yɥ́-lam.
Ulla, Ul'ɑ.
Ummah, Um'ɑ.
Unni, Un'ɩ.
Upharsin, Yɥ-fą́r-sin.
Uphaz, Yɥ́-faz.
Urbane, Ur'ba-nε.
Uri, Yɥ́-rɩ.
Uriah, Yɥ-rɩ-ɑ.
Urias, Yɥ-rɩ-as.
Uriel, Yɥ́-ri-el, *or* Yɥ-rɩ-el.
Urijah, Yɥ-rɩ-jɑ.
Urim, Yɥ́-rim.
Uta, Yɥ́-tɑ.
Uthai, Yɥ́-ða-ɩ, *or* Yɥ-ðá-ɩ.
Uthi, Yɥ́-ðɩ.
Uzai, Yɥ́-za-ɩ.
Uzal, Yɥ́-zal.
Uzza, Uz'ɑ.
Uzzah, Uz'ɑ.
Uzzen Sherah, Uz'en Σé-rɑ.
Uzzi, Uz'ɩ.
Uzziah, Uz-ɩ-ɑ.
Uzziel, Uz-ɩ-el.
Uzzielites, Uz-ɩ-el-ɩts.

# V.

Vajezatha, Va-jéz-a-ðɑ.
Vaniah, Va-nɩ-ɑ.
Vashni, Váʃ-nɩ.
Vashti, Váʃ-tɩ.
Vophsi, Vóf-sɩ.

# X.

Xagus, Zá-gus.
Xanthicus, Zán-ði-kus.
Xeneas, Ze-nε-as.
Xerolybe, Zε-ról-i-bε.
Xerophagia, Zer-ɷ-fá-ji-ɑ.
Xystus, Zís-tus.

# Z.

Zaaman, Zá-a-man.
Zaanaim, Za-a-ná-im.
Zaanannim, Za-a-nán-im.
Zaavan, Zá-a-van.
Zabad, Zá-bad.
Zabadæans, Zab-a-dé-anz.
Zabadaias, Zab-a-dá-yas.
Zabbai, Záb-a.
Zabdeus, Zab-dé-us.
Zabdi, Záb-dɩ.
Zabdiel, Záb-di-el.
Zabina, Za-bɩ-nɑ.
Zabud, Zá-bud.
Zabulon, Záb-yɥ-lon.
Zaccai, Zák-a-ɩ.
Zaccheus, Za-ké-us.
Zaccur, Zák-ur.
Zachariah, Zak-a-rɩ-ɑ.
Zacher, Zá-ker.
Zadok, Zá-dok.
Zaham, Zá-ham.
Zair, Zá-er.
Zalaph, Zá-laf.
Zalmon, Zál-mon.
Zalmonah, Zal-mɷ́-nɑ.
Zalmunah, Zal-mɥ́n-ɑ.
Zambis, Zám-bis.
Zambri, Zám-brɩ.
Zamoth, Zá-moð.
Zamzummims, Zam-zúm-imz.
Zanoah, Za-nɷ́-ɑ.
Zaphnathpaaneah, Zaf-nað-pa-a-né-ɑ.
Zaphon, Zá-fon.
Zara, Zá-rɑ.
Zaraces, Zár-a-sεz.
Zarah, Zá-rɑ.
Zaraias, Zar-a-ɩ-as.
Zareah, Zá-rε-ɑ.
Zareathites, Zá-rε-að-ɩts.
Zared, Zá-red.
Zarephath, Zár-ε-fað.
Zaretan, Zár-ε-tan.
Zareth Shahar, Zá-reð Σá-hɑr.
Zarhites, Zą́r-hɩts.
Zartanah, Zą́r-ta-nɑ.
Zarthan, Zą́r-ðan.
Zathoe, Záð-ɷ-ε.
Zathu, Záð-yɥ.
Zathui, Za-ðɥ́-ɩ.
Zattu, Zát-yɥ.
Zavan, Zá-van.
Zaza, Zá-zɑ.
Zebadiah, Zeb-a-dɩ-ɑ.
Zebah, Zé-bɑ.
Zebaim, Zε-bá-im.
Zebedee, Zéb-ε-dε.
Zebina, Zε-bɩ-nɑ.
Zeboim, Zε-bɷ́-im.
Zebuda, Zε-bɥ́-dɑ.
Zebul, Zé-bul.
Zebulon, Zéb-yɥ-lon.
Zebulonites, Zéb-yɥ-lon-ɩts.
Zechariah, Zek-a-rɩ-ɑ.
Zedad, Zé-dad.
Zedekiah, Zed-ε-kɩ-ɑ.
Zeeb, Zεb, *or* Zé-eb.
Σelah, Zé-lɑ.
Zelek, Zé-lek.
Zelophead, Zε-lɷ́-fε-ad.
Zelotes, Zε-lɷ́-tεz.
Zelzah, Zél-zɑ.
Zemaraim, Zem-a-rá-im.
Zemarite, Zém-a-rɩt.
Zemira, Zε-mɩ-rɑ.
Zenan, Zé-nan.
Zenas, Zé-nas.
Zeorim, Zε-ór-im.
Zephaniah, Zef-a-nɩ-ɑ.
Zephath, Zé-fað.
Zephathah, Zéf-a-ðɑ.
Zephi, Zé-fɩ.
Zepho, Zé-fɷ.

Zephon, Zé-fon.
Zephonites, Zéf-on-ịts.
Zer, Zẹr.
Zerah, Zé-rɑ.
Zerahiah, Zer-a-hị-ɑ.
Zeraia, Zer-a-ị-ɑ.
Zerau, Zé-rɵ.
Zered, Zé-red.
Zereda, Zér-ɛ-dɋ.
Zeredah, Zér-ɛ-dɋ.
Zeredathah, Zɛ-réd-a-ŧɋ.
Zererath, Zér-ɛ-raŧ.
Zeresh, Zé-reʃ.
Zereth, Zé-reŧ.
Zeri, Zé-rị.
Zeror, Zé-ror.
Zeruah, Zɛ-rṓ-ɑ.
Zerubbabel, Zɛ-rúb-a-bel.
Zeruiah, Zer-yų-ị-ɑ.
Zerviah, Zer-vị-ɑ.
Zetham, Zé-ŧam.
Zethan, Zé-ŧan.
Zethar, Zé-ŧɑr.
Zia, Zị-ɑ.
Ziba, Zị-bɑ.
Zibeon, Zíb-ɛ-on.
Zichri, Zík-rị.
Ziddim, Zíd-im.

Zidkijah, Zid-kị-jɑ.
Zidon, Zị-don, *or*
  Sidon, Sị-don.
Zidonians, Zi-dṓ-ni-anz.
Zif, Zif.
Ziha, Zị-hɑ.
Ziklag, Zík-lag.
Zillah, Zíl-ɑ.
Zilpah, Zíl-pɑ.
Zilthai, Zíl-ŧɑ.
Zimmah, Zím-ɑ.
Zimram, Zím-ram, *or*
Zimran, Zím-ran.
Zimri, Zím-rị.
Zin, Zin.
Zina, Zị-nɑ.
Zion, Zị-on, *or*
  Sion, Sị-on.
Zior, Zị-or.
Ziph, Zif.
Ziphah, Zị-fɑ.
Ziphion, Zíf-i-on.
Ziphites, Zíf-ịts.
Ziphron, Zị-fron.
Zippor, Zip-or.
Zipporah, Zi-pṓ-rɑ.
Zithri, Zíŧ-rị.

Ziz, Ziz.
Ziza, Zị-zɑ.
Zizah, Zị-zɑ́.
Zoan, Zṓ-an.
Zoar, Zṓ-ɑr.
Zoba, Zṓ-bɑ, *or*
Zobah, Zṓ-bɑ.
Zobebah, Zɷ-bé-bɑ́.
Zohar, Zṓ-hɑr.
Zoheleth, Zṓ-hɛ-leŧ.
Zonaras, Zón-a-ras.
Zopeth, Zṓ-peŧ.
Zophah, Zṓ-fɑ.
Zophai, Zṓ-fa.
Zophar, Zṓ-fɑr.
Zophim, Zṓ-fim.
Zorah, Zṓ-rɑ.
Zorathites, Zṓ-raŧ-ịts.
Zoreah, Zṓ-rɛ-ɋ.
Zorites, Zṓ-rịts.
Zorobabel, Zɷ-rób-a-bel.
Zuar, Zų́-ɑr.
Zuph, Zuf.
Zur, Zur.
Zuriel, Zų́-ri-el.
Zurishaddai, Zų-ri-ʃád-a-ị.
Zuzims, Zų́-zimz.

## THE UNITED STATES.

| States and Territories. | Capitals. | Population in 1850. | | | |
|---|---|---|---|---|---|
| | | Whites. | Fr. Col. | Slaves. | Total. |
| Maine, ............ | Augusta, ......... | 581,813 | 1,356 | ....... | 583,169 |
| New Hampshire, ... | Concord, ......... | 317,456 | 520 | ....... | 317,976 |
| Vermont, ......... | Montpelier, ....... | 313,402 | 718 | ....... | 314,120 |
| Massachusetts, ..... | Boston, .......... | 985,450 | 9,064 | ....... | 994,514 |
| Rhode Island, ..... | Newport & Prov'e, . | 143,875 | 3,670 | ....... | 147,545 |
| Connecticut, ...... | Hartford & N. H'n, | 369,099 | 7,693 | ....... | 370,792 |
| New York, ....... | Albany, .......... | 3,048,325 | 49,069 | ....... | 3,097,394 |
| New Jersey, ....... | Trenton, ......... | 465,509 | 23,810 | 236 | 489,555 |
| Pennsylvania, ..... | Harrisburg, ....... | 2,258,160 | 53,626 | ....... | 2,311,786 |
| Delaware, ........ | Dover, ........... | 71,169 | 18,073 | 2,290 | 91,532 |
| Maryland, ........ | Annapolis, ........ | 417,943 | 74,723 | 90,368 | 583,034 |
| Dist. of Columbia, . | Washington City, . | 37,941 | 10,059 | 3,687 | 51,687 |
| Virginia, ......... | Richmond, ........ | 894,800 | 54,333 | 472,528 | 1,421,661 |
| North Carolina, .... | Raleigh, .......... | 553,028 | 27,463 | 288,548 | 869,039 |
| South Carolina, ... | Columbia, ........ | 274,563 | 8,960 | 384,984 | 668,507 |
| Georgia, .......... | Milledgeville, ..... | 521,572 | 2,931 | 381,682 | 906,185 |
| Florida, ..... ..... | Tallahasse, ....... | 47,203 | 932 | 39,310 | 87,445 |
| Alabama, ........ | Montgomery, ...... | 426,514 | 2,265 | 342,844 | 771,623 |
| Mississippi, ....... | Jackson, .......... | 295,718 | 930 | 309,878 | 606,526 |
| Louisiana, ........ | Baton Rouge, ..... | 255,491 | 17,462 | 244,809 | 517,762 |
| Texas, ............ | Austin, .......... | 154,034 | 397 | 58,161 | 212,592 |
| Arkansas, ........ | Little Rock, ...... | 162,189 | 608 | 47,100 | 209,897 |
| Tennessee, ....... | Nashville, ... .... | 756,836 | 6,422 | 239,459 | 1,002,717 |
| Kentucky, ....... | Frankfort, ....... | 761,413 | 10,011 | 210,981 | 982,405 |
| Ohio, ............ | Columbus, ........ | 1,955,050 | 25,279 | ....... | 1,980,329 |
| Michigan, ......... | Lansing, ......... | 395,071 | 2,583 | ....... | 397,654 |
| Indiana, .......... | Indianapolis, ...... | 977,154 | 11,262 | ....... | 988,416 |
| Illinois, ........... | Springfield, ...... | 846,034 | 5,436 | ....... | 851,470 |
| Missouri, .......... | Jefferson City, .... | 592,004 | 2,618 | 87,422 | 682,044 |
| Iowa, ............ | Iowa City, ....... | 191,881 | 333 | ....... | 192,214 |
| Wisconsin, ....... | Madison, ......... | 304,756 | 635 | ....... | 305,391 |
| California, ....... | Sacramento, ...... | 91,655 | 962 | ....... | 92,597 |
| Kansas Territory, .. | Topeka, .......... | ...... | ..... | ....... | ........ |
| Nebraska Territory, | Omaha City, ...... | ...... | ..... | ....... | ........ |
| Minnesota Territory, | St. Paul, ......... | 6,038 | 39 | ....... | 6,077 |
| N. Mexico Territory, | Santa Fe, ........ | 61,525 | 22 | ....... | 61,547 |
| Utah Territory, .... | Salt Lake City, ... | 11,330 | 24 | 26 | 11,380 |
| Oregon Territory, .. | Salem, ........... | 13,087 | 207 | ....... | 13,294 |
| Washington Ter., .. | Olympia, ........ | ...... | ..... | ....... | ........ |
| Total, ...... | ............... | 19,553,068 | 434,495 | 3,204,313 | 23,191,876 |

THE MEETING OF THE LEGISLATURES.—California, Mississippi, Ohio and Wisconsin, 1 M. Jan.,—Indiana, January,—Illinois and Virginia, 2 M. Jan.,—Louisiana, 3 M. Jan.,—New-York and Pennsylvania, 1 Tu. Jan.,—New-Jersey, 2 Tu. Jan.,—Maine, Maryland, Massachusetts and Michigan, 1 W. Jan.,—Connecticut, 1 W. May,—Rhode Island, May & Oct.,—Delaware, 1 Tu. June,—New-Hampshire, 1 W. June,—Tennessee, 1 M. Oct.,—Vermont, 2 Th. Oct.,—Arkansas, Florida and Georgia, 1 M. Nov.,—Alabama, 2 M. Nov.,—N. Carolina, 3 M. Nov.,—South Carolina, 4 M. Nov.,—Jowa and Kentucky, 1 M. Dec.,—Texas, December, Missouri, Last M. Dec.

## PRESIDENTS AND VICE-PRESIDENTS OF THE UNITED STATES.

| Year. | Presidents and Vice-Presidents. | Vote | Opposition. | vote | Sct |
|---|---|---|---|---|---|
| 1789 | George Washington, *Virginia.* | 69 | ——— ——— | — | — |
| 1793 | John Adams, *Massachusetts.* | 34 | ——— ——— | — | 35 |
| 1793 | George Washington, *Virginia.* | 132 | ——— ——— | — | — |
| 1797 | John Adams, *Massachusetts.* | 77 | Geo. Clinton, *N-Y.* | 50 | 5 |
| 1697 | John Adams, *Massachusetts.* | 71 | ——— ——— | | 137 |
| 1801 | Thomas Jefferson, *Virginia.* | 68 | ——— ——— | | |
| 1801 | Thomas Jefferson, *Virginia.* | 73 | John Adams, *Mass.* | 65 | — |
| 1805 | Aaron Burr, *New-York.* | 73 | C. C. Pinkney, —— | 64 | 1 |
| 1805 | Thomas Jefferson, *Virginia.* | 162 | C. C. Pinkney, —— | 14 | — |
| 1809 | George Clinton, *New-York.* | 163 | Rufus King, *Maine.* | 14 | — |
| 1809 | James Madison, *Virginia.* | 152 | C. C. Pinkney, —— | 49 | 6 |
| 1813 | Geo. Clinton, *New-York.* | 118 | Rufus King, *Maine.* | 47 | 15 |
| 1813 | James Madison, *Virginia.* | 128 | Dewitt Clinton, *N-Y.* | 89 | — |
| 1817 | Elbridge Gerry, *Massachusetts.* | 131 | Jared Ingersoll, *Pa.* | 86 | — |
| 1817 | James Monroe, *Virginia.* | 183 | Rufus King, *Maine.* | 34 | — |
| 1821 | D. D. Tompkins. *New-York.* | 113 | ——— ——— | — | 134 |
| 1821 | James Monroe, *Virginia.* | 231 | J. Q. Adams, *Mass.* | 1 | — |
| 1825 | D. D. Tompkins, *New-York.* | 212 | ——— ——— | — | 20 |
| 1825 | J. Q. Adams, *Massachusetts.* | 84 | Andrew Jackson, *Tenn.* | 99 | 78 |
| 1829 | John Calhoun, *S. Carolina.* | 182 | ——— ——— | — | 79 |
| 1829 | Andrew Jackson, *Tennessee.* | 178 | J. Q. Adams, *Mass.* | 83 | — |
| 1833 | J. C. Calhoun, *S. Carolina.* | 171 | R. Rush, *Pa.* | 83 | — |
| 1833 | Andrew Jackson, *Tennessee.* | 219 | Henry Clay, *Ky.* | 49 | 18 |
| 1837 | Martin Van Buren, *New-York.* | 189 | John Sergeant, *Pa.* | 49 | 48 |
| 1837 | Martin Van Buren, *New-York.* | 170 | William H. Harrison, *Ohio.* | 73 | 51 |
| 1841 | R. M. Johnston, *Kentucky.* | 147 | Francis Granger, *N-Y.* | 68 | 84 |
| 1841 | William H. Harrison, *Ohio.* | 234 | Martin Van Buren, *N-Y.* | 60 | — |
| 1845 | John Tyler, *Virginia.* | 234 | R. M. Johnston, *Ky.* | 48 | 12 |
| 1845 | James K. Polk, *Tennessee.* | 170 | Henry Clay, *Ky.* | 105 | — |
| 1849 | Geo. M. Dallas. *Pennsylvania.* | 170 | J. Frielinghuyzen, *N-Y.* | 105 | — |
| 1849 | Zachary Taylor, *Louisiana.* | 163 | Lewis Cass, *Mich.* | 127 | — |
| 1853 | Millard Fillmore, *New-York.* | 163 | W. O. Butler, *Ky.* | 127 | — |
| 1853 | Franklin Pierce, *N-Hampshire.* | 254 | Winfield Scott, *Md.* | 43 | — |
| 1857 | W. R. King, *North Carolina.* | 254 | W. A. Graham, *Pa.* | 43 | — |
| 1857 | Jas. Buchanan, *Pennsylvania.* | 173 | J. C. Fremont, *Cal.* | 115 | 8 |
| 1861 | J. C. Breckinridge, *Kentucky.* | 173 | W. L. Dayton, *N-J.* | 115 | 8 |

## TIME OF ELECTIONS AND ELECTORAL VOTES.

| States. | Gen. Election. | E. V. | States. | Gen. Election. | E. V. |
|---|---|---|---|---|---|
| Maine, | 2 M. Sept. | 8 | Alabama, | 1 M. Aug. | 9 |
| New Hampshire, | 2 Tu. March. | 5 | Mississippi, | 1 M. & Tu. N. | 9 |
| Vermont, | 1 Tu. Sept. | 5 | Louisiana, | 1 M. Nov. | 5 |
| Massachusetts, | 2 M. Nov. | 13 | Texas, | 1 M. Aug. | 4 |
| Rhode Island, | 1 W. April. | 4 | Arkansas, | 1 M. Aug. | 4 |
| Connecticut, | 1 M. April. | 6 | Tennessee, | 1 Th. Aug. | 12 |
| New York, | 1 Tu. Nov. | 35 | Kentucky, | 1 M. Aug. | 12 |
| New Jersey, | 1 Tu. Nov. | 7 | Ohio, | 2 Tu. Oct. | 23 |
| Pennsylvania, | 2 Tu. Oct. | 27 | Michigan, | 1 Tu. Nov. | 5 |
| Delaware, | 2 Tu. Nov. | 3 | Indiana, | 2 Tu. Oct. | 13 |
| Maryland, | 1 W. Nov. | 8 | Illinois, | 1 Tu. Nov. | 11 |
| Virginia, | 4 Th. April. | 15 | Missouri, | 1 M. Aug. | 9 |
| North Carolina, | 2 Th. Aug. | 10 | Iowa, | 1 M. Aug. | 4 |
| South Carolina, | 2 M. Oct. | 8 | Wisconsin, | 1 Th. Nov. | 5 |
| Georgia, | 1 M. Oct. | 10 | California, | 1 Th. Sept. | 4 |
| Florida, | 1 M. Oct. | 3 | Total. | .......... | 296 |

# COLLEGES AND PROFESSIONAL SCHOOLS IN THE UNITED STATES.

| Name. | Place. | Founded. | Students. | Vols. in Libraries. |
|---|---|---|---|---|
| Alleghany,‡ | Meadville, Pa. | 1817 | 98 | 9,700 |
| Amherst, | Amherst, Mass. | 1821 | 237 | 20,000 |
| Antioch College, | Yellow Springs, Ohio. | 1852 | 300 | ...... |
| Augusta,‡ | Augusta, Ky. | 1825 | 51 | 2,500 |
| Bacon, | Harrodsburg, Ky. | 1836 | 75 | 1,200 |
| Baton Rouge, | Baton Rouge, La. | 1838 | 45 | 300 |
| Beloit, | Beloit, Rock co., Wis. | 1847 | 30 | 2,500 |
| Bethany College, | Bethany, Va. | 1841 | 141 | 3,500 |
| Bowdoin, | Brunswick, Me. | 1802 | 177 | 27,650 |
| Brown University,* | Providence, R. I. | 1764 | 252 | 32,000 |
| Burlington,† | Burlington, N. J. | 1846 | 118 | 1,200 |
| Centenary,‡ | Jackson, La. | 1839 | 102 | 5,000 |
| Centre, | Danville, Ky. | 1820 | 189 | 5,500 |
| Charleston, | Charleston, S. C. | 1785 | 70 | 2,000 |
| College of New Jersey, | Princeton, N. J. | 1747 | 225 | 17,800 |
| Columbia,† | New-York, N. Y. | 1754 | 148 | 14,000 |
| Columbian,* | Washington, D. C. | 1821 | 55 | 6,000 |
| Cumberland University, | Lebanon, Tenn. | 1844 | 164 | 5,000 |
| Dartmouth, | Hanover, N. H. | 1769 | 252 | 30,798 |
| Davidson, | Mecklenburg co., N. C. | 1838 | 81 | 5,000 |
| Delaware, | Newark, Del. | 1833 | 37 | 7,500 |
| Dickinson,‡ | Carlisle, Pa. | 1783 | 123 | 15,500 |
| East Tennessee, | Knoxville, Tenn. | 1792 | 57 | 4,500 |
| Emory,‡ | Oxford, Ga. | 1837 | 115 | 1,700 |
| Emory and Henry,‡ | Emory, Va. | 1838 | 54 | 8,470 |
| Fayette, | Fayette, Ia. | .... | 75 | ...... |
| Franklin, | Athens, Ga. | 1785 | 182 | 15,500 |
| Franklin, | Opelousas, La. | 1839 | 70 | ..... |
| Franklin, | Near Nashville, Tenn. | 1845 | 106 | 3,500 |
| Franklin, | New Athens, Ohio. | 1824 | 110 | 5,000 |
| Genesee College, | Genesee, N. Y. | | 78 | |
| Georgetown,§ | Georgetown, D. C. | 1789 | 160 | 26,000 |
| Georgetown,* | Georgetown, Ky. | 1840 | 83 | 6,600 |
| Granville,* | Granville, Ohio. | 1831 | 44 | 7,000 |
| Green Mount College, | Richmond, Ia. | 1852 | | |
| Hamilton, | Clinton, N. Y. | 1812 | 140 | 12,000 |
| Hampden Sidney, | Prince Edward co., Va. | 1783 | 25 | 8,000 |
| Hanover College, | Hanover, Ia. | 1832 | 100 | 5,000 |
| Harvard University, | Cambridge, Mass. | 1636 | 339 | 98,100 |
| Hobart Free College,† | Geneva, N. Y. | 1823 | 67 | 7,000 |
| Holy Cross,§ | Worcester, Mass. | 1843 | 120 | 4,220 |
| Howard,* | Marion, Ala. | 1841 | 88 | 2,200 |
| Illinois, | Jacksonville, Ill. | 1830 | 48 | 3,660 |
| Indiana Asbury University,‡ | Greencastle, Ia. | 1837 | 120 | 4,000 |
| Indiana State University, | Bloomington, Ia. | 1816 | 175 | 4,200 |
| Jackson, | Columbia, Tenn. | 1833 | 75 | 4,100 |
| Jefferson, | Canonsburg, Pa. | 1802 | 251 | 10,000 |

| Name. | Place. | Founded. | Students. | Vols. in Libraries. |
|---|---|---|---|---|
| Kenyon,† | Gambier, Ohio. | 1827 | 163 | 7,000 |
| Knox, | Galesburg, Ill. | 1837 | 56 | 3,300 |
| Lafayette, | Easton, Pa. | 1832 | 53 | 5,000 |
| La Grange,‡ | La Grange, Ala. | 1830 | 86 | 4,000 |
| Madison University,* | Hamilton, N. Y. | 1820 | 74 | 12,990 |
| Marietta, | Marietta, Ohio. | 1835 | 68 | 13,700 |
| Marshall, | Mercersburg, Pa. | 1835 | 58 | 6,000 |
| Masonic, | Marion co., Mo. | 1831 | 45 | ...... |
| McKendree,‡ | Lebanon, Ill. | 1835 | 79 | 7,000 |
| Mercer University,* | Penfield, Ga. | 1838 | 106 | 3,400 |
| Miami University, | Oxford, Ohio. | 1809 | 119 | 8,000 |
| Middlebury, | Middlebury, Vt. | 1800 | 55 | 6,000 |
| Mississippi College, | Clinton, Miss. | 1851 | 16 | 300 |
| Missouri University, | Columbia, Mo. | 1842 | 180 | 1,700 |
| Mount St. Mary's,§ | Emmetsburg, Md. | 1830 | 126 | 4,000 |
| Norwich University, | Norwich, Vt. | 1834 | 60 | 1,400 |
| Oakland, | Claiborne co., Miss. | 1830 | 70 | 6,000 |
| Oberlin College, | Oberlin, Ohio. | 1833 | 1,327 | 5,000 |
| Oglethorpe, | Milledgeville, Ga. | 1836 | 69 | 4,500 |
| Ohio University, | Athens, Ohio. | 1804 | 41 | 5,000 |
| Ohio Wesleyan University,‡ | Delaware, Ohio. | 1842 | 57 | 5,400 |
| Pennsylvania, | Gettysburg, Pa. | 1832 | 74 | 6,721 |
| Randolph Macon,‡ | Mecklenburg co., Va. | 1832 | 135 | 8,000 |
| Rector,* | Taylor co., Va. | 1839 | 50 | 2,500 |
| Richmond,* | Richmond, Va. | 1832 | 50 | 1,200 |
| Rutgers, | New Brunswick, N. J. | 1770 | 85 | 10,000 |
| Shelby, | Shelbyville, Ky. | 1841 | 44 | 300 |
| Shurtleff,* | Upper Alton, Ill. | 1835 | 40 | 2,000 |
| South Carolina, | Columbia, S. C. | 1804 | 120 | 21,800 |
| Spring Hill,§ | Spring Hill, Ala. | 1830 | 30 | 7,000 |
| St. Charles,§ | Grand Coteau, La. | 1838 | 103 | 4,000 |
| St. Charles,‡ | St. Charles, Mo. | 1837 | 20 | 900 |
| St. James's,† | Washington co., Md. | 1842 | 72 | 6,800 |
| St. John's,§ | Fordham, N. Y. | 1841 | 141 | 12,600 |
| St. John's, | Annapolis, Md. | 1784 | 43 | 3,292 |
| St. Joseph's,§ | Bardstown, Ky. | 1819 | 80 | 6,600 |
| St. Mary's,§ | Baltimore, Md. | 1805 | 122 | 19,600 |
| St. Phillip's,§ | Near Detroit, Mich. | 1839 | 30 | 3,000 |
| St. Vincent's, | Cape Girardeau, Mo. | 1843 | ... | 5,500 |
| St. Xavier,§ | Cincinnati, Ohio. | 1842 | 18 | 7,500 |
| Transylvania, | Lexington, Ky. | 1798 | 50 | 14,000 |
| Trinity,† | Hartford, Conn. | 1824 | 79 | 15,000 |
| Tufts College, | Somerville, Mass. | 1855 | | |
| Tusculum, | Near Greenville, Tenn. | 1843 | 36 | ...... |
| Union, | Schenectady, N. Y. | 1795 | 225 | 15,000 |
| Union,* | Murfreesboro' Tenn. | 1848 | 111 | 1,300 |
| University at Lewisburg,* | Lewisburg, Pa. | 1849 | 83 | 2,680 |
| University of Alabama, | Tuscaloosa, Ala. | 1831 | 116 | 8,140 |
| " Louisiana, | New Orleans, La. | 1849 | ... | ...... |
| " Michigan, | Ann Arbor, Mich. | 1837 | 64 | 6,400 |
| " Mississippi, | Oxford, Miss. | 1844 | 134 | 2,450 |
| " Nashville, | Nashville, Tenn. | 1806 | 75 | 10,207 |
| " New York, | New-York, N. Y. | 1831 | 65 | 4,000 |
| " N. Carolina, | Chapel Hill, N. C. | 1789 | 270 | 13,700 |
| " Pennsylvania, | Philadelphia, Pa. | 1755 | 88 | 5,000 |
| " Rochester,* | Rochester, N. Y. | 1850 | 123 | 3,000 |
| " St. Louis,§ | St. Louis, Mo. | 1832 | 225 | 15,000 |
| " Vermont, | Burlington, Vt. | 1791 | 107 | 13,000 |

| Name. | Place. | Founded. | Students. | Vols. in Libraries. |
|---|---|---|---|---|
| University of Virginia, | Charlottesville, Va. | 1819 | 466 | 19,500 |
| Urbanna University, | Urbanna, Ohio. | 1850 | ... | 1,000 |
| Virginia Military Institute, | Lexington, Va. | 1839 | 130 | 5,000 |
| Wabash, | Crawfordsville, Ia. | 1834 | 43 | 6,400 |
| Wake Forest,* | Wake Forest, N. C. | 1838 | 76 | 5,000 |
| Washington, | Washington, Pa. | 1806 | 112 | 3,300 |
| Washington, | Chestertown, Md. | 1783 | 70 | 1,200 |
| Washington, | Lexington, Va. | 1798 | 62 | 6,105 |
| Washington, | Washington co., Tenn. | 1795 | 22 | 1,800 |
| Waterville,* | Waterville, Me. | 1820 | 88 | 15,500 |
| Wesleyan Female, | Macon, Ga. | 1839 | 140 | 800 |
| Western Military Institute, | Drennon Springs, Ky. | 1847 | 121 | 1,000 |
| Western Reserve, | Hudson, Ohio. | 1826 | 57 | 8,000 |
| Wesleyan University,‡ | Middletown, Conn. | 1831 | 116 | 12,170 |
| William and Mary,† | Williamsburg, Va, | 1692 | 55 | 5,000 |
| Williams, | Williamstown, Mass. | 1793 | 231 | 17,643 |
| Wisconsin University, | Madison, Wis. | 1848 | 23 | 1,200 |
| Wittenberg, | Springfield, Ohio. | 1845 | 37 | 4,500 |
| Yale, | New Haven, Conn. | 1700 | 443 | 54,000 |

☞ The Colleges marked thus (*) are subject to the control of the *Baptists;* thus (†) *Episcopalians;* thus (‡) *Methodists;* thus (§) *Catholics.*

# Advantages of Phonography.

PHONOGRAPHY has been defined as a philosophical method of writing the English language, with an alphabet composed of the simplest geometrical signs, which accurately represent the sounds of spoken words. It may be written six times as fast as the ordinary longhand, and is equally legible. Aside from the scientific propriety of the system, as made manifest in the Introduction which follows, the following practical advantages are worthy of consideration:

1. To professors of scientific and literary institutions—to gentlemen of the bench or the bar—to legislators in the halls of representation—to ministers of religion—to lecturers on the various arts and sciences—it presents the most invaluable aid, in enabling them to arrange, condense, and fix their thoughts, facts, arguments and proofs, in the briefest period of *time* and the shortest possible *space*, presenting, in the condensed schedule of a *small page*, a full and complete synopsis of their most elaborate speeches, orations, or discourses.

2. By its aid, the advocates in the courts of justice or the halls of trial, will be enabled to write, with ease and accuracy, either the full depositions of important witnesses, or the facts, proofs, evidences, and arguments of legal opponents, and thus be in a position, not only to meet them with readiness and strength, but eventually to thoroughly overthrow and refute them.

3. The student in the halls of science can transcribe with faithfulness, and preserve in the smallest compass, the valuable lessons of professors, and thus preserve, for the meditation of his leisure hours, a *connected whole*, instead of broken, detached, and uncertain fragments, that often serve to confuse, bewilder, or perplex.

4. Merchants, and clerks of mercantile houses, to whom *time* and *space* are really a desideratum, will find Phonography a most invaluable auxiliary; as the ease with which it can

be learned and acquired, and the facility and readiness with which it can be *written* and *read*, will enable them to transcribe their accounts, to note their memoranda, to post up their bills, and even to conduct their correspondence, in less than *one-fifth* of the ordinary time, and in a considerable reduction of the ordinary space; and as " time is *money*," it presents to them indeed a most invaluable gain.

5. To the author, editor, or general writer—to the orator, legislator, or minister—how invaluable must it be, when they reflect how many of their most brilliant thoughts and most glowing conceptions, how many of the most sparkling gems of their imaginations and the most radiant pearls of their thoughts, that in moments of genius and enthusiasm flash like electric sparks from the mind, are *forever* lost for the want of some *Daguerrean* process, like the one we present, to catch and transfix them *on the wing*, recording them on the glowing page in *all* the freshness, vigor, and brilliancy of their first conception, as rapidly as they are presented to the mind! and for the lack of which, alas! like the dazzling flash of the evanescent meteor, they fade and expire as rapidly as they are kindled, and leave but the indistinct memory of their trace behind.

6. A practical acquaintance with this art is highly favorable to the improvement of the mind, invigorating all its faculties, and drawing forth all its resources. The close attention requisite in following the voice of the speaker (in reporting) induces habits of patience, perseverance and watchfulness, which will gradually extend, till they form habits that will be found useful through life. The close attention to the words and thoughts of the speaker which is necessary in writing them down, will naturally have a tendency to endue the mind with quickness of apprehension and distinctness of perception, whereby the judgment will be strengthened and the taste refined.

7. The memory is also improved by the practice of Phonography. The necessity for the writer to retain in his

mind the last sentence of the speaker, while he is attending at the same time to what follows, and also to penning down his words, must be highly beneficial to that faculty, which is more than any other improved by exercise. It draws out and improves all the faculties of the mind.

"Phonography," says Messrs. FOWLERS & WELLS, "we regard as one of the most important inventions of the age, and one which should be open to every person desirous of being considered educated. As a system of reporting, general correspondence, and memoranda, it is unparalleled in usefulness. In chirography, it is what the telegraphs are in agencies for transmitting thought. We employ three reporters, one in our office and two who travel with lecturers from our house. In *ten minutes* we can dictate an article for publication which we could not compose and write in two hours; besides it contains more spirit and freshness than if labored through at the slow pace of ordinary composition. Every scholar should by all means learn it."

Professor HART, Principal of the Philadelphia High School, says: "Phonography has been introduced into this institution two years and a half, and has been learned by about four hundred. Two hundred are studying it now. It is one of the regular branches of the course, being attended to three times a week during the whole of the first year. Had I not supposed it to be of much practical value, I should not have urged its introduction, a measure which I have seen no occasion to regret. Such of our students as have made Phonographic Reporting a profession, have got along in life faster, by all odds, than those in any other kind of business, and that without the possession of any special brilliancy of talents. Some of them, not yet turned twenty, are now making more money by Phonographic Reporting than the Principal of the High School, after having given himself for more than twenty years to his profession."

Said the Hon. Thomas Benton: "Had this art been known forty years ago, it would have saved me twenty years of hard labor."

"It is my humble opinion that it will eventually supersede the present system of writing, as the steam carriage train supersedes the old eight inch wheeled wagon."—*Rev. Dunbar.*

Such are the tendencies of the art this book is designed to unfold.

# TESTIMONIALS ON PHONOGRAPHY.

A course of lessons in Phonography, in addition to the practical utility of the art, will prove highly advantageous to all young men who contemplate becoming public speakers ; as the practice it will give them in the analysis and pronunciation of words will greatly improve their ability to read and speak accurately and distinctly. It will drill them thoroughly in the fundamental principles of the art of Elocution, an art most essential to all well educated persons.

For the information of those not acquainted with the science of Phonetics, nor with the utility of the phonographic art, a few extracts are given on the following pages, taken from the "Report of the Committee appointed by the Board of Controllers of the Public Schools of Philadelphia, to examine into the principles of the art and its capacity for usefulness."

## TO TEACHERS AND STUDENTS.

The Committee, after styling it a "simple, beautiful and labor-saving art," proceed to say they "are satisfied of the practical value of Phonography, not only as applicable to verbatim reporting, and of its eminent utility and admirable adaptation to the purposes of business and professional life, but of great importance as a branch of popular education."

*The Principal of the Philadelphia High School, John S. Hart, says:*—Could a suitable amount of instruction be given to the latter study (Phonography,) I have no doubt every student, with rare exceptions, would become sc proficient in the art as to make it practically useful in whatever business he shall follow; besides having at command a ready and certain means of support in default of other occupations. Such of our students as have made Phonographic Reporting a profession, have got along in life faster, by all odds, than those in any other kind of business, and that without the possession of any special brilliancy of talents. Some of them, not yet turned of twenty, are now making more money by phenographic reporting, than the Principal of the High School, after having given himself for more than twenty years to his profession.

*From Francis Wharton, formerly Prosecuting Attorney:*—Sooner or later, it will supercede the present method of writing; and the result will be a great saving of time and economy of labor. As it stands now, there is no way of so soon making a boy self-supporting as by teaching him Phonography. In one case under my immediate observation, a lad hardly seventeen, was able in the course of three years, not only to support himself, but to establish a fund of nearly three thousand dollars; the income of which is ample to support him during the rest of his professional training. At present, the demand in the Courts and in private business is great and increasing.

*Dr. James W. Stone, of Boston, Mass., says:*—One can always compose, when writing in Phonography, much more readily than while using the longhand ; and this for two reasons : first, because he is not obliged to think of the spelling, so difficult for those most accustomed to write English ; second, because the more rapid transmission of his thoughts to paper enables him to preserve them, without that loss of them so common to those accustomed to write only in the longhand.

# Phonetic Publications.

## Published and Sold by Longley Brothers, Cincinnati, O.

THE SPELLING REFORM—Instituted to make universal education possible, by rendering the arts of Reading and Writing pleasant and easy to acquire. PHONOTYPY is a rational system of spelling words as they are pronounced, by employing an enlarged alphabet containing a separate letter for each sound, by which means the drudgery of learning to spell is entirely dispensed with, and learning to read is accomplished in one-fourth of the time required in the old way. PHONOGRAPHY is a truly philosophical method of writing the English Language, by an alphabet composed of the simplest geometrical signs, which accurately represent the sounds of spoken words. It may be written six times as fast as ordinary longhand, and is equally legible, and such is the simplicity of the art that its principles may be easily mastered even without the aid of a teacher.

*The first price is that charged at the counter; the second includes the prepayment of postage; a liberal reduction by the quantity.*

### Phonotypic Works.

**Chart of the Phonotypic Alphabet, on a sheet 28** by 42 inches, with a Key, 25—25

The same, 36 by 50, with explanatory matter, and remarks on the acquisition of Good Reading, 50—54

The same, on canvas and roller, 1,50

**Phonetic Primer, each letter illustrated with a** letter suggestive of its sound, 10—11

**First Phonetic Reader, containing simple and in**teresting reading lessons, 20—25

*With these books teachers and parents can commence a course of Phonetic instruction, in all confidence that other books will follow as fast as they may be wanted.*

**The Transition Reader, or a Course of Inductive** Romanic Reading Lessons. For the use of Phonetic Readers in learning to read Romanically, 20—25

**Biographies of the Presidents, with their Portraits.** In paper covers, 30—35; in cloth, gilt lettering, 40—48

**New Testament, 12mo. edition, according to the** authorized version. In cloth, 75—90; dark sheep, 85—1,00; morocco, gilt, $1,25—1,40

**Money-Getting and Money-Spending; a Prize Es**say of twenty-four chapters; a serious and reformatory work. In paper, 25—30; cloth, 40—46

**Phonetic Dictionary of the English Language;** a complete work of 800 octavo pages, embracing also lists of Classical, Geographical and Scriptural Names. $3,50—4,00

**Pronouncing Medical Lexicon, the definitions in** the common spelling. An invaluable companion to Medical Students, readers of physiological and hygienic works. Cloth, 75—85; sheep, 85—1,00

**Phonetic Almanac, and Register of the Spelling** and Writing Reform, together with a list of the American Phonetic Society, for the years 1852, 1853, 1854, 1855 and 1856. 10

Phonetic Longhand Writer; exhibiting various styles of Penmanship, 10—11

Longhand Alphabet, in slips, to be used as a key by enclosing in letters written in phonetic longhand. Per dozen, 6—7

School Credit Tickets.—A handsome and useful form of Credit Tickets, in Phonetic dress. The Ticket is adapted for Primary and District Schools. Per hundred, 40

Type of the Times; a journal of the Writing and Spelling Reform. Printed in the new orthography. Semi-monthly. Per year, in advance, $1,00

The Youth's Friend; an elegant monthly paper, devoted to the improvement of the young. Embellished with Portraits and Historical Illustrations, partly in the phonetic orthography. 50 cents a year; three copies, $1,00; ten copies, $3,00; twenty copies, $5,00

## Phonographic Works.

First Lesson in Phonography; Containing the Alphabet and a simple reading lesson. Useful for lecturers to distribute in an audience, &c. 1 ct. Per hundred, 50—60

American Manual of Phonography; being a complete exposition of Phonetic Shorthand, especially arranged so as to give the fullest instruction to those who have not the assistance of the oral teacher. In paper, 40—42; cloth, 50—56

☞ *This instruction book is just published, and differs from any other work of the kind in this important particular: It thoroughly explains the Phonotypic or new printing alphabet, and its exercises for writing are printed phonetically, which enables the pupil to progress more correctly and rapidly than if printed in the ordinary orthography.*

BENN PITMAN'S PHONOGRAPHIC PUBLICATIONS.

Manual of Phonography, 50—57, extra cloth, 60—67
Phonographic Reader, engraved exercises, 25
Cruise of the Tomtit; Second Reader, ditto, 25
Manners Book, corresponding style, do. 75—81
Teacher, a Treatise on Lecturing and Teaching Phonography, 1,00—1,07
Copy Slips, a series of Phonographic exercises, 10—11
Phonographer's Song, richly illustrated, 25—27
Phon. Mag., for 1854, '55, '56, per vol, 1,25—1,36
Phonographic Chart, in colors, 75—80
Reporter's Companion; the adaptation of Phon. to verbatim reporting, 75—81, cloth, 1,00—1,07
History of Shorthand, reporting style, 75—81
Manners Book, in easy reporting, 75—81
Phon. Reporter for 1854, '55, '56, per vol, 1,25—1,36

## Phonetic Works in the Common Spelling.

Introduction to Phonography, 16 pp.: an excellent document for presenting to a friend or a stranger to Phonography, 2—3

Report on Phonetic Teaching, by the Committee of the Ohio State Teachers Association. 16 pages; single copy 2—3; per dozen, 18—30

Lecture on the Spelling Reform, delivered at the first meeting of the Ohio Phonetic Association, held at Columbus, Dec. 20th, 1851. By L. A. Hine, Esq. Single copy, 2—3 cts.; per dozen, 30

The Four Ways of Teaching to Read. By Rev. Thos. Hill, Chairman of the School Committee of Waltham, Mass. 16 pp., single copy 3 cts; per dozen, 25—35

Report of the Philadelphia High School on Phonography.—On a motion to discontinue the teaching of Phonography in the Philadelphia High School, an able report was made by the Committee who had the subject under consideration, in opposition thereto. This is the most complete and overpowering document in favor of the system ever published. 40 octavo pages, covered, 10—11

---

## Phonetic Stationery.

Phonetic Copy-Books, for Common Schools, (romanic or phonetic,) containing on the last page of cover, the shorthand alphabet and an explanation of the system. Small size, 5—6 cts.; large, 10—12; by the dozen, one-fourth less.

Reporting Paper, double-ruled especially for Phonography. This is a heavy article, and indispensable for convenience in reporting. Per quire, 10—12. Bound into blank books of 84 pages, for preserving reports, &c. 50—63

Phonographic Letter Paper, (the size of an envelope); for Circulating Magazines, closely ruled. Per quire, 10—12

Phonographic Pencils, of a superior quality, and adapted for general use. 5 cts. Extra, for Reporting, 10 cts.

Phonographic Gold Pens, that cannot be excelled anywhere; manufactured for Longley Brothers, Cincinnati, who pledge themselves to suit customers. If a pen bought of them prove too hard or too soft, if returned immediately, it will be exchanged for one of a different flexibility. Price, without holder, $1,50; ditto, warranted, $1,75; extra size, $2,00, warranted. [By warranting a pen we mean, that if the point comes off, by fair usage, within six months, by returning the pen a new one will be supplied. The manufacturer never repoints pens.] Long holder, with pencil apparatus, 75 cts; sliding or extension holder, ditto, $1,25. Sent by mail free of postage.

Reporting Covers, Morocco, 75—80; Sheep, 30—35.

Phonographic Breast Pin; a neat gold emblem, consisting of the word-sign for Phonography, the wearing of which will often be the means of inducing an inquiry in reference to Phonetics, and of introducing Phonographers to each other, as they pass up and down the earth. $1,00

Phonetic Envelopes, medium size; containing a statement of the nature of Phonography and Phonotypy, with a specimen of the latter. Per hundred, 30—40

## Miscellaneous Publications.

Pronouncing Vocabulary of Geographical and Personal Names. The Geographical list embraces all the names worthy of note in the known world, accompanied with such Descriptive and Statistical Facts as are usual in Gazetteers. The Personal Names comprise those of the most celebrated men of Ancient and Modern Times, down to the present day, which are likely to be met with in general reading. Appended to each name are such Biographical Facts as are necessary in a Book of Reference. To which is added a Complete List of Scriptural Names. Concluding with Tables which show at a glance the Population of the several States, the meeting of their Legislatures, the Succession of the Presidents, and a List of all the Colleges and Professional Schools in the United States. By Elias Longley. 210 pp. In boards, 40—50; cloth, 50—60

Earth and Man; being a Vindication of Man's relations to the Soil. By L. A. Hine, 224 pp. 50—56

Science and Man; being a Vindication of Man's Educational relations. By L. A. Hine. 208 pp. 50—56

Currie Cummings; or, Love's Labor not Lost. A singularly interesting Reform Story. By L. A. Hine. 96 pp., 25—30

The Practical Cook-Book, containing recipes and directions for plain and superior Cookery on Hygienic principles. By Mrs. Sylvia Campbell. A valuable kitchen companion. In paper, 25—27, cloth, 40—47

Parents and Teachers' Guide, in the Physical, Intellectual, and Moral Education of Children. By Charles Morley. —15

Young Folks' American Troubadour; a Collection of Glees, Quartets, Trios, Duets, and Songs, with Piano accompaniments, comprising many of the most popular pieces of the day. —10

Intemperance; or the use of Intoxicating Liquors, Chemically, Physiologically, and Statistically Considered. By Dr. J. G. Buckly, —15

Philosophy of Health, Disease and Cure: Reasons for not using Drugs, and an explanation of the different kinds of Baths used in Water-Treatment. By Dr. J. G. Buckly, —15

## Children's Illustrated Toy-Books.

The Hobby-Horse. The song of a happy boy, about his Hobby-Horse; each verse illustrated with a beautiful picture. In plain print, 5c.; per doz. 40. In various colors, 8c.; per doz. 50c.

Harry O'Hum and his big round Drum. The adventures of a little fellow who had a Drum given him for his amusement. Illustrated as the above. In plain print, 8c.; per doz. 50c.; in various colors, 10c., per doz. 75c.

The Little Big Man. The story of a Discontented Boy, who, trying to improve his condition, made the matter worse, and learned a useful lesson. Illustrated az the others. In plain print, 10c., per doz. 75cts. In various colors, 15c., per doz. $1,00.

The Young Hero; or, Money never makes the Man. By Mabel. A capital story for Boys. 160 pages, with a graphic frontispiece. Price, retail, in paper covers, 25 cts.; cloth, 40—50

www.ingramcontent.com/pod-product-compliance
Lightning Source LLC
LaVergne TN
LVHW011204110826
845150LV00006B/1316